Fodor's 2012

SAN FRANCISCO

W9-BLB-734

Fodor's Travel Publications   New York, Toronto, London, Sydney, Auckland
www.fodors.com

Eugene Fodor:
The Spy Who Loved Travel

As Fodor's celebrates our 75th anniversary, we are honoring the colorful and adventurous life of Eugene Fodor, who revolutionized guidebook publishing in 1936 with his first book, *On the Continent: The Entertaining Travel Annual.*

Eugene Fodor's life seemed to leap off the pages of a great spy novel. Born in Hungary, he spoke six languages and graduated from the Sorbonne and the London School of Economics. During World War II he joined the Office of Strategic Services, the budding spy agency for the United States. He commanded the team that went behind enemy lines to liberate Prague, and recommended to Generals Eisenhower, Bradley, and Patton that Allied troops move to the capital city. After the war, Fodor worked as a spy in Austria, posing as a U.S. diplomat.

In 1949 Eugene Fodor—with the help of the CIA—established Fodor's Modern Guides. He was passionate about travel and wanted to bring his insider's knowledge of Europe to a new generation of sophisticated Americans who wanted to explore and seek out experiences beyond their borders. Among his innovations were annual updates, consulting local experts, and including cultural and historical perspectives and an emphasis on people—not just sites. As Fodor described it, "The main interest and enjoyment of foreign travel lies not only in 'the sites,' . . . but in contact with people whose customs, habits, and general outlook are different from your own."

Eugene Fodor died in 1991, but his legacy, Fodor's Travel, continues. It is now one of the world's largest and most trusted brands in travel information, covering more than 600 destinations worldwide in guidebooks, on Fodors.com, and in ebooks and iPhone apps. Technology and the accessibility of travel may be changing, but Eugene Fodor's unique storytelling skills and reporting style are behind every word of today's Fodor's guides.

Our editors and writers continue to embrace Eugene Fodor's vision of building personal relationships through travel. We invite you to join the Fodor's community at fodors.com/community and share your experiences with like-minded travelers. Tell us when we're right. Tell us when we're wrong. And share fantastic travel secrets that aren't yet in Fodor's. Together, we will continue to deepen our understanding of our world.

Happy 75th Anniversary, Fodor's! Here's to many more.

Tim Jarrell, Publisher

FODOR'S SAN FRANCISCO 2012

Editor: Maria Teresa Hart, Carolyn Galgano (Restaurants and Hotels)

Writers: Michele Bigley, Marcia Gagliardi, Denise M. Leto, Fiona G. Parrott, Sharron Wood, Sura Wood

Production Editor: Carrie Parker
Maps & Illustrations: David Lindroth, Mark Stroud, *cartographers;* Bob Blake, Rebecca Baer, *map editors;* William Wu, *information graphics*
Design: Fabrizio La Rocca, *creative director;* Guido Caroti, Siobhan O'Hare, *art directors;* Tina Malaney, Nora Rosansky, Chie Ushio, *designers;* Melanie Marin, *senior picture editor*
Cover Photo: Golden Gate Bridge: Siegfried Stolzfuss/eStock Photo
Production Manager: Angela L. McLean

ISBN 978-0-679-00945-0

ISSN 1525-1829

SPECIAL SALES

This book is available at special discounts for bulk purchases for sales promotions or premiums. Special editions, including personalized covers, excerpts of existing books, and corporate imprints, can be created in large quantities for special needs. For more information, write to Special Markets/Premium Sales, 1745 Broadway, MD 3-2, New York, NY 10019, or e-mail specialmarkets@randomhouse.com.

AN IMPORTANT TIP & AN INVITATION

Although all prices, opening times, and other details in this book are based on information supplied to us at press time, changes occur all the time in the travel world, and Fodor's cannot accept responsibility for facts that become outdated or for inadvertent errors or omissions. So **always confirm information when it matters,** especially if you're making a detour to visit a specific place. Your experiences—positive and negative—matter to us. If we have missed or misstated something, **please write to us.** Share your opinion instantly through our online feedback center at fodors.com/contact-us.

PRINTED IN SINGAPORE

10 9 8 7 6 5 4 3 2 1

CONTENTS

Fodor's Features

CONTENTS

MAPS

ABOUT
THIS BOOK

Our Ratings

At Fodor's, we spend considerable time choosing the best places in a destination so you don't have to. By default, anything we recommend in this book is worth visiting. But some sights, properties, and experiences are so great that we've recognized them with additional accolades. Orange **Fodor's Choice** stars indicate our top recommendations; black stars highlight places we deem **Highly Recommended**; and **Best Bets** call attention to top properties in various categories. Disagree with any of our choices? Care to nominate a new place? Visit our feedback center at www.fodors.com/feedback.

TripAdvisor 🔵🔵

Fodor's partnership with TripAdvisor helps to ensure that our hotel selections are timely and relevant, taking into account the latest customer feedback about each property. Our team of expert writers selects what we believe will be the top choices for lodging in a destination. Then, those choices are reinforced by TripAdvisor reviews, so only the best properties make the cut.

> For expanded hotel reviews, visit **Fodors.com**

Hotels

Hotels have private bath, phone, TV, and air-conditioning, and do not offer meals unless we specify that in the review. We always list facilities but not whether you'll be charged an extra fee to use them.

Restaurants

Unless we state otherwise, restaurants are open for lunch and dinner daily. We mention dress only when there's a specific requirement and reservations only when they're essential or not accepted—it's always best to book ahead.

Credit Cards

We assume that restaurants and hotels accept credit cards. If not, we'll note it in the review.

Budget Well

Hotel and restaurant price categories from ¢ to $$$$ are defined in the opening pages of the respective chapters. For attractions, we always give standard adult admission fees; reductions are usually available for children, students, and senior citizens.

Listings		Hotels & Restaurants	Outdoors
★ Fodor's Choice	✉ E-mail	🏨 Hotel	🏌 Golf
★ Highly recommended	💲 Admission fee	🛏 Number of rooms	⛺ Camping
⊠ Physical address	☉ Open/closed times	🛁 Facilities	**Other**
✛ Directions or Map coordinates	Ⓜ Metro stations	🍴 Meal plans	🕑 Family-friendly
🕮 Mailing address	⊟ No credit cards	✗ Restaurant	⇨ See also
🖃 Telephone		🍴 Reservations	⊠ Branch address
🖷 Fax		🏛 Dress code	☞ Take note
🌐 On the Web		⌇ Smoking	

Experience
San Francisco

SAN FRANCISCO TODAY

The quintessential boomtown, San Francisco has been alternately riding high and crashing since the gold rush. Those bearish during the heady days of the dot-com bubble had barely finished dancing on the grave of the Internet economy when biotech rode into town, turning bust to boom once again before the housing market downturn brought the city's previously stratospheric median home price right back down to earth. So which San Francisco will you find when you come to town? A reversal of fortune is always possible, but here's a snapshot of what the city's like—for now, anyway.

Today's San Francisco:

. . . is just as liberal as you've heard. Baghdad by the Bay, Sodom by the Sea: prudish types have been pegging San Francisco as a bastion of sexy liberalism since the town first rolled out the welcome mat. And we do tend to espouse a pretty live-and-let-live attitude here. Health insurance for city employees has covered gender-reassignment surgery since 2001. We voted in 2005 to ban handguns and city supervisors banned Happy Meals (nutritionally deficient meals with toys) in 2010; we have a female fire chief, Joanne Hayes-White; and our biggest bash of the year is June's Gay Pride celebration, when roughly a million people descend on the city to party. Conservatives may celebrate Nancy Pelosi's replacement as Speaker of the House, but she can still count on a huge popular majority at home.

Lieutenant Governor Gavin Newsom, our dashing young former mayor and a raging metrosexual, won the eternal devotion of gay San Franciscans when he decided to issue marriage licenses to same-sex couples in 2004, helping to shove the issue onto the Supreme Court docket as well as the ballot. And in this town he's considered a moderate.

. . . embraces its eccentrics. If a 6-foot-tall transvestite in evening wear doesn't merit a second look, just what does it take to stand out in this town? If history serves, it takes quirkiness and staying power. For instance, back in the 19th century a San Francisco businessman declared himself Norton I, Emperor of the United States and Protector of Mexico. Instead of shipping him off to a nice, quiet place, San Franciscans became his willing subjects, police officers saluted him, and newspapers printed his proclamations (among them that the Democrats and Republicans be abolished for bickering).

WHAT WE'RE TALKING ABOUT

You know the economy is bad when San Franciscans start curbing their dining-out expenditures. Sure, we still eat out, but we're spending less when we do. For the practice of ordering appetizers to share instead of entrées, waiters have dubbed us "non'trées." Ouch.

We love to hate Muni. Grousing about Muni's slow and diminishing service and accident rates is a rite of passage. Commuters unite to share the good, the bad, and the dangerous on Web sites like munidiaries.com and munihaiku.com, with poetry divided by line.

What's that rumble under Chinatown? The city has finally secured federal funding for the controversial Central Subway, a 1.7-mi connection of BART with Soma's CalTrain line and the T-Third. Why "controversial"? That $1.6 billion price tag could buy a lot of Muni improvements.

Today the Brown Twins, ladies of a certain age who dress alike in eye-catching outfits and are always together, have their own place on the list of San Francisco icons. There's also Pink Man, who rides a unicycle wearing a hot pink unitard and cape. (He says you can tell someone's a local when "they don't balk at Pink Man.")

One of the most celebrated eccentrics is Frank Chu, a middle-aged guy in a frumpy suit who's been faithfully carrying a picket sign around the Financial District since the 1990s. He accuses various politicians of being in cahoots and keeping millions of dollars from him and the population of the "12 galaxies." The city's response? Politicians and local businesses buy ad space on the back of his sign, and fans named a (now defunct) bar 12 Galaxies in tribute and created an online Frank Chu–style sign generator (*acme.com/chumaker*).

. . . may be pushing back panhandling. The sight of homeless folks camped out in doorways and parks has long been familiar in the city, but voters are apparently at the end of their ropes. In 2010 they narrowly passed a law, aimed straight at panhandlers and the kids that line Haight Street, that makes it illegal to sit or lie on city sidewalks between 7 am and 11 pm. Looks like even laid-back San Franciscans have a limit to their tolerance.

. . . is reshaping its downtown. Limited by its geography, San Francisco simply has nowhere to go but up. The sprawling area south of Market Street was long an industrial center, but since that industry has dried up, new high-rise developments are under way. Plot the nascent high-rises on a map and you can see a radical shift southward, stretching from Mission Street to Mission Bay (where UCSF's 43-acre medical and biotech campus is rising). More than 20 towers are in the works, several of which will eclipse the city's current tallest building, the 853-foot Transamerica Pyramid.

Got your bearings? Then join the locals as they constantly check the pulse of the city. Although the frenzied adrenaline rush of the dot-com era has died down, a new wave of energy is gathering.

The food-cart scene continues to boom. Watch out for local favorites the Sexy Soup Cart, the Bacon Dog Cart, and, for dessert, the ever-popular Crème Brûlée Cart. Or find them all together at Off the Grid, a roaming food-cart marketplace.

Are we taking back the term "Frisco"? From Emperor Norton to legendary *Chronicle* columnist Herb Caen, residents have harangued against calling the city "Frisco." But lately some locals are rebelling, showing off hoodies and tattoos festooned with the F-word.

There's lots of hand wringing and gnashing of teeth in the Bay Area these days over the economic meltdown and the slipping housing market. Though the city hasn't been hit nearly as hard as most other Bay Area towns, the median home price is at a startling low and finally in range for mere mortals: $440,000 (and dropping).

SAN FRANCISCO PLANNER

When to Go

You can visit San Francisco comfortably any time of year. Possibly the best time is September and October, when the city's summerlike weather brings outdoor concerts and festivals. The climate here always feels Mediterranean and moderate—with a foggy, sometimes chilly bite. The temperature rarely drops below 40°F, and anything warmer than 80°F is considered a heat wave. Be prepared for rain in winter, especially December and January. Winds off the ocean can add to the chill factor. That old joke about summer in SF feeling like winter is true at heart, but once you move inland, it gets warmer. (And some locals swear that the thermostat has inched up in recent years.)

SAN FRANCISCO
TEMPERATURES

Weather

Thanks to its proximity to the Pacific Ocean, San Francisco has remarkably consistent weather throughout the year. The average high is 63°F and the average low is 51°F. Summer comes late in San Francisco, which sees its warmest days in September and October. On average, the city gets 20 inches of rainfall a year, most of it in the December-to-March period.

Getting Around

Walking: San Francisco dearly rewards walking, and the areas that most visitors cover are easy (and safe) to reach on foot. However, many neighborhoods have steep—make that *steep*—hills. In some areas the sidewalk is carved into steps; a place that seems just a few blocks away might be a real hike, depending on the grade. When your calves ache, you're that much closer to being a local. *Check the Safety section in the Travel Smart chapter for a summary on areas through which it may be best to avoid walking.*

By Subway: BART is San Francisco's subway, limited to one straight line through the city. Within the city, it's a handy way to get to the Mission or perhaps Civic Center. BART is most useful for reaching the East Bay or the airport. There are no special visitor passes for BART; within town a ticket runs $1.75.

On Muni: Muni includes the city's extensive system of buses, electric streetcars, nostalgic F-line trolleys, and cable cars. The trolleys and cable cars are a pleasure for the ride alone, and they run in well-traveled areas like Market Street and, in the case of the cable cars, the hills from Union Square to Fisherman's Wharf. Basic fare for the bus, streetcars, and trolleys is $2; cable-car tickets cost $5 one-way. At $13, a one-day Muni Passport that includes cable car rides is a great deal.

By Car or Taxi: Considering its precipitous hills, one-way streets, and infuriating dearth of parking, San Francisco is not a good place to drive yourself. Taxis, however, can come in very handy. Call one or hail one on the street; they tend to cluster around downtown hotels.

Festivals and Parades

San Francisco's major parades and festivals are notoriously creative, energetic, and often off-the-wall. Among the hundreds of events on the city's annual calendar, here are the ones that are especially characteristic and fun.

Chinese New Year, February. This celebration in North America's largest Chinatown lasts for almost three weeks. The grand finale is the spectacularly loud, crowded, and colorful Golden Dragon Parade, which rocks with firecrackers. If you don't want to wait on the sidewalk for hours in advance, buy bleacher seats. Contact the **Chinese Chamber of Commerce** (☎ 415/982–3071 ⊕ www.chineseparade.com) for more info.

St. Stupid's Day Parade, April. The First Church of the Last Laugh (⊕ www.saintstupid.com) holds this fantastically funny event on—when else—April 1. It wanders through the Financial District, with hundreds of people dressed up in elaborate costumes (although there are fewer drag queens than on Halloween). Parade-goers toss socks at the Stock Exchange, throw pennies at the angular sculpture in front of the Bank of America building called the "banker's heart," and sing their way down Columbus Avenue.

San Francisco International Film Festival, April–May. The country's longest-running film festival packs in audiences with premieres, international films, and rarities. Check their listings (☎ 415/561–5000 ⊕ www.sfiff.org) well in advance for tickets.

Cinco de Mayo Festival, May. On the Sunday closest to May 5, the Mission District boils with activity, including a vibrant parade, Mexican music, and dancing in the streets.

Lesbian, Gay, Bisexual, and Transgender Pride Celebration, June. More than half a million people come to join the world's largest pride event, with a downtown parade roaring to a start by leather-clad Dykes on Bikes. If you're visiting around this time, book your hotel *far* ahead (☎ 415/864–0831 ⊕ www.sfpride.org).

San Francisco Open Studios, October. More than 700 artists open their studios to the public. It's a great window into the local fine-arts scene (☎ 415/861–9838 ⊕ www.artspan.org).

Dance-Along Nutcracker, December. This fabulous holiday tradition, part spoof and part warmhearted family event, was started by the San Francisco Lesbian/Gay Freedom Band (⊕ www.sflgfb.org). You can join the dancers onstage for some free-form choreography, or simply toss snowflakes from the audience.

5 Helpful SF Web Sites

Check out these online options—besides our own www.fodors.com.

www.onlyinsanfrancisco.com for the San Francisco visitor bureau.

www.sfgate.com/chronicle from the major daily newspaper, especially www.sfgate.com/sfguide (for city neighborhoods and events) and www.sfgate.com/entertainment (for entertainment articles and listings).

www.sfist.com for a daily feed of local news, gossip, and SF preoccupations.

http://mistersf.com for a passionate local's rundown on favorite local spots and city FAQs.

www.sfstation.com for daily listings on all sorts of events, restaurants, clubs, etc.

. . . and three more just for ha-has

www.burritoeater.com for opinionated reviews of Bay Area burritos.

www.ibabuzz.com/bottomsup for all things beer and wine in the city.

www.quirkysanfrancisco.com for gorgeous photos of off-the-beaten-path gems.

WHAT'S WHERE

1 Union Square. Home to a tourism trifecta: hotels, public transportation, and shopping. There are more hotel beds here than in any other neighborhood in the city; several transit options converge, including the cable cars. The square itself is dominated by flagship stores—but if you're not a shopper, this area may bore you.

2 Chinatown. Live fish flopping around on ice; the scent of incense, cigarettes, and vanilla; bargains announced in myriad Chinese dialects... you'll feel like you should have brought your passport.

3 SoMa. Anchored by SFMOMA and Yerba Buena Gardens, SoMa is a once-industrial neighborhood that's in transition. Luxury condos are going up and there are several cool dance clubs and restaurants, but some parts are still quite gritty.

4 Civic Center. Monumental city government buildings and performing-arts venues dominate, but it's also a chronic homeless magnet. Locals love Hayes Valley, the chic little neighborhood to the west.

5 Nob Hill. Topped by staid and elegant behemoths, hotels that ooze reserve and breeding, Nob Hill is old-money San Francisco.

6 Russian Hill. These steep streets hold a vibrant, classy neighborhood that's very au courant. Locals flock to Polk and Hyde streets, the hill's main commercial avenues, for excellent neighborhood eateries and fantastic window-shopping.

7 North Beach. z8 The Embarcadero. The city's northeastern waterfront is anchored at the foot of Market Street by the exquisitely restored Ferry Building. The promenade that starts in back has great views of the bay and the Bay Bridge.

9 The Northern Waterfront. Wandering the shops and so-called attractions of Fisherman's Wharf, Pier 39, and Ghirardelli Square, the only locals you'll meet will be the ones with visitors in tow. Everything here is designed for tourists, so if you're looking for a souvenir shop...

10 Jackson Square. For history buffs and antiques lovers, this upscale corner of the Financial District is a pleasant diversion.

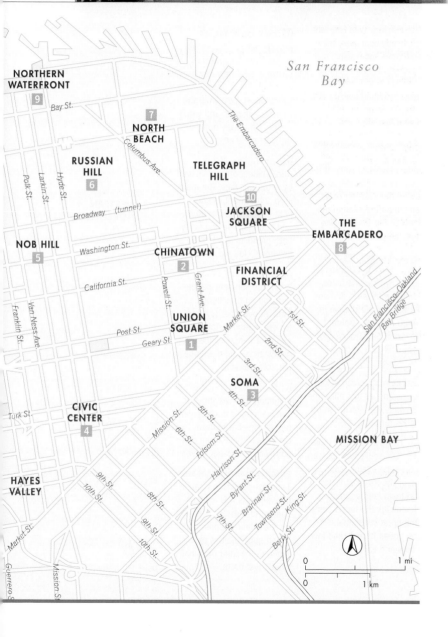

NORTHERN
WATERFRONT
9

Bay St.

7
NORTH
BEACH

Columbus Ave.

RUSSIAN
HILL
6

TELEGRAPH
HILL

*San Francisco
Bay*

The Embarcadero

Broadway   (tunnel)

10
JACKSON
SQUARE

NOB HILL
5

Washington St.

CHINATOWN
2

THE
EMBARCADERO
8

California St.

FINANCIAL
DISTRICT

San Francisco–Oakland
Bay Bridge

Powell St.

Grant Ave.

UNION
SQUARE

Market St.

1st St.

Post St.

Geary St.

1

2nd St.

3rd St.

SOMA
3

4th St.

CIVIC
CENTER
4

Turk St.

5th St.

6th St.

Folsom St.

Mission St.

MISSION BAY

HAYES
VALLEY

9th St.

10th St.

8th St.

9th St.

10th St.

Harrison St.

7th St.

Bryant St.

Brannan St.

Townsend St.

King St.

Berry St.

0   1 mi

0   1 km

Polk St.

Larkin St.

Hyde St.

Van Ness Ave.

Franklin St.

Market St.

Guerrero St.

Mission St.

WHAT'S WHERE

11 The Marina. With fine-wine shops, trendy boutiques, fashionable cafés and restaurants, and pricey waterfront homes, the Marina is San Francisco's yuppiest neighborhood. It's also home to the exquisite 1915 Palace of Fine Arts.

12 The Presidio. Locals come to the Presidio, the wooded shoreline park just west of the Marina, for a quick in-town getaway, the spirit lift only an amble on the sand in the shadow of the Golden Gate Bridge can provide.

13 Golden Gate Park. Covering more than 1,000 acres of greenery, with sports fields, windmills, museums, gardens, and a few buffalo thrown in for good measure, Golden Gate Park is San Francisco's backyard.

14 The Western Shoreline. A natural gem underappreciated by locals and visitors alike, the city's windswept Pacific shore stretches for miles.

15 The Haight. If you're looking for '60s souvenirs, you can find them here, along with some of the loveliest Victorians in town (and aggressive panhandling). Hip locals come for the great secondhand shops, cheap brunch, and low-key bars and cafés.

16 The Castro. Yes, it's proudly rainbow-flag-waving, in-your-face fab, but the Castro is a friendly neighborhood that welcomes visitors of all stripes. Shop the trendy boutiques, and catch a film at the truly noteworthy Castro Theatre.

17 Noe Valley. A cute, pricey neighborhood favored by young families. The main strip, 24th Street, is lined with coffee shops, eateries, and boutiques selling fancy bath products and trendy children's clothing.

18 The Mission District. When the sun sets, people descend on the Mission from all over the Bay Area for destination restaurants, excellent bargain-price ethnic eateries, and the hippest bar scene around.

19 Pacific Heights. This neighborhood has some of San Francisco's most opulent real estate—but in most cases you'll have to be content with an exterior view.

20 Japantown. A tight-knit Japanese-American population supports this area, of interest to outsiders mostly for the ethnic shopping and dining opportunities of the Japan Center and the small streets just north.

PACIFIC OCEAN

Lincoln Park

WESTERN SHORELINE
14

OCEAN BEACH

GOLDEN

GATE

NATIONAL

RECREATION

AREA

43rd Ave.

34th Ave.

Kennedy Dr.

41st Ave.

Sunset Blvd.

Great Highway

Skyli

0   1 mi
0   1 km

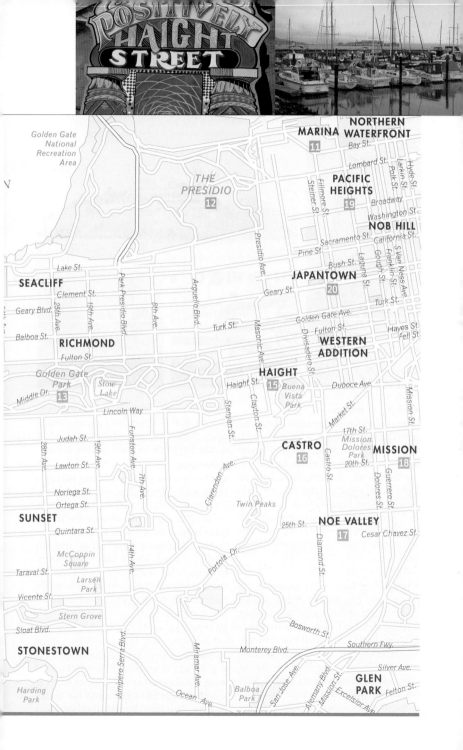

SAN FRANCISCO TOP ATTRACTIONS

Golden Gate Bridge

(A) San Francisco's signature International Orange entryway is the city's majestic background, and about 10 million people a year head to the bridge for an up-close look. Walking the 1.7 mi to Marin County—inches from roaring traffic, steel shaking beneath your feet, and a far-too-low railing between you and the water 200 feet below—is much more than a superlative photo op (though it's that, too).

Alcatraz

(B) Considering how many movies have been set here, you might feel like you've already "been there, done that"—but you really shouldn't miss a trip to America's most infamous federal pen. Husky-throated onetime inmates and grizzled former guards bring the Rock to life on the wonderful audio tour; you'll hear yarns about desperate escape attempts and notorious crooks like Al Capone while you walk the cold cement cellblock. But it's not all doom and gloom: you'll enjoy stunning views of the city skyline on the ferry ride to and from the island.

Fisherman's Wharf

(C) Once part of a thriving fishing industry, Fisherman's Wharf has deteriorated into a giant harpoon aimed straight at your wallet. Throngs from all over the world come to hear the sea lions bark; buy cheap T-shirts; and chow down on overpriced, mediocre food. It's all an utter mystery to locals, who don't come here. Ever. See the magnificent historic ships at the Hyde Street Pier, then take your money and run.

Golden Gate Park

(D) It may be world famous, but first and foremost the park is the city's backyard. Come here any day of the week and you'll find a microcosm of San Francisco, from the Russian senior citizens feeding the pigeons at Stow Lake and the moms pushing strollers through the botanical

gardens to science fans exploring the fabulous California Academy of Sciences and arts boosters checking out the latest at the de Young Museum. Be sure to visit the park's iconic treasures, including the serene Japanese Tea Garden and the beautiful Victorian Conservatory of Flowers. If you have the time to venture farther into this urban oasis, you'll discover less accessible gems like the Beach Chalet and the wild western shores of Ocean Beach.

Cable Cars

(E) You've already seen them (on the big screen, in magazines, and, admit it, on the Rice-a-Roni box). And considering a ticket costs $5 a pop, do you really need to ride a cable car? Yes, you do, at least once during your visit. Flag down a Powell–Hyde car along Powell Street, grab the pole, and clatter and jiggle up mansion-topped Nob Hill. Crest the hill, and hold on for the hair-raising descent to Fisherman's Wharf, with sun glittering off the bay and Alcatraz bobbing in the distance. Don't deny it—this would be a deal at twice the price.

Palace of Fine Arts

(F) Perched on a swan-filled lagoon near the Marina's yacht harbor, this stirringly beautiful terra-cotta-color dome has an otherworldly quality about it. Built for the 1915 Panama-Pacific International Exhibition, the palace is a San Francisco architect's version of a Roman ruin, and it's been eliciting gasps for almost a century. Try to see it from the water.

Coit Tower

(G) Most people assume that this stubby white tower atop Telegraph Hill is supposed to look like a fire-hose nozzle. And considering that a fire truck–chasing, cross-dressing 19th-century socialite donated the funds to build it, maybe it is. The tower itself is of vague interest—it does house the history of San Francisco in murals—but the "park"(ing lot) at its

base has fantastic views of the city and the bay. The tower sits at the top of Telegraph Hill's Filbert Steps, a steep stairway through glorious gardens with vistas of transcendent beauty, an only–in–San Francisco spot locals cherish.

Ferry Building

(H) Foodies rejoice! The historic Ferry Building is stuffed to the brim with all things tasty, including cafés, restaurants, a farmers' market, and merchants peddling everything from wine and olive oil to oysters and mushrooms. The building backs up to the bay, so the views are great—but they're even better from the decks of the departing ferries.

California Academy of Sciences

(I) One look at the building's monumental exterior—glass, glass, and more glass, all topped with 2½ acres of native plants on its undulating living roof—and you'll know this isn't just another science museum. Superfunky architecture and

"green" everything (denim as insulation and rechargeable vehicle stations) enclose a full day's diversions. Visit Claude, the languid albino crocodile, a waddle of penguins, a four-story walk-through rain forest complete with free-flying butterflies, a planetarium, and a good, old-fashioned natural-history hall.

Wine Country

(J) You don't need to be a connoisseur to enjoy a trip to Napa or Sonoma . . . or both (hey, you're on vacation). But there's more to a Wine Country visit than vineyard tours and tastings: landmark restaurants, breathtaking scenery, fantastic artwork, hot-air-balloon rides, and secluded boutique hotels. And when you're ready for a break, a great glass of wine is never that far out of reach.

LOCAL FOR A DAY

Want to get a slice of local life by just hanging out, skipping the sightseeing? These experiences will let you pretend you're a San Franciscan, without a whopping rent check.

Shop the Ferry Plaza Farmers' Market
Roll out of bed and make your way to the Ferry Building—preferably on a Saturday—to join locals and celebrity chefs on a taste bud–driven raid. Out front, farmer-run stands showcase the Bay Area's finest organic, free-range, locavore goods. The indoor stalls will keep your mouth watering with artisanal cheeses, chocolates, and luscious pastries. Snag some takeaway food plus some perfectly ripe fruit for a picnic.

Stretch Your Legs in the Presidio
Spend a few hours wandering around this former military base at the foot of the Golden Gate Bridge. The park is redeveloping the old military buildings, along with ball fields and other rec areas. Join people walking their dogs on the wooded hiking trails, or amble the paths along the sand of Crissy Field, then get in line for a cocoa at the Warming Hut.

Hang Out in Hayes Valley
Long beloved of artsy, cutting-edge locals, this quarter of cool cafés and high-design boutiques is either coming into its own or getting too big for its britches, depending on who you ask. The renovation of Octavia Boulevard, one of this neighborhood's main arteries, makes Hayes Valley even busier. Grab a coffee from local cult microroasters Blue Bottle Coffee and check out the latest temporary art installation in Patricia's Green, the petite community park.

Find a Quiet Beach
Leave the beach near Fisherman's Wharf far behind and seek out these two instead. Breezy Baker Beach, tucked against the cliffs just south of the Golden Gate Bridge, is known for its bridge and ocean views—and its nudists, those hardy souls. A bit farther south, nestled in ultrapricey Seacliff, is China Beach, a smaller, more secluded spot that's never crowded.

Linger over Breakfast
Notoriously food-centric San Franciscans are big on the most important meal of the day. The lines at popular breakfast places can be just as long as those at the hottest nightspots. Some longtime favorites include:

Mama's (⊠ 1701 Stockton St., at Filbert St., North Beach ☎ 415/362–6421) tried-and-true diner, where the line forms early.

Kate's Kitchen (⊠ 471 Haight St., near Fillmore St., Lower Haight ☎ 415/626–3984), where heaping plates of Southern-inspired fare take the edge off a hairy-tongued Lower Haight morning after.

Ella's (⊠ 500 Presidio Ave., at California St., Pacific Heights ☎ 415/441–5669), where oatmeal and chicken hash are served alongside gussied-up standbys like brandied French toast.

Nurse a Coffee
Spend a few hours in the right independent café or coffeehouse and you'll feel like you're in a neighborhood living room. Come for a jolt of java, sometimes a reasonably priced meal, and usually Wi-Fi. Stay all afternoon—nobody minds—and you'll see the best reflection of a microcommunity.

SAN FRANCISCO WITH KIDS

On the Move

Cable Cars. This one's a no-brainer. But don't miss the **Cable Car Terminus** at Powell and Market streets, where conductors push the iconic cars on giant turntables, and the **Cable Car Museum**, where you can see how cable cars work.

Adventure Cat Sailing. Them: playing on the trampoline at the bow of this 55-foot catamaran. You: enjoying a drink and the bay sunset on the stern deck.

F-Line Trolleys. Thomas the Tank Engine fan in tow? Hop on one of the F-line's neat historic streetcars. ■TIP➔ Bonus: this line connects other kid-friendly sights, like Fisherman's Wharf and the Ferry Building.

Sneak in Some Culture

Stern Grove Festival. Enjoying a delicious picnic in a eucalyptus grove, your kids might not even complain that they're listening to—gasp—classical music.

ODC/San Francisco. Best known for its holiday production of *The Velveteen Rabbit,* the dance troupe also holds other performances throughout the year.

San Francisco Mime Troupe. We know, it sounds lame. But these aren't your father's mimes. In fact, they're a vocal political theater troupe that gives family-friendly outdoor performances.

The Great Outdoors

Muir Woods. If these massive trees look tall to you, imagine seeing them from 2 or 4 feet lower.

Stow Lake. When feeding bread to the ducks gets old (like that's ever going to happen), you can rent a rowboat or paddleboat.

Golden Gate Promenade. If your kids can handle a 3.3-mi walk, this one's a beauty—winding from Aquatic Park Beach, through the Presidio, to Fort Point Pier near the base of the Golden Gate Bridge.

Aquatic Park Beach. Does your brood include a wannabe Michael Phelps? Then head to this popular beach, one of the few places around the city where it's safe to swim. ■TIP➔ Many other Bay Area beaches have powerful currents that make swimming dangerous.

Just Plain Fun

AT&T Park. Emerald grass, a sun-kissed day, a hot dog in your hand . . . and suddenly, you're 10 again, too.

Dim Sum. A rolling buffet for which kids point and pick—likely an instant hit.

Fisherman's Wharf, Hyde Street Pier, Ghirardelli Square, and Pier 39. The phrase "tourist trap" may come to mind, but in this area you can get a shrimp cocktail, clamber around old ships, snack on chocolate, and laugh at the sea lions.

Musée Mécanique. What did people do before Wii? Come here to find out.

Rooftop @ Yerba Buena Gardens. Head here for ice-skating, bowling, a carousel, a playground, and Zeum, an interactive arts-and-technology center.

San Francisco Zoo. Between Grizzly Gulch, Lemur Forest, and Koala Crossing, you can make a day of it.

Learn a Thing or Two

California Academy of Sciences. Dinosaurs, penguins, free-flying rain-forest butterflies, giant snakes . . . what's not to like?

Exploratorium. A very hands-on science museum, including the full-immersion Tactile Dome.

TOP WALKING TOURS

■ **All About Chinatown** (☎ 415/982–8839 ⊕ www.allaboutchinatown.com). A delightful "behind-the-scenes" look at the neighborhood. Owner Linda Lee and her guides stop in Ross Alley and at a Buddhist temple. At herbal and food markets you'll learn the therapeutic yield of fish stomachs and ponder uses for live partridges.

■ **Chinatown Alleyway Tours** (☎ 415/984–1478 ⊕ www.chinatownalleywaytours.org). To learn about the modern Chinatown community, join up with one of these young guides. Tour leaders, who all grew up here, discuss not only Chinatown's history but also current social issues.

■ **Don Herron's Dashiell Hammett Tour** (⊕ www.donherron.com). Brush up on your noir slang and join trench-coated guide Herron for a walk by the mystery writer's haunts and the locations from some of Hammett's novels.

■ **Foot! Comedy Walking Tours** (☎ 415/793–5378 ⊕ www.foottours.com). You'll likely find yourself breathless with laughter, not just gasping after a steep hill. The tour leaders are all moonlighting pro comedians; they've got offerings like "Nude, Lewd and Crude" North Beach.

■ **Local Tastes of the City Tours** (☎ 415/665–0480 or 888/358–8687 ⊕ www.localtastesofthecitytours.com). If you want to aggressively snack your way through a neighborhood as you walk it, consider hanging with cookbook author Tom Medin. You'll learn why certain things just taste better in San Francisco—like coffee and anything baked with sourdough—and you'll get tips about how to find good food once you get back home. Along the way, you'll gradually gorge yourself into oblivion: the North Beach tour, for instance, might include multiple stops for coffee and baked goods.

■ **Precita Eyes Mural Walks** (☎ 415/285–2287 ⊕ www.precitaeyes.org). For an insider's look at the vibrant murals in the Mission District, this is the place to call. The nonprofit organization has nurtured this local art form from the get-go, and they stay on top of all the latest additions. ⇨ *See the Mission District Chapter 11 for more details.*

■ **San Francisco City Guides** (☎ 415/557–4266 ⊕ www.sfcityguides.org). An outstanding free service supported by the San Francisco Public Library. Walking-tour themes range from individual neighborhoods to local history (the gold rush, the 1906 quake, ghost walks) to architecture. Each May and October additional walks are offered. Although the tours are free and the knowledgeable guides are volunteers, it's appropriate to make a $5 donation for these nonprofit programs. Tour schedules are available at library branches and at the **San Francisco Visitor Information Center** (✉ *Hallidie Plaza, lower level, Powell and Market Sts., Union Square* ☎ 415/391–2000, 415/392–0328 TDD ⊕ www.sfvisitor.org).

■ **Wok Wiz Chinatown Tour** (☎ 650/355–9657 ⊕ www.wokwiz.com). Cookbook author Shirley Fong-Torres and her team lead these walks. Conversation topics include folklore and, of course, food. One version called "I Can't Believe I Ate My Way Through Chinatown!" includes breakfast and lunch.

A WATERFRONT WALK: THE FERRY BUILDING TO FISHERMAN'S WHARF

One of the great pleasures of San Francisco is a stroll along the bay, with its briny scent, the cry of the gulls, and boats bobbing on the waves. The flat, 2-mi walk along the Embarcadero from the Ferry Building offers a chance to take in some of the city's blockbuster sights along with spectacular bay vistas.

The Ferry Building: Foodie Mecca

Standing sentry at the foot of Market Street, the **Ferry Building** offers organic, seasonal delights from such local treasures as Cowgirl Creamery and Prather Ranch Meat Company. Take your picnic to a bench out back and take in the bay and the Bay Bridge.

Embarcadero: New Life for Old Piers

Heading north on the Embarcadero as the piers go up in number, watch for a mélange of historical info on black-and-white pillars, engraved in the sidewalk, and on plaques. These line **Pier 1**, where the giant paddle wheeler *San Francisco Belle* docks. **Pier 7** juts out far into the bay; an evening stroll here is lovely (if chilly) under the street lamps.

Just two blocks beyond at Pier 15, the city's excellent hands-on science museum, the **Exploratorium**, will reopen in 2013. Meanwhile, stop by local chocolatier **Tcho**, at Pier 17, for free samples and hot cocoa.

North Beach Detour: Levi's and Coit Tower

Near Pier 17, a left on Union and a right on Battery leads to **Levi Strauss headquarters**, where visitors can peruse The Vault, with miners' jeans from the 1880s. Back across Battery, **Levi's Plaza** is one of the most manicured parks in town.

Consider heading west on Filbert or Greenwich and ascending one of the steep staircases clinging to **Telegraph Hill** for spectacular views and a peek into the lush stairway gardens along the way up to **Coit Tower**. Then return down the stairs to continue along the Embarcadero.

Embarcadero North End: Tourist San Francisco

Continuing north up the Embarcadero, **Alcatraz Landing** (Pier 33) is a good spot to pick up souvenirs even if you're not taking the highly recommended tour. **Pier 39** is just around the corner, with its cornucopia of souvenir vendors; thankfully, sea lion–watching is still free.

A few blocks farther north is **Fisherman's Wharf**, at Pier 45. Bypass the wax museum and make a beeline for the fabulous vintage arcade **Musée Mécanique** (at the foot of Taylor Street). For crab- and bunny-shape sourdough loaves, stop by Boudin Bakery just down Taylor.

Last Stop: Historic Vessels at the Hyde Street Pier

Follow the towering masts to the foot of Hyde Street and the collection of exquisitely restored ships there. Afterward, head up Hyde to the **cable-car turnaround**, where you can grab an Irish coffee at the **Buena Vista**.

—Denise M. Leto

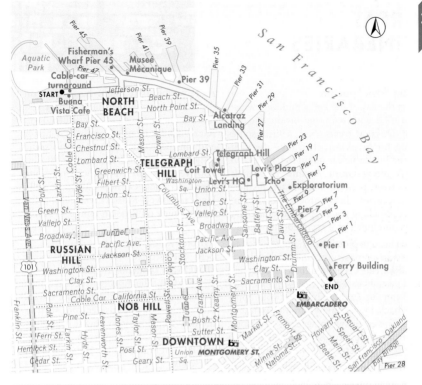

Where to Start:	In front of the Ferry Building.
Time/Length:	30–60 minutes at a moderate pace, without stops. With a picnic and park breaks, this walk could be a 3-hour affair. The total distance in 2 mi.
Where to Stop:	At the cable-car turnaround or resting your feet at Buena Vista.
Best Time to Go:	Sunny days are best for strolling the waterfront. Start off at the Ferry Building in the morning, ideally on a Saturday, when farmers' market stalls fill the plaza. The street-theater scene from Pier 39 to Fisherman's Wharf is liveliest on weekends, too.
Worst Time to Go:	Rain puts a huge damper on this walk, which is all about being outside. Weekends are bustling, but they can mean huge crowds at the big-ticket attractions—Alcatraz and Fisherman's Wharf.
Getting Around:	If you're driving, park at the north end—it's much cheaper—and do the walk backward from north to south. Pedicabs will offer rides along the way, and the F-line is always available for the weary.

GREAT ITINERARIES

Bring Your Appetite

Start the day at the Ferry Building, which is stuffed with tempting produce, cafés, and artisanal treats. Nab a little something for breakfast, then take the California line cable car uphill to Chinatown. Walk along Grant Avenue and Stockton Street, peeking into mysterious herb apothecaries, live-seafood stores, and sweet-smelling tea shops before having a dim sum lunch or a steamed-bun snack.

Then head to North Beach for a post-meal espresso or pastry at one of the classic outdoor cafés. The Italian delis, bakeries, and pasta houses are worth visiting even if you can't eat another bite. Get your appetite back by making your way uphill to Coit Tower for sweeping views of the bay. (Climbing the steep stairways is a tough but scenically stunning way to do this.)

At the end of the day, either head back to North Beach's Columbus Avenue and let one of the restaurant hawkers talk you into coming in for pasta, or make the trip to the Mission District for fantastic, inexpensive ethnic food.

Work the Wharf

Fisherman's Wharf and the surrounding attractions may be touristy with a capital T, but there are some fun experiences to be had. With your pre-reserved ticket in hand (do this in advance, since tours frequently sell out), set out for Alcatraz. When the ferry docks back at Pier 33, head north along the waterfront to Pier 39. If you're on a kitschy-souvenir hunt, browse through the pier's overpriced stores. Otherwise, see if you can spot sea lions basking on floating platforms next to the pier. Take a step back in time to early-20th-century San Francisco at delightful Musée Mécanique, then grab an Irish coffee at the Buena Vista.

As tempting as it might be to dine on the water, most Fisherman's Wharf restaurants have less-than-spectacular food (Gary Danko is an exception). A better and cheaper option is to pick up some to-go Dungeness crab from one of the outdoor vendors and eat as you stroll along the waterfront. Or hop on the Powell–Hyde or Powell–Mason cable-car line for better dining on Russian Hill or in North Beach.

Art and Retail Therapy

Beat the crowds in the morning at SFMOMA (remember that it's closed Wednesday). The modern art collection is SoMa's main magnet, but there are several other museums to consider, too, such as the new Contemporary Jewish Museum, the Museum of the African Diaspora, and the San Francisco Craft and Folk Art Museum.

Take a break from exhibits across the street from SFMOMA in the expansive Yerba Buena Gardens. If you have kids in tow, drop by the game- and gadget-heavy Metreon. Otherwise, head up 4th Street and join the masses at the Bloomingdale's-anchored Westfield San Francisco Shopping Centre (and its spectacular dining court) and the shops around Union Square. This area isn't known for great restaurants, so when you're ready for dinner, head to Belden Place. This bistro-lined alley (many places here are closed Sunday) is one of the few places around Union Square where locals dine.

To top off the evening, gaze down on the city lights from one of the square's skyview lounges like Harry Denton's Starlight Lounge.

Golden Gate Park

Golden Gate Park is better than usual on Sunday, when its main arteries are closed to cars. Start your day at the glorious Conservatory of Flowers (closed Monday). Be sure to take in the scenes ingeniously rendered in flowers out front. Pace the wooden bridges and stone pathways of the Japanese Tea Garden before hitting the San Francisco Botanical Garden at Strybing Arboretum. Next up: the striking, controversial de Young Museum (closed Monday) and the glorious reopened California Academy of Sciences. Make your way west, stopping at Stow Lake, where you can rent a boat and paddle near Strawberry Hill. Back on land, continue west toward Ocean Beach and the endless Pacific. Cap off your tour by kicking back with a pint to enjoy the sunset ocean view at the Beach Chalet.

Find the Funky Neighborhoods

Ride the antique trolleys to the western end of the F-line in the Castro. Stroll down Castro Street, past the art-deco Castro Theatre, window-shopping and stopping at any café that tempts you. Head east on 16th Street to Dolores Street and Mission Dolores, and wander rows of centuries-old gravestones in its tiny cemetery.

Then hit the "Valencia Corridor" (Valencia Street between 16th and 20th streets), dipping into independent bookstores, hipster cafés, and quirky shops. Seek out the area's vibrant, often politically charged murals, either on your own or on a tour with the Precita Eyes organization. Stay in the Mission for dinner and drinks; this is one of the city's best neighborhoods for restaurants and watering holes.

Take It to the Bridge

Start with a stroll and a search for picnic supplies in the Marina, before heading to the gorgeous Palace of Fine Arts. If you're traveling with kids, be sure to visit the Exploratorium (closed Monday) next door. Don't miss its bizarre-but-cool Tactile Dome.

Continue west into the Presidio and make for Crissy Field, the marshland and sandy beach along the northern shore, for your picnic. With the Golden Gate Bridge view to inspire you, head onto or over the bridge itself. Be sure to wear comfortable shoes; the bridge is 1.7 mi across. Save this for a sunny day—and don't forget your jacket!

Bay Views and Real Estate Envy

Start at terraced Ina Coolbrith Park on Russian Hill for broad vistas of the bay. Ascend the Vallejo Steps and you're within easy reach of many of Russian Hill's hidden lanes. Explore famous Macondray Lane; then head around the corner to Leavenworth Street just north of Union Street and look left for the steps to equally lovely but virtually unknown Havens Place. Continue north to zigzag down crooked Lombard Street. If you still have some stamina, head west to Pacific Heights, where you can check out the Haas-Lilienthal House, a Queen Anne treasure, and scads of other Victorians. Want to snap a picture of that iconic row of "painted ladies" with the city's skyline in the background? You'll need to head to Alamo Square in the Western Addition (Hayes and Steiner streets). Finally, head back to Hyde Street for dinner at one of Russian Hill's trendy eateries.

FREE AND
ALMOST FREE

Despite—or perhaps because of—the astronomical cost of living here, San Francisco offers loads of free diversions. Here are our picks for the best free things to do in the city, in alphabetical order. (That is, in addition to the free theater that is life in San Francisco's neighborhoods, parks, beaches, churches, and other public spaces.) Also check out ⊕ *sf.funcheap. com* for a calendar of random, offbeat, and often free one-offs.

Museums and Galleries That Are Always Free

- Chinese Culture Center
- Creativity Explored
- Fort Point National Historic Site
- Museo Italo-Americano
- Octagon House
- Randall Museum
- San Francisco Cable Car Museum
- San Francisco Railway Museum
- SFMOMA Artists Gallery
- Tattoo Art Museum
- Walter & McBean Galleries at the San Francisco Art Institute
- Wells Fargo History Museum

Free Museum Times

The first week of every month brings a bonanza of free museum times.

- Asian Art Museum, first Sunday of every month
- Cartoon Art Museum, first Tuesday of every month is pay-what-you-wish
- Chinese Historical Society of America, first Thursday of every month
- de Young Museum, first Tuesday of every month
- Exploratorium, first Wednesday of every month
- Legion of Honor, first Tuesday of every month
- Museum of Craft and Folk Art, first Tuesday of every month
- San Francisco Museum of Modern Art, first Tuesday of every month
- Yerba Buena Center for the Arts (galleries), first Tuesday of every month

Free Concerts

- The Golden Gate Park Band plays free public concerts on Sunday afternoon, April through October, on the Music Concourse in the namesake park. You might hear anything from Sousa marches to show tunes.

- The San Francisco Conservatory of Music offers frequent free recitals year-round at its Civic Center home.

- Stern Grove Festival concerts, held on Sunday afternoon from June through August, are a long-standing city tradition. Performances range from opera to jazz to pop music. The amphitheater is in a beautiful eucalyptus grove, so come early and picnic before the show.

- Yerba Buena Gardens Festival hosts many concerts and performances from May through October (sometimes almost daily), including Latin jazz, global music, dance, even puppet shows.

Free Tours

- The San Francisco City Guides walking tours are easily one of the best deals going. Knowledgeable, enthusiastic guides lead walks that focus on a particular neighborhood, theme, or historical period, like Victorian architecture in Alamo Square or the bawdy days of the Barbary Coast. The tours are free, though a $5 donation is welcome.

- City Hall offers free tours of its grandiose HQ on weekdays.

More Great Experiences for $5 or Less

■ See some baseball at AT&T Park, for free! Go to the stadium's Portwalk, beyond the outfield wall, and you'll have a standing-room view of the game through the open fence. The fans who watch here are known as the Knothole Gang. BYO peanuts.

■ Visit the Golden Gate Fortune Cookie Factory in Chinatown. This is technically free, although you'll have to resist the temptation to take photos (a 50¢ fee) and buy cookies. There are several nearby spots where you can get a delicious snack for just a dollar or two, like the custard tarts at Golden Gate Bakery. Stop in one or two of Chinatown's incense-filled temples, too—it's best to give a small donation, but you'll feel a world away.

■ Do your own walking tour of the Mission District's fantastic outdoor murals, then grab a bite at a taquería or taco truck.

■ Walk across the Golden Gate Bridge—an obvious but breathtaking choice.

■ Choose a perfect treat at the Ferry Building's fabulous marketplace—maybe a scoop of Ciao Bello gelato or a croissant from Miette—and stroll the waterfront promenade toward the Bay Bridge to Cupid's Span, the giant bow-and-arrow sculpture impaling Rincon Park.

■ Visit the Diego Rivera mural at the San Francisco Art Institute, then sip a cuppa at the school's café and check out the million-dollar view from its North Beach perch.

■ Tour the grounds around the Palace of Fine Arts, circling its swan-filled lagoon. Next, walk through the Presidio to the Letterman Digital Arts Center campus.

Visit the Yoda fountain, then peek inside the building beyond to see a life-size Darth Vader figure. To further explore the Presidio, you can hop the free PresidiGo shuttle. (The Presidio also has lots of free parking.)

■ Check out the offerings at lively El Rio bar in the Mission District. They often have free live music and very cheap drink specials.

■ Hike up to the top of Telegraph Hill for sweeping city and bay views. Since the surrounding trees aren't often trimmed back, the view isn't quite as terrific as the one from the hill's Coit Tower, but it's still a knockout.

■ If you're in town on the second Thursday of the month between April and October, head to the Mission for Dolores Park Movie Night. Screenings, which start at dusk, are free—check the schedule at ⊕ www.doloresparkmovie.org. Saturday screenings happen at Dolores Park, Union Square, and Washington Square Park; see ⊕ www.sfntf.org.

■ Ride a cable car. We hate to harp on this, but you gotta do it at least once.

OFFBEAT SF

Looking for an unusual San Francisco experience that'll give you bragging rights? Try one of these quirky choices—even a local would be impressed.

16th Avenue Steps. Just standing at the base of this glorious mosaic of a stairway in the Inner Sunset is a treat: its underwater theme gives way to daytime dragonflies and butterflies, eventually transitioning to a starry, bat-studded night sky. Hike to the top, and you may have tiny Grand View Park all to yourself. The view is, well, grand. (⊠ *Moraga St., between 15th and 16th Aves.*)

ATA. Dedicated to getting anyone's art in front of an audience, Artists' Television Access has been showing films by local artists for more than 20 years. An open-minded crowd comes to ATA's tiny space, where $5 to $10 gets you a peek at what might be the next groundbreaker. ⊕ *www.atasite.org*

Audium. Billed as a "theater of sound-sculptured space," Audium is an experience like no other. Every Friday and Saturday a few dozen participants sit in concentric circles in a completely sound-proofed room in utter darkness, and music plays over the 169 speakers strategically placed, well, everywhere. ⊕ *www.audium.org*

Mt. Davidson. Ask most San Franciscans what the highest point in town is and they'll likely say Twin Peaks, but it's actually this "mountain," the next hill over. Visible from all over town but rarely visited, Mt. Davidson is topped with a eucalyptus-filled park. Finding the road up here is tricky (entrance at Dalewood and Myra ways), but once you get there you'll have amazing views—while all those tourists are still waiting for a parking space on Twin Peaks.

Nightlife at the Cal Academy of Sciences Supersize snakes, waddling penguins, and taxidermy are cool anytime, but throw in a cash bar and a DJ and this science club gets even cooler. Join the trendiest of geek crowds knocking back drinks and getting up close and personal with wild animals (with help from the academy's staffers) Thursdays from 6 pm to 10 pm; 21 and over. ⊕ *www.calacademy.org*

Nontraditional holiday celebrations. If you find yourself in town on a holiday, chances are the locals are commemorating it in an unorthodox way. Valentine's Day and you want to do something special with your honey? How about the mass pillow fight at Ferry Plaza? Easter Sunday after Mass? Check out BYOBW; at Bring Your Own Big Wheel—yes, those giant plastic ride-ons from grade-school days—often costumed grown-ups fly down the windy bit of Vermont Street with knees akimbo. Celebrations here are a bit of a non sequitur, but that's all part of the fun.

Red Hots Burlesque. Divey Mission hotspot El Rio is hopping most any night, but the saucy ladies of Red Hots Burlesque absolutely pack the house Friday evenings with their sexy, funny, body-positive show. You can even visit their School of Shimmy and take some new moves home with you.

Slides at AT&T Park. The massive Coke bottle looming over the AT&T ballpark is a familiar sight, but most people don't know that you can slide inside. The Coca-Cola Superslide has a series of slides twisting and turning down the bottle's contours. Kids aren't the only ones who get a kick out of the 56-foot "Guzzlers" and the 20-foot "Twist-Offs." It's open for free on some nongame days.

CABLE CARS

The moment it dawns on you that you severely underestimated the steepness of the San Francisco hills will likely be the same moment you look down and realize those tracks aren't just for show—or just for tourists.

Sure, locals rarely use the cable cars for commuting these days. (That's partially due to the $5 fare—hear that, Muni?) So you'll likely be packed in with plenty of fellow sightseers. You may even be approaching cable-car fatigue after seeing its image on so many souvenirs. But if you fear the magic is gone, simply climb on board, and those jaded thoughts will dissolve. Grab the pole and gawk at the view as the car clanks down an insanely steep grade toward the bay. Listen to the humming cable, the clang of the bell, and the occasional quip from the gripman. It's an experience you shouldn't pass up, whether on your first trip or your fiftieth.

HOW CABLE CARS WORK

The mechanics are pretty simple: cable cars grab a moving subterranean cable with a "grip" to go. To stop, they release the grip and apply one or more types of brakes. Four cables, totaling 9 miles, power the city's three lines. If the gripman doesn't adjust the grip just right when going up a steep hill, the cable will start to slip and the car will have to back down the hill and try again. This is an extremely rare occurrence— imagine the ribbing the gripman gets back at the cable car barn!

Gripman: Stands in front and operates the grip, brakes, and bell. Favorite joke, especially at the peak of a steep hill: "This is my first day on the job folks..."

Conductor: Moves around the car, deals with tickets, alerts the grip about what's coming up, and operates the rear wheel brakes.

❶ **Cable:** Steel wrapped around flexible sisal core; 2 inches thick; runs at a constant 9½ mph.

❷ **Bells:** Used for crew communication; alerts other drivers and pedestrians.

❸ **Grip:** Vice-like lever extends through the center slot in the track to grab or release the cable.

❹ **Grip Lever:** Left-hand lever; operates grip.

❺ **Car:** Entire car weighs 8 tons.

❻ **Wheel Brake:** Steel brake pads on each wheel.

❼ **Wheel Brake Lever:** Foot pedal; operates wheel brakes.

❽ **Rear Wheel Brake Lever:** Applied for extra traction on hills.

❾ **Track Brake:** 2-foot long sections of Monterey pine push down against the track to help stop the car.

❿ **Track Brake Lever:** Middle lever; operates track brakes.

⓫ **Emergency Brake:** 18-inch steel wedge, jams into street slot to bring car to an immediate stop.

⓬ **Emergency Brake Lever:** Right-hand lever, red; operates emergency brake.

ROUTES

Cars run at least every 15 minutes, from around 6 AM to about 1 AM.

Powell–Hyde line: Most scenic, with classic Bay views. Begins at Powell and Market streets, then crosses Nob Hill and Russian Hill before a white-knuckle descent down Hyde Street, ending near the Hyde Street Pier.

Powell–Mason line: Also begins at Powell and Market streets, but winds through North Beach to Bay and Taylor streets, a few blocks from Fisherman's Wharf.

California line: Runs from the foot of Market Street, at Drumm Street, up Nob Hill and back. Great views (and aromas and sounds) of Chinatown on the way up. Sit in back to catch glimpses of the Bay. ■TIP➜ Take the California line if it's just the cable-car experience you're after—the lines are shorter, and the grips and conductors say it's friendlier and has a slower pace.

RULES OF THE RIDE

Tickets. A whopping $5 each way. There are ticket booths at all three turnarounds, or you can pay the conductor after you board (they can make change). Try not to grumble about the price—they're embarrassed enough as it is.

■TIP➜ If you're planning to use public transit a few times, or if you'd like to ride back and forth on the cable car without worrying about the price, consider a one-day Muni passport ($14). You can get passports online, at the Powell Street turnaround, the TIX booth on Union Square, or the Fisherman's Wharf cable-car ticket booth at Beach and Hyde streets.

All Aboard. You can board on either side of the cable car. It's legal to stand on the running boards and hang on to the pole, but keep your ears open for the gripman's warnings. ■TIP➜ Grab a seat on the outside bench for the best views.

Most people wait (and wait) in line at one of the cable car turnarounds, but you can also hop on along the route. Board wherever you see a white sign showing a figure climbing aboard a brown cable car; wave to the approaching driver, and wait until the car stops.

Riding on the running boards can be part of the thrill.

CABLE CAR HISTORY

HALLIDIE FREES THE HORSES

In the 1850s and '60s, San Francisco's streetcars were drawn by horses. Legend has it that the horrible sight of a car dragging a team of horses downhill to their deaths roused Andrew Smith Hallidie to action. The English immigrant had invented the "Hallidie Ropeway," essentially a cable car for mined ore, and he was convinced that his invention could also move people. In 1873, Hallidie and his intrepid crew prepared to test the first cable car high on Russian Hill. The anxious engineer peered down into the foggy darkness, failed to see the bottom of the hill, and promptly turned the controls over to Hallidie. Needless to say, the thing worked . . . but rides were free for the first two days because people were afraid to get on.

SEE IT FOR YOURSELF

The **Cable Car Museum** is one of the city's best free offerings and an absolute must for kids. (You can even ride a cable car there, since all three lines stop between Russian Hill and Nob Hill.) The museum, which is inside the city's last cable-car barn, takes the top off the system to let you see how it all works.

Eternally humming and squealing, the massive powerhouse cable wheels steal the show. You can also climb aboard a vintage car and take the grip, let the kids ring a cable-car bell (briefly, please!), and check out vintage gear dating from 1873.

✉ *1201 Mason St., at Washington St., Nob Hill* ☎ *415/474–1887* ⊕ *www. cablecarmuseum.com* ⊠ *Free* ⊙ *Oct.– Mar., daily 10–5; Apr.–Sept., daily 10–6*

■ **TIP→** The gift shop sells cable car paraphernalia, including an authentic gripman's bell for $600 (it'll sound like Powell Street in your house every day). For significantly less, you can pick up a key chain made from a piece of worn-out cable.

CHAMPION OF THE CABLE CAR BELL

Each June the city's best and brightest come together to crown a bell-ringing champion at Union Square. The crowd cheers gripmen and conductors as they stomp, shake, and riff with the rope. But it's not a popularity contest; the ringers are judged by former bell-ringing champions who take each ping and gong very seriously.

Union Square and Chinatown

WORD OF MOUTH

"Grant Street is the 'tourist's' Chinatown. The 'real one' is one block west on Stockton."

— StuDudley

GETTING ORIENTED

TOP 5 REASONS TO GO

Ross Alley, Chinatown: Breathe in the scented air as you watch the nimble hands at Golden Gate Fortune Cookie Factory, then kick back with a cocktail at Li Po around the corner, rumored to be haunted by the ghost of an opium junkie still looking to score.

Return to noir San Francisco: Have a late martini lunch under the gaze of the Maltese Falcon at John's Grill, then swing through the lobby of the Flood Building and nod to the other Maltese Falcon there.

Shop the Square: Prime your credit cards and dive right in, from Bloomie's to the boutiques of Maiden Lane.

Tin How Temple: Climb the narrow stairway to this space with hundreds of red lanterns, then step onto the tiny balcony and take in the alley scene below.

Elevator at the St. Francis: Ride a glass elevator to the sky (or the 32nd floor) for a gorgeous view of the cityscape, especially in the evening when the lights come up.

QUICK BITES

It's a hardy soul that can pass by **Cako Bakery** (⊠ *211 O'Farrell St., Union Square* ☎ *415/404–7303*) without succumbing to the siren call of the perfect cupcake.

Eastern Bakery (⊠ *720 Grant Ave., Chinatown* ☎ *415/433–7973*) claims to be the oldest bakery in Chinatown. The packed little space has become a must-stop on the tourist trail. But it's not a tourist trap, since their goods back up their rep, and the dirt-cheap steamed pork buns make a terrific lunch on the go.

If you're after a substantial bite to eat, duck into the **Irish Bank** (⊠ *10 Mark La., Union Square* ☎ *415/788–7152*), across from the Chinatown Gate, for fish-and-chips.

GETTING THERE

In these two neighborhoods, cars equal hassle. Traffic is slow and parking is pricey. Save yourself the frustration and take advantage of the confluence of public transit at Powell and Market streets; buses, BART (Powell Street Station), cable cars, and F-line streetcars run here.

For the love of Buddha, don't drive in Chinatown! The steep, narrow, one-way streets are notoriously difficult to navigate by car. Both Powell lines of the cable-car system pass through. You can also take the 30–Stockton bus; this route is a virtual "Chinatown Express," running from Fisherman's Wharf down Stockton Street through Chinatown to Union Square.

MAKING THE MOST OF YOUR TIME

Set aside at least an hour to scope out the stores and sights in and around Union Square—or most of the day if you're a shopper—but don't bother arriving before 10 am, when the first shops open. Sunday is a bit quieter.

Give yourself at least two hours to see compact Chinatown. If possible, come on a weekday (less crowded) and before lunchtime (busiest with locals). You won't need more than 15 or 20 minutes at any of the sights themselves, but exploring the shops and alleys is, indeed, the whole point.

2

Sightseeing
★★★
Nightlife
★
Dining
★★★
Lodging
★★★★★
Shopping
★★★★★

The Union Square area bristles with big-city bravado, while just a stone's throw away is a place that feels like a city unto itself, Chinatown. The two areas share a strong commercial streak, although manifested very differently. In Union Square the crowds zigzag among international brands, trailing glossy shopping bags. A few blocks north, people dash between small neighborhood stores, their arms draped with plastic totes filled with groceries or souvenirs.

Updated by
Denise M. Leto

The city's finest department stores put on their best faces in Union Square, along with such exclusive emporiums as Tiffany & Co. and Prada, and such big-name franchises as Niketown, Apple Store, H&M, and Barney's. Visitors lay their heads at several dozen hotels within a three-block walk of the square, and the downtown theater district and many fine-arts galleries are nearby. By any measure, Union Square is shop-centric; if you're not that into shopping, you can find little beyond buildings of vague historical interest to entice you here.

A few blocks uphill is the abrupt beginning of dense and insular Chinatown—the oldest such community in the country. When the street signs have Chinese characters, produce stalls crowd pedestrians off the sidewalk, and folks scurry by with telltale pink plastic shopping bags, you'll know you're there. (The neighborhood huddles together in the 17 blocks and 41 alleys bordered roughly by Bush, Kearny, and Powell streets and Broadway.) Chinatown has been attracting the curious for more than 100 years, and no neighborhood in the city absorbs as many tourists without seeming to forfeit its character. Join the flow and step into another world. Good-luck banners of crimson and gold hang beside dragon-entwined lampposts and pagoda roofs, while honking cars chime in with shoppers bargaining loudly in Cantonese or Mandarin.

UNION SQUARE

TOP ATTRACTIONS

Maiden Lane. Known as Morton Street in the raffish Barbary Coast era, this former red-light district reported at least one murder a week during the late 19th century. Things cooled down after the 1906 fire destroyed the brothels, and these days Maiden Lane is a chic, boutique-lined pedestrian mall stretching two blocks, between Stockton and Kearny streets. Wrought-iron gates close the street to traffic most days between 11 and 5, when the lane becomes a patchwork of umbrella-shaded tables.

At **140 Maiden Lane** you can see the only Frank Lloyd Wright building in San Francisco. Walking through the brick archway and recessed entry feels a bit like entering a glowing cave. The interior's graceful, curving ramp and skylights are said to have been his model for the Guggenheim Museum in New York. Xanadu Gallery, which showcases Baltic, Latin American, and African folk art, now occupies the space. ⊠ *Between Stockton and Kearny Sts., Union Square.*

Union Square. Ground zero for big-name shopping in the city and within walking distance of most hotels, Union Square is home base for many visitors. The St. Francis and Macy's line two sides of the square, with Saks, Neiman-Marcus, and the Levi's Store bordering the other sides, and the shopping titan that is Bloomie's just a few blocks down the cable-car tracks. Considered the heart of San Francisco's downtown since 1850, the landscaped, 2½-acre square is about the only place you can sit for free in this part of town. Back in 2002, the public responded to Union Square's redesign with a resounding shrug. With its pretty landscaping, easier street access, and the addition of a café (welcome, but nothing special), it certainly was an improvement over the previous concrete wasteland. Four globular lamp sculptures by the artist R.M. Fischer preside over the space; there's also a café, an open-air stage, a visitor information booth, and a front-row seat to the cable-car tracks. And there's a familiar kaleidoscope of characters: office workers sunning and brown-bagging, street musicians, shoppers taking a rest, kids chasing pigeons, and a fair number of homeless people.

The square takes its name from the violent pro-Union demonstrations staged here before the Civil War. At center stage, Robert Ingersoll Aitken's *Victory Monument* commemorates Commodore George Dewey's victory over the Spanish fleet at Manila in 1898. The 97-foot Corinthian column, topped by a

CABLE CAR TERMINUS

Two of the three cable-car lines begin and end their runs at Powell and Market streets, a couple of blocks south of Union Square. These two lines are the most scenic, and both pass near Fisherman's Wharf, so they're usually clogged with first-time sightseers. The wait to board a cable car at this intersection is longer than at any other stop in the system. If you'd rather avoid the mob, board the less-touristy California line at the bottom of Market Street, at Drumm Street. ⇨ *For more info on the cable cars, see the Experience San Francisco chapter.*

The epicenter of high-end shopping, Union Square is lined with department stores.

bronze figure symbolizing naval conquest, was dedicated by Theodore Roosevelt in 1903 and withstood the 1906 earthquake. After the earthquake and fire of 1906, the square was dubbed Little St. Francis because of the temporary shelter erected for residents of the St. Francis Hotel. Actor John Barrymore (grandfather of actress Drew Barrymore and a notorious carouser) was among the guests pressed into volunteering to stack bricks in the square. His uncle, thespian John Drew, remarked, "It took an act of God to get John out of bed and the United States Army to get him to work."

On the eastern edge of Union Square, **TIX Bay Area** (☎ *415/433–7827 info only* ⊕ *www.theatrebayarea.org*) provides half-price day-of-performance tickets to all types of performing-arts events, as well as regular full-price box-office services. Union Square covers a convenient four-level garage, allegedly the first underground garage in the world. ⊠ *Bordered by Powell, Stockton, Post, and Geary Sts., Union Square.*

WORTH NOTING

American Conservatory Theater. The 1906 earthquake destroyed all eight of downtown San Francisco's theaters, and this one, a neoclassical stunner, stepped up to the plate a year later. Today it's inextricably linked with its eponymous repertory company, known for award-winning productions by major playwrights such as Tony Kushner (*Angels in America*) and Tom Stoppard (premieres of *Indian Ink*, *The Invention of Love*), and cutting-edge works such as *The Black Rider* by Tom Waits, William S. Burroughs, and Robert Wilson. Damaged heavily in the 1989 earthquake, the building has been beautifully restored. ⊠ *415 Geary St., box office at 405 Geary St., Union Square* ☎ *415/749–2228.*

2

Hallidie Building. Named for cable-car inventor Andrew S. Hallidie, this 1918 structure is best viewed from across the street. Willis Polk's revolutionary glass-curtain wall—believed to be the world's first such facade—hangs a foot beyond the reinforced concrete of the frame. The reflecting glass, decorative exterior fire escapes that appear to be metal balconies, and Venetian Gothic cornice are notably lovely. ⊠ *130 Sutter St., between Kearny and Montgomery Sts., Union Square.*

Lotta's Fountain. Saucy gold rush–era actress, singer, and dancer Lotta Crabtree so aroused the city's miners that they were known to shower her with gold nuggets and silver dollars after her performances. The peculiar, rather clunky fountain was her way of saying thanks to her fans. Given to the city in 1875, the fountain became a meeting place for survivors after the 1906 earthquake. Each April 18, the anniversary of the quake, San Franciscans gather at this quirky monument. You can see an image of Lotta herself in one of the Anton Refregier murals in Rincon Center. ⊠ *Traffic triangle at intersection of 3rd, Market, Kearny, and Geary Sts., Union Square.*

San Francisco Visitor Information Center. A multilingual staff operates this facility below the cable-car terminus. Staffers answer questions and provide maps and pamphlets. You can also pick up discount coupons—the savings can be significant, especially for families—and hotel brochures here. If you're planning to hit the big-ticket stops like the California Academy of Sciences, the Exploratorium, and SFMOMA, and ride the cable cars, consider picking up a CityPass here (or at any of the attractions it covers). ■TIP➔ The CityPass ($64, $39 ages 5–12), good for nine days including seven days of transit, will save you about 50%. Also buy your Muni Passport here. ⊠ *Hallidie Plaza, lower level, Powell and Market Sts., Union Square* ☎ *415/391–2000 or 415/283–0177* ⊕ *www.onlyinsanfrancisco.com* ⊙ *Weekdays 9–5, Sat. 9–3; also Sun. 9–3 May–Oct.*

Westin St. Francis Hotel. The second-oldest hotel in the city, established in 1904, was conceived by railroad baron and financier Charles Crocker and his associates as a hostelry for their millionaire friends. Swift service and sumptuous surroundings have always been hallmarks of the property. After the hotel was ravaged by the 1906 fire, a larger, more luxurious Italian Renaissance–style residence was opened in 1907 to attract loyal

> **LOOK UP!**
>
> When wandering around Chinatown, don't forget to look up! Above the chintziest souvenir shop might loom an ornate balcony or a curly pagoda roof. The best examples are on the 900 block of Grant Avenue (at Washington Street) and at Waverly Place.

clients from among the world's rich and powerful. The hotel's checkered past includes the ill-fated 1921 bash in the suite of the silent-film comedian Fatty Arbuckle, at which a woman became ill and later died. Arbuckle endured three sensational trials for rape and murder before being acquitted, by which time his career was kaput. In 1975 Sara Jane Moore, standing among a crowd outside the hotel, attempted to shoot then-president Gerald Ford. As might be imagined, no plaques in the lobby commemorate these events. ■TIP➜ One of the best views in the city is from the glass elevators here—and best of all, a ride is free. Zip up to the 32nd floor for a bird's-eye view; the lights of the nighttime cityscape are particularly lovely. Don't be shy if you're not a guest: some visitors make this a stop every time they're in town. Every November the hotel's pastry chef creates a spectacular, rotating 12-foot gingerbread castle, on display in the grand lobby—a fun holiday treat for families. ✉ *335 Powell St., at Geary St., Union Square* ☎ *415/397–7000* ⊕ *www. westinstfrancis.com.*

CHINATOWN

TOP ATTRACTIONS

Chinatown Gate. This is the official entrance to Chinatown. Stone lions flank the base of the pagoda-topped gate; the lions, dragons, and fish up top symbolize wealth, prosperity, and other good things. The four Chinese characters immediately beneath the pagoda represent the philosophy of Sun Yat-sen (1866–1925), the leader who unified China in the early 20th century. Sun Yat-sen, who lived in exile in San Francisco for a few years, promoted the notion of friendship and peace among all nations based on equality, justice, and goodwill. The vertical characters under the left pagoda read "peace" and "trust," the ones under the right pagoda "respect" and "love." The whole shebang usually telegraphs the internationally understood message of "photo op." ✉ *Grant Ave. at Bush St., Chinatown.*

Tin How Temple. Duck into the inconspicuous doorway, climb three flights of stairs—on the second floor is a mah-jongg parlor whose patrons hope the spirits above will favor them—and be assaulted by the aroma of incense in this tiny, altar-filled room. Day Ju, one of the first three Chinese to arrive in San Francisco, dedicated this temple to

Where can I find . . . ?

PARKING	**Sutter-Stockton Garage** (444 Stockton St.) Reasonable prices and not too crowded.	**North Beach Parking Garage** (735 Vallejo St.) Relatively clean and roomy.
A DRUGSTORE	**Walgreens** (459 Powell St.) Open 24 hours.	**Walgreens** (776 Market St.) Open 7 am–9 pm.
A NIGHTCAP	**The Hidden Vine Wine Bar** (620 Post St.) A quiet spot that pours mostly California wines.	**Bourbon & Branch** (501 Jones St.) Worth calling ahead to sip such outstanding cocktails.

the Queen of the Heavens and the Goddess of the Seven Seas in 1852. In the temple's entryway, elderly ladies can often be seen preparing "money" to be burned as offerings to various Buddhist gods or as funds for ancestors to use in the afterlife. Hundreds of red-and-gold lanterns cover the ceiling; the larger the lamp, the larger its donor's contribution to the temple. Gifts of oranges, dim sum, and money left by the faithful, who kneel mumbling prayers, rest on altars to various gods. Tin How presides over the middle back of the temple, flanked by one red and one green lesser god. Take a good look around, since taking photographs is not allowed. ⊠ *125 Waverly Pl., Chinatown* ☎ *No phone* ✉ *Free, donations accepted* ⊙ *Daily 9–4.*

WORTH NOTING

Chinese Culture Center. Mostly a place for the community to gather for calligraphy and Mandarin classes, the center also houses a gallery with occasionally interesting temporary exhibits by Chinese and Chinese-American artists. ⊠ *Hilton, 750 Kearny St., 3rd fl., Chinatown* ☎ *415/986–1822* ⊕ *www.c-c-c.org* ✉ *Free* ⊙ *Tues.–Sat. 11–4.*

Chinese Historical Society of America Museum and Learning Center. This airy, light-filled gallery has displays about the Chinese-American experience from 19th-century agriculture to 21st-century food and fashion trends, including a moving collection of racist games and toys. A separate room hosts rotating exhibits by contemporary Chinese-American artists. ⊠ *965 Clay St., Chinatown* ☎ *415/391–1188* ⊕ *www.chsa.org* ✉ *$3, free 1st Thurs. of month* ⊙ *Tues.–Fri. noon–5, Sat. 11–4.*

Chinese Six Companies. Once the White House of Chinatown, this striking building has balconies and lion-supported columns. Begun as an umbrella group for the many family and regional *tongs* (mutual-aid and fraternal organizations) that sprang up to help gold-rush immigrants, the Chinese Six Companies functioned as a government within Chinatown, settling disputes among members and fighting against anti-Chinese laws. The business leaders who ran the six companies (which

Chinatown bursts into color and light on Chinese New Year.

still exist) dominated the neighborhood's political and economic life for decades. The building is closed to the public. ✉ *843 Stockton St., Chinatown.*

🅒 **Golden Gate Fortune Cookie Factory.** Follow your nose down Ross Alley to this tiny but fragrant cookie factory. Workers sit at circular motorized griddles and wait for dollops of batter to drop onto a tiny metal plate, which rotates into an oven. A few moments later out comes a cookie that's pliable and ready for folding. It's easy to peek in for a moment, and hard to leave without a few free samples. A bagful of cookies—with mildly racy "adult" fortunes or more benign ones—costs about $4. You can also purchase the cookies "fortuneless" in their waferlike unfolded state, which makes snacking that much more efficient. Being allowed to photograph the cookie makers at work will set you back 50¢. ✉ *56 Ross Alley, west of and parallel to Grant Ave., between Washington and Jackson Sts., Chinatown* ☎ *415/781–3956* ✆ *Free* ☽ *Daily 9–8.*

Kong Chow Temple. This ornate temple sets a somber, spiritual tone right away with a sign warning visitors not to touch *anything.* The god to whom the members of this temple pray represents honesty and trust. Chinese stores and restaurants often display his image because he's thought to bring good luck in business. Chinese immigrants established the temple in 1851; its congregation moved to this building in 1977. Take the elevator up to the fourth floor, where incense fills the air. You can show respect by placing a dollar or two in the donation box and by leaving your camera in its case. Amid the statuary, flowers, and richly colored altars (red wards off evil spirits and signifies virility, green symbolizes longevity, and gold connotes majesty), a couple of

CLOSE UP

Chinatown Tongs

If you take it from Hollywood, Chinese *tongs* (secretive fraternal associations) rank right up there with the Italian Mafia and the Japanese yakuza. The general public perception is one of an honor-bound brotherhood with an impenetrable code of silence; fortunes amassed through prostitution and narcotics; and disputes settled in a hail of gunfire, preferably in a crowded restaurant. In fact, the tongs began as an innocent community service—but for roughly a century there's been more than a little truth to the sensational image.

When Chinese immigrants first arrived in San Francisco during the gold rush, they made a beeline for an appropriate tong. These benevolent organizations welcomed people from specific regions of China, or those with certain family names, and helped new arrivals get a foothold. For thousands of men otherwise alone in the city, these tongs were a vital social connection. It didn't take long, however, until offers of protection services ushered in a new criminal element, casting a sinister shadow over all the tongs, legitimate or not.

As gambling parlors, illegal lotteries, opium dens, and brothels took root, many tongs became the go-to sources for turf protection and retribution. Early on, the muscles behind the tongs became known as "hatchet men" for their weapons of choice. (They believed guns made too much noise.)

"Tong wars" regularly broke out between competing groups, with especially blood-soaked periods in the 1920s and 1970s. Today the tongs are less influential than at the turn of the 20th century, but they remain a major part of Chinatown life, as they own large swaths of real estate and provide care for the elderly. The criminal side is alive and well, profiting from prostitution and drugs and doing a brisk business in pirated music and DVDs. Violence still erupts, too. In 2006 Allen Leung, a prominent community leader, was shot dead in his shop on Jackson Street. Among his activities, Leung was a very influential "dragon head" of the Hop Sing tong, a group involved in prostitution, the heroin trade, and other underground activities. And just as in the movies, no one's talking.

—Denise M. Leto

plaques announce that "Mrs. Harry S. Truman came to this temple in June 1948 for a prediction on the outcome of the election . . . this fortune came true." The temple's balcony has a good view of Chinatown. ⊠ *855 Stockton St., Chinatown* ☎ *No phone* 🖭 *Free* ☉ *Mon.–Sat. 9–4.*

Old Chinese Telephone Exchange. After the 1906 earthquake, many Chinatown buildings were rebuilt in Western style with pagoda roof and fancy balconies slapped on. This building—today the Bank of Canton—is the exception, an example of top-to-bottom Chinese architecture. The intricate three-tier pagoda was built in 1909. The exchange's operators were renowned for their prodigious memories, about which the San Francisco Chamber of Commerce boasted in 1914: "These girls respond all day with hardly a mistake to calls that are given (in English or one of five Chinese dialects) by the name of the subscriber instead of by his number—a mental feat that would be practically impossible to most high-schooled American misses." ⊠ *Bank of Canton, 743 Washington St., Chinatown.*

Old St. Mary's Cathedral. Dedicated in 1854, this served as the city's Catholic cathedral until 1891. The verse below the massive clock face beseeched naughty Barbary Coast boys: "Son, observe the time and fly from evil." Across the street from the church in **St. Mary's Square,** a statue of Sun Yat-sen towers over the site of the Chinese leader's favorite reading spot during his years in San Francisco. ■TIP→ A surprisingly peaceful spot, St. Mary's Square also has a couple of small, well-kept playgrounds, perfect for a break from the hustle and bustle of Chinatown. ⊠ *Grant Ave. and California St., Chinatown.*

GOSPEL CONCERTS

For a rockin' gospel concert and inclusive, feel-good vibe, head to **Glide Memorial Church** (⊠ *Ellis and Taylor Sts., Tenderloin*) on the edge of the sketchy Tenderloin, Sunday morning at 9 and 11. Reverend Cecil Williams, a bear of a man, is a local celeb do-gooder who leads a hand-clapping, shout-it-out, get-on-your-feet "celebration" that attracts a diverse and enthusiastic crowd. Visitors—gay and straight, all colors of the rainbow, religious or not—are welcome (and plentiful). You might recognize the church from the film *The Pursuit of Happyness.*

Portsmouth Square. Chinatown's living room buzzes with activity. The square, with its pagoda-shape structures, is a favorite spot for morning tai chi; by noon dozens of men huddle around Chinese chess tables, engaged in not-always-legal competition. Kids scamper about the square's two grungy playgrounds (warning: the bathrooms are sketchy). Back in the late 19th century this land was near the waterfront, and Robert Louis Stevenson, the author of *Treasure Island,* often dropped by, chatting up the sailors who hung out here. Some of the information he gleaned about life at sea found its way into his fiction. A bronze galleon sculpture, a tribute to Stevenson, is anchored in a corner of the square. ⊠ *Bordered by Walter Lum Pl. and Kearny, Washington, and Clay Sts., Chinatown.*

CHINATOWN

Chinatown's streets flood the senses. Incense and cigarette smoke mingle with the scents of briny fish and sweet vanilla. Rooflines flare outward, pagoda-style. Loud Cantonese bargaining and honking car horns rise above the sharp clack of mah-jongg tiles and the eternally humming cables beneath the street.

Most Chinatown visitors march down Grant Avenue, buy a few trinkets, and call it a day. Do yourself a favor and dig deeper. This is one of the largest Chinese communities outside Asia, and there is far more to it than buying a back-scratcher near Chinatown Gate. To get a real feel for the neighborhood, wander off the main drag. Step into a temple or an herb shop and wander down a flag-draped alley. And don't be shy: residents welcome guests warmly, though rarely in English.

Whatever you do, don't leave without eating something. Noodle houses, bakeries, tea houses, and dim sum shops seem to occupy every other storefront. There's a feast for your eyes as well: in the market windows on Stockton and Grant, you'll see hanging whole roast ducks, fish, and shellfish swimming in tanks, and strips of shiny, pink-glazed Chinese-style barbecued pork. (For the scoop on dim sum, *see* the Union Square and Chinatown spotlight in the Where to Eat chapter.)

CHINATOWN'S HISTORY

Sam Brannan's 1848 cry of "Gold!" didn't take long to reach across the world to China. Struggling with famine, drought, and political upheaval at home, thousands of Chinese jumped at the chance to try their luck in California. Most came from the Pearl River Delta region, in the Guangdong province, and spoke Cantonese dialects. From the start, Chinese businesses circled around Portsmouth Square, which was conveniently central. Bachelor rooming houses sprang up, since the vast majority of new arrivals were men. By 1853, the area was called Chinatown.

The Street of Gamblers (Ross Alley), 1898 (top). The first Chinese telephone operator in Chinatown (bottom).

COLD WELCOME

The Chinese faced discrimination from the get-go. Harrassment became outright hostility as first the gold rush, then the work on the Transcontinental Railroad petered out. Special taxes were imposed to shoulder aside competing "coolie labor." Laws forbidding the Chinese from moving outside Chinatown kept the residents packed in like sardines, with nowhere to go but up and down—thus the many basement establishments in the neighborhood. State and federal laws passed in the 1870s deterred Chinese women from immigrating, deeming them prostitutes. In the late 1870s, looting and arson attacks on Chinatown businesses soared.

The coup de grace, though, was the Chinese Exclusion Act, passed by the U.S.

Chinatown's Grant Avenue.

Women and children flooded into the neighborhood after the Great Quake.

Congress in 1882, which slammed the doors to America for "Asiatics." This was the country's first significant restriction on immigration. The law also prevented the existing Chinese residents, including American-born children, from becoming naturalized citizens. With a society of mostly men (forbidden, of course, from marrying white women), San Francisco hoped that Chinatown would simply die out.

OUT OF THE ASHES
When the devastating 1906 earthquake and fire hit, city fathers thought they'd seize the opportunity to kick the Chinese out of Chinatown and get their hands on that desirable piece of downtown real estate. Then Chinatown businessman Look Tin Eli had a brainstorm of Disneyesque proportions.

He proposed that Chinatown be rebuilt, but in a tourist-friendly, stylized, "Oriental" way. Anglo-American architects would design new buildings with pagoda roofs and dragon-covered columns. Chinatown would attract more tourists—the curious had been visiting on the sly

for decades—and add more tax money to the city's coffers. Ka-ching: the sales pitch worked.

PAPER SONS
For the Chinese, the 1906 earthquake turned the virtual "no entry" sign into a flashing neon "welcome!" All the city's immigration records went up in smoke, and the Chinese quickly began to apply for passports as U.S. citizens, claiming their old ones were lost in the fire. Not only did thousands of Chinese become legal overnight, but so did their sons in China, or "sons," if they weren't really related. Whole families in Chinatown had passports in names that weren't their own; these "paper sons" were not only a windfall but also an uncomfortable neighborhood conspiracy. The city caught on eventually and set up an immigration center on Angel Island in 1910. Immigrants spent weeks or months being inspected and interrogated while their papers were checked. Roughly 250,000 people made it through. With this influx, including women and children, Chinatown finally became a more complete community.

A GREAT WALK THROUGH CHINATOWN

■ Start at the Chinatown Gate and walk ahead on Grant Avenue, entering the souvenir gauntlet. (You'll also pass Old St. Mary's Cathedral.)

■ Make a right on Clay Street and walk to Portsmouth Square. Sometimes it feels like the whole neighborhood's here, playing chess and exercising.

■ Head up Washington Street to the elaborately pagodaed Old Chinese Telephone Exchange building, now the Bank of Canton. Across Grant, look left for Waverly Place. Here Republic of China flags flap over some of the neighborhood's most striking buildings, including Tin How Temple.

■ At the Sacramento Street end of Waverly Place stands the oddly beautiful brick First Chinese Baptist Church of 1908. Just across the way, the Clarion Music Center is chock-full of unusual instruments, as well as exquisite lion-dance sets.

■ Head back to Washington Street and check out the herb shops, like the Superior Trading Company (No. 839) and the Great China Herb Co. (No. 857).

■ Follow the scent of vanilla from Washington Street down Ross Alley (entrance across from Superior Trading Company) to the Golden Gate Fortune Cookie Factory. Then head across the alley to Sam Bo Trading Co., where religious items are stacked chockablock in the narrow space. Tell the friendly owners your troubles and they'll prepare a package of joss papers, joss sticks, and candles, and tell you how and when to offer them up.

■ Turn left on Jackson Street; ahead is the real Chinatown's main artery, Stockton Street. This is where most residents do their grocery shopping; if it's Saturday, get ready for throngs (and their elbows). Look toward the back of stores for Buddhist altars with offerings of oranges and grapefruit. From here you can loop one block east back to Grant.

ALL THE TEA IN CHINATOWN

Preparing a perfect brew at Red Blossom Tea.

San Francisco's close ties to Asia have always made it more tea-conscious than other American burgs, but these days the city is in the throes of a tea renaissance, with new tasting rooms popping up in every neighborhood. Below are our favorite spots for every tea under the sun.

Red Blossom Tea. A light and modern shop—the staff really know their stuff. It's a favorite among younger tea enthusiasts, who swear by its excellent bang-for-the-buck value. While Red Blossom doesn't do formal tastings or sell tea by the cup, they'll gladly brew up perfect samples of the teas you're interested in. ✉ *831 Grant Ave.* ☎ *415/395–0868.*

Vital Tea Leaf. Tastings here work like those for wine—one of the gregarious, knowledgeable servers chooses the teas and describes them as you sample. It's a great spot for tea newbies to get their feet wet without a hard sell, but local connoisseurs grumble about the high prices and the self-promotion. ✉ *1044 Grant Ave.* ☎ *415/981–2388.*

Imperial Tea Court. If you want to visit the most respected of traditional tea purveyors, you'll need to venture outside of Chinatown. Imperial Tea Court's serene Powell Street oasis closed unexpectedly in 2007, but you'll find the same great selection and expertise at their fancy new digs in the Ferry Building. ☎ *415/544–9830.*

WAITING FOR CUSTARD

As you're strolling down Grant Avenue, past the plastic Buddhas and yin/yang balls, be sure to stop at the Golden Gate Bakery (No. 1029) for some delicious eggy *dan tat* (custard tarts). These flaky-crusted treats are heaven for just a buck. There's often a line, but it's worth the wait.

DON'T-MISS SHOPS

Locals snap up flowers from an outdoor vendor.

If you're in the market for a pair of chirping metal crickets (oh you'll hear them, trust us), you can duck into any of the obvious souvenir-stuffed storefronts. But if you're looking for something special, head for these tempting sources. ■TIP➔ Fierce neighborhood competition keeps prices within reason, but for popular wares like jade, it pays to shop around before making a serious investment. Many stores accept cash only.

Chinatown Kite Shop. Family-run shop selling bright, fun-shaped kites—dragons, butterflies, sharks—since the 1960s. ✉ *717 Grant Ave.* ☎ *415/989–5182.*

Dragon House. A veritable museum: the store sells authentic, centuries-old antiques like ivory carvings. ✉ *455 Grant Ave.* ☎ *415/421–3693.*

Old Shanghai. One of the largest selections of hand-painted robes, formal dresses, and jackets in Chinatown, plus chic Asian-inspired pieces. ✉ *645 Grant Ave.* ☎ *415/986–1222.*

CHINATOWN WITH KIDS

It can be tough for the little ones to keep their hands to themselves, especially when all sorts of curios spill out onto the sidewalk at just the right height. To burn off some steam (in them) and relieve some stress (in you), take them to the small but spruce playground in St. Mary's Square, across California from Old St. Mary's. If that setting's too tranquil, head to the more boisterous Willie Wong Playground, on Sacramento Street at Waverly Place.

SoMa and Civic Center

WORD OF MOUTH

"The Asian Art Museum was fantastic! I wouldn't characterize myself as someone who's into Asian art, but I was pleasantly surprised and really enjoyed myself. . . . If you only have an hour to spare, you can see most of the museum."

—CarolM

GETTING ORIENTED

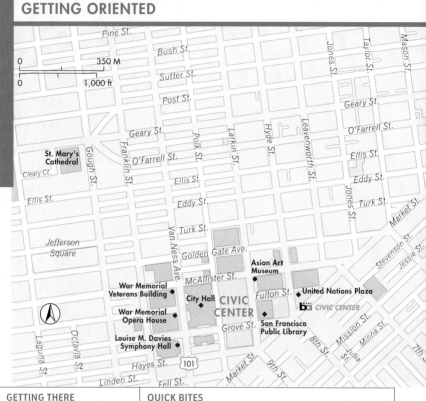

GETTING THERE	QUICK BITES
For most SoMa visitors, who stick close to SFMOMA and the Yerba Buena Gardens, getting here is a matter of walking roughly 10 minutes from Union Square, less from the Market Street transit.	Above the Martin Luther King Jr. memorial in the Yerba Buena Gardens, the **Samovar Tea Lounge** (⊠ *730 Howard St., SoMa* 🖀 *415/227–9400*) is a serene retreat with glass walls overlooking an infinity pool. Especially on a blustery day, the organic and fair-trade teas hit the spot.
It's best to reach Civic Center by BART, bus, or F-line. Hoofing it from Union Square requires walking through the unsavory Tenderloin area, and from SoMa it's a long, ugly haul.	Metreon's **Taste of San Francisco** (⊠ *101 4th St., between Mission and Howard Sts., SoMa*) is the perfect spot to grab all the fixings for an alfresco lunch. Choose sushi from Sanraku or a generous burrito from Luna Azul and stake out a spot in the Yerba Buena Gardens.
After dark, safety concerns dictate a cab for both neighborhoods.	If you see a clutch of people gathered around what looks like a garage in Hayes Valley, chances are you've stumbled upon **Blue Bottle Coffee** (⊠ *315 Linden St., Hayes Valley* 🖀 *415/252–7535*), a tiny stand selling what many claim is the best organic coffee on the planet. The "artisanal microroasting" philosophy says that all coffee should be brewed within 24 hours of roasting, and yes, they are Very Serious.

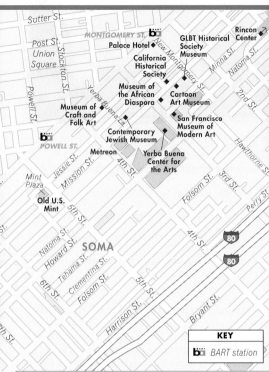

3

TOP 5 REASONS TO GO

SFMOMA: Big-name modern art exhibits in a durably cool building.

Asian Art Museum: Stand face-to-face with a massive gold Buddha in one of the world's largest collections of Asian art.

Club-hopping in SoMa: Shake it with the cool, friendly crowd that fills SoMa's dance clubs until the wee hours, and all weekend long at the EndUp.

Yerba Buena Gardens: Gather picnic provisions and choose a spot on the grass in downtown's oasis.

Hanging out at Patricia's Green: Grab a cup of coffee (Blue Bottle's just around the corner) and head to the narrow swath of park that serves as hopping Hayes Valley's living room. Check out the monumental temporary art exhibit—it always has an interactive element—and the little ones clambering on the fantastic climbing dome.

MAKING THE MOST OF YOUR TIME

You could spend all day museum-hopping in SoMa. Allow two hours to see SFMOMA; if there's a big show on, avoid the line by buying tickets online and arrive early to beat the throngs. An hour each should do it for the Museum of the African Diaspora, the Contemporary Jewish Museum, and the Center for the Arts, less than that for the minor museums.

SoMa after dark is another adventure entirely. More interested in merlot or megaclubs than Matisse? Start here around 8 pm for dinner, then move on to a bar or dance spot. *See the Where to Eat and Nightlife chapters for our top recommendations.*

Don't be suckered by visions of grand architecture and "important" performing-arts venues in Civic Center. Unless you have tickets to the opera, ballet, or a concert, there's no good reason for you to spend much time here.

Sightseeing
★★★
Nightlife
★★★★
Dining
★★★
Lodging
★★★★
Shopping
★

To a newcomer, SoMa (short for "south of Market") and Civic Center may look like cheek-by-jowl neighbors—they're divided by Market Street. To locals, though, these areas are firmly separate entities, especially since Market Street itself is considered such a strong demarcation line. Both neighborhoods have a core of cultural sights but more than their share of sketchy blocks.

Updated by
Denise M. Leto

SoMa is less a neighborhood than a sprawling area of wide, traffic-heavy boulevards lined with office high-rises and pricey live-work lofts. Aside from the fact that many of them work in the area, locals are drawn to the cultural offerings, smattering of destination restaurants, and concentration of dance clubs. In terms of sightseeing, SoMa holds a few points of interest—SFMOMA and the museums of the Yerba Buena District top the list—and these are conveniently close together.

SoMa was once known as South of the Slot (read: the Wrong Side of the Tracks) in reference to the cable-car slot that ran up Market Street. Ever since gold-rush miners set up their tents in 1848, SoMa has played a major role in housing immigrants to the city. Industry took over much of the area when the 1906 earthquake collapsed most of the homes.

SoMa's emergence as a focal point of San Francisco's cultural life was more than three decades in the making. Huge sections of the then-industrial neighborhood were razed in the 1960s, and alternative artists and the gay leather crowd set up shop. A dozen bars and bathhouses frequented by the latter group cropped up; some survive today, and the legacy of that time is the still-raucous annual Folsom Street Fair. The neighborhood lost many artists to the far reaches of SoMa and to the Mission District when urban renewal finally began in earnest in the 1970s; still more fled when the dot-com heyday sent prices here skyrocketing.

Life in the SoMa of the mid- to late 1990s was what the gold rush must have felt like. Young prospectors flooded in to take their pick of well-paying jobs at high-tech startups. Companies with hot (or not) ideas filled their $100-plus-per-square-foot offices with recent college grads, foosball tables, $1,000 ergonomic chairs, and free catered meals. Gaggles of gadget-toting twentysomethings spent their evenings wandering from launch party to marketing event, loading up on swag. Rents—commercial in SoMa and residential citywide—went through the roof, but the dot-commers could still pony up while waiting for the holy grail of the IPO. South Park, the green oval anchored by high-tech hangout Caffè Centro, briefly became the center of the universe.

The electric buzz of the dot-com boom, when venture capitalists couldn't give their money away fast enough, changed the face of the neighborhood forever. Today's

HAYES VALLEY

Hayes Valley, right next door to the Civic Center, is an offbeat neighborhood with terrific eateries, cool watering holes, and great browsing in its funky clothing and home-decor boutiques. Swing down main drag Hayes Street, between Franklin and Laguna, and you can hit the highlights, including two very popular restaurants, Absinthe and Suppenküche. Comfy Place Pigalle (at Hayes and Octavia streets) is also a favorite for its living-room atmosphere, wines, and microbrews. Locals love this quarter, but without any big-name draws it remains off the radar for most visitors.

post-boom SoMa is sobered up and on the rise; the thousands of kids rich on paper have been replaced with substantially wealthy people staking out luxury high-rises in striking residential towers, such as 62-story One Rincon Hill, the pencil-thin building at the end of the Bay Bridge, that will dwarf what are now the city's tallest buildings. The area may still have more than its share of seedy pockets, but even in earthquake town, the 60th-story penthouse at the ultrachic Millennium sold for $11 million in 2008 (and condo prices continued to hover around $825,000 on average in 2010).

Across Market Street from the western edge of SoMa is another of the city's patchy neighborhoods, the Civic Center, between McAllister and Grove streets and Franklin and Hyde streets. The optimistic "City Beautiful" movement of the early 20th century produced the beaux arts–style complex for which this area is named, including the War Memorial Opera House, the Veterans Building, and the old public library, now home of the Asian Art Museum. The centerpiece is the eye-catching, gold-dome City Hall. The current Main Library on Larkin Street between Fulton and Grove streets is a modern variation on the Civic Center's architectural theme.

The Civic Center area may have been set up on City Beautiful principles, but illusion soon gives way to reality. The buildings are grand, but there's a stark juxtaposition of the powerful and the powerless here. On the streets and plazas of Civic Center, many of the city's most destitute residents eke out an existence.

Despite the evidence of social problems, there are areas of interest on either side of City Hall. East of City Hall is United Nations Plaza, which hosts a poor man's version of the Ferry Building's glorious farmers'

The glass-domed Garden Court contributes to the majestic feel of the Palace Hotel.

market twice weekly. On the west side of City Hall are the War Memorial Opera House, Davies Symphony Hall, and other cultural institutions. A few upscale restaurants in the surrounding blocks cater to the theater-symphony crowd. Tickets to a show at one of the grand performance halls are the main reason to venture here. Otherwise, unless you have a hankering to gawk at gray-stone, monumental structures, a glimpse of the gold-veined dome of City Hall as you drive down the street should be enough, especially for first-time visitors.

SOMA

TOP ATTRACTIONS

Contemporary Jewish Museum. Fascinating museum buildings are sprouting up all over the city, and this Daniel Liebeskind–designed CJM is a real coup for SoMa. It's impossible to ignore that diagonal blue cube. The all-new addition jutting into a painstakingly restored power substation is a physical manifestation of the Hebrew phrase *l'chaim* (to life). And even if the architectural philosophy behind the design seems a bit esoteric, the blue, steel-clad cube—one of the most striking structures in town—creates a unique, light-filled space that merits a stroll through the lobby even if current exhibits don't entice you into the galleries. Be sure to check out the seam where old building meets new. ⊠ *736 Mission St., between 3rd and 4th Sts., SoMa* ☎ *415/655–7800* ⊕ *www. thejcm.org* ☞ *$10, $5 Thurs. after 5 pm* ⊗ *Thurs. 1–8, Fri.–Tues. 11–5.*

Fodor'sChoice
★ **San Francisco Museum of Modern Art** *(SFMOMA).* With its brick facade and a striped central tower lopped at a lipstick-like angle, architect Mario Botta's SFMOMA building fairly screams "modern-art museum."

Indeed it is. The stripes continue inside, from the black marble and gray granite of the floors right up the imposing staircase to the wooden slats on the ceiling. ■TIP→ Taking in all of SFMOMA's four exhibit floors can be overwhelming, so having a plan is helpful. Keep in mind that the museum's heavy hitters are on floors 2 and 3. Floor 2 gets the big-name traveling exhibits and collection highlights such as Matisse's *Woman with the Hat,* Diego Rivera's *The Flower Carrier,* and Georgia O'Keeffe's *Black Place 1.* Photography buffs should hustle up to floor 3, with its works by Ansel Adams and Alfred Stieglitz. The large-scale contemporary exhibits on floors 4 and 5 can usually be seen quickly (or skipped). If it's on display, don't miss sculptor Jeff Koons' memorably creepy, life-size gilded porcelain *Michael Jackson and Bubbles,* on the fifth floor at the end of the Turret Bridge, a vertiginous catwalk dangling under the central tower. The window at the bridge's other end offers a great view over the Yerba Buena Gardens below. In 2009 the museum opened its fifth-floor, garage-top sculpture garden.

Seating in the museum can be scarce, so luckily Caffè Museo, accessible from the street, provides a refuge for quite good, reasonably priced drinks and light meals. It's easy to drop a fortune at the museum's large store, chockablock with fun gadgets, artsy doodads of all kinds, very modern furniture, and possibly the best selection of kids' books in town. ■TIP→ No ticket is required to visit the lobby, so if it's the architecture you're interested in, save yourself the admission and have a gander for free. ⊠ *151 3rd St., SoMa* ☎ *415/357–4000* ⊕ *www.sfmoma.org* ✆ *$18, free 1st Tues. of month, ½ price Thurs. 6–9* ⊗ *Labor Day–Memorial Day, Fri.–Tues. 11–5:45, Thurs. 11–8:45; Memorial Day–Labor Day, Fri.–Tues. 10–5:45, Thurs. 10–8:45.*

☺ **Yerba Buena Gardens.** There's not much south of Market that encourages
★ lingering outdoors, or indeed walking at all, with this notable exception. These two blocks encompass the **Center for the Arts, Metreon, Moscone Convention Center,** and the convention center's rooftop **Children's Creativity Museum,** but the gardens themselves are the everyday draw. Office workers escape to the green swath of the East Garden. The memorial to Martin Luther King Jr. is the focal point here. Powerful streams of water surge over large, jagged stone columns, mirroring the enduring force of King's words that are carved on the stone walls and on glass blocks behind the waterfall. Moscone North is behind the memorial, and an overhead walkway leads to Moscone South and its rooftop attractions. ■TIP→ The gardens are liveliest during the week and especially during the Yerba Buena Gardens Festival (May through October, www.ybgf.org), when free performances run from Latin music to Balinese dance.

Atop the Moscone Convention Center perch a few lures for kids. The historic Looff carousel ($3 for two rides) twirls daily 11 to 6. South of the carousel is the Children's Creativity Museum (☎ *415/820–3320* ⊕ *www.zeum.org*), a high-tech, interactive arts-and-technology center (adults, $10; kids 3–18, $8) geared to children ages eight and over. Kids can walk through a model of San Francisco complete with hologram landmarks, make Claymation videos, work in a computer lab, and view exhibits and performances. The museum is open 1–5 Wednesday through Friday and 11–5 weekends during the school year and Tuesday

Above the Yerba Buena Gardens, SFMOMA's striped "eye" can be spotted.

through Sunday 11–5 when school's out. Also part of the rooftop complex are gardens, an ice-skating rink, and a bowling alley. ⊠ *Bordered by 3rd, 4th, Mission, and Folsom Sts., SoMa* ☎ *No phone* ⊕ *www. yerbabuenagardens.org* 🔁 *Free* ☉ *Daily sunrise–10 pm.*

WORTH NOTING

California Historical Society. If you're not a history buff, the CHS might seem like an obvious skip—who wants to look at fading old photographs and musty artifacts? If the answer is an indignant "I do!" or if you're just curious, these airy galleries are well worth a stop. A rotating selection draws from the society's vast repository of Californiana—hundreds of thousands of photographs, publications, paintings, and gold-rush paraphernalia. ■TIP➜ From out front, take a look across the street: this is the best view of the three-story photo mosaic at the Museum of African Diaspora. ⊠ *678 Mission St., SoMa* ☎ *415/357-1848* ⊕ *www. californiahistoricalsociety.org* 🔁 *$3* ☉ *Wed.–Sat. noon–4:30; galleries close between exhibitions.*

Cartoon Art Museum. Krazy Kat, Zippy the Pinhead, Batman, and other colorful cartoon icons greet you at the Cartoon Art Museum, established with an endowment from cartoonist-icon Charles M. Schulz. The museum's strength is its changing exhibits, which explore such topics as America from the perspective of international political cartoons, and the output of women and African-American cartoonists. Serious fans of cartoons—especially those on the quirky underground side—will likely enjoy the exhibits; those with a casual interest may be disappointed. The museum store carries loads of cool titles to add to your collection. ✉ *655 Mission St., SoMa* ☎ *415/227–8666* ⊕ *www.cartoonart. org* 🖾 *$7, pay what you wish 1st Tues. of month* ⊙ *Tues.–Sun. 11–5.*

OFF THE
BEATEN
PATH

GLBT Historical Society Museum. Tucked away in a small exhibit space on the third floor, the Gay, Lesbian, Bisexual, and Transgender (GLBT) Historical Society Museum presents rotating multimedia exhibits on themes such as the Gay Olympics, Harvey Milk, and GLBT military service. Though perhaps not for the faint of heart (those offended by photos of lustily frolicking naked people may, well, be offended), this thoughtful display offers an inside look at these communities so integral to the fabric of San Francisco life. The upstairs location and tiny space mean you may well be the only visitor; a helpful docent from the GLBT Historical Society's office next door will gladly show you around and answer any questions. ✉ *657 Mission St., 3rd fl., SoMa* ☎ *415/777–5455* ⊕ *www.glbthistory.org* 🖾 *$4 donation* ⊙ *Tues.–Sat. 1–5.*

3

OFF THE
BEATEN
PATH

Mint Plaza. Arising from what had long been a gritty, windswept cut-through behind the abandoned Old Mint, L-shape Mint Plaza is that vibrant mix that urban planners always aim for but often miss: stylish urban residences (that are actually occupied) cheek-by-jowl with thriving local businesses, all combining to produce a happening street scene. The secret, tucked-away feel of the alley—which is mere feet from Mission Street—will make you feel like an insider when you visit. Stop by Blue Bottle Café for coffee and a nosh or grab a table at Chez Papa, one of the city's favorite French bistros. Even the mint itself is being reinvented: the Museum of San Francisco is slated to open inside the renovated structure in the next few years. ✉ *Jessie and Mint Sts., near Mission and 5th Sts., SoMa.*

Museum of the African Diaspora (MoAD). Dedicated to the influence that people of African descent have had all over the world, MoAD provokes discussion from the get-go with the question, "When did you discover you are African?" painted on the wall at the entrance. With no permanent collection, the museum is light on displays and heavy on interactive exhibits. For instance, you can sit in a darkened theater and listen to the moving life stories of slaves; hear snippets of music that helped create genres from gospel to hip-hop; and see videos about the Civil Rights movement or the Haitian Revolution. Some grumble that sweeping generalities replace specific information, but almost everyone can appreciate the museum's most striking exhibit in the front window. The three-story mosaic, made from thousands of photographs, forms the image of a little girl's face. Walk up the stairs inside the museum and view the photographs up close—Malcolm X is there, Muhammad Ali, too, along with everyday folks—but the best view is from across the street. ✉ *685 Mission St., SoMa* ☎ *415/358–7200* ⊕ *www.moadsf. org* 🖾 *$10* ⊙ *Wed.–Sat. 11–6, Sun. noon–5.*

Museum of Craft and Folk Art. If you're in the area, this one-room museum is a great way to spend a half hour. Its bright space hosts five rotating exhibits per year showcasing American folk art, tribal art, and contemporary crafts. One exhibit saw the museum transformed into a forest of plants, trees, and a river, all created from paper by an artisan in Japan. Another was devoted entirely to the art of the ukulele. Its tiny front space houses a shop with high-end, sometimes whimsical crafts from around the world. ⊠ *51 Yerba Buena La., SoMa* ☎ *415/227–4888* ⊕ *www.mocfa.org* ⊡ *$5, free 1st Tues.* ⊙ *Wed.–Sat. 11–6.*

Palace Hotel. The city's oldest hotel, a Sheraton property, has a storied past. It opened in 1875, but fire destroyed the original Palace after the 1906 earthquake, despite the hotel's 28,000-gallon reservoir. (The current building dates from 1909.) President Warren Harding died at the Palace while still in office in 1923, and the body of King Kalakaua of Hawaii spent a night here after he died in San Francisco in 1891. The managers play up this ghoulish history with talk of a haunted guest room, but the real draw is simply the Palace's opulent surroundings. **San Francisco City Guides** (☎ *415/557–4266* ⊙ *Tours Tues. and Sat. at 10, Thurs. at 2*) offers free guided tours of the Palace Hotel's grand interior. You see the glass-dome Garden Court restaurant, mosaic-tile floors in Oriental rug designs, and Maxfield Parrish's wall-size painting *The Pied Piper,* the centerpiece of the Pied Piper Bar. Glass cases off the main lobby contain memorabilia of the hotel's glory days. ⊠ *2 New Montgomery St., SoMa* ☎ *415/512–1111* ⊕ *www.sfpalace.com.*

Rincon Center. The only reason to visit what is basically a modern office building is the striking Works Project Administration mural by Anton Refregier in the lobby of the streamlined moderne–style former post office on the building's Mission Street side. The 27 panels depict California life from the days when Native Americans were the state's sole inhabitants through World War I. Completion of this significant work was interrupted by World War II (which explains the swastika in the final panel) and political infighting. The latter led to some alteration in Refregier's "radical" historical interpretations; they exuded too much populist sentiment for some of the politicians who opposed the artist. A permanent exhibit below the murals contains photographs and artifacts of life in the Rincon area in the 1800s. A sheer five-story column of water resembling a mini-rainstorm is the centerpiece of the indoor arcade around the corner from the mural. ⊠ *Bordered by Steuart, Spear, Mission, and Howard Sts., SoMa.*

Yerba Buena Center for the Arts. If SFMOMA's for your parents, this Center is for you. You never know what's going to be on at this facility in the Yerba Buena Gardens, but whether it's an exhibit of Mexican street art (graffiti to laypeople), innovative modern dance, or baffling video installations, it's likely to be memorable. The productions here tend to draw a young, energetic crowd, and lean hard toward the cutting edge. ⊠ *701 Mission St., SoMa* ☎ *415/978–2787* ⊕ *www.ybca.org* ⊡ *Galleries $7, free 1st Tues. of month* ⊙ *Thurs.–Sat. noon–8, Sun. noon–6, 1st Tues. of the month noon–8.*

CIVIC CENTER

TOP ATTRACTIONS

★ **Asian Art Museum.** Expecting a building full of Buddhas and jade? Well, yeah, you can find plenty of that here. Happily, though, you don't have to be a connoisseur of Asian art to appreciate a visit to this splendidly renovated museum, whose monumental exterior conceals a light, open,

Where can I find . . . ?

PARKING	**Civic Center Plaza Garage** (355 McAllister St.) Most convenient place to use if you're here for a performance.	**Jesse Square Garage** (223 Stevenson St.) A SoMa secret with good rates and plenty of space.
A GAS STATION	**76** (390 1st St.) Near I–80, with middling prices.	**Chevron** (1298 Howard St.) In SoMa but relatively close to Civic Center.
PRETHEATER DRINKS	**Hôtel Biron** (45 Rose St.) Have a glass of wine in this tiny, arty Hayes Valley spot.	**Olive** (743 Larkin St.) Stylish cocktail bar/restaurant on the edge of the Tenderloin.

3

and welcoming space. The fraction of the museum's items on display (about 2,500 pieces from a 15,000-plus-piece collection) is laid out thematically and by region, making it easy to follow developments.

Begin on the third floor, where highlights of Buddhist art in Southeast Asia and early China include a large, jewel-encrusted, exquisitely painted 19th-century Burmese Buddha and clothed rod puppets from Java. On the second floor you can find later Chinese works, as well as pieces from Korea and Japan. Look for a cobalt tiger jauntily smoking a pipe on a whimsical Korean jar and delicate Japanese tea implements. The ground floor displays rotating exhibits, including contemporary and traveling shows. ■TIP→ If you'd like to attend one of the occasional tea ceremonies and tastings at the Japanese Teahouse, call ahead, since preregistration is required. ✉ *200 Larkin St., between McAllister and Fulton Sts., Civic Center* ☎ *415/581–3500* ⊕ *www.asianart.org* ✍ *$12, free 1st Sun. of month; $10 some Thurs. 5–9; tea ceremony $27, includes museum* ☉ *Tues.–Sun. 10–5; Feb.–Sept., Thurs. until 9.*

QUICK BITES   **Miette Confiserie** (✉ *449 Octavia St., Hayes Valley* ☎ *415/626–6221*) are so beautiful it's hard to imagine eating them. Happily, they taste as good as they look. For lunch on the go, don't submit to fast food when you've got **Arlequin** (✉ *384 Hayes St., Hayes Valley* ☎ *415/626–1211*), the café offshoot of trendy Absinthe. Grab a reasonably priced hot or cold sandwich to go, or linger at the donut case on your way to the lovely outdoor patio.

WORTH NOTING

City Hall. This imposing 1915 structure with its massive gold-leaf dome—higher than the U.S. Capitol's—is about as close to a palace as you're going to get in San Francisco. (Alas, the metal detectors take something away from the grandeur.) The classic granite-and-marble behemoth was modeled after St. Peter's Cathedral in Rome. Architect Arthur Brown Jr., who also designed Coit Tower and the War Memorial

Opera House, designed an interior
with grand columns and a sweeping central staircase. San Franciscans were thrilled, and probably a
bit surprised, when his firm built
City Hall in just a few years. The
building it replaced, dubbed "the
new City Hall ruin," had lined the
pockets of corrupt builders and
politicians during its 27 years of construction. That 1899 structure
collapsed in about 27 seconds in the 1906 earthquake, revealing trash
and newspapers mixed into the building materials.

City Hall was spruced up and seismically retrofitted in the late 1990s,
but the sense of history remains palpable. Some noteworthy events
that have taken place here include the marriage of Marilyn Monroe
and Joe DiMaggio (1954); the hosing—down the central staircase—
of civil-rights and freedom-of-speech protesters (1960); the murders
of Mayor George Moscone and openly gay supervisor Harvey Milk
(1978); the torching of the lobby by angry members of the gay community in response to the light sentence given to the former supervisor who
killed both men (1979); and the registrations of scores of gay couples
in celebration of the passage of San Francisco's Domestic Partners Act
(1991). February 2004 has come to be known as the Winter of Love:
thousands of gay and lesbian couples responded to Mayor Gavin Newsom's decision to issue marriage licenses to same-sex partners, turning
City Hall into the site of raucous celebration and joyful nuptials for a
month before the state Supreme Court ordered the practice stopped.
That celebratory scene replayed during 2008, when scores of couples
were wed between the court's June ruling that everyone enjoys the civil
right to marry and the November passage of California's ballot proposi-
tion banning same-sex marriage. (Stay tuned . . .) Free tours are offered
weekdays at 10, noon, and 2.

The South Light Court houses a modest, rotating display from the collection of the **Museum of the City of San Francisco** (⊕ *www.sfmuseum.
org*), including historical items, maps, and photographs. That enormous, 700-pound iron head once crowned the *Goddess of Progress*
statue, which topped the old City Hall building when it crumbled during
the 1906 earthquake. Unlike the building, the statue survived the earthquake in one piece, but the subsequent removal proved too much for it.

Across Polk Street is **Civic Center Plaza,** with lawns, walkways, seasonal
flower beds, a playground, and an underground parking garage. This
sprawling space is generally clean but somewhat grim. A large part of
the city's homeless population hangs out here, despite frequently being
shunted away, so the plaza can feel dodgy. ⊠ *Bordered by Van Ness Ave.
and Polk, Grove, and McAllister Sts., Civic Center* ☏ *415/554–6023*
⊕ *www.sfgov.org/site/cityhall* ≊ *Free* ⊙ *Weekdays 8–8.*

Louise M. Davies Symphony Hall. Fascinating and futuristic looking, this
2,750-seat hall is the home of the San Francisco Symphony. The glass
wraparound lobby and pop-out balcony high on the southeast corner

are visible from outside, as is the Henry Moore bronze sculpture that sits on the sidewalk at Van Ness Avenue and Grove Street. The hall's 59 adjustable Plexiglas acoustical disks cascade from the ceiling like hanging windshields. Concerts range from typical symphonic fare to more unusual combinations, such as performers like Al Green and Arlo Guthrie. Scheduled tours (75 minutes), which meet at the Grove Street entrance, take in Davies and the nearby War Memorial Opera House and Herbst Theatre. ⊠ *201 Van Ness Ave., Civic Center* ☎ *415/552–8338* ⊕ *www.sfwmpac.org* ✉ *Tours $5* ☉ *Tours Mon. on the hr 10–2.*

San Francisco Public Library. Topped with a swirl like an art-deco nautilus, the library's seven-level glass atrium fills the building with light. Opened in 1996, the New Main (as Herb Caen dubbed it) is a modernized version of the old beaux arts–style library. Local researchers take advantage of centers dedicated to gay-and-lesbian, African-American, Chinese, and Filipino history, and everyone appreciates the basement-level café, Wi-Fi, and 15-minute Internet terminal access. On the sixth floor an exhibit inside the San Francisco History Center includes doodads from the 1894 Mid-Winter Fair and the 1915 Pan-Pacific Exhibition, as well as the "valuable emeralds" philanthropist Helene Strybing left to the city—alas merely green glass. ■TIP➔ Noir fans should head to the back of the center; you can see "Maltese Falcon" statues in the Flood Building and at John's Grill, but this is the only place to see novelist Dashiell Hammett's typewriter. Free tours of the library are conducted the second Wednesday of the month at 2:30. ⊠ *100 Larkin St., at Grove St., Civic Center* ☎ *415/557–4400* ⊕ *sfpl.lib.ca.us* ☉ *Mon. and Sat. 10–6, Tues.–Thurs. 9–8, Fri. noon–6, Sun. noon–5.*

United Nations Plaza. Locals know this plaza for two things: its Wednesday and Sunday farmers' market—cheap and earthy to the Ferry Building's pricey and beautiful—and its homeless population, which seems to return no matter how many times the city tries to shunt them aside. Brick pillars listing various nations and the dates of their admittance into the United Nations line the plaza, and its floor is inscribed with the goals and philosophy of the United Nations charter, which was signed at the War Memorial Opera House in 1945. ⊠ *Fulton St. between Hyde and Market Sts., Civic Center.*

War Memorial Opera House. During San Francisco's Barbary Coast days, operagoers smoked cigars, didn't check their revolvers, and expressed their appreciation with "shrill whistles and savage yells," as one observer put it. All the old opera houses were destroyed in the 1906 quake, but lusty support for opera continued. The San Francisco Opera didn't have a permanent home until the War Memorial Opera House was inaugurated in 1932 with a performance of *Tosca*. Modeled after its European counterparts, the building has a vaulted and coffered ceiling, marble foyer, two balconies, and a huge silver art-deco chandelier that resembles a sunburst. The San Francisco Opera performs here from September through December and in summer; the opera house hosts the San Francisco Ballet from February through May, with December *Nutcracker* performances. ⊠ *301 Van Ness Ave., Civic Center* ☎ *415/621–6600* ⊕ *www.sfwmpac.org.*

War Memorial Veterans Building. Performing- and visual-arts organizations occupy much of this 1930s structure. **Herbst Theatre** (☎ *415/392–4400*) hosts classical ensembles, dance performances, and City Arts and Lectures events. Past City Arts speakers have included author Salman Rushdie and senator and author Al Franken. Also in the building are two galleries that charge no admission. The street-level **San Francisco Arts Commission Gallery** (☎ *415/554–6080* ▢ *Free* ⊙ *Wed.–Sat. noon–5*) displays the works of Bay Area artists. The **Museum of Performance & Design** (☎ *415/255–4800* ▢ *Free* ⊙ *Wed.–Sat. noon–5*) occupies part of the fourth floor. A small gallery hosts interesting exhibitions, but the organization functions mainly as a library and research center for the San Francisco Bay Area's rich performing-arts legacy. ✉ *401 Van Ness Ave., Civic Center* ⊕ *www.sfwmpac.org.*

Nob Hill and Russian Hill

WORD OF MOUTH

"Another thing I like is the little surprise walkways that you come across; you can be walking down a street and suddenly will come to public steps leading somewhere. Follow them, you never know what you might find."

—Miramar

GETTING ORIENTED

TOP 5 REASONS TO GO

Macondray Lane: Duck into this secret, lush garden lane and walk its narrow, uneven cobblestones.

Vallejo Steps area: Make the steep climb up to lovely Ina Coolbrith Park, then continue up along the glorious garden path of the Vallejo Steps to a spectacular view at the top.

San Francisco Art Institute: Contemplate a Diego Rivera mural and stop at the café for cheap organic coffee and a priceless view of the city and the bay. It may be the best way to spend an hour for a buck in town.

Cable Car Museum: Ride a cable car all the way back to the barn, hanging on tight as it clack-clack-clacks its way up Nob Hill, then go behind the scenes at the museum.

Play "Bullitt" on the steepest streets: For the ride of your life, take a drive up and down the city's steepest streets on Russian Hill. A trip over the precipice of Filbert or Jones will make you feel like you're falling off the edge of the world.

QUICK BITES

A harpist plays the classics and other tunes during afternoon tea at the **Ritz-Carlton, San Francisco** (✉ *600 Stockton St., at California St., Nob Hill* ☎ *415/296–7465* ⊕ *www. ritzcarlton.com*), served weekends 1–4:30. A holiday tradition, afternoon tea is served daily between Thanksgiving and Christmas.

Take a break from walking the hills at the original **Swensen's Ice Cream** (✉ *1999 Hyde St., at Union St., Russian Hill* ☎ *415/775–6818*), a neighborhood favorite since it opened in 1948. An antique sign still fronts the tiny shop, which has just a single counter inside, but concessions to the times include such ice-cream flavors as green tea and lychee.

GETTING THERE

The thing about Russian Hill and Nob Hill is that they're both especially steep hills. If you're not up for the hike, a cable car is certainly the most exciting way to reach the top. Take the California line for Nob Hill and the Powell–Hyde line for Russian Hill. There is some bus service as well, such as the 1–California bus for Nob Hill, but the routes only run east–west. Only the cable cars tackle the steeper north–south streets. Driving yourself is a hassle, since parking is a challenge on these crowded, precipitous streets.

MAKING THE MOST OF YOUR TIME

Since walking Nob Hill is (almost) all about gazing at exteriors, touring the neighborhood during daylight hours is a must. The sights here don't require a lot of visiting time—say a half hour each at the Cable Car Museum and Grace Cathedral—but allow plenty of time for the walk itself. An afternoon visit is ideal for Russian Hill, so you can browse the shops. You could cover both neighborhoods in three or four hours. If you time it just right, you can finish up with a sunset cocktail at one of the überswanky hotel lounges or the retro tiki Tonga Room.

4

Sightseeing
★ ★
Nightlife
★
Dining
★ ★ ★
Lodging
★ ★ ★
Shopping
★ ★

In place of the quirky charm and cultural diversity that mark other San Francisco neighborhoods, Nob Hill exudes history and good breeding. Topped with some of the city's most elegant hotels, Gothic Grace Cathedral, and private blue-blood clubs, it's the pinnacle of privilege. One hill over, across Pacific Avenue, is another old-family bastion, Russian Hill. It may not be quite as wealthy as Nob Hill, but it's no slouch—and it's known for its jaw-dropping views.

Updated by
Denise M. Leto

Nob Hill was officially dubbed during the 1870s when "the Big Four"— Charles Crocker, Leland Stanford, Mark Hopkins, and Collis Huntington, who were involved in the construction of the transcontinental railroad—built their hilltop estates. The lingo is thick from this era: those on the hilltop were referred to as "nabobs" (originally meaning a provincial governor from India) and "swells," and the hill itself was called Snob Hill, a term that survives to this day. By 1882 so many estates had sprung up on Nob Hill that Robert Louis Stevenson called it "the hill of palaces." But the 1906 earthquake and fire destroyed all the palatial mansions except for portions of the James Flood brownstone. History buffs may choose to linger here, but for most visitors, a casual glimpse from a cable car will be enough.

Essentially a tony residential neighborhood of spiffy pieds-à-terre, Victorian flats, Edwardian cottages, and boxlike condos, Russian Hill also has some of the city's loveliest stairway walks, hidden garden ways, and steepest streets—brave drivers can really have some fun here—not to mention those bay views. Several stories explain the origin of Russian Hill's name. One legend has it that Russian farmers raised vegetables here for Farallon Islands seal hunters; another attributes the name to a Russian sailor of prodigious drinking habits who drowned when he fell into a well on the hill. A plaque at the top of the Vallejo Steps gives credence to the version that says sailors of the Russian-American company were buried here in the 1840s. Be sure to visit the sign for yourself—its location offers perhaps the finest vantage point on the hill.

NOB HILL

For details on the Cable Car Museum, see the Cable Cars feature in the Experience San Francisco chapter.

TOP ATTRACTIONS

Grace Cathedral. Not many churches can boast a Keith Haring sculpture and not one but two labyrinths. The seat of the Episcopal Church in San Francisco, this soaring Gothic-style structure, erected on the site of Charles Crocker's mansion, took 53 years to build, wrapping up in 1964. The gilded bronze doors at the east entrance were taken from casts of Lorenzo Ghiberti's incredible Gates of Paradise, which are on the Baptistery in Florence, Italy. A black-and-bronze stone sculpture of St. Francis by Beniamino Bufano greets you as you enter.

The 35-foot-wide labyrinth, a large, purplish rug with a looping pattern, is a replica of the 13th-century stone maze on the floor of Chartres Cathedral. All are encouraged to walk the ¼-mi-long labyrinth, a ritual based on the tradition of meditative walking. There's also a terrazzo outdoor labyrinth on the church's north side. The AIDS Interfaith Chapel, to the right as you enter Grace, contains a metal tryptich sculpture by the late artist Keith Haring and panels from the AIDS Memorial Quilt. ■TIP→ Especially dramatic times to view the cathedral are during Thursday-night evensong (5:15) and during special holiday programs. ⊠ 1100 California St., at Taylor St., Nob Hill ☏ 415/749–6300 ⊕ www.gracecathedral.org ☉ Weekdays 7–6, Sat. 8–6, Sun. 8–7.

WORTH NOTING

Fairmont San Francisco. The hotel's dazzling opening was delayed a year by the 1906 quake, but since then the marble palace has hosted presidents, royalty, movie stars, and local nabobs. Things have changed since its early days, however: on the eve of World War I you could get a room for as low as $2.50 per night, meals included. Nowadays, prices go as high as $8,000, which buys a night in the eight-room, Persian-art-filled penthouse suite. Swing through the opulent lobby on your way to tea (served weekends 1:30–3:30) at the **Laurel Court** restaurant. Don't miss an evening cocktail (a mai tai is in order) in the kitschy **Tonga Room,** complete with tiki huts, a sporadic tropical rainstorm, and a floating bandstand. ⊠ 950 Mason St., Nob Hill ☏ 415/772–5000 ⊕ www.fairmont.com.

InterContinental Mark Hopkins Hotel. Built on the ashes of railroad tycoon Mark Hopkins's grand estate (constructed at his wife's urging; Hopkins himself preferred to live frugally), this 19-story hotel went up in 1926. A combination of French château and Spanish Renaissance architecture, with noteworthy terra-cotta detailing, it has hosted statesmen, royalty, and

CLOSE UPS ON THE BROCKLEBANK

The grand Brocklebank Apartments, on the northeast corner of Sacramento and Mason streets across from the Fairmont hotel, might look eerily familiar. In 1958 the complex was showcased in Alfred Hitchcock's *Vertigo* (Jimmy Stewart starts trailing Kim Novak here) and in the 1990s it popped up in the miniseries *Tales of the City.*

WALKING THE HILLS

Start a tour of Nob Hill and Russian Hill with a cable-car ride up to **California** and **Powell streets** on Nob Hill (all lines go here). Walking two blocks east you can pass all the Big Four mansions-cum-hotels on the hill. Peek at the Keith Haring triptych in impressive **Grace Cathedral**; grab a Peet's coffee in the basement café if you need a lift. Next, head down to the **Cable Car Museum** to see the machinery in action. Then make your way to Russian Hill—a cable car is a fine way to reach the peak—to visit some of the city's loveliest hidden lanes and stairways. At **Mason** and **Vallejo streets,** head up the **Vallejo Steps,** passing contemplative, terraced **Ina Coolbrith Park** and beautifully tended private gardens. Take in the sweeping city and bay view from the top of the hill, then head right on **Jones Street** and duck right under the trellis to wooded and shady **Macondray Lane.** From here it's a six-block hike to crooked **Lombard Street.** If you've still got some steam, be sure to go another block to see **Diego Rivera's mural** and the surprise panoramic view from the **San Francisco Art Institute.**

Hollywood celebrities. The 11-room penthouse was turned into a glass-wall cocktail lounge in 1939: the **Top of the Mark** is remembered fondly by thousands of World War II veterans who jammed the lounge before leaving for overseas duty. Wives and sweethearts watching the ships depart gave the room's northwest nook its name—Weepers' Corner. With its 360-degree views, the lounge is a wonderful spot for a night-time drink. ⊠ *999 California St., at Mason St., Nob Hill* ☎ *415/392–3434* ⊕ *www.markhopkins.net.*

Nob Hill Masonic Center. Erected by Freemasons in 1957, the hall is familiar to locals mostly as a concert and lecture venue, where such notables as Van Morrison and Al Gore have appeared. The recent Dan Brown–led spate of interest in the Masons and other secret fraternities unfortunately hasn't done anything to improve the sight lines or the seats here, but those interested in Masonic history can check out the impressive lobby mosaic. On the eve of his mosaic's renovation in 2005, artist Emile Norman wondered aloud, "How the hell did I do that?" Mainly in rich greens and yellows, the mosaic depicts the Masons' role in California history. There's also an intricate model of King Solomon's Temple in the lobby. ⊠ *1111 California St., Nob Hill* ☎ *415/776–7457* ⊕ *www.sfmasoniccenter.com* ☾ *Lobby weekdays 9–5.*

Pacific Union Club. The former home of silver baron James Flood cost a whopping $1.5 million in 1886, when even a stylish Victorian like the Haas-Lilienthal House cost less than $20,000. All that cash did buy some structural stability. The Flood residence (to be precise, its shell) was the only Nob Hill mansion to survive the 1906 earthquake and fire. The Pacific Union Club, a bastion of the wealthy and powerful, purchased the house in 1907 and commissioned Willis Polk to redesign it; the architect added the semicircular wings and third floor. (The ornate fence design dates from the mansion's construction.) West of the house, Huntington Park is the site of the Huntington mansion, destroyed in 1906. Mrs. Huntington donated the land to the city for use as a park; the Crockers purchased the Fountain of the Tortoises, based on the original in Rome. ■TIP➜ The benches around the fountain offer a welcome break after climbing Nob Hill. It's hard to get the skinny on the club itself; its 700 or so members allegedly follow the directive "no women, no Democrats, no reporters." Those who join usually spend years on the waiting list and undergo a stringent vetting process, the rigors of which might embarrass the NSA. Needless to say, the club is closed to the public. ✉ *1000 California St., Nob Hill.*

The Stanford Court Hotel. In 1876 trendsetter Leland Stanford, a California governor and founder of Stanford University, was the first to build an estate on Nob Hill. The only part that survived the earthquake was a basalt-and-granite wall that's been restored; check it out from the eastern side of the hotel. In 1912 an apartment house was built on the site of the former estate, and in 1972 the present-day hotel was constructed from the shell of that building. The lobby has a stained-glass dome and sepia-tone murals depicting scenes of early San Francisco. ✉ *905 California St., Nob Hill* ☎ *415/989–3500* ⊕ *www.marriott.com.*

RUSSIAN HILL

TOP ATTRACTIONS

★ **Ina Coolbrith Park.** If you make it all the way up here, you may have the place all to yourself, or at least feel like you do. The park's terraces are carved from a hill so steep that it's difficult to see if anyone else is there or not. Locals love this park because it feels like a secret no one else knows about—one of the city's magic hidden gardens, with a meditative setting and spectacular views of the bay peeking out from among the trees. A poet, Oakland librarian, and niece of Mormon prophet Joseph Smith, Ina Coolbrith (1842–1928) introduced Jack London and Isadora Duncan to the world of books. For years she entertained literary greats in her Macondray Lane home near the park. In 1915 she was named poet laureate of California. ✉ *Vallejo St. between Mason and Taylor Sts., Russian Hill.*

★ **Lombard Street.** The block-long "Crookedest Street in the World" makes eight switchbacks down the east face of Russian Hill between Hyde and Leavenworth streets. Residents bemoan the traffic jam outside their front doors, and occasionally the city attempts to discourage drivers by posting a traffic cop near the top of the hill, but the determined can find a way around. If no one is standing guard, join the line of cars waiting to drive down the steep hill, or avoid the whole mess and walk down the steps on either side of Lombard. You take in super views of North Beach and Coit Tower whether you walk or drive—though if you're the one behind the wheel, you'd better keep your eye on the road lest you become yet another of the many folks who ram the garden barriers. ■TIP➜ Can't stand the throngs? Thrill seekers of a different stripe may want to head two blocks south of Lombard to Filbert Street. At a gradient of 31.5%, the hair-raising descent between Hyde and Leavenworth streets is the city's steepest. Go slowly! ✉ *Lombard St. between Hyde and Leavenworth Sts., Russian Hill.*

Where can I find . . . ?

PARKING	State Garage (818 Leavenworth St.) Won't get you to the top of Nob Hill, but decent rates.	Lombardi Parking Garage (1600 Jackson St.) Relatively close to the parking desert of Russian Hill.
A CUP OF COFFEE	Nook (1500 Hyde St.) Coffee, chai tea, and healthy light meals.	Chameleon Café (1299 Pacific Ave.) Retro Russian Hill spot with potent coffee and free Wi-Fi.
A DRUGSTORE	Walgreens (1300 Bush St.) Grab a drink here if the hills are getting to you.	Walgreens (1524 Polk St.) Open Monday through Saturday until midnight, Sunday until 11 pm.

Fodor's Choice
★

Macondray Lane. San Francisco has no shortage of impressive, grand homes, but it's the tiny fairy-tale lanes that make most folks want to move here, and Macondray Lane is the quintessential hidden garden. Enter under a lovely wooden trellis and proceed down a quiet, cobbled pedestrian lane lined with Edwardian cottages and flowering plants and trees. ■TIP→ Watch your step—the cobblestones are quite uneven in spots. A flight of steep wooden stairs at the end of the lane leads to Taylor Street—on the way down you can't miss the bay views. If you've read any of Armistead Maupin's *Tales of the City* books, you may find the lane vaguely familiar. It's the thinly disguised setting for part of the series' action. ⊠ *Between Jones and Taylor Sts., and Union and Green Sts., Russian Hill.*

★

San Francisco Art Institute. A Moorish-tile fountain in a tree-shaded courtyard draws the eye as soon as you enter the institute. The number-one reason for a visit is Mexican master Diego Rivera's *Making of a Fresco Showing the Building of a City* (1931), in the student gallery to your immediate left inside the entrance. Rivera himself is in the fresco—his broad behind is to the viewer—and he's surrounded by his assistants. They in turn are surrounded by a construction scene, laborers, and city notables such as sculptor Robert Stackpole and architect Timothy Pfleuger. *The Making of a Fresco* is one of three San Francisco murals painted by Rivera. The number-two reason to come here is the café, or more precisely the eye-popping, panoramic view from the café, which serves surprisingly decent food for a song.

The older portions of the Art Institute, including the lovely Mission-style bell tower, were erected in 1926. To this day, otherwise pragmatic people claim that ghostly footsteps can be heard in the tower at night. Ansel Adams created the school's fine-arts photography department in 1946, and school directors established the country's first fine-arts film program. Notable faculty and alumni have included painter Richard Diebenkorn and photographers Dorothea Lange, Edward Weston, and Annie Leibovitz. The **Walter & McBean Galleries** (☎ *415/749– 4563 ☉ Tues.–Sat. 11–6*) exhibit the often provocative works of established artists. ✉ *800 Chestnut St., North Beach* ☎ *415/771–7020* ⊕ *www.sfai.edu* 🖻 *Galleries free ☉ Student gallery daily 8:30–8:30.*

WORTH NOTING

Feusier House. Octagonal houses were once thought to make the best use of space and enhance the physical and mental well-being of their occupants. A brief mid-19th-century craze inspired the construction of several in San Francisco. Only the Feusier House, built in 1857, and the Octagon House in Pacific Heights remain standing. A private residence, the Feusier House is easy to overlook unless you look closely—it's dwarfed by the large-scale apartments around it. Across from the Feusier House is the **1907 Firehouse** (✉ *1088 Green St., Russian Hill*). Louise M. Davies, the local art patron for whom Symphony Hall is named, bought it from the city in 1957. The firehouse is closed to the public, but it's worth taking in the exterior. ✉ *1067 Green St., Russian Hill.*

Vallejo Steps area. Several Russian Hill buildings survived the 1906 earthquake and fire and remain standing. Patriotic firefighters saved what's come to be known as the **Flag House** (✉ *1652–56 Taylor St., Russian Hill*) when they spotted the American flag on the property and doused the flames with seltzer water and wet sand. The owner, a flag collector, fearing the house would burn to the ground, wanted it to go down in style, with "all flags flying." The Flag House, at the southwest corner of Ina Coolbrith Park, is one of a number of California Shingle–style homes in this neighborhood, several of which were designed by Willis Polk. Polk also laid out the Vallejo Steps, which climb the steep ridge across Taylor Street from the Flag House. If the walk up the steps themselves is too steep for you, it's possible to park at the top of the steps by heading east on Vallejo from Jones. The **Polk-Williams House** (✉ *Taylor and Vallejo Sts., Russian Hill*) was designed by Polk, who lived in one of its finer sections. The architect also designed **1034–1036 Vallejo,** across the street from the Polk-Williams House. ✉ *Taylor and Vallejo Sts., steps lead up toward Jones St., Russian Hill.*

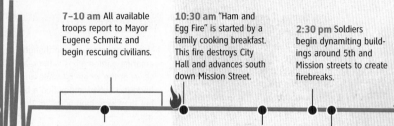

7–10 am All available troops report to Mayor Eugene Schmitz and begin rescuing civilians.

10:30 am "Ham and Egg Fire" is started by a family cooking breakfast. This fire destroys City Hall and advances south down Mission Street.

2:30 pm Soldiers begin dynamiting buildings around 5th and Mission streets to create firebreaks.

8:15 am A major aftershock hits; many damaged buildings collapse.

1 pm The entire Financial District is in flames.

3 pm Mayor Schmitz issues "shoot to kill" order to police to quell looting and other crimes.

WEDNESDAY, APRIL 18, 1906

5:12 am The brunt of the earthquake hits, with sharp shocks and violent shaking lasting up to a minute. Fifty-two fires start across the city.

EARTHQUAKE CITY

San Franciscans know that they are, quite literally, living on the edge. Multiple fault lines run through the Bay Area. Small, undetectable earthquakes rumble beneath the surface here every few days; a few each year are strong enough to feel. Yet residents are willing to tempt fate to live in this vibrant city, and usually the gamble pays off. But if you roll the dice often enough, eventually they come up snake eyes.

9 pm Firefighters attempt to stop fires from advancing up Nob Hill; they are unsuccessful.

5 am Nob Hill mansions are engulfed in flames. Fire reaches Van Ness, where the army has dynamited mansions along the wide avenue to create a firebreak.

Firebreak at Van Ness is successful in the early morning, and the fire's westward movement is halted.

FRIDAY, APRIL 20

THURSDAY, APRIL 19
4 am Secretary of War William Howard Taft orders rations, supplies, and "all the tents in the U.S. Army" sent to San Francisco.

SATURDAY, APRIL 21
Fire in the Mission is stopped at 20th and Dolores streets.

April 1906: A view of Sacramento Street looking east from Powell Street showing the destruction after the great earthquake.

1906: THE GREAT QUAKE AND FIRE

It was dark at 5:12 AM on Wednesday, April 18, 1906—a peaceful midweek morning. A few early risers had just rolled out of bed to put a kettle on. High-society revelers, having attended the much-anticipated Metropolitan Opera of New York performance of *Carmen* Tuesday night, had only just shut their eyes. Night-shifters were still trudging home along the cobblestone avenues.

Seconds later, the face of San Francisco would change forever, after the most severe urban earthquake in known history and four days of uncontrollable fires ravaged the city. The toll would be massive: 28,188 buildings destroyed; $500 million in damages ($8–$12 billion in today's dollars); more than 3,000 dead; and, in a city of 400,000, approximately 225,000 residents left homeless.

Contrary to popular belief, the 1906 earthquake left many landmarks relatively unharmed—it was the subsequent fires that reduced San Francisco to rubble. Nearly all of the city's water mains were severed by the quake, leaving fires to rage unchecked for four days. By the time the flames subsided on Saturday, April 21, burned areas of the city extended more than 500 city blocks, from the bay west to Van Ness and south to 7th and Townsend streets. SoMa, the Financial District, North Beach, and other center-city neighborhoods were beyond repair. The death toll was estimated at just under 500 people—a number that stood until quite recently. But over the past 20 years, dogged research has upped that number to about 3,400. Most of the disaster's victims were consumed by the fires, buried in rubble, or were left uncounted because of their immigrant status.

BY THE NUMBERS

Magnitude: Estimated 7.9 on the moment magnitude scale. The energy unleashed was roughly the equivalent of 15 million tons of dynamite.

Area: Felt in an area of approximately 375,000 square miles, from Coquille, Oregon in the north (390 mi), to Los Angeles in the south (370 mi), to central Nevada in the east (340 mi).

Epicenter: 2 mi offshore, under the Pacific Ocean. **Speed:** Ruptures began at 14,000 mph, but slowed to 8,000 mph by the time they hit the city.

> "As soon as I reached the curb a second shock hit. . . . I was thrown flat and the cobblestones danced like corn in a popper."
>
> —Thomas Jefferson Chase,
> a Ferry Building ticket clerk

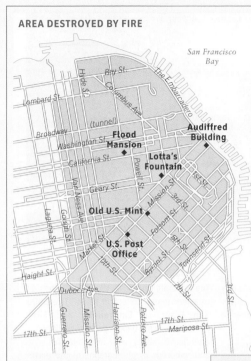

AREA DESTROYED BY FIRE

San Francisco Bay

Bay St.
Hyde St.
The Embarcadero
Columbus Ave.
Lombard St.
(tunnel)
Broadway
Flood Mansion
Audiffred Building
Washington St.
California St.
Lotta's Fountain
Van Ness Ave.
Powell St.
Geary St.
1st St.
Mission St.
3rd St.
Old U.S. Mint
Golden St.
Laguna St.
Folsom St.
5th St.
U.S. Post Office
Market St.
9th St.
Bryant St.
Townsend St.
3rd St.
Haight St.
Duboce Ave.
7th St.
Guerrero St.
Mission St.
Potrero Ave.
Harrison St.
17th St.
Mariposa St.
17th St.

(top) Fire on Market Street.
(bottom) Clay Street in ruins.

LANDMARKS THAT REMAIN

Lotta's Fountain, at the intersection of Kearny and Market streets, was dedicated to the city in 1875; it's the oldest standing monument in San Francisco. A ceremony commemorating the Great Quake is held here every April 18 at 5:12 AM.

The 1889 **Audiffred Building** (Mission St. and the Embarcadero) was the only waterfront structure standing after the fires.

The exterior wall of the 42-room brownstone **Flood mansion** (1000 California St.), now the private Pacific Union Club, is the only intact pre-1906 building on Nob Hill.

The Italian renaissance palazzo–style **U.S. Post Office** (7th and Mission Sts.), completed in 1905, still stands.

Employees dramatically rescued the 1874 **Old U.S. Mint** (88 5th St.)—and the $300,000,000 in its vaults—from within, pumping water from an artesian well.

"The glass in our windows . . . melted down like butter; the sandstone and granite, of which the building was constructed, began to flake off with explosive noises like the firing of artillery."

—U.S. Mint Superintendent Frank Aleomon Leach

THE LITTLE HYDRANT THAT COULD

On Friday, April 20, 1906, fires raged through the Mission. The situation looked bleak, until locals alerted firemen to a working hydrant at 20th and Church streets. With help from refugees and "the Little Giant," firefighters were able to halt the fire's advance at 20th and Dolores streets, steps from Mission Dolores. Each April, locals paint the hydrant gold in celebration.

Removing debris at Third, Kearney, and Market streets.

LOST TREASURES

The **Palace Hotel** (Market and Montgomery Sts.), built in 1876, was the city's most elegant and prestigious hotel, with 800 rooms, marble balconies, and elevators.

The huge, Beaux-Arts **City Hall**, finished in 1899, took 26 years and $6 million (about $130 million in today's dollars) to build. It collapsed in about a minute.

The most ostentatious displays of wealth in San Francisco were the **Nob Hill mansions** owned by railroad magnates Charles Crocker, Mark Hopkins, Leland Stanford, and Collis Huntington—San Francisco's "Big Four." Some considered the homes' destruction to be retribution for the millionaires' corrupt dealings.

REBUILDING

Grand plans to re-create San Francisco in the image of Paris or Washington were short-lived. Residents and business-owners, eager to erase the scars of the disaster, hastily rebuilt the city. Formerly opulent structures, such as City Hall, were reconstructed quickly, with simpler designs and cheaper materials. Graft scandals engulfed Mayor Schmitz, who was removed from office in summer 1907. By then, the last refugee houses were being pulled down. Two years later, about 20,000 new buildings had gone up.

LEARN MORE

The Bancroft Library, at UC Berkeley, has an excellent digital collection titled "**The 1906 San Francisco Earthquake and Fire**" (⊕ http://bancroft.berkeley.edu/collections/earthquakeandfire), with an interactive map and hundreds of photographs of the earthquake and fire.

The Virtual Museum of the City of San Francisco (⊕ www.sfmuseum.org) has the city's best collection of photographs and information about the event; it's available online only, except during special exhibitions.

The *San Francisco Chronicle's* coverage (⊕ www.sfgate.com/greatquake) includes first-person accounts, overview articles, and current-day assessments.

San Francisco City Guides (☎ 415/577-4266 ⊕ www.sfcityguides.org) gives earthquake and fire walking tours year-round.

> "They held on longest to their trunks, and over these trunks many a strong man broke his heart that night. The hills of San Francisco are steep, and up these hills, mile after mile, were the trunks dragged."
>
> —Jack London, for *Collier's* national weekly

1989: THE LOMA PRIETA QUAKE

Excitement filled the Bay Area on October 17, 1989—it was Game 3 of the World Series between the Oakland Athletics and the San Francisco Giants. But as the players took the field of Candlestick Park, exhilaration turned to shock when, at 5:04 pm, a 6.9-magnitude earthquake shook the region.

At first, the thousands of fans in the ballpark thought it might be a joke, but then the field began to roll. The Giants' pitcher, Mike Krukow, said "It felt like a 600-pound gopher going underneath my feet at 40 miles an hour."

The Giants' stadium resisted damage, as did much of San Francisco, but the Marina district was not so lucky. It was built on filled-in marshland, which liquefied as it shook. (Liquefaction occurs when un-compacted soil is jolted and loosens, sinks, and shifts.) Parking garages below buildings collapsed. Fires broke out. To the east, a fifty-foot section of the Bay Bridge collapsed onto the lower deck, claiming one motorist's life. In Oakland, the top deck of the Cypress freeway crashed down, killing 42 drivers. In all, 62 people lost their lives in the earthquake, and 12,000 lost their homes.

The lack of damage from Loma Prieta was mainly due to luck. A blimp covering the World Series game filmed the Marina fires, alerting the fire chief to their existence since phone lines were down. Water lines were ruptured, but the Marina fires were put out by a fireboat that happened to be in the harbor. Winds were light, so the fires didn't spread. And traffic was light on the Bay Bridge, thanks to the World Series.

BY THE NUMBERS

Magnitude: 6.9 on the moment magnitude scale—about $\frac{1}{32}$ the force of the 1906 quake. The shaking lasted for about 15 seconds.

Area: Felt throughout central California and into western Nevada.

Epicenter: About 60 mi south-southeast of San Francisco, near Loma Prieta peak in the Santa Cruz Mountains.

Cost: Over $6 billion in damages (about $3 billion in San Francisco alone).

> "It was like something out of a Godzilla movie. There were people screaming, hollering, waving, every hellish sight you could imagine, every rescue you could imagine."
>
> —Oakland firefighter Mike Hill

SCIENTIFICALLY SPEAKING

Modern earthquake science was born after the 1906 quake. Geologists were stunned by the size and the massive north/south shift of the earth (nearly 20 feet in places), which could not be explained by the prevailing scientific belief that earthquakes themselves created faults. Subsequent studies led to the development of the theory of plate tectonics in the 1950s and 60s, now generally accepted as the cause of earthquakes.

THE NEXT BIG ONE

In 2002, the U.S. Geological Survey reported that there was a 62% chance that an earthquake of magnitude 6.7 or higher would hit the Bay Area before 2032, most likely occurring at the San Andreas Fault (which cuts the peninsula at its "neck") or at the Hayward Fault (which runs through Oakland and Berkeley).

Small quakes hit the Bay Area every few days, but are usually only magnitude 2 or 3, which most people don't even feel. Fewer than five quakes per year are large enough to be felt, but these are usually akin to the rumble of a tractor-trailer passing, and last only a few seconds. Since 1800, only 11 quakes have been categorized as "major," at a magnitude of 7.0 or higher.

Berkeley Digital Seismic Network, Northern California Seismic Network, USGS Low-Frequency Geophysical Network, and Parkfield High-Resolution Seismic Network all have instruments spread around the Bay Area: surface motion sensors, borehole geophones and accelerometers, tensor strain meters, GPS receivers, and ocean-bottom observatories are monitoring the area's shaky ground.

WHAT HAVE WE LEARNED?

Every earthquake teaches engineers a bit more, and modern building codes are such that it's unlikely that a new building would topple in an earthquake. In the Loma Prieta quake, newer up-to-code structures like the Transamerica Pyramid survived with barely a scrape. Unfortunately, modern building codes don't apply to older buildings unless they undergo renovation.

BART tunnels under the bay are not strong enough to withstand a major quake. The new, earthquake-ready eastern section of the Bay Bridge isn't scheduled for completion until 2013—more than 20 years after the Loma Prieta quake. Water pipeline upgrades are a work in progress, but are far from done. About 85% of the city's hospitals are not retrofitted. The entire Sunset neighborhood is on unstable ground and could collapse in a major quake, as buildings did in 1989. And an earthquake on the Hayward fault could destroy the Delta levee system, which supplies water to at least a third of the state of California.

Progress is being made, albeit slowly. Schools have been retrofitted for the most part, and other public buildings, like hospitals, have deadlines for retrofitting. By 2030, all hospitals must be fully functional in an earthquake.

The U.S. Geological Survey posts real-time earthquake maps and 24-hour forecasts on its Web site (⊕ http://quake.wr.usgs.gov/recent/index.html).

North Beach

WORD OF MOUTH

"Wednesday morning was our last day in San Francisco. It was pretty nice out too. We took the bus to Washington Park and walked up the hill to the Coit Tower. I wanted to see the murals which were amazing!!! We both loved them."

—AGM_Cape_Cod

GETTING ORIENTED

0 _____ 350

0 _____ 1,000 ft

Pier 43

Pier 41

Pier 39

Pier 35

Pier 33

Pier 31

Pier 29

San Francisco Bay

The Embarcadero

◆ Fisherman's Wharf

NORTH BEACH

Beach St.

North Point St.

Bay St.

Taylor St. Cable Car

Mason St.

Powell St.

Stockton St.

Kearny St.

Pfeiffer St.

Chestnut St.

Chestnut St.

TELEGRAPH HILL

Lombard St.

Lombard St.

◆ Telegraph Hill

◇ Coit Tower

Greenwich Step

Napier La.

Tattoo Art Museum ◆

Greenwich St.

Filbert Steps

Levi Strau Headquart ◆

Saints Peter and Paul Catholic Church ◆

Medau Pl.

Genoa Pl.

◆ 1360 Montgomery St.

Union

Filbert St.

Union St.

Washington Square ◆

Columbus Ave.

Grant Ave.

Kearny St.

Green St.

Montgomery St.

Sansome St.

Jones St.

Taylor St.

Macondray La.

Green St.

Vallejo St.

Broadway

Cable Car

Tunnel

Stockton St.

Romolo Pl.

◆ Beat Museum

Kerouac Al.

City Lights Bookstore ◆

Jackson Square Historic District

Pacific Ave.

John St.

Sentinel Building ◆

Cable Car

Jackson St.

CHINATOWN

Portsmouth Square

M. Twain Pl.

Washington St.

Clay St.

Commercial St.

TOP 5 REASONS TO GO

Espresso, espresso, espresso: Or cappuccino, Americano, mocha—however you take your caffeine, this is the neighborhood for it. Hanging out in a café constitutes sightseeing here, so find a chair and get to work.

Colorful watering holes: The high concentration of bars with character, like Tosca Café and Vesuvio, makes North Beach the perfect neighborhood for a pub crawl.

Filbert Steps: Walk down this dizzying stairway from Telegraph Hill's Coit Tower, past lush private gardens and jaw-dropping bay views—and listen for the hill's famous screeching parrots.

Grant Avenue: Check out vanguard boutiques, rambling antiques shops, and cavernous old-time bars, all chockablock on narrow Grant Avenue. The best stuff is crowded into the four blocks between Columbus Avenue and Filbert Street.

Browsing books at City Lights: Illuminate your mind at this Beat-era landmark. Its great book selection, author events, and keen staff make it just as cool as ever.

QUICK BITES

Many consider the fresh-from-the-oven focaccia from **Liguria Bakery** (⊠ *1700 Stockton St., at Filbert St., North Beach* ☎ *415/421–3786*) to be the best in the neighborhood. Get there early, before noon—when the focaccia is gone, the place usually closes.

The friendly *paesans* behind the counter at **Molinari Delicatessen** (⊠ *373 Columbus Ave., North Beach* ☎ *415/421–2337*) serve up the most delicious, and quite possibly the biggest, sandwiches in town. Take a number, grab your bread from the bin, and gaze upon the sandwich board. If you want to eat in, say a prayer to the patron saint of table nabbing—there are all of three tables, outside. Fortunately, Washington Square Park is close by.

GETTING THERE

The Powell–Mason cable-car line can drop you within a block of Washington Square Park, in the heart of North Beach. The 30–Stockton and 15–3rd Street buses run to the neighborhood from Market Street. Once you're here, North Beach is a snap to explore on foot. It's mostly relatively flat—but climbing Telegraph Hill to reach Coit Tower is another story entirely.

MAKING THE MOST OF YOUR TIME

There's no bad time of day to visit this quarter. The cafés buzz morning to night, the shops along main drags Columbus Avenue and Broadway tend to stay open until at least 6 or 7 pm, and late-night revelers don't start checking their watches until about 2 am. Sunday is quieter, since some shops close (though City Lights is open daily, until midnight).

Plan to spend a few hours here—it's all about lingering, and the only major "sightseeing" spot is Coit Tower. The walk up to the tower is strenuous but rewarding; if you can tough it, make time for it. If you're driving, keep in mind that parking is difficult, especially at night.

5

Sightseeing
★★

Nightlife
★★★★

Dining
★★★

Lodging
★

Shopping
★★★

San Francisco novelist Herbert Gold calls North Beach "the longest-running, most glorious American bohemian operetta outside Greenwich Village." Indeed, to anyone who's spent some time in its eccentric old bars and cafés, North Beach evokes everything from the Barbary Coast days to the no-less-rowdy Beatnik era.

Updated by
Denise M. Leto

Italian bakeries appear frozen in time, homages to Jack Kerouac and Allen Ginsberg pop up everywhere, and the modern equivalent of the Barbary Coast's "houses of ill repute," strip joints, do business on Broadway. With its outdoor café tables, throngs of tourists, and holiday vibe, this is probably the part of town Europeans are thinking of when they say San Francisco is the most European city in America.

The neighborhood truly was a beach at the time of the gold rush—the bay extended into the hollow between Telegraph and Russian hills. Among the first immigrants to Yerba Buena during the early 1840s were young men from the northern provinces of Italy. The Genoese started the fishing industry in the newly renamed boomtown of San Francisco, as well as a much-needed produce business. Later, Sicilians emerged as leaders of the fishing fleets and eventually as proprietors of the seafood restaurants lining Fisherman's Wharf. Meanwhile, their Genoese cousins established banking and manufacturing empires.

Once almost exclusively Italian-American, today North Beach is a mixture of Italian (many of them elderly), Chinese, and San Francisco yuppie. But walk down narrow Romolo Place (off Broadway east of Columbus) or Genoa Place (off Union west of Kearny) or Medau Place (off Filbert west of Grant) and you can feel the immigrant Italian roots of this neighborhood. Locals know that most of the city's finest Italian restaurants are elsewhere, but North Beach is the place that puts folks in mind of Italian food, and there are many decent options to choose from. Bakeries sell focaccia fresh from the oven; eaten warm or cold, it's the perfect portable food. Many other aromas fill the air: coffee beans, deli meats and cheeses, Italian pastries, and—always—pungent garlic. ⇨ *For more on the North Beach food scene, see the Where to Eat chapter.*

A NORTH BEACH WALK

To hit the highlights of the neighborhood, start off with a browse at Beat landmark **City Lights Bookstore**. For cool boutique shopping, head north up **Grant Avenue**. Otherwise, it's time to get down to the serious business of hanging out. Make a left onto **Columbus Avenue** when you leave the bookstore and walk the strip until you find a café table or pastry display that calls your name.

Fortified, continue down Columbus to **Washington Square**, where you can walk or take the 39 bus up **Telegraph Hill** to Coit Tower's views. Be sure to take in the gorgeous gardens along the **Filbert Steps** on the way down. Finally, reward yourself by returning to **Columbus Avenue** for a drink at one of the atmosphere-steeped watering holes like **Tosca**, which is run by a woman Sean Penn calls "the last of the great saloon mistresses."

TOP ATTRACTIONS

★ **City Lights Bookstore.** Take a look at the exterior of the store: the replica of a revolutionary mural destroyed in Chiapas, Mexico, by military forces; the poetry in the windows; and the sign that says "Turn your sell [sic] phone off. Be here now." This place isn't just doling out best sellers. Designated a city landmark, the hangout of Beat-era writers—Allen Ginsberg and store founder Lawrence Ferlinghetti among them—remains a vital part of San Francisco's literary scene. Browse the three levels of sometimes haphazardly arranged poetry, philosophy, politics, fiction, history, and local zines, to the tune of creaking wood floors. ■TIP➔ Be sure to check their calendar of literary events.

Back in the day, the basement was a kind of literary living room, where writers like Ginsberg and Kerouac would read and even receive mail. Ferlinghetti cemented City Lights' place in history by publishing Ginsberg's *Howl and Other Poems* in 1956. The small volume was ignored in the mainstream . . . until Ferlinghetti and the bookstore manager were arrested for corruption of youth and obscenity. In the landmark First Amendment trial that followed, the judge exonerated both, saying a work that has "redeeming social significance" can't be obscene. *Howl* went on to become a classic.

Kerouac Alley, branching off Columbus Avenue next to City Lights, was rehabbed in 2007. Embedded in the pavement are quotes from Lawrence Ferlinghetti, Maya Angelou, Confucius, John Steinbeck, and of course, the namesake himself. ✉ *261 Columbus Ave., North Beach* ☎ *415/362–8193* ⊕ *www.citylights. com* ⊙ *Daily 10 am–midnight.*

★ **Coit Tower.** Whether you think it resembles a fire-hose nozzle or something more, ahem, adult, this 210-foot tower is among San Francisco's most distinctive skyline

WORD OF MOUTH

"One of my favorite things to do in North Beach is to have a picnic in Washington Square Park. Pick up a panino on Columbus Ave. and then sit in the park and eat it. On a nice day, this is some of the best people watching in town."

—erin74

View of North Beach and Coit Tower as seen from Lombard Street.

sights. Although the monument wasn't intended as a tribute to firemen, it's often considered as such because of the donor's special attachment to the local fire company. As the story goes, a young gold rush–era girl, Lillie Hitchcock Coit (known as Miss Lil), was a fervent admirer of her local fire company—so much so that she once deserted a wedding party and chased down the street after her favorite engine, Knickerbocker No. 5, while clad in her bridesmaid finery. She became the Knickerbocker Company's mascot and always signed her name "Lillie Coit 5." When Lillie died in 1929 she left the city $125,000 to "expend in an appropriate manner . . . to the beauty of San Francisco."

You can ride the elevator to the top of the tower—the only thing you have to pay for here—to enjoy the view of the Bay Bridge and the Golden Gate Bridge; due north is Alcatraz Island. ■TIP→ The views from the base of the tower are also expansive—and free. Parking at Coit Tower is limited; in fact, you may have to wait (and wait) for a space. Save yourself some frustration and take the 39 bus, which goes all the way up to the tower's base, or, if you're in good shape, hike up. ⇨ *For more details on the lovely stairway walk, see the Telegraph Hill listing.*

Inside the tower, 19 Depression-era murals depict California's economic and political life. The federal government commissioned the paintings from 25 local artists, and ended up funding quite a controversy. The radical Mexican painter Diego Rivera inspired the murals' socialist-realist style, with its biting cultural commentary, particularly about the exploitation of workers. At the time the murals were painted, clashes between management and labor along the waterfront and elsewhere in San Francisco were widespread. ⊠ *Telegraph Hill Blvd. at Greenwich*

CLOSE UP

Top 3 Espresso Spots in North Beach

Cafés are a way of life in North Beach, and if you're as serious about your coffee as the average San Franciscan (or Fodor's editor), you might want to stop in at all three of these spots.

The Giotta family celebrates the art of a good espresso as well as a good tune at **Caffè Trieste** (⊠ *601 Vallejo St., at Grant Ave., North Beach* ☎ *415/392–6739*). Every Saturday (as they have since 1971) from noon to 2 pm, the family presents a weekly musical. Arrive early to secure seats. The program ranges from Italian pop and folk music to operas, and patrons are encouraged to participate. If you're one of the few people in creation who haven't gotten started on a screenplay, you may take inspiration from the fact that Francis Ford Coppola reportedly wrote the screenplay for *The Godfather* here.

Intimate, triangular **Mario's Bohemian Cigar Store** (⊠ *566 Columbus Ave., North Beach* ☎ *415/362–0536*) serves up great hot focaccia sandwiches and North Beach–worthy espresso at its few tables and beautiful antique oak bar under old-time posters. On sunny days, take your order across the street to Washington Square for a classic San Francisco picnic.

A glance at the menu board—"Espresso: $1.80, Espresso with lemon: $10"—will clue you in that **Caffè Roma** (⊠ *526 Columbus Ave., North Beach* ☎ *415/296–7942*) takes its coffee a lot more seriously than it takes itself. And if you've got a problem with that, owner Tony Azzollini will convince you, from his refusal to make your coffee extra hot to his insistence that you drink your espresso the moment it's brewed. Airy and decidedly undistracting—black and white marble is the predominant theme—Roma is a no-nonsense coffee drinker's pit stop for a hot cup as well as coffee drinks, pastries, and wine. Spot the massive red roaster in the window and you'll know you're here. And if you insist on the lemon twist, you deserve to pay.

5

St. or Lombard St., North Beach ☎ 415/362–0808 🖾 Free; elevator to top $5 ⊙ Daily 10–6.

OFF THE BEATEN PATH

Tattoo Art Museum. Legendary tattoo artist and historian Lyle Tuttle's collection of tattoo memorabilia fills half this crowded tattoo parlor on the edge of North Beach. Exhibits, including equipment, photographs, newspaper clippings, and a stuffed bat, cover everything from primitive tattooing in Samoa (where the bat comes in) to tattooing in San Francisco in the 1960s. ⊠ 841 Columbus Ave., near Lombard St., North Beach ☎ 415/775–4991 🖾 Free ⊙ Daily noon–8.

Fodor's Choice ★

Telegraph Hill. Hill residents have some of the best views in the city, as well as the most difficult ascents to their aeries. The hill rises from the east end of Lombard Street to a height of 284 feet and is capped by Coit Tower *(see above)*. Imagine lugging your groceries up that! If you brave the slope, though, you can be rewarded with a "secret treasure" SF moment. Filbert Street starts up the hill, then becomes the Filbert Steps when the going gets too steep. You can cut between the Filbert Steps and another flight, the Greenwich Steps, on up to the hilltop. As

Where can I find . . . ?

PARKING	**North Beach Garage** (735 Vallejo St.) Open 24 hours, and each space is printed with a fortune.	**Vallejo Street Garage** (766 Vallejo St.) Bonus: great view from the top floor.
SOMETHING SWEET	**Stella Pastry & Café** (446 Columbus Ave.) It's all about the creamy sacripantina cake.	**Victoria Pastry Co.** (1362 Stockton St.) Look for the custardy St. Honoré cake, cooked in a brick oven.
A NIGHTCAP	**Tosca Café** (242 Columbus Ave.) A time-warp saloon, with brandy-spiked cappuccino.	**Vesuvio** (255 Columbus Ave.) A true 1960s boho hangout.

you climb, you can pass some of the city's oldest houses and be surrounded by beautiful, flowering private gardens. In some places the trees grow over the stairs so they feel like a green tunnel; elsewhere, you'll have wide-open views of the bay. And the telegraphic name? It comes from the hill's status as the first Morse code signal station back in 1853. ⊠ *Bordered by Lombard, Filbert, Kearny, and Sansome Sts., North Beach.*

WORTH NOTING

Beat Museum. It's hard to tell whether the folks who opened this small museum in 2006 are serious—what would the counterculture say about the $18 "Beat beret"? But if you're truly Beat-curious, stop by. Check out the "Beat pad," a mock-up of one of the cheap, tiny North Beach apartments the writers and artists populated in the 1950s, complete with bongos and bottle-as-candleholder. Memorabilia include the shirt Neal Cassady wore while driving Ken Kesey's Merry Prankster bus, "Further." An early photo of the legendary bus is juxtaposed with a more current picture showing it covered with moss and overgrowth, labeled "Nothing lasts." Indeed. There are also manuscripts, letters, and early editions by Jack Kerouac, Allen Ginsberg, and Lawrence Ferlinghetti. The gift store has a good selection of Beat philosophy, though it's nothing you won't find across the street at City Lights. ⊠ *540 Broadway, North Beach* ☎ *800/537–6822* ⊕ *www.thebeatmuseum.org* 💷 *$5* ⊙ *Daily 10–7.*

Grant Avenue. Originally called Calle de la Fundación, Grant Avenue is the oldest street in the city, but it's got plenty of young blood. Here dusty bars such as the Saloon and perennial favorites like the Savoy Tivoli mix with hotshot boutiques, odd curio shops like the antique jumble that is Aria, atmospheric cafés such as the boho haven Caffè Trieste, and authentic Italian delis. While the street runs from Union Square through Chinatown, North Beach, and beyond, the fun stuff in

CLOSE UP

The Birds

While on Telegraph Hill, you might be startled by a chorus of piercing squawks and a rushing sound of wings. No, you're not about to have a Hitchcock bird-attack moment. These small, vivid green parrots with cherry-red heads number in the hundreds; they're descendants of former pets that escaped or were released by their owners. (The birds dislike cages and they bite if bothered...must've been some disillusioned owners along the way.)

The parrots like to roost high in the aging cypress trees on the hill, chattering and fluttering, sometimes taking wing en masse. They're not popular with most residents, but they did find a champion in local bohemian Mark Bittner, a former street musician. Bittner began chronicling their habits, publishing a book and battling the homeowners who wanted to cut down the cypresses. A documentary, *The Wild Parrots of Telegraph Hill*, made the issue a cause célèbre. In 2007 City Hall, which recognizes a golden goose when it sees one, stepped in and brokered a solution to keep the celebrity birds in town. The city will cover the homeowners' insurance worries and plant new trees for the next generation of wild parrots.

—Denise M. Leto

this neighborhood is crowded into the four blocks between Columbus Avenue and Filbert Street. ⊠ *North Beach*.

Levi Strauss headquarters. The carefully landscaped complex appears so collegiate that it's affectionately known as LSU—short for Levi Strauss University. Lawns complement the redbrick buildings, and gurgling fountains drown out the sounds of traffic, providing a perfect environment for brown-bag and picnic lunches. The lobby visitor center has displays focusing on the history of the company, including a vintage-ad exhibit and tons of Levi products. The Filbert Steps to Coit Tower are across the street. ⊠ *Levi's Plaza, 1155 Battery St., North Beach*.

Saints Peter and Paul Catholic Church. Camera-toting visitors focus their lenses on the Romanesque splendor of what's often called the Italian Cathedral. Completed in 1924, the church has Disneyesque stone-white towers that are local landmarks. Mass reflects the neighborhood; it's given in English, Italian, and Chinese. (It's one of the few churches in town where you can hear mass in Italian.) Following their 1954 City Hall wedding, Marilyn Monroe and Joe DiMaggio had their wedding photos snapped here. ■TIP➔ On the first Sunday of October a mass followed by a parade to Fisherman's Wharf celebrates the Blessing of the Fleet. Another popular event is the Columbus Day pageant in North Beach, with a parade that ends at the church. ⊠ *666 Filbert St., at Washington Sq., North*

WORD OF MOUTH

"One strong point is that [North Beach] is often sunny and warm when other parts of SF are cold and/or foggy. It is low-keyed and casual. Well, maybe not low-key on weekend nights, but it is fun."

—LoveItaly

Beach ☎ *415/421–0809* ⊕ *www. stspeterpaul.san-francisco.ca.us.*

Sentinel Building. A striking triangular shape and a gorgeous green patina make this 1907 building at the end of Columbus Avenue a visual knockout. In the 1970s local filmmaker Francis Ford Coppola bought the building to use for his production company. The ground floor is now Coppola's stylish wine bar, **Café Zoetrope**. Stop in for wines from the Coppola vineyards in Napa and Sonoma, simple Italian dishes, and foodie gifts. ✉ *916 Kearny St., at Columbus Ave., North Beach.*

O PIONEERS!

The corner of Broadway and Columbus Avenue witnessed an unusual historic breakthrough. Here stood the Condor Club, where in 1964 Carol Doda became the country's first dancer to break the topless barrier. A bronze plaque honors the milestone (only in SF). And Doda, naturally, now owns a lingerie store in Cow Hollow.

OFF THE BEATEN PATH

1360 Montgomery Street. In the 1947 film *Dark Passage* Humphrey Bogart plays an escaped prisoner from San Quentin convicted of killing his wife. His real-life wife, Lauren Bacall, befriends him and lets him hole up in her apartment, inside this fantastic art-deco building. From the street you can view the etched-glass gazelles and palms counterpointing a silvered fresco of a heroic bridge worker. ✉ *Montgomery St. between Union and Filbert Sts., near top of Filbert Steps, North Beach.*

Washington Square. Once the daytime social heart of Little Italy, this grassy patch has changed character numerous times over the years. The Beats hung out in the 1950s, hippies camped out in the 1960s and early 70s, and nowadays you're just as likely to see kids of Southeast Asian descent tossing a Frisbee as Italian men or women chatting about their children and the old country. In the morning elderly Asians perform the motions of tai chi, but by mid-morning groups of conservatively dressed Italian men in their seventies and eighties begin to arrive. Any time of day, the park may attract a number of homeless people, who stretch out to rest on the benches and grass, and young locals sunbathing or running their dogs. Lillie Hitchcock Coit, in yet another show of affection for San Francisco's firefighters, donated the statue of two firemen with a child they rescued. ■TIP➔ The North Beach Festival, the city's oldest street fair, celebrates the area's Italian culture here each June. ✉ *Bordered by Columbus Ave. and Stockton, Filbert, and Union Sts., North Beach.*

CRAB STATION AT FISHERMA
SEAFOOD COCKTAIL
CRAB 4.95
SHRIMP 3.75
PRAWN 3.95
OYSTER 3.95
SQUID 4.95
CRAB & SHRIMP COMBO 7.60
PRAWN PLATE 6.50
1/2 LOBSTER 13.50
FRIED ITEMS
FISH-N-CHIPS 5.75
SHRIMP-N-CHIPS 7.75
CALAMARI-N-CHIPS 6.75
CLAM STRIPS-N-CHIPS 6.75
2 ITEMS COMBO 8.65
CRAB CAKES 2.75
HOT DOGS 2.50
CORN DOGS 2.50
BURGERS 3.95
CLAM CHOWDER

6

On the Waterfront

WORD OF MOUTH

"Alcatraz Night Tour. . . . This was awesome!!!!!! It was really a great information tour. So spooky to be walking around Alcatraz at night. There was a gorgeous night time view of San Francisco . . . at the end the demonstrations of the cells being locked and opened . . . the noise it made. Chilling. . . ."

—LizaMarie

GETTING ORIENTED

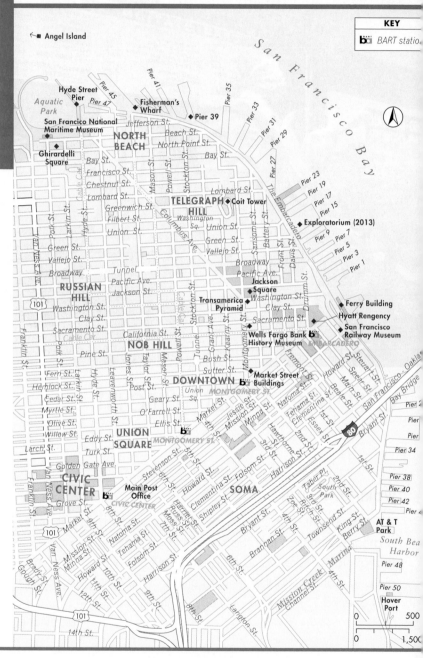

KEY
🅱 BART statio.

← Angel Island

GETTING THERE

The Powell–Hyde and Powell–Mason cable-car lines both end near Fisherman's Wharf. The walk from downtown through North Beach to the northern waterfront is lovely, and if you stick to Columbus Avenue, the incline is relatively gentle. F-line trolleys, often packed to capacity, run all the way down Market to the Embarcadero, then north to the Wharf.

TOP 5 REASONS TO GO

Ferry Building: Join locals eyeing luscious produce and foods prepared by some of the city's best chefs at San Francisco's premier farmers' market on Saturday morning.

Hyde Street Pier: Sing sea chanteys and raise the sails aboard the gorgeously restored 19th-century square-rigged ship *Balclutha*, then head to the Buena Vista for an Irish coffee.

Alcatraz: Go from a scenic bay tour to "the hole"—solitary confinement in absolute darkness—while inmates and guards tell you stories about what life was really like on the Rock.

F-line: Grab a polished wooden seat aboard one of the city's lovingly restored vintage streetcars and clatter down the tracks toward the Ferry Building's spire.

Musée Mécanique: Take a pocketful of quarters and step through the gaping mouth of Laffing Sal to this arcade of vintage machines.

QUICK BITES

The Ferry Building is everyone's favorite spot for a bite on the Embarcadero. Gather bread, cheese, and fruit for a picnic, or grab something to go from **Out the Door** (⊠ *1 Ferry Plaza, Embarcadero* ☎ *415/321–3740*), beloved Vietnamese restaurant Slanted Door's takeout counter. If you need a sweet treat, head to pink **Miette** (⊠ *1 Ferry Plaza, Embarcadero* ☎ *415/837–0300*), where the cakes and pastries are absolute organic perfection.

MAKING THE MOST OF YOUR TIME

If you're planning to go to Alcatraz, be sure to buy your tickets in advance, as tours frequently sell out. Alcatraz ferries leave from Pier 33—so there isn't a single good reason to suffer Pier 39's tacky, overpriced attractions. If you're a sailor at heart, definitely spend an hour with the historic ships of the Hyde Street Pier.

FERRIES

The bay is a huge part of San Francisco's charm, and getting out on the water gives you an attractive and unique (though windy) perspective on the city. Keep in mind that a ride on a commuter ferry is cheaper than a cruise, and just as lovely. The **Red and White Fleet** (⊠ *Pier 43½, Fisherman's Wharf* ☎ *415/ 673-2900* ⊕ *www.redandwhite. com*) has the widest range of tour options, including sunset cruises from April to October. The **Blue & Gold Fleet** (⊠ *Pier 39, Fisherman's Wharf* ☎ *415/705– 5555* ⊕ *www.blueandgoldfleet. com*) offers bay cruises and, in summer, high-speed RocketBoat rides, as well as ferry service to Oakland, Alameda, Tiburon, Sausalito, Vallejo, and Angel Island.

6

Sightseeing
★★
Nightlife
⁻
Dining
★★★
Lodging
★★★★
Shopping
★★

San Francisco's waterfront neighborhoods have fabulous views and utterly different personalities. Kitschy, overpriced Fisherman's Wharf struggles to maintain the last shreds of its existence as a working wharf, while Pier 39 is a full-fledged consumer circus. The Ferry Building draws well-heeled locals with its culinary pleasures, firmly reconnecting the Embarcadero to downtown. Between the Ferry Building and Pier 39 a former maritime no-man's-land is filling in with Alcatraz Landing's fashionable waterfront restaurants, restored pedestrian-friendly piers, and in 2013, the new Exploratorium.

Updated by
Denise M. Leto

Today's shoreline was once Yerba Buena Cove, filled in during the latter half of the 19th century, when San Francisco was a brawling, extravagant gold-rush town. Jackson Square, now a genteel and upscale corner of the inland Financial District, was the heart of the Barbary Coast, bordering some of the roughest wharves in the world. Below Montgomery Street (in today's Financial District), between California Street and Broadway, lies a remnant of these wild days: more than 100 ships abandoned by frantic crews and passengers caught up in gold fever lie under the foundations of buildings here.

TOP ATTRACTIONS

Fodor'sChoice
★

Ferry Building. Renovated in 2003, the Ferry Building is the jewel of the Embarcadero. The beacon of the port area, erected in 1896, has a 230-foot clock tower modeled after the campanile of the cathedral in Seville, Spain. On the morning of April 18, 1906, the tower's four clock faces, powered by the swinging of a 14-foot pendulum, stopped at 5:17—the moment the great earthquake struck—and stayed still for 12 months.

Today San Franciscans flock to the street-level Market Hall, stocking up on supplies from local favorites such as Acme Bread, Scharffen Berger

Chocolate, Cowgirl Creamery, and Blue Bottle Coffee. Lucky diners claim a coveted table at Slanted Door, the city's beloved high-end Vietnamese restaurant. The seafood bars at Hog Island Oyster Company and Ferry Plaza Seafood have fantastic city panoramas—or you can take your purchases around to the building's bay side, where benches face views of the Bay Bridge. Saturday mornings the plaza in front of the building buzzes with an upscale, celebrity-chef-studded farmers' market. Extending from the piers on the north side of the building south to the Bay Bridge, the waterfront promenade is a favorite among joggers and picnickers, with a front-row view of the sailboats slipping by. The Ferry Building also serves actual ferries: from behind the building they sail to Sausalito, Larkspur, Tiburon, and the East Bay. ⊠ *Embarcadero at foot of Market St., Embarcadero* ⊕ *www.ferrybuildingmarketplace.com.*

> ### F-LINE TROLLEYS
>
> The **F-line**, the city's system of vintage electric trolleys, gives the cable cars a run for their money as San Francisco's best-loved mode of transportation. These beautifully restored streetcars—some dating from the 19th century—run from the Castro all the way down Market Street to the Embarcadero, then north to Fisherman's Wharf. Each car is unique, restored to the colors of its city of origin, from New Orleans and Philadelphia to Moscow and Milan. Purchase tickets on board; exact change is required. ⊕ *www.streetcar.org* ⚑ *$2.*

6

QUICK BITES   Even locals love the cheery **Buena Vista Café** (⊠ *2765 Hyde St., Fisherman's Wharf* ☎ *415/474–5044*), which claims to be the first place in the United States to have served Irish coffee. The café opens at 9 am weekdays (8 am weekends) and dishes up a great breakfast. They serve about 2,000 Irish coffees a day, so it's always crowded; try for a table overlooking nostalgic Victorian Park and its cable-car turntable.

☺ **Fisherman's Wharf.** It may be one of the city's best-known attractions, but the Wharf is a no-go zone for most locals, who shy away from the difficult parking, overpriced food, and cheesy shops at third-rate shopping centers like the Cannery at Del Monte Square. If you just can't resist a visit here, come early to avoid the crowds and get a sense of the Wharf's functional role—it's not just an amusement park replica.

Most of the entertainment at the Wharf is schlocky and overpriced, with one notable exception: the splendid **Musée Mécanique** (☎ *415/346–2000* ⏱ *Weekdays 10–7, weekends 10–8*), a time-warped arcade with antique mechanical contrivances, including peep shows and nickelodeons. Some favorites are the giant and rather creepy "Laffing Sal" (you enter the museum through his gaping mouth), an arm-wrestling machine, the world's only steam-powered motorcycle, and mechanical fortune-telling figures that speak from their curtained boxes. Note the depictions of race that betray the prejudices of the time: stoned Chinese figures in the "Opium-Den" and clown-faced African-Americans eating watermelon in the "Mechanical Farm." Admission is free, but you'll need quarters to bring the machines to life.

Among the two floors of exhibits at **Ripley's Believe It or Not! Museum** (✉ *175 Jefferson St., Fisherman's Wharf* ☎ *415/771–6188* ⊕ *www.ripleysf.com* ✑ *$16.99* ⊙ *Late June–Labor Day, Sun.–Thurs. 9 am–11 pm, Fri. and Sat. 9 am–midnight; Labor Day–early June, Sun.–Thurs. 10–10, Fri. and Sat., 10 am–midnight*) is a tribute to San Francisco—an 8-foot-long scale model of a cable car, made entirely of matchsticks.

Notables from local boy Robin Williams to King Tut await at the **Wax Museum** (✉ *145 Jefferson St., Fisherman's Wharf* ☎ *415/202–0400 or 800/439–4305* ⊕ *www.waxmuseum.com*), open daily 10–9. Admission is $14.

The USS *Pampanito* (✉ *Pier 45, Fisherman's Wharf* ☎ *415/775–1943* ⊕ *www.maritime.org/pamphome.htm* ⊙ *Oct.–Memorial Day, Sun.–Thurs. 9–6, Fri. and Sat. 9–8; Memorial Day–Sept., Thurs.–Tues. 9–8, Wed. 9–6*) provides an intriguing if mildly claustrophobic glimpse into life on a submarine during World War II. The sub sank six Japanese warships and damaged four others. Admission is $10; the family pass is a great deal at $20 for two adults and up to four kids. ✉ *Jefferson St. between Leavenworth St. and Pier 39, Fisherman's Wharf.*

⊙ ★ **Hyde Street Pier.** Cotton candy and souvenirs are all well and good, but if you want to get to the heart of the Wharf—boats—there's no better place to do it than at this pier, by far one of the Wharf area's best bargains. Depending on the time of day, you might see boatbuilders at work or children pretending to man an early-1900s ship.

Don't pass up the centerpiece collection of historic vessels, part of the **San Francisco Maritime National Historic Park,** almost all of which can be boarded. The newly restored *Balclutha,* an 1886 full-rigged three-masted sailing vessel that's more than 250 feet long, sailed around Cape Horn 17 times; kids especially love the *Eureka,* a side-wheel passenger and car ferry, for her onboard collection of vintage cars; the *Hercules* is a steam-powered tugboat. The *C. A. Thayer,* a three-masted schooner, recently underwent a painstaking restoration and is back on display. Across the street from the pier and almost a museum in itself is the San Francisco Maritime National Historic Park's **Visitor Center** (✉ *499 Jefferson St., at Hyde St., Fisherman's Wharf* ☎ *415/447–5000* ⊙ *June–Aug., daily 9:30–5:30; Sept.–May, daily 9:30–5*), happily free of mind-numbing, text-heavy displays. Instead, fun large-scale exhibits, such as a huge First Order Fresnel lighthouse lens and a shipwrecked boat, make this an engaging and relatively quick stop. Though it's still undergoing long-term restoration, the **Maritime Museum** (✉ *900 Beach St., at Polk St., Fisherman's Wharf* ⊙ *Lobby daily 10–4*) is worth a peek now to see its lobby mural, a gorgeous underwater dreamscape. ✉ *Hyde and Jefferson Sts., Fisherman's Wharf* ☎ *415/561–7100* ⊕ *www.nps.gov/safr* ✑ *Ships $5* ⊙ *June–Aug., daily 9:30–5:30; Sept.–May, daily 9:30–5.*

S.S. *Jeremiah O'Brien*. A participant in the D-Day landing in Normandy during World War II, this Liberty Ship freighter is one of two such vessels (out of 2,500 built) still in working order. To keep the 1943 ship in sailing shape, the steam engine—which appears in the film *Titanic*—is operated dockside seven times a year on special "steaming weekends." Cruises take place several times a year between May and October, and the vessel is open to visitors daily. ⊠ *Pier 45, Fisherman's Wharf* ☎ *415/544–0100* ⊕ *www.ssjeremiahobrien.org* 🎟 *$10* ☉ *Daily 9–4.*

Pier 39. The city's most popular waterfront attraction draws millions of visitors each year who come to browse through its vertiginous array of shops and concessions hawking every conceivable form of souvenir. The pier can be quite crowded, and the numerous street performers may leave you feeling more harassed than entertained. Arriving early in the morning ensures you a front-row view of the sea lions, but if you're here to shop—and make no mistake about it, Pier 39 wants your money—be aware that most stores don't open until 9:30 or 10 (later in winter).

Pick up a buckwheat hull–filled otter neck wrap or a plush sea lion to snuggle at the **Marine Mammal Center Store** (☎ *415/289–7373*), whose proceeds benefit Sausalito's respected wild-animal hospital, the Marine Mammal Center.

6

Sales of the excellent books, maps, and collectibles—including a series of gorgeous, distinctive art-deco posters for Alcatraz, the Presidio, Fort Point, and the other members of the Golden Gate National Recreation Area—at the **National Park Store** (☎ *415/433–7221*) help to support the National Park Service.

Brilliant colors enliven the double-decker **San Francisco Carousel** (🎟 *$3 per ride*), decorated with images of such city landmarks as the Golden Gate Bridge and Lombard Street.

Follow the sound of barking to the northwest side of the pier to view the sea lions that flop about the floating docks.

At **Aquarium of the Bay** (☎ *415/623–5300 or 888/732–3483* ⊕ *www.aquariumofthebay.org* 🎟 *$16.95* ☉ *June–Sept., daily 9–8; Mar.–May and Oct., Mon.–Thurs. 10–7, Fri.–Sun. 10–8; Nov.–Feb., daily 10–7)* moving walkways transport you through a space surrounded on three sides by water filled with indigenous San Francisco Bay marine life, from fish and plankton to sharks. Many find the aquarium overpriced; if you can, take advantage of the family rate ($39.95 for two adults and two kids under 12).

The **California Welcome Center** (☎ *415/981–1280* ⊕ *www.visitcwc.com* ☉ *Daily 10–6*), on Pier 39's second level, offers Internet use for $5 per half hour.

ALCATRAZ'S FUTURE

Alcatraz is currently undergoing an extensive restoration, and funds are being raised to renovate and reopen outbuildings that have been closed for years. The jail cells' vintage locks have also been repaired. Tours of the island once included briefly locking members into cells—but this hasn't been a part of the program since corroded lock mechanisms began sticking, *really* locking some people in!

Parking (free with validation from a Pier 39 restaurant) is at the Pier 39 Garage, off Powell Street at the Embarcadero. ⊠ *Beach St. at Embarcadero, Fisherman's Wharf ⊕ www.pier39.com.*

WORTH NOTING

Angel Island. For an outdoorsy adventure, consider a day at this island northwest of Alcatraz. Discovered by Spaniards in 1775 and declared a U.S. military reserve 75 years later, the island was used as a screening ground for Asian immigrants—who were often held for months, even years, before being granted entry—from 1910 until 1940. Since 2009 you can visit the restored Immigration Station, from the dock where detainees landed to the barracks where you can see the poems in Japanese script they etched onto the walls. In 1963 the government designated Angel Island a state park. Today people come for picnics, hikes along the scenic 5-mi path that winds around the island's perimeter, and tram tours that explain the park's history; venture inland and you'll likely see evidence of the 2008 fire that swept more than a third of the island's 740 acres. Twenty-five bicycles are permitted on the ferry on a first-come, first-served basis, and you can rent mountain bikes for $10 an hour or $35 a day at the landing (daily April through October; call during other times). There are also a dozen primitive campsites. Blue and Gold Fleet is the only Angel Island ferry service with departures from San Francisco. Boats leave from Pier 41 and the Ferry Building. ⊠ *Pier 41, Fisherman's Wharf* ☎ *415/435–1915 park information and ferry schedules, 415/705–5555, 800/426–8687 tickets* ⊕ *www.angelisland.com* ✉ *$16* ⊙ *Daily 8 am–sunset.*

Ghirardelli Square. Most of the redbrick buildings in this early-20th-century complex were once part of the Ghirardelli factory. Now tourists come here to pick up the famous chocolate, though you can purchase it all over town and save yourself a trip to what is essentially a mall. But this is the only place to watch the cool chocolate manufactory in action. (If you're a chocoholic, this definitely beats the Cannery.) There are no fewer than three Ghirardelli stores here, as well as gift shops and a couple of restaurants—including Ana Mandara—that even locals love. Fairmont recently opened an upscale urban time-share directly on the square. Placards throughout the square describe the factory's history. ⊠ *900 N. Point St., Fisherman's Wharf* ☎ *415/775–5500* ⊕ *www.ghirardellisq.com.*

Hyatt Regency. John Portman designed this hotel noted for its 17-story hanging garden, a delightful interior green space you'd never expect from the unwelcoming, imposing exterior. The garden glows at Christmas, when strands of tiny white lights dangle over the cavernous atrium lobby. The four glass elevators facing the lobby are fun to ride, unless you suffer from vertigo. ⊠ *5 Embarcadero Center, Embarcadero* ☎ *415/788–1234* ⊕ *sanfranciscoregency.hyatt.com.*

> **WORD OF MOUTH**
>
> "Alcatraz is truly amazing…I think it's one of the best sites I've seen and I've been all over the world and I live in San Francisco. I always take people there."
>
> —galaxygrrl200

Where can I find . . . ?

PARKING	Beach and Hyde Garage (655 Beach St.) Steps away from Fisherman's Wharf attractions.	Embarcadero Center (Battery St. near Broadway) Four hours free on nights and weekends with validation.
A DRUGSTORE	Walgreens (320 Bay St.) Stop in for sunscreen on your way to your Alcatraz cruise.	Safeway (145 Jackson St.) Need some aspirin after walking the Embarcadero?
A DRINK	Harrington's (245 Front St.) Irish saloon with a good selection of imported beers.	Hog Island Oyster Bar (Ferry Bldg.) Wine and oysters with a bay view.

Jackson Square. This was the heart of the Barbary Coast of the Gay 90s (the 1890s, that is). Although most of the red-light district was destroyed in the fire that followed the 1906 earthquake, old redbrick buildings and narrow alleys recall the romance and rowdiness of San Francisco's early days. The days of brothels and bar fights are long gone—now Jackson Square is a genteel, quiet corner of the Financial District. It's of interest to the historically inclined and antiques-shop browsers, but otherwise safely skipped.

Some of the city's first business buildings, survivors of the 1906 quake, still stand between Montgomery and Sansome streets. After a few decades of neglect, these old-timers were adopted by preservation-minded interior designers and wholesale furniture dealers for use as showrooms. In 1972 the city officially designated the area—bordered by Columbus Avenue on the west, Broadway and Pacific Avenue on the north, Washington Street on the south, and Sansome Street on the east—San Francisco's first historic district. When property values soared, many of the fabric and furniture outlets fled to Potrero Hill. Advertising agencies, attorneys, and antiques dealers now occupy the Jackson Square–area structures.

It takes a bit of conjuring to evoke the wild Barbary Coast days when checking out the now-gentrified gold rush–era buildings in the 700 block of **Montgomery Street.** But this was an especially colorful block. Author Mark Twain was a reporter for the spunky *Golden Era* newspaper, which occupied No. 732 (now part of the building at No. 744). From 1959 to 1996 the late ambulance-chaser extraordinaire, lawyer Melvin Belli, had his headquarters there. There was never a dull moment in Belli's world; he represented clients from Mae West to Gloria Sykes (who in 1964 claimed that a cable-car accident turned her into a nymphomaniac) to Jim and Tammy Faye Bakker. Whenever he won a case, he fired a cannon and raised the Jolly Roger. Belli was also known

ESCAPE FROM ALCATRAZ

Federal prison officials liked to claim that it was impossible to escape Alcatraz, and for the most part, that assertion was true. For seasoned swimmers, though, the trip has never posed a problem—in fact, it's been downright popular.

In the 1930s, in an attempt to dissuade the feds from converting Alcatraz into a prison, a handful of schoolgirls made the swim to the city. At age sixty, native son Jack LaLanne did it (for the second time) while shackled and towing a 1,000-pound rowboat. Every year a couple of thousand participants take the plunge during the annual Escape from Alcatraz Triathlon. Heck, a dog made the crossing in 2005 and finished well ahead of most of the (human) pack. And in 2006 seven-year-old Braxton Bilbrey became the youngest "escapee" on record. Incidentally, those reports of shark-infested waters are true—but the sharks aren't a dangerous species.

for receiving a letter from the never-caught Zodiac killer. It seems fitting that the building sat for years, deteriorating and moldering, while the late attorney's sons fought wife number five (joined with Belli in holy matrimony just three months before his death). She eventually won, but today the dilapidated building is for sale.

Restored 19th-century brick buildings line Hotaling Place, which connects Washington and Jackson streets. The lane is named for the head of the **A.P. Hotaling Company whiskey distillery** (⊠ *451 Jackson St., at Hotaling Pl.*), which was the largest liquor repository on the West Coast in its day. (Hotaling whiskey is still made in the city, by the way; look for their single malts for a sip of truly local flavor.) ⊠ *Jackson Sq. district, bordered by Broadway and Washington, Kearny, and Sansome Sts., Financial District.*

Market Street buildings. The street, which bisects the city at an angle, has consistently challenged San Francisco's architects. One of the most intriguing responses to this challenge sits diagonally across Market Street from the Palace Hotel. The tower of the **Hobart Building** (No. 582) combines a flat facade and oval sides and is considered one of Willis Polk's best works in the city. East on Market Street is Charles Havens's triangular **Flatiron Building** (Nos. 540–548), another classic solution. At Bush Street, the **Donahue Monument** holds its own against the skyscrapers that tower over the intersection. This homage to waterfront mechanics, which survived the 1906 earthquake (a famous photograph shows Market Street in ruins around the sculpture), was designed by Douglas Tilden, a noted California sculptor. The plaque in the sidewalk next to the monument marks the spot as the location of the San Francisco Bay shoreline in 1848. Telltale nautical details such as anchors, ropes, and shells adorn the gracefully detailed **Matson Building** (No. 215), built in the 1920s for the shipping line Matson Navigation. ⊠ *Between New Montgomery and Beale Sts., Financial District.*

🐚 **San Francisco National Maritime Museum.** You'll feel as if you're out to sea when you step aboard, er, inside this sturdy, round, ship-shape structure dubbed the Bathhouse. The museum, part of the **San Francisco Maritime National Historical Park,** is in the midst of a multiyear renovation. At this writing, only the veranda and the lobby, with its stunningly restored undersea dreamscape mural, were open to the public; call ahead for updates. When restoration is complete, you'll be able to view the

museum's three floors of intricate ship models, beautifully restored figureheads, photographs of life at sea, and other artifacts chronicling the maritime history of San Francisco and the West Coast. The views from the top floor are stunning, as are those from the first-floor balcony, which overlooks the beach; also check out the lovely WPA-era tile designs on your way to the steamships exhibit. ✉ *Aquatic Park, foot of Polk St., Fisherman's Wharf* ☎ *415/447–5000* ⊕ *www.nps.gov/safr* 🔖 *Donation suggested* ☉ *Daily 10–4.*

🐚 **San Francisco Railway Museum.** A labor of love brought to you by the same vintage-transit enthusiasts responsible for the F-line's revival, this one-room museum and store celebrates the city's storied streetcars and cable cars with photographs, models, and artifacts. The permanent exhibit includes the replicated end of a streetcar with a working cab—complete with controls and a bell—for kids to explore; the cool, antique Wiley birdcage traffic signal; and models and display cases to view. Right on the F-line track, just across from the Ferry Building, this is a great quick stop. ✉ *77 Steuart St., Embarcadero* ☎ *415/974–1948* ⊕ *www.streetcar.org* 🔖 *Free* ☉ *Tues.–Sun. 10–6.*

Transamerica Pyramid. It's neither owned by Transamerica nor is it a pyramid, but this 853-foot-tall obelisk *is* the most photographed of the city's high-rises. Excoriated in the design stages as "the world's largest architectural folly," the icon was quickly hailed as a masterpiece when it opened in 1972. Today it's probably the city's most recognized structure after the Golden Gate Bridge. A fragrant redwood grove along the east side of the building, replete with benches and a cheerful fountain, is a placid patch in which to unwind. ✉ *600 Montgomery St., Financial District* ⊕ *www.transamerica.com.*

Wells Fargo Bank History Museum. There were no formal banks in San Francisco during the early years of the gold rush, and miners often entrusted their gold dust to saloon keepers. In 1852 Wells Fargo opened its first bank in the city, and the company soon established banking offices in mother-lode camps throughout California. Stagecoaches and pony-express riders connected points around the burgeoning state,

CLOSE UP

Alcatraz as Native Land

In the 1960s Native Americans attempted to reclaim Alcatraz, citing an 1868 treaty that granted Native Americans any surplus federal land. Their activism crested in 1969, when several dozen Native Americans began a 19-month occupation, supported by public opinion and friendly media.

The group offered to buy the island from the government for $24 worth of beads and other goods—exactly what Native Americans had been paid for Manhattan in 1626. In their Proclamation to the Great White Father and His People, the group laid out the 10 reasons why Alcatraz would make an ideal Indian reservation, among them: "There is no industry and so unemployment is very great," and "The soil is rocky and nonproductive, and the land does not support game." The last holdouts were removed by federal agents in 1971, but today's visitors are still greeted with the huge graffitied message: "Indians Welcome. Indian Land."

where the population boomed from 15,000 to 200,000 between 1848 and 1852. The museum displays samples of nuggets and gold dust from mines, a mural-size map of the Mother Lode, mementos of the poet bandit Black Bart (who signed his poems "Po8"), and an old telegraph machine on which you can practice sending codes. The showpiece is a red Concord stagecoach, the likes of which carried passengers from St. Joseph, Missouri, to San Francisco in just three weeks during the 1850s. ✉ *420 Montgomery St., Financial District* ☎ *415/396–2619* ⊕ *www. wellsfargohistory.com* ☎ *Free* ☉ *Weekdays 9–5.*

ALCATRAZ

"They made that place purely for punishment, where men would rot. It was designed to systematically destroy human beings . . . Cold, gray, and lonely, it had a weird way of haunting you—there were those dungeons that you heard about, but there was also the city . . . only a mile and a quarter away, so close you could almost touch it. Sometimes the wind would blow a certain way and you could smell the Italian cooking in North Beach and hear the laughter of people, of women and kids. That made it worse than hell."

—Jim Quillen, former Alcatraz inmate

Gripping the rail as the ferryboat pitches gently in the chilly breeze, you watch formidable Alcatraz rising ahead. Imagine making this trip shackled at the ankle and waist, the looming fortress on the craggy island ahead, waiting to swallow you whole. Thousands of visitors come every day to walk in the footsteps of Alcatraz's notorious criminals. The stories of life and death on "the Rock" may sometimes be exaggerated, but it's almost impossible to resist the chance to wander the cellblock that tamed the country's toughest gangsters and saw daring escape attempts of tremendous desperation.

LIFE ON THE ROCK

The federal penitentiary's first warden, James A. Johnston, was largely responsible for Alcatraz's (mostly false) hell-on-earth reputation. A tough but relatively humane disciplinarian, Johnston strictly limited the information flow to and from the prison when it opened in 1934. Prisoners' letters were censored, newspapers and radios were forbidden, and no visits were allowed during a convict's first three months in the slammer. Understandably, imaginations ran wild on the mainland.

A LIFE OF PRIVILEGE

Monotony was an understatement on Alcatraz; the same precise schedule was kept daily. The rulebook stated, "You are entitled to food, clothing, shelter, and medical attention. Anything else you get is a privilege." These privileges, from the right to work to the ability to receive mail, were earned by following the prison's rules. A relatively minor infraction meant losing privileges. A serious breach, like fighting, brought severe punishments like time in the Hole (a.k.a. the Strip Cell, since the prisoner had to strip) or the Oriental (an absolutely dark, silent cell with a hole in the ground for a toilet).

THE SPAGHETTI RIOT

Johnston knew that poor food was one of the major causes of prison riots, so he insisted that Alcatraz serve the best chow in the prison system. But the next warden at Alcatraz slacked off, and in 1950, one spaghetti meal too many sent the inmates over the edge. Guards deployed tear gas to subdue the rioters.

A PRISONER'S DAY

6:30 AM: Wake-up call. Prisoners get up, get dressed, and clean cells.

6:50 AM: Prisoners stand at cell doors to be counted.

7:00 AM: Prisoners march single-file to mess hall for breakfast.

7:20 AM: Prisoners head to work or industries detail; count.

9:30 AM: 8-minute break; count.

11:30 AM: Count; prisoners march to mess hall for lunch.

12:00 PM: Prisoners march to cells; count; break in cells.

12:20 PM: Prisoners leave cells, march single-file back to work; count.

2:30 PM: 8-minute break; count.

4:15 PM: Prisoners stop work, two counts.

4:25 PM: Prisoners march into mess hall and are counted; dinner.

4:45 PM: Prisoners return to cells and are locked in.

5:00 PM: Prisoners stand at their doors to be counted.

8:00 PM: Count.

9:30 PM: Count; lights out.

12:01 AM—5 AM: Three counts.

INFAMOUS INMATES

Fewer than 2,000 inmates ever did time on the Rock; though they weren't necessarily the worst criminals, they were definitely the worst prisoners. Most were escape artists, and others, like Al Capone, had corrupted the prison system from the inside with bribes.

Name Al "Scarface" Capone

On the Rock 1934–1939

In for Tax evasion

Claim to fame Notorious Chicago gangster and bootlegger who arranged the 1929 St. Valentine's Day Massacre.

Hard fact Capone was among the first transfers to the Rock and arrived smiling and joking. He soon realized the party was over. Capone endured a few stints in the Hole and Warden Johnston's early enforced-silence policy; he was also stabbed by a fellow inmate. The gangster eventually caved, saying "it looks like Alcatraz has got me licked," thus cementing the prison's reputation.

Name Robert "The Birdman" Stroud

On the Rock 1942–1959

In for Murder, including the fatal stabbing of a prison guard

Claim to fame Subject of the acclaimed but largely fictitious 1962 film *Birdman of Alcatraz.*

Hard fact Stroud was actually known as the "Bird Doctor of Leavenworth." While incarcerated in Leavenworth prison through the 1920s and 30s, he became an expert on birds, tending an aviary and writing two books. The stench and mess in his cell discouraged the guards from searching it—and finding Stroud's homemade still. His years on the Rock were birdless.

Name George "Machine Gun" Kelly

On the Rock 1934–1951

In for Kidnapping

Claim to fame Became an expert with a machine gun at the urging of his wife, Kathryn. Kathryn also encouraged his string of bank robberies and the kidnapping for ransom of oilman Charles Urschel. Insert "ball and chain" joke here . . . While stashed in Leavenworth on a life sentence, Kelly boasted that he would escape and then free Kathryn. That got him a one-way ticket to Alcatraz.

Hard fact Was an altar boy on Alcatraz and was generally considered a model prisoner.

NO ESCAPE

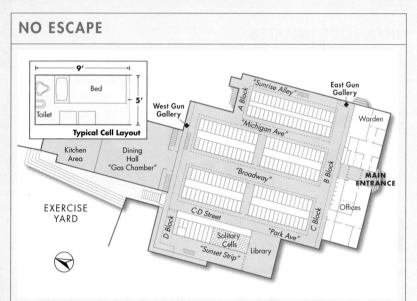

Alcatraz was a maximum-security federal penitentiary with one guard for every three prisoners. The biggest deterrent to escape, though, was the 1.4-mi of icy bay waters separating the Rock from the city. Only a few prisoners made it off the island, and only one is known to have survived. And that story about the shark-infested waters? There are sharks in the bay, but they're not the man-eating kind.

Bloodiest Attempt: In 1946, six prisoners hatched a plan to surprise a guard, seize weapons, and escape through the recreation yard. They succeeded up to a point, arming themselves and locking several guards into cells, but things got ugly when the group couldn't find the key that opened the door to the prison yard. Desperate, they opened fire on the trapped guards. Warden Johnston called in the Marines, who shelled the cell house for two days in the so-called Battle of Alcatraz. Three ringleaders were killed in the fighting; two were executed for murder; and one, who was just 19 years old, got 99 years slapped on to his sentence.

Craftiest Attempt: Over six months, three convicts stole bits and pieces from the kitchen and machine shop to make drills and digging pieces. They used these basic tools to widen a vent into the utility corridor. They also gathered bits of cardboard, toilet paper, and hair from the prison's barbershop to make crude models of their own heads. Then, like teenagers sneaking out, they put the decoy heads in their cots and walked away—up the pipes in the utility corridor to the roof, then down a drainpipe to the ground. They apparently swam for it, equipped with life vests made from prison raincoats, and are officially presumed dead.

Most Anticlimactic: In 1962, one prisoner spent an entire year loosening the bars in a window. Then he slipped through and managed to swim all the way to Fort Point, near the Golden Gate Bridge. He promptly fell asleep there and was found an hour later by some teenagers.

6 TIPS FOR ESCAPING TO ALCATRAZ

"Broadway," once the cell blocks' busiest corridor.

1. Buy your ticket in advance. Visit the Web site for Alcatraz Cruises (☎ 415/981–7625 ⊕ www.alcatrazcruises.com) to scout out available departure times for the ferry. Prepay by credit card—the ticket price covers the boat ride and the audio tour—and print your ticket at home. Bring it to Pier 33 up to an hour before sailing and experience just a touch of schadenfreude as you over-hear attendants tell scores of too-late passengers that your tour is sold out.

2. Dress smart. Bring that pullover you packed to ward off the chill from the boat ride and Alcatraz Island. Also: sneakers. Some Alcatraz guides are fanatical about making excellent time.

3. Go for the evening tour. You'll get even more out of the experience if you do it at night. The evening tour has programs not offered during the day, the bridge-to-bridge view of the city twinkles at night, and your "prison experience" will be amplified as darkness mourn-fully falls while you shuffle around the cell block.

4. Unplug and go against the flow. If you miss a cue on the excellent audio tour and find yourself out of synch, don't sweat it—use it as an opportunity to switch off the tape and walk against the grain of the people following the tour. No one will stop you if you walk back through a cell block on your own, taking the time to listen to the haunting sound of your own footsteps on the concrete floor.

5. Be mindful of scheduled and limited-capacity talks. Some programs only happen once a day (the schedule is posted in the cell house). Certain talks have limited capacity seating, so keep an eye out for a cell house staffer handing out passes shortly before the start time.

6. Talk to the staff. One of the island's greatest resources is its staff, who practically bubble over with information. Pick their brains, and draw them out about what they know.

PRACTICALITIES

Visitors at the Alcatraz dock waiting to depart "Uncle Sam's Devil's Island."

GETTING THERE

All cruises are operated by Alcatraz Cruises, the park's authorized concessionaire.

✉ *Pier 33, Fisherman's Wharf* ☎ *415/ 981–7625* 💺 *$26, including audio tour; $33 evening tour, including audio* ⏱ *Ferry departures every 30–45 mins Sept.–late May, daily 9:30–2:15, 4:20 for evening tour Thurs.–Mon. only; late May–Aug., daily 9:30–4:15, 6:10 and 6:45 for evening tour* 🌐 *www.nps.gov/ alca, www.parksconservancy.org/visit/ alcatraz, www.alcatrazcruises.com*

TIMING

The boat ride to Alcatraz is only about 15 minutes long, but you should allow about three hours for your entire visit. The delightful F-line vintage streetcars are the most direct public transit to the dock; on weekdays the 10-Townsend bus will get you within a few blocks of Pier 33.

FOOD

The prisoners might have enjoyed good food on Alcatraz, but you won't—unless you pack a picnic. Food is not available on the island, so be sure to stock up before you board the boat. Sandwich fare is available at Alcatraz Landing, at Pier 33, and the Ferry Building's bounty is just a 20-minute walk from Pier 33. In a pinch, you can also pony up for the underwhelming snacks on the boat.

KIDS ON THE ROCK

Parents should be aware that the audio tour, while engaging and worthwhile, includes some startlingly realistic sound effects. (Some children might not get a kick out of the gunshots from the Battle of Alcatraz—or the guards' screams, for that matter.) If you stay just one minute ahead in the program, you can always fast forward through the violent moments on your little one's audio tour.

STORM TROOPER ALERT!

When he was filming *Star Wars*, George Lucas recorded the sound of Alcatraz's cell doors slamming shut and used the sound bite in the movie whenever Darth Vader's star cruiser closed its doors.

The Marina and the Presidio

WORD OF MOUTH

"It's hard to describe but as you walk towards the city [on the Golden Gate Bridge], all you hear and feel is the wind across the bridge and the rushing traffic. Then you hit center span and are struck by both the majesty of the view and the overwhelming quiet. It really is spectacular."

—bk3

GETTING ORIENTED

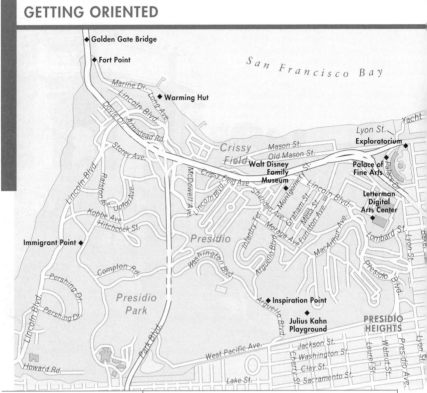

<table>
<tr><td>

MAKING THE MOST OF YOUR TIME

Allow two hours for the Exploratorium, plus 15 minutes to stroll around the Palace of Fine Arts. Walking across the Golden Gate Bridge takes about 30 minutes, but leave some time to take in the view on the other side. If you aren't in a hurry, plan to spend at least two to three hours in the Presidio. In a pinch, make a 30- to 45-minute swing-through for the views. Shoppers can burn up an entire day browsing the Marina's Chestnut Street and Cow Hollow's Union Street. Weekends are liveliest, while Mondays are quiet, since some shops close.

</td><td>

TOP 5 REASONS TO GO

Golden Gate Bridge: Get a good look at the iconic span from the Presidio, then bundle up and walk over the water.

Shop Cow Hollow and the Marina: Browse hip boutiques and lavish antiques shops on Union Street, Cow Hollow's main drag. Then head north across Lombard Street to the Marina's shopping hot spot, Chestnut Street.

Exploratorium and the Palace of Fine Arts: The hands-on Exploratorium is a perennial kids' fave. Just outside is the stunning Palace of Fine Arts.

Crissy Field: Try to spot egrets and herons from the bayside wooden boardwalk over this restored tidal marshland under the Golden Gate Bridge.

Presidio wanderings: Lace up your walking shoes and follow one of the wooded trails; the city will feel a hundred miles away. If you have a car, take a meandering drive, stopping at any and all ocean lookouts—Inspiration Point and Immigrant Point will take your breath away.

</td></tr>
</table>

GETTING THERE

The only public transportation to this part of town is the bus, so if you don't have your own wheels, take the 30–Stockton to Chestnut and Laguna in the Marina, two blocks south of Fort Mason.

The Marina and the Presidio are great for biking (though the Presidio has some hills) and easily reached along the Embarcadero.

The Presidio, vast and with plenty of free parking, is one area where it pays to have a car. If you're driving to either the Marina or the Presidio, parking isn't too bad—the Exploratorium and Palace of Fine Arts and Crissy Field all have free lots; parking at Fort Mason is free for one hour.

For those without wheels, the free year-round shuttle PresidiGo, which loops through the Presidio every half hour, is a dream; ride the whole route for a good 45-minute overview. Pick it up at the transit center at Lincoln Boulevard and Graham Street. For a map and schedule, check ⊕ *www.presidio.gov*.

QUICK BITES

Greens to Go (✉ *Fort Mason, Bldg. A, Marina* ☎ *415/771–6330*), the take-out wing of the famous Greens vegetarian restaurant, carries mouthwatering premade salads, sandwiches, and soups. There aren't any seats, but a steep flight of stairs leads up to a grassy picnicking area with splendid views of the Marina.

If you're after something sweet, look for the periwinkle awning at **La Boulange** (✉ *1909 Union St., Cow Hollow* ☎ *415/440–4450*), which serves tartines (open-faced sandwiches) in addition to perfect pastries and cakes. Free refills of organic coffee and a welcoming interior encourage lingering.

Sightseeing
★★★★
Nightlife
★★
Dining
★★★
Lodging
★★★
Shopping
★★★★

Yachts bob at their moorings, satisfied-looking folks jog along the Marina Green, and multimillion-dollar homes overlook the bay in this picturesque, if somewhat sterile, neighborhood. Does it all seem a bit too perfect? Well, it got this way after the hard knock of Loma Prieta—the current pretty face was put on after hundreds of homes collapsed in the 1989 earthquake. Just west of this waterfront area is a more natural beauty: the Presidio. Once a military base, this beautiful, sprawling park is mostly green space, with hills, woods, and the marshlands of Crissy Field.

Updated by
Denise M. Leto

It's often said that the Marina's 1989 disaster was literally built on the legacy of the Great Quake. Local legend has it that rubble from the 1906 catastrophe was used to fill in the area—unstable landfill that then liquefied when the Loma Prieta temblor struck. That story was disproved in 2004, but regardless of the origin of Marina land, its shaky character stays the same. The district suffered the worst damage in the city from the 1989 quake, and many residents fled in search of more-solid ground. Others stayed put. "I realize that we're sitting on Jell-O," said one local. "[But] how many areas are as beautiful as the Marina? At some point, you just have to pick your poison . . ."

Well-funded postcollegiates and the nouveau riche quickly replaced those who left, changing the tenor of this formerly low-key neighborhood. The number of yuppie coffee emporiums skyrocketed, a bank became a Williams-Sonoma, and the local grocer gave way to a Pottery Barn. On weekends a young, fairly homogeneous, well-to-do crowd floods the cafés and bars. (Some things don't change—even before the quake, the Marina Safeway was a famed pickup place for straight singles, hence the nickname "Dateway.") One unquestionable improvement has been the influx of contemporary cuisine into this former bastion of outdated Italian fare. South of Lombard Street is the Marina's affluent neighbor, Cow Hollow, whose main drag, Union

Street, has some of the city's best boutique shopping and a good selection of fun, fine restaurants and cafés. Joggers and kite-flyers head to the Marina Green, the strip of lawn between the yacht club and the mansions of Marina Boulevard.

The Presidio, meanwhile, is going through some shake-ups, too. Back in 1996 President Clinton signed a bill placing the Presidio in the hands of a trust corporation as part of a novel money-generating experiment. The trust manages most of the Presidio land, leasing buildings and allowing limited development with the goal of making enough money to cover the Presidio's operating costs. The National Park Service oversees the coastal sections. Whether this arrangement is a worthy model for national parks of the future, or the first step in the crass commercialization of a public resource, is the subject of debate and due to be officially evaluated in 2013. Whatever the outcome, the Presidio will still have superb views and the best hiking and biking areas in San Francisco; a drive through the lush area is also a treat.

THE MARINA

TOP ATTRACTIONS

Exploratorium. Walking into this fascinating "museum of science, art, and human perception" is like visiting a mad scientist's laboratory. Most of the exhibits are supersize, and you can play with everything. Get an Alice in Wonderland feeling in the distortion room, where you seem to shrink and grow as you walk across the slanted, checkered floor. In the shadow room, a powerful flash freezes an image of your shadow on the wall; jumping is a favorite pose. "Pushover" demonstrates cow-tipping, but for people: stand on one foot and try to keep your balance while a friend swings a striped panel in front of you (trust us, you're going to fall).

More than 650 other exhibits focus on sea and insect life, computers, electricity, patterns and light, language, the weather, and much more. "Explainers"—usually high-school students on their days off—demonstrate cool scientific tools and procedures, like DNA sample-collection and cow-eye dissection. One surefire hit is the pitch-black, touchy-feely Tactile Dome. In this geodesic dome strewn with textured objects, you crawl through a course of ladders, slides, and tunnels, relying solely on your sense of touch. Not surprisingly, lovey-dovey couples sometimes linger in the "grope dome," but be forewarned: the staff will turn on the lights if they have to. ■TIP➔ Reservations are required for the Tactile Dome, and will get you 75 minutes of access. You have to be at least seven years old to go through the dome, and the space is not for the claustrophobic. The Exploratorium is preparing to move into its new home at Pier 15 in 2013. ⊠ *3601 Lyon St., at Marina Blvd., Marina* ☎ *415/561–0360 general information, 415/561–0362 Tactile Dome reservations* ⊕ *www. exploratorium.edu* ⊡ *$15, free 1st Wed. of month; Tactile Dome $5 extra* ☉ *Tues.–Sun. 10–5.*

Fodor's Choice **Palace of Fine Arts.** At first glance this stunning, rosy rococo palace seems
★ to be from another world, and indeed, it's the sole survivor of the many tinted-plaster structures (a temporary classical city of sorts) built for

the 1915 Panama-Pacific International Exposition, the world's fair that celebrated San Francisco's recovery from the 1906 earthquake and fire. The expo buildings originally extended about a mile along the shore. Bernard Maybeck designed this faux–Roman classic beauty, which was reconstructed in concrete and reopened in 1967.

A victim of the elements, the Palace completed a piece-by-piece renovation in 2008, though the pseudo-Latin language adorning the exterior urns continues to stump scholars. The massive columns (each topped with four "weeping maidens"), great rotunda, and swan-filled lagoon have been used in countless fashion layouts, films, and wedding photo shoots. After admiring the lagoon, look across the street to the house at 3460 Baker Street. If the maidens out front look familiar, they should—they're original casts of the lovely "garland ladies" you can see in the Palace's colonnade. The house was on the market in 2007; if you'd had a cool $8 million, it could've been yours. ⊠ *Baker and Beach Sts., Marina* ☎ *415/561–0364 Palace history tours* ⊕ *www.exploratorium. edu/palace* ⊠ *Free* ⊙ *Daily 24 hrs.*

OFF THE BEATEN PATH

Wave Organ. Conceived by environmental artist Peter Richards and fashioned by master stonecutter George Gonzales, this unusual wave-activated acoustic sculpture gives off subtle harmonic sounds produced by seawater as it passes through 25 tubes. The sound is loudest at high tide. The granite and marble used for walkways, benches, and alcoves that are part of the piece were salvaged from a gold rush–era cemetery. ⊠ *North of Marina Green at end of jetty by Yacht Rd., park in lot north of Marina Blvd. at Lyon St., Marina.*

WORTH NOTING

Fort Mason Center. Originally a depot for the shipment of supplies to the Pacific during World War II, the fort was converted into a cultural center in 1977. Here you can find the vegetarian restaurant Greens and shops, galleries, and performance spaces, most of which are closed Monday. There's also plentiful free parking—a rarity in the city.

You have to be seriously into Italian-American culture to appreciate the text- and photograph-heavy exhibits at the **Museo Italo-Americano** (⊠ *Bldg. C* ☎ *415/673–2200* ⊕ *museoitaloamericano.org* ⊙ *Tues.–Sun. noon–4*), but depending on the exhibit, it might be worth a glance if you're already at Fort Mason. Plus, it's free. The temporary exhibits downstairs at the free **SFMOMA Artists Gallery** (⊠ *Bldg. A* ☎ *415/441–4777*) can be great, but head upstairs and check out the paintings, sculptures, prints, and photographs for sale and for rent. It's a fun scene, with folks flipping through the works like posters. You won't find a Picasso or a Rembrandt here, but you can find works of high quality by emerging Northern California artists—and where else can you get a $50,000 work of art to hang on your wall for $400 (a month)? It's open Tuesday through Saturday 11:30–5:30. ⊠ *Buchanan St. and Marina Blvd., Marina* ☎ *415/345–7500 event information* ⊕ *www.fortmason.org.*

PRESIDIO

TOP ATTRACTIONS

Fodor's Choice
★

Golden Gate Bridge. The suspension bridge that connects San Francisco with Marin County has long wowed sightseers with its simple but powerful art-deco design. Completed in 1937 after four years of construction, the 2-mi span and its 750-foot towers were built to withstand winds of more than 100 mph. It's also not a bad place to be in an earthquake: designed to sway up to 27.7 feet, the Golden Gate Bridge, unlike the Bay Bridge, was undamaged by the 1989 Loma Prieta quake. (If you're on the bridge when it's windy, stand still and you can feel it swaying a bit.) Though it's frequently gusty and misty—always bring a jacket, no matter what the weather's like—the bridge provides unparalleled views of the Bay Area. Muni buses 28 and 76 make stops at the Golden Gate Bridge toll plaza, on the San Francisco side. However, drive to fully appreciate the bridge from multiple vantage points in and around the Presidio; you'll be able to park at designated areas.

From the bridge's eastern-side walkway—the only side pedestrians are allowed on—you can take in the San Francisco skyline and the bay islands; look west for the wild hills of the Marin Headlands, the curving coast south to Land's End, and the Pacific Ocean. On sunny days sailboats dot the water, and brave windsurfers test the often-treacherous tides beneath the bridge. A vista point on the Marin side gives you a spectacular city panorama. ■TIP➔ May 27, 2012, marks the bridge's 75th anniversary. Officials have decided against closing the bridge to traffic for a bridge walk, but look for some official celebration nonetheless.

But there's a well-known, darker side to the bridge's story, too. The bridge is perhaps the world's most popular suicide platform, with an average of about 20 jumpers per year. (The first leaped just three months after the bridge's completion, and the official count was stopped in 1995 as the 1,000th jump approached.) Signs along the bridge read "There is hope. Make the call," referring the disconsolate to the special telephones on the bridge. Bridge officers, who patrol the walkway and watch by security camera to spot potential jumpers, successfully talk down two-thirds to three-quarters of them each year. Documentary filmmaker Eric Steel's controversial 2006 movie *The Bridge* once again put pressure on the Golden Gate Bridge Highway and Transportation District to install a suicide barrier; various options are being considered, with most locals supporting an unobtrusive net. ⊠ *Lincoln Blvd. near Doyle Dr. and Fort Point, Presidio* ☎ *415/921–5858* ⊕ *www.goldengatebridge.org* ☉ *Pedestrians Mar.–Oct., daily 5 am–9 pm; Nov.–Feb., daily 5 am–6 pm; hrs change with daylight saving time. Bicyclists daily 24 hrs.*

7

DON'T LOOK DOWN

Armed only with helmets, safety harnesses, and painting equipment, a full-time crew of 38 painters keeps the Golden Gate Bridge clad in International Orange. Contrary to a favorite bit of local lore, they don't actually sweep on an entire coat of paint from one end of the bridge to the other, but instead scrape, prime, and repaint small sections that have rusted from exposure to the elements.

Where can I find . . . ?

PARKING	**Marina Green Park** (Marina Blvd.) The price is right: free!	**Lombard Street Garage** (2055 Lombard St.) City-owned, with reasonable rates.
A DRUGSTORE	**Walgreens** (3201 Divisadero, at Lombard St.) Open 24 hours.	**Safeway** (15 Marina Blvd.) The infamous "Dateway" has a pharmacy.
A BAR	**MatrixFillmore** (3138 Fillmore St.) On the prowl and looking fabulous? Stop in for a martini.	**Bus Stop** (1901 Union St.) Not dressed up? Drop by this Cow Hollow sports bar.

★ **Presidio.** When San Franciscans want to spend a day in the woods, they head here. The Presidio has 1,400 acres of hills and majestic woods, two small beaches, and—the one thing Golden Gate Park doesn't have—stunning views of the bay, the Golden Gate Bridge, and Marin County. Famed environmental artist Andy Goldsworthy's sculpture greets visitors at the Arguello Gate entrance. Erected at the end of 2008, the 100-plus-foot *Spire*, made of 37 cypress logs reclaimed from the Presidio, looks like a rough, natural version of a church spire. ■TIP→ The best lookout points lie along Washington Boulevard, which meanders through the park.

Part of the **Golden Gate National Recreation Area,** the Presidio was a military post for more than 200 years. Don Juan Bautista de Anza and a band of Spanish settlers first claimed the area in 1776. It became a Mexican garrison in 1822, when Mexico gained its independence from Spain; U.S. troops forcibly occupied the Presidio in 1846. The U.S. Sixth Army was stationed here until October 1994, when the coveted space was transferred into civilian hands.

Today the area is being transformed into a self-sustaining national park with a combination of public, commercial, and residential projects. In 2005 Bay Area filmmaker George Lucas opened the **Letterman Digital Arts Center,** his 23-acre digital studio "campus," along the eastern edge of the land. Seventeen of those acres are exquisitely landscaped and open to the public, but not even landscaping this perfect can compete with the wilds of the Presidio.

The battle over the fate of the rest of the Presidio is ongoing. Many older buildings have been reconstructed; the issue now is how to fill them. The original plan described a nexus for arts, education, and environmental groups. Since the Presidio's overseeing trust must make the park financially self-sufficient by 2013, which means generating enough revenue to keep afloat without the federal government's monthly $20 million checks, many fear that money will trump culture. The Asian-theme SenSpa and a new Walt Disney museum have opened, and a lodge at the Main Post is in the planning stages. With old military housing now repurposed as apartments and homes with rents up to $10,000 a month, there's some concern that the Presidio will become an incoherent mix of pricey real estate. Still, the $6 million that Lucas shells out annually for rent does plant a lot of saplings.

The Presidio also has two beaches, a golf course, a visitor center, and picnic sites; the views from the many overlooks are sublime.

FORT MASON'S OUTDOOR EXHIBITIONS

Dotting the shoreline along Fort Mason are 20 outdoor exhibits, revealed in 2009, that together make up San Francisco's first Outdoor Exploratorium site. The creative folks at the city's stellar, hands-on science museum are moving outside, using a series of flags to create a wind observatory, bringing nature to your tongue with drinking fountains designed to simulate the varying salinity of the bay, and using the Golden Gate Bridge as a thermometer.

☼ ★ Especially popular is **Crissy Field,** a stretch of restored marshland along the sand of the bay. Kids on bikes, folks walking dogs, and joggers share the paved path along the shore, often winding up at the Warming Hut, a combination café and fun gift store at the end of the path, for a hot chocolate in the shadow of the Golden Gate Bridge. Midway along the Golden Gate Promenade that winds along the shore is the Gulf of the Farallones National Marine Sanctuary Visitor Center, where kids can get a close-up view of small sea creatures and learn about the rich ecosystem offshore. Temporarily relocated to East Beach, just across from the Exploratorium, Crissy Field Center offers great children's programs and has cool science displays; grab lunch at the Beach Hut Café next door. West of the Golden Gate Bridge is sandy **Baker Beach,** beloved for its spectacular views and laid-back vibe (read: you'll see naked people here). This is one of those places that inspires local pride. ⊠ *Between Marina and Lincoln Park, Presidio* ⊕ *www.nps.gov/prsf and www.presidio.gov.*

WORTH NOTING

☼ **Fort Point.** Dwarfed today by the Golden Gate Bridge, this brick fortress constructed between 1853 and 1861 was designed to protect San Francisco from a Civil War sea attack that never materialized. It was also used as a coastal-defense fortification post during World War II, when soldiers stood watch here. This National Historic Site is now a sprawling museum filled with military memorabilia, surrounding a lonely, windswept courtyard. The building has a gloomy air and is suitably atmospheric. (It's usually chilly and windy, too, so bring a jacket.) On days when Fort Point is staffed, guided group tours and cannon drills take place. The top floor affords a unique angle on the bay. ■TIP→ Take care when walking along the front side of the building, as it's slippery, and the waves have a dizzying effect. Note that the fort is open only Friday through Sunday. The fort's popular guided candlelight tours, available only in winter, sell out in advance, so be sure to book ahead.

CLOSE UP

The Presidio with Kids

If you're in town with children (and you have a car), the sprawling, bayside Presidio offers enough kid-friendly diversions for one very full day. Start off at **Julius Kahn Park**, on the Presidio's southern edge, which has a disproportionate number of structures that spin. Swing by George Lucas's **Letterman Digital Arts Center** to check out the Yoda fountain; then head to the **Immigrant Point Lookout** on Washington Boulevard, with views of the bay and the ocean. Children love the pet cemetery, with its sweet, leaning headstones; it's near the stables, where you might glimpse some of the park police's equestrian members. Older kids might enjoy

a stop at the **Walt Disney Family Museum** (⊠ *104 Montgomery St.* ☎ *415/345–6800*) to see the model of Disneyland and a replica of the ambu-lance jeep Disney drove during World War I. The last stop is **Crissy Field**, where kids can ride bikes, skate, or run along the beach and clamber over the rocks; the view of the Golden Gate Bridge from below is captivating. Two nature centers here have fun, hands-on exhibits for kids. Finally, stop by the **Warming Hut**, at the western end of Crissy Field, for sandwiches and hot chocolate. You can also do a version of this day using the PresidiGo shuttle, but you'll need to adapt your route according to the shuttle stops.

Southeast of this structure is the **Fort Point Mine Depot,** an army facility that functioned as the headquarters for underwater mining operations throughout World War II. Today it's the Warming Hut, a National Park Service café and bookstore. ⊠ *Marine Dr. off Lincoln Blvd., Presidio* ☎ *415/556–1693* ⊕ *www.nps.gov/fopo* ✉ *Free* ☉ *Fri.–Sun. 10–5.*

The Western Shoreline

WORD OF MOUTH

"Thank you so much for the Lands End trail recommendation! We walked from the Cliff House to the end . . . listening to the fog horns the entire walk. . . . Great experience and what a work out on the legs! All those steps! We loved it."

—AnnMarie_C

GETTING ORIENTED

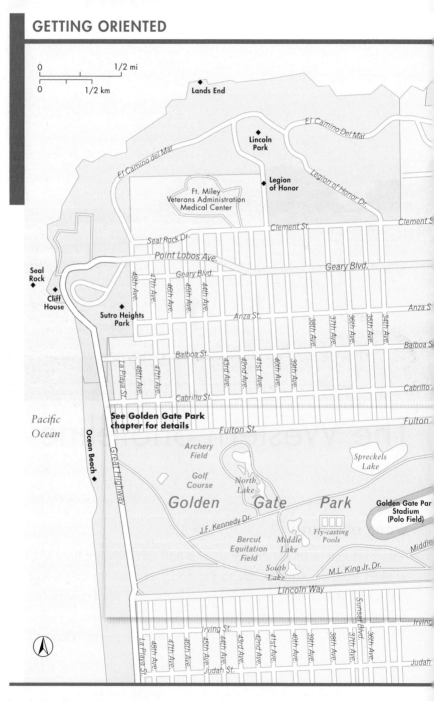

0   1/2 mi

0   1/2 km

Lands End

El Camino Del Mar

Lincoln Park

El Camino del Mar

Legion of Honor Dr.

Ft. Miley Veterans Administration Medical Center

Legion of Honor

Clement S

Clement St.

Seal Rock Dr.

Point Lobos Ave.

Geary Blvd.

Seal Rock

Geary Blvd.

Cliff House

48th Ave.
47th Ave.
46th Ave.
45th Ave.
44th Ave.

38th Ave.
37th Ave.
36th Ave.
35th Ave.
34th Ave.

Anza S

Sutro Heights Park

Anza St.

La Playa St.

48th Ave.
47th Ave.

Balboa St.

43rd Ave.
42nd Ave.
41st Ave.
40th Ave.
39th Ave.

Balboa S

Cabrillo St.

Cabrillo

See Golden Gate Park chapter for details

Fulton St.

Fulton

Pacific Ocean

Ocean Beach

Great Highway

Archery Field

Golf Course

North Lake

Spreckels Lake

Golden   Gate   Park

Golden Gate Par Stadium (Polo Field)

J.F. Kennedy Dr.

Bercut Equitation Field

Middle Lake

Fly-casting Pools

Middle

South Lake

M.L. King Jr. Dr.

Lincoln Way

Sunset Blvd.

Irving St.

Irving

La Playa St.
48th Ave.
47th Ave.
46th Ave.
45th Ave.
44th Ave.
43rd Ave.
42nd Ave.
41st Ave.
40th Ave.
39th Ave.
38th Ave.
37th Ave.
36th Ave.

Judah St.

Judah

MAKING THE MOST OF YOUR TIME

Despite low-lying fog and often biting chill, the premier sights of the Western Shoreline are outdoors—gorgeous hiking trails and sandy stretches of coastline. Bundle up and start off on the Coastal Trail, which passes by the Legion of Honor; time it to arrive at the museum in the afternoon to avoid buses of schoolchildren. Continue west to catch the sunset from the Cliff House or the Beach Chalet. If you don't want to do the entire 3-mi hike, you can spend an hour touring the museum, catch the stunning views just below it, and head to the beach.

TOP 5 REASONS TO GO

Lands End: Head down the freshly restored Coastal Trail near the Cliff House; you'll quickly find yourself in a forest with unparalleled views of the Golden Gate Bridge.

Toast the sunset at the Beach Chalet: Top off a day of exploring with a cocktail overlooking Ocean Beach.

Legion of Honor: Tear yourself away from the spectacular setting and eye-popping view and travel back to 18th-century Europe through the paintings, drawings, and porcelain collected here.

Ocean Beach: Wrap up warm and stroll along the strand on a brisk, cloudy day and you'll feel like a gritty local. Then thaw out over a bowl of steaming pho in the Richmond.

Old-time San Francisco: Wandering among the ruins of the Sutro Baths below the Cliff House, close your eyes and imagine vintage San Francisco: the monumental baths, popular amusement park Playland at the Beach, and that great old teetering, Victorian Cliff House of days gone by.

GETTING THERE

To reach the Western Shoreline from downtown by bus, nab the 38–Geary, which runs all the way to 48th and Point Lobos avenues, just east of the Cliff House. Along the Western Shoreline, the 18–46th Avenue bus runs between the Legion of Honor and the zoo (and beyond).

WORD OF MOUTH

"The Legion of Honor is in the most terrific setting with its views to the Golden Gate Bridge and the headlands. The porcelain on the lower level is beautifully displayed—sort of like being at Gump's except you can't buy anything!" —dovima

QUICK BITES

The gorgeous setting often overshadows the upscale comfort food at the **Beach Chalet** and **Park Chalet** (✉ *1000 Great Hwy.* ☎ *415/386–8439*), across from Ocean Beach, on the western edge of Golden Gate Park. With its plain-wrap storefront, mom-and-pop shop **Hunan Café 2** (✉ *4450 Cabrillo St., Outer Richmond* ☎ *415/751–1283*) may not look like much, but the friendly folks here serve superfresh, delicious Chinese food; favorites include the ginger-and-onion chicken, Mongolian beef, and hot-and-sour soup.

8

Sightseeing
★★★

Nightlife
–

Dining
★

Lodging
–

Shopping
–

Few American cities provide a more intimate and dramatic view of the power and fury of the surf attacking the shore than San Francisco does along its wild Western Shoreline. From Lincoln Park in the north, along Ocean Beach from the Richmond south to the Sunset, a different breed of San Franciscan chooses to live in this area: surfers who brave the heaviest fog to ride the waves; writers who seek solace and inspiration in this city outpost; dog lovers committed to giving their pets a good workout each day.

Updated by
Denise M. Leto

From Lands End in Lincoln Park you have some of the best views of the Golden Gate (the name was given to the opening of San Francisco Bay long before the bridge was built) and the Marin Headlands. From the historic Cliff House south to the sprawling San Francisco Zoo, the Great Highway and Ocean Beach run along the western edge of the city. (If you're here in winter or spring, keep your eyes peeled for migrating gray whales.) The wind is often strong along the shoreline, summer fog can blanket the ocean beaches, and the water is cold and usually too rough for swimming. Don't forget your jacket!

TOP ATTRACTIONS

Fodor's Choice
★

Legion of Honor. The old adage of real estate—location, location, location—is at full force here. You can't beat the site of this museum of European art atop cliffs overlooking the ocean, the Golden Gate Bridge, and the Marin Headlands. A pyramidal glass skylight in the entrance court illuminates the lower-level galleries, which exhibit prints and drawings, English and European porcelain, and ancient Assyrian, Greek, Roman, and Egyptian art. The 20-plus galleries on the upper level display the permanent collection of European art (paintings, sculpture, decorative arts, and tapestries) from the 14th century to the present day.

The noteworthy Auguste Rodin collection includes two galleries devoted to the master and a third with works by Rodin and other 19th-century sculptors. An original cast of Rodin's *The Thinker* welcomes you as you walk through the courtyard. As fine as the museum is, the setting and view outshine the collection and make a trip here worthwhile.

The **Legion Café,** on the lower level, serves tasty light meals (soup, sandwiches, grilled chicken) inside and on a garden terrace. (Unfortunately, there's no view.) Just north of the museum's parking lot is George Segal's *The Holocaust,* a stark white installation that evokes life in concentration camps during World War II. It's haunting at night, when backlighted by lights in the Legion's parking lot. ■ TIP➔ Admission to the Legion also counts as same-day admission to the de Young Museum. ⊠ *34th Ave. at Clement St., Outer Richmond* ☎ *415/750–3600* ⊕ *legionofhonor.famsf.org* ✉ *$10, $2 off with Muni transfer, free 1st Tues. of month* ⊗ *Tues.–Sun. 9:30–5:15.*

★ **Lincoln Park**. Although many of the city's green spaces are gentle and welcoming, Lincoln Park is a wild 275-acre park with windswept cliffs and panoramic views. The newly renovated Coastal Trail, the park's most dramatic one, leads out to **Lands End**; pick it up west of the Legion of Honor (at the end of El Camino del Mar) or from the parking lot at Point Lobos and El Camino del Mar. Time your hike to hit Mile Rock at low tide, and you might catch a glimpse of two wrecked ships peeking up from their watery graves. ⚠ Do be careful if you hike here; landslides are frequent, and many people have fallen into the sea by standing too close to the edge of a crumbling bluff top.

On the tamer side, large Monterey cypresses line the fairways at Lincoln Park's 18-hole golf course, near the Legion of Honor. At one time this land was the Golden Gate Cemetery, where the dead were segregated by nationality; most were indigent and interred without ceremony in the potter's field. In 1900 the Board of Supervisors voted to ban burials within city limits, and all but two city cemeteries (at Mission Dolores and the Presidio) were moved to Colma, a small town just south of San Francisco. When digging has to be done in the park, bones occasionally surface again. ⊠ *Entrance at 34th Ave. at Clement St., Outer Richmond.*

WORTH NOTING

Cliff House. A meal at the Cliff House isn't about the food—the spectacular ocean view is what brings folks here. The vistas, which include offshore Seal Rock (the barking marine mammals who reside there are actually sea lions), can be 30 mi or more on a clear day—or less than a mile on foggy days. ■ TIP➔ Come for drinks just before sunset; then head back into town for dinner.

Three buildings have occupied this site since 1863. The current building dates from 1909; a 2004 renovation has left a strikingly attractive restaurant and a squat concrete viewing platform out back. The complex, owned by the National Park Service, includes a gift shop.

Sitting on the observation deck is the **Giant Camera,** a camera obscura with its lens pointing skyward housed in a cute yellow-painted wooden shack. Built in the 1940s and threatened many times with demolition, it's now on the National Register of Historic Places. Step into the dark, tiny room inside (for a $3 fee); a fascinating 360-degree image of the surrounding area—which rotates as the "lens" on the roof rotates—is

8

Where can I find . . . ?

A CUP OF COFFEE	**Java Beach Café** (1396 La Playa St.) Strong, organic coffee and outdoor tables.	**Trouble Coffee Company** (4033 Judah St.) Coffee, cinnamon toast, and coconuts (yes, coconuts).
A GAS STATION	**Sunset 76** (1700 Noriega St.) Head here to get a flat patched, or to gas up.	**19th Ave. 76 Station** (1401 19th Ave.) Stop by for gas and auto repairs.
A DRUGSTORE	**Walgreens** (25 Point Lobos Ave., near 43rd Ave.) Open until midnight.	**Walgreens** (199 Parnassus Ave.) Just two blocks from Golden Gate Park's southeast corner.

projected on a large, circular table. ■ TIP➜ In winter and spring you may also glimpse migrating gray whales from the observation deck.

To the north of the Cliff House are the ruins of the once-grand glass-roof **Sutro Baths,** which you can explore on your own (they look a bit like water-storage receptacles). Adolf Sutro, eccentric onetime San Francisco mayor and Cliff House owner, built the bath complex, including a train out to the site, in 1896, so that everyday folks could enjoy the benefits of swimming. Six enormous baths (some freshwater and some seawater), more than 500 dressing rooms, and several restaurants covered 3 acres north of the Cliff House and accommodated 25,000 bathers. Likened to Roman baths in a European glass palace, the baths were for decades the favorite destination of San Franciscans in search of entertainment. The complex fell into disuse after World War II, was closed in 1952, and burned down (under officially questionable circumstances, wink wink) during demolition in 1966. ✉ *1090 Point Lobos Ave., Outer Richmond* ☎ *415/386–3330* ⊕ *www.cliffhouse.com* ✆ *Free* ☾ *Weekdays 9 am–9:30 pm, weekends 9 am–10 pm.*

Ocean Beach. Stretching 3 mi along the western side of the city from the Richmond to the Sunset, this sandy swath of the Pacific coast is good for jogging or walking the dog—but not for swimming. The water is so cold that surfers wear wet suits year-round, and riptides are strong. As for sunbathing, it's rarely warm enough here; think meditative walking instead of sun worshiping.

Paths on both sides of the Great Highway lead from Lincoln Way to Sloat Boulevard (near the zoo); the beachside path winds through landscaped sand dunes, and the paved path across the highway is good for biking and in-line skating. (Though you have to rent bikes elsewhere.) The **Beach Chalet** restaurant and brewpub is across the Great Highway from Ocean Beach, about five blocks south of the Cliff House. ✉ *Along Great Hwy. from Cliff House to Sloat Blvd. and beyond.*

Visitors enjoy the rough beauty of the Pacific from the Cliff House.

San Francisco Zoo. Ever since one of its tigers escaped its enclosure and killed a visitor on Christmas Day 2007, the city's zoo has concentrated on polishing its image, raising funds to update its habitats, and restoring its reputation with animal welfare organizations. Occupying prime oceanfront property, the zoo—which some have accused of caring more about human entertainment than the welfare of its wards—is touting its metamorphosis into the "New Zoo," a wildlife-focused recreation center that inspires visitors to become conservationists. Integrated exhibits group different species of animals from the same geographic areas together in enclosures that don't look like cages. More than 250 species reside here, including endangered species such as the snow leopard, Sumatran tiger, and grizzly bear.

The zoo's superstar exhibit is **Grizzly Gulch,** where orphaned sisters Kachina and Kiona enchant visitors with their frolicking and swimming. When the bears are in the water, the only thing between you and them is (thankfully thick) glass. Grizzly feedings are 11 am daily.

The **Lemur Forest** has five varieties of the bug-eyed, long-tailed primates from Madagascar. You can help hoist food into the lemurs' feeding towers and watch the fuzzy creatures climb up to chow down. African Kikuyu grass carpets the circular outer area of **Gorilla Preserve,** one of the largest and most natural gorilla habitats of any zoo in the world. Trees and shrubs create communal play areas.

Ten species of rare monkeys—including black howler monkeys, black-and-white ruffed lemurs, and macaques—live and play at the two-tier **Primate Discovery Center,** which contains 23 interactive learning exhibits on the ground level.

Magellanic penguins waddle about the rather sad concrete **Penguin Island,** splashing and frolicking in its 200-foot pool. Feeding times are 10:15 and 3:30. Koalas peer out from among the trees in **Koala Crossing,** and kangaroos and wallabies headline the **Australian Walkabout** exhibit. The 7-acre **Puente al Sur** (Bridge to the South) re-creates habitats in South America, replete with giant anteaters and capybaras.

An **African Savanna** exhibit mixes giraffes, zebras, kudus, ostriches, and many other species, all living together in a 3-acre section with a central viewing spot accessed by a covered passageway.

The 6-acre **Children's Zoo** has about 300 mammals, birds, and reptiles, plus an insect zoo, a meerkat and prairie-dog exhibit, a nature trail, a nature theater, a restored 1921 Dentzel carousel, and a mini–steam train. A ride on the train costs $4, and you can hop astride one of the carousel's 52 hand-carved menagerie animals for $2. ⊠ *Sloat Blvd. and 47th Ave., Sunset ✛ Muni L–Taraval streetcar from downtown* ☎ *415/753–7080* ⊕ *www.sfzoo.org* ⊠ *$15, $1 off with Muni transfer* ☻ *Mid-Mar.–Oct., daily 10–5; Nov.–mid-Mar., daily 10–4.*

Sutro Heights Park. Crows and other large birds battle the heady breezes at this cliff-top park on what were once the grounds of the home of Adolph Sutro, an eccentric mining engineer and former San Francisco mayor. An extremely wealthy man, Sutro may have owned about 10% of San Francisco at one point, but he couldn't buy good taste: a few remnants of his gaudy, faux-classical statue collection still stand (including the lions at what was the main gate). Monterey cypresses and Canary Island palms dot the park, and photos on placards depict what things looked like before the house burned down in 1896, from the greenhouse to the ornate carpet-bed designs.

All that remains of the main house is its foundation. Climb up for a sweeping view of the Pacific Ocean and the Cliff House below (which Sutro owned), and try to imagine what the perspective might have been like from one of the upper floors. San Francisco City Guides (☎ *415/557–4266*) runs a free Saturday tour of the park that starts at 2 (meet at the lion statue at 48th and Point Lobos avenues). ⊠ *Point Lobos and 48th Aves., Outer Richmond.*

Golden Gate Park

WORD OF MOUTH

"My husband and I are visiting [with our kids] . . . and I want to see Golden Gate Park . . . hear JFK Dr. is closed to cars on Sundays—will this make it hard to get to the things we want to see?"

—dimpi213

"You might consider renting bikes with a kid trailer in order to avoid the whole search for parking. This is how many locals with small kids enjoy the park on Sundays."

—SAB

A GREEN RETREAT

Stretching more than 1,000 acres from the ocean to the Haight, Golden Gate Park is a place to slow down and smell the eucalyptus. Stockbrokers and gadget-laden parents stroll the Music Concourse, while speedy tattooed cyclists and wobbly, training-wheeled kids cruise along shaded paths. Stooped seniors warm the garden benches, hikers search for waterfalls, and picnickers lounge in the Rhododendron Dell. San Franciscans love their city streets, but the park is where they come to breathe.

PLANNING A PARK VISIT

ORIENTATION

The park breaks down naturally into three chunks. The eastern end attracts the biggest crowds with its cluster of blockbuster sights. It's also the easiest place to dip into the park for a quick trip. Water hobbyists come to the middle section's lake-speckled open space, home to fly-casting pools and the Model Yacht Club. Sporty types head west to the coastal end for its soccer fields, golf course, and archery range. This windswept western end is the park's least visited and most naturally landscaped part. ☉ Daily 6 am–10pm ⊕ www.parks.sfgov.org

WALKING TOURS

San Francisco Botanical Garden (☎ 415/661–1316) has free botanical tours every day. Tours start near the main gate weekdays at 1:30 pm, weekends at 10:30 am and 1:30 pm. Meet at the Friend Gate (at the northern entrance) Wednesday, Friday, and Sunday at 2 pm.
San Francisco City Guides (☎ 415/557–4266) offers free year-round tours of the eastern end and the western end of the park.

San Francisco Parks Trust (☎ 415/263–0991) offers tours of many park features, including historically minded tours of the Japanese Tea Garden Monday at 9:30 am and Wednesday and Sunday at 1. The hour-long tours are free but don't include garden admission.

BEST TIMES TO VISIT

Time of day: It's best to arrive early at the Conservatory of Flowers, the de Young Museum, and the Japanese Tea Garden to avoid crowds. At sunset, the only place to be is the park's western end, watching the sun dip into the Pacific.

Time of year: Visit during the week if you can. The long, Indian summer days of September and October are the warmest times to visit, and many special weekend events are held then.

Blooms: The rhododendrons burst into billowy bloom between February and May. The Queen Wilhelmina Tulip Garden blossoms in February and March. Cherry trees in the Japanese Tea Garden bloom in April, and the Rose Garden is at its best from mid-May to mid-June, in the beginning of July, and during September.

(opposite) Conservatory of Flowers. (top left) The Strybing Arboretum in bloom.

TIPS

BEST WAYS TO SPEND YOUR TIME

The park stretches 3 mi east to west and is a half-mile wide, so it's possible to cover the whole thing in a day—by car, public transportation, bike, or even on foot. But to do so might feel more like a forced march than a pleasure jaunt. Weigh your time and your interests, choose your top picks, then leave at least an extra hour to just enjoy being outdoors.

Two hours: Swing by the exquisite Conservatory of Flowers for a 20-minute peek, then head to the de Young Museum. Spend a few minutes assessing its controversial exterior and perhaps glide through some of the galleries before heading to the observation tower for a panoramic view of the city. Cross the music concourse to the spectacular Academy of Sciences.

Half day: Spend a little extra time at the sights described above, then head to the nearby Japanese Tea Garden to enjoy its perfectionist landscape. Next, cross the street to the San Francisco Botanical Garden at Strybing Arboretum and check out the intriguing Primitive Garden. If you brought supplies, this is a great place for a picnic; you can also grab lunch at the de Young Café.

Full day: After the half-day (above) continue on to the children's playground if you have kids in tow. Once your little ones see the playground's tree house–like play structures and climbing opportunities, you may be here for the rest of the day. Alternatively, make your way to the serene National AIDS Memorial Grove. Then head west, stopping at Stow Lake to climb Strawberry Hill. Wind up at the Beach Chalet for a sunset drink.

(top) Amateur musicians entertain passersby. (middle) Sundays are ideal biking days. (bottom) The meandering paths are perfect for strolling.

GETTING AROUND THE PARK

WALKING

The most convenient entry point is on the eastern edge at Stanyan and Kezar streets, which points you directly toward the Conservatory of Flowers. It's a 10-minute walk there; allow another 10–15 minutes to reach the California Academy of Sciences, de Young Museum, Japanese Tea Garden, and San Francisco Botanical Garden. Stow Lake is another 10 minutes west from these three sights.

BY BIKE

The park is fantastic for cycling, especially on Sunday when cars are barred from John F. Kennedy Drive. Biking the park round trip is about a 7-mi trip, which usually takes 1–2 hours. The route down John F. Kennedy Drive takes you past the prettiest, well-maintained sections of the park on a mostly flat circuit. The most popular route continues all the way to the beach. Keep in mind that the ride is downhill toward the ocean, uphill heading east.

BY CAR

If you have a car, you'll have no trouble hopping from sight to sight. (But remember, the main road, John F. Kennedy Drive, is closed to cars on Sunday.) Parking within the park is often free and is usually easy to find especially beyond the eastern end. On Sundays or anytime the eastern end is crowded, head for the residential streets north of the park or the underground parking lot; enter on 10th and Fulton (northern edge of the park) or MLK and Concourse (in the park).

BY SHUTTLE

If you're visiting on a weekend between May and October, you can ride the free Golden Gate Park shuttle. This loops through the park every 15 minutes, roughly between 10 AM and 6 PM, stopping at 15 sights from McLaren Lodge to the Beach Chalet. Maps are posted at each stop.

WHERE TO RENT

Golden Gate Park Bike & Skate (✉ *3038 Fulton St.* ☎ *415/668–1117*). On the northern edge of the park; has good deals on rentals.

Blazing Saddles (✉ *1095 Columbus Ave., North Beach* ☎ *415/202–8888*). The biggest rental outfit in town. Although their branches aren't close to the park, the company is worth considering since they have tons of bikes in good condition. They're very helpful when it comes to route recommendations, too.

BEST PLACES TO PICNIC ON WEEKENDS

- Lawn in front of the Conservatory of Flowers.
- By the pond in the San Francisco Botanical Garden.
- The benches overlooking the Rustic Bridge at Stow Lake.
- Rhododendron Dell.

(top) Water lilies adorn the Japanese Tea Garden.

DON'T-MISS SIGHTS

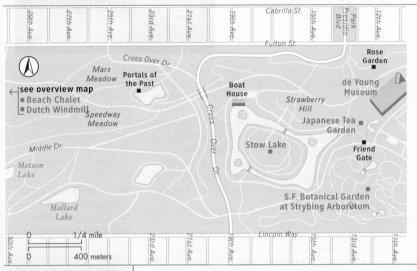

Conservatory of Flowers

✉ John F. Kennedy Dr. at Conservatory Dr.

☎ 415/666-7001

💲 $7, free 1st Tues. of month

🕐 Tues.–Sun. 9–5; 10–4:30 in winter

🌐 www.conservatoryof flowers.org

CONSERVATORY OF FLOWERS

Whatever you do, be sure to at least drive by the Conservatory of Flowers—it's just too darn pretty to miss. The gorgeous, white-framed, 1878 glass structure is topped with a 14-ton glass dome. Stepping inside the giant greenhouse is like taking a quick trip to the rainforest; it's humid, warm, and smells earthy. The undeniable highlight is the Aquatic Plants section, where lily pads float and carnivorous plants dine on bugs to the sounds of rushing water. On the east side of the conservatory (to the right as you face the building), cypress, pine, and redwood trees surround the **Dahlia Garden,** which blooms in summer and fall. To the west is the **Rhododendron Dell,** which contains 850 varieties, more than any other garden in the country. It's a favorite local Mother's Day picnic spot.

STOW LAKE

Russian seniors feed the pigeons, kids watch turtles sunning themselves, and joggers circle this placid body of water, Golden Gate Park's largest lake. Early park superintendent John McLaren may have snarked that manmade Stow Lake was "a shoestring around a watermelon," but for more than a century visitors have come to walk its paths and bridges, paddle boats, and climb Strawberry Hill (the "watermelon"). Cross one of the bridges—the 19th-century stone bridge on the southwest side is lovely—and ascend the hill; keep your eyes open for the waterfall and an elaborate Chinese Pavilion.

Map

10th Ave.
8th Ave.
6th Ave.
4th Ave.
Arguello Blvd.
Conservatory

J.F. Kennedy Dr.

Conservatory of Flowers ■

Rhododendron ■ Dell

Dahlia Garden ■

McLaren Lodge (Park HQ) ■

■ Music Concourse

California Academy of Sciences   Middle Dr. E.

Shakespeare Garden

National AIDS ■ Memorial Grove

Bowling Green Dr.

Stanyan St.

ookstore

S.F. County Fair Bldg.

M.L. King Jr. Dr.

Koret Children's ■ Quarter
Kezar Dr.

■ Main Gate

9th Ave.
7th Ave.
5th Ave.
3rd Ave.

Kezar Stadium

Stow Lake

✉ Off John F. Kennedy Dr.

☎ Boat rental 415/752–0347; surrey and bike rental 415/668–6699

🕐 Boat rentals daily 10–4, surrey and bicycle rentals daily 9–dusk.

San Francisco Japanese Tea Garden

✉ Hagiwara Tea Garden Dr.

☎ 415/752–4227

💲 $7, free Mon., Wed., and Fri. with entry by 10 am

🕐 Mar.–Oct., daily 9–6; Nov.–Feb., daily 9–4:45.

SAN FRANCISCO JAPANESE TEA GARDEN

As you amble through the manicured landscape, past Japanese sculptures and perfect miniature pagodas, over ponds of carp that have been there since before the 1906 quake, you may be transported to a more peaceful plane. Or maybe the shrieks of kids clambering over the almost vertical "humpback" bridges will keep you firmly in the here and now. Either way, this garden is one of those tourist spots that's truly worth a stop (a half-hour will do). And at 5 acres, it's large enough that you'll always be able to find a bit of serenity, even when the tour buses drop by. ■TIP➜ The garden is especially lovely in April, when the cherry blossoms are in bloom.

KORET CHILDREN'S QUARTER

The country's first public children's playground reopened in 2007 after a spectacular renovation, with wave-shaped climbing walls, old-fashioned cement slides, and a 20-plus-foot rope climbing structure that kids love and parents fear. Thankfully, one holdover is the beautiful, handcrafted 1912 Herschell-Spillman Carousel. The lovely stone Sharon Building, next to the playground, offers kids' art classes. Bring a picnic or pick up grub nearby on 9th Avenue and you could spend the entire day here. Be aware that the playground, which has separate areas for toddlers and bigger kids, is unenclosed and sightlines can be obstructed.

Koret Children's Quarter

✉ Bowling Green Dr., off Martin Luther King Jr. Dr

☎ 415/831–2700

💲 Playground free, carousel $2, kids 6–12 $1

🕐 Playground daily dawn-dusk; carousel Memorial Day–Labor Day, daily 10–4:30, Labor Day–Memorial Day, Fri.–Sun. 10–4:30.

DE YOUNG MUSEUM

⊠ 50 Hagiwara Tea Garden Dr.

☎ 415/750–3600

⊕ deyoung.famsf.org

💳 $10; free 1st Tues. of month

🕐 Tues.–Sun. 9:30–5:15

TIPS

■ Admission at the de Young is good for same-day admission to the Legion of Honor and vice-versa.

■ The de Young is famous these days first and foremost for its striking and controversial new building and tree-topping tower. These are accessible to the public for free, so if it's not the art you're interested in seeing, save the cost of admission and head up the elevator to 360-degree views from the glass-walled observation floor.

■ When it's time for a nosh, head to the de Young Café and dine in the lovely outdoor sculpture garden on tableware fit for MOMA.

Everyone in town has a strong opinion about the new de Young. Some adore the striking copper façade, while others grimace and hope that the green patina of age will mellow the effect. The building almost overshadows the museum's respected collection of American, African, and Oceanic art.

HIGHLIGHTS

Head through the sprawling concourse level and begin your visit on the upper level, where you'll find textiles; art from Africa, Oceana, and New Guinea; and highlights of the 20th-century American painting collection (such as Wayne Thiebaud, John Singer Sargent, Winslow Homer, and Richard Diebenkorn). These are the don't-miss items, so take your time. Then head back downstairs to see art from the Americas and contemporary work.

The de Young has had some major international coups, scoring exhibits such as Tutankhamun and the Golden Age of the Pharoahs; Van Gogh, Gauguin, Cezanne, and Beyond: Post-Impressionist Masterpieces from the Musée d'Orsay; and Picasso from Musée National Picasso, Paris. Be sure to check for traveling exhibits while you're visiting.

CALIFORNIA ACADEMY OF SCIENCES

⊠ 55 Music Concourse Dr.

☎ 415/379-8000

⊕ www.calacademy.org

✉ $29.95, free 3rd Wed. of month

🕑 Mon.–Sat. 9:30–5, Sun. 11–5

TIPS

■ The academy often hosts gaggles of schoolchildren. Arrive early and allow plenty of time to wait in line.

■ Plan ahead: check Planetarium show times, animal feeding times, etc, before you arrive.

■ Visitors complain about the high cost of food here; consider bringing a picnic.

■ Free days are tempting, but the tradeoff includes extremely long lines and the possibility that you won't get in.

■ With antsy kids, visit Early Explorers Cove and use the academy's in-and-out privileges to run around outside.

■ Take time to examine the structure itself, from denim insulation to weather sensors.

With its native plant–covered living roof, retractable ceiling, three-story rainforest, gigantic planetarium, living coral reef, and frolicking penguins, the Cal Academy is one of the city's most spectacular treasures. Dramatically designed by Renzo Piano, it's an eco-friendly, energy-efficient adventure in biodiversity and green architecture. The roof's large mounds and hills mirror the local topography, and Piano's audacious design completes the dramatic transformation of the park's Music Concourse. Moving away from a restrictive role as a backward-looking museum that catalogued natural history, the new academy is all about sustainability and the future, but you'll still find those beloved dioramas in African Hall.

HIGHLIGHTS

By the time you arrive, hopefully you've decided which shows and programs to attend, looked at the academy's floorplan, and designed a plan to cover it all in the time you have. And if not, here's the quick version: Head left from the entrance to the wooden walkway over otherworldly leopard rays in the Philippine Coral Reef, then continue to the Swamp to see the famous albino alligator. Swing through African Hall and gander at the penguins, take the elevator up to the living roof, then return to the main floor and get in line to explore the Rainforests of the World, ducking free-flying butterflies and watching for other live surprises. You'll end up below ground in the Amazonian Flooded Rainforest, where you can explore the academy's other aquarium exhibits. Phew.

ALSO WORTH SEEING

San Francisco Botanical Garden at Strybing Arboretum

SAN FRANCISCO BOTANICAL GARDEN AT STRYBING ARBORETUM

One of the best picnic spots in a very picnic-friendly park, the 55-acre arboretum specializes in plants from areas with climates similar to that of the Bay Area. Walk the Eastern Australian garden to see tough, pokey shrubs and plants with cartoon-like names, such as the hilly-pilly tree. Kids gravitate toward the large shallow fountain and the pond with ducks, turtles, and egrets. ✉ *Enter the park at 9th Ave. at Lincoln Way* ☎ *415/661–1316* ⊕ *www.sfbotanicalgarden.org* ✉ *$7* ☉ *Apr.–Oct., daily 9–6; Nov.–Mar., daily 10–5.*

NATIONAL AIDS MEMORIAL GROVE

This lush, serene 7-acre grove was conceived as a living memorial to the disease's victims. Coast live oaks, Monterey pines, coast redwoods, and other trees flank the grove. There are also two stone circles, one recording the names of the dead and their loved ones, the other engraved with a poem. Free 20-minute tours are available some Saturdays. ✉ *Middle Dr. E, west of tennis courts* ☎ *415/765–0497* ⊕ *www.aidsmemorial.org.*

Beach Chalet

BEACH CHALET

Hugging the park's western border, this 1925 Willis Polk–designed structure houses gorgeous depression-era murals of familiar San Francisco scenes, while verses by local poets adorn niches here and there. Stop by the ground-floor visitors center on your way to indulge in a microbrew upstairs, ideally at sunset. ✉ *1000 Great Hwy.* ☎ *restaurant 415/386–8439* ⊕ *www.beachchalet.com* ☉ *Restaurant Mon.–Thurs. 9 am–10 pm, Fri. 9 am–11 pm, Sat. 8 am–11 pm, Sun. 8 am–10 pm.*

DUTCH WINDMILL

It may not pump water anymore, but this carefully restored windmill, built in 1903 to irrigate the park, continues to enchant visitors. The Queen Wilhelmina Tulip Garden here is a welcoming respite, particularly lovely during its February and March bloom. Fund-raising is underway to restore the Murphy Windmill, just south; swing by for an interesting comparison. ✉ *Northwest corner of the park* ☎ *No phone* ☉ *Dawn–dusk.*

Dutch Windmill

The Haight, the Castro, and Noe Valley

WORD OF MOUTH

"When I walk around the Haight, I rarely set foot on Haight St. itself. I wander around Page St. looking at the Victorians . . . I'll hit a few streets between Page & Haight or Page & Oak. I might even wander on the Panhandle side of Oak to admire the Victorians."

—StuDudley

GETTING ORIENTED

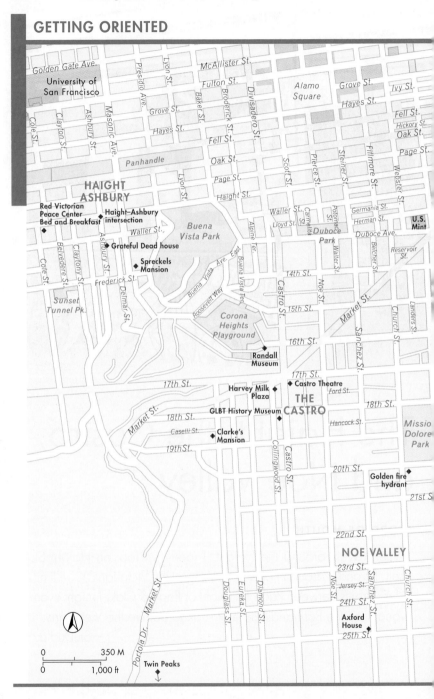

MAKING THE MOST OF YOUR TIME

The Upper Haight is only a few blocks long, and although there are plenty of shops and amusements, an hour or so should be enough. Many restaurants here cater to the morning-after crowd, so this is a great place for brunch. With the prevalence of panhandling in this area, you may be most comfortable here during the day.

The Castro, with its fun storefronts, invites unhurried exploration; allot at least 60 to 90 minutes. Visit in the evening to check out the lively nightlife, or in the late morning—especially on weekends—when the street scene is hopping.

A loop through Noe Valley takes about an hour. With its popular breakfast spots and cafés, this neighborhood is a good place for a morning stroll. After you've filled up, browse the shops along 24th and Church streets.

TOP 5 REASONS TO GO

Castro Theatre: Take in a film at this gorgeous throwback and join the audience shouting out lines, commentary, and songs. Come early and let the Wurlitzer set the mood.

Sunday brunch in the Castro: Recover from Saturday night (with the entire community) at one of the Castro's top three brunch destinations: Lime (⊠ 2247 Market), 2223 (⊠ 2223 Market), or Caffè Luna Piena (⊠ 558 Castro St.).

Vintage shopping in the Haight: Find the perfect chiffon dress at La Rosa, a pristine faux-leopard coat at Held Over, or the motorcycle jacket of your dreams at Buffalo Exchange.

24th Street stroll: Take a leisurely ramble down lovable Noe Valley's main drag, lined with unpretentious cafés, comfy eateries, and cute one-of-a-kind shops.

Cliff's Variety: Stroll the aisles of the Castro's "hardware" store (⊠ 479 Castro St.) for lightbulbs, hammers, and pipes (as well as false eyelashes, tiaras, and feather boas) to get a feel for this neighborhood's full-tilt flair.

QUICK BITES

Lovejoy's Antiques & Tea Room (⊠ 1351 Church St., at Clipper St., Noe Valley ☎ 415/648–5895) is a homey jumble, with its lace-covered tables, couches, and mismatched chairs set among the antiques for sale. High tea and cream tea are served, along with traditional English-tearoom "fayre."

Get a jolt of organic fair-trade caffeine and a bit of revolutionary spirit at book-filled **Coffee to the People** (⊠ 1206 Masonic Ave., Haight ☎ 415/626–2435).

The aroma alone might lure you into **Philz Coffee** (⊠ 4023 18th St., Castro ☎ 415/875–9656), just off the main drag of Castro Street. Its fedora-hung, cramped space gives off a casual vibe, but don't be fooled: the city's second most-popular place for the über-serious coffee drinker (after Blue Bottle) serves up the strongest handcrafted cup of joe in town.

GETTING THERE

The Castro is the end of the line for the F-line, and both the Castro and Noe Valley are served by the J–Church Metro. The only public transit that runs to the Haight is the bus; take the 7–Haight from Civic Center or the 6–Parnassus from Polk and Market. If you're on foot, keep in mind that the hill between the Castro and Noe Valley is very steep.

10

Sightseeing
★
Nightlife
★★★
Dining
★★★
Lodging
★
Shopping
★★★

These distinct neighborhoods are where the city's soul resides. They wear their personalities large and proud, and all are perfect for just strolling around. Like a slide show of San Franciscan history, you can move from the Haight's residue of 1960s counterculture to the Castro's connection to 1970s and '80s gay life to 1990s gentrification in Noe Valley. Although historic events thrust the Haight and the Castro onto the international stage, both are anything but stagnant—they're still dynamic areas well worth exploring.

Updated by
Denise M. Leto

During the 1960s the siren song of free love, peace, and mind-altering substances lured thousands of young people to the Haight, a neighborhood just east of Golden Gate Park. By 1966 the area had become a hot spot for rock artists, including the Grateful Dead, Jefferson Airplane, and Janis Joplin. Some of the most infamous flower children, including Charles Manson and People's Temple founder Jim Jones, also called the Haight home.

Today the '60s message of peace, civil rights, and higher consciousness has been distilled into a successful blend of commercialism and progressive causes: the Haight Ashbury Free Medical Clinic, founded in 1967, survives at the corner of Haight and Clayton, while throwbacks like Bound Together Books (the anarchist book collective), the head shop Pipe Dreams, and a bevy of tie-dye shops all keep the Summer of Love alive in their own way. The Haight's famous political spirit— it was the first neighborhood in the nation to lead a freeway revolt, and it continues to host regular boycotts against chain stores—survives alongside some of the finest Victorian-lined streets in the city. And the kids continue to come: this is where young people who end up on San Francisco's streets most often gather. Visitors tend to find the Haight either edgy and exhilarating or scummy and intimidating (the panhandling here can be aggressive).

CLOSE UP

Hippie History

The eternal lure for twentysome-things, cheap rent, first helped spawn an indelible part of SF's history and public image. In the early 1960s young people started streaming into the sprawling, inexpensive Victorians in the area around the University of San Francisco. The new Haight locals earnestly planned a new era of communal living, individual empowerment, and expanded consciousness.

Golden Gate Park's Panhandle, a thin strip of green on the Haight's northern edge, was their public gathering spot—the site of protests, concerts, food giveaways, and general hanging out. In 1967 George Harrison strolled up the park's Hippie Hill, borrowed a guitar, and played for a while before someone finally recognized him. He led the crowd, Pied Piper–style, into the Haight.

At first the counterculture was all about sharing and taking care of one another—a good thing, considering most hippies were either broke or had renounced money. They hadn't renounced food, though, and the daily free "feeds" in the Panhandle were a staple for many. The Diggers, an anarchist street-theater group, were known for handing out bread shaped like the big coffee cans they baked it in. (The Diggers also gave us immortal phrases such as "Do your own thing.")

At the time, the U.S. government, Harvard professor Timothy Leary, a Stanford student named Ken Kesey, and the kids in the Haight were all experimenting with LSD. Acid was legal, widely available, and usually given away for free. At Kesey's all-night parties, called "acid tests," a buck got you a cup of "electric" Kool-Aid, a preview of psychedelic art, and an earful of

the house band, the Grateful Dead. LSD was deemed illegal in 1966, and the kids responded by staging a Love Pageant Rally, where they dropped acid tabs en masse and rocked out to Janis Joplin and the Dead.

Things crested early in 1967, when between 10,000 and 50,000 people ("depending on whether you were a policeman or a hippie," according to one hippie) gathered at the Polo Field in Golden Gate Park for the Human Be-In of the Gathering of the Tribes. Allen Ginsberg and Timothy Leary spoke, the Dead and Jefferson Airplane played, and people costumed with beads and feathers waved flags, clanged cymbals, and beat drums. A parachutist dropped onto the field, tossing fistfuls of acid tabs to the crowd. America watched via satellite, gape-mouthed—it was every conservative parent's nightmare.

Later that year, thousands heeded Scott McKenzie's song "San Francisco," which promised "For those who come to San Francisco, Summertime will be a love-in there." The Summer of Love swelled the Haight's population from 7,000 to 75,000; people came both to join in and to ogle the nutty subculture. But degenerates soon joined the gentle people, heroin replaced LSD, crime was rampant, and the Haight began a fast slide.

Hippies will tell you the Human Be-In was the pinnacle of their scene, while the Summer of Love came from outside—a media creation that turned their movement into a monster. Still, the idea of that fictional summer still lingers, and to this day pilgrims from all over the world come to the Haight to search for a past that never was.

CASTRO AND NOE WALK

The Castro and Noe Valley are both neighborhoods that beg to be walked—or ambled through, really, without time pressure or an absolute destination. Hit the Castro first, beginning at **Harvey Milk Plaza** under the gigantic rainbow flag. If you're going on to Noe Valley, first head east down **Market Street** for the cafés, bistros, and shops, then go back to **Castro Street** and head south, past the glorious art-deco **Castro Theatre**, checking out boutiques and cafés along the way (Cliff's Variety, at 479 Castro Street, is a must). To tour Noe Valley, go east down **18th Street** to Church (at Dolores Park), and then either strap on your hiking boots and head south over the hill or hop the J–Church to **24th Street**, the center of this rambling neighborhood.

Just over Buena Vista Hill from Haight Street, nestled at the base of Twin Peaks, lies the brash and sassy Castro District—the social, political, and cultural center of San Francisco's thriving gay (and, to a lesser extent, lesbian) community. This neighborhood is one of the city's liveliest and most welcoming, especially on weekends. Streets teem with folks out shopping, pushing political causes, heading to art films, and lingering in bars and cafés. Hard-bodied men in painted-on tees cruise the cutting-edge clothing and novelty stores, and pairs of all genders and sexual persuasions hold hands. Brightly painted, intricately restored Victorians line the streets here, making the Castro a good place to view striking examples of the architecture San Francisco is famous for.

Still farther south lies Noe Valley—also known as Stroller Valley for its relatively high concentration of little ones—an upscale but relaxed enclave that's one of the city's most desirable places to live. Church Street and 24th Street, the neighborhood's main thoroughfares, teem with laid-back cafés, kid-friendly restaurants, and comfortable, old-time shops. You can also see remnants of Noe Valley's agricultural beginnings: Billy Goat Hill (at Castro and 30th streets), a wild-grass hill often draped in fog, is named for the goats that grazed here right into the 20th century.

10

THE HAIGHT

TOP ATTRACTIONS

Haight-Ashbury Intersection. On October 6, 1967, hippies took over the intersection of Haight and Ashbury streets to proclaim the "Death of Hip." If they thought hip was dead then, they'd find absolute confirmation of it today, what with the only tie-dye in sight on the famed corner being Ben & Jerry's storefront.

Everyone knows the Summer of Love had something to do with free love and LSD, but the drugs and other excesses of that period have tended to obscure the residents' serious attempts to create an America that was more spiritually oriented, more environmentally aware, and less caught up in commercialism. The Diggers, a radical group of actors and populist agitators, for example, operated a free shop a few blocks

TWO HAIGHTS

The Haight is actually composed of two distinct neighborhoods: the Lower Haight runs from Divisadero to Webster; the Upper Haight, immediately east of Golden Gate Park, is the part people tend to call Haight-Ashbury (and the part that's covered here). San Franciscans come to the Upper Haight for the myriad vintage clothing stores concentrated in its few blocks, bars with character, restaurants where huge breakfast portions take the edge off a hangover, and Amoeba, the best place in town for new and used CDs and vinyl. The Lower Haight is a lively, grittier stretch with several well-loved pubs and a smattering of niche music shops.

off Haight Street. Everything really was free at the free shop; people brought in things they didn't need and took things they did. (The group also coined immortal phrases like "Do your own thing.")

Among the folks who hung out in or near the Haight during the late 1960s were writers Richard Brautigan, Allen Ginsberg, Ken Kesey, and Gary Snyder; anarchist Abbie Hoffman; rock performers Marty Balin, Jerry Garcia, Janis Joplin, and Grace Slick; LSD champion Timothy Leary; and filmmaker Kenneth Anger. If you're keen to feel something resembling the hippie spirit these days, there's always Hippie Hill, just inside the Haight Street entrance of Golden Gate Park. Think drum circles, guitar players, and whiffs of pot smoke.

WORTH NOTING

Buena Vista Park. If you can manage the steep climb, this eucalyptus-filled park has great city views. Be sure to scan the stone rain gutters lining many of the park's walkways for inscribed names and dates; these are the remains of gravestones left unclaimed when the city closed the Laurel Hill cemetery around 1940. You might also come across used needles and condoms; definitely avoid the park after dark, when these items are left behind. ⊠ *Haight St. between Lyon St. and Buena Vista Ave. W, Haight.*

QUICK
BITES

Boisterous Cha Cha Cha (⊠ *1801 Haight St., at Shrader St., Haight* ☏ *415/386–7670*) serves island cuisine, a mix of Cajun, Southwestern, and Caribbean influences. The decor is Technicolor tropical plastic, and the food is hot and spicy. Try the fried calamari or chili-spiked shrimp, and wash everything down with a pitcher of Cha Cha Cha's signature sangria. Reservations are not accepted, so expect a wait for dinner.

Grateful Dead House. On the outside, this is just one more well-kept Victorian on a street that's full of them—but true fans of the Dead may find some inspiration at this legendary structure. The three-story house (closed to the public) is tastefully painted in sedate mauves, tans, and teals (no bright tie-dye colors here). ⊠ *710 Ashbury St., just past Waller St., Haight.*

A colorful mosaic mural in the Castro

Red Victorian Bed & Breakfast Inn and Peace Center. By even the most generous accounts, the Summer of Love quickly crashed and burned, and the Haight veered sharply away from the higher goals that inspired that fabled summer. In 1977 Sami Sunchild acquired the Red Vic, built as a hotel in 1904, with the aim of preserving the best of 1960s ideals. She decorated her rooms with 1960s themes—one chamber is called the Flower Child Room—and opened the Peace Arts Gallery on the ground floor. Here you can buy her paintings, T-shirts, and "meditative art," along with books about the Haight and prayer flags. Simple, cheap vegan and vegetarian fare is available in the Peace Café, and there's also a meditation room. ✉ *1665 Haight St., Haight* ☎ *415/864–1978* ⊕ *www.redvic.com.*

Spreckels Mansion. Not to be confused with the Spreckels Mansion of Pacific Heights, this house was built for sugar baron Richard Spreckels in 1887. Jack London and Ambrose Bierce both lived and wrote here, while more recent residents included musician Graham Nash and actor Danny Glover. The boxy, putty-color Victorian—today a private home—is in mint condition. ✉ *737 Buena Vista Ave. W, Haight.*

THE CASTRO

TOP ATTRACTIONS

★ **Castro Theatre.** Here's a classic way to join in the Castro community: grab some popcorn and catch a flick at this gorgeous, 1,500-seat art-deco theater; opened in 1922, it's the grandest of San Francisco's few remaining movie palaces. The neon marquee, which stands at the top of the Castro strip, is the neighborhood's great landmark. The Castro was

CLOSE UP

The Evolution of Gay San Francisco

San Francisco's gay community has been a part of the city since its earliest days. As a port city and a major hub during the 19th-century gold rush, it became known for its sexual openness along with all its other liberalities. But a major catalyst for the rise of a gay community was World War II.

During the war, hundreds of thousands of servicemen cycled through "Sodom by the Sea," and for most, San Francisco's permissive atmosphere was an eye-opening experience. The army's "off-limits" lists of forbidden establishments unintentionally (but effectively) pointed the way to the city's gay bars. When soldiers were dishonorably discharged for homosexual activity, many stayed on.

Scores of these newcomers found homes in what was then called Eureka Valley. When the war ended, the predominantly Irish-Catholic families in that neighborhood began to move out, heading for the 'burbs. The new arrivals snapped up the Victorians on the main drag, Castro Street.

The establishment pushed back. In the 1950s San Francisco's police chief vowed to crack down on "perverts," and the city's gay, lesbian, bisexual, and transgender residents lived in fear of getting caught in police raids. (Arrest meant being outed in the morning paper.) But harassment helped galvanize the community. The Daughters of Bilitis lesbian organization was founded in the city in 1955; the gay male Mattachine Society, started in Los Angeles in 1950, followed suit with an SF branch.

By the mid-1960s these clashing interests gave the growing gay population a national profile. The police

upped their policy of harassment, but overplayed their hand. In 1965 they dramatically raided a New Year's benefit event, and the tide of public opinion began to turn. The police were forced to appoint the first-ever liaison to the gay community. Local gay organizations began to lobby openly. As one gay participant noted, "We didn't go back into the woodwork."

The 1970s—thumping disco, raucous street parties, and gay bashing—were a tumultuous time for the gay community. Thousands from across the country flocked to San Francisco's gay scene. Eureka Valley had more than 60 gay bars, the bathhouse scene in SoMa (where the leather crowd held court) was thriving, and graffiti around town read "Save San Francisco—Kill a Fag." When the Eureka Valley Merchants Association refused to admit gay-owned businesses in 1974, camera shop owner Harvey Milk founded the Castro Valley Association, and the neighborhood's new moniker was born. Milk was elected to the city's Board of Supervisors in 1977, its first openly gay official (and the inspirational figure for the Oscar-winning film *Milk*).

San Francisco's gay community was getting serious about politics, civil rights, and self-preservation, but it still loved a party: 350,000 people attended the 1978 Gay Freedom Day Parade, where the rainbow flag debuted. But on November 27, 1978, Milk and Mayor George Moscone were gunned down in City Hall by enraged former city council member Dan White. Thousands marched in silent tribute out of the Castro down to City Hall.

CLOSE UP

When the killer got a relatively light conviction of manslaughter, the next march was not silent. Another crowd of thousands converged on City Hall, this time smashing windows, burning 12 police cars, and fighting with police in what became known as the White Night Riot. The police retaliated by storming the Castro.

The gay community recovered, even thrived—especially economically—but in 1981 the first medical and journalistic reports of a dangerous new disease surfaced. A notice appeared in a Castro pharmacy's window warning people about "the gay cancer," later named AIDS. By 1983 the populations most vulnerable to the burgeoning epidemic were publicly identified as gay men in San Francisco and New York City.

San Francisco gay activists were quick to mobilize, starting foundations as early as 1982 to care for the sick, along with public memorials to raise awareness nationwide. By 1990 the disease had killed 10,000 San

Franciscans. Local organizations lobbied hard to speed up drug development and FDA approvals. In the past decade the city's network of volunteer organizations and public outreach has been recognized as one of the best global models for combating the disease.

Today the Castro is still the heart of San Francisco's gay life—though many young hetero families have also moved in. As the gay mecca becomes diluted, debate about the neighborhood's character and future continues. But the legacy remains, as is evident when a Harvey Milk bust was unveiled in City Hall on May 22, 2008, Milk's birthday.

10

Where can I find . . . ?

A NIGHTCAP	**Trax** (437 Haight St.) A laid-back gay bar with good beer specials.	**Pilsner Inn** (225 Church St.) A casual neighborhood joint with a nice patio.
A CUP OF COFFEE	**Peet's** (2257 Market St.) One cup, and you could become a Peetnik.	**Cole Valley Café** (701 Cole St., at Waller St.) Good coffee and free Wi-Fi. What's not to like?
A PARKING SPACE	**Metered Lot** (Castro St. and 17th St.) City-owned lot.	**Metered Lot** (Collingwood and 18th Sts.) Another city-owned lot.

the fitting host of 2008's red-carpet preview of Gus Van Sant's film *Milk*, starring Sean Penn as openly gay San Francisco supervisor Harvey Milk. The theater's elaborate Spanish baroque interior is fairly well preserved. Before many shows the theater's pipe organ rises from the orchestra pit and an organist plays pop and movie tunes, usually ending with the Jeanette McDonald standard "San Francisco" (go ahead, sing along). The crowd can be enthusiastic and vocal, talking back to the screen as loudly as it talks to them. Classics such as *Who's Afraid of Virginia Woolf?* take on a whole new life, with the assembled beating the actors to the punch and fashioning even snappier comebacks for Elizabeth Taylor. Head here to catch classics, a Fellini film retrospective, or the latest take on same-sex love. ☒ *429 Castro St., Castro* ☎ *415/621–6120.*

OFF THE BEATEN PATH Branching out from its small, third-floor exhibit space South of Market, the **Gay, Lesbian, Bisexual and Transgender (GLBT) History Museum** opened its new home in the Castro, a block from the site of Harvey Milk's camera shop, in 2010. Swing by 4127 18th Street to see displays on the community's history (Tues.–Sat 11–7 and Sun.–Mon. noon–5). Admission is $5, free the first Wednesday of the month.

WORTH NOTING

Clarke's Mansion. Built for attorney Alfred "Nobby" Clarke, this 1892 off-white baroque Queen Anne home was dubbed Clarke's Folly. (His wife refused to inhabit it because it was in an unfashionable part of town—at the time, anyone who was anyone lived on Nob Hill.) The greenery-shrouded house (now apartments) is a beauty, with dormers, cupolas, rounded bay windows, and huge turrets topped by gold-leaf spheres. ☒ *250 Douglass St., between 18th and 19th Sts., Castro.*

QUICK BITES Sometimes referred to as Café Floorshow because it's such a see-and-be-seen place, Café Flore (☒ *2298 Market St., Castro* ☎ *415/621–8579*) serves coffee drinks, beer, and tasty café fare. It's a good place to catch the latest Castro gossip.

Harvey Milk Plaza. An 18-foot-long rainbow flag, the symbol of gay pride, flies above this plaza named for the man who electrified the city in 1977 by being elected to its Board of Supervisors as an openly gay candidate. In the early 1970s Milk had opened a camera store on the block of Castro Street between 18th and 19th streets. The store became the center for his campaign to open San Francisco's social and political life to gays and lesbians.

The liberal Milk hadn't served a full year of his term before he and Mayor George Moscone, also a liberal, were shot in November 1978 at City Hall. The murderer was a conservative ex-supervisor named Dan White, who had recently resigned his post and then became enraged when Moscone wouldn't reinstate him. Milk and White had often been at odds on the board, and White thought Milk had been part of a cabal to keep him from returning to his post. Milk's assassination shocked the gay community, which became infuriated when the infamous "Twinkie defense"—that junk food had led to diminished mental capacity—resulted in a manslaughter verdict for White. During the so-called White Night Riot of May 21, 1979, gays and their allies stormed City Hall, torching its lobby and several police cars.

Milk, who had feared assassination, left behind a tape recording in which he urged the community to continue the work he had begun. His legacy is the high visibility of gay people throughout city government; a bust of him was unveiled at City Hall on his birthday in 2008, and the 2008 film *Milk* gives insight into his life. A plaque at the base of the flagpole lists the names of past and present openly gay and lesbian state and local officials. ⊠ *Southwest corner of Castro and Market Sts., Castro.*

10

☾ **Randall Museum.** The best thing about visiting this free nature museum for kids may be its tremendous views of San Francisco. Younger kids who are still excited about petting a rabbit, touching a snakeskin, or seeing a live hawk will enjoy a trip here. (Many of the creatures here can't be released into the wild due to injury or other problems.) The museum sits

PINK TRIANGLE PARK

Pink Triangle Park. On a median near the Castro's huge rainbow flag stands this memorial to the gays, lesbians, and bisexual and transgender people whom the Nazis forced to wear pink triangles. Fifteen triangular granite columns, one for every 1,000 gays, lesbians, bisexual, and transgender people estimated to have been killed during and after the Holocaust, stand at the tip of a pink-rock-filled triangle—a reminder of the gay community's past and ongoing struggle for civil rights. ⊠ *Corner of Market, Castro, and 17th Sts., Castro.*

SISTER ACT!

If you're lucky enough to happen upon a cluster of cheeky cross-dressing nuns while in the Castro, meet the legendary Sisters of Perpetual Indulgence. They're decked out in white face-paint, glitter, and fabulous jewels. Renowned for their wit and charity fund-raising bashes, the Sisters—Sister Mary MaeHimm, Sister Bea Attitude, Sister Farrah Moans, and the gang—are the pinnacle of Castro color.

beneath a hill variously known as Red Rock, Museum Hill, and, correctly, Corona Heights; hike up the steep but short trail for great, unobstructed city views. ■ TIP→ It's a great resource for local families, but if you're going to take the kids to just one museum in town, make it the Exploratorium (see ch. 7). ✉ *199 Museum Way, off Roosevelt Way, Castro* ☎ *415/554–9600* ⊕ *www.randallmuseum.org* ✉ *Free* ⊘ *Tues.–Sat. 10–5.*

NOE VALLEY

WORTH NOTING

Axford House. This mauve house was built in 1877, when Noe Valley was still a rural area, as evidenced by the hayloft in the gable of the adjacent carriage house. The house is perched several feet above the sidewalk. Various types of roses grow in the well-maintained garden that surrounds the house, which is a private home. ✉ *1190 Noe St., at 25th St., Noe Valley.*

Golden fire hydrant. When all the other fire hydrants went dry during the fire that followed the 1906 earthquake, this one kept pumping. Noe Valley and the Mission District were thus spared the devastation wrought elsewhere in the city, which explains the large number of pre-quake homes here. Every year on April 18 (the anniversary of the quake) folks gather here to share stories about the earthquake, and the famous hydrant gets a fresh coat of gold paint. ✉ *Church and 20th Sts., southeast corner, across from Dolores Park, Noe Valley.*

OFF THE
BEATEN
PATH

Twin Peaks. Windswept and desolate Twin Peaks yields sweeping vistas of San Francisco and the neighboring East and North Bay counties. You can get a real feel for the city's layout here; arrive before the late-afternoon fog turns the view into pea soup in summer. To drive here, head west from Castro Street up Market Street, which eventually becomes Portola Drive. Turn right (north) on Twin Peaks Boulevard and follow the signs to the top. Muni Bus 37–Corbett heads west to Twin Peaks from Market Street. Catch this bus above the Castro Street Muni light-rail station on the island west of Castro at Market Street.

Mission District

WORD OF MOUTH

"We had a great time looking at the murals in a couple of the famous alleyways [in the Mission], and in other random places. It was also fun walking around an area that didn't feel quite as polished as the rest of the city."

—sunny16

GETTING ORIENTED

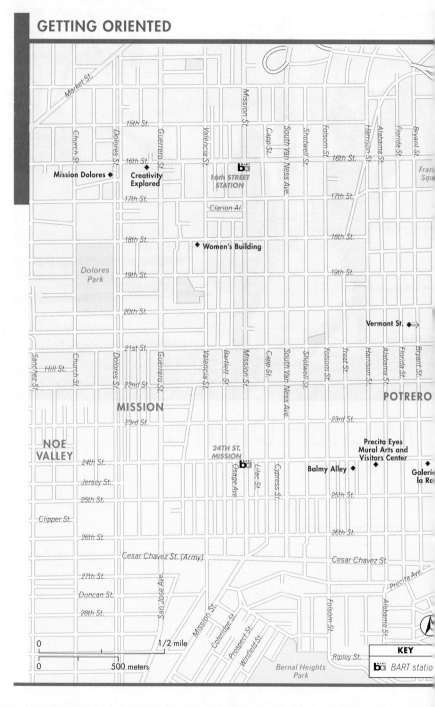

Market St.

Church St.

Dolores St.

15th St.

Guerrero St.

Valencia St.

16th St.

Mission St.

Capp St.

South Van Ness Ave.

Shotwell St.

Folsom St.

Harrison St.

Alabama St.

Florida St.

Bryant St.

Mission Dolores ◆

Creativity Explored

16th STREET STATION

17th St.

Franl Squa

Clarion Al.

18th St.

◆ Women's Building

18th St.

Dolores Park

19th St.

19th St.

20th St.

Sanchez St.

Hill St.

21st St.

Vermont St. ◆→

Church St.

Dolores St.

22nd St.

Guerrero St.

Valencia St.

Bartlett St.

Mission St.

Capp St.

South Van Ness Ave.

Shotwell St.

Folsom St.

Treat St.

Harrison St.

Alabama St.

Florida St.

Bryant St.

MISSION

23rd St.

POTRERO

NOE VALLEY

23rd St.

24th St.

24TH ST. MISSION

Precita Eyes Mural Arts and Visitors Center

Osage Ave.

Lilac St.

Cypress St.

Balmy Alley ◆

Galeri la Ro

Jersey St.

25th St.

25th St.

Clipper St.

26th St.

26th St.

Cesar Chavez St. (Army)

Cesar Chavez St.

Precita Ave.

27th St.

San Jose Ave.

Duncan St.

Folsom St.

Alabama St.

28th St.

Mission St.

Coleridge St.

Prospect St.

Winfield St.

0   1/2 mile

0   500 meters

Ripley St.

Bernal Heights Park

KEY

BART statio

11

TOP 5 REASONS TO GO

Bar-hop: Embrace your inner (or not-so-inner) hipster. Start off at Medjool's rare rooftop deck, then move up to the stylish Nihon Whisky Lounge or pull up a chair in pretension-free Truck. Round the night off in the company of the 150+ beers available at the Monk's Kettle.

Chow down on phenomenal, cheap ethnic food: Keen appetites and thin wallets will meet their match here. Just try to decide between deliciously fresh burritos, garlicky falafel, thin-crust pizza, savory crepes, and more.

One-of-a-kind shopping: Barter for buried treasure at 826 Valencia and its Pirate Supply Store, then hop next door and say hello to the giraffe's head at the mad taxidermy–cum–garden store hodgepodge that is Paxton Gate.

Vivid murals: Check out dozens of energetic, colorful public artworks in alleyways and on building exteriors.

Hang out in Dolores Park: Join Mission locals and their dogs on this hilly expanse of green with a glorious view of downtown and, if you're lucky, the Bay Bridge.

QUICK BITES

Latin-American pastries are the specialty at **La Victoria** (✉ 2937 24th St., at Alabama St., Mission ☎ 415/642–7120). You can also pick up a coffee, piñatas, and votive candles.

For an old-fashioned soda or homemade ice cream, stop into the **St. Francis Fountain and Candy Store** (✉ 2801 24th St., at York St., Mission ☎ 415/826–4200).

Muddy Waters (✉ 521 Valencia St., at 16th St., Mission ☎ 415/863–8006) is a welcome stop near the 16th Street Mission BART station. You'll get an eyeful of the neighborhood culture here—some oddball characters and very casual housekeeping—but the coffee, chai, and wireless crackle at full capacity.

GETTING THERE

After climbing the hills downtown, you'll find the Mission to be welcomingly flat. BART's two Mission District stations drop you right in the heart of the action. Get off at 16th Street for Mission Dolores, shopping, nightlife, and restaurants, or 24th Street to see the neighborhood murals. The busy 14–Mission bus runs all the way from downtown into the neighborhood, but BART is a much faster and more direct route. Parking can be a drag, especially on weekend evenings. If you're heading out in the evening, your safest bet would be taking a cab, since some blocks are sketchy.

MAKING THE MOST OF YOUR TIME

A walk that includes Mission Dolores and the neighborhood's murals takes about two hours. If you plan to go on a mural walk with the Precita Eyes organization or if you're a window-shopper, add at least another hour. The Mission is a neighborhood that sleeps in. In the afternoon and evening the main drags really come to life.

Sunday through Tuesday is relatively quiet here, especially in the evening—a great time to get a café table with no wait. If you're getting bummed out by fog elsewhere in the city, come here—the Mission wins out in San Francisco's system of microclimates.

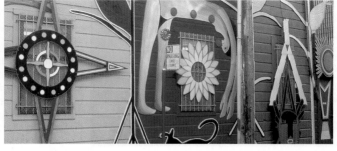

Sightseeing
★★
Nightlife
★★★★★
Dining
★★★★★
Lodging
—
Shopping
★★★

The Mission has a number of distinct personalities: it's the Latino neighborhood, where working-class folks raise their families and where gangs occasionally clash; it's the hipster hood, where tattooed and pierced twenty- and thirtysome-things hold court in the coolest cafés and bars in town; it's a culinary epicenter, with the strongest concentration of destination restaurants and affordable ethnic cuisine; and it's the artists' quarter, where murals adorn literally blocks of walls. It's also the city's equivalent of the Sunshine State—this neighborhood's always the last to succumb to fog.

Updated by
Denise M Leto

The eight blocks of Valencia Street between 16th and 24th streets—what's come to be known as the Valencia Corridor—typify the neighborhood's diversity. Businesses on the block between 16th and 17th streets, for instance, include an upscale Peruvian restaurant, an Indian grocery and sundries store, a tattoo parlor, the yuppie-chic bar Blondie's, a handful of funky home-decor stores, a pizzeria, a taquería, a Turkish restaurant, a sushi bar, bargain and pricey thrift shops, and the Puerto Alegre restaurant, a hole-in-the-wall with pack-a-punch margaritas locals revere. On the other hand, Mission Street itself, three blocks east, is mostly a down-at-the-heels row of check-cashing places, dollar stores, and residential hotels—but there are more than a few great taquerías. And the farther east you go, the sketchier the neighborhood gets.

Italian and Irish in the early 20th century, the Mission became heavily Latino in the late 1960s, when immigrants from Mexico and Central America began arriving. An influx of Chinese, Vietnamese, Arabic, and other immigrants, along with a young bohemian crowd enticed by cheap rents and the burgeoning arts-and-nightlife scene, followed in the 1980s and early 1990s. The skyrocketing rents of the late 1990s have leveled off and the district is yet again in transition. The Mission is still quite scruffy in patches, so as you plan your explorations, take

DID YOU KNOW?

San Francisco is chockablock with murals—about 600 by recent count—and the Mission District is the epicenter of all that artistic fervor.

Touring the Mission's Murals

San Francisco fairly teems with murals. Since the 1970s, groups of artists have worked to transform the city's walls into canvases, art accessible to everyone. Muralists here fall into two loose categories: those in the Latin American tradition of addressing political and social justice issues through art, and everyone else (those who simply paint on a large scale and like lots of people to see it).

Rediscovering the work of Mexican liberal artist and muralist Diego Rivera in the 1960s, Latino muralists began to address public issues on the community's walls. Heavily Latino since the 1970s, the Mission District became the collective canvas for these artists. The Precita Eyes Mural Arts Center emerged to support those artists and galvanize collaborative projects in the neighborhood. Early on, the San Francisco Arts Commission hired the center to create murals all over town. Of the 800-plus murals that adorn city surfaces, a good quarter of them were painted by muralists associated with Precita Eyes.

Bright Sunbelt colors reflect the medium's historical geography; in contemporary work, look for anime and woodblock cuts along with traditional Latino symbols. Murals are considered permanent, and aren't painted over without consulting the artist. Keep your eyes peeled as you wander the city and you'll begin to discover art everywhere. Here are the best and brightest of the Mission District:

■ **826 Valencia.** Fans of graphic novelist Chris Ware will want to take a good look at the facade here. Ware designed the intricate mural for the storefront, a meditation on the evolution of human communication.

■ **Balmy Alley.** The most famous of the Mission's murals—a vivid sweep from end to end. This group series began in 1971 and still gets new additions.

■ **Clarion Alley.** A new generation of muralists is creating a fresh alley-cum-gallery here, between Valencia and Mission streets and 17th and 18th streets. The loosely connected artists of the Clarion Alley Mural Project (CAMP) represent a broad range of style and imagery. Carpet-draped Indonesian elephants plod calmly down the block; kung fu movie-style headlines shout slogans. The works here offer a dense glimpse at the Mission's contemporary art scene.

■ **Shotwell Street grocery.** A bit off the beaten path but well worth the detour is Brian Barneclo's gigantic *Food Chain.* This adorns the grocery store on Shotwell Street between 14th and 15th streets. It's a retro, 1950s-style celebration of the city's many neighborhoods (and the food chain), complete with an ant birthday party and worms finishing off a human skull. But in a cute way. Barneclo fans can see more of his work at cool watering hole Rye and hipster restaurant Nopa.

■ **24th Street.** Several murals in the Mexican political tradition adorn the buildings along 24th Street, including St. Peter's (at Alabama Street) and even McDonald's (at Mission Street).

■ **Women's Building.** *Maestrapeace*—the impressive, towering mural that seems to enclose this building—celebrates women around the world who work for peace.

—Denise M. Leto

Where can I find . . . ?

A CAFÉ WITH FREE WI-FI	**Philz Coffee** (3101 24th St.) Potent joe with a loyal following.	**Ritual Roasters** (1026 Valencia St.) Strong coffee, very sceney.
A GAS STATION	**Arco** (1798 Mission St.) Close to the neighborhood core.	**Potrero Hill 76** (401 Potrero Ave.) Average prices, near the 101.
A DRUGSTORE	**Community Pharmacy** (2462 Mission St.) All the OTC standbys.	**Walgreens** (1979 Mission St.) Right by the 16th Street BART station.

into account your comfort zone. ■TIP→ If raucous bar-hoppers are a bit intimidating to you, an afternoon trip to the Valencia Corridor may be your best bet.

TOP ATTRACTIONS

Balmy Alley. Mission District artists have transformed the walls of their neighborhood with paintings, and Balmy Alley is one of the best-executed examples. Murals fill the one-block alley, with newer ones continually filling in the blank spaces. Local children working with adults started the project in 1971. Since then dozens of artists have steadily added to it, with the aim of promoting peace in Central America, as well as community spirit and AIDS awareness. ■TIP→ Be alert here: the 25th Street end of the alley adjoins a somewhat dangerous area. ⊠ *24th St. between and parallel to Harrison and Treat Sts., alley runs south to 25th St., Mission.*

★ **Mission Dolores.** Two churches stand side by side at this mission, including the small adobe **Mission San Francisco de Asís,** the oldest standing structure in San Francisco. Completed in 1791, it's the sixth of the 21 California missions founded by Father Junípero Serra in the 18th and early 19th centuries. Its ceiling depicts original Ohlone Indian basket designs, executed in vegetable dyes. The tiny chapel includes frescoes and a hand-painted wooden altar. There's a hidden treasure here, too. In 2004 an archaeologist and an artist crawling along the ceiling's rafters opened a trap door behind the altar and rediscovered the mission's original mural, painted with natural dyes by Native Americans in 1791. The centuries have taken their toll, so the team photographed the 20-by-22-foot mural and began digitally restoring the photographic version. Among the images is a dagger-pierced Sacred Heart of Jesus. There's a small museum covering the mission's founding and history, and the pretty little mission cemetery (made famous by a scene in Alfred Hitchcock's *Vertigo*) maintains the graves of mid-19th-century European immigrants. (The remains of an estimated 5,000 Native Americans

Vivid public art provides a backdrop for the Mission District.

lie in unmarked graves.) Services are held in both the Mission San Francisco de Asís and next door in the handsome multi-dome basilica. ✉ *Dolores and 16th Sts., Mission* ☎ *415/621–8203* ⊕ *www.missiondolores. org* ⊠ *$5 donation, audio tour $7* ☯ *Nov.–Apr., daily 9–4; May–Oct., daily 9–4:30.*

WORTH NOTING

Creativity Explored. Joyous, if chaotic, creativity pervades the workshops of this art-education center and gallery for developmentally disabled adults. Several dozen adults work at the center each day—guided by a staff of working artists—painting, working in the darkroom, producing videos, and crafting prints, textiles, and ceramics. On weekdays you can drop by and see the artists at work. The art produced here is striking, and some of it is for sale; this is a great place to find a unique San Francisco masterpiece to take home. ✉ *3245 16th St., Mission* ☎ *415/863–2108* ⊕ *www.creativityexplored.org* ⊠ *Free* ☯ *Mon.–Wed. and Fri. 10–3, Thurs. 10–7, Sat. 1–6.*

Galería de la Raza. San Francisco's premier showcase for contemporary Latino art, the gallery exhibits the works of mostly local artists. Events include readings and spoken word by local poets and writers, screenings of Latin American and Spanish films, and theater works by local minority theater troupes. Just across the street, amazing art festoons the 24th Street/York Street Minipark, a tiny urban playground. A mosaic-covered Quetzalcoatl serpent plunges into the ground and rises, creating hills for little ones to clamber over, and mural-covered walls surround the space. ✉ *2857 24th St., at Bryant St., Mission* ☎ *415/826–8009* ⊕ *www.galeriadelaraza.org* ☯ *Gallery Tues. 1–7, Wed.–Sat. noon–6.*

San Francisco on Film

11

With its spectacular cityscape, atmospheric fog, and a camera-ready iconic bridge, it's little wonder that San Francisco has been the setting for hundreds of films. While you're running around town, you might have the occasional sense of déjà vu, sparked by a scene from a Hitchcock or Clint Eastwood thriller. Below are a few of the city's favorite cinematic sites:

■ *Zodiac*, a 2007 drama about a legendary Bay Area serial killer, filmed scenes at the real-life locations where victims were gunned down. It also re-created the San Francisco Chronicle offices, but down south in L.A.

■ City Hall shows up in the Clint Eastwood cop thrillers *Dirty Harry* and *Magnum Force*, and is set aflame in the James Bond flick *A View to a Kill*. Its domed interior became a nightclub for Robin Williams' *Bicentennial Man* and a courthouse in *Tucker: The Man and His Dream*.

■ Streets in Russian Hill, Potrero Hill, and North Beach were used for the supreme car-chase sequence in *Bullitt*. The namesake detective, played by Steve McQueen, lived in Nob Hill at 1153–57 Taylor Street. And the "King of Cool" did much of his own stunt driving, thank you very much.

■ Brocklebank Apartments, at Mason and Sacramento streets in Nob Hill, appears in several films, most notably as the posh residence of Kim Novak in Alfred Hitchcock's *Vertigo*. Other key *Vertigo* locations include the cemetery of Mission Dolores and the waterfront at Fort Point.

■ The great Bogie-and-Bacall noir film *Dark Passage* revolves around the art-deco apartment building at 1360 Montgomery Street and the nearby Filbert Steps.

■ Dashiell Hammett's "Thin Man" characters, Nick and Nora Charles, do much of their sleuthing in the city, especially in films like *After the Thin Man*, in which the base of Coit Tower stands in as the entrance to the Charles' home.

■ North Beach's Tosca Café, at 242 Columbus Avenue, is the bar where Michael Douglas unwinds in *Basic Instinct*.

■ The Hilton Hotel at 333 O'Farrell Street became the "Hotel Bristol," the scene of much of the mayhem caused by Barbra Streisand in *What's Up, Doc?*

■ At 2640 Steiner Street in Pacific Heights is the elegant home that Robin Williams infiltrates while disguised as a nanny in *Mrs. Doubtfire*.

■ The Castro of the 1970s comes alive in *Milk*, Gus Van Sant's film starring Sean Penn as slain San Francisco supervisor Harvey Milk.

■ And, of course, there are plenty of movies about the notorious federal prison on Alcatraz Island, including Burt Lancaster's redemption drama *Birdman of Alcatraz*, Clint Eastwood's suspenseful *Escape from Alcatraz*, the goofy *So I Married an Axe Murderer*, and the Sean Connery and Nicolas Cage action flick, *The Rock*.

—Jim Van Buskirk

Precita Eyes Mural Arts and Visitors Center. Founded by muralists, this nonprofit arts organization designs and creates murals. The artists themselves lead informative guided walks of murals in the area. Most tours start with a 45-minute slide presentation. The bike and walking trips, which take between one and three hours, pass several dozen murals. May is Mural Awareness Month, with visits to murals-in-progress and presentations by artists. You can pick up a map of 24th Street's murals at the center and buy art supplies, T-shirts, postcards, and other mural-related items. Bike tours are available by appointment; Saturday's 11 am walking tour meets at Cafe Venice, at 24th and Mission streets. (All other tours meet at the center.) ⊠ *2981 24th St., Mission* ☎ *415/285–2287* ⊕ *www.precitaeyes.org* ⊠ *Center free, tours $12–$15* ⊙ *Center weekdays 10–5, Sat. 10–4, Sun. noon–4; walks weekends at 11 and 1:30 or by appointment.*

> **SAFETY IN THE MISSION**
>
> The Mission is a vibrant area, but it does have dodgy zones. The safest area is bordered by Mission, Dolores, 16th, and 20th streets—where everything is happening anyway. Even here, plenty of homeless people crash in doorways, and robberies and assaults can happen. After dark, the areas east of Mission Street and south of 24th Street can feel unsafe, with empty stretches or groups of loitering toughs. If you're in this area after dark, stick to main drags like Mission and 24th streets. If you keep your wits about you and stick to well-lighted areas, you're unlikely to run into trouble.

OFF THE BEATEN PATH

Vermont Street. With a similar series of switchbacks, this Potrero Hill street is a kind of blue-collar Lombard Street, but minus the throngs (and the spectacular gardens and views). It's on the east side of the 101 from the Mission. To check it out, head down 24th Street to the end, go left on Vermont, right on 23rd Street past the freeway, left on Rhode Island Street, left on 20th Street, and finally head left down the curvy stretch of Vermont. Bring a city map along! ⊠ *Between 20th and 22nd Sts., Potrero Hill.*

Women's Building. The cornerstone of the female-owned and -run businesses in the neighborhood, this place has held workshops and conferences of particular interest to women since 1979. The exterior is the reason to visit: its two stories are completely covered with an impressive mural, *Maestrapeace*, depicting women's peacekeeping efforts over the centuries. Inside are offices for many social and political organizations; the center also sponsors talks and readings by writers such as Alice Walker and Angela Davis. Head inside to pick up a key to the murals' figures and symbols. ⊠ *3543 18th St., Mission* ☎ *415/431–1180* ⊕ *www.womensbuilding.org* ⊙ *Mon.–Thurs. 9–5, Fri. 10–6.*

Pacific Heights and Japantown

WORD OF MOUTH

"[For rainy day activities] you can grab a bowl of steaming Japanese Noodles in the Kabuki Mall and/or sign yourselves up for some really good Japanese baths at Kabuki Hot Springs."

—PamSF

GETTING ORIENTED

Gashouse Cove

Fort Mason

North Point St.

Beach St.

Beach St.

Cervantes Blvd.

North Point St.

Bay St.

Capra Way

Avila St.

MARINA

George R. Moscone Rec. Center

Francisco St.

Chestnut St.

Toledo Way

Lombard St.

FILLMORE

Magnolia St.

101

RUSSIAN HILL

Lombard St.

Moulton St.

Greenwich St.

Greenwich St.

Pixley St.

Filbert St.

Filbert St.

Wedding Houses ◆

Laguna St.

Octavia St.

101

Polk St.

Larkin St.

Vedanta Society ◆

◆ Octagon House

Green St.

Union St.

Gough St.

Franklin St.

Van Ness Ave.

Vallejo St.

Green St.

Scott St.

Pierce St.

Steiner St.

Fillmore St.

Webster St.

Buchanan St.

PACIFIC HEIGHTS

Broadway

Broadway

◆ ◆

Broadway and Webster Street estates

Whittier Mansion

Pacific Ave.

Jackson St.

Haas-Lilienthal ◆ House

NOB HILL

Spreckels Mansion ◆

Washington St.

Clay St.

WEBSTER ST. HISTORIC DISTRICT

Lafayette Park ◆

Franklin Street ◆ buildings

Alta Plaza Park ◆

Clay St.

Sacramento St.

California St.

California St. ◆ Noteworthy Victorians

Pine St.

Austin St.

Bush St.

Perine Pl.

California St.

Webster St.

Laguna St.

Octavia St.

Van Ness Ave.

Fern St.

Sutter St.

Hemlock St.

Pine St.

Wilmot St.

Bush St.

JAPANTOWN

Gough St.

Franklin St.

Cedar St.

Geary St.

Divisadero St.

Sutter St.

◆ Japan Center Mall

◆ New People

Myrtle St.

O'Farrell

Post St.

Kabuki Springs & Spa ◆

◆ Japan Center

Geary Blvd.

Starr King Way

Olive St.

Ellis St.

St. Francis Square

Ellis St.

101

Willow St.

Eddy St.

O'Farrell St.

Steiner St.

Fillmore St.

Willow St.

Laguna St.

Jefferson Square

Gough St.

Franklin St.

Larch St.

Elm St.

Polk St.

Ellis St.

Scott St.

Pierce St.

Broderick St.

Turk St.

Elm St.

Golden Gate Ave.

McAllister St.

0   1/4 mile

0   400 meters

12

TOP 5 REASONS TO GO

Chic shopping on Fillmore Street: Browse the superfine shops along Pacific Heights' main drag.

Picnic with a view at Lafayette Park: Gather supplies along Fillmore Street and climb to the top of this park. It's surrounded by grand homes and has a sweeping view of the city.

Asian food galore in the Japan Center: Graze your way through the mall, from sushi boat offerings at Isobune to quick bean-paste snacks at May's Coffee Shop, decked out like an open-air Japanese restaurant.

Spa serenity at Kabuki Springs: Enter the peaceful lobby and prepare to be transported at the Japanese-style communal baths.

See how the other half lives: Check out the grand, historic homes along the tree-lined streets of Pacific Heights.

QUICK BITES

Swing by **La Boulangerie** (⊠ *2325 Pine St., at Fillmore St., Pacific Heights* ☎ *415/440-0356*), an oh-so-French bakery and patisserie whose patrons swoon for its perfect baguettes, rounds, croissants, and tartlets. Flaky-crust savory tarts filled with veggies and cheese or leeks and prosciutto make perfect picnic fare for Lafayette Park.

Red-and-white lanterns adorn the room at the Japan Center's **Isobune** (⊠ *Kintetsu Bldg., 1737 Post St., Japantown* ☎ *415/563-1030*), where "sushi boats" float around the counter. Crowds of customers take what they want and pay per dish at the end of the meal.

GETTING THERE

Steep streets in Pacific Heights make for impressive views and rough walking; unless you're in decent shape, consider taking a car or taxi to this neighborhood.

The only public transit that runs through the area is the bus. For Pacific Heights proper, take the 12–Folsom to the area just north of Lafayette Park. For shopping on Union Street in Cow Hollow (lower Pacific Heights), catch the 41– or the 45–Union bus.

Buses that run to Japantown from downtown include the 2–Clement, 3–Jackson, and the very busy 38–Geary.

MAKING THE MOST OF YOUR TIME

Give yourself an hour to wander Fillmore Street, more if you're planning to have a meal here or picnic in Lafayette or Alta Plaza parks. Checking out the stunning homes in Pacific Heights is best done by car, unless you have serious stamina; a half hour should be enough.

Since the Japan Center is the main highlight of Japantown, plan a daytime visit for a meal and some window-shopping; lunchtime is ideal.

Sightseeing
★★
Nightlife
★★
Dining
★★★
Lodging
★
Shopping
★★★

Pacific Heights and Japantown are something of an odd couple: privileged, old-school San Francisco and the workaday commercial center of Japanese-American life in the city, stacked virtually on top of each other. The sprawling, extravagant mansions of Pacific Heights gradually give way to the more modest Victorians and unassuming housing tracts of Japantown. The most interesting spots in Japantown huddle in the Japan Center, the neighborhood's two-block centerpiece, and along Post Street. You can find plenty of authentic Japanese treats in the shops and restaurants, if you have a special interest in these.

Updated by
Denise M. Leto

Pacific Heights defines San Francisco's most expensive and dramatic real estate. Grand Victorians line the streets, mansions and town houses are priced in the millions, and there are magnificent views from almost any point in the neighborhood. Old money and new, personalities in the limelight, and those who prefer absolute media anonymity live here, and few outsiders see anything other than the pleasing facades of Queen Anne charmers, English Tudor imports, and baroque bastions. Nancy Pelosi and Dianne Feinstein, Larry Ellison, and Gordon Getty all own impressive homes here, but not even pockets as deep as those can buy a large garden—space in the city is simply at too much of a premium. The boutiques and restaurants along Fillmore, which range from glam to funky, have become a draw for the whole city.

Japantown, on the other hand, feels somewhat adrift. (Also called Nihonmachi, it's centered on the southern slope of Pacific Heights, north of Geary Boulevard between Fillmore and Laguna streets.) The Japan Center mall, for instance, comes across as rather sterile. Where Chinatown is densely populated and still largely Chinese, Japantown struggles to retain its unique character.

A PACIFIC HEIGHTS WALK

Start at **Broadway and Webster Street**, where four notable estates stand within a block of one another. Two are on the north side of Broadway to the west of the intersection, one is on the same side to the east, and the last is half a block south on Webster Street. Head south down Webster and hang a right onto Clay to **Alta Plaza Park**, or skip the park and turn left on Jackson to the **Whittier Mansion**, on the corner of Jackson and Laguna streets. Head south down Laguna and cross Washington Street to **Lafayette Park**. Walk on Washington along the edge of Lafayette Park, past the formal French **Spreckels Mansion** at the corner of Octavia Street, and continue east two more blocks to Franklin Street. Turn left (north); halfway down the block stands the handsome **Haas-Lilienthal House**. Head back south on Franklin Street, stopping to view several **Franklin Street buildings**. At California Street, turn right (west) to see more **noteworthy Victorians** on that street and Laguna Street. Beyond Laguna, continue three blocks west back to Fillmore Street.

The Japanese community in San Francisco started around 1860; after the 1906 earthquake and fire many of these newcomers settled in the Western Addition. By the 1930s they had opened shops, markets, meeting halls, and restaurants and established Shinto and Buddhist temples. But during World War II the area was virtually gutted, when many of its residents, including second- and third-generation Americans, were forced into so-called relocation camps. During the 1960s and '70s redevelopment further eroded the neighborhood, and most Japanese-Americans now live elsewhere in the city.

Still, when several key properties in the neighborhood were sold in 2007, a vocal group rallied to "save Japantown," and some new blood is finally infusing the neighborhood with energy: Robert Redford's Sundance corporation turned the venerable Kabuki Theatre into a destination cinema-restaurant combo; local hotel group Joie de Vivre took over the Hotel Kabuki; and the new J-Pop Center, New People, brings Japanese pop culture and a long-missing youthful vibe to the neighborhood. ■TIP➜ Japantown is a relatively safe area, but the Western Addition, south of Geary Boulevard, can be dangerous even during the daytime. Avoid going too far west of Fillmore Street on either side of Geary.

PACIFIC HEIGHTS

TOP ATTRACTIONS

Haas-Lilienthal House. A small display of photographs on the bottom floor of this elaborate, gray 1886 Queen Anne house makes clear that despite its lofty stature and striking, round third-story tower, the house was modest compared with some of the giants that fell victim to the 1906 earthquake and fire. The Foundation for San Francisco's Architectural Heritage operates the home, whose carefully kept rooms provide an intriguing glimpse into late-19th-century life through period furniture, authentic details (antique dishes in the kitchen built-in), and photos of

the family who occupied the house until 1972. Volunteers conduct one-hour house tours three days a week and informative two-hour walking tours ($8) of the Civic Center, Broadway, and Union Street areas on Saturday afternoon, and of the eastern portion of Pacific Heights on Sunday afternoon (call or check Web site for schedule). ✉ *2007 Franklin St., between Washington and Jackson Sts., Pacific Heights* ☎ *415/441–3004* ⊕ *www.sfheritage.org* 🎫 *Entry $8* ⊙ *1-hr tour Wed. and Sat. noon–3, Sun. 11–4; 2-hr tour Sun. at 12:30.*

Noteworthy Victorians. Two **Italianate Victorians** (✉ *1818 and 1834 California St., Pacific Heights*) stand out on the 1800 block of California. A block west is the Victorian-era **Atherton House** (✉ *1990 California St., Pacific Heights*), whose mildly daffy design incorporates Queen Anne, Stick-Eastlake, and other architectural elements. Many claim the house—now apartments—is haunted by the ghosts of its 19th-century residents, who regularly whisper, glow, and generally cause a mild fuss. The oft-photographed **Laguna Street Victorians,** on the west side of the 1800 block of Laguna Street, cost between $2,000 and $2,600 when they were built in the 1870s. No bright colors here though—most of the paint jobs are in soft beiges or pastels. ✉ *California St. between Franklin and Octavia Sts., and Laguna St. between Pine and Bush Sts., Pacific Heights.*

WORTH NOTING

☾ **Alta Plaza Park.** Golden Gate Park's fierce longtime superintendent, John McLaren, designed Alta Plaza in 1910, modeling its terracing on that of the Grand Casino in Monte Carlo, Monaco. From the top you can see Marin to the north, downtown to the east, Twin Peaks to the south, and Golden Gate Park to the west. Kids love the many play structures at the large, enclosed playground at the top; everywhere else is dog territory. ✉ *Bordered by Clay, Steiner, Jackson, and Scott Sts., Pacific Heights.*

Broadway and Webster Street estates. Broadway uptown, unlike its garish North Beach stretch, has plenty of prestigious addresses. The three-story palace at 2222 Broadway, which has an intricately filigreed doorway, was built by Comstock silver-mine heir James Flood and later donated to a religious order. The Convent of the Sacred Heart purchased the **Grant House** at 2220 Broadway. These two buildings, along with a Flood property at 2120 Broadway, are used as school quarters. A gold-mine heir, William Bourn II, commissioned Willis Polk to build the nearby brick mansion at 2550 Webster Street.

Franklin Street buildings. What at first looks like a stone facade on the **Golden Gate Church** (✉ *1901 Franklin St., Pacific Heights*) is actually redwood painted white. A Georgian-style residence built in the early 1900s for a coffee merchant sits at 1735 Franklin. On the northeast corner of Franklin and California streets is a **Christian Science church**; built in the Tuscan revival style, it's noteworthy for its terra-cotta detailing. The **Coleman House** (✉ *1701 Franklin St., Pacific Heights*) is an impressive twin-turret Queen Anne mansion that was built for a gold-rush mining and lumber baron. Don't miss the large, brilliant-purple stained-glass window on the house's north side. ✉ *Franklin St. between Washington and California Sts., Pacific Heights.*

Lafayette Park. Clusters of trees dot this four-block-square oasis for sun-bathers and dog-and-Frisbee teams. On the south side of the park, squat but elegant **2151 Sacramento,** a private condominium, is the site of a home occupied by Sir Arthur Conan Doyle in the late 19th century. Coats of arms blaze in the front stained-glass windows. The park itself is a lovely neighborhood space, where Pacific Heights residents laze in the sun or exercise their pedigreed canines while gazing at downtown's skyline in the distance. ⊠ *Bordered by Laguna, Gough, Sacramento, and Washington Sts., Pacific Heights.*

Octagon House. This eight-sided home sits across the street from its original site on Gough Street; it's one of two remaining octagonal houses in the city (the other is on Russian Hill), and the only one open to the public. White quoins accent each of the eight corners of the pretty blue-gray exterior, and a colonial-style garden completes the picture. Inside, it's full of antique American furniture, decorative arts (paintings, silver, rugs), and documents from the 18th and 19th centuries. A deck of Revolutionary-era hand-painted playing cards takes an antimonarchist position: in place of kings, queens, and jacks, the American upstarts substituted American statesmen, Roman goddesses, and Indian chiefs. ⊠ *2645 Gough St., Pacific Heights* ☎ *415/441–7512* ⊠ *Free, donations encouraged* ⊙ *Feb.–Dec., 2nd Sun. and 2nd and 4th Thurs. of month noon–3; group tours weekdays by appointment.*

Spreckels Mansion. Shrouded behind tall juniper hedges at the corner of lovely winding, brick Octavia Street, overlooking Lafayette Park, the estate was built for sugar heir Adolph Spreckels and his wife Alma. Mrs. Spreckels was so pleased with her house that she commissioned George Applegarth to design another building in a similar vein: the Legion of Honor. One of the city's great iconoclasts, Alma Spreckels was the model for the bronze figure atop the Victory Monument in Union Square. Today this house belongs to prolific romance novelist Danielle Steel. ⊠ *2080 Washington St., at Octavia St., Pacific Heights.*

Vedanta Society. A pastiche of colonial, Queen Anne, Moorish, and Hindu opulence, lavender with turrets battling red-top onion domes, and Victorian detailing everywhere, this 1905 structure was the first Hindu temple in the West. Vedanta, an underlying philosophy of Hinduism, maintains that all religions are paths to one goal. Although the Vedanta Society's main location is the temple at Vallejo and Fillmore streets (closed Tuesday), *this* temple (open only Friday evening 8–9) is the organization's heart. ⊠ *2963 Webster St., Pacific Heights* ☎ *415/922–2323* ⊕ *www.sfvedanta.org.*

Wedding Houses. These identical white double-peak homes (joined in the middle) were erected in the late 1870s or early 1880s by dairy rancher James Cudworth as wedding gifts for his two daughters. These days the buildings house an English-style pub and a pizzeria. ⊠ *1980 Union St., Pacific Heights.*

Whittier Mansion. With a Spanish-tile roof and scrolled bay windows on all four sides, this is one of the most elegant 19th-century houses in the state. Unlike other grand mansions lost in the 1906 quake, the Whittier

Mansion was built so solidly that only a chimney toppled over during the disaster. ⊠ *2090 Jackson St., Pacific Heights.*

JAPANTOWN

TOP ATTRACTIONS

★ **Japan Center.** Cool and curious trinkets, noodle houses and sushi joints, a destination bookstore, and a peek at Japanese culture high and low await at this 5-acre complex designed in 1968 by noted American architect Minoru Yamasaki. The Japan Center includes the shop- and restaurant-filled Kintetsu and Kinokuniya buildings; the excellent Kabuki Springs & Spa; the Hotel Kabuki; and the Sundance Kabuki, Robert Redford's fancy, reserved-seating cinema/restaurant complex. Unfortunately, the development hasn't aged well, and its Peace Plaza, where seasonal festivals are held, is an unwelcoming sea of cement.

The Kinokuniya Bookstores, in the Kinokuniya Building, have an extensive selection of Japanese-language books, *manga* (graphic novels), books on design, and English-language translations and books on Japanese topics. Just outside, follow the Japanese teenagers to Pika Pika, where you and your friends can step into a photo booth and then use special effects and stickers to decorate your creation. On the bridge connecting the center's two buildings, check out Shige Antiques for *yukata* (lightweight cotton kimonos) for kids and lovely silk kimonos, and Asakichi and its tiny incense shop for tinkling wind chimes and display-worthy teakettles. Continue into the Kintetsu Building for a selection of Japanese restaurants.

Between the Miyako Mall and Kintetsu Building are the five-tier, 100-foot-tall **Peace Pagoda** and the Peace Plaza. Continue into the Miyako Mall to Ichiban Kan, a Japanese dollar store where you can pick up fun Japanese kitchenware, tote bags decorated with hedgehogs, and erasers shaped like food. ⊠ *Bordered by Geary Blvd. and Fillmore, Post, and Laguna Sts., Japantown* ☎ *No phone.*

★ **Kabuki Springs & Spa.** This serene spa is one Japantown destination that draws locals from all over town, from hipster to grandma, Japanese-American or not. Balinese urns decorate the communal bath area of this house of tranquillity.

The massage menu has also expanded well beyond traditional shiatsu technique. The experience is no less relaxing, however, and the treatment regimen includes facials, salt scrubs, and mud and seaweed wraps. You can take your massage in a private room with a bath or in a curtained-off area. The communal baths ($22 weekdays, $25 weekends) contain hot and cold tubs, a large Japanese-style bath, a sauna, a steam room, and showers. Bang the gong for quiet if your fellow bathers are speaking too loudly.

The clothing-optional baths are open for men only on Monday, Thursday, and Saturday; women bathe on Wednesday, Friday, and Sunday. Bathing suits are required on Tuesday, when the baths are coed. Men and women can reserve private rooms daily. An 80-minute massage-and-bath package with a private room costs $110; a package that

Where can I find . . . ?

A DRUGSTORE	**Walgreens** (1899 Fillmore St.) Open until 10 pm Monday through Sat., 9 pm on Sunday.	**Safeway** (1335 Webster St., at Geary St.) Open daily until midnight.
A COFFEE SHOP	**Peet's Coffee and Tea** (2197 Fillmore St.) The Berkeley Peet's was the inspiration for Starbucks.	**Murata's Café Hana** (1737 Post St., #368) Gorgeous fruit tarts and outdoor seating.
A PARKING SPACE	**Japan Center Garage** (1610 Geary Blvd.) Validation available through many Japan Center proprietors.	**California and Steiner** (2450 California St.) Outdoor parking lot with metered spaces.

includes a 50-minute massage and the use of the communal baths costs $100. ⊠ *1750 Geary Blvd., Japantown* ☎ *415/922–6000* ⊕ *www. kabukisprings.com* ☽ *Daily 10–10.*

WORTH NOTING

Japan Center Mall. The buildings lining this open-air mall are of the shoji school of architecture. The shops are geared more toward locals—travel agencies, electronics shops—but there are some fun Japanese-goods stores. Arrive early in the day and you may score some fabulous *mochi* (a soft, sweet Japanese rice treat) at **Benkyodo** (⊠ *1747 Buchanan St., Japantown* ☎ *415/922–1244*). It's easy to spend hours among the fabulous origami and craft papers at **Paper Tree** (⊠ *1743 Buchanan St., Japantown* ☎ *415/921–7100*), open since the 1960s. Be sure to swing around the corner, just off the mall, to **Super 7** (⊠ *1628 Post St., Japantown* ☎ *415/409–4700*), home of many large plastic Godzillas, glow-in-the-dark robots, and cool graphic tees. You can have a seat on local artist Ruth Asawa's twin origami-style fountains, which sit in the middle of the mall; they're squat circular structures made of fieldstone, with three levels for sitting and a brick floor. ⊠ *Buchanan St. between Post and Sutter Sts., Japantown* ☎ *No phone.*

New People. The kids' counterpart to the Japan Center, this fresh shopping center combines a cinema, café, shopping, and a gallery with a successful synergy. Ground-floor VIZ Cinema shows classic and cutting-edge Asian (largely Japanese) films. Grab a bento box and a cup of Blue Bottle at the café before perusing the coolest collection of Japanese pop-culture fun stuff and fashion in town at New People: The Store and in the Fashion Floor Boutiques, then be sure to check out what's on display in the tiny gallery space upstairs. ⊠ *1746 Post St., Japantown* ☎ *415/525–8630 Store, 415/525–8600 VIZ Cinema* ⊕ *www. newpeopleworld.com* ☽ *Mon.–Sat. 11–8, Sun. 11–7.*

EYE ON ARCHITECTURE

San Francisco's architecture scene has been going through a dramatic growth spurt—with the growing pains to match. Boldface international architects seem to be everywhere, spearheading major projects like the de Young Museum (Herzog & de Meuron of Switzerland), the California Academy of Sciences (Renzo Piano of Italy), and the Contemporary Jewish Museum (Polish New Yorker Daniel Libeskind). As the hard hats multiply, so do the heated local debates.

The development flurry is thrown into relief by the previous decades spent carefully preserving the city's historic buildings. Genteel Victorian homes are a city signature, and this residential legacy has been fiercely protected. But some critics complain of the lack of a current, strong, homegrown style and the trend for "imported talent."

Residents aren't shy about voicing opinions on the "starchitect" plans, either. As high-profile designs unfold and new condo neighborhoods break ground, criticism will surely escalate. (One thing that gratifies everyone: The impressive advances made in eco-friendly building practices.) As *Chronicle* columnist John King put it, SF is getting "a crash course in contemporary architecture. One that is long, long overdue."

Previous exhibition at the San Francisco Museum of Modern Art (SFMOMA)

SAN FRANCISCO'S SIGNATURE BUILDINGS

❶ OCTAGONAL HOUSES
c. 1850–60s

Only a few examples of this fad remain; the preserved home on Gough Street is a prime specimen. The style was promoted as being particularly healthy, as it would bring in more light and fresh air. Inside the Gough Street house (open to the public) are square rooms divided by triangular storage spaces. The builder, William McElroy, hid a "time capsule" letter under its stairway.

❷ QUEEN ANNE HOUSES
c. 1885–1890s

The most richly decorated, over-the-top style for Victorian town houses. Known for steep, shingled roofs, slanted bay windows, gingerbread adornments, and "witch's-cap" towers. (The ornamentation was mostly mass-produced, then added to façades.) One of the best is the Haas-Lilienthal home in Pacific Heights, now a public museum.

❸ PAINTED LADIES
c. 1870–1900, paint jobs in the 1960s

The nickname for Victorian houses with vivid, polychrome paint jobs. The original colors were neutrals, but hippies slathered on buttercup yellow, purple, fuschia, you name it. Examples of all the Victorian architectural variations have gotten the Easter-egg treatment, from the pointed arches of the Gothic Revival to the angular bay windows of the Stick-Eastlake look. The most scenic collection of painted ladies can be found along "Postcard Row," a stretch of six candy-colored homes on Steiner Street opposite Alamo Square.

Octagonal Houses

Haas-Lilienthal House

Painted Ladies

WALKING TOURS

For architecture-centric walking tours, check out the offerings from **San Francisco Architectural Heritage** (☎ 415/441–3000 ⊕ www.sfheritage.org). **San Francisco City Guides** (☎ 415/557–4266 ⊕ www.sfcityguides.org) has some cool tours focusing on specific buildings, like the Ferry Building or the Yerba Buena Complex.

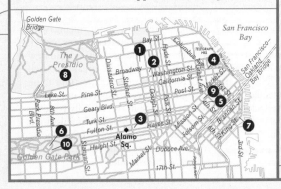

❹ TRANSAMERICA PYRAMID
c. 1972

At 853 feet, this tapering skyscraper, long synonymous with San Francisco, is the tallest building in the city (though Sutro Tower, topping 981 feet, is the tallest *structure*). Initially the pyramid, designed by William Pereira, ignited a storm of protest, with then-Assemblyman John Burton claiming it would "rape the skyline."

Now it's considered an icon. Although the building isn't open to the public, you can walk among the redwood trees on the east side of the tower.

❺ SAN FRANCISCO MUSEUM OF MODERN ART (SFMOMA)
c. 1995

Renowned Swiss architect Mario Botta's first shot at designing a museum. The distinctive, sturdy geometrical forms reflect his signature style. Here a black-and-white cylindrical tower anchors the brick structure. Botta called the huge, slanted skylight the city's "eye, like the Cyclops." A new wing, designed by Snøhetta, a Norwegian architecture firm noted for its cultural projects, is slated to open in 2016. The expansion, which adds over 100,000 square feet of gallery and public space, will accommodate the recently acquired modern art collection of late Gap founder, Don Fisher, a must for modern art lovers.

❻ DE YOUNG MUSEUM OF FINE ART
c. 2005

Love it or hate it, the structure is a must-see destination in Golden Gate Park. After the original Egyptian-revival edifice was deemed seismically unsafe following the Loma Prieta quake in 1989, the Pritzker prize–winning Swiss team Herzog & de Meuron won the commission to rebuild. Their design's copper façade and, in particular, the 144-foot observation tower—a twisted parallelogram grazing the treetops—drew fire from critics, who compared the design to a "rusty aircraft carrier." But the copper hue is mellowing with age, and the panoramic view from the ninth-floor observation deck is a hit—shifting any controversy to the museum's internal politics.

Transamerica Pyramid

SFMOMA

de Young Museum of Fine Art

WORD OF MOUTH

"At what time of day are the Painted Ladies at their best? Many of the photos that I see appear to have the houses in partial shade or dusk with the city behind in late sunshine or with lights on in the buildings. Is late afternoon/early evening the best time to view this sight?"—kiwi_rob

"The views are best in the late afternoon—since the Queen Anne Victorians all face west. That series of Victorians is called Postcard Row."—StuDudley

NEW STARS AND COMING ATTRACTIONS

❼ MISSION BAY, RINCON HILL, AND THE TRANSBAY DISTRICT
Ongoing

Tremendous changes are coming to San Francisco's cityscape, especially moving south from Market Street along the waterfront. Don't expect old-school gingerbread. Instead, glass-sheathed, condo-crammed high-rises are taking over what was a working-class area of warehouses and lofts, studded by the AT&T Ballpark. A new University of California, San Francisco (UCSF) campus is springing up in Mission Bay, with a blocky Campus Community Center by Mexican architect Ricardo Legorreta now open for business.

❽ PRESIDIO
Ongoing

The development of this parkland continues at a relatively slow pace. Its historic military-base buildings are being put to new uses—everything from a printing press to a spa. Filmmaker George Lucas built a digital arts center here, and a Walt Disney museum opened in October 2009.

❾ CONTEMPORARY JEWISH MUSEUM
Opened June 2008

Architect Daniel Libeskind, known for his work on the World Trade Center site, designed this new arrival in the vibrant Yerba Buena Arts corridor. The multi-use building retains original features of Willis Polk's 1907 power substation—exposed brick, skylights, trusses, exterior arches, and moldings—while incorporating a dramatic two-storey gallery space and blue-steel panels forming rectangle-like structures.

❿ CALIFORNIA ACADEMY OF SCIENCES
Opened September 2008

An eco-friendly, energy-efficient adventure in biodiversity, Renzo Piano's audacious design for this natural history museum comes equipped with a rain forest, a planetarium, skylights, and a retractable ceiling over the central courtyard. But it's the "living roof," covered in native plants, that's generating comment. Dotted with large mounds and hills (Piano's tribute to local topography) the roof looks like an alien launchpad.

The UCSF Community Center

Contemporary Jewish Museum

California Academy of Sciences

ARCHI-FEST

Are you craving more? The American Institute of Architects' SF chapter organizes an **Architecture and the City festival** each September. The event includes tours, lectures, films, and what's been called "domestic modernist porn," a home-tour weekend. Check www.aiasf.org for details.

For an incredibly rich trove of architecture and design publications, head to **William Stout Architectural Books** (⇨ the Shopping chapter).

Where to Eat

WORD OF MOUTH

"There is only one place for a true, quintessential San Francisco experience with cioppino—Tadich Grill. It's on California Street, an easy walk from Union Square."

—DebitNM

Updated
by Marcia
Gagliardi

You can find just about any food in San Francisco, a place where trends are set and culinary diversity rules. Since the 1849 gold rush flooded the city with foreign flavors, residents' appetites for exotic eats haven't diminished by even one bite.

Today San Francisco remains a vital culinary crossroads, with nearly every ethnic cuisine represented, from Afghan to Vietnamese. You don't just go out for Chinese here: regional offerings range from the classic Cantonese to the obscure Hakka cuisine of southern China. And although locals have long headed to the Mission District for Latin food, Chinatown for Asian food, and North Beach for Italian food, they also know that every part of the city offers dining experiences beyond the neighborhood tradition. One of the biggest trends to hit San Francisco is pizza—from obsessive *pizzaiolos* making authentic Neapolitan pies in imported Italian ovens, to chefs doing their own California spin—you'll be able to find quality pizzas in practically every neighborhood. And with the recent explosion of food trucks, renegade street-food stands, and pop-up restaurants, the local dining scene has become even more varied, creative, and exciting.

Diners also have grown increasingly serious about what they're sipping. In response, restaurateurs are offering more sophisticated wine lists, emphasizing new vintners, lesser-known varietals, and emerging wine-making regions, in addition to more environmental choices like biodynamic and organic wines. And cocktail lovers have been treated to an explosion of innovative drinks that are keeping the city's much-admired bartenders busy pouring, stirring, and shaking from one end of town to the other. Last but not least, beer is also gaining a foothold around the city, from new brewpubs brewing their own beer, to quality beers showing up on beverage lists.

SAN FRANCISCO DINING PLANNER

EATING OUT STRATEGY

Where should we eat? With hundreds, even thousands, of San Francisco eateries competing for your attention, it may seem like a daunting question. But fret not. Our expert writers and editors have done most of the legwork. The selections here represent the best this city has to offer. *Search the Best Bets section for top recommendations by price, cuisine, and experience.* Sample local flavor in the neighborhood features. Delve in, and enjoy!

13

RESERVATIONS

If you're determined to snag a table at a restaurant with lots of buzz, call and make a reservation as far in advance as possible—try dining there earlier in the week if the Friday and Saturday tables are all full. You can also get lucky at the last minute if you're flexible—and friendly. Most restaurants keep at least a few tables (and sometimes more) open for walk-ins and VIPs, and you should always ask if there's a bar or counter you can dine at. Show up for dinner early (5:30 pm) or late (after 9 pm) and politely inquire about any last-minute vacancies or cancellations—you can also try calling a restaurant in the early afternoon, because that's when they're making their reservation confirmation calls. If you're calling a few days ahead of time, ask if you can be put on a waiting list. Occasionally, an eatery may ask you to call the day before your scheduled meal to reconfirm: don't forget, or you could lose out.

HOURS

Unless otherwise noted, the restaurants listed in this guide are open daily for lunch and dinner. Prime time for dinner is around 7:30 or 8 pm, and although there are places for night owls to fuel up, most restaurants stop serving around 10 pm. Restaurants, along with bars and clubs, may serve alcohol between the hours of 6 am and 2 am. The legal age to buy alcoholic beverages in California is 21.

WHAT TO WEAR

In general, San Franciscans are neat but casual dressers; only at the top-notch dining rooms do you see a more formal style. But the way you look can influence how you're treated—and where you're seated. Generally speaking, jeans will suffice at most table-service restaurants in the $ to $$ range. Moving up from there, many pricier restaurants require jackets, and some insist on ties. In reviews, we mention dress only when men are required to wear a jacket or a jacket and tie. Note that shorts, sweatpants, and sports jerseys are rarely appropriate. When in doubt, call the restaurant and ask.

PRICES

If you're watching your budget, be sure to ask the price of daily specials. The charge for these dishes can sometimes be out of line with the menu. And always review your bill. If you eat early or late you may be able to take advantage of a prix-fixe deal not offered at peak hours. Many upscale restaurants offer lunch deals with special menus at bargain prices. Credit cards are widely accepted, but some restaurants

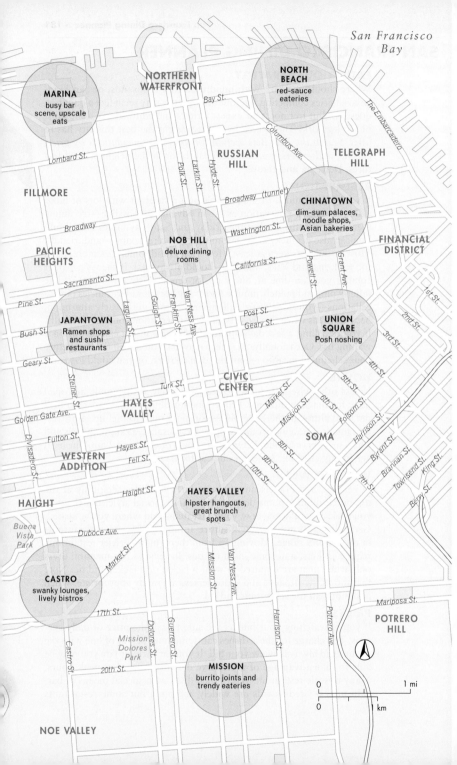

San Francisco Bay

MARINA
busy bar scene, upscale eats

NORTHERN WATERFRONT

NORTH BEACH
red-sauce eateries

Bay St.

Columbus Ave.

The Embarcadero

RUSSIAN HILL

TELEGRAPH HILL

FILLMORE

Polk St.

Larkin St.

Hyde St.

Broadway (tunnel)

CHINATOWN
dim-sum palaces, noodle shops, Asian bakeries

FINANCIAL DISTRICT

Lombard St.

Broadway

Washington St.

PACIFIC HEIGHTS

NOB HILL
deluxe dining rooms

California St.

Powell St.

Grant Ave.

Sacramento St.

Franklin St.

Van Ness Ave.

1st St.

Pine St.

JAPANTOWN
Ramen shops and sushi restaurants

Laguna St.

Gough St.

Post St.

Geary St.

UNION SQUARE
Posh noshing

2nd St.

Bush St.

3rd St.

Geary St.

Steiner St.

Turk St.

4th St.

Golden Gate Ave.

CIVIC CENTER

5th St.

Divisadero St.

Fulton St.

HAYES VALLEY

Market St.

Mission St.

6th St.

Folsom St.

Harrison St.

Bryant St.

WESTERN ADDITION

Hayes St.

Fell St.

8th St.

SOMA

Brannan St.

Townsend St.

King St.

HAIGHT

Haight St.

9th St.

10th St.

7th St.

Berry St.

Buena Vista Park

Duboce Ave.

HAYES VALLEY
hipster hangouts, great brunch spots

Mission St.

Van Ness Ave.

Market St.

CASTRO
swanky lounges, lively bistros

17th St.

Mission Dolores Park

Dolores St.

Guerrero St.

Harrison St.

Mariposa St.

Potrero Ave.

POTRERO HILL

Castro St.

20th St.

MISSION
burrito joints and trendy eateries

0   1 mi

0   1 km

NOE VALLEY

(particularly smaller ones) accept only cash. If you plan to use a credit card, it's a good idea to double-check its acceptability when making reservations or before sitting down to eat. Also, keep in mind that a restaurant listed as $$$ may actually have a good deal or two, such as an early prix-fixe dinner or a great bar scene and good, reasonably priced bar food to go with it.

WHAT IT COSTS					
	¢	$	$$	$$$	$$$$
Restaurants	under $10	$10–$14	$15–$22	$23–$30	over $30

Prices are per person for a typical main course or equivalent combination of smaller dishes. Note: If a restaurant offers only prix-fixe (set-price) meals, it has been given the price category that reflects the full prix-fixe price.

TIPPING AND TAXES
In most restaurants, tip the waiter 16%–20%. (To figure out a 20% tip quickly, just move the decimal spot one place to the left and double that.)

Bills for parties of six or more sometimes include the tip. Tip at least $1 per drink at the bar. Tipping the maître d' is not necessary unless you're trying to pave your way to being a regular. Also be aware that many restaurants, now required to fund the city's new universal health-care ordinance, are passing these costs along to their customers—usually in the form of a 3%–4% surcharge or a $1–$1.50-per-head charge. (SF sales tax has climbed to 9.5%, too.)

CHILDREN
Dining with youngsters in the city does not have to mean culinary exile. Many of the restaurants reviewed in this chapter are excellent choices for families and are marked with a ☾ symbol.

SMOKING
Smoking is banned in all city restaurants and bars, and is now banned in all restaurant outdoor areas, from sidewalk seating to patios

PARKING
Most upper-end restaurants offer valet parking—worth considering in crowded neighborhoods such as North Beach, Russian Hill, Union Square, and the Mission. There's often a nominal charge and a time restriction on validated parking.

USING THE MAPS
Throughout the chapter, you'll see mapping symbols and coordinates (✛ 3:F2) after property names or reviews. To locate the property on a map, turn to the San Francisco Dining and Lodging Atlas at the end of the chapter. The first number after the ✛ symbol indicates the map number. Following that is the property's coordinate on the map grid.

BEST BETS FOR SAN FRANCISCO DINING

With thousands of restaurants to choose from, how will you decide where to eat? Fodor's writers and editors have selected their favorite restaurants by price, cuisine, and experience in the Best Bets lists below. In the first column, Fodor's Choice designations represent the "best of the best" in every price category. You can also search by neighborhood for excellent eats—just peruse the following pages.

Fodor's Choice★

A16, $$$, p. 219
Acquerello, $$$$, p. 211
Aziza, $$$, p. 232
Boulevard, $$$$, p. 215
Coi, $$$$, p. 213
Delfina, $$$, p. 225
Gary Danko, $$$$, p. 215
L'Osteria del Forno, $, p. 214
Quince, $$$, p. 208
Swan Oyster Depot, $$, p. 213
Zuni Café, $$$, p. 206

By Price

¢

Burger Joint, p. 224
Mijita Cocina Mexicana, p. 217
Naan 'N' Curry, p. 208
Pho Hoa Clement, p. 232

$

Dosa, p. 226
Lers Ros, $, p. 212
L'Osteria del Forno, p. 214
SanJalisco, p. 228
Ti Couz, p. 229

$$

Barbacco, p. 207
Nopalito, p. 221
Out the Door, p. 230
SPQR, p. 230
Swan Oyster Depot, p. 213

$$$

A16, p. 219
Aziza, p. 232
Canteen, p. 200
Delfina, p. 225
One Market, p. 217
Perbacco, p. 208
Quince, p. 208
Range, p. 228
Zuni Café, p. 206

$$$$

Acquerello, p. 211
Boulevard, p. 215
Coi, p. 213
Gary Danko, p. 215
Saison, p. 228

By Cuisine

AMERICAN

Bar Tartine, $$$, p. 224
Canteen, $$$, p. 200
Coco500, $$$, p. 202
Nopa, $$$, p. 221
One Market, $$$, p. 217
Town Hall, $$$, p. 204

CHINESE

R&G Lounge, $$, p. 202
San Tung, $$, p. 233
Ton Kiang, $$, p. 233
Yank Sing, $$, p. 209

FRENCH

Absinthe, $$$, p. 205
Bar Jules, $$$, p. 205

Café Claude, $$, p. 207
Chez Spencer, $$$, p. 225
Frances, $$$, p. 222
Ti Couz, $, p. 229

INDIAN

Dosa, $, p. 226
Dosa on Fillmore, $$, p. 231
Indian Oven, $$, p. 221

ITALIAN

A16, $$$, p. 219
Delfina, $$$, p. 225
Farina, $$$$, p. 226
Incanto, $$$, p. 223
La Ciccia, $$$, p. 223
SPQR, $$, p. 230
Zero Zero, $$, p. 205

JAPANESE

Maki, $$, p. 231
Mifune, $, p. 231

LATIN AMERICAN

Charanga, $$, p. 225
La Mar Cebicheria Peruana, $$$, p. 216
La Santaneca de la Mission, $, p. 227
Limón Rotisserie, $, p. 227
Mijita Cocina Mexicana, ¢, p. 217

MEDITERRANEAN

The Moss Room, $$$, p. 233
Terzo, $$$, p. 220
Zaré at Fly Trap, $$$, p. 204

13

MEXICAN

Mijita Cocina Mexicana, ¢, p. 217
Nopalito, $$, p. 221
SanJalisco, $, p. 228

SEAFOOD

Hog Island Oyster Company, $$, p. 216
Plouf, $$, p. 208
Swan Oyster Depot, $$, p. 213
Woodhouse Fish Co., $$, p. 223

STEAK HOUSE

Epic Roasthouse, $$$$, p. 216
Harris', $$$$, p. 212

THAI

Lers Ros, $, p. 212
Thep Phanom, $$, p. 221

VIETNAMESE

Bodega Bistro, $$, p. 212
Out the Door, $$, p. 230
Pagolac, $, p. 213
Slanted Door, $$$, p. 218

By Experience

BAR MENU

Absinthe, $$$, p. 205
Farallon, $$$$, p. 200
Jardinière, $$$$, p. 206
Kokkari, $$$, p. 207

BAY VIEWS

Epic Roasthouse, $$$$, p. 216
Greens Restaurant, $$, p. 219
Slanted Door, $$$, p. 218
Waterbar, $$$$, p. 218

BRUNCH

Bar Jules, $$$, p. 205
Bar Tartine, $$$, p. 224
Canteen, $$$, p. 200
Foreign Cinema, $$$, p. 226
Rose's Café, $$, p. 220

BUSINESS DINING

Boulevard, $$$$, p. 215
Epic Roasthouse, $$$$, p. 216
One Market, $$$, p. 217
Perbacco, $$$, p. 208

CHILD-FRIENDLY

Burger Joint, ¢, p. 224
Capp's Corner, $$, p. 213
Mijita Cocina Mexicana, ¢, p. 217
Nopalito, $$, p. 221
Park Chow, $, p. 233
San Tung, $$, p. 233
Ti Couz, $, p. 229
Tommaso's, $$, p. 215
Yank Sing, $$, p. 209

COMMUNAL TABLE

Bocadillos, $$$, p. 207
Marlowe, $$$, p. 203

Nopa, $$$, p. 221
Out the Door, $$, p. 230
Salt House, $$$, p. 204
Tommaso's, $$, p. 215
Zaré at Fly Trap, $$$, p. 204

HISTORIC INTEREST

Boulevard, $$$$, p. 215
Swan Oyster Depot, $$, p. 213
Tadich Grill, $$$, p. 209
Tommaso's, $$, p. 215

HOT SPOTS

A16, $$$, p. 219
Dosa on Fillmore, $$, p. 231
Frances, $$$, p. 222
Nopa, $$$, p. 221
Nopalito, $$, p. 221
SPQR, $$, p. 230
Zero Zero, $$, p. 205

HOTEL DINING

Fifth Floor, $$$$, p. 203
Scala's Bistro, $$$, p. 201

LATE-NIGHT BITES

Absinthe, $$$, p. 205
Chow, $, p. 222
Nopa, $$$, p. 221
Scala's Bistro, $$$, p. 201
Zuni Café, $$$, p. 206

PRE-THEATER MEAL

Canteen, $$$, p. 200
Farallon, $$$$, p. 200
Le Colonial, $$$$, p. 201
Scala's Bistro, $$$, p. 201

QUIET MEAL

Acquerello, $$$$, p. 211
Coi, $$$$, p. 213
Fleur de Lys, $$$$, p. 200
Katia's, $$, p. 232
Quince, $$$, p. 208

SINGLES SCENE

Beretta, $$, p. 224
Nopa, $$$, p. 221
Salt House, $$$, p. 204
Tacolicious, $$, p. 219

SMALL PLATES

Barbacco, $$, p. 207
Bocadillos, $$$, p. 207
Coco500, $$$, p. 202
Terzo, $$$, p. 220

SPECIAL OCCASION

Acquerello, $$$$, p. 211
Boulevard, $$$$, p. 215
Gary Danko, $$$$, p. 215
Jardinière, $$$$, p. 206
Quince, $$$, p. 208
Saison, $$$$, p. 228

UNION SQUARE, FINANCIAL DISTRIC, AND CHINATOWN

Fashion, business, and history collide in this broad swatch of the city, where you can eat for pennies or spend your rent in a single sitting.

Around Union Square, *pictured above*, department stores and boutiques rule, and hotels—from Campton Place to the Sir Francis Drake with its **Scala's Bistro** (⊠ *432 Powell St.* ☎ *415/395–8555* ✛ *4:F3*)—pull diners in for pricey lunches and pricier dinners. Here and in the nearby Financial District, CEOs can hide away in old-school dining rooms, like the red walls and tufted booths at **Alfred's Steak House** (⊠ *659 Merchant St.* ☎ *415/781–7058* ✛ *1:E4*), while ladies who lunch pop into **Café Claude** (⊠ *7 Claude La.* ☎ *415/392–3505* ✛ *4:H2*).

But budget-minded locals know to slip into sandwich shops that line Kearny, Montgomery, and Bush streets (and the adjoining alleys), or to head to Sutter and Post streets, where modest storefronts dish up well-priced Burmese, Japanese, Thai, and Indonesian plates. Or you can hotfoot it over to the narrow lanes of Chinatown, where a bowl of wonton soup or a rice plate in dozens of storefront eateries along Jackson, Clay, or Washington streets will bring change from a five-dollar bill.

EURO FLAVOR

San Franciscans like to brag about their city's European atmosphere, citing Belden Place as evidence of that claim. The charming pedestrian-only street is anchored by the historic **Sam's Grill** (⊠ *374 Bush St.* ☎ *415/421–0594* ✛ *1:E5*), a seafood institution for more than 70 years. Beyond Sam's, the possibilities are a delicious mix of European tables (but don't be surprised by the hawkers—competition is fierce), with French favorites like **Plouf** (⊠ *40 Belden Pl.* ☎ *415/986–6491* ✛ *4:H2*), **Café Bastille** (⊠ *22 Belden Pl.* ☎ *415/986–5673* ✛ *4:H2*), and the Italian **Café Tiramisu** (⊠ *28 Belden Pl.* ☎ *415/421–7044* ✛ *4:H2*).

DIVING INTO DIM SUM

The popular Cantonese midday custom of going out for dim sum—small dishes, both savory and sweet, hot and cold—can be explored on nearly every block in Chinatown. In big restaurants servers push dish-laden carts around the dining room, and diners select what they want. Smaller places dispense with the carts in favor of more easily managed trays. You won't always know what you're choosing, so embrace the mystery.

New Asia (⊠ 772 Pacific Ave. ☎ 415/391–6666 ✛ 1:D3) is perfect for dim sum newbies—English is spoken here, and the sprawling room means you won't stick out like a sore thumb. For the best selection, try for a table near the kitchen; by the time the carts make their way upstairs, they're picked over.

For more-adventurous spirits, **Dol Ho** (⊠ 808 Pacific Ave. ☎ 415/392–2828 ✛ 1:D3) is a hole-in-the-wall serving up good dim sum at great prices. Neighborhood regulars fill the small space, snapping up the best items from the single cart. There's not much English spoken here, but the authenticity and low tab make any sign-language efforts pay off.

When you walk downstairs into **Hang Ah** (⊠ 1 Pagoda Pl., at Stockton St. ☎ 415/982–5686 ✛ 4:G1), you'll feel like you've discovered a long-hidden gem, where you can fill up on conventional dim sum for a song.

If you're in a rush, stop at friendly **You's** (⊠ 675 Broadway ☎ 415/788–7028 ✛ 1:D3), a busy take-out spot famous for its barbecued pork buns.

Many locals like **Great Eastern** (⊠ 649 Jackson St. ☎ 415/986–2500 ✛ 1:D4) because they can check off what they want on dim sum menus instead of waiting for a cart. Others, especially Financial District workers on weekdays and families on weekends, migrate to **City View Restaurant** (⊠ 622 Commercial St. ☎ 415/398–2838 ✛ 1:E4) for its relatively quiet dining room, ample choices, and atmospheric location.

AND FOR DESSERT

13

Chinatown's **Eastern Bakery** (⊠ 720 Grant Ave., near Sacramento St. ☎ 415/982–5157 ✛ 1:D4) is the neighborhood's oldest bakery and best-known outpost for traditional mooncakes, in some two dozen styles, from winter melon to yellow bean to coconut. If you're not tempted by mooncakes, try the tiny egg custard tartlets (often still warm) or the coffee crunch cake, with coffee-flavor pastry cream between sponge-cake layers and crunchy toffee on top. If you're willing to head a little bit into the "TenderNob," that mini-neighborhood where the lower part of Nob Hill meets the Tenderloin, you'll be rewarded at **Hooker's Sweet Treats** (⊠ 442 Hyde St., near Ellis St. ✛ 1:B5), a stylish and small oasis known for its house-made salted chocolate-caramels, chocolate-banana bread pudding with hard sauce, cookies, and locally roasted coffee drinks. The owner (Hooker) is from New Orleans, which shows in the bohemian aesthetic.

SOMA, CIVIC CENTER, AND HAYES VALLEY

These areas prove that terrific restaurants can spring up in gritty surroundings—and often they'll help spur a general neighborhood improvement. This serving of gentrification comes with tempting menus and stylish dining rooms.

The hip SoMa once was a warehouse district punctuated by blue-collar households. Nowadays, the same streets are chockablock with residential lofts, trendy bars and clubs, and scores of restaurants that fuel the mostly young and single local crowd (or business types in town for a convention).

The Civic Center is heavy with government buildings and grand performance spaces. Its dining scene is geared for people grabbing a bite before or after *La Bohème* or Mahler.

Hayes Valley is sprouting several hip and haute dining destinations along its main stem, Hayes Street. The low-key vibe in its wine bars and cafés makes it easy to feel like a local.

WAKE UP

One of the better locals' secrets is at **Arlequin Café & Food To Go** (⊠ *384 Hayes St., near Gough St.* ☎ *415/626–1211* ⊕ *3:E2*), the little sister to the classy Absinthe restaurant. The casual place has plenty of self-serve items, plus homemade granola or oatmeal for the healthy set; egg lovers should go for the egg sandwiches that come on a bagel, levain, or a croissant. The best part? There's a garden patio in the back with tables among the trees. It's so comfortable, you might even stay for lunch. And why wouldn't you, with choices like Indian-spiced lamb burger and a three-cheese mac 'n cheese.

EAT CHEAP OR DINE CHIC

SNACKING AROUND . . .

SoMa: Tree-lined South Park is a charming green oasis. The park is bordered by 2nd and 3rd streets, and Brannan and Bryant streets. One of our favorite cafés is **The Butler & the Chef** (⊠ *155 S. Park St.* ☎ *415/896–2075* ⊹ *1:G6*), which offers organic breakfast and lunch items, including croissants and *croque monsieurs* (grilled ham-and-cheese sandwichs) that will make you think you're in Paris. Take your pick of inventive grilled-cheese sandwiches (with soup on the side) at **The American Grilled Cheese Kitchen** (⊠ *1 S. Park Ave., Suite 103A, at 2nd St.* ☎ *415/243–0107* ⊹ *1:G6*). Closer to Market Street, the takeaway-only **Sentinel** sandwich shop (⊠ *35 New Montgomery St.* ☎ *415/284–9960* ⊹ *1:E5*), with Canteen's star chef Dennis Leary at the helm, builds and wraps the city's best Reuben.

Civic Center: For something quick before a show at Symphony Hall or the Opera House, head to **Arlequin Café & Food To Go** (⊠ *384 Hayes St., near Gough St.* ☎ *415/626–1211* ⊹ *3:E2*), a casual café famous for its lamb burger, and grilled ham-and-Gruyère-cheese sandwich on *pain levain*.

Hayes Valley: You can enjoy meatballs or sliders off the J Lounge menu at **Jardinière** (⊠ *300 Grove St., at Franklin St.* ☎ *415/861–5555* ⊹ *3:F2*) or sit at the bar at **Absinthe** (⊠ *398 Hayes St., at Gough St.* ☎ *415/551–1590* ⊹ *3:E2*), which has an excellent and filling French onion soup for under $10. At **Frjtz** (⊠ *581 Hayes St., near Laguna St.* ☎ *415/864–7654* ⊹ *3:E2*) you can opt for Belgian fries with a wild array of dips or six different kinds of Belgian waffles.

SOMA SOPHISTICATES

Around Brannan and 4th streets and nearby South Park, several classy restaurants dish up eats, including the Japanese-influenced **Alexander's Steakhouse** (⊠ *448 Brannan St.* ☎ *415/495–1111* ⊹ *1:E6*), the lively small-plates **Coco500** (⊠ *500 Brannan St.* ☎ *415/543–2222* ⊹ *4:H6*), and the very French **South Park Café** (⊠ *108 S. Park St.* ☎ *415/495–7275* ⊹ *1:G6*).

AND FOR DESSERT

13

We hope you're up for a French macarons tasting, because the neighborhood is full of these brightly colored treats. First stop is **Paulette** (⊠ 437 Hayes St., near Gough St. ☎ 415/864–2400 ⊹ 3:E2), a store originally from Beverly Hills with a French pastry chef and full of flavors like Sicilian pistachio, Earl Grey tea, and violet cassis. Head to the nearby **Miette Confiserie** (⊠ 449 Octavia St., near Hayes St. ☎ 415/626–6221 ⊹ 3:E2) and sample their ladylike cakes—try the best-selling gingerbread cupcakes topped with a swirl of cream-cheese frosting, or get a couple of their cream-filled macarons to nibble as you stroll. SoMa's **Patisserie Philippe** (⊠ 655 Townsend St., between 7th and 8th Sts. ☎ 415/558–8016 ⊹ 1:E6), good for both walkabout and sit-down, is no slouch either when it comes to perfect French macarons— or to tarts, cakes, pastries, croissants, and more, for that matter.

NORTH BEACH, NOB HILL, AND RUSSIAN HILL

One of the city's oldest neighborhoods, North Beach continues to speak Italian, albeit in fewer households than it did when Joe DiMaggio was hitting home runs at the local playground. But the Italian presence in the markets and cafés is deliciously unmissable.

North Beach is the perfect spot to grab an outdoor table and watch passersby while you feast on classic Italian food.

Columbus Avenue, North Beach's primary commercial artery, and nearby side streets boast dozens of moderately priced Italian restaurants and coffee bars that San Franciscans flock to for a dose of strong community feeling.

Nob Hill, the most famous hill in a city of hills, is known for its iconic hotels—the Fairmont, the Mark, the Ritz-Carlton, the Huntington—though only the Ritz-Carlton is a destination for serious diners nowadays.

Nearby Russian Hill, which rises from Columbus Avenue, has few restaurants on its peak and higher slopes, but packs in scores of kitchens and cafés, especially around Polk and Larkin streets, as it descends to Van Ness Avenue.

BOB'S DONUTS

OK, doughnuts aren't the healthiest food, but if you're gonna splurge, why not make it count with the award-winning dough rings at the no-frills **Bob's Donuts** (✉ *1621 Polk St., near Clay St.* ☎ *415/776–3141* ✛ *2:H5*). However you like 'em—cake, glazed, raised, sugared, or apple-studded—Bob's makes them 24 hours a day. They're fried in small batches, guaranteeing that every bite is fresh and delicious.

ON THE CHEAP: BIG FLAVORS IN . . .

LITTLE ITALY
The casual bites in this neighborhood are almost always first-rate. The century-old **Molinari's** (✉ 373 Columbus Ave., at Vallejo St. ☎ 415/421–2337 ✣ 1:D3) makes delicious Italian sandwiches to order—mortadella, salami, prosciutto—that are great for toting to a bench in nearby Washington Square Park. So, too, does the aptly named **Petite Deli** (✉ 752 Columbus Ave., between Filbert and Greenwich Sts. ☎ 415/398–1682 ✣ 3:C2), a one-woman operation where the customers rave about the egg-salad sandwich and the turkey club. You can also grab hot Italian beef sandwiches, house-made corned beef, or a New York–style slice from the city's only coal-fired pizza oven at **Tony's Coal Fired Pizza & Slice House** (✉ 1556 Stockton St., near Union St. ☎ 415/835–9888 ✣ 1:D3). If you prefer to eat indoors, grab a table at the modest **Mario's Bohemian Cigar Store** (✉ 566 Columbus Ave., at Union St. ☎ 415/362–0536 ✣ 1:D3), which no longer sells cigars but does offer a legendary meatball sandwich on focaccia.

For good coffee, take a seat at the more than half-century-old **Caffè Trieste** (✉ 609 Vallejo St., at Grant Ave. ☎ 415/982–2605 ✣ 1:D3), where you may also be serenaded by local opera singers; or grab a sidewalk table at **Caffè Greco** (✉ 423 Columbus Ave., near Vallejo St. ☎ 415/397–6261 ✣ 1:D3), pictured below, to enjoy espresso and one of the better versions of tiramisu in the neighborhood.

LITTLE SAIGON
The southern edge of Nob Hill bleeds into the mean streets of the Tenderloin. But hidden here are some Vietnamese culinary gems, especially on Larkin Street. That's where you can find **Bodega Bistro** (✉ 607 Larkin St. ☎ 415/921–1218 ✣ 2:H6), one of the neighborhood's most popular Vietnamese restaurants, along with **Pagolac** (✉ 655 Larkin St. ☎ 415/776–3234 ✣ 4:A6), and the famous chicken pho ga at **Turtle Tower** (✉ 631 Larkin St. ☎ 415/409–3333 ✣ 4:A6).

AND FOR DESSERT

13

Jacqueline Margulis makes only one thing at her small, charming **Café Jacqueline** (✉ 1454 Grant Ave., between Union and Green Sts. ☎ 415/981–5565 ✣ 1:D3): tall, airy, gorgeous soufflés, both savory and sweet. She changes the menu regularly, offering such irresistible classics as bittersweet-chocolate, strawberry, or Grand Marnier, all of them with creamy centers. For more creamy goodness, grab a buttery scoop of gelato at the venerable **Gelato Classico** (✉ 576 Union St., between Stockton St. and Grant Ave. ☎ 415/391–6667 ✣ 1:D3), a slim spot with just a counter and no place to sit. Every flavor—and there are many—looks delicious, and the patient staff hands over a taste to curious customers—which, face it, is everyone. The coppa mista, a wild swirl of vanilla, chocolate, pistachio, and rum gelatos, is a house specialty, and a good way to satisfy the craving for multiple flavors.

THE WATERFRONT

Locals and visitors alike flock here for gorgeous bay views, a world-class waterfront esplanade, and a Ferry Building that is much better known for its food than its boat rides.

Not surprisingly, both restaurateurs and diners appreciate proximity to the water, and a slew of restaurants, including the award-winning **Boulevard** (⊠ *1 Mission St.* ☎ *415/543–6084* ✛ *1:G4*), Hotel Vitale's sleek **Americano** (⊠ *8 Mission St.* ☎ *415/278–3777* ✛ *1:G4*), the splashy **Waterbar** (⊠ *399 Embarcadero* ☎ *415/284–9922* ✛ *1:H5*), the meat-driven **Epic Roasthouse** (⊠ *369 Embarcadero* ☎ *415/369–9955* ✛ *1:H5*), and the Tokyo-chic **Ozumo** (⊠ *161 Steuart St.* ☎ *415/882–1333* ✛ *1:G4*).

To the north of the Ferry Building lies Fisherman's Wharf, a jumbled mix of seafood dining rooms, sidewalk vendors, and trinket shops that visitors religiously trudge through and San Franciscans invariably dismiss as a tourist trap. But even disdainful locals are sometimes seen making their way home from the Wharf with a cracked crab tucked under one arm and a loaf of sourdough bread under the other.

DUNGENESS CRAB

The local Dungeness season runs from November through June, which is when San Franciscans descend on the more than half dozen crab stands at the Wharf. Buy an expertly cracked and cooked-to-order Dungeness at the stand in front of **Fisherman's Grotto #9** (⊠ *2847 Jefferson St., at Taylor* ☎ *415/673–7025* ✛ *1:B1*), pick up a loaf of sourdough bread, and feast on a true San Francisco tradition.

If you happen to be in town in February, you're in for a treat: events honoring the celebrated crustacean occur throughout the month at restaurants citywide, as part of the annual San Francisco Crab Festival.

A MOVABLE FEAST

The **Ferry Building Marketplace** (✉ *1 Ferry Bldg., Embarcadero* ✛ *1:G4*) is located at the foot of Market Street on the Embarcadero, with a magnetic pull that makes even the most jaded foodies go weak in the knees. It has just about everything: you can slurp stellar oysters at **Hog Island Oyster Bar** (☎ *415/391–7117*), snack on Baja fish tacos at **Mijita** (☎ *415/399–0814*) or the sublime egg salad sandwich at Il Cane Rosso (☎ *415/391–7599*).

Hungry for Asian fare? The Japan-based **Delica rf1** (☎ *415/834–0344*) offers an irresistible daily bento, and sushi at their new counter. Looking for a panino packed with house-made salame pepato, sweet basil, roasted peppers, and creamy mozzarella? **Boccalone Salumeria** (☎ *415/433–6500*) will build it for you. Happy with just a cheese sandwich? Stop in at **Sidekick** (☎ *415/392–4000*), the new snack counter with gougères, cheese sandwiches, and more from the ladies behind **Cowgirl Creamery** (☎ *415/362–9354*)—or just stop at the original Cowgirl shop for a wedge of artisanal blue, and then grab a crusty baguette at the **Acme Bread Company** (☎ *415/288–2978*) a few steps away. Or order a burger at **Gott's Roadside Tray Gourmet** (☎ *415/328–3663*), a Vietnamese spring roll at **Out the Door** (☎ *415/321–3740*), or a glass of vintage cabernet at the **Ferry Plaza Wine Merchant** (☎ *415/391–9400*). Have a sweet tooth? There are chocolates at **Recchiuti Confections** (☎ *415/834–9494*), cookies and cupcakes at **Miette** (☎ *415/837–0300*), and creamy gelato at **Ciao Bella** (☎ *415/834–9330*).

LOCAL FAVORITE: BOULETTE'S LARDER

Long before you get to **Boulette's Larder** (✉ *Ferry Bldg.* ☎ *415/399–1155*), you know something is cooking. The aromas that rise from this retail food shop and daytime dining spot waft through the Ferry Building Marketplace, drawing people to the southern end of the complex. Breakfast might be poached eggs and Dungeness crab, while lunch is whatever is on the stove that day.

AND FOR DESSERT

13

Want to act civilized and sit down for high tea? Then make your way to the playfully stylish **Crown & Crumpet** (☎ *900 N. Point St., Ghirardelli Sq.* ☎ *415/771–4252* ✛ *1:A1*) for a tower on your table of sweets and treats, including the namesake crumpets. If you're a fan of cupcakes, then beeline to **Kara's Cupcakes** (✉ *900 N. Point St., Ghirardelli Sq.* ☎ *415/351–2253* ✛ *1:A1*), where a long glass case holds about a dozen flavors, including the excellent java version (chocolate cake with espresso buttercream). To accompany your cupcakes: cold milk or hot French-press coffee. Or go traditional and stop at the **Ghirardelli Ice Cream and Chocolate Shop** (✉ *900 N. Point St., Ghirardelli Sq.* ☎ *415/474–3938* ✛ *1:A1*), where you can first see equipment that was used to make chocolate in 19th-century San Francisco and then sit down to a luscious hot-fudge sundae, banana split, or cup of hot cocoa topped with whipped cream.

THE MISSION, THE CASTRO, AND NOE VALLEY

You'll never go hungry here, in some of San Francisco's most jam-packed restaurant neighborhoods. From dirt-cheap taquerías to hip tapas joints, city dwellers know this sector as the go-to area for a great meal.

The city's best Mexican food can be found in the Mission. A pile of hot, salty chips and fiery salsa often arrives gratis with your meal. A filling super burrito goes for about $6.

Head over to the Mission to dig into Mexican and Latin American menus. In recent years the Latino community has been sharing the neighborhood with legions of twenty- and thirtysomethings who pack the dozens of eateries along Valencia Street, between 16th and 24th streets, and Mission Street from 19th to 24th streets. East of the Mission, Potrero Hill is home to a cluster of casual dining rooms in the blocks around Connecticut and 18th streets.

The Castro neighborhood, the epicenter of the city's gay community, is chockablock with restaurants and bars. Market Street between Church and Castro streets is a great stretch for people-watching and restaurant-hopping. Just south, in Noe Valley, everyone seems to be pushing a baby carriage, but they're all eating out too, mostly along 24th Street from Church to Castro streets, and on Church Street from 24th to 30th streets.

> ## WAKE UP
>
> A placard at the door says to sign in and wait to be seated at homey **Chloe's Café** (⊠ 1399 Church St., between 26th and Clipper Sts. ✛ 3:D6.). That wait for your croissant French toast or avocado-and-cheese scramble is bound to be long on weekends—hey, everyone else has the same delicious idea—so come with your patience. Come with cash in your pocket, too, as no credit cards are taken.

MISSION DINING TWO WAYS

	MEXICAN:	ITALIAN:
Grab-and-go	**Two El Tonayense Taco Trucks** (⊠14th St. and Harrison St. ✛ 3:G4 ⊠ 19th St. and Harrison St. ✛ 3:G6) serve up the city's most authentic tacos, stuffed with a variety of meats and spicy salsa.	The no-frills **Arinell** (⊠ 509 Valencia St., near 16th St. ☎415/255–1303 ✛ 3:E5) is famous for its floppy New York–style slices handed across a walk-up counter, late into the night.
Cheap eats	**Pancho Villa Taqueria** (⊠ 3071 16th St., between Mission and Valencia Sts. ☎415/864–8840 ✛ 3:E5) is a Mission institution. The bulging burritos, heavy with beans, rice, meat, and salsa, are just $7.	The superbusy **Little Star Pizza** (⊠ 400 Valencia St., at 15th St. ☎415/551–7827 ✛ 3:F4) doles out cornmeal-crusted pizzas, deep-dish or thin, with toppings like spinach and feta, pesto, and chicken.
Casual chic	**Velvet Cantina** (⊠ 3349 23rd St., at Bartlett St. ☎415/648–4142 ✛ 3:F6) offers a modern take on Mexican cuisine, in a dimly lighted, bordello-themed room filled with tipsy hipsters. Try the avocado-cactus enchiladas with cilantro pesto, washed down with a memorable margarita.	Stop in at the ever-busy **Pizzeria Delfina** (⊠ 3611 18th St., at Guerrero St. ☎415/437–6800 ✛ 3:E6), the casual offshoot of upscale Delfina, for top-notch Neapolitan pies, antipasti (eggplant caponata, fresh-stretched mozzarella), and some 20 wines by the glass.

MEXICAN VS ITALIAN

For years the Mission was where San Franciscans went to eat burritos and tacos, enchiladas, and tamales. But in the mid-1990s new Italian eateries began to open up in this Mexican stronghold, with Parmesan and pasta becoming as common as queso fresco and frijoles. (And the number of Italian places opening just keeps growing.) Thankfully for diners, there are plenty of tasty choices on both sides of the menu.

13

AND FOR DESSERT

The Mission has ice cream in every flavor imaginable. **Bi-Rite Creamery** (⊠ *3692 18th St., near Valencia St.* ☎ *415/626–5600* ✛ *3:E6*) balances orbs of salted caramel or soft serve in organic cones. And the venerable **Mitchell's** (⊠ *668 San Jose St., at 29th St.* ☎ *415/648–2300* ✛ *3:E6*) has been scooping out creamy lemon custard and Mexican chocolate for over 50 years. Cult ice-cream shop **Humphry Slocombe** (⊠ *2790 Harrison St., near 24th St.* ☎ *415/550–6971* ✛ *3:G6*) is famous for irreverent flavors like balsamic caramel, prosciutto, and Thai chili lime sorbet. For something baked, hit **Tartine Bakery** (⊠ *600 Guerrero St., at 18th St.* ☎ *415/487–2600* ✛ *3:E6*), where the staff pulls devil's food cakes, lemon bars, banana-cream tarts, brownies, and shortbread from the oven daily. And if doughnuts and coffee are your thing, head to **Dynamo Donut & Coffee** (⊠ *2760 24th St., between Potrero and York Sts.* ☎ *415/920–1978* ✛ *3:H6*), and dunk a *dulce de leche* doughnut in a cup of strong drip-to-order coffee.

PACIFIC HEIGHTS, THE MARINA, AND JAPANTOWN

One of the city's best public transit rides is on the 22–Fillmore trolley bus, from the edge of Japantown at Geary Boulevard and Fillmore Street, up through mansion-lined Pacific Heights, then down to Cow Hollow and the Marina. We recommend jumping on and off the trolley, stopping for treats along the way.

In Japantown, which covers about six city blocks, start with a green tea latte at the pillbox-size **Café Tan Tan** in the Japan Center (⌂ *Kinokuniya Bldg.* ☎ *415/346–6260* ✢ *2:F6*), or an ice-cream-and-fruit-filled crepe next door at **Sophie's Crepes** (☎ *415/929–7732* ✢ *2:F6*).

Up the hill, Lower Pacific Heights is all about shopping. But growling stomachs can find relief in a Vietnamese lunch at the chic Out the Door (⌂ *2232 Bush St., near Fillmore St.* ☎ *415/923–9575* ✢ *2:E6*) or a baguette sandwich at **Bay Bread Boulangerie** (⌂ *2325 Pine St.* ☎ *415/440–0356* ✢ *2:F5*).

ITALIAN WINE BAR

A simple bite and a glass of Dolcetto d'Alba may be all you want after a long day of scaling San Francisco's hills. The small, delightfully rustic **Ottimista Enoteca** (⌂ *1838 Union St.* ☎ *415/674–8400* ✢ *2:G3*), *pictured at upper right*, offers just that, with more than two dozen wines by the glass and small plates like baked olives, saffron-scented *arancine* (deep-fried, fontina-stuffed rice balls), and bruschetta with seasonal toppings. For something more substantial, try the pappardelle or braised pork with polenta. If you're out late, end on a sweet note with a glass of *vin santo* and biscotti, served until 2 am on weekends (it can be quite the hot spot).

TASTE OF TOKYO, WEST-COAST STYLE

At San Francisco's three-building Japan Center mall, bordered by Geary Boulevard and Post, Fillmore, and Laguna streets, you can eat as they do in Tokyo, stopping in at the sleek **Juban** (✉ *Kinokuniya Bldg.* ☎ *415/776–5822* ✛ *2:F6*) for *yakiniku*, meat grilled at your table, including American Kobe rib eye; at the homey **Izumiya** (✉ *Kinokuniya Bldg.* ☎ *415/441–6867* ✛ *2:F6*), where *okonomiyaki*, a design-your-own savory pancake studded with pork or squid, is the draw; or at the refined (and rather serious) **Ino Sushi** (✉ *Mikyako Bldg.* ☎ *415/922–3121* ✛ *2:F6*), with its 10-seat sushi bar and handful of tables.

Noodle aficionados will want to try the house-made ramen at **Sapporo-ya** (✉ *Kinokuniya Bldg.* ☎ *415/563–7400* ✛ *2:F6*) or the soba and udon at **Mifune** (✉ *Kintetsu Bldg.* ☎ *415/922–0337* ✛ *2:F6*). If your group wants a mix of specialties, wend your way to **Takara** (✉ *Miyako Bldg.* ☎ *415/921–2000* ✛ *2:F6*), a *shokuji dokoro*, or Japanese bistro, which offers a mix of choices, from sushi to tempura (the cooked dishes are especially delicious).

BRUNCHING LIKE A LOCAL

Don't be surprised on weekend mornings to find San Franciscans of all ages waiting in line—rain or shine—at eateries around town. Like attending church or watching Sunday football, going out to brunch is a revered weekend ritual here, a time for friends and family to gather and gab. And, of course, to eat.

The ever-popular **Ella's** (✉ *500 Presidio Ave.* ☎ *415/441–5669* ✛ *2:C6*) is well known for its sticky buns and chicken hash with eggs. If you're feeling adventurous, try the homey breakfast porridge or pho at **Out the Door** (✉ *2232 Bush St., near Fillmore St.* ☎ *415/923–9575* ✛ *2:E6*)—but don't worry, there are some egg dishes as well. For classic diner flavor, grab a seat at **Home Plate** (✉ *2274 Lombard St.* ☎ *415/922–4663* ✛ *2:E3*), where the scones are free and the atmosphere is low-key.

AND FOR DESSERT

13

The father-daughter team at Fillmore Bakeshop (✉ *1890 Fillmore St., at Bush St.* ☎ *415/923–0711* ✛ *2:F6*) is baking contemporary European-American treats, and winning over the neighborhood with their danishes and almond-pear croissants. There isn't much seating—so you may have to nab something portable. Another pastry case that will tempt your willpower is at **La Boulangerie** (✉ *2325 Pine St., at Fillmore St.* ☎ *415/440–0356* ✛ *2:F5*), chock-full of classic French pastries and cookies like cannelés de Bordeaux, madeleines, and grab-and-go sandwiches. Just look for the bright blue exterior. Or, if you want to rest your feet in a spiffier environment, continue up Fillmore Street to **Citizen Cake** (✉ *2125 Fillmore St., between Sacramento and California Sts.* ☎ *415/861–2228* ✛ *2:F5*), where pastry chef Elizabeth Falkner has a patisserie case of treats to tempt you (think éclairs, petit gateaus, and macarons), along with edgier treats, like ice cream made with liquid nitrogen.

HAIGHT, RICHMOND, AND SUNSET

The Haight-Ashbury was home base for the country's famed 1960s counterculture, and its café scene still reflects that colorful past. For ethnic flavors, go to the neighborhoods on either side of Golden Gate Park.

Over time, the Haight has become two distinct neighborhoods. The Upper Haight is an energetic commercial stretch from Masonic Avenue to Stanyan Street, where head shops and tofu-burger joints still thrive. There are a few upscale restaurants, like the sizzling Caribbean kitchen of **Cha Cha Cha** (✉ *1801 Haight St.* ☎ *415/386–5758* ✛ *3:A4*), *pictured below right*. Meanwhile, the modestly gritty Lower Haight has emerged as a lively bohemian quarter of sorts, with mostly ethnic eateries lining the blocks between Webster and Pierce streets.

The Richmond and Sunset neighborhoods encompass the land on both sides of Golden Gate Park, running all the way to the ocean's edge. Both districts have welcomed a dramatic increase in Asian families. And not surprisingly, scores of Asian restaurants have opened up.

HAUTE PIES

The shoebox-size **Pizzetta 211** (✉ *211 23rd Ave., near Clement St., Richmond* ☎ *415/379–9880* ✛ *3:B1*) puts together thin-crust pies topped with the kinds of ingredients that are worth the (almost) constant wait. The selection changes daily—the tomato, basil, and mozzarella pizza is the only constant—but our favorites include the Sardinian cheese, pine nut, and rosemary pie (the white anchovies that top the pizzas here are also stellar). Pizzetta 211 is open nightly for dinner, and for lunch Wednesday through Sunday, and doesn't take reservations. Go early to avoid a long wait.

EXPLORING THE RICHMOND DISTRICT

NEW CHINATOWN

Since the early 20th century the Richmond District has been a desirable family address. Today those families are primarily Asian, and the neighborhood has been dubbed New China-town, though its dining choices go far beyond the People's Republic. Locals in search of a meal head to four main areas: Clement Street from Arguello Boulevard to 26th Avenue, Geary Boulevard from Masonic Avenue to 26th Avenue, and Balboa Street from 5th to 8th avenues and 33rd to 39th avenues. Clement Street is a sea of temptation. If you'd like to try the complex curries and salads at the always-busy **Burma SuperStar** (⊠ *309 Clement St., near 3rd Ave.* ☎ *415/387–2147* ⊹ *2:A6*), put your name and cell phone number on the waiting list as soon as you get to the neighborhood. A cluster of plain-Jane storefronts fire up smoky charcoal braziers on Geary Boulevard between Arguello Boulevard and 10th Avenue, including the **Wooden Charcoal Barbecue House** (⊠ *4611 Geary Blvd.* ☎ *415/751–6336* ⊹ *3:B1*), which serves up Korean *bulkogi,* or grilled beef ribs.

OLD RUSSIA

Nostalgia hangs heavy in the dining room of the half-century-old **Cinderella Bakery and Restaurant** (⊠ *436 Balboa St., near 5th Ave.* ☎ *415/751–9690* ⊹ *3:B1*), where diners tuck into borscht and cabbage rolls while sipping *kvass,* or beer brewed from bread. Be sure to stop at the bakery counter on your way out for a flaky napoleon or cheese pastries. The homey **Katia's** (⊠ *600 5th Ave., at Balboa St.* ☎ *415/668–9292* ⊹ *3:A2*) has samovars ready for Russian tea service, along with hearty *pel'meni* (dumplings) and excellent pies during the holidays. Not far away, at **Moscow and Tblisi Bakery** (⊠ *5540 Geary Blvd., near 19th Ave.* ☎ *415/668–6959* ⊹ *3:B1*), locals line up for some of those same old-country tastes, including *piroshki* (meat- and vegetable-filled pastries) and poppy-seed rolls.

AND FOR DESSERT   13

Out in the Richmond, you would be hard-pressed to find a longtime resident who didn't spend some of his or her youth in the truly kitschy **Toy Boat Dessert Cafe** (⊠ *401 Clement St., between 5th and 6th Aves.* ☎ *415/751–7505* ⊹ *2:A6*), where Double Rainbow ice cream competes with a battalion of vintage toys. No toys compete with the scoops at the funky **Joe's Ice Cream** (⊠ *5420 Geary Blvd., at 18th Ave.* ☎ *415/751–1950* ⊹ *3:B1*), and no Joe is there now, either. But Mutsuhiko and Aki Murashige have been keeping Joe's name hon-est since 1979, when they bought the business. They fashion thick milk shakes, make a mean banana split, and put together their own It's-It, San Francisco's iconic ice-cream sand-wich—all with their house-made ice cream.

RESTAURANT REVIEWS

Listed alphabetically within neighborhood.

UNION SQUARE AND CHINATOWN

UNION SQUARE

$$$
AMERICAN

✕ **Canteen.** Blink, and you'll miss this place. Chef-owner Dennis Leary has transformed this narrow coffee shop into one of the most sought-after dinner reservations in town. The homey place has just 20 counter seats and a quartet of wooden booths. But that's all Leary, with a modest open kitchen and a single assistant, can handle. The dinner menu, which changes often, offers only four first courses, four mains, and three or four desserts. A typical meal might start with veal meatballs with fennel-artichoke puree, followed by a gratin of chanterelles and tomatoes, or pork tenderloin with braised cranberry beans and fig-olive jus, and then a dreamy vanilla soufflé or almond torte. On Tuesday night a three-course prix-fixe menu is in force (no choices within each course) for $35 (seatings are at 6 pm and 8 pm). Because this is a one-man band, there are set times to dine other nights in the week: 6 pm, 7:30 pm, and 9:15 pm. ⊠ *817 Sutter St., Union Square* ☎ *415/928–8870* ⊕ *www.sfcanteen.com* ⌿ *Reservations essential* ⊙ *Closed Mon. No lunch Tues.–Thurs. or weekends* ✛ *4:C3.*

$$$$
SEAFOOD

✕ **Farallon.** Sculpted jellyfish chandeliers, kelp-covered columns, and sea-urchin lights give this swanky Pat Kuleto–designed restaurant a decidedly quirky look. But there's nothing quirky about chef Mark Franz's impeccable seafood, which reels in serious diners from coast to coast. The extensive raw bar includes chilled Maine lobster with a trio of dipping sauces. The menu changes daily, but you might find prawn and scallop quenelles, cedar plank–grilled trout, and scallops with truffled potato ravioli. Meat eaters aren't ignored, with such choices as fillet of beef and a pork chop. If you want to enjoy the surroundings but not pay the price, you can take a seat at the French-style oyster bar and fill up on oyster shooters, a shrimp cocktail, crab cakes, french fries with aioli, and more from the less expensive bar menu. The carrot cake shouldn't be missed. ⊠ *450 Post St., Union Square* ☎ *415/956–6969* ⊕ *www.farallonrestaurant.com* ⊙ *No lunch* ✛ *4:E3.*

$$$$
FRENCH

✕ **Fleur de Lys.** The creative cooking of chef-owner Hubert Keller has brought every conceivable culinary award to this romantic spot. His three-, four-, and five-course prix-fixe menus (each course with many choices), priced from $72 to $95, include plenty of foie gras, squab, lobster, and truffles to satisfy palates geared to fancy French plates. Choosing some items will boost your tab, such as $25 extra for filet mignon with foie gras, $75 extra for an ounce of domestic osetra caviar, and even $6 extra for chocolate soufflé. The dining room, with its dramatic tented ceiling of 900 yards of draped and swathed fabric, is as showy as the food (and is special occasion central). These days some regulars have grumbled that Keller is paying more attention to his growing gourmet burger-bar and steak-house chain than his San Francisco dining room, citing less-than-stellar service and a stagnant menu as evidence of their claims. ⊠ *777 Sutter St., Union Square* ☎ *415/673–7779* ⊕ *www.*

fleurdelyssf.com ⌣ *Reservations essential* 🏛 *Jacket required* ⊘ *Closed Sun. No lunch* ✛ *4:D3.*

$$$$
VIETNAMESE
✗ **Le Colonial.** This is high-style Vietnamese food served up in a French-colonial time machine: stamped-tin ceiling, period photographs, slow-moving fans, and tropical plants. Local society types who can't be bothered with dining in Little Saigon come for the sea bass steamed in banana leaves, green papaya salad, and lamb chops with grilled eggplant salad. They also like to pick from among the big selection of fried or fresh appetizer rolls, filled with everything from shredded duck to Dungeness crab. Downstairs are two large and rather formal dining rooms. Anything goes upstairs in the lively lounge: you can eat appetizers, you can dance (Wednesday through Saturday nights), or you can just sip a cocktail at the bar and take in the scene. Plenty of locals find the dining room stuffy—and expensive—but are quick to defend the lounge. It's full of atmosphere during weekend brunch. ✉ *20 Cosmo Pl., Union Square* ☎ *415/931–3600* ⊕ *www.lecolonialsf.com* ⊘ *No lunch* ✛ *4:D3.*

$$$
VEGETARIAN
✗ **Millennium.** This big, wood-lined dining room in the Hotel California is *the* gourmet dining destination for visiting vegans. The seasonal menu of "animal-free" dishes made with organic ingredients includes flat bread with caramelized onion and cherry tomatoes, chickpea flour–crusted oyster mushrooms with sea vegetable noodle salad, mirin-glazed sesame rice balls, and maple-roasted squash with hazelnut-farro risotto. All dishes are dressed up with bold flavors, and numerous ingredients (sometimes a few too many). Come dessert, you may find the chocolate almond midnight (mocha chocolate filling in an almond-cashew crust) hard to resist. A long list of organic wines is available, and a five-course tasting menu ($69) is offered for when your wallet is full, or a "Frugal Foodie" three-course menu Sunday through Wednesday for $39. ✉ *Hotel California, 580 Geary St., Union Square* ☎ *415/345–3900* ⊕ *www.millenniumrestaurant.com* ⊘ *No lunch* ✛ *4:D4.*

$$$
ITALIAN
✗ **Scala's Bistro.** Smart leather-and-wood booths, a pressed-tin ceiling, a menu of rustic Italian (and a few French) dishes, a steady hum of activity—it's hard not to like the big-city feel of this hotel dining room. Fritto misto of shrimp, squid, and fennel; orecchiette with spicy sausage and broccoli; and salmon with buttermilk mashed potatoes are among the evening's hearty choices. The room is open late, making it a welcome dessert destination—with sweet successes like the Bostini cream pie and Chocolate! Chocolate! Chocolate! (a chocolate creation of mousse, pecan crust, gelato, and sauce). ✉ *Sir Francis Drake Hotel, 432 Powell St., Union Square* ☎ *415/395–8555* ⊕ *www.scalasbistro.com* ✛ *4:F3.*

CHINATOWN

$$
CHINESE
☺
✗ **Great Eastern.** Don't be tempted to order a Szechuan or Beijing dish here or you'll leave unhappy. This is a Cantonese restaurant, and that means fresh, simply prepared seafood, quickly cooked vegetables and meats, clear soups, and no fiery chilies. Tanks filled with crabs, black bass, catfish, shrimp, and other freshwater- and saltwater creatures occupy a corner of the street-level main dining room. Look to them for your meal, but check prices, as swimming seafood isn't cheap. Kids will find their Chinese-restaurant favorites here: stir-fried noodles, cashew

13

chicken, fried rice. Dim sum is also popular here (there aren't any carts, however—you order off a paper sheet). Avoid the basement dining room, which is brightly lighted but also claustrophobic. Toward midnight, Chinese night owls drop in for a plate of noodles or a bowl of *congee* (rice porridge). ⊠ *649 Jackson St., Chinatown* ☎ *415/986–2500* ✛ *1:D4.*

$$

CHINESE

☺

✗ **R&G Lounge.** The name conjures up an image of a dark, smoky bar with a piano player, but this Cantonese restaurant is actually as bright as a new penny. On the lower level (entrance on Kearny Street) is a notablecloth dining room that's packed at lunch and dinner. The classy upstairs space (entrance on Commercial Street) is a favorite stop for Chinese businessmen on expense accounts and special-occasion banquets. The street-level room on Kearny is a comfortable spot to wait for an open table. A menu with photographs helps you pick from the many wonderful, sometimes pricey, always authentic dishes, such as the famous salt-and-pepper Dungeness crab, roast squab, and shrimp-stuffed tofu (and much of the seafood is fresh from the tank). You can sip a lychee- or watermelon-flavor martini while waiting for your table. ⊠ *631 Kearny St., Chinatown* ☎ *415/982–7877 or 415/982–3811* ⊕ *www.rnglounge.com* ✛ *1:E4.*

SOMA AND CIVIC CENTER

$$$$

ECLECTIC

✗ **Ame.** America and Japan, along with France and Italy, converge in high style on the plates of chef Hiro Sone. Indeed, his food, from *cha-wan mushi* (egg custard) with matsutake mushrooms and lobster, to a napoleon of foie gras and eel, to sake-marinated black cod, is almost too beautiful to eat. The dishes from the sushi bar offer additional delights. He serves it in an equally stunning, modern space in the handsome St. Regis, which shelters both hotel guest rooms and condominium residences, including one that Al Gore makes his West Coast home. Not surprisingly, the space and the plates attract members of the local—and, some would say, stuffy—elite who know food and have the means to pay a lofty price for it. ⊠ *St. Regis Hotel, 689 Mission St., SoMa* ☎ *415/284–4040* ⊕ *www.amerestaurant.com* ☽ *No lunch* ✛ *1:E6.*

$$$

FRENCH

✗ **Chez Papa Resto.** Downtown's newish Mint Plaza, tucked behind the city's long-decommissioned, but recently renovated 1874 federal mint, is home to this utterly urban 70-seat restaurant, with its exposed concrete, bare-wood-topped tables, and high black ceiling. The contemporary French menu—beef tartare, roasted bone marrow, duck confit, seared scallop bouillabaisse, profiteroles filled with pistachio ice cream and drizzled with warm chocolate sauce—will have you dreaming of the Left Bank. A three-course prix-fixe business lunch ($23.95), with a few choices in each category, is available. And for the impecunious after-work crowd, happy hour delivers six-buck cocktails and some nibbles from 5 to 7 pm weekdays. ⊠ *4 Mint Plaza, SoMa* ☎ *415/546–4134* ⊕ *www.chezpapasf.com* ☽ *Closed Sun.* ✛ *4:F6.*

$$$

NEW AMERICAN

✗ **Coco500.** Chef-owner Loretta Keller knows how to change with the times. She shuttered her long-admired Bizou restaurant and reopened in the same spot with this up-to-the-minute small-plates and not-so-small-plates venue. Menu categories like "small starts," "leaf (salads)," and "California dirt (local organic vegetables)" reflect Keller's modern outlook, as do dishes like the COCOmole taco, which pairs tortilla triangles with beef cheeks and a chili-chocolate mole sauce. You'll also find duck-liver terrine, truffled flat bread, Sonoma duck breast, milk-braised pork shoulder with fingerling potatoes, and a signature *vacherin* (crème anglaise, Swiss meringue, coffee ice cream, and chocolate sauce) from Bizou days. For a simpler and smaller sweet ending, order the chocolate-dipped frozen banana. That delicious menu mix pulls in young hipsters and sophisticated oldsters, all cheerfully grazing the menu, whether it's a business lunch, happy hour, or dinnertime. ⊠ *500 Brannan St., SoMa* ☏ *415/543–2222* ⊕ *www.coco500.com* ☉ *Closed Sun. No lunch Sat.* ✢ *4:H6.*

$$$$ ╳ **Fifth Floor.** A clubhouse for well-off diners, this swanky spot is tucked
FRENCH away in the Palomar Hotel. It has seen toques come and go in the last few years, but at least they've always been talented. Dressed up in sandy beige walls, hardwood floors, sleek dark-wood tables, and modern club chairs, the dining room is the stylish setting for a dinner of New American dishes like octopus in a pimentón marinade, rabbit crepinette, and roasted lamb with pistou and favas. You can order dishes à la carte, but the menu is structured as a four-course affair—or enjoy a six-course tasting menu ($72). The extensive wine list is also of note. If you want to see how the other half eats, enjoy a burger or lamb meatballs in the more casual—and more affordable—lounge next door to the dining room, along with excellent cocktails. ⊠ *Palomar Hotel, 12 4th St., SoMa* ☏ *415/348–1555* ⊕ *www.fifthfloorrestaurant. com* ☉ *Closed Sun. No lunch* ✢ *4:G5.*

$$$ ╳ **LuLu.** In its early years LuLu was a magnet for dot-commers, but
MEDITERRANEAN now it seems to have more of an appeal for conventioneers at nearby Moscone Center and business diners (although there are some locals who consider it a fave). It's rustic cuisine that's easy for large groups to share, like mixed antipasti platters (you pick three items); mussels roasted in an iron skillet; wood-oven roasted poultry, meats, and shellfish; and a small selection of pizzas and pastas. There is a well-supplied raw bar, and main-course specials include a rotisserie-cooked option that changes daily; Friday brings a succulent suckling pig. Sharing dishes is the custom here, and portions are typically bountiful. Wine drinkers will appreciate the long list of choices by the glass. When LuLu is packed, service can suffer. ⊠ *816 Folsom St., SoMa* ☏ *415/495–5775* ⊕ *www.restaurantlulu.com* ✢ *1:E6.*

$$$ ╳ **Marlowe.** Formerly an Australian restaurant, this tucked-away little
AMERICAN spot is now drawing in the crowds for its menu of American bistro fare, like roasted bone marrow, steak tartare, and a crave-worthy burger. Lunchtime brings five different sandwiches (try the fried chicken), and any time is a good time for the crisp Brussels sprouts. There's a small bar in the back, and diners also gather around the communal table. The space has a classic aesthetic, with penny tile floors, wood tables, and a navy-blue-and-white color scheme. It's a bit small—with tables close together, and a high volume—so don't come on a romantic dinner. But do come hungry; and thirsty—there's plenty on the wine list to choose

13

from. ✉ *330 Townsend St., SoMa* ☎ *415/974–5599* ⊕ *www.marlowesf. com* ⊗ *Closed Sun. No lunch Sat.* ✛ *1:E6.*

$$$ ✕**Orson.** Edgy California cuisine—that's what chef Elizabeth Falkner
NEW AMERICAN has dubbed the fare at her chic South of Market restaurant. This self-proclaimed edginess translates into some creative touches, like king salmon with bamboo rice and Lapsang tea butter, or blue-cheese ice cream with a fried-chicken ballontine. But there are also many familiar but delicious dishes, like wood-fired mussels with chorizo, house-made mozzarella with eggplant caponata, half a dozen pizzas nicely crisp from the wood-burning oven, and short ribs. The Orson burger and duck-fat fries also have their own fan club. The after-work crowd takes over the circular bar and lounge Tuesday to Saturday with five-buck cocktails from 5 to 7. Lunch and brunch both have the kinds of menus that will make you a repeat customer. ✉ *508 4th St., at Bryant, SoMa* ☎ *415/777–1508* ⊕ *www.orsonsf.com* ⊗ *No dinner Sun. and Mon.* ✛ *4:H6.*

$$$ ✕**Salt House.** A boisterous crowd packs this high-ceiling, brick-lined
NEW AMERICAN dining space that once housed a printing press. Rusted girders, chandeliers fashioned from old postcard racks, and water poured from vintage milk bottles set a casual mood. The small plates, like crisp shrimp atop spicy green beans, almonds, and serrano ham; a popular (and rich) poutine; and foie gras with sautéed quince, are so appealing that most diners find it hard to move to the mains. Such flawed logic means missing out on a first-rate roast chicken with fingerlings or Sonoma rabbit with Lady apples. Single diners can grab a seat at the big communal table. ✉ *545 Mission St., SoMa* ☎ *415/543–8900* ⊕ *www.salthousesf. com* ⊗ *No lunch weekends* ✛ *1:E6.*

$$$ ✕**Town Hall.** Well-known chefs Mitchell and Steven Rosenthal are the
NEW AMERICAN culinary brains behind this way station for the city's powerbrokers and their acolytes. The fare is sophisticated American with some Southern flair—roasted veal meatballs, spicy shrimp, juicy fried chicken, a thick pork chop, butterscotch-and-chocolate *pot de crème*—with plenty of variety to satisfy nearly everyone. The converted-warehouse space, with dark-wood floors, exposed brick walls, white wainscoting, and contemporary art, comfortably blends old with new. You can cool your heels with a cocktail on the heated patio (like a perfect Sazerac) while you wait for your table. The decibel level here can wear down your vocal chords, so ask for a quieter table. ✉ *342 Howard St., SoMa* ☎ *415/908–3900* ⊕ *www.townhallsf.com* ⊗ *No lunch weekends* ✛ *1:F5.*

$$$ ✕**Zaré at Fly Trap.** Chef-owner Hoss Zaré has brought vitality and per-
MEDITERRANEAN sonality to this classic San Francisco locale, while still maintaining its air of history and class. Both the bar and communal table fill up with an after-work crowd, hungry for the lamb burger and other flavorful bites on the Mediterranean menu. A sit-down dinner here is ideal for friends, dates, dinner with the parents, and business—the non-table-cloth environment keeps things feeling comfortable. The menu features many exotic ingredients from the chef's Persian upbringing, while still maintaining a California vibe. Pistachio meatballs, oxtail penne, and the lamb-shank *abgusht* (stew) are more on the hearty side, while grilled salmon with toasted fregola and a variety of vegetable dishes keep

things light (vegetarians will find plenty to dine on here). The bar is welcoming to solo diners. ☒ *606 Folsom St., SoMa* ☎ *415/243–0580* ⊕ *www.zareflytrap.com* ☻ *Closed Sun. No lunch* ✛ *1:F6.*

$$ ✗ **Zero Zero.** Chef-owner Bruce Hill (of Bix and Picco fame) has created
ITALIAN a popular and comfortable California-Italian restaurant where you can go almost any time of day, whether you're craving one of his standout thin-crust "Cali-politan" pizzas for lunch, a cocktail after work, house-made pasta for dinner, or flavorful skillet-fried chicken thighs with a waffle for brunch. Ingredients are fresh and seasonal, and portions are affordable and easy to share (large groups can also order punch bowls for the table). Choose-your-own-toppings soft serve for dessert is a hit. There's a lengthy downstairs bar and lounge, with another second smaller bar upstairs that are both packed in the evenings with diners and drinkers alike. ☒ *826 Folsom St., SoMa* ☎ *415/348–8800* ⊕ *www. zerozerosf.com* ✛ *1:E6.*

HAYES VALLEY

$$$ ✗ **Absinthe.** In 2007 this restaurant's long-notorious namesake could
FRENCH once again be poured legally in the United States, after nearly a century in exile. Not surprisingly, regular customers turned up in big numbers to sample the legendary Green Fairy, and then stayed on to enjoy Absinthe's brasserie-inspired fare of onion soup, cold seafood platters, beef tartare, and Kurobuta pork rib eye, all served in an upscale dark wood–lined, white-tablecloth dining room. The bar, reminiscent of a Belle Époque Parisian café, offers a late-night bar menu—oysters, croque monsieur, grass-fed-beef burgers, *steak frites,* addictive spicy fried chickpeas—that fuels neighborhood night owls. A hearty weekend brunch is designed to heal—ditto on the excellent cocktails here. ☒ *398 Hayes St., Hayes Valley* ☎ *415/551–1590* ⊕ *www.absinthe.com* ☻ *Closed Mon.* ✛ *3:E2.*

$$$ ✗ **Bar Jules.** An open kitchen, a counter lined with red-topped stools, a
FRENCH dozen or so small tables, and a generally young crowd are tucked into this cozy, bright eatery on the edge of trendy Hayes Valley. The daily-changing blackboard menu is small and invariably appealing, with seasonal dishes like butternut squash soup with pumpkin seed, cauliflower and sunchoke gratin with Gruyère and thyme, and wood-grilled steak with caper butter sauce. Desserts range from plum tart to butterscotch pudding to the famed Chocolate Nemesis. Sunday brunch draws a neighborhood crowd to the sunny storefront. On the downside: service can be slow, and the sea of hard surfaces can make quiet conversation impossible. ☒ *609 Hayes St., Hayes Valley* ☎ *415/621–5482* ⊕ *www. barjules.com* ☻ *Closed Mon. No lunch Tues. No dinner Sun.* ✛ *3:E2.*

$$$ ✗ **Hayes Street Grill.** Arrive here just as local music lovers are folding their
SEAFOOD napkins and heading off for the 8 pm curtain at the nearby Opera House and you'll snag a table and some perfectly fresh (and local) seafood. Much of the fish—sea bass, yellowfin tuna, swordfish—is simply grilled and served with a choice of sauces from beurre blanc to lemon-and-caper butter. A pile of crisp, thin Belgian frites rides alongside the grilled offerings. Brass coat hooks, white tablecloths, a long bar, and a mix of banquettes and tables define the traditional San Francisco look of this

three-decades-old seafood stronghold. Folks who eschew water-based fare will be happy to know a flat-iron steak and thick pork chops are on the menu, in addition to an excellent burger. Anyone on a budget will want to come after 7:30 for the three-course prix-fixe menu priced at just $33. ✉ *320 Hayes St., Hayes Valley* ☎ *415/863–5545* ⊕ *www. hayesstreetgrill.com* ⊘ *No lunch weekends* ✛ *3:F2.*

$$$$
NEW AMERICAN

✕ **Jardinière.** A special anniversary? An important business dinner? A fat tax refund? These are the reasons you book a table at Jardinière. The restaurant takes its name from its chef-owner, Traci Des Jardins, and the sophisticated interior, with its eye-catching oval atrium and curving staircase, fills nightly with locals and out-of-towners alike. The equally sophisticated French-cum-Californian dining-room menu, served upstairs in the atrium, changes daily, but regularly includes such high-priced adornments as caviar, foie gras, and truffles. Downstairs, the lounge menu, with smaller plates and smaller prices ($8 to $18), is ideal for when you want to eat light while visiting with friends or tame your hunger before or after the nearby opera or symphony. Cheese lovers will appreciate the wide variety of choices—both Old World and New—housed in the glassed-in cheese-aging chamber in the rear of the restaurant. ✉ *300 Grove St., Hayes Valley* ☎ *415/861–5555* ⊕ *www. jardiniere.com* ⌂ *Reservations essential* ⊘ *No lunch* ✛ *3:F2.*

$$
GERMAN

✕ **Suppenküche.** Nobody goes hungry—and no beer drinker goes thirsty—at this lively, hip outpost of simple German cooking in the trendy Hayes Valley corridor. When the room gets crowded, which it regularly does, strangers sit together at unfinished pine tables. Servers are quick and efficient, and keep the pace moving along. The hearty food—bratwurst and red cabbage, potato pancakes with house-made applesauce, meat loaf, braised beef, pork loin, schnitzel, strudel—is tasty and kind to your pocketbook, and the imported brews are first-rate. There's also a popular Sunday brunch, with appealing fare such as gravlax with mustard-dill sauce and pancakes with brandied raisins. ✉ *525 Laguna St., Hayes Valley* ☎ *415/252–9289* ⊕ *www.suppenkuche. com* ⊘ *No lunch* ✛ *3:E2.*

$$$
MEDITERRANEAN
Fodor's Choice
★

✕ **Zuni Café.** After one bite of chef Judy Rodgers' succulent brick-oven-roasted whole chicken with Tuscan bread salad, you'll understand why she's a national star. Food is served here on two floors; the rabbit warren of rooms on the second level includes a balcony overlooking the main dining room. The crowd is a disparate mix that reflects the makeup of the city: casual and dressy, young and old, hip and staid. At the long copper bar, trays of briny-fresh oysters on the half shell are dispensed along with cocktails and wine. The southern French–Italian menu changes daily (though the signature chicken, prepared for two, is a fixture—sadly its already-dear cost is what keeps rising). Rotating dishes include house-cured anchovies with Parmigiano-Reggiano, deep-fried squid and lemons, ricotta gnocchi with seasonal vegetables, and brick-oven squab with polenta. Desserts are simple and satisfying, and include crumbly crusted tarts and an addictive cream-laced coffee granita. The lunchtime (and late-night) burger on rosemary focaccia with a side of shoestring potatoes is a favorite with locals. ✉ *1658 Market St., Hayes Valley* ☎ *415/552–2522* ⊕ *www.zunicafe.com* ⊘ *Closed Mon.* ✛ *3:F3.*

FINANCIAL DISTRICT

$$ ✕ **Barbacco.** This busy sister restaurant to neighboring Perbacco is all
ITALIAN about affordable smaller plates that are big on flavor. Financial District
workers crowd in for lunch or happy hour at the communal tables and
long counter, while diners from all over town make their reservations
for the evening. The room has a chic Milanese look to it, but the food
is soulful and rustic. Start with the *ascolane* (stuffed olives) and *arancini*
(risotto croquettes), and move on to plates of the excellent house-made
charcuterie, a variety of bruschette, hearty pastas, delicious "angry mus-
sels," and larger plates like Sicilian meatballs. There are plenty of Ital-
ian wines to explore by the glass, and a well-informed staff to tell you
about them. ✉ *220 California St., Financial District* ☎ *415/955–1919*
⊕ *www.barbaccosf.com* ✆ *No lunch weekends* ✢ *1:E4.*

$$$ ✕ **Bocadillos.** The name means "sandwiches," but that's only half the
SPANISH story here. You'll find 13 bocadillos at lunchtime: plump rolls filled
with everything from serrano ham to Catalan sausage with arugula to a
memorable lamb burger. But at night chef-owner Gerald Hirigoyen, who
also owns the high-profile Piperade, focuses on tapas, offering some two
dozen choices, including a savory octopus carpaccio, an equally superb
pig's trotters with herbs, and *patatas bravas* (potatoes) with *romesco*
sauce (a thick combination of red pepper, tomato, almonds, and garlic).
His wine list is well matched to the food. A youngish crowd typically
piles into the modern, red-brick-wall dining space, so be prepared to
wait for a seat. A large communal table is a good perch for singles. If
you're in the neighborhood at breakfast time, there is plenty here to
keep you happy, including a scrambled-eggs-and-cheese bocadillo or
house-made chorizo and eggs. ✉ *710 Montgomery St., Financial District* ☎ *415/982–2622* ⊕ *www.bocasf.com* ⌘ *Reservations not accepted*
✆ *Closed Sun. No lunch Sat.* ✢ *1:E4.*

$$ ✕ **Café Claude.** If you think this place looks like it could be in Paris,
FRENCH you're right. Nearly everything, from the zinc bar and the banquettes to
the light fixtures and cinema posters, was shipped from a defunct café in
the City of Light to this atmospheric downtown alley. Order a croque
monsieur or niçoise salad at lunchtime. The francophone kitchen sends
out even more French staples for dinner, like escargots, steak tartare,
coquilles Saint-Jacques, and roast lamb. Grab a table outdoors (heat
lamps keep you warm on cool nights) and pretend you are in Paris
at a sidewalk café. Stop by Thursday, Friday, and Saturday nights to
enjoy live jazz along with your meal. ✉ *7 Claude La., Financial District*
☎ *415/392–3515* ⊕ *www.cafeclaude.com* ✆ *No lunch Sun.* ✢ *4:H2.*

$$$ ✕ **Kokkari.** The interior of this classy restaurant won't recall homey
GREEK tavernas just steps from the Acropolis. But its menu will satisfy your
craving for good Greek taverna food—albeit at steak-house prices.
Most savvy diners start off with a trio of dips—eggplant, yogurt, and
cucumber—and *taramosalata*, fish roe puréed with olive oil and bread
crumbs. Main courses showcase such Athenian standards as moussaka,
a mixed seafood grill, braised lamb shank, lemon-oregano chicken, and
outstanding grilled lamb chops. A bar menu of small plates—crispy
smelts, feta-stuffed phyllo, grilled octopus—satisfies weekday afternoon
customers—and it's a lively after-work scene. Desserts like semolina

custard wrapped in phyllo (it has a dedicated following) and yogurt with walnuts and honey make for a light, sweet finish. ⊠ *200 Jackson St., Financial District* ☎ *415/981–0983* ⊕ *www.kokkari.com* ⊘ *No lunch weekends* ✛ *1:E3.*

¢   ✕ **Naan 'N' Curry.** You will find no frills here—and minimal service and INDIAN   housekeeping—but you will find food fresh off the fire at rock-bottom prices. This is just one location in a local mini-chain of Indian-Pakistani eateries that cater primarily to starving students, poorly paid office workers, local South Asians, and anyone else who likes spicy food but doesn't give a damn about ambience. The tandoor-fired chicken *tikka masala, bhindi* (okra with onion and spices), garlic naan, and tongue-scorching tandoori lamb chops are favorites. The Bollywood music is too loud, but the naan is the size of a hubcap and the chai (milk) tea is free. ⊠ *533 Jackson St., Financial District* ☎ *415/693–0499* ⊕ *www. naanncurry.com* ✛ *1:D4.*

$$$ ✕ **Perbacco.** With its long marble bar and open kitchen, this brick-lined ITALIAN   two-story space oozes big-city charm. The arrival of skinny, brittle bread sticks is the first sign that the kitchen understands the cuisine of northern Italy, specifically Piedmont. And if the breadbasket doesn't convince you, try the antipasto of house-made cured meats (chef Staffan Terjeis known for making some of the city's finest *salumi*) or *burrata* (cream-filled mozzarella) with seasonal vegetables, the delicate *agnolotti dal plin* (veal-stuffed pasta with a cabbage-laced meat sauce), or *pappardelle* with full-flavored duck *ragù.* The clientele, a mix of business types and Italian food aficionados, appreciates the big, smart wine list along with the superb food. ⊠ *230 California St., Financial District* ☎ *415/955–0663* ⊕ *www.perbaccosf.com* ⊘ *Closed Sun. No lunch Sat.* ✛ *1:E4.*

$$ ✕ **Plouf.** This French-friendly spot is a gold mine for mussel lovers, with SEAFOOD   six preparations to choose from, plus a mussels and clams combo, all at a modest price. Among the best are *marinière* (white wine, garlic, and parsley) and one combining coconut milk, lime juice, and chili. Add a side of the skinny fries and that's all most appetites need. The menu changes seasonally, and includes lamb shank and filet mignon to satisfy any unrepentant carnivores. Many of the appetizers—oysters on the half shell, clam croquettes, ceviche—stick to seafood, as well. The tables are squeezed together in the bright, lively dining room, so you might overhear neighboring conversations. On temperate days and nights, try for one of the outdoor tables. ⊠ *40 Belden Pl., Financial District* ☎ *415/986–6491* ⊕ *www.ploufsf.com* ⊘ *Closed Sun. No lunch Sat.* ✛ *4:H2.*

$$$ ✕ **Quince.** Previously housed in a small, almost quaint, former apoth-ITALIAN   ecary in Pacific Heights, this smart, wildly praised restaurant has taken Fodor's Choice   up residence in a much bigger, high-design, and elegant space in Jackson ★   Square. Michael Tusk, who has cooked at the legendary Chez Panisse and Oliveto, oversees the kitchen, where he uses only the finest local ingredients to turn out his Italian-inspired cuisine. The menu changes regularly, featuring a delicious selection of their famed pastas and seasonal dishes, such as chestnut tagliatelle with squab sugo, rabbit with flageolet beans, and fig crostata with burnt-honey ice cream. Don't

pass up the cheese course—it's one of the city's finer selections. The 800-bottle-strong wine list is top-notch, but can get pricey (the $35 corkage means you won't save much by bringing your own bottle), and the service is both refined and friendly. (You can also slink next door to Quince's new casual offshoot, Cotogna, for an affordable and rustic meal, both for lunch and dinner.) ✉ *470 Pacific St., Financial District* ☎ *415/775–8500* ⊕ *www.quincerestaurant.com* ⚖ *Reservations essential* ☯ *No lunch* ✛ *1:E3*

13

$$$
SEAFOOD

✗ **Tadich Grill.** Locations and owners have changed more than once since this old-timer started as a coffee stand on the waterfront in 1849, but the crowds keep coming. Generations of regulars advise that simple grills, sautés, and panfries are the best choices. Try the Dungeness crab cocktail and cioppino during crab season (November to May), the Pacific halibut between January and May, and iconic San Francisco sand dabs year-round. Happily, the old-fashioned house-made tartar sauce doesn't change with the seasons. There's counter seating, a few tables, and private booths (complete with a bell to summon the waiter), and a long line of business types at noon is inevitable. The crusty, white-coated waiters are a throwback to another time, and the old-school bartenders serve up martinis as good as the mollusks. Finish the night with the Tadich rice custard pudding, topped with bourbon hard sauce. ✉ *240 California St., Financial District* ☎ *415/391–1849* ⚖ *Reservations not accepted* ☯ *Closed Sun.* ✛ *1:F4.*

$$
CHINESE
☕

✗ **Yank Sing.** This is the granddaddy of the city's dim sum teahouses. It opened in a plain-Jane storefront in Chinatown in 1959, but left its Cantonese neighbors behind for the high-rises of downtown by the 1970s. This brightly decorated location on quiet Stevenson Street (there's also a big, brassy branch in the Rincon Center) serves some of San Francisco's best dim sum to office workers on weekdays and to big, boisterous families on weekends. The kitchen cooks up some 100 varieties of dim sum on a rotating basis, offering 60 different types daily. These include both the classic (steamed pork buns, shrimp dumplings, egg custard tartlets) and the creative (scallion-skewered prawns tied with bacon, lobster and *tobiko* roe dumplings, basil seafood dumplings). The Shanghai soup dumplings are a classic—and some of the best in the city. A take-out counter makes a meal on the run a satisfying and pennywise compromise when office duties—or touring—won't wait. ✉ *49 Stevenson St., Financial District* ☎ *415/541–4949* ⊕ *www.yanksing. com* ☯ *No dinner* ✛ *1:E5.*

NOB HILL AND RUSSIAN HILL

NOB HILL

$$$$
FRENCH

✗ **Masa's.** Although the toque has been passed to several chefs since the death of founding chef Masataka Kobayashi, this 25-year-old restaurant, with its chocolate-brown walls, white fabric ceiling, and red-silk-shaded lanterns, is still one of the country's most celebrated food temples. Chef Gregory Short, who worked alongside Thomas Keller at the famed French Laundry for seven years, is at the helm these days, and his tasting menus of three, four, and seven courses, including a vegetarian option, are pleasing both diners and critics. The fare is dubbed

Eating with Kids

Kids can be fussy eaters, but parents can be, too, so picking places that will satisfy both is important. Fortunately, there are plenty of excellent possibilities all over town.

If you're downtown for breakfast, stop at the touristy but venerable **Sears Fine Food** (⊠ *439 Powell St., near Post St.* ☏ *415/986–0700* ✛ *4:F3*), home of "the world-famous Swedish pancakes." Eighteen of the silver-dollar-size beauties cost less than a movie ticket. Nearby in Chinatown, **City View Restaurant** (⊠ *662 Commercial St., near Kearny St.* ☏ *415/398–2838* ✛ *1:E4*) serves a varied selection of dim sum, with tasty pork buns for kids and more-exotic fare for adults.

If you found yourself dragging the kids through SFMOMA, you can win them back with lunch at the nearby **Crêpe O Chocolate** (⊠ *75 O'Farrell St., between Stockton St. and Grant Ave.* ☏ *415/362–0255* ✛ *4:G4*), where they can fill up on a turkey-and-cheese sandwich and a crepe filled with peanut butter and chocolate—and you can, too. Try **Pluto's** (⊠ *627 Irving St., between 7th and 8th Sts.* ☏ *415/753–8867* ✛ *2:A6*) after a visit to Golden Gate Park. Small kids love the chicken nuggets, which arrive with good-for-you carrot and celery sticks, whereas bigger kids will likely opt for one of the two-fisted sandwiches or make-your-own salads. Everyone will want a double fudge brownie for dessert. **Barney's Gourmet Burgers** (⊠ *3344 Steiner St., near Union St.* ☏ *415/563–0307* ✛ *3:C6*), not far from Fort Mason and the Exploratorium, caters to older kids and their parents with mile-high burgers and giant salads. But Barney's doesn't forget "kids under 8," who have their own menu featuring a burger, an all-beef frank, chicken strips with ranch dressing, and more. The Ferry Building (✛ *1:G4*) on the Embarcadero has plenty of kid-friendly options, from **Mijita Cocina Mexicana**, which has its own kids' menu, to **Gott's Roadside Tray Gourmet**, for burgers, shakes, and more. (And the outdoor access can help keep the little ones entertained.) The Mission has dozens of no-frills taco-and-burrito parlors; especially worthy is bustling **La Corneta** (⊠ *2731 Mission St., between 23rd and 24th Sts.* ☏ *415/252–9560* ✛ *2:F6*), which has a baby burrito. Banana splits and hot-fudge sundaes are what **St. Francis Fountain** (⊠ *2801 24th St., at York St.* ☏ *415/826–4200* ✛ *3:H6*) is known for, along with its vintage decor (and popularity with hipsters for weekend brunch). Opened in 1918, it recalls the early 1950s, and the menu, with its burgers, BLTs, grilled-cheese sandwiches, and chili with corn bread, is timeless. In Lower Haight, the small **Rosamunde Sausage Grill** (⊠ *545 Haight St., between Steiner and Fillmore Sts.* ☏ *415/437–6851* ✛ *3:D3*) serves just that—a slew of different sausages, from Polish to duck to Weisswurst (Bavarian veal). You get your choice of two toppings, like grilled onions, sauerkraut, and chili, and since there are only six stools, plan on takeout. Hint: head to nearby Duboce Park, with its cute playground.

Finally, both kids and adults love to be by the ocean, and the **Park Chalet** (⊠ *1000 Great Hwy., at Fulton St.* ☏ *415/386–8439* ✛ *3:A3*), hidden behind the two-story Beach Chalet, offers pizza, mac and cheese, sticky ribs, and a big banana split.

New French, and all the dishes are laced with fancy ingredients, leaving diners struggling to choose between foie gras, langoustines, and squab. In fall, when northern Italy's exquisite white truffles are in season, Short typically puts together a tasting menu that tucks them into every course, including dessert, which in a past season featured a white-truffle ice-cream float. Wine drinkers are bound to find something that suits them, with an award-winning list that includes many small-production wines from around the globe. Be prepared for a decidedly stuffy, though not suffocating, atmosphere (a jacket is preferred for gentlemen). ☒ *Hotel Vintage Court, 648 Bush St., Nob Hill* ☎ *415/989–7154* ⊕ *www. masasrestaurant.com* ⚄ *Reservations essential* ☼ *Closed Sun. and Mon. No lunch* ✛ *4:F2.*

$$$$ ✕ **Ritz-Carlton Dining Room.** The Ritz's formal Dining Room, with French
FRENCH windows, fine linens, and an encyclopedic wine list, serves only prix-fixe French seasonal dinners with a Japanese accent, priced by the number of courses (three and nine: $74 and $125; reservations essential for nine-course menu). The tariff is ski-slope steep, but the food—abalone, foie gras with huckleberries, salsify ravioli with lobster mushrooms—and service are worth it. ☒ *600 Stockton St., Nob Hill* ☎ *415/773–6198* ⌂ *Jacket required* ☼ *Closed Sun. and Mon. No lunch* ✛ *4:F6.*

RUSSIAN HILL

$$$$ ✕ **La Folie.** This small, *très* Parisian establishment has long been a favor-
FRENCH ite of Francophiles (and anyone who loves foie gras). The restaurant, outfitted in warm woods, copper tones, and white linens, is smartly designed to let chef-owner Roland Passot's whimsical cuisine take center stage. Choose from well-apportioned prix-fixe menus of three, four, or five courses ($75, $85, and $95, respectively). The dishes, such as a napoleon of Dungeness crab salad with a coconut and curry panna cotta or the rôti of squab and quail wrapped in crisp and thin potato, are artfully presented and delicious. Vegetarians will be happy to discover a menu of their own ($75). Such rarefied preparation is costly, of course, so you may want to save La Folie for a special occasion. Everyone will enjoy the complimentary petit fours that arrive at the end of the meal. (La Folie Lounge just next door has cocktails and small plates on the menu—you can also order à la carte off La Folie's menu.) ☒ *2316 Polk St., Russian Hill* ☎ *415/776–5577* ⊕ *www.lafolie.com* ☼ *Closed Sun. No lunch* ✛ *2:H3.*

VAN NESS/POLK

$$$$ ✕ **Acquerello.** For years, devotees of chef-owner Suzette Gresham-
ITALIAN Tognetti's high-end but soulful Italian cooking have been swooning
Fodor's Choice over her incomparable Parmesan *budino* (pudding), ridged pasta with
★ foie gras and truffles, and veal loin rolled and stuffed with seasonal vegetables. Dishes are complex, refined, and also feature some cutting-edge touches and techniques. Dinners are prix-fixe, with three ($64), four ($78), or five ($90) courses and at least six choices within each course. Tognetti also tempts with a chef's eight-course tasting menu ($180, with wine pairings). The cheese course is definitely worth saving room for. Co-owner Giancarlo Paterlini (and his son) oversee the

13

service and the list of Italian wines, both of which are superb. The room, with its vaulted ceiling and terra-cotta and pale-ocher palette, suits the refined food. This is a true San Francisco dining gem that is worth every penny. ✉ *1722 Sacramento St., Van Ness/Polk* ☎ *415/567–5432* ⊕ *www.acquerello.com* ⊗ *Closed Sun. and Mon. No lunch* ✢ *2:H5.*

$$
VIETNAMESE

✕ **Bodega Bistro.** This casual Vietnamese bistro, located on the mildly sketchy edge of the Tenderloin, brims at lunchtime with savvy eaters from Civic Center offices who come in for steaming bowls of pho (the beef versions are some of the best in town). For dinner, groups of diners overload their tables with green papaya salad, roast squab, *bun cha Hanoi* (broiled pork, herbs, rice vermicelli, and lettuce wrapped in rice paper), and salt-and-pepper Dungeness crab with garlic noodles, the latter priced for a special occasion. You'll see many French touches on the extensive Vietnamese menu here. ✉ *607 Larkin St., Van Ness/Polk* ☎ *415/921–1218* ✢ *4:A6.*

$$$$
STEAKHOUSE

✕ **Harris'.** Red-meat connoisseurs will appreciate this old-school restaurant, home to some of the best dry-aged steaks in town, including pricey American Kobe rib eye. Harris' ages all of its beef for 21 days; proof of the process is visible from the street through a window where large cuts are displayed. There are a dozen steaks to choose from, plus grilled chops, chicken, and a couple of seafood dishes for anyone who wants to steer clear of beef. Don't overlook the classic sides: creamed spinach, caramelized onions, and sautéed mushrooms. If you're a martini or Manhattan drinker, take this opportunity to enjoy an artful example of the legendary cocktails. (The lounge is also a fun scene for a cocktail and a steak.) And if you want to try to cook this top-notch beef yourself, you can pick up raw steaks to go at the well-stocked beef counter. ✉ *2100 Van Ness Ave., Van Ness/Polk* ☎ *415/673–1888* ⊕ *www. harrisrestaurant.com* ⌂ *Reservations essential* ⊗ *No lunch* ✢ *2:H4.*

$$
MIDDLE EASTERN

✕ **Helmand Palace.** In late 2007 this popular—and popularly priced—restaurant moved from a scruffy block of Broadway in North Beach to a smaller Van Ness address and added "Palace" to its name, but kept everything else—authentic Afghan cooking and a handsomely outfitted dining room—intact. Highlights of the reasonably priced menu include *aushak* (leek-filled ravioli served with yogurt and ground beef), pumpkin with yogurt-and-garlic sauce, and the half lamb rack with sautéed eggplant and rice served on Afghan flat bread. Basmati rice pudding, perfumed with cardamom and pistachio, is an exotic finish. ✉ *2424 Van Ness Ave., Van Ness/Polk* ☎ *415/362–0641* ⊕ *www.helmandpalace. com* ⊗ *No lunch* ✢ *2:F3.*

$
THAI

✕ **Lers Ros.** Diners who navigate a somewhat sketchy neighborhood to get to one of the city's most authentic Thai restaurants are richly rewarded. Skip the "same old" familiar dishes like pad thai and take this opportunity to try something new—Thai herb sausage and sliced pork shoulder are good appetizers to share. The pork belly with crispy rind and basil leaves and *duck larb* (meat salad) come packed with flavor—speaking of which, the menu is full of sinus-clearing dishes, so be sure to specify how hot you can really handle it. If you come in a group, you'll be able to try more dishes on the lengthy menu. There are nightly late hours and free delivery as well. The room is a bit nondescript, but is contemporary and clean (with some quirky pop music playing in the background). ✉ *730 Larkin St., Van Ness/Polk* ☎ *415/931–6917* 🌐 *www.lersros.com* ✣ *4:A5.*

$ VIETNAMESE ✕ **Pagolac.** Savvy diners know that Pagolac serves a great "seven-way beef" dinner, the classic south Vietnamese feast of seven different beef dishes for an unbelievable $16 per person (two-person minimum). This is also a good place for lotus-root salad with pink shrimp, all kinds of rolls, the shrimp with sugarcane, aromatic clay pots, and noodles or rice topped with protein—pork, beef, shrimp, chicken—in all forms—fried, shredded, grilled. The narrow space is decorated in dark-wood tables and chairs and a few nice pieces of Vietnamese art, and the service, though sometimes a little ragged, is always friendly. Of course, such low prices and good food haven't remained a secret, so come before 6 or after 9 to avoid a long wait. ✉ *655 Larkin St., Van Ness/Polk* ☎ *415/776–3234* ▭ *No credit cards* ⏲ *Closed Mon. No lunch* ✣ *4:A6.*

$$ SEAFOOD Fodor's Choice ★ ✕ **Swan Oyster Depot.** Half fish market and half diner, this small, slim, family-run seafood operation, open since 1912, has no tables, only a narrow marble counter with about a dozen-and-a-half stools. Most people come in to buy perfectly fresh salmon, halibut, crabs, and other seafood to take home. Everyone else hops onto one of the rickety stools to enjoy a bowl of clam chowder—the only hot food served—a dozen oysters, half a cracked crab, a slice of crusty sourdough, a big shrimp salad, or a smaller shrimp cocktail. Come early or late to avoid a long wait. ✉ *1517 Polk St., Van Ness/Polk* ☎ *415/673–1101* ✍ *Reservations not accepted* ▭ *No credit cards* ⏲ *Closed Sun. No dinner* ✣ *2:H5.*

NORTH BEACH

$$ ITALIAN ✕ **Capp's Corner.** One of North Beach's last family-style trattorias, Capp's is steadfastly old-fashioned. The men at the bar still roll dice for drinks, celebrity photos line the walls, and diners sit elbow-to-elbow at long, oilcloth-covered tables. The fare is packaged in bountiful five-course family-style dinners for $20.50, with pasta dishes like veal tortellini, and the roast lamb a good choice for the main (the tasty osso buco and polenta is $5 more). The food isn't award-winning, but a meal here won't break the bank either. A three-course option, good for smaller appetites—and smaller budgets ($18)—includes minestrone, salad, and choice of pasta (or you can skip the family-style format and get the trio of courses for $15.50). For $4 more, you can finish with an order of spumoni. Kids under 10 will be happy with their own menu priced at $13. ✉ *1600 Powell St., North Beach* ☎ *415/989–2589* 🌐 *www.cappscorner.com* ✣ *1:C3.*

$$$$ NEW AMERICAN Fodor's Choice ★ ✕ **Coi.** Daniel Patterson, who has made a name for himself both as a chef and as a pundit on contemporary restaurant trends, has created a destination restaurant, an intriguing 50-seat spot on the gritty end of Broadway. Coi (pronounced *kwa*) is really two restaurants. One is an intimate 30-seat formal dining room—ascetic gold-taupe banquettes on two walls—that offers an 11-course tasting menu ($135). The highly seasonal and obsessively sourced food matches the space in sophistication, with such inspired dishes as chilled fennel consommé with sea urchin and purslane, Prather Ranch beef with black garlic, and

Monterey Bay abalone with nettle-dandelion salsa verde. The menu in the more casual—and more casually priced—lounge is à la carte, with fewer than a dozen items, including a crisp-skinned roast chicken, a bowl of udon noodles, and a grilled Gruyère cheese sandwich (and you don't need reservations to nab a seat). ⊠ *373 Broadway, North Beach* ☎ *415/393–9000* ⊕ *www.coirestaurant.com* ⚲ *Reservations not accepted for lounge* ⊘ *Closed Sun. and Mon. No lunch* ✚ *1:E3.*

$

ITALIAN

☺

Fodor'sChoice

★

✕ **L'Osteria del Forno.** A staff chattering in Italian and seductive aromas drifting from the open kitchen make customers who pass through the door of this modest storefront, with its sunny yellow walls and friendly waitstaff, feel as if they've stumbled into a homey trattoria in Italy. Each day the kitchen produces small plates of simply cooked vegetables (grilled radicchio wrapped in prosciutto, roasted carrots, and fennel), a few pastas, a daily special or two, milk-braised pork, a roast of the day, creamy polenta, and thin-crust pizzas—including a memorable "white" pie topped with porcini mushrooms and mozzarella. (All the hot dishes come out of an oven—no stove here, so don't come expecting a large selection of pastas.) Wine drinkers will find a good match for any dish they order on the all-Italian list, which showcases gems from limited-production vineyards. At lunch try one of North Beach's best focaccia sandwiches. ⊠ *519 Columbus Ave., North Beach* ☎ *415/982–1124* ⊕ *www.losteriadelforno.com* ▭ *No credit cards* ⊘ *Closed Tues.* ✚ *1:D3.*

$$

MIDDLE EASTERN

✕ **Maykadeh.** Although it sits in an Italian neighborhood, this authentic Persian restaurant has a large and faithful following of homesick Iranian émigrés. Lamb dishes with rice are the specialties, served in an attractive but not showy dining room. Among the many appetizers are traditional dishes such as eggplant with mint sauce, pickled vegetables, and saffron-and-lime-spiced lamb tongue. Along with the requisite—and tasty—kebabs, the restaurant serves a variety of poultry and meats marinated in olive oil, lime juice, and herbs (the tender chicken joojeh kebab is particularly delicious). Anyone looking for a hearty, traditional main dish should order *ghorme sabzee,* lamb shank braised with a bouquet of Middle Eastern spices, or *baghali polo,* lamb shank with fava beans and rice served only on Sunday. Give yourself plenty of time here, as service occasionally slows to a crawl. The affordable valet parking is a bonus. ⊠ *470 Green St., North Beach* ☎ *415/362–8286* ⊕ *www.maykadehrestaurant.com* ✚ *1:D3.*

$$$

ITALIAN

✕ **Rose Pistola.** This busy spot is named for one of North Beach's most revered barkeeps (and fortunately the cocktails here are excellent), while the food celebrates the neighborhood's early Ligurian settlers. The menu changes daily, but a large assortment of antipasti—grilled octopus with fennel and arugula; bruschetta with figs and prosciutto—and pizzas from the wood-burning oven are favorites, as are the cioppino and the fresh fish of the day, served in various ways. A big bar area opens onto the sidewalk, and an exhibition kitchen lets you keep an eye on your order. Even though the kitchen has had trouble holding on to a good chef, the service sometimes arrives with attitude, and the tab can shoot up pretty fast, the style and sometimes-winning items on the menu seem to keep the tourist-heavy crowds coming. ⊠ *532 Columbus Ave., North Beach* ☎ *415/399–0499* ⊕ *www.rosepistolasf.com* ✢ *1:D3.*

$$ ✕**Tommaso's.** This is the site of San Francisco's first wood-fired pizza
PIZZA oven, installed in 1935 when the restaurant opened. The oven is still
☺ here, and the restaurant, with its coat hooks, boothlike dining nooks,
and communal table running the length of the basement dining room,
has changed little since those early days. The pizzas' delightfully chewy
crusts, creamy mozzarella, and full-bodied house-made sauce have kept
legions of happy eaters returning for decades. Pair one of the hearty pies
with a salad of grilled sweet peppers, green beans, or broccoli dressed
in lemon juice and olive oil and a bottle of the house wine. There are
also a variety of classic pasta dishes, and baked chicken and veal dishes.
If you have room—and you may not if you ordered a small pizza for
yourself—treat yourself to tiramisu. ⊠ *1042 Kearny St., North Beach*
☎ *415/398–9696* ⊕ *www.tomassos.com* ⌕ *Reservations not accepted*
☽ *Closed Mon. No lunch* ✢ *1:D3.*

THE WATERFRONT

FISHERMAN'S WHARF

$$$$ ✕**Gary Danko.** Be prepared to wait your turn for a table behind chef
NEW AMERICAN Gary Danko's legion of loyal fans, who typically keep the reservation
Fodor'sChoice book chock-full here (plan on reserving two months in advance). The
★ cost of a meal ($68–$102) is pegged to the number of courses, from
three to five. The decadent menu, which changes seasonally, may include
risotto with lobster and rock shrimp, seared foie gras with Fuji apples,
braised veal breast with sweetbreads, and quail stuffed with mushrooms
and quinoa. A diet-destroying chocolate soufflé with two sauces is usu-
ally among the desserts. So, too, is a "no-cholesterol" Grand Marnier
soufflé with raspberry sorbet, perfect for diners with a conscience or a
heart problem. The wine list is the size of a small-town phone book,
and the banquette-lined room, with beautiful wood floors and stunning
(but restrained) floral arrangements, is as memorable as the food. ⊠ *800
N. Point St., Fisherman's Wharf* ☎ *415/749–2060* ⊕ *www.garydanko.
com* ⌕ *Reservations essential* ☽ *No lunch* ✢ *1:A1.*

EMBARCADERO

$$$$ ✕**Boulevard.** Two of San Francisco's top restaurant celebrities—chef
AMERICAN Nancy Oakes and designer Pat Kuleto—are responsible for this high-
Fodor'sChoice profile, high-priced eatery in the magnificent 1889 Audiffred Build-
★ ing, a Parisian look-alike and one of the few downtown structures
to survive the 1906 earthquake. Kuleto's Belle Époque interior and
Oakes's sophisticated American food with a French accent attract well-
dressed locals and flush out-of-towners. The menu changes seasonally,
but count on standout appetizers and generous portions of dishes like
gnocchi and Maine lobster, pan-roasted halibut with three side dishes
(grains, squash blossoms, and spinach), and wood-grilled extra-thick
pork chop with roasted heirloom apples. Save room (and calories) for
one of the dynamite desserts, such as caramelized apple brioche pud-
ding. There's counter seating for folks too hungry to wait for a table,
and an American Kobe and Chianina beef burger at lunchtime that lets

13

you eat with the swells without raiding your piggy bank. The well-chosen wine list and excellent service are also hallmarks here. ⊠ *1 Mission St., Embarcadero* ☎ *415/543–6084* ⊕ *www.boulevardrestaurant.com* ⌒ *Reservations essential* ⊘ *No lunch weekends* ✛ *1:G4.*

$$$$
STEAKHOUSE

✕ **Epic Roasthouse.** "Epic" describes it all: the outsize dining room, the 7-foot flywheel and pulley that sits in the middle of it (an homage to old bay-side pump houses), the mile-wide bay view, the huge metal fireplace, the hearty slabs of meat, and, alas, the prices. This is the latest venture, along with the seafood-theme Waterbar right next door, of famed restaurant architect-owner Pat Kuleto. Chef Jan Birnbaum, who made his name first in San Francisco and later in the Napa Valley, is in charge of putting $46 New York strip steaks and $20 burgers on the fire. There are also seafood, duck, and plenty of other non-beef dishes. For sides, he has opted for sautéed spinach with garlic confit over classic creamed spinach, and you can take your pick from five different preparations of potatoes. If you don't have a Texas-size wallet but still want an Epic experience, head upstairs to the Quiver bar and graze from the rather extensive bar menu, served only until 8 pm. Weekend brunch has a variety of options, and that expansive view of the bay. ⊠ *369 Embarcadero, between Folsom and Harrison Sts., Embarcadero* ☎ *415/369–9955* ⊕ *www.epicroasthousesf.com* ⊘ *No lunch weekends* ✛ *1:H5.*

$$
AMERICAN
☾

✕ **Fog City Diner.** This fully chromed destination is a far cry from the no-frills diner of Edward Hopper's *Nighthawks*. Fog City has all the trappings of a luxurious railroad car: wood paneling, huge windows, comfortable booths, and attentive staff. The menu is both classic and contemporary, and includes cheddar biscuits; mac-and-cheese made with three cheeses; cornmeal-crusted oysters with sriracha rémoulade; a pork T-bone; cioppino; a half-pound burger with a choice of cheese; and milk shakes and root-beer floats. Locals complain of too many out-of-towners, but plenty of folks who call San Francisco home fill the booths at lunch and dinner. ⊠ *1300 Battery St., Embarcadero* ☎ *415/982–2000* ⊕ *www.fogcitydiner.com* ✛ *1:E2.*

$$
SEAFOOD

✕ **Hog Island Oyster Company.** Hog Island, a thriving oyster farm in Tomales Bay, north of San Francisco, serves up its harvest at this attractive raw bar and retail shop in the busy Ferry Building. The U-shape counter and a handful of tables seat no more than three dozen diners, who come here for impeccably fresh oysters (from Hog Island and elsewhere) or clams (from Hog Island) on the half shell. Other mollusk-centered options include a first-rate oyster stew, clam chowder, and "steamer" clams with Israeli couscous. The bar also turns out what is arguably the best grilled-cheese sandwich (with three artisanal cheeses on artisanal bread) this side of Wisconsin. You need to eat early, however, as the bar closes at 8 on weekdays and 6 on weekends. Happy hour, 5 to 7 on Monday and Thursday, is an oyster lover's dream and jam-packed: chef's choice of oysters for a buck apiece and beer for $3.50. ⊠ *Ferry Bldg., Embarcadero at Market St., Embarcadero* ☎ *415/391–7117* ⊕ *www.hogislandoysters.com* ✛ *1:G4.*

$$$
LATIN AMERICAN

✕ **La Mar Cebicheria Peruana.** This casually chic restaurant, set right on the water's edge, is divided into three areas: a lounge with a long ceviche

13

bar where diners watch chefs put together their plates; the savvy Pisco Bar facing the Embarcadero, where mixologists make a dozen different cocktails based on Peru's famed Pisco brandy; and a bright blue and whitewashed dining room overlooking an outdoor patio and the bay. The waiter starts you out with a pile of potato and plantain chips with three dipping sauces, but then you're on your own, choosing from a long list of ceviches, can't-miss *causas* (whipped potatoes topped with a choice of fish, shellfish, or vegetable salads), and everything from crisp, lightly deep-fried fish and shellfish to soups and stews and rice dishes, many spiked with Peruvian chilies. The original La Mar is in Lima, Peru. San Francisco is the first stop in its campaign to open a string of cebicherias across the United States and Latin America. ⊠ *Pier 1½ between Washington and Jackson Sts., Embarcadero* ☎ *415/397–8880* ⊕ *www.lamarcebicheria.com* ✛ *1:F3.*

¢   ✗ **Mijita Cocina Mexicana**. Famed local chef Traci Des Jardins is the culi-
MEXICAN   nary powerhouse behind one of the city's best-known white-tablecloth
☯   restaurants, Jardinière. But to honor her Latin roots, she chose Mexican hot chocolate over martinis when she opened this casual taquería and weekend brunch spot. The tacos feature handmade corn tortillas and fillings like *carnitas* (slow-cooked pork), mahimahi, and *carne asada* (grilled strips of marinated meat). The superb meatball soup and Oaxacan chicken tamales are served daily, and the weekend brings breakfast favorites like *chilaquiles* and *huevos rancheros*, classic Mexican dishes with eggs, tortillas, and salsa. Kid-size burritos (beans and cheese) and quesadillas will keep your niños happy. Ingredients are purchased from suppliers whose foods are produced in a sustainable manner, making prices here a bit higher than at many Mexican eateries, but you can feel good about where those pennies go. Seating is simple—wooden tables and benches—but some outside tables offer a perfect perch for watching gulls on the bay. Plan to eat dinner early; Mijita closes at 7 on weekdays, 8 on weekends. (There is a second location with a full bar and later hours near the AT&T Park.) ⊠ *Ferry Bldg., Embarcadero at Market St., Embarcadero* ☎ *415/399–0814* ⊕ *www.mijitasf.com* ☾ *No dinner Sun.* ✛ *1:G4.*

$$$ ✗ **One Market**. A giant among American chefs, Bradley Ogden runs an
AMERICAN   upscale mini–restaurant chain that stretches from Marin County to San Diego. This large space with a bay view and a grown-up ambience is his well-known San Francisco outpost. (He also boasts a steak house in the downtown Westfield Centre.) The two-tier dining room seats 170— many of them suits brokering deals—and serves a seasonal, wonderfully homey yet refined menu that might include tender bacon-wrapped pork tenderloin with dandelion greens, olive oil–poached black cod, and roasted Liberty Farms duck breast and leg confit. Folks who want only a small sweet to finish can choose from a half dozen mini-desserts, such as chocolate toffee almond cake, a mint chip ice-cream bar, or butterscotch pudding. The wine list includes the best California labels, many by the glass. Hearty appetites will appreciate the three-course market menu for just $39. Business types on a budget can opt for the two-course lunch for $22.50. ⊠ *1 Market St., Embarcadero* ☎ *415/777–5577* ⊕ *www. onemarket.com* ☾ *Closed Sun. No lunch Sat.* ✛ *1:F4.*

$$$
SPANISH

✕ **Piperade.** Longtime San Francisco chef Gerald Hirogoyen serves a French Basque menu full of the rustic dishes of his childhood. Among them are garlic soup with rock shrimp, bacon, bread, and egg; cold poached foie gras with apple compote; *pipérade* (cooked peppers and tomatoes served with serrano ham and poached egg); warm sheep's-milk cheese–and-ham terrine; and lamb chops with white beans. Try a Basque wine from the impressive list, and don't miss the featherweight orange-blossom beignets or the pastry cream–filled gâteau basque with cherry preserves. Service in the typically packed dining room is professional without being stuffy. Hirogoyen also operates a small café and take-out operation around the corner and the small-plates Bocadillos in the Financial District. ⊠ *1015 Battery St., Embarcadero* ☎ *415/391-2555* ⊕ *www.piperade.com* ☉ *Closed Sun. No lunch Sat.* ✚ *1:E3.*

$$$
VIETNAMESE

✕ **Slanted Door.** If you're looking for homey Vietnamese food served in a down-to-earth dining room at a decent price, *don't* stop here. Celebrated chef-owner Charles Phan has mastered the upmarket, Western-accented Vietnamese menu. To showcase his cuisine, he chose a big space with sleek wooden tables and chairs, white marble floors, a cocktail lounge, a bar, and an enviable bay view. Among his popular dishes are green papaya salad, daikon rice cakes, cellophane crab noodles, chicken clay pot, and shaking beef (tender beef cubes with garlic and onion). Alas, the crush of fame means that no one speaking in a normal voice can be heard. To avoid the midday and evening crowds (and to save some bucks), stop in for the afternoon-tea menu (spring rolls, grilled pork over rice noodles), or visit Out the Door, Phan's take-out counter around the corner from the restaurant. A second Out the Door, complete with table service, is in the Westfield Centre downtown, and a third one, again with table service, is a popular location in the Lower Pacific Heights. ⊠ *Ferry Bldg., Embarcadero at Market St., Embarcadero* ☎ *415/861–8032* ⊕ *www.slanteddoor.com* ◿ *Reservations essential* ✚ *1:G4.*

$$$$
SEAFOOD

✕ **Waterbar.** When you walk in the door of Waterbar, there's no mistaking what's on the menu. The 200-seat dining room is dominated by sky-high aquariums filled with candidates—or at least cousins of candidates (the kitchen has its own aquariums)—for your dinner plate. Every fin and shell is sustainably sourced, so there's no guilt in sitting down to a plate of roasted petrale sole, pan-seared scallops, or grilled Pacific swordfish. Waterbar, like its next-door neighbor, Epic Roasthouse, is part of the steadily expanding empire of high-energy architect-restaurateur Pat Kuleto. Chef Parke Ulrich, who spent a decade at the city's celebrated seafood palace Farallon, dishes up the catch raw, cured, and cooked in dozens of ways, while nationally acclaimed pastry chef Emily Luchetti handles the sweet end of the menu. If you want to experience this watery world and can't afford the spendy seafood, grab a seat in the bar, where you can snack off the bar menu and take in the drop-dead bay view (there's also a $1 oyster happy hour daily 11:30 am–6 pm). ⊠ *399 Embarcadero, between Folsom and Harrison Sts., Embarcadero* ☎ *415/284–9922* ⊕ *www.waterbarsf.com* ✚ *1:H5.*

THE MARINA AND THE PRESIDIO

$$$
ITALIAN
Fodor's Choice
★

✕ **A16.** Marina residents—and, judging from the crowds, everybody else—gravitate to this lively trattoria, named for the autostrada that winds through Italy's sunny south. The kitchen serves the food of Naples and surrounding Campania, such as burrata with olive oil and crostini and crisp-crust pizzas, including a classic Neapolitan Margherita (mozzarella, tomato, and basil). Among the regularly changing mains are rustic pastas like *maccaronara* with *ragu napoletana* and house-made ricotta salata, and grilled yellowtail with cherry tomato and fennel *agrodolce* (sweet-and-sour sauce). A big wine list of primarily southern Italian with some California wines suits the fare perfectly. The long space includes an animated bar scene near the door; ask for a table in the quieter alcove at the far end. Reservations are easier to snag midweek. ⊠ *2355 Chestnut St., Marina* ☎ *415/771–2216* ⊕ *www. a16sf.com* ☉ *No lunch Sat.–Tues.* ✛ *2:D2.*

13

$$
VEGETARIAN

✕ **Greens Restaurant.** Owned and operated by the San Francisco Zen Center, this nonprofit vegetarian restaurant gets some of its fresh produce from the center's famous organic Green Gulch Farm. Floor-to-ceiling windows give diners a sweeping view of the Marina and the Golden Gate Bridge. Despite the lack of meat, hearty dishes like a risotto with seasonal vegetables, or the ample vegetable brochette plate really satisfy. Other standouts include thin-crust pizza with local cheese, potato, and grilled onions; and the salads really are something special, especially the wilted spinach salad with croutons, feta, and olives. An à la carte menu is offered on Sunday and weeknights, but on Saturday a $49 four-course prix-fixe dinner is served. Sunday brunch is a good time to watch boaters on the bay. A small counter just inside the front door stocks sandwiches, soups, and sweets for easy takeout (and it's open in the morning). ⊠ *Bldg. A, Fort Mason, enter across Marina Blvd. from Safeway, Marina* ☎ *415/771–6222* ⊕ *www.greensrestaurant.com* ☉ *No lunch Sun. and Mon.* ✛ *2:G1.*

$$
FRENCH

✕ **Isa.** Past Isa's tiny storefront dining room is a heated, candlelit patio that consistently draws couples on date night, ladies night out, and groups of friends celebrating birthdays. The extensive menu of French-inspired tapas is known for its seared foie gras, flat-iron steak, potato-wrapped sea bass, and veal-sweetbreads-and-mushroom fricassee. Portions are small plates designed to be shared instead of full-size entrées, so hearty appetites can run up a sizable tab. A good way to keep your costs down is to opt for the three-course prix-fixe menu offered Monday through Thursday for $29. The wine list includes some affordable by-the-glass choices. ⊠ *3324 Steiner St., Marina* ☎ *415/567–9588* ⊕ *www.isarestaurant.com* ☉ *Closed Sun. No lunch* ✛ *2:E3.*

$$
SPANISH

✕ **Tacolicious.** This Mexican Marina hotspot draws a young and energetic crowd that fuels up on equal parts tacos and tequila. The menu uses many local and sustainable ingredients, but still keeps it affordable (and crowd pleasing, with chili con carne and taquitos). Tables are usually laden with made-to-order guacamole and platters of well-stuffed tacos (the carnitas and short-rib versions are especially full of flavor). You'll also see groups ordering rounds of "chupitos," easy-to-drink shots of tequila mixed with juices, from prickly pair to passion fruit. The *pan* *con chocolate* is a holdover from the previous restaurant's incarnation for a good reason—it's a delicious finish. If you are hard of hearing or don't want to speak in a raised voice, this is not the restaurant for you, unless you land one of the few outside tables. ⊠ *2031 Chestnut St., Marina* 🕾 *415/346–1966* ⊕ *www.tacolicioussf.com* ⊹ *2:E2.*

COW HOLLOW

$$ ✕**Betelnut.** Most of the primarily young, hip crowd that packs this Union
ASIAN Street landmark probably don't know what a betel nut is (the seed of an Asian palm, chewed for the mild high it delivers). But they do know they like the Pan-Asian cuisine and adventurous drinks (everything from martinis to house-brewed rice beer and sake flights). The menu, divided into big and small plates, noodles, dumplings, and salads, includes chili-crusted calamari, spicy Chinese green beans, sea bass "cha ca la vong" prepared table-side, plus a memorable beggar's chicken baked in clay. Tuesday nights feature a special roast pork dinner. Lacquered walls, bamboo ceiling fans, and period posters create a comfortably exotic mood that matches the food. Patience is required to cope with long wait times and the occasional noise from large parties. ⊠ *2030 Union St., Cow Hollow* 🕾 *415/929–8855* ⊕ *www.betelnutrestaurant.com* ⊹ *2:F3.*

$$ ✕**Rose's Café.** Sleepy-headed locals turn up at Rose's for the break-
ITALIAN fast pizza of smoked ham, eggs, and fontina; house-baked pastries and
🕘 breads; poached eggs with Yukon Gold potato and mushroom hash; or soft polenta with mascarpone and jam. Midday is time for a roasted chicken and fontina sandwich; pizza with eggplant, roasted peppers, and smoked mozzarella; or linguine with clams. Evening hours find customers eating their way through more pizza and pasta if they are on a budget, and skirt steak and roasted chicken if they aren't. The ingredients are top-notch, the service is friendly, and the seating is in comfortable booths, at tables, and at a counter. At the outside tables, overhead heaters keep you toasty when the temperature dips. Expect long lines for Sunday brunch. ⊠ *2298 Union St., Cow Hollow* 🕾 *415/775–2200* ⊕ *www.rosescafesf.com* ⊹ *2:E3.*

$$$ ✕**Terzo.** With its zinc tapas bar, fireplace, big communal table, and mix
MEDITERRANEAN of leather banquettes and oak tables, Terzo has what it takes to pull in the neighborhood social set and everyone else who appreciates expertly prepared Mediterranean fare. The restaurant is known for its small-plates menu, but also offers full-size entrées. On the compact, seasonally shifting menu you might find creamy hummus and warmed-to-order pita, chanterelles with crisp polenta and pecorino, grilled calamari with lentils, chicken spiedini, and wild mahimahi with garbanzos and *charmoula* sauce (spicy Moroccan sauce). But a plate of seriously addictive onion strings is available year-round. The extensive wine list is loaded with interesting vintners and varietals (some of them on the pricey side). Choosing from a handful of aperitifs—Lillet, Dubonnet, sherry, vermouth—is a good way to start your meal. ⊠ *3011 Steiner St., Cow Hollow* 🕾 *415/441–3200* ⊕ *www.terzosf.com* ☽ *No lunch* ⊹ *2:E3.*

THE HAIGHT, THE CASTRO AND NOE VALLEY

THE HAIGHT

$$ ✕**Indian Oven.** This white-tablecloth northern Indian restaurant draws

INDIAN diners from all over the city who come for the tandoori specialties—chicken, lamb, breads. Classics like *saag paneer* (spinach with Indian cheese), *aloo gobhi* (potato, cauliflower, and spices), and *bengan bartha* (roasted eggplant with onions and spices) are also excellent. The chef wants to keep his clientele around for the long haul, too, and puts a little "heart healthy" icon next to some of the menu items. On Friday and Saturday nights famished patrons overflow onto the sidewalk as they wait for open tables. If you try to linger over a mango *lassi* or an order of the excellent *kheer* (rice pudding) on one of these nights, you'll probably be hurried along by a waiter. For better service, come on a slower weeknight. ✉ *233 Fillmore St., Lower Haight* ☎ *415/626–1628* ⊕ *www.indianovensf.com* ✆ *No lunch* ✛ *3:D3.*

$$$ ✕**Nopa.** In the mid-2000s North of the Panhandle became the city's

AMERICAN newest talked-about neighborhood in part because of the big, bustling Nopa, which is cleverly named after it. This casual space, with its high ceilings, concrete floor, long bar, and sea of tables, suits the high-energy crowd of young suits mixed with stylish neighborhood residents that fill it every night (and since the kitchen doesn't close until 1 am, plenty of restaurant industry types come in late into the night). Diners come primarily for the rustic fare, like an irresistible flat bread topped with fennel sausage and chanterelles; the vegetable tagine with lemon yogurt; smoky, crisp-skinned rotisserie chicken; a juicy grass-fed hamburger with thick-cut fries; one of the city's best pork chops; and for dessert, the donutlike sopapillas. But they also love the lively spirit of the place. Unfortunately, that buzz sometimes means that raised voices are the only way to communicate with fellow diners. A big communal table and the friendly bar ease the way for anyone dining out on his or her own. Wine lovers are happily satisfied here, and weekend brunch is another hit. ✉ *560 Divisadero St., Haight* ☎ *415/864–8643* ⊕ *www. nopasf.com* ✆ *No lunch* ✛ *3:B3.*

$$ ✕**Nopalito.** This is one of the more unusual Mexican restaurants in

MEXICAN the city. The menu features authentic recipes prepared skillfully with excellent ingredients, from a bright ceviche and seasonal salads to the succulent pork carnitas and a fulfilling posole. All the tortillas are made from an organic house-ground masa (so good as tortilla chips in the *chilaquiles* during lunchtime). It's a casual space with a variety of tables, communal seating, and a counter; it's a popular spot with families (and the well-selected tequila list keeps the adults happy). Expect a steady wait in the evening—you'll have to leave your name on a wait-list, but you can call before heading over to get your name on the list in advance. There's also a take-out window if the wait proves to be too long. ✉ *306 Broderick St., Haight* ☎ *415/437–0303* ⊕ *www.nopalitosf. com* ✛ *3:B3.*

$$ ✕**Thep Phanom.** Long ago local food critics and restaurant goers began

THAI singing the praises of Thep Phanom. The tune hasn't stopped, except for an occasional sour note on rising prices. Duck is deliciously prepared in several ways—atop a mound of spinach, in a fragrant curry, minced

13

for salad. Seafood (in various guises) is another specialty, along with warm eggplant salad, fried tofu with peanut sauce, spicy beef salad, fried quail, and rich Thai curries. The lengthy regular menu is supplemented by a list of daily specials, which only makes it harder to make a decision. At least you'll be pondering your choices in comfortable surroundings: the cozy dining room is lined with Thai art and artifacts that owner Pathama Parikanont has collected over the years. ⊠ *400 Waller St., Lower Haight* ☎ *415/431–2526* ⊕ *www.thepphanom.com* ⊗ *No lunch* ✣ *3:D3.*

$ ✕ **Uva Enoteca.** A marble counter, a handful of banquettes, tables for two
ITALIAN and four, a long brick wall, a young, savvy staff—Uva has all the trappings of the perfectly casual Italian wine bar. The menu is straightforward: assortments of Italian cured meats and cheeses, about 10 salads and vegetable dishes, and six pizzas. The *piadine*—folded Italian flat breads stuffed with fillings like eggplant caponata, bitter greens, and pecorino—are both delicious and priced right at eight bucks each. Italian wine aficionados appreciate the more than 15 wines by the glass, available in two sizes, *assaggio* (2 ounces) and *quartino* (8 ounces), and a long list of bottles. Many of the vini are from small vineyards and all of them are carefully chosen. Even the gelato is special, made by a local artisan. There's a weekend brunch. ⊠ *568 Haight St., Lower Haight* ☎ *415/829–2024* ⊕ *www.uvaenoteca.com* ⊗ *No lunch.* ✣ *3:D3.*

THE CASTRO

$$ ✕ **2223 Restaurant.** Slip into the urbane 2223 on Tuesday when every
AMERICAN main course is just 12 bucks. The menu shifts with the seasons, with Thai-style lamb spring rolls, herb-roasted chicken with garlic mashed potatoes, and a luscious sour-cherry bread pudding with a scoop of vanilla ice cream among possible offerings. For its popular Sunday brunch, the restaurant spins out updated takes on old favorites, like eggs Benedict with house-smoked salmon and house-made chorizo and pepper-Jack scramble—all of them light enough that you won't be tempted to slink back to your hotel for a nap. ⊠ *2223 Market St., Castro* ☎ *415/431–0692* ⊕ *www.2223restaurant.com* ⊗ *No lunch* ✣ *3:C5.*

$ ✕ **Chow.** Wildly popular and consciously unpretentious, Chow is a
AMERICAN funky yet savvy diner where soporific standards like hamburgers, piz-
♻ zas, and spaghetti with meatballs are treated with culinary respect. A magnet for penny-pinchers, the restaurant has built its top-notch reputation on honest fare made with fresh local ingredients priced to sell. Salads, pastas, and mains come in two sizes to accommodate big and small appetites, there's a daily sandwich special, and kids can peruse their mini-menu. Because reservations are restricted to large parties, folks hoping to snag seats usually surround the doorway. Come early (before 6:30) or late (after 10) to reduce the wait, and don't even think about leaving without trying the ginger cake with caramel sauce. ⊠ *215 Church St., Castro* ☎ *415/552–2469* ⊕ *www.chowfoodbar.com* ✣ *3:C5.*

$$$ ✕ **Frances.** One of the hottest tickets in town is located, ironically, on
FRENCH a sleepy residential street in the Castro. Chef-owner Melissa Perello's menu of California and French cuisine is well executed, balanced, and notably affordable for the high quality. Bacon beignets, tender gnocchi, and a savory bavette steak are becoming favorites on the seasonally

driven menu. The small space is simply designed and casual, with a limited number of close tables (hence the difficulty in landing a reservation). Frances features a well-chosen wine list, and there's a small bar area for desperate diners who want to try their luck for a walk-in spot at the counter. ✉ *3870 17th St., Castro* ☎ *415/621–3870* ⊕ *www.frances-sf.com* ≈ *Reservations essential* ⊘ *Closed Mon. No lunch* ✛ *3:C5.*

$$ ✕ **Woodhouse Fish Co.** New Englanders hungry for a lobster-roll fix need
SEAFOOD look no further than this superfriendly spot, where the utterly authentic lobster rolls, properly served on a buttered top-loaded bun and accompanied with slaw and fries, come in two sizes, a 3-ouncer and a "mega" 6-ouncer. You'll also find fried Ipswich clams, crab cakes, fish-and-chips, clam chowder, and plenty more to keep East Coast seafood partisans smiling. When Dungeness crab season starts, come in for their fresh supply, excellent in a Louie salad. The restaurant's V-shape storefront, which stands on a busy Market Street corner, is all worn wood and paint and comfortably funky. On Tuesday, all day long, oysters are just a buck apiece. It seems like everyone in the neighborhood turns out for this delicious bargain, so be prepared to wait for a table. A second branch has now opened in Lower Pacific Heights. ✉ *2073 Market St., Castro* ☎ *415/437–2722* ⊕ *www.woodhousefish.com* ≈ *Reservations not accepted* ✛ *3:D4.*

NOE VALLEY

$$$ ✕ **Incanto.** The people who run Incanto are thoughtful. They filter, chill,
ITALIAN and carbonate the very good local tap water and serve it in eco-friendly reusable glass carafes. They use sustainably grown and harvested ingredients produced by local farmers. They even grow many of their own herbs in their rooftop garden. They are also adventurous, putting invariably tasty and offal-loaded dishes not found at many other restaurants in town on their daily-changing menu: acorn soup with duck livers and sage; corzetti ("stamped" pasta disks) with pig's trotter, foie gras, and dates; shaved tripe salad with Meyer lemon, chili, and parsley; braised veal breast with wild mushrooms; and bay leaf panna cotta. The recently renovated interior is casual and comfortable—with wood tables and chairs and large photographs on the walls—and is the perfect setting for the inspired fare, while the wine list of obscure Italian labels makes everything taste even better. ✉ *1550 Church St., at Duncan St., Noe Valley* ☎ *415/641–4500* ⊕ *www.incanto.biz* ⊘ *Closed Tues. No lunch* ✛ *3:D6.*

$$$ ✕ **La Ciccia.** Chef Massimiliano Conti quickly won a loyal following
ITALIAN after opening this charming neighborhood trattoria serving Sardinian food. The island's classics are all represented—seafood salad dressed with olive oil and lemon; seared lamb tenderloin; pasta with *bottarga* (salted mullet roe); and *fregola* (pebble-shape pasta) with fresh ricotta and cured tuna heart. The space came with a pizza oven, so Conti also turns out a pair of respectable thin-crust pies. The award-winning, extensive wine list looks no further than Italy, and one-fourth of the choices are Sardinian. The staff is both friendly and efficient, and Conti and his wife regularly circle the room to make sure everyone is

13

happy. ⊠ *291 30th St., Noe Valley* ☎ *415/550–8114* ⊕ *www.laciccia. com* ⊗ *Closed Mon. No lunch* ✛ *3:D6.*

MISSION DISTRICT

¢   ✕ **Angkor Borei**. Aromatic Thai basil, lemongrass, and softly sizzling
CAMBODIAN   chilies perfume this modest neighborhood restaurant, opened by Cambodian refugees in the late 1980s. The menu includes an array of curries; salads of squid or cold noodles with ground fish; a crisp, pork-and-sprout-filled crepe; and lightly curried fish mousse cooked in a banana leaf. Chicken grilled on skewers and served with mild pickled vegetables is a house specialty, as are the green papaya salad and the panfried catfish. Vegetarians will be happy to discover two full pages of selections. Service is friendly though sometimes languid, so don't stop here when you're in a hurry. ⊠ *3471 Mission St., Mission* ☎ *415/550–8417* ⊕ *www.cambodiankitchen.com* ✛ *3:F6.*

$$$ ✕ **Bar Tartine**. This restaurant offshoot of the cultlike Tartine Bakery
NEW AMERICAN   provides one way you can get a taste of their famed (and always sold-out) country loaf. It's a definite neighborhood restaurant, drawing an energetic crowd to the cozy and artsy space. The menu is all about California seasonality with excellent salads, well-executed terrines and charcuterie, a juicy cast-iron-skillet chicken, and a burger that has its own fan club (get it with the marrow supplement if you're feeling decadent). Desserts are homey, and the extensive wine list makes this a fun place to swing by for a glass—if you can find a seat. Weekend brunch rates high on quality—and calories. ⊠ *561 Valencia St., Mission* ☎ *415/487–1600* ⊕ *www.bartartine.com* ⊗ *Closed Mon. No lunch weekdays* ✛ *3:F5.*

$$ ✕ **Beretta**. The formula here works: excellent cocktails, an array of
ITALIAN   affordable antipasti, solid pizzas, risottos, *piatti del giorno* (daily mains), and fantastic late hours. The bartenders are both serious and friendly, smiling when they detail the 10 or so gins you can choose from for your martini. The pizzas respect their Italian heritage (thin crusts, traditional and contemporary toppings) and the antipasti are an appealing mix of vegetables (the eggplant caponatina with burrata is a standout), fish (a light fritto misto or marinated sardines), and locally made artisanal salumi (cured meats). The long, ascetically outfitted room—tin ceiling, white walls, bare wood tables—is casual and smart, and typically filled with a young crowd. What doesn't work here? Conversation, unless you speaking pretty loudly or read lips. The weekend brunch is hit with the neighborhood crowd. Reservations are accepted for groups of six or more only. ⊠ *1199 Valencia St., Mission* ☎ *415/695–1199* ⊕ *www.berettasf.com* ⊗ *No lunch weekdays* ✛ *3:F6.*

¢   ✕ **Burger Joint**. Cross the threshold here and you're back in the days of
BURGER   sock hops and big Chevy sedans. Dressed in red and turquoise, with
⟳   checkered floors and comfy booths, the retro Burger Joint serves Niman Ranch beef burgers, ridiculously thick and creamy milk shakes, big root-beer floats, and crisp, stocky fries. Every burger comes with tomatoes, lettuce, onion, and pickles, a toasted sesame bun, and a pile of fries. A petite appetite? The mini-cheeseburger and fries fit the bill. Cheeseburger partisans can dress up their patties with American, cheddar, Swiss, or Monterey Jack. Non–beef eaters can opt for a gardenburger

or chicken-breast burger. ✉ *807 Valencia St., Mission* ☎ *415/824–3494* ⊕ *www.burgerjointsf.com* ✛ *4:A6.*

$$
LATIN AMERICAN

✕ **Charanga**. It's hard to resist the tropical vibe that weaves its way through this animated tapas depot, with its eclectic mix of Cuban and Caribbean-inspired flavors. Some tapas stay true to their Spanish ancestry, like *patatas bravas*, which are twice-fried potatoes with roast-tomato sauce. Others, like fried yucca with chipotle aioli, are a mix of both the Old and the New World, and some, like Cuban *picadillo*, a minced-beef dish studded with green olives and raisins, and Costa Rican–style arroz con pollo, chicken and rice with peas, cilantro, and olives, are firmly rooted on this side of the Atlantic. Many of the dishes are bigger than typical tapas—more like *raciones*, tapas' traditional big brothers—which means healthy appetites will be satisfied here. The dining room, with walls of exposed brick and soothing green and accents of gold, is small and friendly, so grab—or make—some friends, order a pitcher of sangria, and enjoy yourself. ✉ *2351 Mission St., Mission* ☎ *415/282–1813* ⊕ *www.charangasf.com* ☾ *Closed Mon.* ✛ *3:F6.*

$$
FRENCH

✕ **Chez Papa**. France arrived on Potrero Hill with Chez Papa, which delivers food, waiters, and charm that would be right at home in Provence. The modest corner restaurant, with a Mediterranean blue awning, big windows overlooking the street, and a small heated patio, caters to a lively crowd that makes conversation difficult. Small plates include mussels in pastis, beef tartare, and an heirloom tomato tarte tatin. Big plates range from duck confit, and salmon with a niçoise olive tapenade, to homey lamb daube. Leave space for a typically Gallic crème brûlée or chocolate fondant. The $34.95 prix-fixe is also a good deal for the penny-wise. To accommodate the overflow of Hill residents who have packed this place since day one, the owners opened the tiny (and more casual) Chez Maman (crepes, burgers, salads) a few doors down the block. ✉ *1401 18th St., Potrero Hill* ☎ *415/824–8205* ⊕ *www.chezpapasf.com* ☾ *No lunch Sun.* ✛ *3:H6.*

$$$
FRENCH

✕ **Chez Spencer**. A semi-industrial neighborhood, with an OfficeMax outlet a nearby neighbor, is an unlikely location for an upmarket French restaurant. Yet that's where you'll find Chez Spencer. Tucked into a former warehouse, boasting arched beam ceilings, polished concrete floors, a wood-burning oven, and a full bar, it attracts diners from all over the city. The menu—foie-gras torchon, grilled steak with morels and truffled butter, smoked duck-breast salad with a poached egg at its center, warm chocolate pudding cake—is meticulously prepared. The wine list, small and mostly French, is carefully crafted to match the food. There's patio dining, too, with plenty of heaters to keep you warm. The downside of Chez Spencer? The chef needs to tinker with the menu occasionally to keep regulars interested. ✉ *82 14th St., Mission* ☎ *415/864–2191* ⊕ *www.chezspencer.net* ☾ *No lunch* ✛ *3:G4.*

$$$
ITALIAN
Fodor's Choice
★

✕ **Delfina**. "Irresistible." That's how countless die-hard fans describe Craig and Anne Stoll's Delfina. Such wild enthusiasm has made patience the critical virtue for anyone wanting a reservation here (although walk-ins can find some success at a counter and in the bar area). The interior is comfortable, with hardwood floors, aluminum-top tables, a tile bar, and a casual, friendly atmosphere. The menu changes daily, and among

13

the usual offerings are grilled squid with warm white-bean salad and excellent tripe (they're also known for their spaghetti). If Piemontese fresh white truffles have made their way to San Francisco, you are likely to find hand-cut tagliarini dressed with butter, cream, and the pricey aromatic fungus on the menu alongside dishes built on more-prosaic ingredients. The panna cotta is best in class. The storefront next door is home to pint-size Pizzeria Delfina. And for folks who can't get to the Mission, the Stolls have opened a second pizzeria on California Street in lively Lower Pacific Heights. ✉ *3621 18th St., Mission* ☎ *415/552–4055* ⊕ *www.delfinasf.com* 🍴 *Reservations essential* ⊗ *No lunch* ✛ *3:E6.*

$ ✕ **Dosa.** Like Indian food but crave more than tandoori chicken and
INDIAN   naan? Dosa is your answer. This temple of South Indian cuisine, done in cheerful tones of tangerine and turmeric, serves not only the large, thin savory pancake for which it is named, but also curries, *uttapam* (open-face pancakes), and various starters, breads, rice dishes, and chutneys. You can select from about 10 different dosa fillings, ranging from traditional potatoes, onions, and cashews to spinach and fennel stems. Each comes with tomato and fresh coconut chutneys and *sambar* (lentil curry) for dipping. Lamb curry with fennel and tomatoes and tamarind prawns are popular, as are starters like Chennai chicken (chicken marinated in yogurt and spices and lightly fried), and the new Indian street-food additions, like *vada pav* (a vegetarian slider). The wine and beer lists are top drawer, and both include some Indian labels. Weekend brunch offers a nice change from the usual brunch suspects. Queues for this Mission District spot convinced the owners to open a second, splashier branch on the corner of Fillmore and Post in Japantown. ✉ *995 Valencia St., at 21st St., Mission* ☎ *415/642–3672* ⊕ *www. dosasf.com* ⊗ *No lunch* ✛ *3:F6.*

$$$$ ✕ **Farina.** Locals shed a tear when the longtime Anna's Danish Cookies
ITALIAN   closed in this spot. But anyone who craves the Ligurian fare of northern Italy—the home of pesto, focaccia, and delicate pastas—is bound to be pleased with the offerings at Farina. Here diners fill up on such iconic dishes as focaccia di Recco (paper-thin pizzalike focaccia sandwiching melted stracchino cheese), handmade "handkerchief" pasta dressed with the city's best pesto, corzetti ("stamped" pasta rounds) with tomato meat sauce, and pansotti stuffed with borage and ricotta. Those with slim pocketbooks should stay away from the very pricey secondi and instead choose from the regularly changing array of Ligurian carbs and small dishes of sautéed greens, eggplant parmigiana, or other vegetables. Sunday brunch offerings sometimes include braised eggs with black-truffle butter or sunny-side-up eggs with prosciutto. ✉ *3560 18th St., at Dearborn St., Mission* ☎ *415/565–0360* ⊕ *www. farina-foods.com* ⊗ *No lunch* ✛ *3:E6.*

$$$ ✕ **Foreign Cinema.** Forget popcorn. In this hip, loftlike space "dinner and
NEW AMERICAN   a movie" become one joyous event. Classic films like René Clément's
🕑   noirish 1960 *Purple Noon* and Krzysztof Kieslowski's 1990 *Blue* are projected on a wall in a large inner courtyard while you're served oysters on the half shell, house-cured sardines, their excellent fried chicken, or seafood stew from the dinner menu; or a crab panino or chicken-liver

pâté from the café menu. Fussy filmgoers should call ahead to find out what's playing and arrive in time for a good seat (although it's really more about dining than movie watching here). Kids aren't forgotten, with celery and carrot sticks, pasta with butter and cheese, and two scoops of ice cream for just $7. The adjacent two-level Laszlo Bar has a serious DJ, and the weekend brunch brings big crowds for some of the city's best egg dishes and Bloody Marys. ⊠ *2534 Mission St., Mission* ☎ *415/648–7600* ⊛ *www.foreigncinema.com* ◷ *No lunch* ✛ *3:F6.*

13

$ ╳ **La Santaneca de la Mission.** Lots of El Salvadorans live in the Mission,
LATIN AMERICAN and here they find the *pupusa,* a stuffed cornmeal round that is more or
less the hamburger of their homeland. It usually comes filled with beans, cheese, or meat—sometimes in combination—and is eaten with seasoned shredded cabbage. The kitchen at this friendly, family-run place also makes the more unusual rice-flour pupusa, as well as other dishes popular in Central America, including fried plantains, seafood soup, tamales filled with chicken or pork, *chicharrones* (fried pork skins), and yucca. Accompany your meal with *horchata,* a cooling rice-based drink flavored with cinnamon. Service is sometimes a bit slow, and pupusas are made to order, so don't come here when you're in a rush. ⊠ *2815 Mission St., Mission* ☎ *415/285–2131* ▭ *No credit cards* ✛ *3:F6.*

$$ ╳ **Limón.** Cooks in Peru and Ecuador have long argued over which
PERUVIAN country invented *ceviche,* a dish consisting of raw fish marinated in citrus juices. Most diners at Limón would probably line up with the Peruvians after eating the myriad, delicious versions here (try the red snapper, calamari, and shrimp version), all accompanied by yucca and corn, and prepared by chef-owner Martin Castillo. They also like the *empanadas,* flaky pastries filled with minced beef, olives, and raisins; the hearty *lomo saltado,* beef strips sautéed with onions, tomatoes, and potatoes; the *arroz con mariscos,* mixed seafood with spicy saffron rice; and the crispy whole snapper with coconut rice. Choose from a list of Peruvian beers for sipping with your meal. The three-course prix-fixe menus (plus dessert) at $40 can help you keep your tab under control while exploring the menu. Brunch and lunch prices are also a few ticks lower. ⊠ *524 Valencia St., Mission* ☎ *415/252–0918* ✛ *3:F5*

$ ╳ **Limón Rotisserie.** The kid sister of Limón, this cheery but modest din-
LATIN AMERICAN ing room outfitted with dark-wood tables and brightened with splashes of yellow, orange, and lime-green is just a 10-minute walk from its classier sibling. The neighborhood is a bit bleak, but the friendly prices and even friendlier staff quickly help you forget the street scene. An order of the crisp-skinned citrus-y chicken, which is typically fresh off the rotisserie, comes with a pair of sauces and a choice of two sides, including rice-and-bean cakes called *tacu-tacu,* green salad, grilled vegetables, french fries, and yucca fries. The $20 prix-fixe menu served family style is good for groups. You won't go thirsty, either. The list of beverages includes almost a dozen wines by the glass, half a dozen beers, and even some sake cocktails. ⊠ *1001 S. Van Ness Ave., Mission* ☎ *415/821–2134* ⊛ *www.limonrotisserie.com* ⊿ *Reservations not accepted* ◷ *Closed Sun.* ✛ *3:F6.*

$$ ╳ **Luna Park.** It can be a tight fit on weekend nights in this clangorous
AMERICAN American bistro in the trendy Mission District. The youngish crowd is

here to sip mojitos and nosh on steamed mussels with bacon or goat-cheese fondue with apple wedges. Most of the mains are homey—mac-and-cheese, short ribs and mashed potatoes, grilled salmon, breaded pork cutlet—and priced to sell. An order of s'mores includes cups of melted chocolate and marshmallows and a handful of house-made graham crackers to customize the campfire classic. On weekends a slew of popular brunch dishes are added to the weekday lunch list of salads and sandwiches. ⊠ *694 Valencia St., Mission* ☎ *415/553–8584* ⊕ *www.lunaparksf.com* ✛ *3:F6.*

$$$
AMERICAN

✕ **Range**. The name sounds strictly down-home, but the place looks and feels big city. Just across the threshold is a full bar stocked with the best bottles—and plenty of people to appreciate them. An open kitchen with a line of tables opposite comes next, and then the dining room furnished with roomy banquettes and a chatty crowd. The compact, changing menu is a nice mix of high-end and homey, with cured arctic char with shishito peppers and pickled green tomatoes sharing space with coffee-rubbed pork shoulder on creamy hominy and greens. On the sweeter side, you'll find some excellent seasonal desserts, plus a bittersweet chocolate soufflé that will make you forget your diet. For the more ascetic, there are buckwheat crepes with huckleberries and crème fraîche. Service is smooth—informative but not gushy—in both the dining room and the bar. Adventurous cocktail drinkers will want to dip into the specialty drinks menu before dinner. ⊠ *842 Valencia St., Mission* ☎ *415/282–8283* ⊕ *www.rangesf.com* ☽ *No lunch* ✛ *3:F6.*

$$$$
NEW AMERICAN

✕ **Saison**. One wouldn't expect to find such a stylish restaurant on this dingy street in the Mission, but that's part of the charm of this unique and hidden-away gem. The kitchen and everything that comes out of it is rooted in European style, but made with premium local ingredients (the kitchen even employs a full-time forager). The tasting menu is full of clean flavors and artful plating, with many items cooked on the outdoor hearth. The wine list is carefully curated, so consider springing for the pairing option. The outdoor terrace (overlooking the hearth) is lovely on a warm night, but the natural modern styling of the dining room also charms. This is a nice special-occasion restaurant, but also perfect for those who want a unique experience—the chef is an up-and-comer. The adjoining wine bar, Dcantr, also includes some à la carte choices from the Saison menu. ⊠ *2124 Folsom St., Mission* ☎ *415/828–7990* ⊕ *www.saisonsf.com* ⊜ *Reservations essential* ☽ *Closed Sun. and Mon.* ✛ *3:G5.*

$
MEXICAN
☙

✕ **SanJalisco**. This old-time, sun-filled, colorful, family-run restaurant is a neighborhood gem (and it's not just because it serves breakfast all day). At brunch, try the hearty *chilaquiles,* made from day-old tortillas cut into strips and cooked with cheese, eggs, chilies, and sauce. Or order eggs scrambled with cactus or with *chicharrones* (crisp pork skins) and served with freshly made tortillas. Soup offerings change daily, with Tuesday's *albondigás* (meatballs) comfort food at its best. On weekends, adventurous eaters may opt for *birria,* a spicy goat stew, or *menudo,* a tongue-searing soup made from tripe, calf's foot, and hominy. The latter is a time-honored hangover cure. Bring plenty of

CLOSE UP

Coffee with a Shot of Local Flavor

North Beach may have the highest coffee profile, but fantastic brews can be found all over town. Tear yourself away from Columbus Avenue and head to Hayes Valley's **Blue Bottle Coffee** (⊠ *315 Linden St., near Gough St.* ☎ *415/252–7535* ✛ *3:E2*), a modest kiosk where the organic beans (no more than two days from the roaster) are ground for each cup and the espresso is automatically *ristretto*—a short shot. (Although traditionalists stick to the quirky kiosk, in early 2008 Blue Bottle opened a "proper café" downtown in the newly minted Mint Plaza.) In the Mission District, the owners of the popular **Ritual Coffee Roasters** (⊠ *1026 Valencia St., between 21st and 22nd Sts.* ☎ *415/641–1024* ✛ *3:E6*) have plunked their roaster in the middle of the café, so you know where your beans—usually single-origin, rather than a blend—were roasted when you order your cap or latte. Coffee aficionados should also head farther up Valencia Street to **Four Barrel Coffee** (⊠ *375 Valencia St., between 14th and 15th Sts.* ☎ *415/252–0800* ✛ *3:E4*) for excellent house-roasted coffee in a fun and funky space, packed with Mission hipsters and artists (be sure to look at the selection of Dynamo donuts as well). While you're sipping your inky strong cup at

friendly **Farley's** (⊠ *1315 18th St., at Texas St.* ☎ *415/648–1545* ✛ *3:H5*), a neighborhood institution on sunny Potrero Hill, you can play chess, check out the eclectic magazine selection, or catch up on the local gossip. If you are a serious bicyclist and serious about coffee, the funky **Mojo Bicycle Café** (⊠ *639A Divisadero St., between Grove and Hayes Sts.* ☎ *415/440–2338* ✛ *3:B3*), in the increasingly hip North of the Panhandle neighborhood, is the place for you. You can down an espresso made from locally roasted fair-trade beans, tuck into a great sandwich, and either buy or admire a beautiful new bike or get the one you are riding fixed. In the Lower Haight, sun seekers grab an outside table at **Café du Soleil** (⊠ *200 Fillmore St., at Waller St.* ☎ *415/934–8637* ✛ *3:D3*) and sip bowls of café au lait with their morning croissant. And anyone looking for a real cup of joe in a bare-bones pine shack should join the savvy dock workers, carpenters, and young suits at the more than 80-year-old **Red's Java House** (⊠ *Pier 30, between Embarcadero and Bryant St.* ☎ *415/777–5626* ✛ *1:H6*), where the coffee typically follows a cheeseburger and a Bud and the gorgeous view of the East Bay is priceless.

—Sharon Silva

---

change for the jukebox loaded with Latin hits. ⊠ *901 S. Van Ness Ave., Mission* ☎ *415/648–8383* ⊕ *www.sanjalisco.com* ✛ *3:F6.*

$

FRENCH

☺

✕ **Ti Couz.** Big, thin, square buckwheat crepes just like those found in Brittany are the specialty here, filled with everything from ham to Gruyère to ratatouille to sausage to scallops. You can begin with a green salad, oysters on the half shell, a plate of charcuterie, a hefty seafood salad, or a bowl of soup. Then order a savory crepe from the long list of possibilities—you can create your own filling combination—and end with a divine white chocolate or chestnut crepe. Or, you can skip the sweet crepe and order a gelato doused with espresso or liqueur. The self-consciously rustic dining room—sturdy wood tables, mismatched cutlery, whitewashed walls—welcomes an eclectic crowd late into the night. A full bar serves mixed drinks, but the best—and the traditional—beverage is French hard cider, served in pottery bowls. ⊠ *3108 16th St., Mission* ☎ *415/252–7373* ✣ *3:E5.*

PACIFIC HEIGHTS AND JAPANTOWN

PACIFIC HEIGHTS

$$$ ✗ **Florio.** San Franciscans have always had a weakness for little French
FRENCH bistros, which helped make Florio a hit from the day it opened. It had all the elements: a space that looked like a Paris address, classic charcuterie and roast chicken, and reasonably priced French wines. Since then, this neighborhood favorite has picked up a thick Italian accent, with bruschetta with tuna confit and heirloom tomatoes, chicken-liver crostini, and risotto with chanterelles lining up next to salmon tartare, steamed mussels, *poulet rôti,* and steak frites on the menu. Save room for the kitchen's crème caramel, a neighborhood favorite. The room can get noisy, so don't come here hoping for a quiet tête-à-tête. You can eat at the bar, too, a nice plus if you're out on the town on your own. ⊠ *1915 Fillmore St., Lower Pacific Heights* ☎ *415/775–4300* ⊕ *www.floriosf.com* ⊘ *No lunch* ✣ *2:F6.*

$$ ✗ **Out the Door.** This casual offshoot of Charles Phan's Slanted Door is
VIETNAMESE actually where locals prefer to go for his version of Vietnamese food
☾ made with high-end ingredients. The look is chic and simple, with an open kitchen, a communal table, counter seating, and an eclectic crowd ranging from Pacific Heights ladies to couples on a first date to young parents with their kids in tow. You can find all the Phan classics (spring rolls, daikon rice cake, crab and cellophane noodles, shaking beef), but there are plenty of other standout dishes on the menu. Lunch has some delicious soups, breakfast features porridge (jook) alongside tasty egg dishes, and the weekend brunch is even more hard to resist. There's excellent Vietnamese coffee made with Blue Bottle coffee, and plenty of quality wines and beers on tap to choose from. ⊠ *2232 Bush St., Lower Pacific Heights* ☎ *415/923–9575* ⊕ *www.outthedoors.com* ✣ *2:E6.*

$$ ✗ **SPQR.** If you know your Italian history, you know this acronym
ITALIAN roughly translates to the senate and people of Rome. Brought to you by the same team that operates the Marina's wildly popular A16, SPQR is a casual, friendly spot—bare-topped tables, open kitchen, old travel posters on the walls—with a dedicated neighborhood following of all ages. Of course, that dedication usually means a long wait for a table, unless you made reservations, or turn up after 9 or on a slow Monday. Singles can opt for a seat at the two counters. The loyalists come here for the nearly 15 antipasti and *spuntini* (the chicken liver and crispy pig's ears are favorites), 10 superlative pastas, and savory mains. The appetizing and inventive menu changes constantly with the seasons (and the chef's whims), but the pastas are particularly notable—you'll want to try a few at least, so come hungry. The Italian wine list is also full of gems, with wonderful choices by the glass. ⊠ *1911 Fillmore St., Lower Pacific Heights* ☎ *415/771–7779* ⊕ *www.spqrsf.com* ⊘ *No lunch weekends* ✣ *2:F6.*

$$$$
NEW AMERICAN
✕ **Spruce.** One of the hottest reservations in town from the day it opened, Spruce caters to the city's social set, with the older crowd sliding into the mohair banquettes in the early hours and the younger set taking their places after eight. The large space, a former 1930s auto barn, shelters a high-style dining room and a more casual bar-cum-library lounge. Charcuterie, bavette steak with bordelaise sauce and duck-fat fries, and sweetbreads reflect the French slant of the modern American menu. If you can't wrangle a table, stop in at the take-out café next door, which carries not only sandwiches, salads, and pastries (like the exquisite palmiers) but also anything from the dining room menu to go. And if you are watching your pocketbook, you can graze off the bar menu and watch the swells come and go. ⊠ *3640 Sacramento St., Pacific Heights* ☎ *415/931–5100* ⊕ *www.sprucesf.com* ⌷ *Reservations essential* ☉ *No lunch weekends* ✢ *2:B5.*

JAPANTOWN

$$
INDIAN
✕ **Dosa on Fillmore.** As soon as the large door swings open to this happening two-level space, diners are greeted with a sexy atmosphere with bright colors, vivid artwork, upbeat music, a lively bar scene, and the smell of spices in the air. This is the second location of the popular Dosa on Valencia, but it's definitely the glamorous younger sister, with a full bar, an expanded menu, and much more room. The menu entices with savory fish dishes, fall-off-the-bone pepper chicken, and papery dosas stuffed with a variety of fillings. The restaurant handles group dining often, and has a special menu you can customize. Return for lunch and indulge in the Indian street-food selections, and the famed *pani puri* (little crisp puffs you fill with mint and tamarind water and pop all at once into your mouth). ⊠ *1700 Fillmore St., Japantown* ☎ *415/441–3672* ⊕ *www.dosasf.com* ☉ *No lunch Mon. and Tues.* ✢ *2:F6.*

$$
JAPANESE
✕ **Maki.** *Wappa-meshi,* rice topped with meat or fish and steamed in a bamboo basket, is the specialty at this diminutive and quiet restaurant featuring the refined Kansai cuisine of Osaka and Kyoto. The sashimi, sukiyaki, udon (try the shrimp tempura version), *chawan mushi* custard, and freshwater eel on rice in a lacquer box are also first-rate. Everything is served on beautiful tableware, from the smallest *sunomono* salad to a big lunchtime *donburi,* protein-topped rice. Maki stocks an impressive assortment of sakes, which it serves in exquisite decanters. If you don't know your sake, the helpful staff will lead you in the right direction. ⊠ *Japan Center, Kinokuniya Bldg., 1825 Post St., Japantown* ☎ *415/921–5215* ☉ *Closed Mon. No lunch Tues.–Fri.* ✢ *2:F6.*

$
JAPANESE
☾
✕ **Mifune.** Thin brown soba and thick white udon are the stars at this long-popular North American outpost of an Osaka-based noodle empire. A line regularly snakes out the door, but the house-made noodles, served both hot and cold and with a score of toppings, are worth the wait. Seating is at wooden tables, where diners of every age can be heard slurping down big bowls of such traditional Japanese combinations as *nabeyaki udon,* wheat noodles topped with tempura, chicken, and fish cake; and *tenzaru,* cold noodles and hot tempura with gingery dipping sauce served on lacquered trays. The noodle-phobic can choose from a few rice dishes and sushi. ⊠ *Japan Center, Kintetsu Bldg., 1737 Post St., Japantown* ☎ *415/922–0337* ⊕ *www.mifune.com* ✢ *2:F6.*

13

$$$
JAPANESE

✕**Yoshi's.** San Franciscans were long envious of Oakland jazz lovers who had Yoshi's restaurant and nationally known jazz club at their doorstep. But with the late 2007 opening of Yoshi's in San Francisco's slowly rising jazz district on the edge of Japantown, that envy quickly became history. While talented musicians do their thing in a separate space, the equally talented chef Shotaro Kamio serves some of the city's finest—and priciest—Japanese food: exquisite sashimi, memorable robata, crisp tempura, exotic maki-sushi (rolls), pristine nigiri sushi. The big, handsome restaurant harbors stylish booths, a sushi bar, small tables, a tatami room, a mezzanine lounge, and a bar, ensuring a comfortable perch for every diner. When funds are tight, you can order from the pub menu in the bar. ✉ *1330 Fillmore St., Japantown* ☎ *415/655–5600* ⊕ *www.yoshis.com/sanfrancisco* ☽ *No lunch* ✛ *3:D1.*

RICHMOND

$$$
MOROCCAN
Fodor's Choice
★

✕**Aziza.** Chef-owner Mourad Lahlou's California-Moroccan food boasts a healthy dose of modernity that keeps locals coming back for his unique flavors. Diners enjoy inspired and gorgeously plated first courses like sardines with green charmoula and black garlic, or duck liver with chestnut, persimmon, and *ras el hanout* (African spice blend). The main courses are equally elegant, ranging from squab with smoked farro to lamb shank with apricot, turnips, and barley. Desserts here are a can't-miss. The attractive three-room dining area, done in blue, saffron, and white, is a warm, inviting sea of tiles, arches, and candlelight. The wine list is very food-friendly, with some organic and biodynamic options, while cocktail enthusiasts can pick from more than two dozen inspired potions. ✉ *5800 Geary Blvd., Richmond* ☎ *415/752–2222* ⊕ *www.aziza-sf.com* ☽ *Closed Tues. No lunch* ✛ *3:B1.*

$$
RUSSIAN

✕**Katia's.** This cozy Richmond District gem serves Russian food guaranteed to make former Muscovites smile. Small dishes of eggplant, caviar, marinated mushrooms, blini and smoked salmon, and meat- or vegetable-filled *piroshki* are delicious ways to start a meal. Follow up with hearty beef Stroganoff, delicate chicken cutlets, or homey *pelmeni,* meat-filled dumplings in broth. You can sip a Russian beer—the porter is good—or a cup of Russian tea (Assam and Keemun blend) with milk or lemon. If you can put together a group, make a reservation for one of Katia's afternoon tea parties, complete with sweets and savories and tea dispensed from a handsome samovar. ✉ *600 5th Ave., Inner Richmond* ☎ *415/668–9292* ⊕ *www.katias.com* ☽ *Closed Mon. and Tues. No lunch weekends* ✛ *3:A2.*

¢
VIETNAMESE

✕**Pho Hoa Clement.** The menu at this homey Formica-and-linoleum spot is big and remarkably cheap. You can order everything from sandwiches and salads to rice dishes and noodle plates. But the soups are what shine, from the two dozen varieties of *pho,* rice noodles in beef broth, to a dozen types of *hu tieu,* seafood and pork noodle soups. All of them are served in three sizes—small, medium, and large—usually separated by just 75¢, and no bowl is skimpy. Regulars, many of whom hail from Southeast Asia, favor the shrimp, fish ball, and pork slices soup with clear noodles and the special combo *pho* with rare steak, well-done brisket, tendon, and tripe. ⊠ *239 Clement St., Inner Richmond* ☎ *415/379–9008* ✥ *2:A6.*

$$ ✕ **Ton Kiang.** This restaurant introduced the lightly seasoned Hakka cui-
CHINESE sine of southern China, rarely found in this country and even obscure
🕲 to many Chinese. Salt-baked chicken, stuffed bean curd, steamed fresh
bacon with dried mustard greens, chicken in wine sauce, and clay pots
of meats and seafood are among the hallmarks of the Hakka kitchen,
and all of them are done well here, as the tables packed with local Chinese families and others prove. Don't overlook the excellent seafood
offerings like salt-and-pepper shrimp, catfish in black-bean sauce, or
stir-fried crab with ginger and scallions. A local favorite for dim sum—
delicate dumplings of pea shoots and shrimp, scallops and shrimp, pork
and greens—means you should expect a noontime or weekend rush (a
small selection is available at night, too). ⊠ *5821 Geary Blvd., Richmond* ☎ *415/387–8273* ⊕ *www.tonkiang.net* ✥ *3:B1.*

SUNSET DISTRICT

$$$ ✕ **The Moss Room.** Loretta Keller of Coco500 is behind this subterranean
MEDITERRANEAN restaurant under the California Academy of Sciences. You reach the
coolly ascetic dining room by entering the museum and then descend-
ing a staircase lined with a moss-covered wall, a live reminder of the
thoroughly green building. The menu sticks with the cuisine Keller is
known for, an easy mix of Mediterranean and Californian, and some
dishes have strong Asian influences, like barbecue octopus and pork
belly with pickled burdock, *chawan mushi* custard with Manila clams
and shimeji mushrooms, and mains like goat-cheese agnolotti with kale
and short ribs for two. Save room for warm tarte tatin with crème
fraîche ice cream, and save your money for the wine list, which leans
heavily on your pocketbook. During the day a museum admission is
the only way to enter the Moss Room; at night, when the museum is
closed, a staffer stationed on the patio directs you through the only
open door. It can be an inky, foggy trek to the entrance, so watch
your step. ⊠ *California Academy of Sciences in Golden Gate Park, 55
Music Concourse Dr., Sunset* ☎ *415/876–6121* ⊕ *www.themossroom.
com* ⚑ *Reservations essential* ✥ *3:A5.*

$ ✕ **Park Chow.** What do spaghetti and meatballs, Thai noodles with
AMERICAN chicken and shrimp, and big burgers have in common? They're all on
🕲 the eclectic comfort-food menu at Park Chow, and offered at unbeatable
prices. This neighborhood standby is also known for its desserts: fresh-
baked pies and ginger cake with pumpkin ice cream are standouts. Kids
get their own menu, with items such as a burger, grilled-cheese sand-
wich, chicken, fish, and pizza to choose from. In cool weather there's
a roaring fire in the dining-room fireplace; in warm weather, get there
early to snag an outdoor table. Up early? You can sit down to breakfast
on weekdays and brunch on weekends. The original location is in the
Castro neighborhood. ⊠ *1240 9th Ave., Inner Sunset* ☎ *415/665–9912*
⊕ *www.chowfoodbar.com* ✥ *3:A5.*

$$ ✕ **San Tung.** Many of the best chefs in Beijing's imperial kitchens hailed
CHINESE from China's northeastern province of Shandong. San Franciscans,
🕲 with or without imperial ancestry, regularly enjoy dishes of the same

province at this bare-bones storefront restaurant. Specialties include steamed dumplings—shrimp and leek dumplings are the most popular—and hand-pulled noodles, in soup or stir-fried. Among the typical accompaniments are a salad of jellyfish, seaweed, or sliced cucumbers and a plate of cold, poached chicken marinated in Shaoxing wine. Parents and kids regularly fight over platters of dry-fried chicken wings. To get a table without a wait, come before or after the noon or dinner rush. ✉ *1031 Irving St., Inner Sunset* ☎ *415/242–0828* ⊕ *www. santungrestaurant.com* ☉ *Closed Wed.* ✛ *3:A5.*

Dining and Lodging Atlas

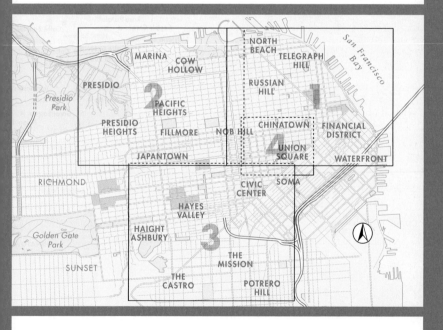

KEY	
☐	Hotels
■	Restaurants
■	Restaurant in Hotel
Embarcadero	
ᖯᖆ	BART Station
	Bay Area Rapid Transit

A   **B**   **C**   **D**

Pier 47

Pier 45   **FISHERMAN'S**
        WHARF

Pier 39

Pier 35

Aquatic Park

Argonaut Hotel

Jefferson St.

Fisherman's Grotto #9

Beach St.

1

MARITIME
MUSEUM
Crown &
Crumpet

Kara's
Cupcakes

Hyatt at
Fisherman's
Wharf

Sheraton Fisherman's
Wharf Hotel

North Point St.

Kearny St.

Beach St.

Best Western Tuscan Inn

Ghirardelli
Square

Gary Danko

North Point St.

Bay St.

Stockton St.

Powell St.

Fairmont
Heritage
Place

Ghirardelli Ice Cream
& Chocolate Shop

San Francisco
Marriott
Fisherman's
Wharf

Jones St.

Taylor St.

Mason St.

Pfeiffer St.

Russian
Hill Park

Francisco St.

San Remo
Hotel

TELEGRAPH
HILL

2

SAN FRANCISCO
ART INSTITUTE

Chestnut St.

NORTH
BEACH

COIT
TOWER

Lombard St.

Jansen St.

Columbus Ave.

Petite Deli

Gelato
Classico

Cafe
Jacqueline

Grant Ave.

Sonoma St.

Varennes St.

Greenwich St.

Washington
Square Inn

Washington
Square

Filbert St.

Jones St.

Taylor St.

Mario's Bohemian Cigar Store

Rose Pistola

Tony's Coal-Fired
Pizza

Maykadeh

Leavenworth St.

Union St.

Capp's Corner

Hotel Bohème

Caffè BaoNecci

3

Macondray La.

L'Osteria del Forno

Caffè Greco

Caffè Puccini

Caffè Trieste

Green St.

RUSSIAN
HILL

Vallejo St.

Molinari's

Kearny St.

Van Ness Ave.

Polk St.

Larkin St.

Hyde St.

Tunnel

Broadway

SW Hotel

Tommaso's

101

Broadway

Bernard St.

Pacific Ave.

Cable Car

John St.

Dol Ho

New Asia

Great Eastern

Stockton St.

Naan 'N'
Curry

Hilton San Francisco
Financial District

Jackson St.

CABLE CAR
MUSEUM

Mason St.

Portsmouth
Square

4

NOB HILL

Washington St.

Commercial St.

Eastern Bakery

See Map 4
Union Square area

Pleasant St.

CHINATOWN

Clay St.

Bob's Donuts

Huntington
Park

California St.

St.
Mary's
Sq.

Sacramento St.

Cable Car

CHINATOWN
GATE

Tunnel

5

California St.

Bush St.

Grant Ave.

Pine St.

Polk St.

Larkin St.

Hyde St.

Leavenworth St.

Jones St.

Taylor St.

Mason St.

Powell St.

Sutter St.

Franklin St.

Bush St.

Post St.

Fern St.

Sutter St.

Union
Square

Maiden Ln.

Hemlock St.

Post St.

Cedar St.

Geary St.

UNION
SQUARE

6

Geary St.

Myrtle St.

O'Farrell St.

O'Farrell St.

Jones St.

Olive St.

Ellis St.

Leavenworth St.

Hyde St.

Ellis St.

Eddy St.

POWELL ST. b

4th St.

A   **B**   **C**   **D**

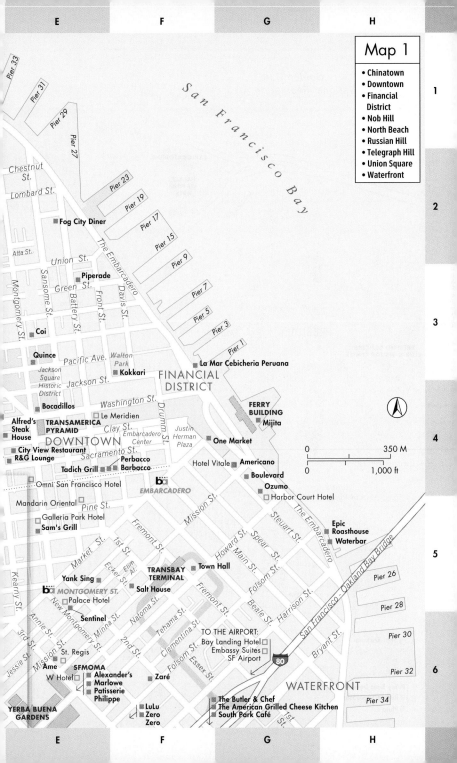

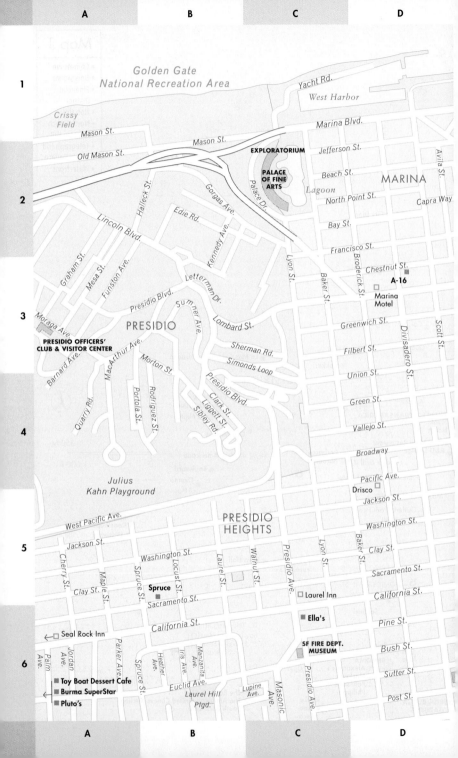

Map 2

- Cow Hollow
- Fillmore
- Japantown
- Marina
- Pacific Heights
- Presidio Heights

E   F   G   H

1

Marina Small
Craft Harbor

East
Harbor

Fort
Mason

Gashouse
Cove

■ Greens

Russian
Hill Park

Casa Way Way

Retiro Way

Rico Way

Cervantes Blvd.

Marina Blvd.

Beach St.

North Point St.

Bay St.

2

COW
HOLLOW

George R.
Moscone
Recreation
Center

Francisco St.

Chestnut St.

Polk St.

Larkin St.

Alhambra St.

Mallorca Way

Toledo Way

■ Tacolicious

Magnolia St.

Marina Inn □

Lombard St.

101

■ Isa
□ Cow Hollow Motor
Inn and Suites   □ Coventry Motor Inn

Greenwich St.

Lombard St.

Moulton St.

■ Home Plate

Fillmore St.

Hotel
Del Sol

Buchanan St.

Laguna St.

Harris Pl.

Octavia St.

Pacific Heights Inn □

Union St.

Franklin St.

Van Ness Ave.

■ Helmand
Palace

■ La Folie

3

■ Rose's Café
Terzo ■

Union Street
Inn

Webster St.

■ Betelnut

■ Ottimista Enoteca

Green St.

Gough St.

101

Pierce St.

Steiner St.

Broadway

Pacific Ave.

Harris' ■

4

PACIFIC
HEIGHTS

Jackson St.

Bromley
Pl.

Washington St.

Alta Plaza

PACIFIC
MED. CTR.

Lafayette
Park

Clay St.

■ Bob's Donuts

Acquerello ■

Sacramento St.

Swan Oyster Depot ■

Cable Car

5

FILLMORE

■ Citizen Cake

California St.

Webster St.

Buchanan St.

Laguna St.

Octavia St.

Gough St.

Franklin St.

Pine St.

■ La Boulangerie

Florio ■

Bush St.

Fern St.

Out the Door ■   ■ SPQR

Sutter St.

■ Fillmore Bakeshop   □ Best Western
Hotel Tomo

Queen Anne □

□ Majestic

Post St.

□ Kabuki Hotel

6

■ Dosa on Fillmore

MT. ZION
HOSP.

Hamilton
Square

Maki ■

JAPAN CENTER,
MIYAKO BUILDING

Geary St.

Myrtle St.

O'Farrell St.

ST. MARY'S
CATHEDRAL

Olive St.

JAPANTOWN

St. Francis
Square

Cleary Ct.

E   F   G   H

Map 3

- The Castro
- Civic Center
- Haight Ashbury
- Hayes Valley
- Mission District
- SOMA

Geary Blvd.
Kimball Playground
St. Francis Square
Hollis
Willow St.

■ Joe's Ice Cream
■ Aziza
■ Ton Kiang
■ Wooden Charcoal Barbecue House
■ Moscow and Tblisi Bakery
■ Pizzetta 211

O'Farrell St.

Terra Vista Ave.
Ellis St.
■ Yoshi's
WESTERN ADDITION

Cinderella Bakery and Restaurant

Fortuna Ave.
Baker St.
Josepha Ave.

Eddy St.
Pierce St.

Anza Vista Ave.
Turk St.
Elm St.

Golden Gate Ave.

McAllister St.

← ■ Katia's

Fulton St.
Alamo Square
Steiner St.
Fillmore St.
Webster St.
Grove St.
Ivy St.

Lyon St.
Baker St.
Broderick St.
Divisadero St.
Scott St.
Hayes St.
Linden

Grove St.
Presidio Ave.
Fell St.

Hayes St.
■ Mojo Bicycle Café
■ Nopa
Hickory St.
Oak St.

Fell St.
Page St.

← ■ Park Chalet
Panhandle
Oak St.
■ Nopalito
Pierce St.

Page St.
■ Uva Enoteca

HAIGHT ASHBURY
Page St.
■ Indian Oven
Rosamunde Sausage Grill ■
■ Thep Phanom

Lyon St.
Haight St.

← ■ The Alembic
← ■ Cha Cha Cha

Waller St.
Germania St.
U.S. MINT

Masonic Ave.
Waller St.
Lloyd St.
Carmelita St.
Alpine Ter.
Potomac St.
Duboce Park
Herman St.

Duboce Ave.

Buena Vista Park
Buena Vista Ave. East
Buena Vista Ter.
Walter St.
Belcher St.
■ Woodhouse Fish Company ■

14th St.
Castro St.
Noe St.
Market St.
■ Chow
Dolores St.

15th St.
Church St.
Landers St.

Corona Heights Playground

16th St.
■ 2223 Restaurant
MISSION DOLORES

■ The Moss Room
■ Park Chow
■ San Tung
17th St.
■ Frances

17th St.

THE CASTRO
Ford St.
Dorland St.

Market St.
18th St.
Douglass St.
Eureka St.
Diamond St.
Collingwood St.
Castro St.
18th St.
Hancock St.
Mission Dolores Park

0   350 M
0   1,000 ft
19th St.
Barney's Gourmet Burger ■
■ Incanto
Chloe's Café ■
La Ciccia ■

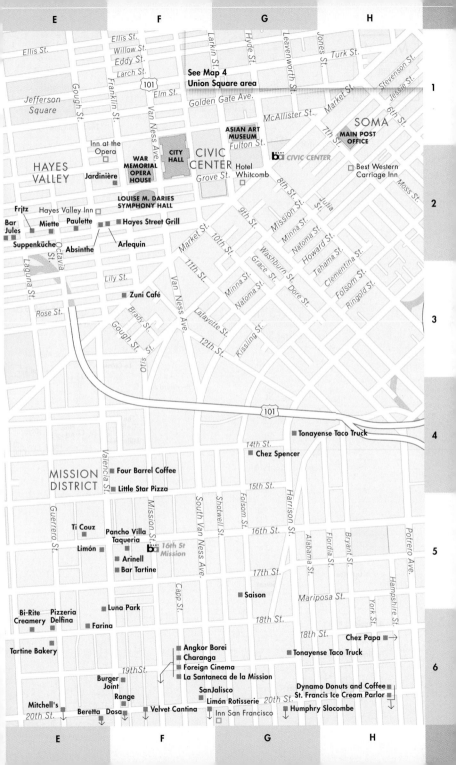

E **F** **G** **H**

Ellis St.
Willow St.
Eddy St.
Larch St.
Ellis St.

101 Elm St.
Golden Gate Ave.

See Map 4
Union Square area

Jefferson
Square

McAllister St.

ASIAN ART
MUSEUM

Fulton St.

SOMA

MAIN POST
OFFICE

CIVIC
CENTER

CIVIC CENTER

HAYES
VALLEY

WAR
MEMORIAL
OPERA
HOUSE

CITY
HALL

Hotel
Whitcomb

Grove St.

□ **Best Western**
Carriage Inn

Inn at the
Opera

Jardinière

Moss St.

LOUISE M. DARIES
SYMPHONY HALL

Fritz ■ Hayes Valley Inn □

Bar
Jules ■ **Miette** ■ **Paulette** ■ ■ **Hayes Street Grill**

Suppenküche ■

Absinthe **Arlequin**

Market St.

9th St.

Mission St.

Minna St.

Natoma St.

Howard St.

Tehama St.

Clementina St.

Folsom St.

10th St.

Washburn St.

Grace St.

Dore St.

Ringold St.

Lily St.

■ **Zuni Café**

11th St.

Minna St.

Natoma St.

Lafayette St.

Kissling St.

Rose St.

Brady St.

Gough St.

Otis St.

12th St.

101

■ **Tonayense Taco Truck**

14th St.

■ **Chez Spencer**

MISSION
DISTRICT

■ **Four Barrel Coffee**

■ **Little Star Pizza**

15th St.

Ti Couz ■

Pancho Villa
Taqueria ■

Limón ■

16th St
Mission

16th St.

■ **Arinell**

■ **Bar Tartine**

17th St.

■ **Saison**

Mariposa St.

Bi-Rite **Pizzeria**
Creamery ■ **Delfina**

■ **Luna Park**

■ **Farina**

18th St.

18th St.

Chez Papa ■→

Tartine Bakery ■

■ **Angkor Borei**
■ **Charanga**
■ **Foreign Cinema**
■ **La Santaneca de la Mission**

■ **Tonayense Taco Truck**

19th St.

Burger
Joint ■

Range ■

SanJalisco ■

Dynamo Donuts and Coffee ■
St. Francis Ice Cream Parlor ■

Mitchell's ■

20th St.

Beretta **Dosa** ■

■ **Velvet Cantina**

Limón Rotisserie ■ 20th St.

Inn San Francisco □

■ **Humphry Slocombe**

E **F** **G** **H**

1

2

3

4

5

6

Map 4

- Nob Hill
- SoMa
- Union Square

A **B** **C** **D**

1

Kimball Pl.
Taylor St.
Cushman St.
Sacramento St.
Golden Ct.
Leroy Pl.
Lysette St.
Huntington Park
Cable Car
The Huntington Hotel
Acorn Al.
California St.
Helen St.

2

Pine St.
Leavenworth St.
Touchard St.
Jones St.
Taylor St.
Mulford Al.
Hyde St.
Bush St.

3

Hotel Beresford □
Hotel Vertigo □
■ Fleur de Lys
■ Canteen
Sutter St.
Cosmo Pl.
Andrews □
Le Colonial ■
Prescott □
Shannon St.
Beresford Arms □
Colin Pl.
Post St.
Meacham Pl.
Larkin St.

4

The Hotel California
Hotel Diva □
□ Hotel Adagio
Millennium ■
Hotel Monaco □
□ Clift
Geary St.
Amity Al.
Harlem Al.
Ada Ct.

5

Myrtle St.
O'Farrell St.
Steveloe Pl.
Antonio St.
■ Lers Ros
Olive St.
■ Hooker's Sweet Treats

6

Ellis St.
Cohen Pl.
■ Pagolac
■ Turtle Tower
Willow St.
■ Bodega Bistro
□ Phoenix Hotel
Eddy St.
Wagner Al.
■ Saigon Sandwiches
Turk St.

A **B** **C** **D**

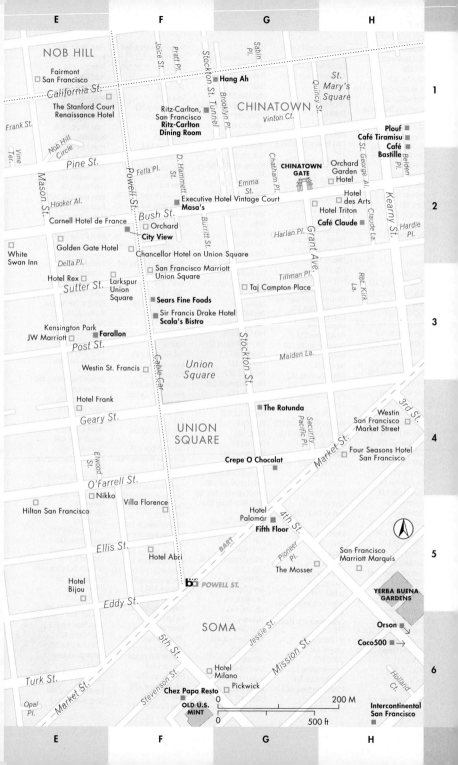

Where to Stay

WORD OF MOUTH

"I love the Monaco. Okay, I REALLY love the Monaco. It's a Kimpton boutique hotel and I love their hotels, but the Monaco SF is my very favorite hotel anywhere. I just love the vibe of the place."

—starrs

Updated by
Michele Bigley

San Francisco serves up a dizzying array of lodging choices. Whether you're seeking a cozy inn, a kitschy motel, a chic boutique, or a grande-dame hotel, it is not difficult to find the perfect fit for any budget.

If you're searching for a centrally located, classy hotel, check out Union Square's dramatic Clift, a property with surrealistic flavor, conjured by maverick star-designer Philippe Starck, or perched atop Nob Hill the newly renovated Huntington Hotel has housed celebrities, railroad barons, and royalty.

Now is a great time to go: hotel deals are easier to come by, upgrades and renovations are taking place at properties throughout the city, and both new and established properties are trending toward the eco-friendly—SF hotels are "going green" in a big way. Although the Orchard Garden boasts San Francisco's first all-new green construction, many other local properties are installing ecological upgrades. Most of the city's hotels are non-smoking.

Wherever you stay, be sure to ask what's included in your room rate. And when you settle into your perfect room, remember this tip: When in doubt, ask the concierge. This holds true for almost any request, whether you have special needs or burning desires (if anyone can get you tickets to a sold-out show or reservations at a fully booked restaurant, it's the concierge). You'll likely be impressed by the lengths hoteliers are willing to go to please their guests.

Finally, consider timing: If you're flexible on dates, ask the reservationist if there's a cheaper time to stay in your preferred travel window.

SAN FRANCISCO LODGING PLANNER

LODGING STRATEGY

Where should we stay? With hundreds of San Francisco hotels, it may seem like a daunting question. But fret not—our expert writers and editors have done most of the legwork. The selections here represent the best this city has to offer—from the best budget motels to the sleekest designer hotels. Scan "Best Bets" for top recommendations by price and

WHERE SHOULD I STAY?

	Neighborhood Vibe	Pros	Cons
Union Square/ Downtown	Union Square is square one for visitors; you'll find a wide range of choices—and prices—for lodging.	Excellent shopping and dining. Home to the theater district, great transit access to other neighborhoods.	Often crowded and noisy. Close to Tenderloin, a still-seedy part of town. Take cabs at night.
SoMa	The "new heart of the city," adjacent to the developing Mission Bay neighborhood, offers luxury high-rises, old classics, and a few bargains.	Near the cultural magnet of the San Francisco Museum of Modern Art and Yerba Buena Gardens, as well as a growing number of eateries.	Lots of construction may mean traffic snarls. As with many changing neighborhoods, street life takes many forms. Be cautious walking around at night.
Financial District	A mini midtown Manhattan where properties cater to business travelers.	Excellent city and bay views, which are spectacular by night. Easy access to restaurants and nightclubs.	Some streets are iffy at night. Street parking takes some work. Hotels are on the pricey side.
Nob Hill	Synonymous with San Francisco's high society, this area contains some of the city's best-known luxury hotels.	Many hotels boast gorgeous views and notable restaurants. Easy access to Union Square and Chinatown.	Hotels here will test your wallet, while the area's steep hills may test your endurance.
Civic Center/ Van Ness	A wide mix of lodgings scattered throughout this area.	Asian Art Museum, opera house, symphony hall, and government offices surround this central hub. Close to busy Fillmore Street and not far from Union Square.	Away from touristy areas, public transportation can sometimes be a challenge. There's a large homeless population in the Civic Center area.
Fisherman's Wharf/North Beach	Mostly chain hotels by the Wharf; lodgings get funkier and smaller in North Beach.	Near attractions like Ghirardelli Square, Pier 39, and the Cannery. Cable-car lines and piers for bay cruises are nearby.	City ordinances limit Wharf hotels to four stories, so good views are out. Very hilly area.
Pacific Heights/Cow Hollow/The Marina	A few tony accommodations in the quietly residential Pacific Heights. Mostly motels along Lombard Street, the major traffic corridor leading to the Golden Gate Bridge.	Away from the more tourist-oriented areas, visitors have a chance to explore where locals eat and shop. Lots of free parking.	Getting downtown can be challenging via public transportation. Some complain of the fraternity-like bar scene.
By the Airport	Construction booms near San Francisco International Airport have added several luxury hotels to this rather prosaic area.	Rates are about 20% lower than in-town hotels, and weekend prices are often slashed because clients tend to be midweek business travelers.	The drive from the airport area to downtown San Francisco takes 20 to 30 minutes, so what you gain in value you may lose in convenience.

14

experience. Or find a review quickly in the listings. Search by neighbor-hood, then alphabetically. Happy hunting!

RESERVATIONS

Reservations are always advised, especially during the peak seasons—August through November, weekends in December, and celebrations like Pride, Mother's Day, and Chinese New Year. The San Francisco Convention and Visitors Bureau publishes a free lodging guide with a map and listings of San Francisco and Bay Area hotels. You can reserve a room, by phone or via the Internet, at more than 60 Bureau-recom-mended hotels. San Francisco Reservations, in business since 1986, can arrange reservations at more than 200 Bay Area hotels, often at special discounted rates.

Booking: San Francisco Convention and Visitors Bureau (☎ 415/391–2000 general information, 415/283–0177, 888/782–9673 lodging service ⊕ www. onlyinsanfrancisco.com). **San Francisco Reservations** (☎ 800/677–1500 ⊕ www.hotelres.com). **Bed & Breakfast San Francisco** (☎ 415/899–0060 ⊕ www.bbsf.com).

FACILITIES

In each hotel review we list what facilities are available, but we don't always specify whether they cost extra. When pricing accommodations, always ask what's included and what entails an additional charge. All the hotels listed have private baths, central heating, and private phones unless otherwise noted. Many places don't have air-conditioning, but you probably won't need it. Even in September and October, when the city sees its warmest days, the temperature rarely climbs above 70°F.

Many hotels now have wireless Internet (Wi-Fi) available, although it's not always free. Larger hotels often have video or high-speed checkout capability, and many can arrange babysitting. Pools are a rarity, but most large properties have gyms or health clubs, and sometimes full-scale spas; hotels without facilities usually have arrangements for guests at nearby gyms, sometimes for a fee. At the end of each review, we state whether any meals are included in the room rate.

PARKING

Several properties on Lombard Street and in the Civic Center area have free parking (but not always in a covered garage). Hotels in the Union Square and Nob Hill areas almost invariably charge $25 to $50-plus per day for a spot in their garages; note that if you are renting a car many hotels charge extra fees for SUVs. Occasionally hotel package deals include parking. Some B&Bs have limited free parking available, but many don't, and require you to park on the street. Depending on the neighborhood and the time, this can be easy or akin to whipping up dinner for 37 picky eaters on a dime, so ask for realistic parking information when you call. Some hotels with paid parking offer a choice of valet parking with unlimited in-out privileges or self-parking (where the fee is less expensive and there's no tipping).

FAMILY TRAVEL

San Francisco has gone to great lengths to attract family vacationers, and hotels have followed the family-friendly trend. Some properties provide diversions like in-room video games, suites with kitchenettes and fold-out sofa beds; some, like Hotel Diva, have even decked out special kid's suites with toys, games, and karaoke machines. Most full-service San Francisco hotels provide roll-away beds, babysitting, and stroller rentals, but be sure to make arrangements when booking the room, not when you arrive.

PRICES

San Francisco hotel prices, among the highest in the United States, may come as an unpleasant surprise. But as at most hotels, prices are starting to soften. Weekend rates for double rooms in high season average about $160 a night citywide. Rates may vary widely according to room availability; always inquire about special rates and packages when making reservations; call the property directly, but also check its Web site and try Internet booking agencies. The lodgings we list are the cream of the crop in each price category.

14

WHAT IT COSTS					
	¢	$	$$	$$$	$$$$
For two people	under $90	$90–$149	$150–$199	$200–$250	over $250

Prices are for two people in a standard double room in high season, excluding 14% tax.

USING THE MAPS

Throughout the chapter, you'll see mapping symbols and coordinates (✛ 3:F2) after property names or reviews. To locate the property on a map, turn to the San Francisco Dining and Lodging Atlas at the end of the Where to Eat chapter. The first number after the ✛ symbol indicates the map number. Following that is the property's coordinate on the map grid.

LODGING REVIEWS

Listed alphabetically within neighborhoods. The following reviews have been condensed for this book. Please go to Fodors.com for full reviews of each property.

UNION SQUARE AND CHINATOWN

UNION SQUARE

$–$$ ▣ **The Andrews Hotel.** Two blocks west of Union Square, this Queen Anne–style abode began its life in 1904 as the Sultan Turkish Baths; today newly renovated rooms and bathrooms are small, but well decorated with Victorian reproductions, old-fashioned floral curtains with lace sheers, iron bedsteads draped with soft bedding, ceiling fans, and large closets. **Pros:** intimate; decor has character; moderately priced; free Wi-Fi. **Cons:** smallish rooms. **TripAdvisor:** "very friendly and helpful,"

BEST BETS FOR
SAN FRANCISCO LODGING

Fodor's offers a selective listing of quality lodging experiences at every price range, from the city's best budget motel to its most sophisticated luxury hotel. Here we've compiled our top recommendations by price and experience. The very best properties—in other words, those that provide a particularly remarkable experience in their price range—are designated in the listings with the Fodor's Choice logo.

Fodor's Choice★

Argonaut Hotel, $$$, p. 268
Best Western Hotel Tomo, $–$$, p. 273
Cow Hollow Motor Inn and Suites, $, p. 271
Four Seasons Hotel San Francisco, $$$$, p. 259
Hotel Drisco, $$$–$$$$, p. 273
Hotel Monaco, San Francisco, $$$–$$$$, p. 253
Hotel Nikko, San Francisco, $$$$, p. 255
InterContinental San Francisco, $$$$, p. 259
Mandarin Oriental, San Francisco, $$$$, p. 264
Orchard Hotel, $$$–$$$$, p. 256
Palace Hotel, San Francisco, $$$$, p. 261
Ritz-Carlton, San Francisco $$$$, p. 266

San Remo Hotel, ¢, p. 267
Union Street Inn, $$–$$$, p. 272

By Price

¢
Hotel des Arts, p. 253
Marina Inn, p. 271
San Remo Hotel, p. 267

$
Best Western Hotel Tomo, p. 273
Cornell Hotel de France, p. 251
Cow Hollow Motor Inn and Suites, p. 271
Queen Anne Hotel, p. 273

$$
Beresford Arms, p. 251
Hotel Diva, p. 253
Union Street Inn, p. 272

$$$
Hotel Drisco, p. 273
Hotel Monaco, San Francisco, p. 253
Orchard Hotel, p. 256

$$$$
Four Seasons Hotel San Francisco, p. 259
Hotel Nikko, San Francisco, p. 255
Huntington Hotel, p. 266
InterContinental San Francisco, p. 259
Mandarin Oriental, San Francisco, p. 264
Palace Hotel, San Francisco, p. 261
Ritz-Carlton, San Francisco, p. 266

By Experience

BUSINESS TRAVELERS
Hilton San Franscisco Financial District, p. 263

Hotel Nikko, p. 255
Hotel Vitale, p. 271
Le Méridien San Francisco, p. 264

HISTORIC INTEREST
Fairmont San Fransisco, p. 264
Hotel Vertigo, p. 266
Inn at San Francisco, p. 272
Palace Hotel, San Francisco p. 261
Westin St. Francis, p. 257

MOST KID-FRIENDLY
Argonaut Hotel, p. 268
Hilton San Francisco, p. 252
Hotel del Sol, p. 271
Hotel Diva, p. 253
Seal Rock Inn, p. 274

MOST ROMANTIC
Fairmont San Francisco, p. 264
Hotel Drisco, p. 273
Hotel Majestic, p. 273
Huntington Hotel, p. 266
Union Street Inn, p. 272

BEST SPAS
Hilton San Francisco Financial District, p. 263
Huntington Hotel, p. 266
St. Regis San Francisco, p. 261

"location is great," "rooms are small." ✉ *624 Post St., Union Square* ☎ *415/563–6877 or 800/926–3739* ⊕ *www.andrewshotel.com* ⇗ *48 rooms, 5 suites* △ *In-room: no a/c, Wi-Fi. In-hotel: restaurant, parking* ⵀⵔ *Breakfast* ✛ *4:D3.*

$$ 　**Beresford Arms.** Surrounded by fancy molding and 10-foot-tall win-
☺ 　dows, the red-carpet lobby of this brick Victorian explains why the building is on the National Register of Historic Places. **Pros:** moderately priced; suites with kitchenettes and Murphy beds are a plus for families with kids; excellent service. **Cons:** no air-conditioning; cramped standard rooms; can be noisy at night. **TripAdvisor:** "very friendly and helpful," "bathroom was spotless," "good location." ✉ *701 Post St., Union Square* ☎ *415/673–2600 or 800/533–6533* ⊕ *www.beresford. com* ⇗ *83 rooms, 12 suites* △ *In-room: no a/c, kitchen (some), Wi-Fi. In-hotel: parking, some pets allowed* ⵀⵔ *Breakfast* ✛ *4:C3.*

$$$ 　**Chancellor Hotel on Union Square.** Built to accommodate visitors to the 1915 Panama Pacific International Exposition, this busy hotel is considered by many to be one of the best bets on Union Square for comfort without extravagance. **Pros:** huge walk-in closets; great value for Union Square; clean rooms. **Cons:** older building with dark hallways and rooms; small bathrooms; noise from cable cars. **TripAdvisor:** "staff is extremely friendly and helpful," "rooms are small but very clean," "comfortable beds." ✉ *433 Powell St., Union Square* ☎ *415/362–2004 or 800/428–4748* ⊕ *www.chancellorhotel.com* ⇗ *135 rooms, 2 suites* △ *In-room: no a/c, Wi-Fi. In-hotel: restaurant, room service, bar, business center, parking* ⵀⵔ *No meals* ✛ *4:F3.*

$$$$ 　**Clift San Francisco.** A favorite of hipsters, music industry types, and celebrities fleeing the media onslaught—security discreetly keeps photographers and other heat-seekers away—this sexy hotel, whose entrance is so nondescript you can walk right past it without a hint of what's inside, is the brainchild of entrepreneur Ian Schrager and artist-designer Philippe Starck. **Pros:** good rates compared to similar top-tier hotels in San Fran; surreal moody interior design; ideal location for shopping and theaters; close to public transportation; discreet and helpful staff. **Cons:** some guests note thin walls; street noise. **TripAdvisor:** "very friendly and helpful," "great service and gym," "great location." ✉ *495 Geary St., Union Square* ☎ *415/775–4700 or 800/606–6090* ⊕ *www. clifthotel.com* ⇗ *337 rooms, 26 suites* △ *In-room: Internet, Wi-Fi. In-hotel: restaurant, room service, bar, gym, business center, parking, some pets allowed* ⵀⵔ *No meals* ✛ *4:D4.*

$–$$ 　**Cornell Hotel de France.** Discovering this French family-operated hotel is like finding a bit of Paris near Union Square. Charming hosts Claude and Micheline Lambert arrived from their native Orléans 40 years ago, and over the years have renovated and decorated each room with prints of paintings by Picasso, Chagall, and Gustav Klimt. **Pros:** special packages and discounts available online; a little bit of France in San Fran. **Cons:** several blocks from the center of things; surrounding area can be dodgy after dark. **TripAdvisor:** "clean and comfortable," "rooms are quite nice," "great location." ✉ *715 Bush St., Union Square* ☎ *415/421–3154 or 800/232–9698* ⊕ *www.cornellhotel.com* ⇗ *55 rooms* △ *In-room: no a/c, Wi-Fi. In-hotel: restaurant, parking* ⵀⵔ *Breakfast* ✛ *4:F2.*

14

$$ 🏨 **Executive Hotel Vintage Court.** This Napa Valley–inspired hotel two blocks from Union Square has newly renovated rooms named after California wineries. Some have sunny window seats, and all have large writing desks and dark-wood venetian blinds. **Pros:** complimentary local wines. **Cons:** small bathrooms; far from downtown and many tourist spots. **TripAdvisor:** "friendly and helpful," "very clean and spacious," "great location and price." ⊠ *650 Bush St., Union Square* ☎ *415/392–4666 or 800/654–1100* ⊕ *www.executivehotels.net/vintagecourt* 🛏 *106 rooms, 1 suite* △ *In-room: Internet, Wi-Fi. In-hotel: restaurant, bar, business center, parking* ¶◎| *Breakfast* ✛ *4:F2.*

$–$$ 🏨 **Golden Gate Hotel.** Families looking for accommodations in the Union Square area will delight in this homey, family-run B&B. Built in 1913, the four-story Edwardian building has front and back bay windows and an original "birdcage" elevator that transports you to hallways lined with nostalgic historical photographs. **Pros:** friendly staff; spotless rooms; comfortable bedding; good location if you're a walker. **Cons:** only some of the rooms have private baths. **TripAdvisor:** "very friendly and helpful," "small but well appointed," "great location." ⊠ *775 Bush St., Union Square* ☎ *415/392–3702 or 800/835–1118* ⊕ *www.goldengatehotel.com* 🛏 *25 rooms, 14 with bath* △ *In-room: no a/c, Internet, Wi-Fi. In-hotel: business center, parking, some pets allowed* ¶◎| *Breakfast* ✛ *4:E2.*

$$$–$$$$ 🏨 **Hilton San Francisco.** With 1,908 renovated rooms and suites, this is the largest hotel in California—its lobby can sometimes feel like downtown at rush hour; its silvery tower rises 46 floors to a penthouse event space with awe-inspiring 360-degree panoramic views that rank among the finest in San Francisco. **Pros:** super views; excellent service; full-service spa. **Cons:** area is dodgy after dark; there can be a wait at check-in. **TripAdvisor:** "staff was friendly and helpful," "rooms were clean and modern," "great location." ⊠ *333 O'Farrell St., Union Square* ☎ *415/771–1400* ⊕ *www.hiltonsanfranciscohotel.com* 🛏 *1,824 rooms, 84 suites* △ *In-hotel: restaurant, room service, bar, pool, gym, parking* ¶◎| *No meals* ✛ *4:E5.*

$$$$ 🏨 **Hotel Adagio.** The Spanish-colonial facade of this 16-story, theater-row hotel complements its chic, modern interior. **Pros:** close to theater district; on a bus route; good on-site restaurant. **Cons:** street noise; side streets can be dodgy at night. **TripAdvisor:** "very helpful and courteous," "modern and spacious," "location is excellent." ⊠ *550 Geary St., Union Square* ☎ *415/775–5000 or 800/228–8830* ⊕ *www.thehoteladagio.com* 🛏 *169 rooms, 2 suites* △ *In-room: Wi-Fi. In-hotel: room service, bar, gym, business center, parking* ¶◎| *No meals* ✛ *4:D4.*

$ 🏨 **Hotel Beresford.** This relatively inexpensive hotel is less than two blocks from Union Square. Well-maintained rooms with traditional furniture have recently received a wash of modernity—with fresh earth-toned linens, flat-screen TVs, and dark-wood furniture. **Pros:** reasonably priced; close to Union Square; friendly staff; free Wi-Fi. **Cons:** no air-conditioning; small rooms. **TripAdvisor:** "staff was pleasant," "small yet clean," "breakfast was basic but very good." ⊠ *635 Sutter St., Union Square* ☎ *415/673–9900 or 800/533–6533* ⊕ *www.beresford.*

com ⚑ *114 rooms* ⚐ *In-room: no a/c, Wi-Fi. In-hotel: bar, business center, parking, some pets allowed* ❘❍❘ *Breakfast* ✢ *4:D3.*

$$ 🛏 **Hotel Bijou.** Dedicated to the city's cinematic history, this hotel's tasteful lobby is filled with black-and-white photographs of local movie houses and reproductions of Tamara De Lempicka's art-deco paintings. **Pros:** near downtown; free nightly movies. **Cons:** close to the Tenderloin; small rooms. **TripAdvisor:** "staff was nice and polite," "great location," "reasonably sized rooms." ✉ *111 Mason St., at Eddy St., Union Square* ☎ *415/771–1200 or 800/771–1022* ⊕ *www.hotelbijou. com* ⚑ *65 rooms* ⚐ *In-room: no a/c, Wi-Fi. In-hotel: business center, parking* ❘❍❘ *Breakfast* ✢ *4:E5.*

¢–$ 🛏 **Hotel des Arts.** You'll need to climb a narrow, nondescript staircase to discover this hotel, which doubles as an art gallery: The hallways and rooms of this small, funky property have been transformed by international artists, who painted the walls and installed site-specific small sculptures. **Pros:** art-gallery atmosphere; good location. **Cons:** only about half of the rooms have private baths; small rooms. **TripAdvisor:** "clean and comfortable," "great location," "excellent service." ✉ *447 Bush St., Union Square* ☎ *415/956–3232 or 800/956–4322* ⊕ *www. sfhoteldesarts.com* ⚑ *43 rooms* ⚐ *In-room: Wi-Fi. In-hotel: parking* ❘❍❘ *Breakfast* ✢ *4:H2.*

$$–$$$ 🛏 **Hotel Diva.** Entering this hotel requires stepping over footprints, handprints, and autographs embedded into the sidewalk by visiting stars; with two major theaters, the Curran and Geary (home of the acclaimed American Conservatory Theater company), just across the street, this hotel has long been a magnet for actors, musicians, writers, and artists. **Pros:** clean; safe; in the heart of the theater district; accommodating service. **Cons:** no frills; tiny bathrooms. **TripAdvisor:** "location was great," "modern décor is nice," "beds were very comfortable." ✉ *440 Geary St., Union Square* ☎ *415/885–0200 or 800/553–1900* ⊕ *www. hoteldiva.com* ⚑ *115 rooms, 3 suites* ⚐ *In-room: Wi-Fi. In-hotel: gym, business center, parking, some pets allowed* ❘❍❘ *No meals* ✢ *4:D4.*

$$–$$$ 🛏 **Hotel Frank.** As if it popped off the pages of *Architectural Digest*, Hotel Frank's fun and business-friendly design is a nod to iPhone-toting urbanities who seek stylish digs in Union Square. **Pros:** hip design; free Wi-Fi; walking distance to theaters, shops, and restaurants. **Cons:** borders the seedy Tenderloin District; stylish design might feel as if you are in a gallery not a hotel room. **TripAdvisor:** "really friendly and helpful," "clean and comfortable," "some street noise." ✉ *386 Geary St., Union Square* ☎ *415/986–2000 or 877/828–4478* ⊕ *www.hotelfranksf.com* ⚑ *150 rooms, 3 suites* ⚐ *In-room: no a/c, Wi-Fi. In-hotel: restaurant, room service, bar, gym (off-site), parking, some pets allowed* ❘❍❘ *No meals* ✢ *4:E4.*

$$$–$$$$ 🛏 **Hotel Monaco, San Francisco.** A cheery 1910 Beaux-Arts facade and
Fodor's Choice snappily dressed doormen welcome you into a plush lobby dominated
★ by a French inglenook fireplace, vaulted ceilings painted with whimsical murals of hot-air balloons, a marble staircase, and a large metal baobab tree dedicated to hotelier Bill Kimpton. **Pros:** amazing service; stylish; full of character; near theater district; staff offers guests a goldfish to keep them company. **Cons:** close to the Tenderloin; some discount-rate

Mandarin Oriental, San Francisco

Argonaut Hotel

rooms are small. **TripAdvisor:** "fantastic customer service," "great location," "a lot of luxury."✉ *501 Geary St., Union Square* ☎*415/292–0100 or 866/622–5284* ⊕ *www.monaco-sf.com* ⇨*181 rooms, 20 suites* ᗡ *In-room: Wi-Fi. In-hotel: restaurant, room service, bar, gym, spa, business center, parking, some pets allowed* ⊚*No meals* ✦*4:D4.*

$$$$

Fodor's Choice

★

⊡ **Hotel Nikko, San Francisco.** The vast surfaces of gray-flecked white marble and gurgling fountains in the neoclassical lobby of this business traveler hotel have the sterility of an airport; however the crisply designed rooms in muted tones, with flat-screen TVs, modern bathrooms with sinks that sit on top of black vanities, plus separate showers and tubs, please jet-setters. **ros:** friendly multilingual staff; ultramodern baths; very clean. **Cons:** rooms and antiseptic lobby lack color; some may find the atmosphere cold; expensive parking. **TripAdvisor:** "staff was very professional," "impressively elegant," "great location."✉ *222 Mason St., Union Square* ☎*415/394–1111 or 800/248–3308* ⊕ *www.hotelnikkosf.com* ⇨*510 rooms, 22 suites* ᗡ *In-room: Internet, Wi-Fi. In-hotel: restaurant, room service, bar, pool, gym, business center, parking, some pets allowed* ⊚*No meals* ✦*4:E5.*

14

$$–$$$

⊡ **Hotel Rex.** At this stylish literary-themed hotel—named after San Francisco Renaissance poet, translator, and essayist Kenneth Rexroth and frequented by artists and writers—paintings and shelves of antiquarian books line the "library," a homey lobby lounge where book readings and roundtable discussions take place. **Pros:** convenient location; literary pedigree. **Cons:** cramped airless rooms; tiny baths and closets; musty hallways. **TripAdvisor:** "friendly and extremely helpful," "room was a good size," "furnished to a high standard."✉ *562 Sutter St., Union Square* ☎*415/433–4434 or 800/433–4434* ⊕ *www.thehotelrex.com* ⇨*92 rooms, 2 suites* ᗡ *In-room: Wi-Fi. In-hotel: restaurant, room service, bar, business center, parking, some pets allowed* ⊚*No meals* ✦*4:E3.*

$$

⊡ **Hotel Triton.** The spirit of fun has taken up full-time residence in this Kimpton property, which has a youngish, superfriendly staff; pink-and-blue-neon elevators; and a colorful psychedelic lobby mural depicting the San Francisco art and music scene—think flower power mixed with Andy Warhol. **Pros:** attentive service; refreshingly funky atmosphere; hip arty environs; good location. **Cons:** rooms and baths are on the small side. **TripAdvisor:** "very friendly and helpful," "location was great," "nice and clean."✉ *342 Grant Ave., Union Square* ☎*415/394–0500 or 800-800-1299* ⊕ *www.hoteltriton.com* ⇨*133 rooms, 7 suites* ᗡ *In-room: Wi-Fi. In-hotel: gym, parking, some pets allowed* ⊚*No meals* ✦*4:H2.*

$$$$

⊡ **JW Marriott San Francisco.** Guests here are whisked skyward in bullet elevators from the rose-and-gray-marble foyer into this John Portman–designed, former Pan Pacific hotel. **Pros:** recently renovated; convenient location; large rooms; luxurious bathrooms. **Cons:** comfortable but lacking character; some readers complain that the showers are too small. **TripAdvisor:** "beautiful and centrally located," "great location," "great rooms."✉ *500 Post St., Union Square* ☎*415/771–8600* ⊕ *www.jwmarriottunionsquare.com* ⇨*329 rooms, 8 suites* ᗡ *In-room: Internet. In-hotel: restaurant, room service, bar, gym, parking, some pets allowed* ⊚*No meals* ✦*4:E3.*

$$ ⛫**Kensington Park Hotel.** Built in the1920s in a Moorish and Gothic style, this intimate boutique hotel, originally designed to house the city's Elks Club, has retained its distinctive period feel and features. **Pros:** friendly personal service; guests rave about great location. **Cons:** some rooms have street noise; standard rooms are on the smallish side. **TripAdvisor:** "extremely helpful and friendly," "clean and comfy," "great location."⊠ *450 Post St., Union Square* ☎ *415/788–6400 or 800/553–1900* ⊕ *www.kensingtonparkhotel.com* ⤳ *92 rooms, 1 suite* ♿ *In-room: no a/c, Wi-Fi. In-hotel: restaurant, room service, bar, business center, parking, some pets allowed* |○| *No meals* ✚ *4:E3.*

$$–$$$ ⛫**Larkspur Union Square.** This compact boutique hotel, housed in a 1913 Edwardian building near Union Square, retains the original period feel throughout rooms, the lobby and in its lively Bar 1915. **Pros:** good location; moderately priced; spacious closets; clean. **Cons:** airless rooms and hallways; small baths. **TripAdvisor:** "great location," "always friendly and helpful," "very clean."⊠ *524 Sutter St., Union Square* ☎ *415/421–2865 or 866/823–4669* ⊕ *www.larkspurhotels.com* ⤳ *109 rooms, 5 suites* ♿ *In-room: a/c, Wi-Fi. In-hotel: bar, parking, some pets allowed* |○| *No meals* ✚ *4:F3.*

$$$$ ⛫**Orchard Garden Hotel.** Feel virtuous and environmentally sensitive at the first San Francisco hotel built to environmentally stringent LEED specifications, exacting standards which mandate the use of eco-friendly features such as chemical-free cleaning agents, recycling bins, and a custom guest-room key card energy-control system. **Pros:** environmentally sensitive; clean rooms; great location close to the Financial District and Chinatown. **Cons:** a bit of a hike from Union Square. **TripAdvisor:** "very comfortable and good location," "sleek and modern," "well run."⊠ *446 Bush St., Union Square* ☎ *415/399–9807 or 888/717–2881* ⊕ *www.theorchardgardenhotel.com* ⤳ *86 rooms* ♿ *In-room: Wi-Fi. In-hotel: restaurant, parking* |○| *Breakfast* ✚ *4:H2.*

$$$–$$$$
Fodor's Choice
★
⛫**Orchard Hotel.** The 104-room hotel embraces state-of-the-art technology—from CD and DVD players in each room to Wi-Fi access throughout the building—mixing cutting-edge Silicon Valley chic with classic European touches. **Pros:** cutting-edge technology; sizable boutique-style rooms; tech-savvy quarters. **Cons:** can be a bit pricey. **TripAdvisor:** "spacious room," "staff were friendly," "very clean."⊠ *665 Bush St., Union Square* ☎ *415/362–8878 or 888/717–2881* ⊕ *www.theorchardhotel. com* ⤳ *104 rooms, 9 suites* ♿ *In-room: Wi-Fi. In-hotel: restaurant, room service, parking, some pets allowed* |○| *No meals* ✚ *4:F2.*

$$$–$$$$ ⛫**The Prescott Hotel.** This relatively small establishment providing extremely personalized service prides itself on offering "good taste on Union Square." **Pros:** good location; excellent café and bar, and restaurant is top-notch, too. **Cons:** off-site valet service can be slow; some guests complain of street noise. **TripAdvisor:** "staff was extremely friendly," "service was fantastic," "a lot of street noise."⊠ *545 Post St., Union Square* ☎ *415/563–0303 or 866/271–3632* ⊕ *www.prescotthotel. com* ⤳ *132 rooms, 32 suites* ♿ *In-room: Wi-Fi. In-hotel: restaurant, room service, bar, gym, business center, parking, some pets allowed* |○| *No meals* ✚ *4:D4.*

$$$$ 🗔 **San Francisco Marriott Union Square.** The former Hotel 480, recently taken over by Marriott, has a prime location near shopping, restaurants, nightspots, and access to public transportation. **Pros:** convenient location; a slew of in-room amenities for business travelers. **Cons:** noisy street; feels corporate. **TripAdvisor:** "staff was friendly," "room service was quick and tasty," "great location and comfortable rooms."✉ *480 Sutter St., Union Square* 🕾 *415/398–8900 or 415/989–9823* ⊕ *www. marriott.com* ⤳ *447 rooms, 53 suites* ♿ *In-room: a/c, Wi-Fi (paid). In-hotel: restaurant, room service, bar, gym, laundry facilities, business center, parking* ⧉ *No meals* ✛ *4:F3.*

$$–$$$ 🗔 **Sir Francis Drake Hotel.** Beefeater-costumed doormen welcome you into the regal, dimly lighted lobby of this 1928 landmark property, decked out with boldly striped banners, wrought-iron balustrades, chandeliers, Italian marble, and leather and velvet furnishings that are a little on the tired side; the cumulative effect is of a Scottish castle that's seen better days. However, the major renovation—completed in 2011—enlivens the property—especially the elderly rooms—and gives this ole gal the energy of a teenager. **Pros:** can't beat the location; free in-room Wi-Fi; on-site restaurant and bar are moderately priced. **Cons:** small baths; lobby furniture looks a bit tired; some complaints about unresponsive service and cleanliness. **TripAdvisor:** "so friendly," "room service was fast," "centrally situated."✉ *450 Powell St., Union Square* 🕾 *415/392– 7755 or 800/795–7129* ⊕ *www.sirfrancisdrake.com* ⤳ *390 rooms, 20 suites* ♿ *In-room: Wi-Fi. In-hotel: restaurant, room service, bar, gym, business center, parking, some pets allowed* ⧉ *No meals* ✛ *4:F3.*

$$$$ 🗔 **Taj Campton Place San Francisco.** Beauty and highly attentive service remain the hallmarks of this exquisite jewel-like, top-tier hotel. **Pros:** attentive service; first-class restaurant; abundant natural light. **Cons:** smallish rooms; pricey (but worth it). **TripAdvisor:** "very friendly," "room service is efficient," "location is first class."✉ *340 Stockton St., Union Square* 🕾 *415/781–5555 or 866/332–1670* ⊕ *www. camptonplace.com* ⤳ *101 rooms, 9 suites* ♿ *In-room: Wi-Fi. In-hotel: restaurant, room service, bar, gym, parking, some pets allowed* ⧉ *No meals* ✛ *4:G3.*

$$$$ 🗔 **Villa Florence.** This newly remodeled, mid-size hotel is indeed a little bit of Italy on Powell Street. Bar Norcini, an Italian café-bar with marble surfaces, is just off the street, and a glass wall separates a wide lobby with high ceilings, comfy furnishings, and Italianate chandeliers from Kuleto's, a boisterous, trendy restaurant often packed with locals. **Pros:** great location for those who want to be in the center of things; easy access to shopping, theater, and public transport. **Cons:** noise from cable cars; crowded street. **TripAdvisor:** "very pleasant," "clean and comfortable," "quality rather than size."✉ *225 Powell St., Union Square* 🕾 *415/397–7700* ⊕ *www.villaflorence.com* ⤳ *154 rooms, 28 suites* ♿ *In-room: Wi-Fi. In-hotel: restaurant, bars, gym, some pets allowed* ⧉ *No meals* ✛ *4:F5.*

$$ 🗔 **Westin St. Francis.** The site of sensational, headline scandals, this hotel's past is shrouded in as much infamy as stardust: This is the place where Sara Jane Moore tried to assassinate Gerald Ford, where Al

14

Jolson died playing poker; Suite 1219–21 was the scene of a massive scandal, which erupted when a 30-year-old aspiring actress died after a night of heavy boozing in the close company of silent film comedian Fatty Arbuckle. **Pros:** fantastic beds; prime location; spacious rooms, some with great views. **Cons:** some guests comment on the long wait at check-in; rooms in original building can be small; glass elevators are not for the faint of heart. **TripAdvisor:** "very friendly and helpful," "room was a good size," "great location." ⌧ *335 Powell St., Union Square* ☎ *415/397–7000 or 800/917–7458* ⊕ *www.westinstfrancis. com* ⤵ *1,157 rooms, 38 suites* ⚹ *In-room: Internet, Wi-Fi. In-hotel: restaurants, room service, bars, spa, business center, parking, some pets allowed* ❑ *No meals* ✛ *4:F4.*

$$–$$$ ▢ **White Swan Inn.** A cozy library with a crackling fireplace is the heart of this inviting, English-style B&B, where patrons rest on comfortable chairs and sofas, lingering in the lounge, where wine, cheese, and tea are served in the afternoon. **Pros:** cozy B&B antidote to sterile chain hotels; nice lounge and patio area. **Cons:** thin walls make for noisy rooms; nearby streets can be a bit rough at night; Union Square is a bit of a hike (about three blocks). **TripAdvisor:** "very friendly and helpful," "fantastic service," "homey." ⌧ *845 Bush St., Union Square* ☎ *415/775–1755 or 800/999–9570* ⊕ *www.jdvhotels. com* ⤵ *25 rooms, 1 suite* ⚹ *In-room: no a/c, Wi-Fi. In-hotel: gym, parking* ❑ *Breakfast* ✛ *4:E2.*

CHINATOWN

$–$$ ▢ **SW Hotel.** Opened in 1913 as the Columbo Hotel, this lodging on the bustling border between Chinatown and North Beach has rooms and suites decorated in a blend of Italian and Chinese styles, with Florentine wall coverings and Ming-style furniture. **Pros:** top-floor views of Coit Tower; multilingual staff; self-serve parking under building. **Cons:** cramped closets and bathrooms. **TripAdvisor:** "very clean and convenient," "gem of a little hotel," "great location and price." ⌧ *615 Broadway, Chinatown* ☎ *415/362–2999 or 888/595–9188* ⊕ *www. swhotel.com* ⤵ *81 rooms, 2 suites* ⚹ *In-room: no a/c (some), Wi-Fi. In-hotel: business center, parking* ❑ *Breakfast* ✛ *1:D3.*

SOMA AND CIVIC CENTER

SOMA

$–$$ ▢ **Best Western Carriage Inn.** The newly rebranded Carriage Inn reminisces about San Francisco's literary, subversive, and comedic history by paying homage to city legends. Upon entering the boisterous lobby, view the framed caricatures of the city's brightest—you'll notice everyone from the sign-toting Frank Chu to the Golden Gate's favorite son, Robin Williams. **Pros:** plenty of character; spacious rooms; free Wi-Fi. **Cons:** not the safest neighborhood; thin walls. **TripAdvisor:** "beautiful remodeled rooms," "sketchy area but good value," "staff was friendly." ⌧ *140 7th St., SoMa* ☎ *415/552–8600 or 866/539–0036* ⊕ *www.carriageinnsf. com* ⤵ *48 rooms* ⚹ *In-room: a/c, Wi-Fi. In-hotel: business center, parking, some pets allowed* ❑ *Breakfast* ✛ *3:H2.*

$$$$ ⬚ **Four Seasons Hotel San Francisco.** Occupying floors 5 through 17 of
♻ a skyscraper, this luxurious (and award-winning) hotel, designated
Fodor's Choice as the "heart of the city," is sandwiched between multimillion-dollar
★ condos, elite shops, and a premier sports-and-fitness complex. **Pros:**
near museums, galleries, restaurants, and clubs; terrific fitness facilities;
luxurious rooms and amenities. **Cons:** pricey. **TripAdvisor:** "friendly
and helpful," "wonderful dining," "great location." ⊠ *757 Market St.,
SoMa* ☎ *415/633–3000, 800/332–3442, or 800/819–5053* ⊕ *www.
fourseasons.com/sanfrancisco* ⇨ *231 rooms, 46 suites* ⟳ *In-room:
Internet, Wi-Fi. In-hotel: restaurant, room service, bar, pool, gym, spa,
business center, parking, some pets allowed* ⧉ *No meals* ✛ *4:H4.*

$-$$ ⬚ **Hotel Milano.** Adjacent to the always hopping Westfield San Francisco
Shopping Centre—whose tenants include Bloomingdale's, a fantastic
food court, and Nordstrom—and close to many of the museums and
attractions south of Market Street, this hotel is a shopping and culture
maven's delight. **Pros:** good value; great location close to shopping
and museums; comfy beds; responsive front desk; stylish arty environs.
Cons: lots of hubbub and traffic; air-conditioning is inconsistent; some
rooms are dark. **TripAdvisor:** "great location," "very friendly and helpful," "comforting experience." ⊠ *55 5th St., SoMa* ☎ *415/543–8555*
⊕ *www.hotelmilanosf.com* ⇨ *108 rooms* ⟳ *In-room: Internet, Wi-Fi.
In-hotel: restaurant, room service, bar, gym, parking* ⧉ *No meals*
✛ *4:F6.*

$$$-$$$$ ⬚ **Hotel Palomar San Francisco.** The top five floors of the green-tile 1908
Pacific Place Building offer a luxurious oasis above the busiest part of
town: a softly lighted lounge area with plush sofas gives way to the
high-end, newly renovated Fifth Floor restaurant-café, renowned for its
adventurous French cuisine. **Pros:** in-room spa service available; first-
class restaurant; good location; refuge from downtown. **Cons:** pricey.
TripAdvisor: "service was great," "restaurant is excellent," "great
location." ⊠ *12 4th St., SoMa* ☎ *415/348–1111 or 866/373–4941*
⊕ *www.hotelpalomar-sf.com* ⇨ *184 rooms, 11 suites* ⟳ *In-room: Wi-Fi.
In-hotel: restaurant, room service, bar, gym, business center, parking,
some pets allowed* ⧉ *No meals* ✛ *4:G5.*

$$$$ ⬚ **InterContinental San Francisco.** The arctic-blue glass exterior and sub-
Fodor's Choice dued, Zen-like lobby of this sparkling new hotel may be as bland as an
★ airport concourse, but it's merely a prelude to the spectacularly light,
expansive, thoughtfully laid-out guest rooms, which have all the ultra-
modern conveniences. **Pros:** a stone's throw from the Moscone Center;
well-equipped gym; near hip clubs and edgy eateries; perfect for a week-
end getaway. **Cons:** conservative decor is a bit short on character; bor-
ders a rough neighborhood; a bit far from many major points of interest
for tourists. **TripAdvisor:** "friendly and helpful staff," "good gym and
pool," "views incredible." ⊠ *888 Howard St., SoMa* ☎ *415/616–6500
or 888/811–4273* ⊕ *www.intercontinentalsanfrancisco.com* ⇨ *536
rooms, 14 suites* ⟳ *In-room: Wi-Fi. In-hotel: restaurant, room service,
bar, pool, gym, spa, parking, some pets allowed* ⧉ *No meals* ✛ *4:H6.*

$-$$ ⬚ **The Mosser Hotel.** Originally built by patron of the arts Alice Phelan
in 1913 as the Keystone, this property was purchased in 1981 by com-
poser Charles W. Mosser and completely renovated in 2003. The result

14

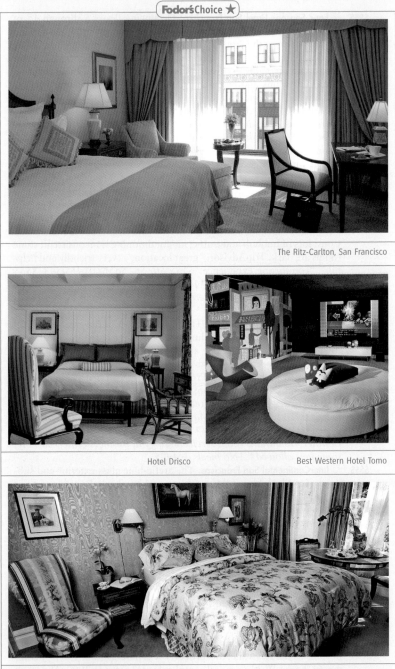

Fodor's Choice ★

The Ritz-Carlton, San Francisco

Hotel Drisco

Best Western Hotel Tomo

Union Street Inn

is a compatible pairing of contemporary decor and original Victorian architectural elements. **Pros:** convenient location; music-themed rooms; lively location in SoMa. **Cons:** a third of the rooms are without private baths; can be loud. **TripAdvisor:** "convenient and clean," "staff was very friendly," "rooms are tastefully modern."☒ *54 4th St., SoMa* ☎ *415/986–4400 or 800/227–3804* ⊕ *www.themosser.com* ⟿ *166 rooms, 112 with bath* ☐ *In-room: Wi-Fi. In-hotel: restaurant, bar, business center, parking* ⎮◯⎮ *Breakfast* ✛ *4:G5.*

$$$$

Fodor's Choice

★

☐ **Palace Hotel, San Francisco.** "Majestic" is the word that best sums up this landmark hotel, which was the world's largest and most luxurious when it opened in 1875. It was completely rebuilt after the 1906 earthquake and fire, and the carriage entrance reemerged as the grand Garden Court restaurant. **Pros:** gracious service; close to Union Square; near BART. **Cons:** design from another era; smallish rooms with even smaller baths; many nearby establishments closed on weekends; west-facing rooms can be warm and stuffy. **TripAdvisor:** "nice and clean," "lobby and restaurant are spectacular," "great location."☒ *2 New Montgomery St., SoMa* ☎ *415/512–1111 or 888/627–7196* ⊕ *www. sfpalace.com* ⟿ *518 rooms, 34 suites* ☐ *In-room: Internet. In-hotel: restaurants, room service, bar, pool, gym, parking* ⎮◯⎮ *No meals* ✛ *1:E5.*

14

$-$$

☐ **The Pickwick Hotel.** This terra-cotta-clad neo-Gothic hotel, built in 1926, is decked out with a can't-miss-it, seven-story corner sign straight out of film noir. Next door to the Westfield San Francisco Centre, which houses Bloomingdale's and Nordstrom, and convenient to Moscone Center, Yerba Buena District, and Union Square, the hotel caters to both business and leisure travelers. **Pros:** multilingual staff; helpful concierge; close to Yerba Buena District. **Cons:** not as opulent as some other options; some rooms dark and on the small side. **TripAdvisor:** "cozy and warm," "rooms are small but charming," "great location."☒ *85 5th St., SoMa* ☎ *415/421–7500 or 800/227–3282* ⊕ *www.thepickwickhotel. com* ⟿ *187 rooms, 2 suites* ☐ *In-room: Wi-Fi. In-hotel: restaurant, bar, parking* ⎮◯⎮ *No meals* ✛ *4:G6.*

$$$–$$$$

☐ **San Francisco Marriott Marquis.** The distinctive design of this 40-story hotel has been compared to a parking meter and a jukebox. Inside, a five-story, glass-top atrium encloses a dining court lush with palm trees, tropical plants, a cascading fountain, and a Starbucks in the lobby. **Pros:** stunning views from some rooms; in the cultural district; centered on business travelers. **Cons:** pricey parking; noisy lobby; some guests find the rooms sterile. **TripAdvisor:** "staff are friendly and helpful," "room service is surprisingly good," "room and bathroom were clean."☒ *55 4th St., SoMa* ☎ *415/896–1600* ⊕ *www.marriott.com/sfodt* ⟿ *1,498 rooms, 134 suites* ☐ *In-room: Internet. In-hotel: restaurants, room service, bars, pool, gym, parking* ⎮◯⎮ *No meals* ✛ *4:H5.*

$$$$

☐ **The St. Regis San Francisco.** This may be the most luxurious hotel in the city. Guests often remark that it's hipper and more modern than other hotels in the St. Regis chain, though the decor is still conservative: rooms have subdued cream-color, leather-texture walls and window seats, and 85% have views of the city. **Pros:** stunning, newly furnished rooms; good location; views. **Cons:** expensive; some guests report inconsistent service; hallway noise; long waits for room service and valet parking. **TripAdvisor:** "very comfortable," "room service was prompt," "a lot of street noise." ⊠ *125 3rd St., SoMa* ☏ *415/284–4000* ⊕ *www.stregis.com/sanfrancisco* ⟳ *214 rooms, 46 suites* ⚷ *In-room: Internet, Wi-Fi. In-hotel: restaurants, room service, bar, pool, gym, spa, business center, parking, some pets allowed* ❒ *No meals* ✦ *1:E6.*

$$$$ ☷ **W San Francisco.** The epitome of cool urban chic and fashion forward
 ☾   in design and clientele, this swanky 31-story Starwood hotel owes some of its cachet to a prime location next door to the San Francisco Museum of Modern Art. **Pros:** hip energy; sophisticated digs; in the heart of the cultural district; hotel is "going green." **Cons:** hotel's signature scents could pose a problem for sensitive noses. **TripAdvisor:** "so nice," "wonderful service," "great location." ⊠ *181 3rd St., SoMa* ☏ *415/777–5300* ⊕ *www.whotels.com/sf* ⟳ *404 rooms, 9 suites* ⚷ *In-room: Internet, Wi-Fi. In-hotel: restaurant, room service, bar, pool, gym, spa, business center, parking, some pets allowed* ❒ *No meals* ✦ *1:F6.*

$$$–$$$$ ☷ **Westin San Francisco Market Street.** Rising 36 stories over the bustling downtown and SoMa areas, this hotel (formerly the Argent) revels in its views. **Pros:** good location; clean rooms; fine restaurant and bar. **Cons:** some street noise; lots of convention and corporate business-types. **TripAdvisor:** "great service," "everything is perfect," "fantastic location." ⊠ *50 3rd St., SoMa* ☏ *415/974–6400 or 877/222–6699* ⊕ *www.westin.com* ⟳ *641 rooms, 26 suites* ⚷ *In-room: Internet, Wi-Fi. In-hotel: restaurant, room service, bar, gym, parking* ❒ *No meals* ✦ *4:H4.*

CIVIC CENTER

$–$$ ☷ **Hotel Whitcomb.** Built in 1910, this historic hotel (formerly the Ramada Plaza) was the temporary seat of city government from 1912 to 1915 before becoming a hotel in 1916. (What was once the mayor's office now serves as the hotel's administrative offices, and the jail cells are still intact in the hotel basement.) **Pros:** good location; rich architectural and historic legacy; opulent lobby; airport shuttle; free Wi-Fi. **Cons:** difficult to find street parking; area can be dodgy at night; rooms are not as flashy as the lobby. **TripAdvisor:** "friendly and helpful," "location was convenient," "rooms were clean." ⊠ *1231 Market St., Civic Center* ☏ *415/626–8000 or 800/227–4747* ⊕ *www.hotelwhitcomb.com* ⟳ *447 rooms, 13 suites* ⚷ *In-room: Wi-Fi. In-hotel: restaurant, room service, bar, gym, parking* ❒ *No meals* ✦ *3:G2.*

THE TENDERLOIN

$$$–$$$$ ☷ **Hotel Abri.** The Larkspur Hotel Collection has renovated the former Monticello Inn into a stylish hotel near Union Square shops, theaters, and restaurants. **Pros:** free Wi-Fi; shouting distance from the cable-car turnaround, shops, and eateries. **Cons:** most rooms have showers only; on-street parking nearly impossible. **TripAdvisor:** "staff was very friendly," "service was excellent," "only drawback is noise." ⊠ *127 Ellis St., Tenderloin* ☏ *866/823–4669 or 415/392–8800* ⊕ *www.hotel-abri.com* ⟳ *63 rooms, 28 suites* ⚷ *In-room: Wi-Fi. In-hotel: restaurant, room service, bar, business center, parking, some pets allowed* ❒ *No meals* ✦ *4:E5.*

$-$$ ⌂ **Phoenix Hotel.** A magnet for the hip at heart and ultracool—Little Richard, Elijah Wood, Sean Lennon, and members of R.E.M. and Pearl Jam have stayed here—so it's not the best choice for those seeking peace and quiet (or anyone put off by the hotel's location, on the fringes of the sketchy Tenderloin District). **Pros:** boho atmosphere; popular with musicians. **Cons:** somewhat seedy location; no elevators. **TripAdvisor:** "kind and very helpful," "coolest hotel in town," "relaxed atmosphere." ⌧ *601 Eddy St., Tenderloin* ☎ *415/776–1380 or 800/248–9466* ⊕ *www.thephoenixhotel.com* ⇆ *41 rooms, 3 suites* ♿ *In-room: no a/c, Wi-Fi. In-hotel: restaurant, bar, pool, parking* ⏹ *Breakfast* ✚ *4:A6.*

HAYES VALLEY

14

¢ ⌂ **Hayes Valley Inn.** Offering "European charm in the heart of Hayes Valley," the modest, clean rooms of this hotel come with sinks and vanities. Unfortunately the bathroom is down the hall. **Pros:** inexpensive; free local calls; close to shopping, restaurants, and theater. **Cons:** no in-room bathroom; no elevator; some street noise. **TripAdvisor:** "always friendly and helpful," "clean and comfortable," "a bit of street noise." ⌧ *417 Gough St., Hayes Valley* ☎ *415/431–9131 or 800/930–7999* ⊕ *www.hayesvalleyinn.com* ⇆ *28 rooms with shared baths* ♿ *In-room: no a/c, Wi-Fi. In-hotel: restaurant, laundry facilities, business center, parking, some pets allowed* ⏹ *Breakfast* ✚ *3:E2.*

$-$$ ⌂ **Inn at the Opera.** Within walking distance of Davies Symphony Hall and the War Memorial Opera House, this homey boutique hotel caters to season-ticket holders for the opera, ballet, and symphony; it has been the venue of choice for stars of the music, dance, and opera worlds, from Luciano Pavarotti to Mikhail Baryshnikov. **Pros:** staff goes the extra mile; intimate restaurant. **Cons:** smallish rooms and bath; sold out far in advance during opera season. **TripAdvisor:** "bed was very comfortable," "extremely friendly and helpful," "service was very good." ⌧ *333 Fulton St., Hayes Valley* ☎ *415/863–8400 or 800/325–2708* ⊕ *www.shellhospitality.com* ⇆ *30 rooms, 18 suites* ♿ *In-room: no a/c, Internet, Wi-Fi. In-hotel: restaurant, room service, bar, parking* ⏹ *Breakfast* ✚ *3:E2.*

FINANCIAL DISTRICT

$$$$ ⌂ **Galleria Park Hotel.** This boutique hotel, which has a dedicated clientele and is particularly packed on weekdays with corporate travelers, is close to BART, the Chinatown Gate, Union Square, and the high-end Crocker Galleria shopping complex. **Pros:** can't beat the location; one block from BART; friendly management; quiet rooms. **Cons:** small rooms and baths. **TripAdvisor:** "limited room service," "bathroom was a good size," "a bit of street noise." ⌧ *191 Sutter St., Financial District* ☎ *415/781–3060 or 800/792–9639* ⊕ *www.galleriapark.com* ⇆ *177 rooms, 8 suites* ♿ *In-room: Internet, Wi-Fi. In-hotel: restaurant, room service, bar, gym, business center, parking, some pets allowed* ⏹ *No meals* ✚ *1:E5.*

$$$-$$$$ ⌂ **Hilton San Francisco Financial District.** Fresh from a $55-million transformation, this stylish hotel now gleams as the crossroad between

Chinatown, the Financial District, and North Beach. **Pros:** abundant parking; bay and city views; award-winning spa; playground across the street. **Cons:** congested area. **TripAdvisor:** "extremely friendly and helpful," "very nicely appointed," "great views of the bay." ⊠ *750 Kearny St., Financial District* ☎ *415/433–6600* ⊕ *www.sanfranciscohiltonhotel. com* 📠 *537 rooms, 7 suites* ⚫ *In-room: Wi-Fi. In-hotel: restaurants, room service, bar, parking* ⦿ *Breakfast* ✛ *1:D4.*

$$$$ ⊞ **Omni San Francisco Hotel.** Although the lobby's glittering crystal chandeliers, dark mahogany paneling, and iron-and-marble staircase may hark back to an old-fashioned gentility, this 1926 redbrick-and-stone building, a former bank, is now home to a modern luxury hotel. **Pros:** outstanding personalized service; cookies and milk for the kids; immaculately clean; historical flavor. **Cons:** so-so air-conditioning; rooftop views are less than inspiring. **TripAdvisor:** "very courteous," "room service was fast," "great location." ⊠ *500 California St., Financial District* ☎ *415/677–9494* ⊕ *www.omnisanfrancisco.com* 📠 *347 rooms, 15 suites* ⚫ *In-room: Internet, Wi-Fi. In-hotel: restaurant, room service, bar, gym, business center, parking, some pets allowed* ⦿ *No meals* ✛ *1:E4.*

$$$$ ⊞ **Le Méridien San Francisco.** Across Battery Street from the Embarcadero Center complex, this hotel (formerly the Park Hyatt) has completed renovating its lounge and lobby area, as well as a style makeover of its standard rooms and suites in an effort to attract both leisure and business visitors. **Pros:** excellent service; ultra-convenient; spacious rooms; great views; top-notch concierge; interesting artwork throughout. **Cons:** strange New Age elevator sound track. **TripAdvisor:** "room service was prompt and tasty," "staff is well-trained and professional," "expect to do some walking." ⊠ *333 Battery St., Financial District* ☎ *415/296–2900* ⊕ *www.lemeridien.com/sanfrancisco* 📠 *281 rooms, 79 suites* ⚫ *In-room: Internet, Wi-Fi. In-hotel: restaurants, room service, bars, gym, business center, parking, some pets allowed* ⦿ *No meals* ✛ *1:E4.*

$$$$

Fodor's Choice

★

⊞ **Mandarin Oriental, San Francisco.** Two towers connected by glass-enclosed sky bridges compose the top 11 floors of San Francisco's third-tallest building, offering spectacular panoramas from every room; the windows open so you can hear that trademark San Francisco sound: the "ding ding" of the cable cars some 40 floors below (and some rooms even include binoculars). **Pros:** spectacular "bridge-to-bridge" views; attentive service; in the running for the most comfy beds in the city. **Cons:** located in a business area that's quiet on weekends; restaurant is excellent but expensive (as is the hotel). **TripAdvisor:** "staff was very friendly," "beds are great," "excellent views." ⊠ *222 Sansome St., Financial District* ☎ *415/276–9600 or 800/622–0404* ⊕ *www. mandarinoriental.com/sanfrancisco* 📠 *151 rooms, 7 suites* ⚫ *In-room: Wi-Fi. In-hotel: restaurant, room service, bar, gym, business center, parking, some pets allowed* ⦿ *No meals* ✛ *1:E4.*

NOB HILL AND RUSSIAN HILL

$$$$ ⊞ **Fairmont San Francisco.** This hotel, which dominates the top of Nob Hill like a European palace, has a rich history that includes surviving the 1906 earthquake and hosting the signing of the United Nations

Fodor'sChoice ★

InterContinental San Francisco

Palace Hotel, San Francisco

Four Seasons Hotel San Francisco

Charter in 1945. **Pros:** huge bathrooms; stunning lobby; great location. **Cons:** some guests have complained about spotty service; hills can be challenging for those on foot. **TripAdvisor:** "staff are very friendly and helpful," "lovely and spacious," "meal was very good."⊠ *950 Mason St., Nob Hill* ☎ *415/772–5000 or 800/257–7544* ⊕ *www.fairmont. com/sanfrancisco* ⋐ *591 rooms, 65 suites* ⌂ *In-room: Internet, Wi-Fi. In-hotel: restaurants, room service, bars, gym (off-site),spa (off-site), parking, some pets allowed* ⦿| *No meals* ✛ *4:E1.*

$ ⊡ **Hotel Vertigo.** Hitchcock's classic thriller *Vertigo* was set and partially shot in this ornate hotel, which was a speakeasy during Prohibition; recently the hotel's interiors have been redesigned to pay tribute to the film. **Pros:** tons of personality; artsy decor. **Cons:** borderline neighborhood; no air-conditioning. **TripAdvisor:** "very nice," "friendly and helpful," "comfortably in safe middle ground."⊠ *940 Sutter St., between Leavenworth and Hyde Sts., Nob Hill* ☎ *415/885–6800 or 800/553–1900* ⊕ *www.hotelvertigosf.coml.com* ⋐ *102 rooms, 8 suites* ⌂ *In-room: no a/c, Internet, Wi-Fi. In-hotel: restaurant, business center, parking* ⦿| *No meals* ✛ *4:B3.*

$$$$ ⊡ **The Huntington Hotel.** The venerable ivy-covered hotel, a family-owned property for three generations, has provided gracious personal service to everyone from Bogart and Bacall to Picasso and Pavarotti. **Pros:** personal service; an aura of old San Francisco; guests have access to the primo spa with city views; cable car passes by right out front. **Cons:** up a steep hill from downtown. **TripAdvisor:** "staff were very friendly," "room service charges steep," "great location."⊠ *1075 California St., Nob Hill* ☎ *415/474–5400 or 800/227–4683* ⊕ *www.huntingtonhotel. com* ⋐ *96 rooms, 40 suites* ⌂ *In-room: kitchen (some), Wi-Fi. In-hotel: restaurant, room service, bar, pool, gym, spa, parking* ⦿| *No meals* ✛ *4:D1.*

$$$$ ⊡ **Ritz-Carlton, San Francisco.** A preferred destination for travel-industry
Fodor's Choice   honchos, movie stars, and visitors alike, this hotel—a stunning tribute
★   to beauty and attentive, professional service—completed a $12.5-million renovation of its guest rooms and meeting spaces. **Pros:** terrific service; all-day food service on Club Level; beautiful surroundings. **Cons:** expensive; hilly location. **TripAdvisor:** "food was very good," "bartenders were very good," "great location."⊠ *600 Stockton St., at California St., Nob Hill* ☎ *415/296–7465* ⊕ *www.ritzcarlton.com* ⋐ *276 rooms, 60 suites* ⌂ *In-room: Wi-Fi. In-hotel: restaurants, room service, bars, pool, gym, business center, parking, some pets allowed* ⦿| *No meals* ✛ *4:F1.*

$$–$$$ ⊡ **The Stanford Court Renaissance Hotel San Francisco Hotel.** A stained-glass dome dominates the lobby of this stately, but comfortable, Marriott-operated hotel, though this initial enchantment is dwarfed by the understated elegance of guest rooms. **Pros:** focus on comfort; classic elegance. **Cons:** up a steep hill from most popular tourist sights; some guests complain that rooms are small. **TripAdvisor:** "staff were very friendly," "food was delicious," "great location."⊠ *905 California St., Nob Hill* ☎ *415/989–3500* ⊕ *www.stanfordcourt.com* ⋐ *389 rooms, 4 suites* ⌂ *In-room: Internet, Wi-Fi. In-hotel: restaurant, room service, bar, gym, business center, parking, some pets allowed* ⦿| *No meals* ✛ *4:F1.*

LODGING ALTERNATIVES

VACATION RENTALS

If you want an alternative to a hotel—one that gives a more authentically San Francisco experience (or at least a slightly more spacious one)— vacation rentals are the way to go. Many families and long-term visitors have found great apartments for reasonable rates by searching online in specific neighborhoods. There are few reputable local vacation rental companies, but you can't go wrong by visiting the San Francisco Convention and Visitors Bureau (⊕ *www. onlyinsanfrancisco.com*), where some property owners list their rentals.

CAMPING

While most travelers do not equate camping with an urban experience, those nutty San Franciscans have toppled that belief. **The Presidio of San Francisco** has recently renovated its **Rob Hill Campground** (☎ 415/561–5444 ⊕ *www.presidio. gov/experiences/camp.htm*)—the only place to pitch a tent in the city. Perched atop the highest hill in San Francisco's largest green space,

beneath a canopy of eucalyptus trees, and with views of Baker Beach, this site may be small (there are two sites that house 30 people each) and expensive ($100 a night with a maximum of two nights), but you can imagine the bragging rights earned for a night spent outdoors in the fog. Book well in advance, as you might expect, sites fill fast. The season closes on October 31.

HOSTELS

No matter your age (or style of luggage), staying at a hostel saves cash. San Francisco's three hostels are members of **Hostelling International** (the massive umbrella organization of thousands of properties all over the world). While members receive priority reservations (and discounts), you don't have to pay the 30 bucks to join in order to stay the night. The San Francisco City Center and San Francisco Downtown hostels offer reasonable rates in the heart of the action. But the real steal is the San Francisco Fisherman's Wharf Hostel, as some rooms offer bay views. w*www.norcalhostels.org.*

14

NORTH BEACH

$$ 🛏 **Hotel Bohème.** This small hotel in historic North Beach takes you back in time with cast-iron beds, large mirrored armoires, and memorabilia recalling the Beat generation—whose leading light, Allen Ginsberg, often stayed here (legend has it that in his later years he could be seen sitting in a window, typing away on his laptop computer). **ros:** North Beach location with literary pedigree; stylish rooms; helpful staff. **Cons:** street parking is scarce; lots of traffic congestion; no air-conditioning; small rooms. **TripAdvisor:** "awesome location," "beautiful room," "in the heart of North Beach."⊠ *444 Columbus Ave., North Beach* ☎ *415/433–9111* ⊕ *www.hotelboheme.com* ⤴ *15 rooms* ⚹ *In-room: no a/c, Internet, Wi-Fi* ⍋⊙ *No meals* ✛ *1:D3.*

¢ 🛏 **San Remo Hotel.** A few blocks from Fisherman's Wharf, this three-
Fodor's Choice story 1906 Italianate Victorian—once home to longshoremen and
★ Beat poets—has a narrow stairway from the street leading to the front desk and labyrinthine hallways; rooms are small but charming, with

lace curtains, forest-green-painted wood floors, brass beds, and other antique furnishings. **Pros:** inexpensive; historic; cozy. **Cons:** some rooms are dark; no private bath; spartan amenities. **TripAdvisor:** "very clean," "great location," "helpful staff." ⊠ *2237 Mason St., North Beach* ☎ *415/776–8688 or 800/352–7366* ⊕ *www.sanremohotel.com* ➫ *64 rooms with shared baths, 1 suite* ⚲ *In-room: no a/c, no TV, Wi-Fi. In-hotel: laundry facilities, parking* ¶◯¶ *No meals* ⊹ *1:C2.*

$$$–$$$$ 🏨 **Washington Square Inn.** Overlooking the tree-lined park of its name-sake and surrounded by fine shops and cafés, this gracious corner B&B sits at the foot of Telegraph Hill in the heart of North Beach. **Pros:** nice rooms; fun location. **Cons:** some guests complain about gruff management; no air-conditioning; street parking is difficult to come by. **TripAdvisor:** "very comfortable," "immaculately clean," "great location." ⊠ *1660 Stockton St., at Filbert St., North Beach* ☎ *415/981–4220 or 800/388–0220* ⊕ *www.wsisf.com* ➫ *15 rooms* ⚲ *In-room: no a/c, Wi-Fi. In-hotel: business center, parking* ¶◯¶ *Breakfast* ⊹ *1:D2.*

THE WATERFRONT

FISHERMAN'S WHARF

$$$ 🏨 **Argonaut Hotel.** When the four-story Haslett Warehouse was a fruit-and-vegetable canning complex in 1907, boats docked right up against the building; today it's a hotel with a nautical decor—think anchors, ropes, compasses, and a row of cruise-ship deck chairs in the lobby—that reflects its unique partnership with the San Francisco Maritime National Historical Park. **Pros:** bay views; near Hyde Street cable car; sofa beds; toys for the kids. **Cons:** nautical theme isn't for everyone; cramped public areas; service can be hit or miss; location is a bit of a trek from other parts of town. **TripAdvisor:** "outstanding breakfast," "very friendly staff," "fabulous view of Alcatraz." ⊠ *495 Jefferson St., at Hyde St., Fisherman's Wharf* ☎ *415/563–0800 or 866/415–0704* ⊕ *www.argonauthotel.com* ➫ *239 rooms, 13 suites* ⚲ *In-room: Internet, Wi-Fi. In-hotel: restaurant, room service, bar, gym, parking, some pets allowed* ¶◯¶ *No meals* ⊹ *1:A1.*

Fodor's Choice
★

$$$ 🏨 **Best Western Tuscan Inn.** Described by some Fodors.com users as a "hidden treasure," this hotel's redbrick facade barely hints at the Tuscan country villa that lies within. **Pros:** wine and beer hour; down-home feeling; great location near Fisherman's Wharf. **Cons:** congested touristy area; small rooms. **TripAdvisor:** "staff are very friendly," "very clean," "comfortable good sized room." ⊠ *425 N. Point St., at Mason St., Fisherman's Wharf* ☎ *415/561–1100 or 800/648–4626* ⊕ *www.tuscaninn.com* ➫ *212 rooms, 12 suites* ⚲ *In-room: Wi-Fi. In-hotel: restaurant, room service, bar, business center, parking, some pets allowed* ¶◯¶ *No meals* ⊹ *1:C1.*

$$$$ 🏨 **Fairmont Heritage Place, Ghirardelli Square.** Housed in the former Ghirardelli chocolate factory, these one-to-three-bedroom serviced apartments might possibly be the most luxurious accommodations in San Francisco. **Pros:** luxury at its finest; gigantic apartments with heaps of amenities; bay views from most apartments; free Lexus SUV hotel car to deliver you within a 2-mi radius. **Cons:** a bit of a trek from downtown; expensive. **TripAdvisor:** "classic hotel service," "home away from home," "great location."✉ *950 Mason St., Fisherman's Wharf* ☎ *415/576–1900* ⊕ *www.fairmont.com/ghirardelli* 🛏 ⅛ *In-room: a/c, kitchen, Wi-Fi. In-hotel: gym, spa, laundry facilities, business center, parking, some pets allowed* ⍾ *Breakfast* ✛ *1:A1.*

$$$–$$$$ 🏨 **Hyatt at Fisherman's Wharf.** The location is key to this hotel's popularity: it's within walking distance of such tourist hot spots as Ghirardelli Square, the Cannery, Pier 39, Aquatic Park, and Alcatraz ferries; bay cruises dock nearby; and it's across the street from a cable-car turnaround. **Pros:** primo sightseeing location; close to cable cars; friendly staff. **Cons:** street noise; crowds; expensive parking. **TripAdvisor:** "staff is friendly and helpful," "room service was fine," "ideal location."✉ *555 N. Point St., Fisherman's Wharf* ☎ *415/563–1234 or 800/233–1234* ⊕ *www.fishermanswharf.hyatt.com* 🛏 *313 rooms, 8 suites* ⅛ *In-room: Wi-Fi. In-hotel: restaurant, room service, bar, pool, gym, laundry facilities, business center, parking* ⍾ *No meals* ✛ *1:B1.*

$$$ 🏨 **San Francisco Marriott Fisherman's Wharf.** Behind the hotel's sand-color facade is a lavish, low-ceiling lobby with marble floors, a double fireplace, and English club–style furniture. Rooms—which have recently been fully remodeled—have either a king-size bed or two double beds; all are triple-sheeted, and the abundance of extra pillows allows for lots of luxurious lounging. **Pros:** near tourist hot spots; comfortable bedding. **Cons:** touristy area; on a busy street. **TripAdvisor:** "friendly and helpful," "beds were comfortable," "very clean and well appointed."✉ *1250 Columbus Ave., Fisherman's Wharf* ☎ *415/775–7555* ⊕ *www.marriott.com* 🛏 *269 rooms, 16 suites* ⅛ *In-room: Internet. In-hotel: restaurant, room service, bar, gym, laundry facilities, business center, parking, some pets allowed* ⍾ *No meals* ✛ *1:B1.*

$$$$ 🏨 **Sheraton Fisherman's Wharf Hotel.** The newly gutted and reimagined Sheraton Fisherman's Wharf might not look like much from outside, but inside she is one festive gal. From the fire pits lining the parking area to the contemporary teal mood lighting in the lobby, guests have taken to the playful design, lounging in common spaces to sip wine, Skype their friends, and catch up on the news. **Pros:** in the heart of Fisherman's Wharf; newly renovated with fun colors; outdoor pool; free Wi-Fi in the Spressi café. **Cons:** touristy area; feels corporate. **TripAdvisor:** "very friendly and helpful," "rooms are clean," "great location." ✉ *2500 Mason St., Fisherman's Wharf* ☎ *415/362–5500 or 888/627–7024* ⊕ *www.sheratonatthewharf.com* 🛏 *524 rooms, 7 suites* ⅛ *In-room: a/c, Wi-Fi (paid). In-hotel: restaurants, room service, bar, pool, gym, business center, parking, some pets allowed* ⍾ *No meals* ✛ *1:C1.*

EMBARCADERO

$$$$ 🏨 **Harbor Court Hotel.** Exemplary service and a friendly staff earn high marks for this cozy hotel, which overlooks the Embarcadero and is within shouting distance of the Bay Bridge. **Pros:** convenient location; quiet; friendly service; cozy. **Cons:** small rooms. **TripAdvisor:** "very well appointed," "rooms are not large," "outstanding hotel."✉ *165 Steuart St., Embarcadero* ☎ *415/882–1300 or 866/792–6283* ⊕ *www.harborcourthotel.com* 🛏 *130 rooms, 1 suite* ⅛ *In-room: Wi-Fi. In-hotel: bar, business center, parking, some pets allowed* ⍾ *No meals* ✛ *1:G4.*

14

Fodor's Choice ★

Hotel Nikko, San Francisco

Orchard Hotel

Hotel Monaco, San Francisco

$$$$ ⚃ **Hotel Vitale.** "Luxury, naturally," the theme of this eight-story ter-
Ↄ raced bayfront hotel, is apparent in every thoughtful detail: little vases
of aromatic herbs mounted outside each room; the penthouse day spa
with soaking tubs set in a rooftop bamboo forest; and the aromatherapy
garden off the patio of restaurant Americano, whose outdoor terrace is
packed Thursday and Friday. **Pros:** family-friendly studios; great views;
recently renovated spa; luxurious amenities throughout. **Cons:** cramped
rooms can be noisy; some guests report inconsistent service from staff
and find the hotel pricey. **TripAdvisor:** "very friendly and helpful,"
"food quality was very good," "well-appointed and clean." ⊠ *8 Mission St., Embarcadero* ☎ *415/278–3700 or 888/890–8688* ⊕ *www.
hotelvitale.com* ⊅ *190 rooms, 9 suites* ⚄ *In-room: Internet, Wi-Fi. In-
hotel: restaurant, room service, bar, gym, spa, business center, parking,
some pets allowed* ⵔ*No meals* ⊹ *1:G4.*

14

THE MARINA AND THE PRESIDIO

$ ⚃ **Cow Hollow Motor Inn and Suites.** Suites at this large, family-owned
Fodor's Choice modern motel are more spacious than average, with sitting and dining
★ areas, dark-wood furniture, and wallpaper with muted yellow, brown,
and green patterns. **Pros:** suites are the size of apartments; good for
families; covered parking in building. **Cons:** congested neighborhood
has a fratty feeling; rooms are on a loud street. **TripAdvisor:** "very clean
and comfortable," "great value," "great location." ⊠ *2190 Lombard
St., Marina* ☎ *415/921–5800* ⊕ *www.cowhollowmotorinn.com* ⊅ *117
rooms, 12 suites* ⚄ *In-room: a/c, kitchen (some), Wi-Fi. In-hotel: parking* ⵔ*No meals* ⊹ *2:E3.*

$$–$$$ ⚃ **Hotel Del Sol.** Go tropical in the Marina District at this colorfully
Ↄ restored three-story 1950s motor lodge. **Pros:** kid-friendly; plenty of
nearby places to eat and shop. **Cons:** congested area; faces a busy
thoroughfare. **TripAdvisor:** "very friendly and helpful," "dynamic
neighborhood," "clean and fun stay." ⊠ *3100 Webster St., Marina*
☎ *415/921–5520 or 877/433–5765* ⊕ *www.thehoteldelsol.com* ⊅ *42
rooms, 15 suites* ⚄ *In-room: kitchen (some), Wi-Fi. In-hotel: pool, parking, some pets allowed* ⵔ*Breakfast* ⊹ *2:F3.*

¢–$ ⚃ **Marina Inn.** Five blocks from the Marina, this four-story 1924 build-
ing feels like a B&B, but is priced like a motel. **Pros:** affordable; daybed
option for kids. **Cons:** street-side rooms can be noisy. **TripAdvisor:**
"always nice," "very clean and comfortable," "great location." ⊠ *3110
Octavia St., at Lombard St., Marina* ☎ *415/928–1000 or 800/274–
1420* ⊕ *www.marinainn.com* ⊅ *40 rooms* ⚄ *In-room: no a/c, Wi-Fi*
ⵔ*Breakfast* ⊹ *2:G2.*

$ ⚃ **Marina Motel.** Reminiscent of the motor courts of yesteryear, this
family-owned motel is an inexpensive option within walking distance
of restaurants, bars, and shops in the Marina District and on the waterfront. **Pros:** staff that accommodates guests with pets; more character
than the chain motels on the same strip. **Cons:** no air-conditioning;
located on a busy street; rooms can be noisy and stuffy; staff can be
gruff. **TripAdvisor:** "very clean," "motel is charming," "lovely flowers everywhere." ⊠ *2576 Lombard St., Marina* ☎ *415/921–9406 or*

800/346–6118 ⊕ *www.marinamotel.com* ⟿ *39 rooms* ⚹ *In-room: no a/c, kitchen (some), Wi-Fi. In-hotel: parking, some pets allowed* ¶○¶ *No meals* ⊹ *2:D3.*

COW HOLLOW

¢–$ ⊡ **Coventry Motor Inn.** Among the many motels on busy Lombard Street, this is one of the cleanest, friendliest, and quietest—especially the rooms that don't face Lombard. **Pros:** clean; friendly; good value; lots of eateries nearby; free parking in building. **Cons:** busy street; few amenities. **TripAdvisor:** "clean and comfortable room," "location is great," "very helpful staff." ⊠ *1901 Lombard St., Cow Hollow* ☎ *415/567– 1200* ⊕ *www.coventrymotorinn.com* ⟿ *69 rooms* ⚹ *In-room: Wi-Fi. In-hotel: parking* ¶○¶ *No meals* ⊹ *2:F3.*

$–$$ ⊡ **Pacific Heights Inn.** One of the most genteel-looking motels in town, this two-story motor court near the busy intersection of Union and Van Ness is dressed up with wrought-iron railings and benches, hanging plants, and pebbled exterior walkways facing the parking lot. **Pros:** kitchenettes; free parking; reasonable rates; close walk to the Marina shopping and dining areas. **Cons:** noisy; crowded parking area. **TripAdvisor:** "great staff," "comfortable and clean," "location not luxury." ⊠ *1555 Union St., Cow Hollow* ☎ *415/776–3310 or 800/523–1801* ⊕ *www.pacificheightsinn.com* ⟿ *28 rooms, 12 suites* ⚹ *In-room: no a/c, kitchen (some), Wi-Fi. In-hotel: parking, some pets allowed* ¶○¶ *Breakfast* ⊹ *2:H3.*

$$–$$$ ⊡ **Union Street Inn.** Precious family antiques and unique artwork helped
FodorsChoice   British innkeepers Jane Bertorelli and David Coyle (former chef for
★   the Duke and Duchess of Bedford) transform this green-and-cream 1902 Edwardian into a delightful B&B. **Pros:** personal service; Jane's excellent full breakfast; romantic setting. **Cons:** on a congested street; no air-conditioning; no elevator. **TripAdvisor:** "warmly welcoming," "comfortable and cozy," "great location." ⊠ *2229 Union St., Cow Hollow* ☎ *415/346–0424* ⊕ *www.unionstreetinn.com* ⟿ *6 rooms* ⚹ *In-room: no a/c, Wi-Fi. In-hotel: parking* ¶○¶ *Breakfast* ⊹ *2:E3.*

MISSION DISTRICT

$–$$ ⊡ **The Inn San Francisco.** No other bed-and-breakfast is as seeped in local lore as the Inn at San Francisco: this Italianate Victorian mansion once belonged to a city commissioner who struck it rich in the potato business, and was then dubbed the city's "Potato King"; for decades the 27-room mansion has welcomed visitors to the vibrant Mission District. **Pros:** lots of charming antiques; helpful staff; located in the sunny side of the city. **Cons:** neighborhood can be sketchy at night; some rooms are very small. **TripAdvisor:** "good place to explore the city," "friendly and helpful staff," "almost southern hospitality." ⊠ *943 S. Van Ness Ave, Mission District* ☎ *415/641–0188 or 800/359–0913* ⊕ *www.innsf.com* ⟿ *21 rooms* ⚹ *In-room: no a/c, Wi-Fi. In-hotel: parking* ¶○¶ *Breakfast* ⊹ *3:G6.*

PACIFIC HEIGHTS AND JAPANTOWN

PACIFIC HEIGHTS

$$$–$$$$
Fodor's Choice
★

Hotel Drisco. Pretend you're a resident of one of the wealthiest and most beautiful residential neighborhoods in San Francisco at this understated, elegant 1903 Edwardian hotel. **Pros:** great service; comfortable rooms; quiet residential retreat. **Cons:** small rooms; far from downtown. **TripAdvisor:** "great Pacific Heights location," "very comfortable," "exceptional staff." ⊠ *2901 Pacific Ave., Pacific Heights* ☎ *415/346–2880 or 800/634–7277* ⊕ *www.hoteldrisco.com* ➦ *29 rooms, 19 suites* ⚲ *In-room: no a/c. In-hotel: business center* ⍩ *Breakfast* ✛ *2:D4.*

$–$$

Hotel Majestic. Built in 1902 as a private residence, this five-story white Edwardian building is the city's oldest continually operating hotel—movie-star sisters Joan Fontaine and Olivia de Havilland, symbols of Old Hollywood royalty, once lived here. **Pros:** quintessential SF hotel; destination café; Victorian flavor; quiet neighborhood; spacious rooms; perfect for a romantic getaway. **Cons:** you'll need a cab to get downtown or walk 15 minutes. **TripAdvisor:** "loved the neighborhood," "friendly and helpful," "small but clean." ⊠ *1500 Sutter St., Pacific Heights* ☎ *415/441–1100 or 800/869–8966* ⊕ *www.thehotelmajestic. com* ➦ *47 rooms, 9 suites* ⚲ *In-room: Wi-Fi (paid). In-hotel: restaurant, room service, bar, business center, parking* ⍩ *No meals* ✛ *2:G6.*

$$$
☾

Laurel Inn. The blue-and-tan Googie-style facade of this stylish inn suggests its 1963 urban-motel origins. Rooms, decorated in black and taupe, are spacious and clean; some have desks and fold-out sofas, and 18 offer convenient kitchenettes. **Pros:** clean; spacious; kid-friendly rooms; close to Sacramento Street shopping and dining. **Cons:** no air-conditioning; far from downtown. **TripAdvisor:** "clean and refreshing service," "quiet and lovely," "very nice view." ⊠ *444 Presidio Ave., Pacific Heights* ☎ *415/567–8467 or 800/552–8735* ⊕ *www. thelaurelinn.com* ➦ *49 rooms* ⚲ *In-room: no a/c, kitchen (some), Wi-Fi (paid). In-hotel: bar, parking, some pets allowed* ⍩ *Breakfast* ✛ *2:C5.*

$–$$

Queen Anne Hotel. Built in the 1890s as a girls' finishing school and located in fashionable Pacific Heights, this Victorian mansion has a large comfortable parlor done up in red brocade, lace, and heirloom antiques. **Pros:** free weekday car service; has lots of character. **Cons:** 15-minute walk to downtown; slightly dated. **TripAdvisor:** "so accommodating," "well-appointed," "rooms were clean." ⊠ *1590 Sutter St., Pacific Heights* ☎ *415/441–2828 or 800/227–3970* ⊕ *www.queenanne.com* ➦ *41 rooms, 7 suites* ⚲ *In-room: Wi-Fi. In-hotel: parking* ⍩ *Breakfast* ✛ *2:G6.*

JAPANTOWN

$–$$
☾
Fodor's Choice
★

Best Western Hotel Tomo. Japanese Pop, or J-Pop as it is known across the pond, comes alive in this newly reinvented Japantown boutique hotel, located just a couple of blocks from the chic Fillmore district, Yoshi's, and the Fillmore Theatre. **Pros:** J-Pop style; anime playing on the lobby TV and manga in your room; great price in a fun neighborhood. **Cons:** small rooms; far from downtown. **TripAdvisor:** "fun hotel," "bargain in the city," "quiet and super clean." ⊠ *1800 Sutter St., Japantown* ☎ *415/921–4000* ⊕ *www.hoteltomo.com* ➦ *125 rooms, 1 suite* ⚲ *In-room: a/c, Internet. In-hotel: restaurant, bar, gym* ⍩ *No meals* ✛ *2:G6.*

14

$$–$$$ 🏨 **Hotel Kabuki.** This pagoda-style boutique hotel, which underwent a $10-million face-lift in 2007, is next door to Japantown and two blocks from Fillmore Street and Pacific Heights. **Pros:** serene environment; locally favored restaurant. **Cons:** a bit of a trek from downtown. **TripAdvisor:** "hotel is definitely shabby," "reasonable value," "room was comfortable." ✉ *1625 Post St., at Laguna St., Japantown* ☎ *415/922–3200 or 800/533–4567* ⊕ *www.jdvhotels.com* ➵ *204 rooms, 14 suites* ⌂ *In-room: Internet, Wi-Fi. In-hotel: restaurant, bar, gym, business center, parking* ⦿*No meals* ✢ *2:G6.*

RICHMOND

$–$$ 🏨 **Seal Rock Inn.** About as far west as you can go in San Francisco with-
☺ out falling into the Pacific, this hotel within easy walking distance of the Cliff House and Ocean Beach is a welcome refuge from the hub-bub of downtown. **Pros:** close to the beach; lots of activities for kids. **Cons:** no air-conditioning; no pets allowed; far from the action of the city; in the foggy part of town. **TripAdvisor:** "great comfort," "won-derful breakfasts," "great views." ✉ *545 Point Lobos Ave., Richmond* ☎ *415/752–8000 or 888/732–5762* ⊕ *www.sealrockinn.com* ➵ *27 rooms* ⌂ *In-room: no a/c, kitchen (some), Internet, Wi-Fi. In-hotel: restaurant, pool, parking* ⦿*No meals* ✢ *2:A6.*

BY THE AIRPORT

$$ 🏨 **Bay Landing Hotel.** For an airport hotel, you can't get much better than this European country-style property with unsurpassed bay views. **Pros:** spectacular bayfront views; friendly staff; breakfast included in rate. **Cons:** a trek from the city. **TripAdvisor:** "very comfortable," "very friendly and helpful," "great view." ✉ *1550 Bayshore Hwy., Burlingame* ☎ *650/259–9000* ⊕ *www.baylandinghotel.com* ➵ *130 rooms, 3 suites* ⌂ *In-room: a/c, Wi-Fi. In-hotel: gym, laundry facilities, business center, parking* ⦿*Breakfast* ✢ *1:G6.*

$$ 🏨 **Embassy Suites San Francisco Airport, Burlingame.** Set on the bay, with clear vistas of airplanes flying above San Francisco in the distance, the building's focal point is a nine-story atrium and tropical garden show-casing exotic towering palms, bamboo and banana plants, and koi-filled ponds all crowned by a waterfall; this is one of the most lavish hotels in the airport corridor. **Pros:** low rates; luxurious accommodations. **Cons:** no standard rooms; no concierge. **TripAdvisor:** "friendly and helpful," "rooms are very spacious," "great value." ✉ *150 Anza Blvd., Burlingame* ☎ *650/342–4600 or 800/362–2779* ⊕ *www.sfoburlingame. embassysuites.com* ➵ *340 suites* ⌂ *In-room: kitchen, Wi-Fi. In-hotel: res-taurant, bar, pool, gym, parking, some pets allowed* ⦿*Breakfast* ✢ *1:G6.*

Performing Arts

WORD OF MOUTH

"I think after New York, this area has the most interesting and varied and unexpected performing arts scene in the country. It ranges from the most experimental theater and dance-theater hybrids imaginable . . . to really lavish (and expensive) professional and commercial shows."

—Jean S.

Updated by
Sura Wood

Sophisticated, offbeat, and ahead of the curve, San Francisco's diverse and vibrant performing arts scene is as eclectic as its inhabitants. After all, this is the city that spawned Tony Kushner's landmark opus *Angels in America.*

Most of San Francisco's major theaters are concentrated on Geary Street west of Union Square, but a number of commercial houses, as well as resident companies, are within walking distance of this theater-centric row, while other seriously quirky, adventurous venues have sprung up in lower-rent districts like the Mission. Just across the bay, Berkeley Rep has developed productions that have won critical acclaim in New York and London.

Music, from jazz to classical, is the lifeblood of the city. The San Francisco Opera offers up both the classics and unconventional collaborative projects, and the San Francisco Ballet likewise presents traditional repertoire while reaching out to hip contemporary choreographers like Mike Morris to infuse the company with new vitality. This has long been a hub for dancers—don't forget, Isadora Duncan danced with abandon in diaphanous costumes in the courtyard of the Palace of the Legion of Honor, and the San Francisco Ballet presented the American debut of *The Nutcracker* here in 1944. Exciting modern and experimental dance companies remain a major part of the city's thriving cultural life.

And as in France, film here is truly considered an art form; San Francisco's cinema-savvy audiences and award-winning resident filmmakers support more local film festivals than any other city aside from Paris.

PERFORMING ARTS PLANNER

TICKETS 101
The opera, symphony, the San Francisco Ballet's *The Nutcracker,* and touring hit musicals are often sold out in advance. Tickets are usually available for other shows within a day of the performance.

City Box Office (⌧ *180 Redwood St., Suite 100, off Van Ness Ave. between Golden Gate Ave. and McAllister St., Civic Center* 🖀 *415/392–4400* ⊕ *www.cityboxoffice.com*), a charge-by-phone service, offers tickets for many performances and lectures. You can buy tickets in person at its downtown location weekdays 9:30–5:30. **San Francisco Performances** (⊠ *500 Sutter St., Suite 710* ☎ *415/398–6449* ⊕ *www. performances.org*) brings an eclectic array of top-flight global music and dance talents to various venues—mostly the Yerba Buena Center for the Arts, Davies Symphony Hall, and Herbst Theatre. Artists have included the Los Angeles Guitar Quartet, Edgar Meyer, the Paul Taylor Dance Company, and Midori. Tickets can be purchased in person, online, or by phone.

You can charge tickets for everything from jazz concerts to Giants games by phone or online through **Tickets.com** (☎ *800/955–5566* ⊕ *www.tickets.com*). Half-price, same-day tickets for many local and touring stage shows go on sale (cash only) at 11 am Tuesday through Saturday at the **TIX Bay Area** (⊠ *Powell St. between Geary and Post Sts., Union Square* ☎ *415/433–7827* ⊕ *www.tixbayarea.com*) booth on Union Square. TIX is also a full-service ticket agency for theater and music events around the Bay Area, open Tuesday through Friday 11–6, Saturday 10–6, and Sunday 10–3.

TOP ARTS PICKS

Berkeley Repertory Theatre. The Bay Area's most satisfying theatrical performances are just a quick BART trip away.

Castro Theatre. This dramatic art-deco palace is the perfect spot for munching buttery popcorn and watching a Judy Garland or Jimmy Stewart flick on the big screen.

Yoshi's. Amazing jazz and great Japanese food in a stylish theater.

Stern Grove Festival. While away a Sunday afternoon listening to opera, jazz, rock, and other musical genres in a gorgeous eucalyptus-enclosed amphitheater.

15

LISTING INFORMATION

The best guide to the arts is the Sunday "Datebook" section (⊕ *www. sfgate.com/datebook*), printed on pink paper, in the *San Francisco Chronicle*. The four-day entertainment supplement "96 Hours" (⊕ *www.sfgate.com/96hours*) is in the Thursday *Chronicle*. Also be sure to check out the city's free alternative weeklies, including *SF Weekly* (⊕ *www.sfweekly.com*) and the more avant-garde *San Francisco Bay Guardian* (⊕ *www.sfbg.com*).

Online, SF Station (⊕ *www.sfstation.com*) has a frequently updated arts and nightlife calendar. San Francisco Arts Monthly (⊕ *www.sfarts.org*), which is published at the end of the month, has arts features and events, plus a helpful "Visiting San Francisco?" section. For offbeat, emerging artist performances, consult CounterPULSE (⊕ *www.counterpulse.org*).

For information on getting around after dark, see Late-Night Transportation in Nightlife.

DANCE

San Francisco continues to gain recognition for its exciting modern and experimental dance companies. Local groups such as Alonzo King's Lines Ballet and ODC/San Francisco tour extensively and are well regarded by national dance critics. The San Francisco Ballet excels at both traditional and contemporary repertoires.

Dancers' Group (⊕ *www.dancersgroup.org*) is a Web site with events and resource listings for dancers and dance aficionados. **Voice of Dance** (⊕ *www.voiceofdance.com*) is a national publication with local calendars. Web-only **DanceView Times** (⊕ *www.danceviewtimes.com*) reviews productions and events.

★ **Alonzo King's Lines Ballet**. Since 1982 this company has been staging the fluid and gorgeous ballets of choreographer and founder Alonzo King, sometimes in collaboration with top-notch world musicians such as Zakir Hussain and Hamza El Din. Ballets incorporate both classical and modern techniques, with experimental set design, costumes, and music. The San Francisco season is in spring. ☎ *415/863–3040* ⊕ *www. linesballet.org*.

Joe Goode Performance Group. Physicality and high-flying style are the hallmarks of this original group, a blend of modern dance and theater. Works include narrative, video projections, and song, and succeed at being both poignant and funny. ☎ *415/561–6565* ⊕ *www.joegoode.org*.

☾ **ODC/San Francisco**. Popular with kids, this 10-member group's annual
★ Yuletide version of *The Velveteen Rabbit* (mid-November–mid-December), at the Yerba Buena Center for the Arts, ranks among the city's best holiday-season performances. The group's main repertory season generally runs intermittently between January and June. ☎ *415/863–6606* ⊕ *www.odcdance.org*.

Fodor's Choice **San Francisco Ballet**. For ballet-lovers, this company is reason alone to
★ come to the Bay Area. Under artistic director Helgi Tomasson, the San Francisco Ballet's works—both classical and contemporary—have won critical raves.The primary season runs from February through May. Its repertoire includes full-length ballets such as *Don Quixote* and *Sleeping Beauty*; the December presentation of *The Nutcracker* is one of the most spectacular in the nation. The company also performs bold new dances from star choreographers such as William Forsythe and Mark Morris, alongside modern classics by George Balanchine and Jerome Robbins. Tickets and information are available at the **War Memorial Opera House**. ✉ *War Memorial Opera House, 301 Van Ness Ave., Civic Center* ☎ *415/865–2000* ⊕ *www.sfballet.org* ☉ *Weekdays 10–4*.

Smuin Ballet/SF. Former San Francisco Ballet director Michael Smuin founded this company, whose works are renowned for their gorgeous fluidity. It regularly integrates popular music—everything from Gershwin to the Beatles and Elton John—into its performances, most of which take place at the Yerba Buena Center for the Arts. ☎ *415/556–5000* ⊕ *www.smuinballet.org*.

FILM

The San Francisco Bay Area, including Berkeley and Marin County, is considered one of the nation's most savvy movie markets. Films of every stripe—3-D blockbusters, art-house indies, classic revivals—find an audience here. The area is also a filmmaking center, where documentaries and experimental works are produced on modest budgets, feature films and television programs are shot on location, and pioneering animation companies like Pixar Animation Studios, which is just across the bay in Emeryville, push the technological envelope. In San Francisco about a third of the theaters regularly show foreign and independent films.

San Francisco Cinematheque (☎ 415/552–1990 ⊕ www.sfcinematheque. org) showcases experimental film and digital media, with most screenings at the Yerba Buena Center for the Arts or at Artists' Television Access.

MOVIE THEATERS

The Bridge. This theater, built in 1939, has been showing films on its single screen since the 1950s. ✉ 3010 Geary Blvd., at Blake St., Western Addition ☎ 415/267–4893.

Fodor's Choice ★ **Castro Theatre.** An art-deco showstopper, this is the most dramatic movie theater in the city, and it hosts revivals, foreign films, independent engagements, local film festivals, and the occasional sing-along movie musical. Just strolling into the space, designed by Timothy Pfleuger and opened in 1922, is worthwhile, but coming for a film is the full experience. Parking is limited in the Castro District, so taking public transportation is advised. ✉ 429 Castro St., near Market St., Castro ☎ 415/621–6120 ⊕ www.castrotheatre.com.

The Clay. This small but comfortable and well-kept single-screen theater dates to 1910 and has first-run art-house films. ✉ 2261 Fillmore St., at Clay St., Pacific Heights ☎ 415/267–4873.

Embarcadero Center Cinemas. Shows often sell out at this modern, extremely popular five-screen theater, which has the best in first-run independent, art house, and foreign films. ✉ 1 Embarcadero Center, promenade level, Embarcadero ☎ 415/267–4893.

Lumière. This three-screen theater tends toward experimental and foreign films, as well as documentaries. ✉ 1572 California St., between Polk and Larkin Sts., Van Ness/Polk ☎ 415/267–4893.

Opera Plaza Cinemas. The four theaters and their screens are small, but this is often the last place you can see an independent or foreign film before it ends its run in the city. It's great for indie-film-loving procrastinators, but if you arrive late for the show, you may have to sit in the front row of the tiny screening room. ✉ 601 Van Ness Ave., between Turk St. and Golden Gate Ave., Civic Center ☎ 415/267–4893.

Red Vic Movie House. An adventurous lineup of hard-to-find contemporary and classic American and foreign indies and documentaries is screened in a funky setting, which is California's only worker-owned and -operated movie house. ✉ 1727 Haight St., between Cole and Shrader Sts., Haight ☎ 415/668–3994 ⊕ www.redvicmoviehouse.com.

Roxie Cinema. Film noir and indie features and documentaries, as well as first-run movies and classic foreign cinema, are the specialties here. ✉ 3117 16th St., between Valencia and Guerrero Sts., Mission ☎ 415/863–1087 ⊕ www.roxie.com.

15

FILM FESTIVALS

Although San Francisco isn't a mainstream movie mecca or company town like Los Angeles, it has long been a center for award-winning documentary filmmaking; and area film festivals, especially the popular San Francisco International Film Festival, attract sell-out crowds to many screenings which feature Q&A sessions with (directors and actors from around the world). Smaller niche festivals, which are proliferating and more intimate, often offer the opportunity to mix it up with filmmakers.

American Indian Film Festival. This event, presented by the American Indian Film Institute, has been based in San Francisco since 1977. Each November the festival takes over various venues, including the Palace of Fine Arts Theatre. ☎ *415/554–0525* ⊕ *www.aifisf.com.*

San Francisco International Asian American Film Festival. Asian and Asian-American cinema is the focus of this March festival, presented by the Center for Asian American Media. The lineup includes feature and short films and videos—everything from animation to documentaries. ☎ *415/863–0814* ⊕ *www.asianamericanmedia.org.*

San Francisco International Film Festival. For two weeks each spring the San Francisco Film Society—which also sponsors year-round screenings and film series—takes over several theaters, including the Castro Theatre, the Sundance Kabuki Cinemas, and Pacific Film Archive.The festival schedules about 200 films, documentaries, and videos from 50 countries; many are U.S. premieres. Tickets and program information can be found on their Web site. ⊕ *www.sffs.org.*

San Francisco Independent Film Festival (Indiefest and Docfest). This popular event presents a slate of movies that are defiantly out of the mainstream. Indiefest, which caters to a younger demographic, specializes in oddball fare rarely programmed at other festivals; Docfest performs the same service for documentaries you won't find at the local multiplex. ☎ *415/820–3907* ⊕ *www.sfindie.com.*

San Francisco International Lesbian & Gay Film Festival. The world's oldest and largest festival of its kind takes place at various venues for two weeks in late June. ☎ *415/703–8650* ⊕ *www.frameline.org/festival.*

San Francisco International South Asian Film Festival. Documentaries, feature films, and Bollywood movies are shown at this weeklong festival in November. ☎ *415/835–4783* ⊕ *www.thirdi.org/festival.*

San Francisco Jewish Film Festival. In late July and early August, the Castro Theatre and other Bay Area venues screen films as part of this event, which was started in 1980. Parties on the opening and closing nights of the festival celebrate the filmmakers. ☎ *415/621–0556* ⊕ *www.sfjff.org.*

MUSIC

San Francisco's symphony and opera perform in the Civic Center area, but musical ensembles can be found all over the city: in churches, museums, restaurants, and parks—not to mention in Berkeley and on the Peninsula.

42nd Street Moon. This group produces delightful "semistaged" concert performances of rare chestnuts from Broadway's golden age of musical theater, such as *L'il Abner* and *The Boys From Syracuse*. The **Eureka Theatre** (✉ *215 Jackson St., between Front and Battery Sts., Financial District*) hosts most 42nd Street Moon shows. ☎ *415/255–8207* ⊕ *www.42ndstmoon.com*.

★ **Chanticleer.** A Bay Area treasure, this all-male a-cappella ensemble stages lively and technically flawless performances that show off a repertoire ranging from sacred medieval music to show tunes to contemporary avant-garde works. ☎ *415/252–8589* ⊕ *www.chanticleer.org*.

★ **Kronos Quartet.** Twentieth-century works and a number of premieres make up the programs for this always entertaining, Grammy Award–winning string ensemble, which spends much of the year traveling throughout the United States and abroad. ⊕ *www.kronosquartet.org*.

Noontime Concerts at Old St. Mary's Cathedral. This Gothic Revival church, completed in 1872 and rebuilt after the 1906 earthquake, hosts a notable chamber-music series on Tuesday at 12:30; suggested donation is $5. ✉ *660 California St., Financial District* ☎ *415/777–3211* ⊕ *www. noontimeconcerts.org*.

Old First Concerts. The well-respected Friday-evening and Sunday-afternoon series includes chamber music, choral works, vocal soloists, new music, and jazz. Tickets are $17. ✉ *Old First Presbyterian Church, 1751 Sacramento St., at Van Ness Ave., Van Ness/Polk* ☎ *415/474–1608* ⊕ *www.oldfirstconcerts.org*.

Fodor'sChoice
★ **San Francisco Symphony.** One of America's top orchestras, the San Francisco Symphony performs from September through May, with additional summer performances of light classical music and show tunes; visiting artists perform here the rest of the year. The orchestra and its charismatic music director, Michael Tilson Thomas, who is known for his daring programming of 20th-century American works (most notably his Grammy Award–winning Mahler cycle), often perform with soloists of the caliber of Andre Watts, Gil Shaham, and Renée Fleming. The adventuresome side of the organization is amply illustrated by this symphony's collaboration with the heavy-metal group Metallica. David Byrne has performed here, as well. Tickets run about $15–$100.

Many members of the San Francisco Symphony perform in the **Summer in the City** (☎ *415/864–6000* ⊕ *www.sfsymphony.org*) concert series, held in the 2,400-seat Davies Symphony Hall. The schedule includes light classics and Broadway, country, and movie music. ✉ *Davies Symphony Hall, 201 Van Ness Ave., at Grove St., Civic Center* ☎ *415/864–6000* ⊕ *www.sfsymphony.org*.

MUSIC FESTIVALS

Hardly Strictly Bluegrass Festival. The city's top free music event, as well as one of the greatest gatherings for bluegrass, country, and roots music in the country, takes place from late September to early October. Roughly 50,000 folks turn out to see the likes of Willie Nelson, Emmylou Harris, Jimmie Dale Gilmore, and Del McCoury at Speedway Meadows in Golden Gate Park. ⊕ *www.strictlybluegrass.com*.

Noise Pop Festival. Widely considered to be one of the country's top showcases for what's new in indie-pop and alt-rock, Noise Pop is a

15

weeklong festival in February or March held at Slim's, the Great American Music Hall, and other cool clubs. Founded in 1993, the low-key festival has helped local fans discover such talented acts as Modest Mouse, Kristin Hersh, and Bettie Serveert. (Phone info on the event is best obtained by calling the individual venues.) ☎ *415/375–3370* ⊕ *www.noisepop.com.*

San Francisco Jazz Festival. Every year starting in October, concert halls, clubs, and churches throughout the city host this acclaimed two-week festival. The popular event, which got its start in 1983, has featured such big-name acts as Ornette Coleman, Sonny Rollins, and McCoy Tyner, as well as talked-about up-and-comers like Brad Mehldau and Chris Botti. ☎ *415/398–5655* ⊕ *www.sfjazz.org.*

San Francisco World Music Festival. Founded in 2000, this respected festival draws musicians from around the world to various venues in the city. Unlike some so-called world music festivals, this event truly *is* a global affair, offering more than just the standard assortment of Celtic acts and Latin jazz players. The event takes place each fall, usually starting in November. ☎ *415/561–6571* ⊕ *www.sfworldmusicfestival.org.*

SFJAZZ Spring Season. The increasingly popular counterpart to the fall festival, the Spring Season is programmed by artistic director Joshua Redman, a saxophone colossus who grew up across the bay in Berkeley. Founded in 2000, the lengthy festival runs roughly from mid-March to early June and features an array of top-notch headliners. ☎ *415/398– 5655* ⊕ *www.sfjazz.org.*

Stern Grove Festival. The nation's oldest continual free summer music festival hosts Sunday-afternoon performances of symphony, opera, jazz, pop music, and dance. The amphitheater is in a beautiful eucalyptus grove below street level, perfect for picnicking before the show. (Dress for cool weather.) ✉ *Sloat Blvd. at 19th Ave., Sunset* ☎ *415/252–6252* ⊕ *www.sterngrove.org.*

OPERA

Fodor's Choice
★

San Francisco Opera. Founded in 1923, this world-renowned company has resided in the Civic Center's War Memorial Opera House since the building's completion in 1932. Over its split season—September through January and June through July—the opera presents about 70 performances of 10 to 12 operas. Translations are projected above the stage during almost all non-English operas. Long considered a major international company and the most important operatic organization in the United States outside New York, the opera frequently embarks on productions with European opera companies and unconventional projects, some with a popular cultural edge designed to attract younger audiences. Ticket prices can range from $25 to $195. The full-time box office (Monday 10–5, Tuesday through Friday 10–6) is at 199 Grove Street, at Van Ness Avenue. ✉ *War Memorial Opera House, 301 Van Ness Ave., at Grove St., Civic Center* ☎ *415/864–3330 tickets* ⊕ *www. sfopera.com.*

PERFORMING ARTS CENTERS

Fodor's Choice ★ **War Memorial Opera House.** With its soaring vaulted ceilings and marble foyer, this elegant 3,146-seat venue, built in 1932, rivals the Old World theaters of Europe. Located in a performing arts complex of buildings that also houses the San Francisco Symphony and Herbst Theatre, it's home to both the San Francisco Opera and the San Francisco Ballet, who perform here during alternating seasons. ⊠ *301 Van Ness Ave., at Grove St. Civic Center* ☎ *415/621–6600* ⊕ *www.sfwmpac.org.*

Fodor's Choice ★ **Yerba Buena Center for the Arts.** Across the street from the Museum of Modern Art and abutting a lovely urban garden, this performing arts complex schedules interdisciplinary art exhibitions, touring and local dance troupes, music, film programs, and contemporary theater events. You can depend on the quality of the productions at Yerba Buena. Film buffs often come here to check out the San Francisco Cinematheque (⊕ *www.sfcinematheque.org*), which showcases experimental film and digital media. And dance enthusiasts can attend concerts by a roster of city companies that perform here including Smuin Ballet/SF (⊕ *www. smuinballet.org*), the ODC/San Francisco (⊕ *www.odcdance.org*), the Margaret Jenkins Dance Company, and Alonzo King's Lines Ballet (⊕ *www.linesballet.org*). The Lamplighters (⊕ *www.lamplighters.org*), an alternative opera that specializes in Gilbert and Sullivan, also has a season here in addition to performing at various venues around town. ⊠ *3rd and Howard Sts., SoMa* ☎ *415/978–2787* ⊕ *www.ybca.org.*

15

SPOKEN WORD AND READINGS

Nearly every night of the week, aspiring and established writers, poets, and performers step up to the mike and put their words and egos on the line. Check "Listings" in the free alternative weekly papers and the *San Francisco Sunday Chronicle* "Book Review" section for other options.

Cafe International. An open-mike session follows one or more featured readers here every Friday night at 8. Spoken-word performances are interspersed with acoustic musical acts. ⊠ *508 Haight St., at Fillmore St., Lower Haight* ☎ *415/552–7390.*

Fodor's Choice ★ **City Arts & Lectures.** Each year this program includes more than 20 fascinating conversations with writers, composers, actors, politicians, scientists, and others. The Herbst Theatre, in the Civic Center area, is usually the venue. Past speakers have included Nora Ephron, Salman Rushdie, Ken Burns, and Linda Ronstadt. ☎ *415/392–4400* ⊕ *www.cityarts.net.*

★ **Commonwealth Club of California.** The nation's oldest public-affairs forum hosts speakers as diverse as Erin Brockovich and Bill Gates; every president since Teddy Roosevelt has addressed the club. Topics range from culture and politics to economics and foreign policy. Events are open to nonmembers; contact the club for the current schedule of events. Venues vary by speaker. Lectures are broadcast on NPR. ⊠ *595 Market St., at 2nd St., Financial District* ☎ *415/597–6700* ⊕ *www. commonwealthclub.org.*

★ **West Coast Live.** Billed as "San Francisco's Live Radio Show to the World," the program invites an audience to its weekly broadcasts, many at Fort Mason's Magic Theater, the Empire Plush Room, and the Freight & Salvage Coffee House in Berkeley. The ever-changing guest list includes authors, musicians, comedians, and pundits. Recent guests have included Dave Barry, Charlie Owen, and Jamaica Kincaid. ☎ *415/664–9500* ⊕ *www.wcl.org.*

Writers With Drinks. This quirky, oft-madcap, and hilariously funny spoken word event is part reading, part circus variety show. Writers range from unknowns to rising stars and the occasional well-known author. Writers With Drinks usually takes place at the Make-Out Room, at 3225 22nd Street in the Mission. ⊕ *www.writerswithdrinks.com.*

THEATER

The three major commercial theaters—Curran, Golden Gate, and Orpheum—are operated by the Shorenstein-Nederlander organization, which books touring plays and musicals, some before they open on Broadway. Theatre Bay Area (⊕ *www.theatrebayarea.org*) lists most Bay Area performances online.

★ **American Conservatory Theater.** Not long after its founding in the mid-1960s, the city's major nonprofit theater company became one of the nation's leading regional theaters. During its season, which runs from early fall to late spring, ACT presents approximately eight plays, from classics to contemporary works, often in rotating repertory. In December ACT stages a much-loved version of Charles Dickens's *A Christmas Carol.* The **ACT ticket office** (✉ *405 Geary St., Union Square* ☎ *415/749–2228*) is next door to **Geary Theater,** the company's home. ✉ *Geary Theater, 415 Geary St., Union Square* ⊕ *www.act-sf.org.*

Asian American Theater Company. This group, which puts on works by Americans of Asian and Pacific Islands descent, is dedicated to working with local actors, directors, and playwrights. Plays tend to be edgy and thought-provoking, and are often funny. ✉ *55 Teresita Blvd., SoMa* ☎ *415/519–2920* ⊕ *www.asianamericantheater.org.*

Curran Theater. Some of the biggest touring shows mount productions at this theater, which has hosted classical music, dance, and stage performances since its 1925 opening. Shows are of the long-running Broadway musical variety, such as *Stomp* and *Jersey Boys*, and the seasonal *A Christmas Carol.* ✉ *445 Geary St., at Mason St., Union Square* ☎ *415/551–2000* ⊕ *www.shnsf.com.*

Exit Theatre. *The* place for absurdist and experimental theater, this three-stage venue also presents the annual **Fringe Festival** in September. ✉ *156 Eddy St., between Mason and Taylor Sts., Union Square* ☎ *415/931–1094* ⊕ *www.sffringe.org.*

Golden Gate Theater. This stylishly refurbished movie theater is now primarily a musical house. Touring productions of popular Broadway shows and revivals are its mainstay. ✉ *Golden Gate Ave. at Taylor St., Tenderloin* ☎ *415/551–2000* ⊕ *www.shnsf.com.*

Lorraine Hansberry Theatre. The performance of plays by black writers such as August Wilson and Langston Hughes is the raison d'être of this company. Though they're currently without a resident theater, an

CLOSE UP

Arts and Culture Beyond the City

Although most folks from outlying areas drive *into* San Francisco to enjoy the performing arts, there are plenty of reasons to head *out* of the city.

FILM
The **Pacific Film Archive** (✉ *2575 Bancroft Way, near Bowditch St., Berkeley* ☎ *510/642-0808* ⊕ *www.bampfa.berkeley.edu*), affiliated with the University of California, screens a comprehensive mix of classics, American, and foreign films. The spectacular art-deco **Paramount Theatre** (✉ *2025 Broadway, near 19th St. BART station, Oakland* ☎ *510/465-6400* ⊕ *www.paramounttheatre.com*) screens a few vintage flicks (*The Sting, Casablanca*) every month and presents live events.

MUSIC
Some of the most talented practitioners of folk, blues, Cajun, and bluegrass perform at the alcohol-free **Freight & Salvage Coffee House** (✉ *2020 Addison St., Berkeley* ☎ *510/644-2020* ⊕ *www.freightandsalvage.org*). Oakland is home to **Yoshi's** (✉ *510 Embarcadero St., between Washington and Clay Sts., Oakland* ☎ *510/238-9200* ⊕ *www.yoshis.com*), one of the nation's best jazz venues.

The East Bay's **Berkeley Symphony Orchestra** (☎ *510/841-2800* ⊕ *www.berkeleysymphony.org*) has risen to considerable prominence under artistic director Kent Nagano's baton. The emphasis is on 20th-century composers. The orchestra plays a handful of concerts each year, in the University of California–Berkeley's Zellerbach Hall and in other locations around Berkeley. ■**TIP→** The acoustics in Zellerbach Hall are notoriously dead; sit in the front or middle orchestra for the best sound.

THEATER
The Tony Award–winning **Berkeley Repertory Theatre** (✉ *2025 Addison St., Berkeley* ☎ *510/647-2949* ⊕ *www.berkeleyrep.org*) is the American Conservatory Theatre's major rival for leadership among the region's resident professional companies. It performs an adventurous mix of classics and new plays from fall to spring in its theater complex, near BART's Downtown Berkeley Station. Parking is at a premium, so plan to arrive early if you're coming by car.

The **Cal Performances** (☎ *510/642-9988* ⊕ *www.calperformances.org*) series, held at various venues on the University of California–Berkeley campus from September through May, offers the Bay Area's most varied bill of internationally acclaimed artists in all disciplines.

15

announcement of a new space is expected this year. Check the Web site for more details.☎ *415/345–3980* ⊕ *www.lorrainehansberrytheatre.com.*

Magic Theatre. Once Sam Shepard's favorite showcase, the pint-size Magic presents works by rising American playwrights, such as Matthew Wells, Karen Hartman, and Claire Chafee. ✉ *Fort Mason, Bldg. D, Laguna St. at Marina Blvd., Marina* ☎ *415/441–8822* ⊕ *www.magictheatre.org.*

The Marsh. Experimental works, including one-man and one-woman shows, works in progress, and new vaudeville shows, can be seen here. ✉ *1062 Valencia St., at 22nd St., Mission* ☎ *800/838–3006 tickets, 415/826–5750 information* ⊕ *www.themarsh.org.*

New Conservatory Theatre Center. This three-stage complex hosts the annual **Pride Season,** focusing on contemporary gay- and lesbian-themed works, as well as other events, including educational plays for young people. ✉ *25 Van Ness Ave., between Fell and Oak Sts., Hayes Valley* ☎ *415/861–8972* ⊕ *www.nctcsf.org.*

☾ **New Pickle Circus**. The acrobatically inclined group generally performs at the Circus Center around Christmastime, with fire-breathing jugglers and high-flying trapeze artists. There are a few smaller productions in San Francisco and the Bay Area throughout the year. ✉ *755 Frederick St.* ☎ *415/759–8123* ⊕ *www.circuscenter.org.*

Orpheum Theater. The biggest touring shows, such as *Hairspray* and *The Lion King,* are performed at this gorgeously restored 2,500-seat venue. The theater, opened in 1926 as a vaudeville stage, is as much an attraction as the shows. It was modeled after the Spanish baroque palaces and is considered one of the most beautiful theaters in the world; the interior walls have ornate cathedral-like stonework, and the gilded plaster ceiling is perforated with tiny lights. ✉ *1192 Market St., at Hyde St., Tenderloin* ☎ *415/551–2000* ⊕ *www.shnsf.com.*

☾ **San Francisco Mime Troupe**. The politically leftist, barbed satires of this
★ Tony Award–winning troupe are hardly mime in the Marcel Marceau sense. The group performs afternoon musicals at area parks from the July 4 weekend through September, and taking one in is a perfect way to spend a sunny summer day. ☎ *415/285–1717* ⊕ *www.sfmt.org.*

Fodor's Choice **Teatro ZinZanni**. Contortionists, chanteuses, jugglers, illusionists, and
★ circus performers ply the audience as you're served a surprisingly good five-course dinner in a fabulous antique Belgian traveling-dance-hall tent (the location of which is moving to a new permanent home this year). Be ready to laugh, and arrive early for a front-and-center table. Reservations are essential; tickets are $125 to $150; call or check the Web site for prices and location. And dress fancy. ☎ *415/438–2668* ⊕ *www.zinzanni.org.*

Theatre Rhinoceros. Gay and lesbian performers and playwrights are showcased in this small Mission theater. ✉ *1360 Mission St., Suite 200, Mission* ☎ *800/838–3006 tickets, 415/552–4100 offices* ⊕ *www. therhino.org.*

Nightlife

WORD OF MOUTH

"San Francisco is an early town but there are endless bars and clubs . . . [Recently I] prowled North Beach, and beyond; drank at Bix (art deco/beautiful wood bar, a must w/champagne). There's also Saloon, the oldest bar in the City w/cheap drinks & many characters."

—JeriO

Updated by
Sura Wood

Downtown cool, trendy, relaxed, quirky, and downright outrageous could all be used to describe San Francisco's diverse collection of bars and clubs. It can be overwhelming to decide where to go in your short time here, but using the neighborhood as a guide can be a helpful way to design the evening you want.

Nob Hill is noted for its old-money mansions; today's plush hotel bars and panoramic skyline lounges, the most famous being Top of the Mark, fit right in here. North Beach's historic bars invoke the city's bohemian past, and its sleek lounges lure diners from the area's mom-and-pop Italian restaurants who seek an après-meal, late-night experience to top off the evening. Fisherman's Wharf, with many of the city's hotels, is probably the most touristy part of the city; but, you could also find yourself here after a trip to the Exploratorium or a ferry ride back from Alcatraz, Angel Island, or Sausalito. Singles bars on tony Union Street and in the nearby Marina attract well-dressed and well-to-do crowds in their twenties and thirties. (Be sure to break out your snazziest threads for the Marina.) South of Market—or SoMa—is a nightlife hub, with a clutch of popular dance clubs, bars, and supper clubs, as well as a few excellent live-music venues. The gay and lesbian scenes are centered in the Castro District and along Polk Street. Twentysomethings and indie types should check out the ever-funky Mission District and Haight Street, although even these two neighborhoods have more upscale cocktail lounges and fewer dive bars every year. An up-and-coming area for swanky clubs and lounges is Union Square and farther up Geary, where several new establishments have opened their doors, drawing well-heeled tourists, hip professionals, and Gen-Exers.

NIGHTLIFE PLANNER

HOURS
Sports bars and hotel bars tend to be open Sunday, but others may be closed. A few establishments—especially wine bars and restaurant bars—also close Monday. Last call is typically 1:30 am; Financial

TOP 5 BARS

■ **Cliff House:** Granted, it's pricey and the interior is ho-hum, but huge picture windows with views of the rolling Pacific create an ambience that's pure Zen.

■ **El Rio:** The perfect dive, with $2.50 drink specials, a stellar patio, and an ever-changing calendar of events (free oysters on Friday, salsa Sunday...).

■ **Hôtel Biron:** Everything a small wine bar should be: intimate, stylish, and slightly hard to find, with an eclectic wine list and good small plates.

■ **Martuni's:** Expertly mixed martinis, a relaxed and friendly clientele, and the off chance that your traveling companion might belt out a Liza Minelli tune after a few drinks. What more could you ask for?

■ **Vesuvio Café:** One of those rare bars with a fleet of regulars that everyone knows about. It's in one of the most touristy parts of town, but still manages to be cool.

District bars catering to the after-work crowd, however, may stop serving as early as 9 or 10 pm, and generally close by midnight at the latest. Bands and performers usually take the stage between 8 and 11 pm. A handful of after-hours clubs are open until 4 am or all night.

LATE-NIGHT TRANSPORTATION

You're better off taking public transportation or taxis on weekend nights, unless you're heading downtown (Financial District or Union Square) and are willing to park in a lot. There's only street parking in North Beach, the Mission, Castro, and the Haight, and finding a spot can be practically impossible. Muni stops running between 1 am and 5 am but has its limited Owl Service on nine lines—including the N, L, 90, 91, 14, and 22—every 30 minutes, though service cuts have made a dent in convenience and frequency; check ⊕ *www.sfmuni.com* for details. You can sometimes hail a taxi on the street in well-trodden nightlife locations (like North Beach or the Mission), but you can also call for one (☎ *415/626–2345 Yellow Cab, 415/648–3181 Arrow*). ■TIP→ Be aware that cabs in SF are more expensive than in other areas in the United States; expect to pay at least $10 to get anywhere within the city. And keep in mind that BART service across the bay stops shortly after midnight.

LOCAL LISTINGS

Entertainment information is printed in the pink Sunday "Datebook" section (⊕ *www.sfgate.com/datebook*) and the more calendar-based Thursday "96 Hours" section (⊕ *www.sfgate.com/96hours*) in the *San Francisco Chronicle*. Also consult any of the free alternative weeklies, notably the *SF Weekly* (⊕ *www.sfweekly.com*), which blurbs nightclubs and music, and the *San Francisco Bay Guardian* (⊕ *www.sfbg.com*), which lists neighborhood, avant-garde, and budget events. SF Station (⊕ *www.sfstation.com*; online only) has an up-to-date calendar of entertainment goings-on.

SMOKING

By law, bars and clubs are smoke-free, except for the very few that are staffed entirely by the owners.

TICKETS AND COVERS

The cover charge at smaller, less popular clubs ranges from $5 to $10, and credit cards are rarely accepted for this. Covers at larger venues may spike to $30, and tickets usually can be purchased through Tickets. com or Ticketweb.com. Bars often have covers for live music—usually $5 to $15.

WHAT TO WEAR

Except for a few skyline lounges, you're not expected to dress up. Still, San Franciscans are a stylish bunch. For women, dressed-up jeans with heels and cute tops are one popular uniform; for guys it's button-up shirts or designer tees and well-tailored jeans. Of course, stylish means a black designer outfit at one place and funky thrift-store togs at another, so you have to use your judgment.

UNION SQUARE AND CHINATOWN

UNION SQUARE

BARS

Le Colonial. Down an easy-to-miss alley off Taylor Street is what appears to be a two-story colonial plantation house in the center of the city. Without being kitschy, the top-floor bar successfully evokes French-colonial Vietnam, thanks to creaky wooden floors, Victorian sofas, a patio with potted palms, and tasty French-Vietnamese food and tropical cocktails. When you arrive, sweep right past the café tables downstairs, past the hostess, and up the stairs to your left (dining is downstairs). The bar occasionally has live, low-key music. ⊠ *20 Cosmo Pl., Union Square* ☎ *415/931–3600* ⊕ *www.lecolonialsf.com.*

Otis. The brainchild of a transplanted New Yorker, this tiny, two-level, art-deco-tinged watering hole that seats 49 is an ideal environment for upscale city denizens, hipsters, and corporate jockeys who have made this their hangout and, for the most part, kept the place a secret. And why shouldn't they? Happy hour (weekdays 5–8 pm) offers light fare and a number of excellent specialty cocktails; the place doesn't get jumping until around 10 pm, especially on weekends. Red lacquered walls, white leather couches optimal for people-watching, and the pièce de résistance—a stuffed peacock above the bar—add a touch of class and sass. Retreat to the cozy upstairs if you need to escape the clamor. ⊠ *25 Maiden La., Union Square* ☎ No phone ⊕ *www.otissf.com.*

The Rrazz Room. Tucked away in the marble lobby of Hotel Nikko, the newly opened Rrazz Room caters primarily to middle-aged business clientele staying at the hotel, though the crowd varies with the entertainment, which ranges from the sweet soulful sounds of local Paula Weston to nostalgia acts like the overripe Keely Smith. Shows are on tap most nights; 7 pm on Sunday, Tuesday through Saturday showtimes vary, with occasional late shows at 10:30. Light cuisine is offered for cabaret seats. A full bar, which serves a raft of specialty cocktails, wines, and coffee, is open daily beginning at 2 pm. Check the Web site for schedules and ticketing info. ⊠ *222 Mason St., Union Square* ☎ *415/394–1189* ⊕ *www.therrazzroom.com.*

Fodor's Choice ★ **Vessel.** A relatively new club/lounge that's enticing, romantic, and ultra-hip in one package, Vessel has a cavalier glamour that embraces you as you descend the staircase into its sleekly designed 5,000-square-foot industrial space made intimate with glowing amber lighting and low-slung benches that line exposed brick walls. New York in attitude and decor, but quintessential San Francisco in its egalitarian mix of casual Gen-Xers, fortysomething professionals, and tourists, Vessel emits a classy, sexy vibe that telegraphs "this is the place to be" without snobbishness. Light food and signature cocktails are served in the lounge weekday evenings 5 to 9. Action picks up after 11 pm, when DJs and live acts take the stage pumping through a multi-million-dollar sound system. You can escape to strategically placed cognac leather love seats or dance on top of the long plank tables spotlighted from below. ⊠ *85 Campton Pl., at Stockton St. Union Square* ☎ *415/433–8585* ⊕ *www.vesselsf.com* ✍ *No cover weeknights; weekends $10–$20; reserved seating $250–$500* ⊘ *Wed. and Sat. 10 pm–2 am, Thurs. 9:30 pm–2 am, Fri. 4 pm–2 am.*

BARS FOR A BALLGAME

Two bars near the Giants' AT&T Park are especially popular on game day.

Stylish American restaurant and trendy bar **MoMo's** (⊠ *760 2nd St., at King St., SoMa* ☎ *415/227–8660* ⊕ *www.sfmomos.com*) has an outdoor patio perfect for sunny days; it's the most popular pre- and postgame bar.

Nova (⊠ *555 2nd St., near Bryant St., SoMa* ☎ *415/543–2282* ⊕ *www.novabar.com*) fills up before and after Giants games with fans thirsty for chic cocktails and hungering for a hearty serving of mac and cheese.

16

SKYLINE AND OCEAN-VIEW BARS ★ **Harry Denton's Starlight Room.** Forget low-key drinks—the only way to experience Harry Denton's is to go for a show. Cough up the cover charge and enjoy the opulent, over-the-top decor and entertainment (some of the best cover bands in the business, usually playing Top 40 hits from the '60s, '70s, and '80s). Velvet booths and romantic lighting help re-create the 1950s high life on the 21st floor of the Sir Francis Drake Hotel, and the small dance floor is packed on Friday and Saturday nights. Jackets are preferred for men. Call ahead—it's sometimes closed for private events on weekdays. ⊠ *Sir Francis Drake Hotel, 450 Powell St., between Post and Sutter Sts., Union Square* ☎ *415/395–8595* ⊕ *www.harrydenton.com.*

WINE BARS **The Hidden Vine.** True to its name, this tiny wine bar is in a little alley (just north of Market Street) and down a set of stairs. The location is part of the appeal, but the wines and amuse-bouches make it truly worthwhile. A jumble of velvet chairs and love seats fills the carpeted space, and the owner, who serves most nights, acts as your sommelier. Another hidden find, Le Colonial *(see Bars, above)* is just across the alley. ⊠ *½ Cosmo Pl., at Taylor St., Union Square* ☎ *415/674–3567* ⊕ *www.thehiddenvine.com.*

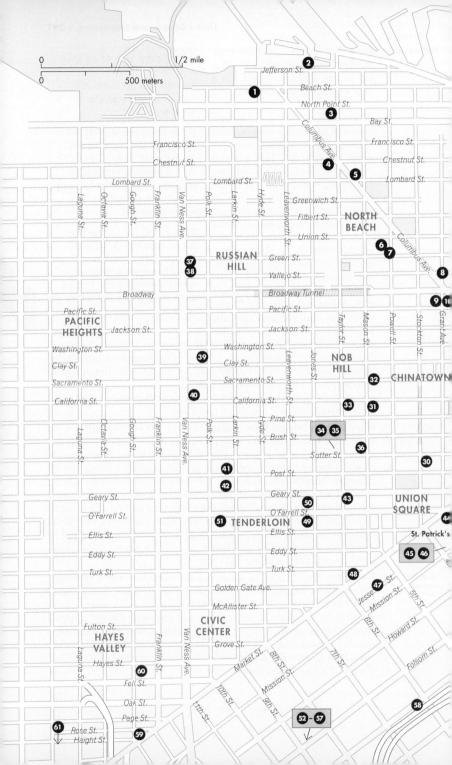

Nightlife In and Around Downtown

16

CLOSE UP

Best Hotel Bars

Big 4 Bar. Dark-wood paneling and green leather banquettes lend a masculine feel to the bar at the Huntington Hotel, where the over-30 crowd orders Scotch and Irish coffee. To accompany your whiskey, try the potpies or Irish stew. This place is a San Francisco history lesson—read up on the Big Four (four of the city's most influential pre-earthquake movers and shakers) before you go to get more out of the experience. ⊠ *The Huntington Hotel, 1075 California St., Nob Hill* ☎ *415/474–5400.*

Pied Piper Bar. Originally opened in 1875 (after being built for the then-extravagant price of $5 million), the Palace Hotel is still one of San Francisco's classiest. Suitably, this watering hole, which takes its name from the Maxfield Parrish mural *The Pied Piper of Hamelin* behind the bar, draws a very affluent and upscale clientele for its excellent two-olive martinis and other libations. ⊠ *2 New Montgomery St., at Market St., SoMa* ☎ *415/512–1111.*

Redwood Room. Opened in 1933 and updated by über-hip designer Philippe Starck in 2001, the Redwood Room at the Clift Hotel is a San Francisco icon. The entire room, floor to ceiling, is paneled with the wood from a single redwood tree, giving the place a rich, monochromatic look. The gorgeous original art-deco sconces and chandeliers still hang, but bizarre video installations on plasma screens also adorn the walls. It's packed on weekend evenings after 10, when young scenesters swarm the hotel; for maximum glamour, visit on a weeknight. ⊠ *Clift Hotel, 495 Geary St., at Taylor St., Union Square* ☎ *415/929–2372 for table reservations, 415/775–4700 for hotel.*

Seasons Bar. The walnut-panel walls, inlaid cherrywood floor, and elegant furnishings of the tiny lobby bar capture the aesthetic of the coolly minimalist Four Seasons. Discreet staff members in dark suits serve top-shelf cocktails and salty nibbles. A piano player entertains Tuesday through Saturday evening in the lobby lounge, where you can relax on overstuffed sofas and chairs. The clientele is, as expected, generally 40-plus and business-suited. The bartender, Sierra Zimei, recently won the Best Mixologist Award, bestowed by *San Francisco* magazine. ⊠ *Four Seasons Hotel San Francisco, 757 Market St., between 3rd and 4th Sts., SoMa* ☎ *415/633–3000.*

Tonga Room. Since 1947 the Tonga Room has given San Francisco a taste of high Polynesian kitsch. Fake palm trees, grass huts, a lagoon (three-piece combos play pop standards on a floating barge), and faux monsoons—courtesy of sprinkler-system rain and simulated thunder and lightning—grow more surreal as you quaff fruity cocktails. ⊠ *Fairmont San Francisco, 950 Mason St., at California St., Nob Hill* ☎ *415/772–5278.*

W Café and XYZ Bar. Floor-to-ceiling blue velvet draperies, black-and-white terrazzo floors, and a thumpin' sound system set the aggressive see-and-be-seen tone of the lobby bar at the W Hotel, where a DJ spins hypnotic beats Wednesday through Friday evenings. Escape the ogling crowd by heading upstairs to the tucked-away XYZ Bar. ⊠ *W Hotel, 181 3rd St., at Howard St., SoMa* ☎ *415/777–5300.*

CHINATOWN
GAY NIGHTLIFE

KARAOKE
BARS

Bow Bow Cocktail Lounge. An inclusive quirky, divey karaoke bar where you can get your kicks performing in front of a sometimes rowdy—but almost always supportive—audience of hip young things and Asian businessmen. ✉ *1155 Grant Ave., near Broadway, Chinatown* ☎ *415/421–6730.*

SOMA AND CIVIC CENTER

SOMA
BARS

21st Amendment. Possibly the best brewpub in SF, 21st Amendment has a good range of beer types (unlike some other spots in town). In the spring season, watermelon wheat gets rave reviews. Nine different brews are on tap at all times. The space has an upmarket warehouse feel, though exposed wooden ceiling beams, framed photos, white-washed brick walls, and hardwood floors make it feel cozy. ✉ *563 2nd St., between Federal and Brannan Sts., SoMa* ☎ *415/369–0900* ⊕ *www.21st-amendment.com.*

16

Gordon Biersch Brewery and Restaurant. This giant microbrewery has outlasted the boutique-beer trend and continues to draw big after-work crowds. Part of a nationwide empire that got its start in nearby Palo Alto, Gordon Biersch is known for its German-style pilsners and brews—as well as what some have called the greatest garlic fries in creation (though regulars give the burgers at this location low marks). ■ TIP➔ The outdoor seating area has killer views of the Bay Bridge, making this an ideal spot for an afternoon drink. ✉ *2 Harrison St., at the Embarcadero, SoMa* ☎ *415/243–8246* ⊕ *www.gordonbiersch.com.*

Nihon. Whiskey-lovers *need* to check this place out, if only to drool over the 150 or so bottles behind the bar. This place has a superswank, youngish scene. The pricey Japanese tapas are pretty good, and whiskey pairs with sushi surprisingly well. The dramatic lighting, close quarters, and blood-red tuffets make Nihon more suitable for romance than business. ✉ *1779 Folsom St., between Eire and 14th Sts., SoMa* ☎ *415/552–4400* ⊕ *www.nihon-sf.com.*

BARS WITH
LIVE MUSIC

The Hotel Utah Saloon. This funky hipster spot offers a mix of local bands and young national touring acts performing rock, indie pop, alt-country, and everything in between. The low-ceiling performance space is small, with a few tables grouped around the stage. (Be sure to grab a Cuban sandwich from the bar before the show.) The bar area takes up about half of this joint and is just as popular as the music. Monday is open-mike night. ✉ *500 4th St., at Bryant St., SoMa* ☎ *415/546–6300* ⊕ *www.thehotelutahsaloon.com.*

SKYLINE AND
OCEAN-VIEW
BARS

View Lounge. Art-deco-influenced floor-to-ceiling windows frame superb views on the 39th floor of the San Francisco Marriott. You won't feel out of place here just getting a drink or two rather than dinner. Note that it can get quite crowded on weekends. ✉ *San Francisco Marriott, 55 4th St., between Mission and Market Sts., SoMa* ☎ *415/896–1600.*

SPORTS BARS   **Fourth Street Bar and Deli**. San Francisco may not be the best sports town in the country, but you'd never guess it by the buzzing scene at this huge, modern sports wonderland on the ground floor of the Marriott Hotel. The bar has 44 beers, 23 televisions, and all the salty, fried snacks you'll need to enjoy the game properly. ✉ *55 4th St., at Mission St., SoMa* ☎ *415/442–6734*.

> ### SHOOK ME ALL NIGHT LONG
>
> The EndUp is San Francisco's only serious after-hours place. It's open nonstop from 10 pm Friday until 4 am Monday, and generally 10 pm–4 am weekdays. People from all walks of life end up here.

CABARET

asiaSF. Saucy, sexy, and fun, this is one of the hottest places in town for a drag-show virgin. (Veterans might try something more specialized, like the Stud's "Trannyshack.") The entertainment, as well as gracious food service, is provided by some of the city's most gorgeous "gender illusionists," who strut in impossibly high heels on top of the catwalk bar, vamping to tunes like "Cabaret" and "Big Spender." The creative Asian-influenced cuisine is surprisingly good. ■**TIP→** Go on a weekday to avoid a deluge of bachelorette parties. Make reservations, or risk being turned away. Oh, and bring a camera. ✉ *201 9th St., at Howard St., SoMa* ☎ *415/255–2742* ⊕ *www.asiasf.com*.

DANCE CLUBS

★   **111 Minna Gallery**. Gallery by day, bar–dance club by night, this unpretentious warehouse space is often full of artsy young San Franciscans who prefer it to glitzier spots. The door is unmarked, and it's on a small side street just south of Mission. Dance events typically take place Friday and Saturday 9 pm–2 am, though the bar opens around 5), It's closed Monday. ✉ *111 Minna St., between 2nd and New Montgomery Sts., SoMa* ☎ *415/974–1719* ⊕ *www.111minnagallery.com*.

330 Ritch Street. One of the city's best parties, the long-running **Popscene** features Brit pop, '60s soul, and New Wave every Thursday. Live acts—such as the Killers, Hot Hot Heat, and Lily Allen—are thrown into the mix. The stylish, modern space also serves pizza and has 16 beers on tap. ✉ *330 Ritch St., between 3rd and 4th Sts., SoMa* ☎ *415/541–9574* ⊕ *www.330ritch.com*.

★   **DNA Lounge**. The music changes nightly at the venerable DNA Lounge, but this club gets a star solely for **Bootie.** Held the second Saturday of each month, this popular mashup unites hard-core and indie rockers, hip-hop devotees, and emo fans. If a DJ mix of Gorillaz, Donna Summer, and Joy Division sounds like your bag, you're in for a treat. **Remedy,** which brings deep-house and hip-hop DJs most Friday nights, is also popular. On other nights, the place can be dead. Three bars and dance floors on two levels mean it's rarely uncomfortably crowded. ✉ *375 11th St., between Harrison and Folsom Sts., SoMa* ☎ *415/626–1409*.

The EndUp. Sometimes 2 am is just too early. The EndUp is by far SF's most popular after-hours place, with possibly the best sound system in the city. ■**TIP→** Said system is cranked. Even the cool kids wear earplugs. It can be a bit of a meat market (which ladies can avoid on Fag

Fridays), but this San Francisco institution doesn't adhere to any particular scene. ✉ *401 6th St., at Harrison St., SoMa* ☎ *415/646–0999* ⊕ *www.theendup.com.*

Mezzanine. If you like megaclubs, then you'll dig this industrial-chic two-story club, which doubles as a gallery and performance venue. Live acts have included Mos Def, the Dandy Warhols, and Def Jux artists. The crowd is generally mixed, straight and gay. If the jam-packed dance floor (which can accommodate nearly 1,000 people) overwhelms you, head upstairs to the quietish mezzanine lounges to converse or to ogle the sexy crowd. ✉ *444 Jessie St., at 5th St., SoMa* ☎ *415/625–8880* ⊕ *www.mezzaninesf.com.*

GAY NIGHTLIFE

GAY MALE BARS

★ **Eagle Tavern**. Bikers are courted with endless drink specials and, increasingly, live rock music at this humongous indoor-outdoor leather bar, one of the few SoMa bars remaining from the days before AIDS and gentrification. The Sunday-afternoon "Beer Busts" (3–6 pm) are a social high point and benefit charitable organizations. It's a surprisingly welcoming place for people from all walks of life. ✉ *398 12th St., at Harrison St., SoMa* ☎ *415/626–0880* ⊕ *www.sfeagle.com.*

★ **The Stud**. Mingle with glam trannies, tight-teed pretty boys, ladies and their ladies, and a handful of straight onlookers who dance to the live DJ and watch world-class drag performers on the small stage. The entertainment is often campy, pee-your-pants funny, and downright talented. Each night's music is different—from funk, soul, and hip-hop to 80s tunes and disco favorites. The club is sometimes closed Sunday. ✉ *1284 Harrison St., at 9th St., SoMa* ☎ *415/863–6623* ⊕ *www.studsf.com.*

ROCK, POP, HIP-HOP, FOLK, AND BLUES CLUBS

Slim's. National touring acts—mostly along the pop-punk and hard- and alt-rock lines but including metal and bluegrass—are the main event at this venue, one of SoMa's most popular nightclubs. If you want it, you can find it here. Co-owner Boz Scaggs helps bring in the crowds and famous headliners like Dressy Bessy and Dead Meadow. ✉ *333 11th St., between Harrison and Folsom Sts., SoMa* ☎ *415/255–0333* ⊕ *www.slims-sf.com.*

CIVIC CENTER
ROCK, POP, HIP-HOP, FOLK, AND BLUES CLUBS

Warfield. This former movie palace—a "palace" in every sense of the word—is now one of the city's largest rock-and-roll venues, with tables and chairs downstairs and theater seating upstairs. The historic venue has booked everyone from Phish and the Grateful Dead to the Pretenders and Green Day. Check schedules and buy tickets at Ticketmaster. com. ✉ *982 Market St., at 6th St., Civic Center* ☎ *415/345–0900.*

THE TENDERLOIN

BARS

Bourbon & Branch. The address and phone are unlisted, the black outer door unmarked, and when you make your reservation (required), you get a password for entry. In short, Bourbon & Branch reeks of

16

Prohibition-era speakeasy cool. It's not exclusive, though: everyone is granted a password. The place has sex appeal, with tin ceilings, bordello-red silk wallpaper, intimate booths, and low lighting; loud conversations and cell phones are not allowed. The menu of expertly mixed cocktails and quality bourbon and whiskey is substantial, but the servers aren't always authorities. ■TIP→ This place is small, so couples or groups of four or fewer are ideal. Your reservation dictates your exit time, which is strictly enforced. ⊠ *501 Jones St., Tenderloin* ☎ *No phone* ⊕ *www.bourbonandbranch.com.*

Edinburgh Castle. Work off your fish-and-chips and Scottish brew with a turn at the dartboard or pool table at this cavernous pub. It's popular with locals and Brits who congregate at the long bar or in the scattered seating areas, downing single-malt Scotch or pints of Fuller's. They have weekly trivia nights, and occasional Scottish cultural events (January's Robert Burns celebration is a favorite). Be aware that the area around the bar is gritty. ⊠ *950 Geary St., between Larkin and Polk Sts., Tenderloin* ☎ *415/885–4074* ⊕ *www.castlenews.com.*

GAY NIGHTLIFE

GAY MALE BARS
Divas. In the rough-and-tumble Tenderloin, around the corner from the Polk Street bars, trannies (transvestites and transsexuals) and their admirers come here for the racy entertainment. (Naughty Schoolgirls night is a fave.) This multilevel space has separate areas for stage performances, dancing, and quiet chats. It's not a drag bar, as there is no sense of irony or camp about the place; the girls here are charming, and the fun is in the titillation. ⊠ *1081 Post St., between Larkin and Polk Sts., Tenderloin* ☎ *415/474–3482* ⊕ *www.divassf.com.*

ROCK, POP, HIP-HOP, FOLK, AND BLUES CLUBS

Fodor'sChoice ★
Great American Music Hall. You can find top-drawer entertainment at this great, eclectic nightclub. Acts range from the best in blues, folk, and jazz to up-and-coming college-radio and American-roots artists to of-the-moment indie rock stars (OK Go, Mates of State) and the establishment (Cowboy Junkies). The colorful marble-pillared emporium (built in 1907 as a bordello) also accommodates dancing at some shows. Pub grub is available most nights. ⊠ *859 O'Farrell St., between Polk and Larkin Sts., Tenderloin* ☎ *415/885–0750* ⊕ *www.gamh.com.*

HAYES VALLEY

BARS

Sugar. Just trendy enough, but never pretentious, Sugar has fun cocktails (lemon drops, grape 'o' tinis), good drink specials, and a low-key vibe. DJs spin world and house music in this small, narrow neighborhood favorite. ⊠ *377 Hayes St., Hayes Valley* ☎ *415/255–7144* ⊕ *www.sugarloungesf.com.*

WINE BARS ★
Hôtel Biron. Sharing an alleylike block with the backs of Market Street restaurants, this tiny, cavelike (in a good way) spot displays rotating artwork of the Mission School aesthetic on its brick walls. The clientele is well-behaved twenty- to thirtysomethings who enjoy the cramped quarters, good range of wines and prices, off-the-beaten path location,

Built as a bordello in 1907, the Great American Music Hall now pulls in top-tier performers.

soft lighting, and hip music. ⊠ *45 Rose St., off Market St., Hayes Valley* ☎ *415/703–0403* ⊕ *www.hotelbiron.com.*

GAY NIGHTLIFE

KARAOKE
BARS

★

The Mint. A mixed gay-straight crowd that's drop-dead serious about its karaoke (to the point where you'd think an *American Idol* casting agent was in the crowd) comes here seven nights a week. Regulars sing everything from Simon and Garfunkel songs to disco classics in front of an attentive audience. Do *not* go here unprepared! Check out the songbook online to perfect your debut before you attempt to take the mike. ⊠ *1942 Market St., between Duboce and Laguna Sts., Hayes Valley* ☎ *415/626–4726* ⊕ *www.themint.net.*

FINANCIAL DISTRICT

BARS

Harrington's. The epicenter for downtown festivities on St. Patrick's Day, this family-owned Irish saloon (closed Sunday) is an attitude-free place for the well-tailored-suit set to have an after-work drink the rest of the year. The restaurant serves American fare, with the occasional Irish special. It has a good selection of imported beers and a patio out back. Another local favorite, the Royal Exchange, is next door and eerily similar. ⊠ *245 Front St., near Sacramento St., Financial District* ☎ *415/392–7595.*

OUTDOOR
BARS

Hog Island Oyster Bar. On a sunny day, is there anything better than sipping wine and eating oysters? Only if it's here, on a waterside patio, with the looming Bay Bridge and the Oakland and Berkeley hills as a backdrop. The oysters are from Marin County, and many of the wines are from Sonoma or Napa. ⊠ *Ferry Bldg., 1 Embarcadero Plaza, Financial District* ☎ *415/391–7117* ⊕ *www.hogislandoysters.com.*

COMEDY

Punch Line. A launch pad for the likes of Jay Leno and Whoopi Goldberg, this place books some of the nation's top talents. Headliners have included Dave Chappelle, Margaret Cho, and Jay Mohr. No one under 18 is admitted. ⊠ *444 Battery St., between Clay and Washington Sts., Financial District* ☎ *415/397–7573* ⊕ *www.punchlinecomedyclub.com.*

NOB HILL AND RUSSIAN HILL

NOB HILL

BARS

SKYLINE AND OCEAN-VIEW BARS

Top of the Mark. A famous magazine photograph immortalized this place, on the 19th floor of the Mark Hopkins InterContinental, as a hot spot for World War II servicemen on leave or about to ship out. Entertainment ranges from solo jazz piano to six-piece jazz ensembles. Cover charges and schedules vary, but tend to be around $10 beginning at 7 pm weekdays and 9 pm weekends. ⊠ *Mark Hopkins InterContinental, 999 California St., at Mason St., Nob Hill* ☎ *415/616–6916* ⊕ *www.topofthemark.com.*

RUSSIAN HILL

BARS

Royal Oak. Tiffany-style lamps and cascading ferns contribute to the clubby feel of this comfortable spot, walkable from other nearby neighborhood bars. Arrive early to snag a seat on one of the antique, swoopback tufted-velvet couches. ⊠ *2201 Polk St., at Vallejo St., Russian Hill* ☎ *415/928–2303.*

VAN NESS/POLK

GAY NIGHTLIFE

GAY MALE BARS

The Cinch. This Wild West–themed neighborhood bar has pinball machines, pool tables, and a smoking patio. It's not the least bit trendy, which is part of the charm for regulars. ⊠ *1723 Polk St., between Washington and Clay Sts., Van Ness/Polk* ☎ *415/776–4162* ⊕ *www.thecinch.com.*

ROCK, POP, HIP-HOP, FOLK, AND BLUES CLUBS

Red Devil Lounge. Local and up-and-coming hip-hop, rap, funk, indie rock, and jazz acts perform at this plush, dimly lighted lounge. Intimate (read: tightly spaced) tables line the narrow balcony overlooking the dance floor. Call ahead for schedules. ⊠ *1695 Polk St., at Clay St., Van Ness/Polk* ☎ *415/921–1695* ⊕ *www.reddevillounge.com.*

SPORTS BARS

Greens Sports Bar. Cramped and packed to the gills with sports memorabilia, Greens is the quintessential old-school neighborhood sports bar, with 18 screens and 18 beers on tap. Seating is on stools at high bar tables, and the HD TVs are positioned just right for optimal viewing. Food is not served here, but the bar has delivery menus. ⊠ *2239 Polk St., at Green St., Van Ness/Polk* ☎ *415/775–4287.*

NORTH BEACH

BARS

Bix. The retro-chic martini-bar craze keeps going strong at glam, gorgeous Bix. Jazz combos provide the backbeat for the cocktail-swilling gadabouts and nattily dressed diners who pack the small bar area of this spirited yet refined supper club. Plenty of regulars stop in just to sip the well-crafted cocktails, so you won't feel out of place if you're not eating—but you will if you're not wearing something chic. ✉ 56 Gold St., off Montgomery St., North Beach ☎ 415/433–6300 ⊕ www.bixrestaurant.com.

Specs Twelve Adler Museum Cafe. If you're bohemian at heart, you can groove on this hidden hangout for artists, poets, and heavy-drinking lefties. It's one of the few remaining old-fashioned watering holes in North Beach that still smack of the Beat years and the 1960s. Though it's just off a busy street, Specs is strangely immune to the hustle and bustle outside. ✉ 12 William Saroyan Pl., off Columbus Ave., between Pacific Ave. and Broadway, North Beach ☎ 415/421–4112.

★ **Tosca Café**. Like Specs and Vesuvio nearby, this historic charmer holds a special place in San Francisco lore. It has an Italian flavor, with opera, big-band, and Italian standards on the jukebox, an antique espresso machine that's nothing less than a work of art, and lived-in red leather booths. With Francis Ford Coppola's Zoetrope just across the street, celebrities and hip film-industry types often stop by when they're in town; locals, like Sean Penn, have been known to shoot pool in the back room. ✉ 242 Columbus Ave., near Broadway, North Beach ☎ 415/391–1244.

★ **Vesuvio Café**. If you're only hitting one bar in North Beach, it should be this one. The low-ceiling second floor of this raucous boho hangout, little altered since its 1960s heyday (when Jack Kerouac frequented the place), is a fine vantage point for watching the colorful Broadway and Columbus Avenue intersection. Another part of Vesuvio's appeal is its diverse, always-mixed clientele (twenties to sixties), from neighborhood regulars and young couples to Bacchanalian posses of friends. ✉ 255 Columbus Ave., at Broadway, North Beach ☎ 415/362–3370 ⊕ www.vesuvio.com.

SPORTS BARS **The Boardroom**. If you've been looking for a bar where you can watch football *and* get a decent martini, this is it. Not your typical sports pub, this small lounge has as many female patrons as male, and it's not superloud and raucous. Due to its size, the Boardroom has only four plasma-screen TVs, which are just as likely to be broadcasting snowboarding as the usual baseball-football-basketball trifecta. The food is better than your average pub grub. ✉ 1609 Powell St., North Beach ☎ 415/982–8898 ⊕ www.boardroomsf.com.

WINE BARS **Bubble Lounge**. Champagne is the specialty at this dark, upscale spot; the selection of bubbly is excellent, with more than 300 types to choose from. Upstairs, young executives nestle into wing chairs and overstuffed couches, and downstairs there's a re-created Champagne cellar. A full bar is available, as are sushi, caviar, desserts, and other delicate nibbles. You won't feel out of place in a suit or slinky dress and heels here. Make

16

table reservations ($30 minimum) on weekends, or you'll be relegated to the tiny bar area. ✉ *714 Montgomery St., at Washington St., North Beach* ☎ *415/434–4204* ⊕ *www.bubblelounge.com.*

CABARET

Fodor'sChoice
★ **Club Fugazi.** Club Fugazi's claim to fame is *Beach Blanket Babylon,* a wacky musical send-up of San Francisco moods and mores that has been going strong since 1974, making it the longest-running musical revue anywhere. Although the choreography is colorful, the singers brassy, and the satirical songs witty, the real stars are the comically exotic costumes and famous ceiling-high "hats"—which are worth the price of admission alone. The revue sells out as early as a month in advance, so order tickets as far ahead as possible. Those under 21 are admitted only to the Sunday matinee. ■TIP➔ If you don't shell out the extra $15–$20 for reserved seating, you won't have an assigned seat—so get your cannoli to go and arrive at least 30 minutes prior to showtime to get in line. ✉ *678 Green St., at Powell St., North Beach* ☎ *415/421–4222* ⊕ *www.beachblanketbabylon.com.*

COMEDY

Cobb's Comedy Club. Stand-up comics such as Bill Maher, Paula Poundstone, and Sarah Silverman have appeared at this club. You can also see sketch comedy and comic singer-songwriters here. No one under 18 is admitted. ✉ *915 Columbus Ave., at Lombard St., North Beach* ☎ *415/928–4320* ⊕ *www.cobbscomedyclub.com.*

Purple Onion. This intimate nightspot ranks right up there with Bimbo's and the Fillmore on the list of San Francisco's most famous clubs, and people seem to love it or hate it. While the Onion is an historic, quintessential San Francisco venue that provided an early platform for both folk-music troubadours such as the Kingston Trio and comedic acts like the Smothers Brothers, it has seen better days. In addition to stand-up, you can catch sketch comedies, open mikes, and improv shows. ✉ *140 Columbus Ave., at Broadway, North Beach* ☎ *415/956–1653* ⊕ *www. purpleonioncomedy.com.*

ROCK, POP, HIP-HOP, FOLK, AND BLUES CLUBS

★ **Bimbo's 365 Club.** The plush main room and adjacent lounge of this club, here since 1951, retain a retro vibe perfect for the "Cocktail Nation" programming that keeps the crowds entertained. For a taste of the old-school San Francisco nightclub scene, you can't beat this place. Indie low-fi and pop bands like Stephen Malkmus and the Jicks and Camera Obscura fill the bill. ✉ *1025 Columbus Ave., at Chestnut St., North Beach* ☎ *415/474–0365* ⊕ *www.bimbos365club.com.*

The Saloon. Hard-drinkin' in-the-know North Beach locals favor this raucous spot, known for great blues. Get the schedule at ⊕ *www. sfblues.net/Saloon.html.* Built in the 1860s, the onetime bordello is purported to be the oldest bar in the city. This is not the place to order a mixed drink. You've been warned. ✉ *1232 Grant Ave., near Columbus Ave., North Beach* ☎ *415/989–7666.*

THE WATERFRONT

FISHERMAN'S WHARF

BARS

★ **Buena Vista Café.** Smack-dab at the end of the Hyde Street cable-car line, the Buena Vista packs 'em in for its famous Irish coffee—which, according to owners, was the first served stateside (in 1952). The place oozes nostalgia, drawing devoted locals as well as out-of-towners relaxing after a day of sightseeing. It's narrow and can get crowded, but this spot is a welcome respite from the overpriced, generic tourist joints nearby. ✉ *2765 Hyde St., at Beach St., Fisherman's Wharf* ☎ *415/474–5044* ⊕ *www.thebuenavista.com.*

SPORTS BARS **Knuckles at the Wharf.** This bar underwent a recent overhaul and toned down its sports motif in an effort to attract more female patrons, but it's still in its historic location, the early-20th-century Joseph Musto Marble Works building. The original exposed beams and brick remain part of the decor. Because it's in Fisherman's Wharf, this lively spot draws a healthy stream of tourists who can view the venue's 28 TVs, including a jumbo screen. ✉ *555 N. Point St., Fisherman's Wharf* ☎ *415/563–1234.*

ROCK, POP, HIP-HOP, FOLK, AND BLUES CLUBS

Lou's Pier 47. Nightly blues accompany the hot Cajun seafood at this waterfront spot. Bands typically start playing in the late afternoon and continue until midnight. If you're staying near the Wharf, this is your best bet for live music without having to take a taxi. ✉ *300 Jefferson St., at Jones St., Fisherman's Wharf* ☎ *415/771–5687* ⊕ *www.louspier47. com.*

EMBARCADERO

BARS

OUTDOOR **Pier 23 Cafe.** Beer arrives at your table in buckets at this waterfront bar,
BARS which has ample seating at plastic tables on a wooden deck. Although you'd expect to sit elbow-to-elbow with fishermen, you're more likely to share the space with twenty- and thirtysomethings drawn by the beer and food specials. ✉ *Pier 23, Embarcadero* ☎ *415/362–5125* ⊕ *www. pier23cafe.com.*

THE MARINA AND THE PRESIDIO

BARS

Balboa Cafe. Here you'll spy young (thirtysomething) and upwardly mobile former frat boys and sorority girls munching on tasty burgers (considered by some to be the best in town) while trying to add a few new names to their Blackberrys. ✉ *3199 Fillmore St., at Greenwich St., Marina* ☎ *415/921–3944* ⊕ *www.balboacafe.com.*

Circa. This classy lounge with shimmering chandeliers is dimly lighted, but fellow patrons will still notice the logo on your purse; dress appropriately (par for the course in the Marina). At the central, square bar, attractive yuppies sip cosmos and nibble pan-seared scallops, while skilled DJs spin downtempo electronica. This place takes tongue-in-cheek chic seriously, down to the lobster-and-truffle mac-and-cheese.

16

As expected, there's a strong list of specialty cocktails. ⊠ *2001 Chestnut St., at Fillmore St., Marina* ☎ *415/351–0175* ⊕ *www.circasf.com.*

★ **MatrixFillmore.** Don a pair of Diesel jeans and a Michael Kors sweater and sip cosmos or Cabernet with the Marina's bon vivants. This is the premier spot in the "Triangle" (short for Bermuda Triangle, named for all of the singles who disappear in the bars clustered at Greenwich and Fillmore streets). Although there's a small dance floor where some folks bump and grind to high-energy DJ-spun dance tracks, the majority of the clientele usually vies for the plush seats near the central open fireplace, flirts at the bar, or huddles for romantic tête-à-têtes in the back. The singles scene can be overwhelming on weekends. ⊠ *3138 Fillmore St., between Greenwich and Filbert Sts., Marina* ☎ *415/563–4180* ⊕ *www.matrixfillmore.com.*

WINE BARS **Nectar.** Classy Nectar has reasonable tasting flights (around $20) and decent food that looks more impressive than it tastes. No complaints about the wine choices, though, which are consistently excellent. The small storefront lounge is warmly lighted, with modern furnishings, including a signature beehive-shape wine display. On weekends the decibel level rises considerably and space is at a premium. ⊠ *3330 Steiner St., Marina* ☎ *415/345–1377* ⊕ *www.nectarwinelounge.com.*

COW HOLLOW

BARS

Perry's. It may be one of San Francisco's oldest singles bars, but Perry's still packs em in. You can dine on great hamburgers as well as more-substantial fare while gabbing about the game with the well-scrubbed, khaki-clad, baseball-cap-wearing crowd. ⊠ *1944 Union St., at Laguna St., Cow Hollow* ☎ *415/922–9022* ⊕ *www.perryssf.com.*

SPORTS BARS **Bus Stop.** Popular with frat boys and stockbrokers alike, this Marina/ Cow Hollow favorite has 18 screens and two pool tables. If you want to meet the local diehards, this is the place. It's also one of the few spots in this neighborhood where you'll feel comfortable dressed down. Order food from neighboring restaurants; the bar provides menus. ⊠ *1901 Union St., at Laguna St., Cow Hollow* ☎ *415/567–6905.*

THE WESTERN SHORELINE

BARS

SKYLINE AND **Cliff House.** A bit classier than the Beach Chalet, with a more impressive,
OCEAN-VIEW sweeping view of Ocean Beach, the Cliff House is our pick if you must
BARS choose just one oceanfront restaurant/bar. Sure, it's the site of many
★ high-school prom dates, and you could argue that the food and drinks are overpriced, and some say the sleek facade looks like a mausoleum— but the views are terrific. The best window seats are reserved for diners, but there's a small upstairs lounge where you can watch gulls sail high above the vast blue Pacific. Come before sunset. ⊠ *1090 Point Lobos, at Great Hwy., Lincoln Park* ☎ *415/386–3330* ⊕ *www.cliffhouse.com.*

GOLDEN GATE PARK

BARS

OUTDOOR BARS
Park Chalet. You'll feel like you're in a cabin in the woods as you relax in an Adirondack chair under a heat lamp, enclosed by the greenery of Golden Gate Park. In addition to serving pub food such as burgers, salads, steaks, and fish-and-chips, the brewery churns out its own beer. The Park Chalet shares a building with the Beach Chalet *(see below)*—but it isn't waterside, so you won't freeze if it's overcast. ✉ *1000 Great Hwy., near Martin Luther King Jr. Dr., Golden Gate Park* ☎ *415/386–8439* ⊕ *www.beachchalet.com.*

> **KEEP IN MIND**
>
> Don't bother going to an ocean-view bar when it's foggy; you'll spend the evening squinting at the skyline.

SKYLINE AND OCEAN-VIEW BARS
Beach Chalet. This restaurant-microbrewery, on the second floor of a historic building filled with 1930s Works Project Administration murals, has a stunning view of the Pacific Ocean, so you may want to time your visit to coincide with the sunset. ■TIP→ Get there at least 30 minutes before sunset to beat the dinner reservations. If you come right at dinnertime or even at lunch on weekends, diners with reservations will be given first dibs on the window seats (and on tables in general). The bar is toward the back, with a so-so view of the action. The American bistro food—which, for appetizers, includes ahi tuna tartare and fried calamari—is decent, the house brews are rich and flavorful, and there's a good selection of California wines by the glass. The seasonal Oktoberfest brew is a highlight of the beer menu. The cheaper Park Chalet *(see above)* on the ground floor has park, rather than ocean, views. ✉ *1000 Great Hwy., near Martin Luther King Jr. Dr., Golden Gate Park* ☎ *415/386–8439* ⊕ *www.beachchalet.com.*

16

THE HAIGHT, THE CASTRO, AND NOE VALLEY

THE HAIGHT

BARS

WINE BARS
★
Eos Restaurant and Wine Bar. Though it's just a few blocks away, Cole Valley is a world apart from funky, grungy Haight Street. Eos, along with the handful of restaurants and bars that line this part of Cole Street, manages to be both sophisticated and unpretentious—and truly fantastic. This narrow and romantically lighted space, with more than 400 wines by the bottle and 40-plus by the glass, offers two different wine flights—one red and one white—every month. The adjoining restaurant's excellent East-meets-West cuisine is available at the bar. ✉ *901 Cole St., at Carl St., Haight* ☎ *415/566–3063* ⊕ *www.eossf.com.*

GAY NIGHTLIFE

GAY MALE BARS
Trax. "Laid back" would be an understatement. Once inside, you won't feel like you're in a gay bar—or in San Francisco. And that's the way the regulars like it. Cheap beer specials draw people from every ilk. And though you don't have to don your cruise wear for this place, it's still social. ✉ *1437 Haight St., Haight* ☎ *415/864–4213.*

THE CASTRO
GAY NIGHTLIFE

GAY MALE
BARS

Badlands. Shirts off! If a sweaty muscle sandwich sounds like your idea of a good time, head to Badlands, where serious party boys come to grind to throbbing music on a packed dance floor. The lines can be ridiculous on weekends; those in the know go on Wednesday or Thursday. Tight-teed patrons range from twenties to forties. ⊠ *4121 18th St., between Castro and Collingwood Sts., Castro* ☎ *415/626–9320* ⊕ *www.sfbadlands.com.*

The Café. Always comfortable and often packed with a mixed gay, lesbian, and straight crowd, this is a place where you can dance to house or disco music, shoot pool, or meet guys in their twenties at the bar. The outdoor deck—a rarity—makes it a favorite destination for smokers. Weekend cover is $3; expect a line to get in. ⊠ *2369 Market St., at 17th St., Castro* ☎ *415/834–5840* ⊕ *www.cafesf.com.*

★ **Lime.** The 1960s mod design of this chic cocktail lounge and restaurant (with rainbow-color Plexiglas at every turn) evokes L.A. more than SF, but it's the top choice for Abercrombie-wearing gay men who swill mojitos by the bucket. There's also a diverse and delicious menu of small plates, good for sharing. ⊠ *2247 Market St., between Noe and Sanchez Sts., Castro* ☎ *415/621–5256.*

Moby Dick. The quintessential neighborhood watering hole, this unpretentious spot has a pool table, pinball machines, and a live "DVJ" mixing pop videos and music. A giant fish tank sits over the bar, giving shy types a place to rest their gaze while they take a shot of liquid courage. An eclectic (in style and age) mix of casually dressed couples and guys with nothing to prove frequents this place, but there's some pick-up potential, too. ⊠ *4049 18th St., at Hartford St., Castro* ☎ *415/861–1199* ⊕ *www.mobydicksf.com.*

Pilsner Inn. Casual and comfortable—yet still hip and cruise-y—Pilsner is the type of neighborhood joint you quickly claim as your own. Kick back with a pint on the fantastic year-round patio (it's covered), and enjoy eye candy of the thirtysomething variety (ranging from conservative yuppie guys to Mission emo boys). Pilsner Inn is technically a sports bar, which means it has a pool table and sponsors some local amateur teams. ⊠ *225 Church St., at Market St., Castro* ☎ *415/621–7058* ⊕ *www.pilsnerinn.com.*

ROCK, POP, HIP-HOP, FOLK, AND BLUES CLUBS

Café du Nord. You can hear some of the coolest jazz, blues, rock, and alternative sounds in town at this basement bar. Built in 1907, it has retained some of its original Victorian features, which contribute to the hip, vaguely illicit feel—reminiscent of its days as a speakeasy. The music, a mix of local talent and indie headliners like Kristin Hersh and Bettie Serveert, is strictly top-notch. ⊠ *2170 Market St., between Church and Sanchez Sts., Castro* ☎ *415/861–5016* ⊕ *www.cafedunord.com.*

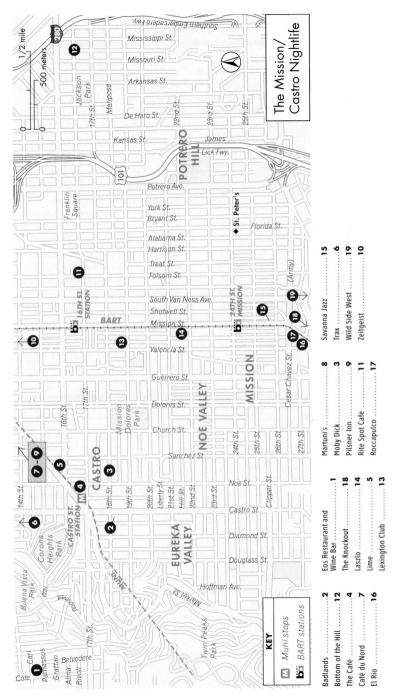

The Mission/
Castro Nightlife

16

KEY

Ⓜ Muni stops
🅱 BART stations

Badlands **2**	Eos Restaurant and
Bottom of the Hill **12**	Wine Bar **1**
The Café **4**	The Knockout **18**
Café du Nord **7**	Laszlo **14**
El Rio **16**	Lime **5**
	Lexington Club **13**

Martuni's **8**	Savanna Jazz **15**
Moby Dick **3**	Trax **6**
Pilsner Inn **9**	Wild Side West **19**
Rite Spot Cafe **11**	Zeitgeist **10**
Roccapulco **17**	

CLOSE UP

Gay and Lesbian Nightlife in San Francisco

In the days before the gay liberation movement, bars were more than mere watering holes—they also served as community centers where members of a mostly underground minority could network and socialize. In the 1960s the bars became hotbeds of political activity; by the 1970s other social opportunities had become available to gay men and lesbians, and the bars' importance as centers of activity decreased.

Old-timers may wax nostalgic about the vibrancy of pre-AIDS, 1970s bar life, but you can still have plenty of fun. The one difference is the one-night-a-week operation of some of the best clubs, which may cater to a different (sometimes straight) clientele on other nights. This type of club tends to come and go, so it's best to pick up one of the two main gay papers to check the latest happenings. The *Bay Area Reporter*

(☎ 415/861–5019 ⊕ www.ebar.com), a biweekly newspaper, lists gay and lesbian events in its calendar and has a special nightlife site (⊕ www.bartabsf.com). The biweekly *San Francisco Bay Times* (☎ 415/626–0260 ⊕ www.sfbaytimes.com) is aimed at gay and lesbian readers.

For a place known as a gay mecca, San Francisco has always suffered from a surprising drought of gay women's bars. The Lexington Club, in the nightlife-filled Mission District, is the best-known bar. The Café is probably the most lesbian-friendly Castro bar, though you'll find queer gals (and many more queer guys) at the Mint and the Stud, too.

The calendar at ⊕ www.hillgirlz.com, one of the best places for detailed information about the city's lesbian scene, covers everything from dance events to social and political gatherings.

MISSION DISTRICT

BARS

Laszlo. Attached to the Foreign Cinema restaurant, Laszlo is a cavernous, classy space with an open, bi-level design; movies are projected onto the walls. Dim lighting, candles, and an upscale selection of cocktails and single-malts make it suitable for romance, but the loud music and cacophonic levels of conversation keep it lively. DJs spin most nights after 9. ⊠ *2532 Mission St., between 21st and 22nd Sts., Mission* ☎ *415/401–0810* ⊕ *www.laszlobar.com.*

Rite Spot Cafe. A Mission tradition for more than 50 years, this classy and casual charmer is like a cabaret club in an aging mobster's garage. Quirky lounge singers and other musicians entertain most nights. A small menu of affordable sandwiches and Italian food beats your average bar fare. Rite Spot is in a mostly residential and somewhat desolate part of the Mission, so you may feel like you're entering a no-man's-land. ⊠ *2099 Folsom St., at 17th St., Mission* ☎ *415/552–6066* ⊕ *www.ritespotcafe.net.*

A DRINK TO RIVAL DINNER

Some of San Francisco's best and most inventive bars are primarily restaurants.

You might be tempted to order wine with your French meal at **Absinthe** (✉ 398 Hayes St., at Gough, Hayes Valley ☎ 415/551–1590). Resist. The 30- plus specialty cocktails— or even just a plain old Manhattan—are too good to pass up. And the food—oh, the food.

The increasingly trendy Haight has been waiting for a place like this. **The Alembic** (✉ 1725 Haight St., Haight ☎ 415/666–0822) is a classy, dark-wood, low-lighted space that buzzes with conversation.

Tsunami Sushi (✉ 1306 Fulton St., Western Addition ☎ 415/567–7664) has a small but very good sushi menu, as well as a list of more than 100 sakes and a staff who knows their stuff—including how to make killer sake-tinis.

BARS WITH LIVE MUSIC
Fodor's Choice
★

El Rio. A dive bar in the best sense, El Rio has a calendar chock-full of events, from free bands and films to Salsa Sunday (seasonal), all of which keep Mission kids coming back. Bands play several nights a week, and there are plenty of popular events. No matter what day you attend, expect to find a diverse gay–straight crowd. The large patio out back is especially popular when the weather's warm. ✉ 3158 Mission St., between César Chavez and Valencia Sts., Mission ☎ 415/282–3325 ⊕ www.elriosf.com.

16

The Knockout. In a grungy but hip section of the Mission, the king of dive bars (with requisite cheap bottled beer and photo booth) is popular with the discerning hipsters who dare to venture south of César Chavez Street. There's usually a cover for bands or DJs on weekends, but it's never more than $10. Bingo on Thursday keeps it real. An added bonus for trekking out to the southern edge of the Mission: some of the city's best taquerías are nearby. ✉ 3223 Mission St., at Valencia, Mission ☎ 415/550–6994 ⊕ www.theknockoutsf.com.

OUTDOOR BARS
Zeitgeist. It's a bit divey, a bit rock and roll, and the port-a-potties are arguably cleaner than the restroom, but Zeitgeist is a good place to relax with a cold one or an ever-popular (and ever-strong) Bloody Mary in the large beer "garden" (there's not much greenery) on a sunny day. Grill food of the burger-and-hot-dog variety is available. If you own a trucker hat, a pair of Vans, and a Pabst Blue Ribbon T-shirt, you'll fit right in. ✉ 199 Valencia St., at Duboce Ave., Mission ☎ 415/255–7505.

DANCE CLUBS

Roccapulco. Salsa, salsa, salsa. With dancing and live music from big-name salsa bands on Friday and Saturday, this cavernous dance hall and restaurant knows how to pack 'em in. Pick up some moves at the Wednesday, Friday, and Saturday evening salsa lessons. The club enforces a dress code, so don't wear sneakers. This place is also a supper club serving Latin-nouveau cuisine. ✉ 3140 Mission St., between Precita and César Chavez Sts., Mission ☎ 415/648–6611 ⊕ www.roccapulco.com.

Rock music one day and salsa the next keeps a diverse crowd coming to El Rio.

GAY NIGHTLIFE

GAY MALE
BARS
★

Martuni's. A mixed crowd enjoys cocktails in the semirefined environ-ment of this elegant bar at the intersection of the Castro, the Mission, and Hayes Valley; variations on the martini are a specialty. In the inti-mate back room a pianist plays nightly, and patrons take turns boister-ously singing show tunes. It's a favorite post-theater spot—especially after the symphony or opera, which are within walking distance. ⌧ *4 Valencia St., at Market St., Mission* ☎ *415/241–0205.*

LESBIAN BARS
★

Lexington Club. According to its slogan, "every night is ladies' night" at this all-girl club geared to urban alterna-dykes in their twenties and thirties (think piercings and tattoos, not lipstick). ■TIP→ **The women's room has awesome graffiti.** ⌧ *3464 19th St., at Lexington St., Mission* ☎ *415/863–2052* ⊕ *www.lexingtonclub.com.*

JAZZ CLUBS

★

Savanna Jazz. Deep in the Outer Mission, this is one of the best jazz joints in SF, an unexpected find in a neighborhood filled with hipster bars. Loungey booths and low lighting set the scene for consistently good old-school Latin and Brazilian jazz acts. Cover is generally $5–$8. ⌧ *2937 Mission St., between 25th and 26th Sts., Mission* ☎ *415/285–3369* ⊕ *www.savannajazz.com.*

POTRERO HILL

ROCK, POP, HIP-HOP, FOLK, AND BLUES CLUBS

★ **Bottom of the Hill**. This is a great live-music dive—in the best sense of the word—and truly the epicenter for independent rock in the Bay Area. The club has hosted some great acts over the years, including the Strokes and the Throwing Muses. Rap and hip-hop acts occasionally make it to the stage. ⊠ *1233 17th St., at Texas St., Potrero Hill* ☎ *415/621–4455* ⊕ *www.bottomofthehill.com.*

PACIFIC HEIGHTS AND JAPANTOWN

PACIFIC HEIGHTS
GAY NIGHTLIFE

GAY MALE BARS **Lion Pub**. With big comfy chairs, cascades of potted plants, and a small fireplace, this bar is so welcoming that—even though it's one of the oldest gay bars in the city—it tends to draw every sort of San Franciscan, young and old, gay and straight. Specialty drinks made with fresh-squeezed fruit juices attract cocktail connoisseurs. ⊠ *2062 Divisadero St., at Sacramento St., Pacific Heights* ☎ *415/567–6565.*

JAPANTOWN
JAZZ CLUBS

16

★ **Yoshi's**. The legendary Oakland club that has pulled in some of the world's best jazz musicians—Pat Martino, Branford Marsalis, Betty Carter, and Dizzy Gillespie, to name just a few—opened a San Francisco location in late 2007. The new club has terrific acoustics, a 9-foot Steinway grand piano (broken in by Chick Corea), and seating for 411; it's been hailed as "simply the best jazz club in the city." Yoshi's also serves Japanese food in an adjoining restaurant set in a soaring two-story space, decorated with blond wood and hanging paper lanterns (you can also order food at café tables in the club). And yes, the coupling of sushi and jazz *is* as elegant as it sounds. Sightlines are good from just about any vantage point, including the back balcony. Yoshi's is located in the Fillmore District, which was known as the "Harlem of the West" in its heyday during the 1940s and '50s. Be advised, the strip where the club is located is part of a new city redevelopment project—it's on a tough block in an even tougher neighborhood; so, take advantage of the valet parking. ⊠ *1330 Fillmore St., at Eddy St., Japantown* ☎ *415/655–5600* ⊕ *www.yoshis.com.*

GAY NIGHTLIFE BEYOND THE BARS

The San Francisco Lesbian, Gay, Bisexual, and Transgender Community Center (⊠ *1800 Market St., Hayes Valley* ☎ *415/865–5555* ⊕ *www.sfcenter.org*) is home to many social activities, from writers' groups to yoga.

Nightlife: Japantown, Pacific Heights and the Marina

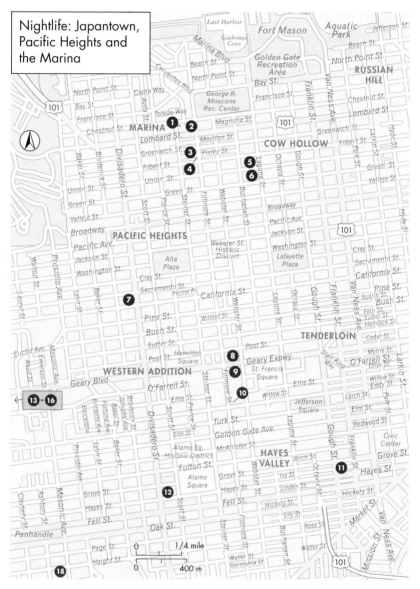

SAFETY AFTER DARK

San Franciscans sometimes seem to get a perverse thrill out of the grittiness of their city. Some of the best nightlife options are in slightly sketchy locations; in the areas we've listed below you're better off cabbing it. Bartenders can call you a ride when you're ready to leave.

■ **Civic Center:** If you're having a nightcap, don't wander north, east, or south. The one safe corridor is west to Gough, which will bring you to Hayes Valley. Especially avoid Market Street between 6th and 10th streets.

■ **SoMa:** More than five blocks or so south of Market is a sort of industrial no-man's-land, though this area becomes more developed and inhab-ited by flashy residential skyscrapers with each passing year.

■ **The Tenderloin:** Plenty of locals walk to bars in the Tenderloin, but if addicts and sketchy dudes hanging out in front of hourly rate motels make you uncomfortable (and really, can't imagine why they wouldn't), you should take a cab. The edges of the Tenderloin, closer to Jones (east) or Sutter (north), aren't too bad.

■ **The Outer Mission (below 24th Street):** If you're feeling out of sorts on Mission Street between 16th and 24th streets, cut over to Valencia.

It's safe to walk around the Financial District, Union Square, Haight Street and Cole Valley, Nob Hill, the Mission (above 24th Street), and SoMa north of Howard.

16

ROCK, POP, HIP-HOP, FOLK, AND BLUES CLUBS

Fodor's Choice ★ **BooM BooM RooM.** John Lee Hooker's old haunt has been an old-school blues haven for years, attracting top-notch acts from all around the country. Luck out with legendary masters like James "Super Chikan" Johnson, or discover new blues and funk artists. ⊠ *1601 Fillmore St., at Geary Blvd., Japantown* ☎ *415/673–8000* ⊕ *www.boomboomblues. com.*

WESTERN ADDITION

ROCK, POP, HIP-HOP, FOLK, AND BLUES CLUBS

The Fillmore. This is *the* club that all the big names, from Coldplay to Clapton, want to play. San Francisco's most famous rock-music hall serves up a varied menu of national and local acts: rock, reggae, grunge, jazz, folk, acid house, and more. Most tickets cost $20–$30, and some shows are open to all ages. ■**TIP**➜ Avoid steep service charges by buying tickets at the Fillmore box office on Sunday (10–4). ⊠ *1805 Geary Blvd., at Fillmore St., Western Addition* ☎ *415/346–6000* ⊕ *www.thefillmore. com.*

The Independent. Originally called the Box for its giant cube-shape interior, this off-the-beaten-path music venue showcases an eclectic mix of rock, heavy metal, folk, soul, reggae, hip-hop, and DJ acts. There's a big dance floor. Recent shows have included Lyrics Born, Sonya Kitchell and The Slip, Testament, and the Dears. ⊠ *628 Divisadero St., at Hayes St., Western Addition* ☎ *415/771–1421* ⊕ *www.theindependentsf.com.*

BERNAL HEIGHTS

GAY NIGHTLIFE

LESBIAN BARS **Wild Side West**. A friendly pool game is always going on at this mellow, slightly out-of-the-way neighborhood hangout, where all are welcome. Outside is a large deck and one of San Francisco's best bar gardens, where acoustic-guitar sing-alongs are not uncommon. ⊠ *424 Cortland Ave., Bernal Heights* ☎ *415/647–3099.*

RICHMOND

ROCK, POP, HIP-HOP, FOLK, AND BLUES CLUBS

The Plough and Stars. This decidedly unglamorous pub, where crusty old-timers swap stories over pints of Guinness, is the city's best bet for traditional Irish music. Bay Area musicians (and, once in a while, big-name bands) perform every night except Monday. Talented locals gather to play on Tuesday and Sunday *seisiúns,* informal "sessions" where musicians sit around a table and drink and eat while chiming in; anyone skilled at Irish traditional music can join in. ⊠ *116 Clement St., at 2nd Ave., Richmond* ☎ *415/751–1122* ⊕ *www.theploughandstars.com.*

Sports and the Outdoors

WORD OF MOUTH

"If you want a long walking day, go all the way Ferry Building (Sat farmers market) and Embarcadero to Aquatic Park, Fort Mason, Crissy Field, on to Ft Point (under the Golden Gate bridge). Or just do the section Crissy Field to Ft Point and visit the historic Ft Point for an interesting perspective, visual and historic, on the city."

—car_free_traveler

Updated by
Fiona G.
Parrott

San Francisco's surroundings—the bay, ocean, mountains, and forests—make getting outdoors away from the city a no-brainer. Muir Woods, Point Reyes, and Stinson Beach in Marin County (⇨ *see Chapter 19*) offer dozens of opportunities for exploring the natural beauty of the Bay Area. But the peninsular city—with its many green spaces, steep inclines, and breathtaking views—has plenty to offer itself.

Bikers and hikers traverse the majestic Golden Gate Bridge, bound for the Marin Headlands or the winding trails of the Presidio. Runners, strollers, in-line skaters, and cyclists head for Golden Gate Park's wooded paths, and water lovers satisfy their addictions by kayaking, sailing, or kite-surfing in the bay and along the rugged Pacific coast. The monthly *Competitor Nor Cal Magazine* (⊕ *www.competitornorcal. com*), available for free at sporting-goods stores, tennis centers, and other recreational sites, lists running and bicycle races, and other participant sports events, in Northern California.

Prefer to watch from the sidelines? The Giants (baseball) and the 49ers (football) are San Francisco's professional sports teams; the Athletics (baseball) and the Golden State Warriors (basketball) play in Oakland. But the city has plenty of other periodic sporting events to watch (including the roving costume party–like Bay to Breakers race). For events listings and local perspectives on Bay Area sports, pick up a copy of the *San Francisco Chronicle* (⊕ *www.sfgate.com*) or the *Examiner* (⊕ *www.examiner.com*), both of which list schedules and scores.

BASEBALL

☾   The National League's New York Giants became the **San Francisco**
Fodor's Choice   **Giants** (✉ *AT&T Park, 24 Willie Mays Plaza, between 2nd and 3rd Sts.,*
★   *SoMa* ☎ *415/972-2000 or 800/734-4268* ⊕ *sanfrancisco.giants.mlb. com*) when they moved to California in 1958, the same year that the Brooklyn Dodgers moved to Los Angeles. Today the beautiful, classic

design of the Giants' AT&T Park, in addition to the team's wining the 2010 World Series, has created a new legion of fans. Buy your tickets in advance—nearly every game sells out.

GETTING TICKETS

The park is small and there are 30,000 season-ticket holders (for 43,000 seats), so Giants tickets for popular games routinely sell out the day they go on sale, and other games sell out quickly. If tickets aren't available at Tickets.com, try the Double Play Ticket Window Web site, or even try showing up on game day—there are usually plenty of scalpers, some selling at reasonable prices.

Tickets.com (☎ 877/473–4849 ⊕ www.tickets.com) sells game tickets over the phone and charges a per-ticket fee of $5–$24, plus a per-call processing fee of up to $3.50. The **Giants Dugout** (⊠ AT&T Park, 24 Willie Mays Plaza, SoMa ☎ 415/972–2000 or 800/734–4268 ⊠ 4 Embarcadero Center, Embarcadero ☎ 415/951–8888) sells tickets in any of its stores (check the Web site, ⊕ sanfrancisco.giants.mlb.com/sf/ballpark/dugout_stores.jsp, for all locations); a surcharge is added at all but the ballpark store.

The Giants' Web-only **Double Play Ticket Window** (⊕ sanfrancisco.giants. mlb.com) allows season-ticket holders to resell their unused tickets. You won't always find a deal, but you might get a seat at an otherwise sold-out game. Click the "Tickets" link on the home page.

A WORLD SERIES WIN FOR THE GIANTS

It was a World Series like no other: In 2010, the San Francisco Giants made headlines, not only for their win over the Texas Rangers, but for winning with unforgettable panache. Pitcher and prankster Brian Wilson dyed his beard to a cartoon-pirate black, and drag queen Donna Sachet sang the national anthem in full regalia, reminded fans that this is a city unlike any other. The victory parades continued in the streets long after the last strike was thrown. Not since 1954 have the SF Giants or their fans had it this good.

17

BEACHES

Taking in a beachside sunset is the perfect way to end a busy day in the city (assuming the fog hasn't blown in for the afternoon). Always bring a sweater—even the sunniest of days can become cold and foggy without warning. Icy temperatures and treacherous currents make most waters too dangerous for swimming without a wet suit, but with a Frisbee, picnic, or some good walking shoes, you can have a fantastic day at the beach without leaving the city.

☉ An urban beach, surrounded by Fort Mason, Ghirardelli Square, and Fisherman's Wharf, **Aquatic Park Beach** (⊕ www.nps.gov/safr) is a tiny, ¼-mi-long strip of sand with gentle water, bordered by docks and piers. The waters near shore are shallow, safe for kids to swim or wade, and fairly clean (admirably so, for a city). Locals—including the seemingly ubiquitous older-man-in-Speedo—come out for quick dips in the frigid water. The Golden Gate Promenade, with dog-walkers, inline-skaters, and cyclists, passes just behind the beach, so this isn't a secluded spot. Facilities include restrooms and showers.

Members of the **Dolphin Club** come every morning for a dip in the ice-cold waters of Aquatic Park; an especially large and raucous crowd braves the cold on New Year's Day.

Baker Beach (⊠ *Gibson Rd. off Bowley St., southwest corner of Presidio*), with gorgeous views of the Golden Gate Bridge and the Marin Headlands, is a local favorite and an established nudist spot. (Never seen nude Frisbee? This is the place.) The pounding surf and strong currents make swimming a dangerous prospect, but the mile-long shoreline is ideal for fishing, building sand castles, or watching sea lions at play. On warm days the entire beach is packed with bodies—including those nudists, who hang out at the north end. Picnic tables, grills, restrooms, and drinking water are available. Rangers give tours of the 95,000-pound cannon at Battery Chamberlin, overlooking the beach, the first weekend of every month.

> **TOP OUTDOOR ACTIVITIES**
>
> ■ Ride a bike over the Golden Gate Bridge to Sausalito, then take the ferry back.
>
> ■ Hike to the top of Angel Island.
>
> ■ Catch a Giants game at AT&T Park.

☺ Sheltered **China Beach,** one of the city's safest swimming beaches, was named for the impoverished Chinese fishermen who once camped here. (Some maps label it James D. Phelan Beach.) This 600-foot strip of sand, south of the Presidio and Baker Beach, has gentle waters as well as changing rooms, restrooms, showers, grills, drinking water, and picnic tables. Despite its humble beginnings, China Beach today is bordered by the multimillion-dollar homes of the Seacliff neighborhood. The hike down to the beach is steep.

☺ The largest—and probably best—of San Francisco's city beaches, **Ocean Beach** stretches for more than 3 mi along the Great Highway south of the Cliff House, making it ideal for long walks and runs. It isn't the cleanest shore, but it's an easy-to-reach place to chill; spot sea lions sunning themselves atop Seal Rock, at the north end of the beach; or watch daredevil surfers riding the roiling waves. Because of extremely dangerous currents, swimming isn't recommended. After the sun sets, bonfires form a string of lights along the beach in summer. (Fires are prohibited north of Fulton Street or south of Lincoln Way, the northern and southern edges of Golden Gate Park.) Restrooms are at the north end.

BICYCLING

San Francisco is known for its treacherously steep hills, so it may be surprising to see so many cyclists. This is actually a great city for biking—there are ample bike lanes, it's not hard to find level ground with great scenery (along the water), and if you're willing to tackle a challenging uphill climb, you're often rewarded with a fabulous view—and a quick trip back down.

AT&T Park: Where Giants Tread

The size of AT&T Park hits you immediately—the field, McCovey Cove, and the Lefty O'Doul drawbridge all look like miniature models. At only 13 acres, the San Francisco Giants' ballpark is one of the country's smallest. After Boston's Fenway, AT&T Park has the shortest distance to the wall; from home plate it's just 309 feet to the right field. But there's something endearing about its petite stature—not to mention its location, with yacht masts poking up over the outfield and the blue bay sparkling beyond.

From 1960 to 2000 the Giants played at Candlestick Park (now Monster Park, the home of the NFL's '49ers). The huge, modern stadium has nice views, but it's also in one of the coldest, windiest parts of the city. (Giants' pitcher Stu Miller was famously "blown off the mound" here in 1961.)

In 2000 the Giants played their first game at AT&T Park (then Pacific Bell Park, later SBC Park—in fact, some locals jokingly call it the Phone Company Park). All told, $357 million was spent on the privately funded park, and it shows in the retro red-brick exterior, the quaint clock tower, handsome bronze statues and murals, above-average food (pad Thai, anyone?), and tiny details like baseball-style lettering on no-smoking signs. There isn't a bad seat in the house, and the park has an unusual level of intimacy and access. Concourses circle the field on two levels—on the field level you can stand inches from players as they exit the locker rooms. On the street level non-ticket-holders can get up close, too, outside a gate behind the visiting team's dugout.

Diehards may miss the grittiness of Candlestick, but it's hard not to love this park. It's a new stadium with an old-time aura, already a San Francisco institution.

THE FAMOUS "SPLASH HIT"

Locals show up in motorboats and inflatable rafts, with fishing nets ready to scoop up home-run balls that clear the right field wall and land in McCovey Cove. Hitting one into the water isn't easy: the ball has to clear a 26-foot wall, the elevated walkway, and the promenade outside. Barry Bonds had the first splash hit on May 1, 2000.

GETTING THERE

Parking is pricey ($30 and up), and 5,000 spaces for 43,000 seats doesn't add up. Take public transportation. Muni line N (to CalTrain/Mission Bay) stops right in front of the park, and Muni bus lines 10, 15, 30, 42, 45, and 47 stop a block away. Or you can arrive in style—take the ferry from Jack London Square in Oakland (⊕ www.eastbayferry.com).

AT&T Park (✉ 24 Willie Mays Plaza, SoMa ☎ 415/972–2000 or 800/734–4268 ⊕ www.attpark.com).

Park Tours (✉ $12.50 ⊙ Daily at 10:30 and 12:30).

The giant Coca-Cola bottle and mitt you see beyond the outfield are part of a **playground**. The bottle is a slide and the mitt actually has decent views of the field. It also alongside a mini-version of the park used for minor-league tryouts and pee-wee baseball.

17

The **San Francisco Bicycle Coalition** (☎ 415/431–2453 ⊕ *www.sfbike. org*) has extensive information about the policies and politics of riding a bicycle in the city and lists local events for cyclists on its Web site. You can also download (but not print) a PDF version of the *San Francisco Bike Map and Walking Guide.*

WHERE TO RENT

Bike and Roll. You can rent bikes here for $8 per hour or $32 per day; discounted weekly rates are available. They have three locations and also have complimentary maps. ⊠ *899 Columbus Ave., North Beach* ⊠ *353 Jefferson St. between Jones and Leavenworth Sts., Fisherman's Wharf* ⊠ *2800 Leavenworth St., Fisherman's Wharf* ☎ *415/229–2000 or 888/245–3929* ⊕ *www. bicyclerental.com.*

Bike Hut. Known for its mom-and-pop–style service, the Hut is a small rental, repair, and used-bike shop. Hourly rentals go for $6, daily rentals for $22. ⊠ *Pier 40, SoMa* ☎ *415/543–4335* ⊕ *www.thebikehut.com* ☉ *Wed.–Sun.*

Blazing Saddles. This outfitter rents bikes for $8 to $9 an hour, depending on the type of bike, or $32 to $88 a day, and shares tips on sights to see along the paths. ⊠ *2715 Hyde St., Fisherman's Wharf* ⊠ *433 Mason St., Union Sq.* ⊠ *Pier 41, Fisherman's Wharf* ⊠ *465 Jefferson St., at Hyde St., Fisherman's Wharf* ⊠ *2555 Powell St., Fisherman's Wharf* ⊠ *1095 Columbus, North Beach* ⊠ *721 Beach St., North Beach* ☎ *415/202–8888* ⊕ *www.blazingsaddles.com.*

San Francisco Cyclery. Rent a bike for $15 for one to two hours, $20 for two to four hours, or $30 for eight hours. ⊠ *672 Stanyan St., between Page and Haight Sts., Haight* ☎ *415/379–3870* ⊕ *www. sanfranciscocyclery.com* ☉ *Wed.–Mon. 10–6.*

From April through October you can rent mountain bikes on **Angel Island** (☎ *415/435–5390* ⊕ *www.angelisland.org*) for $10 an hour or $35 a day.

THE EMBARCADERO

A completely flat, sea-level route, the Embarcadero hugs the eastern and northern bay and gives a clear view of open waters, the Bay Bridge, and sleek high-rises. The route from Pier 40 to Aquatic Park takes about 30 minutes, and there are designated bike lanes the entire way. As you ride along, you can see—from east to west—the Ferry Building, the Bay Bridge, a view of Coit Tower near Pier 19 (look inland), and various ferries and historic ships. At Aquatic Park there's a nice view of Golden Gate Bridge. If you're not tired yet, continue along the Marina and through the Presidio's Crissy Field. You may want to time your

---

NO UPHILL BATTLE

Don't want to get stuck slogging up 30-degree inclines? Then be sure to pick up a copy of the foldout *San Francisco Bike Map and Walking Guide* ($3), which indicates street grades by color and delineates bike routes that avoid major hills and heavy traffic. You can pick up a copy in bicycle shops, select bookstores, or at the San Francisco Bicycle Coalition's Web site (⊕ www.sfbike.org).

ride so you end up at the Ferry Building, where you can refuel with a sandwich, a gelato, or—why not?—fresh oysters.

■ TIP➜ Be sure to keep your eyes open along this route—cars move quickly here, and streetcars and tourist traffic can cause congestion. Near Fisherman's Wharf you can bike on the promenade, but take it slow—we've seen more than one near miss between bicyclist and pedestrian.

CAUTION Streetcar tracks can wreak havoc on skinny bike tires—and the bicyclist perched above them. Watch the ground and cross the tracks perpendicularly.

GOLDEN GATE PARK

A beautiful maze of roads and hidden bike paths crisscrosses San Francisco's most famous park, winding past rose gardens, lakes, waterfalls, museums, horse stables, bison, and, at the park's western edge, spectacular views of the Pacific Ocean. John F. Kennedy Drive is closed to motor vehicles on Sunday (and sometimes Saturday), when it's crowded with people-powered wheels.

■ TIP➜ Get a map of the park before you go—it's huge.

From the eastern entrance of the park between Oak and Fell streets, veer right to begin a 30- to 45-minute, 3-mi ride down John F. Kennedy Drive through the park to the Great Highway, where land meets ocean. Take a break and watch the waves roll in at Ocean Beach, or cross the street for a drink or a bite to eat at the casual, tree-shrouded Park Chalet (behind the Beach Chalet). Extend your ride a few more miles by turning left, riding a few blocks, and connecting with a raised bike path that runs parallel to the Pacific, winds through fields of emerald-green ice plant, and, after 2 mi, leads to Sloat Boulevard and the San Francisco Zoo. ■ TIP➜ On exceptionally windy days, expect to encounter blowing sand along this route.

THE MARINA GREEN AND GOLDEN GATE BRIDGE

The Marina Green, a vast lawn at the edge of the northern bay front, stretches along Marina Boulevard, adjacent to Fort Mason. It's the starting point of a well-used, paved bike path that runs through the Presidio along Crissy Field's waterfront wetlands, then heads for the Golden Gate Bridge and beyond. To do this ride, first take the path from Aquatic Park through Fort Mason to the Marina Green. Continue

LEGS OF STEEL

After crossing the Golden Gate, the superfit can ride alongside triathletes and hard-core cyclists in the Marin Headlands. Take the Alexander Avenue exit off the bridge as if you were going to Sausalito, but turn left instead and double back under the freeway. Just before the road merges with San Francisco–bound traffic, bear right and ascend the steep, rolling hills of the Marin Headlands. Follow the road to the top, where it becomes one-way and drops toward the ocean. Loop around the backside of the hills and through the tunnel, back to the bridge. On a clear day the views along this route are stunning.

17

into the Presidio, and you'll eventually reach the base of the bridge, a 60-minute ride round-trip. To view the bridge from underneath, stay at water level and ride to Fort Point (where Kim Novak leaped into the drink in the film *Vertigo*).

If you want to cross the bridge, take Lincoln Boulevard to reach the road-level viewing area and continue across the bridge (signs indicate which side you must use). Once you're across, turn right on the first road leading northeast, Alexander Avenue. After a 10-minute all-downhill ride, you'll arrive on Bridgeway in downtown Sausalito, where you can rest in a café. After a little shopping, board the Blue & Gold Fleet's ferry (the ferry terminal is at the end of Bridgeway) with your bike for the half-hour ride back to Fisherman's Wharf. ■**TIP→** If it's overcast, foggy, or windy, don't bother doing the Golden Gate Bridge bike ride—the wind can feel downright dangerous on the bridge, and the trip is only awe-inspiring when you can take in the view.

ANGEL ISLAND STATE PARK

A former military garrison and a beautiful wildlife preserve, **Angel Island** has some steep roads and great views of the city and the bay. Bicycles must stay on roadways; there are no single-track trails on the island. A ferry operated by **Blue & Gold Fleet** (☎ 415/705–8200 ⊕ *www.blueandgoldfleet.com*) runs to the island from Pier 41 at Fisherman's Wharf and takes about 20 minutes one way; the fare is $16 round-trip, which includes park admission. Ferries leave once a day at 10 am weekdays and 10:30 am weekends, returning at around 3:30 pm; schedules change, so call for up-to-date info. Twenty-five bicycles are permitted on board on a first-come, first-served basis. The café is closed mid-November through February, so bring your own grub. ☎ 415/435–5390 ⊕ *www.angelisland.org*.

BOATING AND SAILING

San Francisco Bay has year-round sailing, but tricky currents and strong winds make the bay hazardous for inexperienced navigators. Boat rentals and charters are available throughout the Bay Area and are listed under "Boat Renting" in the Yellow Pages.

Near Fisherman's Wharf, from spring through fall, **Adventure Cat Sailing Charters** (✉ *Pier 39, Dock J Fisherman's Wharf* ☎ 800/498–4228 or 415/777–1630 ⊕ *www.adventurecat.com*) takes passengers aboard a 55-foot-long catamaran. The kids can play on the trampoline-like net between the two hulls while you sip drinks on the wind-protected sundeck. A 90-minute bay cruise costs $30; sunset sails with drinks and hors d'oeuvres are $45.

Rendezvous Charters (✉ *Pier 40, South Beach Harbor* ☎ 415/543–7333 ⊕ *www.rendezvouscharters.com*) offers individually ticketed trips on large sailing yachts, including sunset sails ($30) and Sunday brunch cruises on a schooner ($45). **Spinnaker Sailing** (✉ *Pier 40, South Beach Harbor* ☎ 415/543–7333 ⊕ *www.spinnaker-sailing.com*) offers sailing instruction and charters private sailboats with or without a skipper (bring your logbook if you want to captain a boat yourself). Both Rendezvous and Spinnaker are south of the Ferry Building on the eastern waterfront, right next to AT&T Park, *not* next to Pier 39.

🕃 If you prefer calm freshwater, you can rent rowboats ($20 per hour), pedal boats ($25 per hour), and electric motorboats ($35 per hour) at **Stow Lake** (⊠ *Off John F. Kennedy Dr., ½ mi west of 10th Ave., Golden Gate Park* ☎ *415/752–0347*), in Golden Gate Park. They take both cash and credit cards; also remember to bring bread for the ducks. The lake is open daily 10 am–4 pm for boating, weather permitting, but call for seasonal hours.

> ### DID YOU KNOW?
>
> Candlestick Park has gone through several names in recent years, due to various sponsors and naming rights deals—from 3Com Park at Candlestick Point to Monster Park to the San Francisco Stadium at Candlestick Point. Today it has reverted back to its original name: Candlestick Park. But in 2007 the city named the field part of the stadium after Bill Walsh, the late and popular '49ers coach. The entire area is now referred to as the Bill Walsh Field/ Candlestick Park.

FISHING

Fishing boats angle for salmon and halibut outside the bay or striped bass and giant sturgeon within. On land, you can cast your line at the Municipal Pier, Fisherman's Wharf, Baker Beach, or Aquatic Park. Fishing licenses are not necessary when casting from public piers. (The exception is sturgeon fishing, for which you need a Sturgeon Fishing Report Card.) Licenses are required for all other types of fishing, and can be purchased from the **California Department of Fish and Game** (⊕ *www.dfg.ca.gov*). Non-California residents can purchase 1-, 2-, or 10-day licenses for $14, $22, and $43 respectively. Sportfishing charters depart daily from Fisherman's Wharf during the salmon-fishing season (March or April through October), and cost about $95.

Lovely Martha's Sportfishing (⊠ *Fisherman's Wharf, Berth 3, Fisherman's Wharf* ☎ *415/509–5552* ⊕ *www.lovelymartha.com*) has salmon-fishing excursions and bay cruises. **Wacky Jacky** (⊠ *Foot of Jones St. at Jefferson St., Fisherman's Wharf* ☎ *415/586–9800* ⊕ *www. wackyjackysportfishing.com*), skippered by a straight-shootin' woman named Jacky, takes you salmon fishing in a sleek, fast, and comfortable 50-foot boat.

FOOTBALL

The **San Francisco '49ers** (⊠ *Candlestick Park, 490 Jamestown Ave., Bayview Heights* ☎ *415/656–4900* ⊕ *www.sf49ers.com*) play at **Candlestick Park** near the San Mateo County border, just north of the airport. Single-game tickets, available via **Ticketmaster** (☎ *800/745–3000* ⊕ *www.ticketmaster.com*), almost always sell out far in advance.

GOLF

You can get detailed directions to the city's public golf courses or reserve a tee time ($1 reservation fee per player) up to six days in advance through San Francisco's automated **municipal tee times reservation line** (☎ 415/750–4653 ⊕ *www.sfteetimes.com*).

Expect to use every club in your bag to tackle the fast, sloping greens and unpredictable winds at the challenging **Gleneagles International Golf Course** (✉ *McLaren Park, 2100 Sunnydale Ave., Excelsior/Visitacion Valley* ☎ *415/587–2425* ⊕ *www.gleneaglesgolfsf.com*). The 9-hole, par-36 course is a little worse for wear.

> ### TAKE IT TO THE BRIDGE
>
> We prefer biking across the bridge rather than walking, but you can get the same spectacular views either way. Be sure to wear a jacket, and save this for fair-weather days. Set aside four hours if you plan to walk all the way across and back.

Golden Gate Park Golf Course (✉ *970 47th Ave., Golden Gate Park* ☎ *415/751–8987* ⊕ *www.goldengateparkgolf.com*) is a 9-hole, par-27 course in lovely Golden Gate Park, just above Ocean Beach. It's a beginner's paradise, but more-seasoned players might be put off by the lax play and wayward balls. There's first-come, first-served play only (no reservations).

★ **Harding Park Golf Course** (✉ *99 Harding Rd., at Skyline Blvd., Lake Merced* ☎ *415/664–4690* ⊕ *www.harding-park.com*) has an 18-hole, par-72 course and a 9-hole, par-32 Jack Fleming–designed course. The 9-hole course has all the characteristics of a championship course, but is less difficult. Both have fantastic views. About $15 million has been invested into the place over the past few years, and it shows. Book tee times as far in advance as possible.

The 18-hole, par-68 **Lincoln Park Golf Course** (✉ *300 34th Ave., at Clement St., Richmond* ☎ *415/221–9911* ⊕ *www.lincolnparkgc.com*) offers magnificent views of the Golden Gate Bridge, but the somewhat scraggly greens don't hold up well in damp weather. Arnold Palmer Golf Management runs the challenging and well-maintained 18-hole, par-72 **Presidio Golf Course** (✉ *300 Finley Rd., at Arguello Blvd., Presidio* ☎ *415/561–4661* ⊕ *www.presidiogolf.com*). You can book tee times online for an additional $8–$12 fee.

HANG GLIDING AND PARAGLIDING

Paragliding is like hang gliding, but uses a parachute-like nylon glider instead of a fixed wing. **Air Time San Francisco** (☎ 650/638–9463 ⊕ *www.sftandem.com*) offers paragliding instruction ($450 for two days; $550 for two people for two days) and tandem scenic flights ($200 per person; discounts for two or more people) just south of San Francisco in Pacifica, where you can fly over the coastal cliffs and take in spectacular views. The **San Francisco Hang Gliding Center** (☎ 510/528–2300 ⊕ *www.sfhanggliding.com*) specializes in tandem hang gliding ($295–$325).

CLOSE UP

San Francisco's Top Spas

Nestled deep inside the basement of the city's old Italian bank, **Acqua di Roma** (✉ *700 Montgomery St., North Beach* ☎ *415/434–2100* ⊕ *www. acquadiroma.com*) is a haven of harmony and relaxation that's anything but dark. The spa has high windows, warm yellow walls, and smooth brown tiles. The old bank vault has become the ultimate private treatment room with cork floors and trickling water fountains. Try the Deep Tissue Hydromassage that includes an underwater high-pressure hose.

Traditional sit-down Japanese showers and communal bathing are two out-of-the-ordinary features of **Kabuki Springs & Spa** (✉ *1750 Geary Blvd., Japantown* ☎ *415/922–6000* ⊕ *www. kabukisprings.com*). The renowned $155 Javanese Lulur Treatment includes a combination massage with jasmine oil, exfoliation with turmeric and ground rice, yogurt application, and a candlelight soak with rose petals. Men and women are welcome every day for private treatments, but call ahead regarding communal bathing schedules; the baths are coed only on Tuesday. Note that clothing is optional, except on coed days.

Warning: after experiencing the serene and luxurious **Nob Hill Spa** (✉ *1075 California St., Nob Hill* ☎ *415/345–2888* ⊕ *www.huntingtonhotel.com*) at the Huntington Hotel, you'll start to *expect* Champagne with your massage. Unique features include the eucalyptus steam bath and a gorgeous infinity pool that overlooks the city through a glass wall. After your treatments, you can hang here all day: take a yoga or Pilates class, get a green-tea body scrub, or just read on the sundeck.

All treatments at the St. Regis Hotel's très chic **Remède Spa** (✉ *125 3rd St., at Mission St., SoMa* ☎ *415/284–4060* ⊕ *www.remede.com*) incorporate a line of high-end French skin-care products. Offerings include custom skin therapy, massage, body scrubs, seaweed wraps, and a variety of mani–pedi, facial, and waxing options. Prices range from $40 for a manicure to $240 for a massage.

Elegant but casual **Spa Radiance** (✉ *3011 Fillmore St., between Union and Filbert Sts., Cow Hollow* ☎ *415/346–6281* ⊕ *www.sparadiance. com*) specializes in facials and draws the occasional celebrity. Try a vitamin-and-oxygen treatment, or the "super-duper" series—a deep-pore cleaning followed by dermabrasion.

The futuristic **Tru Spa** (✉ *750 Kearney St., Financial District* ☎ *415/339–9700* ⊕ *www.truspa.com*) is a local favorite, and for good reason. Its uncluttered space radiates calm. They offer face, body, and nail treatments, all excellent. Try the Trutherapy75, a beautiful 75-minute, personally tailored full-body massage enhanced with aromatherapy and colored light therapy, bringing the treatment to a whole new level of indulgence. Prices range from $70 to $230 for body treatments.

17

Hang-gliding and paragliding flights leave from giant Mt. Tamalpais in Marin and land on the sands of Stinson Beach, at the base of soft hills. First-timers are welcome. The center also has solo lessons ($160 per lesson).

HIKING

Hills and mountains—including Mt. Tamalpais in Marin County and Mt. Diablo in the East Bay, which has the second-longest sight lines anywhere in the world after Mt. Kilimanjaro—form a ring around the Bay Area. The **Bay Area Ridge Trail** (⊕ *ridgetrail.org*) is an ongoing project to connect all of the region's ridgelines. The trail is currently 300 mi long, but when finished it will extend 500 mi, stretching from San Jose to Napa and encompassing all nine Bay Area counties.

One of the most impressive ridgelines of the Bay Area Ridge Trail can be found on Mt. Tamalpais, in Marin County. The **Rock Spring Trail** starts at the Mountain Theater and gently climbs about 1¾ mi to the **West Point Inn,** once a stop on the Mt. Tam railroad route. Relax at a picnic table and stock up on water before forging ahead, via Old Railroad Grade Fire Road and the Miller Trail, to Mt. Tam's Middle Peak, about 2 mi uphill.

Starting at the Pan Toll Ranger Station, the precipitous **Steep Ravine Trail** brings you past stands of coastal redwoods and, in the springtime, numerous small waterfalls. Take the connecting **Dipsea Trail** to reach the town of Stinson Beach and its swath of golden sand. If you're too weary to make the 3½-mi trek back up, Golden Gate Transit Bus 63 (Saturday, Sunday, and holidays from mid-March through early December) takes you from Stinson Beach back to the ranger station.

But you don't have to leave the city for a nice hike. In the middle of San Francisco you can climb to the top of Mt. Davidson, Bernal Heights, Corona Heights, or Buena Vista Park. Little more than undeveloped hilltops, they offer spectacular views of the city and beautiful shows of wildflowers in spring.

In the Presidio, hiking and biking trails wind through nearly 1,500 acres of woods and hills, past old redbrick military buildings and jaw-dropping scenic overlooks with bay and ocean views. Rangers and docents lead guided hikes and nature walks throughout the year. For a current schedule, pick up a copy of the quarterly *Park News* at the **Presidio Visitor Center** (⊠ *Presidio Officers' Club, Bldg. 50, Moraga Ave., in Main Post area* ☎ *415/561–4323* ⊕ *www.nps.gov/prsf*) or go online.

☾ Stop by the **Warming Hut** (⊠ *Bldg. 983 off Old Mason Rd., facing water just east of Fort Point* ☎ *415/561–3040*) to refuel on snacks and to browse through the extensive selection of books (including good ones for kids) and the many ingenious gifts made from recycled materials.

Fodor'sChoice The Presidio is part of **Golden Gate National Recreation Area (GGNRA)**
★ (☎ *415/561–4700* ⊕ *www.nps.gov/goga*), which also encompasses the San Francisco coastline, the Marin Headlands, and Point Reyes National Seashore. It's veined with hiking trails, and guided walks

are available. You can find current schedules at GGNRA visitor centers in the Presidio and Marin Headlands; they're also online at ⊕ *www.nps.gov/goga/parknews*. For descriptions of each location within the recreation area—along with rich color photographs, hiking information, and maps—pick up a copy of *Guide to the Parks*, available in local bookstores or online from the **Golden Gate National Parks Conservancy** (☎ 415/561–3000 ⊕ *www.parksconservancy. org*).

The **Golden Gate Promenade** is another great walk; it passes through Crissy Field, taking in marshlands, kite-flyers, beachfront, and windsurfers, with the Golden Gate Bridge as a backdrop. The 3.3-mi walk is flat and easy—it should take about two hours round-trip. If you begin at Aquatic Park, you'll end up practically underneath the bridge at Fort Point Pier. ■ TIP➔ If you're driving, park at Fort Point and do the walk from west to east. It can get blustery, even when it's sunny, so be sure to layer.

Hikers head to **Angel Island State Park** (☎ 415/435–1915 ⊕ *www. angelisland.org*) for access to 13-plus mi of sometimes steep foot trails and fire roads that wind through the wildlife preserve. The Northridge/Sunset loop trail to the 788-foot summit of Mt. Livermore rewards with fantastic views; the Perimeter Road gives access to the island's beaches and historic sites. **Blue & Gold Fleet** (☎ 415/705–8200 ⊕ *www. blueandgoldfleet.com*) operates a ferry to the island from Pier 41 at Fisherman's Wharf. The $16 round-trip fare includes park admission. Schedules change frequently, so call for specifics; at this writing, ferries leave at 10 am weekdays and 10:30 am weekends, returning around 3:30 pm.

17

KAYAKING

Surrounded by water on three sides, San Francisco has plenty of opportunities for kayaking enthusiasts of all levels. **City Kayak** (✉ *Pier 39, Embarcadero at Stockton St., Fisherman's Wharf* ✉ *Pier 40, South Beach Harbor, SoMa* ☎ 415/357–1010 ⊕ *www.citykayak.com*), the only kayak-rental outfit in the city, operates bay tours along the waterfront and beneath the Bay Bridge starting from $50; they also run full-moon night paddles and trips to Alcatraz. Rentals are $35 per hour for a single, and $65 for a double. Half-day trips depart at 10 am daily. No prior experience is necessary, but you must watch an instructional video. ■ TIP➔ The Pier 39 location is for tours only, not rentals. Trips run by **Outdoor Programs** (✉ *500 Parnassus Ave., at 3rd Ave., Inner Sunset* ☎ 415/476–2078 ⊕ *www.outdoors.ucsf.edu*) originate in either Sausalito or Mission Bay in San Francisco and range from moonlight paddles from Sausalito (with views of the San Francisco skyline) to daytime sea-kayaking classes for all levels.

Sea Trek Kayaking (☎ 415/488–1000 ⊕ www.seatrekkayak.com) offers trips around Angel Island and the Golden Gate Bridge, moonlight paddles, and many trips in Marin County. Three-hour trips are $65 to $75 and full-day trips are $85 to $130. Most excursions leave from Sausalito (⇨ see Chapter 19), but Angel Island tours leave from the island.

RUNNING

PLACES TO RUN

The *San Francisco Bike Map and Walking Guide (see Bicycling, above)*, which indicates hill grades on city streets by color, is a great resource. Online, check the **San Francisco Road Runners Club** site (⊕ www.sfrrc. org) for some recommended routes and links to several local running clubs.

★ The city is spectacular for running—*Runner's World* magazine named San Francisco number one in its list of the top 25 running cities in 2005. There are more than 7 mi of paved trails in and around **Golden Gate Park**; circling **Stow Lake** and then crossing the bridge and running up the path to the top of Strawberry Hill is a total of 2½ mi. An enormously popular route is the 2-mi raised bike path that runs from Lincoln Way along the ocean, at the southern border of Golden Gate Park, to Sloat Boulevard, which is the northern border of the San Francisco Zoo. (Stick to the park's interior when it's windy, as ocean gusts can kick up sand.) From Sloat Boulevard you can pick up the **Lake Merced** bike path, which loops around the lake and the golf course, to extend your run another 5 mi. The paved path along the **Marina** runs 1½ mi (round-trip) along a flat, well-paved surface and has great bay views.

You can extend your run by jogging the paths through the restored wetlands of Crissy Field (just past the yacht harbor), then up the hill to the Golden Gate Bridge: its walkway is 1.7 mi long.

EVENTS

First run in 1912, the 12K **Bay to Breakers race** (☎ 415/359–2800 ⊕ www.baytobreakers.com), held the third Sunday in May, is one of the world's oldest footraces—but in true San Francisco fashion there's nothing typical about it. About a third of the 50,000 to 100,000 runners are serious athletes; the rest are "fun runners" who wear famously wacky costumes—or no costumes at all (there's a faithful

> **NIGHT SKATE**
>
> If you love in-line skating, you're in luck. Every Friday night anywhere from several dozen to several hundred renegade skaters wend their way en masse through the city streets. Want to join them? Don some sequins and a wig and meet up with the Midnight Rollers Friday Night Skate (☎ 415/752–1967 ⊕ cora.org/ nightskates.html) at the plaza in front of the Ferry Building at 8:30 pm. The event ends by midnight. Rent a pair of skates at Bike and Roll (see their information under Bicycling, above).

nude contingency). The race makes its way from the Embarcadero at the bay to the Pacific Ocean, passing through Golden Gate Park.

The **San Francisco Marathon** (☎ *888/958–6668* ⊕ *www.runsfm.com*), held annually on a Sunday in late July or early August, starts and finishes at the Embarcadero. Up to 7,000 runners pass through downtown, the Marina, the Presidio, and Golden Gate Park, and cross the Golden Gate Bridge, tackling some of the city's milder hills along the way.

SWIMMING

Though San Francisco is right on the ocean, swimming in the rough Pacific waters is unsafe due to strong currents and frigid temperatures—it's c-c-cold. Some locals, including kids, do swim in the slightly warmer (but still often only around 50°F) and much calmer waters of the lagoon at Aquatic Park, between the Marina (next to Fort Mason) and Fisherman's Wharf.

TENNIS

The **San Francisco Recreation and Park Department** (☎ *415/831–2700* ⊕ *www.parks.sfgov.org*) maintains 132 public tennis courts throughout the city. All courts listed here are free except for those in Golden Gate Park. **Golden Gate Park** (⊠ *John F. Kennedy Dr. near 3rd Ave.* ☎ *415/753–7131 reservations, 415/753–7001 information*) has 21 tennis courts. Court fees are $5 to $10. Call for weekend reservations. Weekdays are first come, first served; avoid times after 4 pm on weekdays, when school teams show up for practice. In the southeast corner of the beautiful Presidio, **Julius Kahn Park** (⊠ *W. Pacific Ave. between Spruce and Locust Sts., Presidio*) has four courts; the park and fantastic playground are great distractions for kids if the courts are full when you arrive. **Mission Dolores Park** (⊠ *18th and Dolores Sts., Castro*) has six lighted courts, available on a first-come, first-served basis. **Mountain Lake Park** (⊠ *Lake St. and 8th Ave., Richmond*), on the southern edge of the Presidio, has nice courts; it's an in-the-know tennis spot.

WHALE-WATCHING

Between January and April, hundreds of gray whales migrate along the coast; the rest of the year humpback and blue whales feed offshore at the Farallon Islands. The best place to watch them from shore is Point Reyes, in Marin County *(see Chapter 19).*

For a better view, head out on a whale-watching trip. Seas around San Francisco can be rough, so pack motion-sickness tablets. You should also dress warmly, wear sunscreen, and pack rain gear and sunglasses; binoculars come in handy, too. Tour companies don't provide meals or snacks, so bring your own lunch and water. Make reservations at least a week in advance. Most trips last a full day.

17

California Whale Adventures (☎ *415/760–8613 or 650/579–7777* ⊕ *www. californiawhaleadventures.com*) has year-round whale-watching trips ($95) Friday through Sunday. In October you can take a great-white-shark tour, and seabird tours run July through October; these tours cost $150 per person and are operated on weekends only. All trips leave from Fisherman's Wharf.

★ **The Oceanic Society** (☎ *415/441–1106 or 800/326–7491* ⊕ *www. oceanicsociety.org*) operates year-round full- and half-day whale-watching excursions ($95 Friday, $100 weekends) with top-notch guides. In winter they also run half-day trips ($40 Friday, $45 weekends) from Half Moon Bay. The society also has a whale-watching hotline (☎ *415/474–3385*) and publishes the excellent *Oceanic Society Field Guide to the Gray Whale*. Most trips leave from the San Francisco Yacht Harbor, outside the harbormaster's office in the Marina District.

Shopping

WORD OF MOUTH

"Among our favorite shops on Valencia were Paxton Gate (gardening supply and taxidermy!) and 826 Valencia (a non-profit children's writing project and pirate supply store!). . . . There were also some wonderful independent bookstores. . . . Modern Times and Dog Eared Books, which had unbelievable selections of titles you'd never come across in major chain bookstores."

—CarolM

Updated by
Fiona G.
Parrott

From its grand department stores to its funky secondhand boutiques, San Francisco summons a full range of shopping experiences that rival those of any city. Deep-pocketed buyers and window-shoppers alike mob the dozens of pricey shops packed into the blocks bordering Union Square, while bargain hunters dig through record shops and thrift stores in the Mission District and the Haight. From the anarchist bookstore to the mouthwatering specialty-food purveyors at the gleaming Ferry Building, the local shopping opportunities reflect the city's various personalities.

Visitors with limited time often focus their energies on the high-density Union Square area, where several major department stores tower over big-name boutiques. But if you're keen to find unique local shops, you should definitely move beyond the square's radius. Each neighborhood has its own distinctive finds, whether it's '60s housewares, cheeky stationery, or vintage Levi's.

If shopping in San Francisco has a downside, it's that real bargains can be few and far between. Sure, neighborhoods such as the Lower Haight and the Mission have thrift shops and other inexpensive stores, but you won't find many discount outlets in the city, where rents are sky high and space is at a premium. And the 9.5% sales tax adds up for serious shoppers, though tax is waived if you arrange to have your purchases shipped to an out-of-state address.

Seasonal sales, usually in late January and late July or August, are good opportunities for finding deep discounts on clothing. The *San Francisco Chronicle* and *San Francisco Examiner* advertise sales. For smaller shops, check the two free weeklies the *San Francisco Bay Guardian* and *SF Weekly,* which can be found on street corners every Wednesday. Sample sales are usually held by individual manufacturers, so check your favorite company's site before visiting. Splendora (⊕ *www.splendora.*

com/cityguide/san_francisco) is a good site to check for upcoming sales and promotions around the city.

UNION SQUARE AND CHINATOWN

UNION SQUARE

ART GALLERIES

★ **Fraenkel Gallery.** One of the world's preeminent photography galleries, Fraenkel has represented museum-caliber photographers like Richard Avedon, Garry Winogrand, and Idris Khan since 1979. They usually exhibit one or two of their artists at a time, but each July at their annual exhibit titled "Several Exceptionally Good Recently Acquired Pictures" you can see a full range of their work. ⊠ *49 Geary St., between Kearny St. and Grant Ave., Union Square* ☎ *415/981–2661.*

Hackett-Mill Gallery. This gallery prides itself on its friendly staff, who will educate you about the art or leave you alone—whichever you prefer. Collections include Modern, postwar Abstract Expressionism, and local figurative art. A wide range of international artists exhibit their work here, all incorporating the theme of mid-20th-century historical movements. ⊠ *201 Post St., Suite 1000, Union Square* ☎ *415/362–3377.*

Fodor's Choice
★ **Hang Art.** A spirit of fun imbues this inviting space, where emerging artists display their works. Prices range from a few hundred dollars to several thousand, making it an ideal place for novice art collectors to get their feet wet. A rental program lets you take a piece home before buying it. ⊠ *567 Sutter St., between Mason and Powell Sts., Union Square* ☎ *415/434–4264.*

Hespe Gallery. Priced between 3 and 50 grand, the paintings and sculptures here by mid-career artists like Eric Zener and Kim Cogan, especially Californians, are primarily done in an abstract style. Owner Charles Hespe is an instantly likable art enthusiast who equally delights buyers and browsers. ⊠ *251 Post St., Suite 420, between Stockton and Grant Sts., Union Square* ☎ *415/776–5918.*

John Berggruen Gallery. Twentieth-century American and European paintings are displayed throughout three airy floors here. Works by Bay Area figurative artists such as Richard Diebenkorn are a specialty. ⊠ *228 Grant Ave., at Post St., Union Square* ☎ *415/781–4629.*

Meyerovich Gallery. Sculpture and works on paper by masters such as Pablo Picasso, Robert Motherwell, David Sultan, and Grisha Bruskin are the attraction. Colorful, whimsical sculptures by contemporary artist Guy Dill draw the eye from across the room. ⊠ *251 Post St., 4th fl., between Stockton St. and Grant Ave., Union Square* ☎ *415/421–7171.*

BEAUTY

★ **Lush.** Towers of bulk soap, which can be cut to order, and mountains of baseball-size fizzing "bath bombs" are some of the first items you'll see in this tightly packed and extremely fragrant little boutique, which resembles a cheese shop more than a Sephora. They pride themselves on using the highest-quality ingredients, and some potions are so fresh (and perishable) they're stored in a refrigerator and come with an expi-

18

UNION SQUARE

The tall elegance of the high-rises here radiates a style and grace that vibrates through the busy streets. This is a place for strolling and noticing the intricate details of doorways, quaint cobbled lanes, and unusual sidewalk stalls.

Above) The curated collection of menswear at The Archive. (Right) Macy's decked out in holiday cheer.

Perennially popular, this neighborhood becomes a holiday hub during the wintertime. There's a giant Christmas tree and outdoor ice rink that draws in excited families and love-struck couples. As for stores, anything and everything you would hope to find is here, and then some. From Prada to Banana Republic to Cartier and Macy's, all the big and little shops call this area home. There are dozens of art galleries, indulgent eateries, linen and kitchen stores, as well as hundreds of one-of-a-kind boutiques. The most popular stretch is the physical square that reaches around Stockon, Geary, Powell and Post Streets, but don't limit yourself this small radius; there is so much to shop for north, south, east, and west of its limits. Grant Street, in particular, has dozens of charming shops to get lost in.

BEST TIME TO GO

Aim for Tuesday through Friday afternoons—all the stores and galleries are open, the fog has lifted, and the streets aren't too crowded.

BEST SOUVENIR FOR YOUR FRIENDS

Ginger sugar scrub balls, bohemian lemon soap bars, even vegan coconut shampoo—**Lush** (✉ *240 Powell St.*) makes bathing sound like dessert.

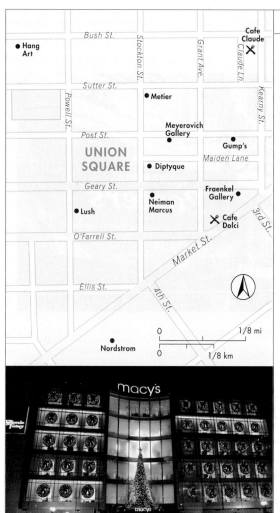

BEST FOR

DEPARTMENT STORES, SF STYLE

Gump's: Elegant and refined, this San Francisco institution sells carefully selected housewares, fine antiques, and jewelry.

Nordstrom: From contemporary to classic to teen fashion, there truly is something here for everyone.

Neiman Marcus: Stunning architecture surrounds this haven of designer clothing, to-die-for shoes, and "it" handbags.

BEAUTIFUL BOUTIQUES

Diptyque: With gorgeous candles and teas in indulgent French country scents, this is a fashion editor's go-to gift shop.

Metier: An eclectic array of clothing and jewelry by well-known and soon-to-be-discovered designers.

The Archive: Distinguished handmade menswear from suits to belt buckles.

GALLERY GAZING

Fraenkel Gallery: Simply one of the best photography galleries in the world.

Hang Art: A good place to view art from local and emerging artists.

Meyerovich Gallery: Impressive sculptures, paintings, and installations.

18

REFUELING

Cafe Claude (✉ *7 Claude La., Sutter and Bush Sts.* ☎ *415/392–3505*) is the perfect place to rest your kitten heels after a morning of hard shopping. This quaint French restaurant is both well priced and wide-ranging, with salads, soups, sandwiches, and cheese plates. But if you're after a faster, more grab-'n-go meal, head for **Cafe Dolci** (✉ *740 Market St., 3rd St. and Grant Ave.* ☎ *415/392–9222*), one of the best Vietnamese sandwich shops in town.

THE HAIGHT

Remembered most for being the epicenter of the '60s Flower Power movement, today's Haight has changed significantly. Incense, music, and musicians still decorate the district, but so do international chains like Starbucks and the Gap.

(Above) Ashbury's colorful street scene. (Right) Digging through Amoeba's encyclopedic music collection.

Locals come to this area for the secondhand clothing and music stores; and there are dozens to choose from. You'll also find one-of-a-kind boutiques that sell funky clothing, toys, instruments, and shoes. Think unusual, big, and fun. The area's laid-back vibe is most definitely represented in the stores, and it's important to take your time in them. Be sure to walk the length and both sides of upper Haight to get a good feel for the area.

Fodorites agree that this area contrast sharply with Union Square. As Leely put it, "Union Square has good shopping, but it's not what I'd consider funky. Hayes Valley, the Mission, and that old standby the Haight are all funkier."

BEST TIME TO GO

Monday through Friday late mornings or early afternoons are most peaceful, although it never really gets hectic.

BEST SOUVENIR FOR MUSIC LOVERS

Come to **Amoeba Music** (✉ *1855 Haight St.*) to score a one-of-a-kind music find. From posters to CDs and DVDs, new and old titles fill the enormous space at extremely low prices.

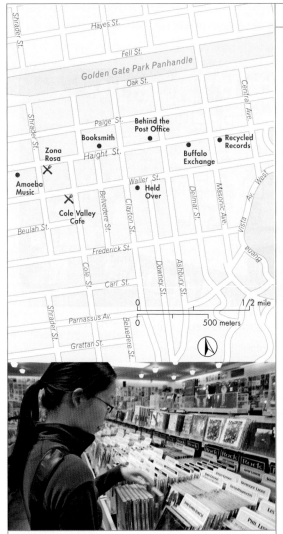

Shrader St.
Hayes St.
Fell St.
Golden Gate Park Panhandle
Oak St.
Central Ave.
Shrader St.
Paige St.
Behind the Post Office
Booksmith
Recycled Records
Zona Rosa
Haight St.
Buffalo Exchange
West
Amoeba Music
Waller St.
Held Over
Belvedere St.
Clayton St.
Delmar St.
Masonic Ave.
Cole Valley Cafe
Beulah St.
Ashbury St.
Frederick St.
Buena Vista
Cole St.
Downey St.
Carl St.
0 **1/2 mile**
Shrader St.
Parnassus Av.
Belvedere St.
0 **500 meters**
Grattan St.

REFUELING

Cole Valley Cafe (✉ *701 Cole St., cross streets Waller and Beulah* ☎ *415/668–5282*), is a bright and warm place to stop for a hearty turkey sandwich, Caesar salad, or latte. If you're looking for something with more of a kick, head for **Zona Rosa** (✉ *1797 Haight St., cross streets Cole and Shrader* ☎ *415/668–7717*), an authentic taquería that serves enormous burritos.

BEST FOR

UNUSUAL CLOTHING
Behind the Post Office: An only-in-SF boutique, home to hip brands and unusual accessories. You can also find some striking children's clothes and handmade toys here, too.

Buffalo Exchange: Fun and fabulous used clothing that's been carefully selected for a second time around. The rails are neatly organized for hassle-free bargain hunting.

Held Over: Pristine clothing from various decades are a hit with vintage shoppers. Here's where '70s suits meet sequin gowns.

FEEDING YOUR HEAD
Amoeba Music: Where music, posters, and films collide inside a space the size of a bowling hall. It's easy to spend an entire day here, especially when you factor in time for people-watching.

Booksmith: A good old-fashioned bookshop; the perfect place to find your favorite novel and get lost in it.

Recycled Records: You thought records were extinct? Think again. Prepare for a vinyl flashback and reunions with classic LPs.

18

THE MISSION

Giant vibrant murals of fields, flowers, and faces decorate building after building here. There is music in the streets, and the sweet smell of baking bread fills the air in the early morning, but at night this is where people come to drink, dance, and celebrate.

(Above) Flights of fancy at Paxton Gate. (Right) Window shopping in the Mission.

Once the artists' hub, today's Mission is quickly gentrifying, as are its shops. Yesterday's thrift stores and vintage furniture shops are slowly being replaced by trendy boutiques and gourmet eateries. These changes have created a patchwork of shopping areas instead of one central hub. Some of the best are along Valencia and Mission Streets; 16th, 17th, and 24th streets are also good places to shop. As dorima on the Fodor's forums put it "for funky, on-of-a-kind shops, my favorite area is Valencia Street, roughly between 16th and 22nd or so. Little artisanal boutiques selling cool clothing, objets d'art, etc. Plus you are in the 'hot belt' of some of San Francisco's most forward-thinking restaurants."

BEST TIME TO GO

Monday through Wednesday afternoons are the most relaxed times. Weekends and late afternoons, particularly on Friday and Saturday, are hectic and full of energy, but that can be nice to tap into, too.

BEST SOUVENIR FOR MOM

The **Ruby Gallery** (✉ *3602 20th St.*) is a small artists' cooperative that sells original jewelry, candleholders, and handmade cards.

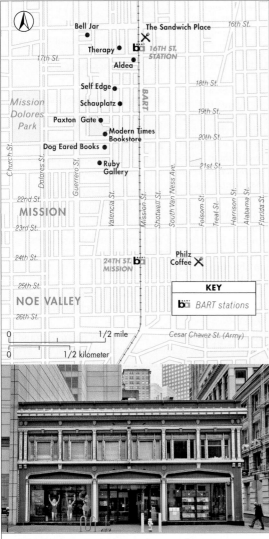

REFUELING

If you're looking for the perfect shopping boost, **Philz Coffee** (✉ *3101 24th St., at Folsom* ☎ *415/875–9370*) is the place. It's full of atmosphere, art, and scrumptious baked goods. Sandwiches at the **Sandwich Place** (✉ *2029 Mission St., between 16th and 17th* ☎ *415/431–3811*) are loaded with fresh ingredients, and they are huge.

BEST FOR

BOOKS, BOOKS, BOOKS

Dog Eared Books: Used, new, travel, food, fiction, poetry—it's all in here.

Get Lost Travel Books, Maps & Gear: More than 9,000 travel titles to choose from. Accessories, too.

Modern Times Bookstore: Hosts readings and literary events for all.

FUNKY FASHION

Bell Jar: Flowing dresses, rhinestone jewelry, paper, and art. This place is full of gorgeous little things.

Schauplatz: Vintage clothing from the '20s through the '80s, from Chanel suits to go-go boots.

Self Edge: Metal rods full of Japanese selvage denim.

FURNITURE, HOUSE-WARES, AND GIFTS

Aldea: From blankets to vases, from plates to cuff links, here you'll find that perfect little something from a far-off corner of the world.

Paxton Gate: Earthenware flowerpots, even outdoor artwork are on offer at this unusual shop inspired by nature and science.

Therapy: Retro kitchenware that's quirky and fun.

18

ration date. ✉ *240 Powell St., between O'Farrell and Geary Sts., Union Square* ☎ *415/693–9633.*

CHILDREN'S CLOTHING

Murik. Those with fashion-forward five-year-olds will be grateful to discover this tiny shop. From Petit Bateau jumpers for infants to linen pants and ruffled shirts for your grade-schooler, the pricey garments are so adorable you might wish you could wear them yourself. ✉ *73 Geary St., between Grant Ave. and Kearny St., Union Square* ☎ *415/395–9200.*

CLOTHING: MEN AND WOMEN

The Archive. The closest thing you'll get to Savile Row in San Francisco, this small and narrow cutting-edge men-only fashion boutique has everything from handmade suits to large handmade silver belt buckles from top-shelf Japanese and Italian designers. ✉ *317 Sutter St., between Grant Ave. and Stockton St., Union Square* ☎ *415/391–5550.*

Gucci. The gold-label designer upped the ante with its palatial, brand-new, 11,000 square feet of black lacquer, bronze, and marble. The first floor is dominated by fine jewelry, handbags, and luggage. Shoes run the show on the second floor, and if you make it to the third floor without maxing out your credit card you'll be rewarded for trying on an evening gown or dinner coat with a flute of champagne. ✉ *240 Stockton St., at Post St., Union Square* ☎ *415/392–2808.*

Harputs of San Francisco. After selling Adidas shoes since 1968 out of its brick-and-mortar digs, Harputs recently opened Harputs of San Francisco. The boutique carries the largest selection of Y-3 (a joint venture between Adidas and avant-garde designer Yohji Yamamoto) on the West Coast. In between vintage Vespas and sewing machines, you can find vintage Christian Dior shades, suits, and accessories by Comme des Garçons, and an impressive collection of vintage Ellesse fluorescent jumpsuits. Still, Harputs of San Francisco stays true to its roots: sneaker fanatics swoon over the display cases of rare Adidas shoes. ✉ *540 Sutter, between Powell and Mason, Union Square* ☎ *415/392–2222.*

Levi's. A massive flagship for 501's, this is quite possibly the biggest place to buy your favorite pair of five-pocket jeans. Every style, size, color, and cut of this original denim brand is here. They even do custom fittings, but book your appointment ahead of time. ✉ *300 Post St., Union Square* ☎ *415/501–0100.*

Marc Jacobs. Fashion's wunderkind peddles his buckled leather bags, bright patent-leather shoes, and shrunken cashmere sweaters at his designer outpost—minus the expected pretense. His less expensive line, Marc by Marc Jacobs, is on Fillmore Street, and has an interesting collection of plastic knick-knacks, key chains, and buttons that make for quirky souvenirs. ✉ *125 Maiden La., at Grant St., Union Square* ☎ *415/362–6500.*

Fodor'sChoice ★ **Margaret O'Leary.** If you can only buy one piece of clothing in San Francisco, make it a hand-loomed, locally made cashmere sweater by this Irish-born local legend. The perfect antidote to the city's wind and fog, the sweaters are so beloved by San Franciscans that some people literally never wear anything else. Pick up an airplane wrap for your trip home and a media cozy to keep your iPod toasty, too. Another store is located in Pacific Heights on Fillmore Street. ✉ *1 Claude La., at Sutter St., Union Square* ☎ *415/391–1010.*

Metier. For boutique shopping that's anything but hit or miss, browse through this unusual selection of clothes by brands like Blumarine and See by Chloe. An even more impressive selection of jewelry by artists like Cathy Waterman and Philip Crangi has won this boutique an obsessively loyal following. ✉ *355 Sutter St., between Stockton and Grant Sts., Union Square* ☎ *415/989–5395.*

Tory Burch. The East Coast socialite–turned–CFDA Accessiories Designer of the Year brightened the notoriously staid Maiden Lane with her new outpost for Bergdorf Blondes. Inspired by designs from the 60s and 70s, the carpet is a rich avocado, walls are magenta among other colors, and velvet curtains frame floor-to-ceiling mirrors in other candy colors. In addition to her ubiquitous ballet flats (even available in toddler sizes), her signature tunics, silk blouses, and suits are on offer. ✉ *50 Maiden La., between Kearney and Grant Sts., Union Square* ☎ *415/398–1525.*

OUTLET AND DISCOUNT CLOTHING

Christine Foley. Discounts of up to 50% apply to the hand-loomed cotton sweaters with fanciful, intricate designs. There's a particularly large selection of colorful sweaters for children. Pillows, stuffed animals, and assorted knickknacks sell at retail prices in the small storefront showroom. ✉ *950 Mason St., between Sacramento and California Sts., Union Square* ☎ *415/399–9938.*

Fodor'sChoice ★ **Loehmann's.** Renovations have tamed the chaos that used to reign among these drastically reduced designer labels, resulting in more-orderly racks and more-spacious changing rooms. Credit is due to their massive inventory, from gym clothes to business wear. The racks for in-season overruns are tidier; the sections of past seasons' clothes are messier but

18

have even deeper discounts. The shoe department is across the street from the main store. ✉ *222 Sutter St., at Kearny St., Union Square* ☎ *415/982–3215.*

Anne Fontaine. Brazilian-born designer Anne Fontaine clearly has a fetish for the white shirt. Her meticulously detailed button-up shirts put a feminine touch on the menswear staple, with flounces at the neckline, impossibly tiny pleats, or ruching at the waist. The spare little store also stocks a small number of pants, skirts, and jackets to complement her famous tops. ✉ *118 Grant Ave., at Maiden La., Union Square* ☎ *415/677–0911.*

TAILORED **Cable Car Clothiers.** This classic British menswear store, open since 1939,
★ is so chock-full of inventory that a whole room is dedicated to hats, pants are cataloged like papers in file cabinets, and entire displays showcase badger-bristle shaving brushes. ■TIP➜ Their cable-car logo gear, from silk ties to pewter banks, makes for dashing souvenirs. ✉ *200 Bush St., at Sansome St., Union Square* ☎ *415/397–4740.*

DEPARTMENT STORES

Barneys New York. Barneys sets itself apart by identifying up-and-coming designers first. Fashion is taken seriously here—a pair of distressed shoes that look like they've been mowed down on the highway can cost you over a grand—but, it's always done with a wink and a smile. Check out the witty touches from their infamous store windows to the details of design (on the third floor copper pennies create a rack for designer ready-to-wear). As you enter Barneys' six-story corner locale, a flight of stairs extends to the mezzanine, where 20,000 shoes make up their infamous shoe salon. Below street level, cosmetics and fragrances reign: there are even state-of-the-art cylindrical sniffing chambers where you can sample new scents. ✉ *77 O'Farrell St., at Stockton St., Union Square* ☎ *415/268–3500.*

Bloomingdales. The black-and-white checkerboard theme, the abundance of glass, and the sheer size might remind you of Vegas. This department store emphasizes American labels like Diane von Furstenberg and Jack Spade. Its well-planned layout defines individual departments without losing the grand and open feel. ✉ *845 Market St., between Grant Ave. and Kearny St., Union Square* ☎ *415/856–5300.*

★ **Gump's.** It's a San Francisco institution, dating to the 19th century, and it's a strikingly luxurious one. The airy store exudes a museum-like vibe, with its large decorative vases, sumptuous housewares, and a gobsmacking Tahitian pearl display. Locals line up to register for weddings here. But it's also a great place to pick up gifts, such as their Golden Gate Bridge note cards or their silver-plated butter spreaders in a signature Gump's box. ✉ *135 Post St., between Grant Ave. and Kearny St., Union Square* ☎ *415/982–1616.*

Macy's. Downtown has two behemoth branches of this retailer, where you can find almost anything you could want, if only you have the patience to find it. One—with entrances on Geary, Stockton, and O'Farrell streets—houses the women's, children's, furniture, and housewares departments. With its large selection and its emphasis on

American designers like DKNY and Marc Jacobs, the department for young women stands out. The men's department occupies its own building across Stockton Street at 50 O'Farrell. During the holidays, pups up for adoption bark in the ground-level windows. ✉ *170 O'Farrell St., at Stockton St., Union Square* ☎ *415/397–3333.*

Neiman Marcus. The surroundings, which include a Philip Johnson–designed checkerboard facade, gilded atrium, and stained-glass skylight, are as ritzy as the goods showcased in them. The mix includes designer men's and women's clothing and accessories as well as posh household wares. ■ **TIP➔** Although the prices may raise an eyebrow or two, Neiman's biannual Last Call sales—in January and July—draw a crowd. After hitting the vast handbag salon, ladies who lunch daintily order consommé and bread laden with strawberry butter in the Rotunda Restaurant. ✉ *150 Stockton St., at Geary Blvd., Union Square* ☎ *415/362–3900.*

★ **Nordstrom.** Somehow Nordstrom manages to be all things to all people, and this location, with spiral escalators circling a four-story atrium, is no exception. Whether you're an elegant lady of a certain age shopping for a new mink coat or a teen on the hunt for a Roxy hoodie, the salespeople are known for being happy to help. While still carrying the best selections in town of new designers like Tory Burch, their own Nordstrom brands have loyal followings. The most recent addition is a Nordstrom Spa. ✉ *San Francisco Shopping Centre, 865 Market St., between 4th and 5th Sts., Union Square* ☎ *415/243–8500.*

Saks Fifth Avenue. As the West Coast counterpart to the New York flagship, this branch claims a prime chunk of Union Square territory and it's chockablock with women swinging the latest "it" handbag. Where the store really outshines the competition is in the incredibly well-stocked Men's Store down the street at 220 Post. The impeccable service will get any casual guy into a suit and tie—and the staff can convince almost anyone to enjoy dressing up. ✉ *384 Post St., at Powell St., Union Square* ☎ *415/986–4300.*

ELECTRONICS

★ **Apple Store San Francisco.** A shiny, stainless-steel box is the setting for San Francisco's flagship Apple store, a high-tech temple to Macs and the people who use them. Play around with iPods, laptops, and hundreds of geeky accessories; then watch a theater presentation or attend an educational workshop. There is, of course, an Internet café, while the "Genius Bar" helps those with computer woes. ✉ *1 Stockton St., at Market St., Union Square* ☎ *415/392–0202.*

FOOD AND DRINK

William Glen. The more than 400 whiskies arranged along the back wall—mostly single-malt Scotches—are organized by their region of origin, so you can easily distinguish those made in Islay from those from Speyside or Lowland. The charming Scottish proprietor can tell you about his favorites, help you with the selection of tartan scarves or cashmere sweaters, or even equip you with a kilt. ✉ *360 Sutter St., Union Square* ☎ *415/989–1030.*

18

FURNITURE, HOUSEWARES, AND GIFTS

Fodor'sChoice **Diptyque.** The original Diptyque boutique in Paris has long attracted a
★ following of celebrities. You can find the full line of scented candles and
fragrances in this chic shop that would be at home on the boulevard
St-Germain. Trademark black-and-white labels adorn the popular L'eau
toilet water, scented with geranium and sandalwood. Candles come in
both traditional and esoteric scents, including lavender, basil, leather,
and fig tree. Also available is a collection of French Mariage Frères teas.
✉ *171 Maiden La., between Grant and Stockton Sts., Union Square*
☎ *415/402–0600.*

Ferrari Store. Even if you can't afford a new Spyder, there's something
for everyone at the new 4,000-square-foot Ferrari Store. You can pick
up a show-stopping, fire engine–red racing jacket, or an actual key
for the ultimate aspirational shopper (or practical joker). Something
for the Mrs.? Purchase signature Ferrari china cups or a pastel argyle
sweater—all complete with the signature prancing stallion. To add to
the fun: A racecar is parked by the front door and the salespeople wear
head-to-toe racing suits. ✉ *2 Stockton St., at Market St., Union Square*
☎ *415/834–9200.*

★ **Scheuer Linens.** Designers and other fans make their way to this store, a
Union Square fixture since 1953, for luxurious bed and bath items and
linens. The pretty tablecloths, runners, and napkins, fragrant candles,
and luxurious bath accessories are popular gifts to indulge loved ones.
✉ *340 Sutter St., at Stockton St., Union Square* ☎ *415/392–2813.*

COOKWARE **Sur la Table.** Everything the home chef could need is here, along with
some things many cooks have never heard of—such as round aspic
cutters and larding needles. Cooking classes and demonstrations are
often held downstairs at the Maiden Lane location. ✉ *77 Maiden La.,
between Grant Ave. and Kearny St., Union Square* ☎ *415/732–7900*

Williams-Sonoma. Behind the striped awnings and historic facade is the
massive mother ship of the Sonoma-founded kitchen-store empire. La
Cornue custom stoves beckon you inward, and two grand staircases
draw you upward to the world of dinnerware, linens, and chefs' tools.
Antique tart tins, eggbeaters, and pastry cutters from the personal collection of founder Chuck Williams line the walls. ✉ *340 Post St., in
between Powell and Stockton Sts., Union Square* ☎ *415/362–9450.*

HANDBAGS, LUGGAGE, AND LEATHER GOODS

Goyard. After more than a century of selling trunks, handbags, and
pet leashes on the rue St-Honoré in Paris, Goyard opened their second
store here to offer San Franciscans a relatively discreet alternative to
Louis Vuitton. Rather than splashing their name everywhere, they signal
luxury with a signature chevron pattern. Even if you walk away empty-
handed, you'll be reminded of what travel used to mean. ✉ *345 Powell
St., between Post and Geary Sts., Union Square* ☎ *415/398–1110.*

Kate Spade. Punchy colors, retro shapes, and a cheeky sense of humor
have made these purses wildly popular among ladies of all ages. Case
in point: the boxy Tarrytown Quinn bag that comes in Kelly green and
features a little price tag that reminds you to "call your mom." The

shop also stocks a few shoes as well as cosmetics cases, date books, and note cards. ✉ *227 Grant Ave., between Post and Sutter Sts., Union Square* ☎ *415/216–0880.*

HANDICRAFTS AND FOLK ART

Fodor'sChoice
★
Xanadu Gallery San Francisco. The spectacular collection of international art and antiquities here includes such treasures as Latin American folk art and masks, sculptures, woven baskets, tapestries, and textiles from Africa, Oceania, and Indonesia. Museum-quality pieces such as a gilt bronze figure of a lama (Tibetan Buddhist holy man) can go for nearly $100,000, but beautiful books on subjects such as Tibetan art make more-affordable souvenirs. ■TIP➜ If nothing else, the shop is worth a visit to see its Frank Lloyd Wright–designed home, where a spiral ramp recalls New York City's Guggenheim Museum. ✉ *140 Maiden La., between Stockton St. and Grant Ave., Union Square* ☎ *415/392–9999.*

JEWELRY AND COLLECTIBLES

De Beers. From one of the world's original diamond miners comes a surprisingly sparse, modern showroom: ebony counters with square glass cases and sheets of etched glass over dark hardwood. Even more surprising: the price is displayed next to each sparkler, a rarity for upscale jewelers. ✉ *185 Post St., between Grant Ave. and Robert Kirk La., Union Square* ☎ *415/391–1400.*

Fodor'sChoice
★
Lang Antiques and Estate Jewelry. Dozens of diamond bracelets in the window attract shoppers to one of the city's best vintage jewelry shops, where rings, brooches, and other glittering items represent a wide spread of eras, from Victorian and Edwardian to art nouveau and Arts and Crafts. The shop has been selling fine jewelry, including engagement rings and a small number of vintage watches, since 1969. ✉ *323 Sutter St., at Grant Ave., Union Square* ☎ *415/982–2213.*

Shreve & Co. Along with gems in dazzling settings, San Francisco's oldest retail store—it's been at this location since 1852—carries lovely watches by Jaeger-LeCoultre and others. On weekends well-heeled couples crowd around the glass cases scoping out hefty diamond engagement rings. ✉ *200 Post St., at Grant Ave., Union Square* ☎ *415/421–2600.*

Tiffany & Co. This gray marble beauty towers over Union Square with almost as much leverage as its signature blue box. The company that all but invented the modern engagement ring makes more than just brides swoon with Elsa Peretti's sinuous silver and architect Frank Gehry's collection using materials like Pernambuco wood and black gold. ✉ *350 Post St., between Powell and Stockton Sts., Union Square* ☎ *415/781–7000.*

SHOES

Camper. The Spanish brand's whimsical footwear is wildly popular with young adults. Unexpected embroidered patterns (leaves, butter-flies) adorn many of the pairs, sometimes beginning on one shoe and continuing on the other. Other styles are reminiscent of bowling and boxing shoes. ✉ *39 Grant Ave., between O'Farrell and Geary Sts., Union Square* ☎ *415/296–1005.*

18

SPORTING GOODS

Niketown. More glitzy multimedia extravaganza than true sporting-goods store, this emporium is nevertheless the best place in town to find anything and everything with the famous swoosh. ⊠ *278 Post St., at Stockton St., Union Square* ☎ *415/392–6453.*

The North Face. The Bay Area–based national retailer is famous for its top-of-the-line tents, sleeping bags, backpacks, and outdoor apparel, including rugged Gore-Tex jackets and pants. ⊠ *180 Post St., between Kearny St. and Grant Ave., Union Square* ☎ *415/433–3223.*

CHINATOWN

FOOD AND DRINK

Great China Herb Co. Since 1922 this aromatic shop has been treating the city with its wide selection of ginseng, tea, and other herbs. You might even hear the click of an abacus as a purchase is tallied up. A Chinese (but English-speaking) doctor is always on hand to recommend the perfect remedy. ⊠ *857 Washington St., between Grant Ave. and Stockton St., Chinatown* ☎ *415/982–2195.*

Vital Tealeaf. Tea enthusiasts will feel at peace in this bright, spacious, hardwood-floor haven for sipping. You'll find more than 400 different varieties of tea here, and the helpful staff is extremely knowledgeable on the health benefits of each and every one. ⊠ *509 Grant Ave., Chinatown* ☎ *415/544–9838.*

FURNITURE, HOUSEWARES, AND GIFTS

COOKWARE **The Wok Shop.** The store carries woks, of course, but also anything else you could need for Chinese cooking—bamboo steamers, ginger graters, wicked-looking cleavers—as well as accessories for Japanese cooking, including sushi paraphernalia and tempura racks. ⊠ *718 Grant Ave., at Sacramento St., Chinatown* ☎ *415/989–3797.*

TOYS AND GADGETS

Chinatown Kite Shop. Kites at this family-owned business (operating since 1969) range from basic diamond shapes to box- and animal-shape configurations. Colorful dragon kites make great Chinatown souvenirs. ⊠ *717 Grant Ave., between Clay and Sacramento Sts., Chinatown* ☎ *415/989–5182.*

SOMA AND CIVIC CENTER

SOMA

ANTIQUES

Grand Central Station Antiques. This large, three-story space stocks mostly 19th- and early-20th-century European and American storage pieces—armoires, highboys, buffets, and the occasional barrister bookcase—with an emphasis on the small and practical. Service is affable. ⊠ *333 9th St., between Folsom and Ringold Sts., SoMa* ☎ *415/252–8155.*

ART GALLERIES

Catharine Clark Gallery. Although nationally known artists—like Masami Teraoka and Nina Katchadourian—display their sculpture, paintings, photographs, and installation artwork here, emerging artists with a Bay Area connection get the spotlight, like Chester Arnold and Josephine

Taylor. ✉ *150 Minna St., between 3rd and New Montgomery Sts., SoMa* ☎ *415/399–1439.*

Crown Point Press. What started as a print workshop in 1962 now includes studios as well as a large, airy gallery where etchings, intaglio prints, engravings, and aquatints by both local and internationally renowned artists are displayed. ✉ *20 Hawthorne St., between 2nd and 3rd Sts., SoMa* ☎ *415/974–6273.*

San Francisco Camerawork. This non-profit artists' organization holds frequently changing thematic exhibits. It's also an excellent photography resource center with a well-stocked bookstore and a reference library. The lecture program includes noted photographers and critics. ✉ *657 Mission St., 2nd fl., between 2nd and New Montgomery Sts., SoMa* ☎ *415/512–2020.*

Yerba Buena Center for the Arts. The gallery within this on-the-pulse arts center should not be overlooked. The artwork is charged, topical, and often controversial. Many of the artists are from the area and incorporate popular culture into their work. ✉ *701 Mission St., SoMa* ☎ *415/978–2700.*

BOOKS

Alexander Book Co. The three floors of titles here are stocked with literature, poetry, and children's books, with a focus on hard-to-find works by men and women of color. ✉ *50 2nd St., between Market and Mission Sts., SoMa* ☎ *415/495–2992.*

CLOTHING: MEN AND WOMEN

OUTLET AND DISCOUNT CLOTHING ★

Jeremy's. A discount store for people who usually wouldn't be caught dead discount shopping, this store offers steep discounts (generally 20% to 50%, with occasional clearance items even more deeply discounted) on top-notch men's and women's apparel by designers such as Prada and Jil Sander. The space is cleanly organized, so you won't need to rack-rake. ✉ *2 S. Park Rd., at 2nd St., SoMa* ☎ *415/882–4929.*

Nordstrom Rack. Items from the Nordstrom department store get discounts of 30% to 75% here. The goods include fragrances, bath and body products, and a few housewares, as well as a good selection of men's and women's clothing and accessories displayed on well-organized racks. Call for the dates of new-arrival events, when savvy shoppers arrive promptly at opening time for the best selection. ✉ *555 9th St., between Bryant and Brannan Sts., SoMa* ☎ *415/934–1211.*

FOOD AND DRINK

Blue Bottle Cafe. After operating from a booth at the farmers' outfit for years and more recently out of a back-alley garage, this highly sought-after Berkeley microroaster has finally quelled its long lines with a roomy and permanent locale. Here they brew their sacred beans in a $20,000 siphon bar from Japan with halogen-lighted glass globes that

18

A San Francisco institution, the farmers' market delivers sensory overload.

resemble a science experiment. Just a stone's throw from the mall, it's the perfect shopping reprieve. Don't forget to take a bag of java home with you. ⊠ *66 Mint St., at Jesse St., SoMa* ☎ *415/495–3394.*

WINES AND SPIRITS

City Beer. Think beer isn't as sophisticated as wine? Think again. At City Beer more than 450 beers are for sale (many refrigerated)—and with six on tap you can imbibe while you shop. You'll get 10% off when you mix and match your six-pack with everything from Allagash Curieux, a dark beer aged in Jim Beam barrels, to Zatec, an authentic Czech beer. ⊠ *1168 Folsom St., Suite 100, between 7th and 8th Sts., SoMa* ☎ *415/503–1033.*

★ **K&L Wine Merchants.** More than any other wine store, the Merchants has an ardent cult following around town. The friendly staffers promise not to sell what they don't taste themselves, and weekly events (Thursday from 5 pm and 6:30 pm and Saturday from noon to 3 pm) open the tastings to customers. Their best-seller list for varietals and regions for both the under- and over-$30 categories appeals to the wine lover in everyone. ⊠ *638 4th St., between Brannan and Townsend Sts., SoMa* ☎ *415/896–1734.*

Wine Club. The large selection of wines at some of the best prices in the city makes up for the bare-bones feel of this place. A self-serve wine bar tucked in the back allows you to taste a wide variety of wines for a modest fee, a great boon to those who'd like to try before they buy. A small collection of caviar and wine paraphernalia, including Riedel wineglasses, books, openers, and decanters, is also available. ⊠ *953 Harrison St., between 5th and 6th Sts., SoMa* ☎ *415/512–9086.*

CLOSE UP

Cool Local Souvenirs

■ Something from McEvoy Ranch's body-care line, like their gardener's hand salve, all made with locally produced, organic olive oil.

■ A book published by City Lights, like one of their new political dynamos or something old-school like Allen Ginsberg's evergreen *Howl.*

■ A phthalates-free EarthLust stainless-steel water bottle overlaid with intricate graphics, available at Spring.

■ A cashmere weekender cardigan from Margaret O'Leary—something to live in every Saturday.

■ A collectible bottle of California wine from K&L Wine Merchants or a rare Armagnac from D&M Wines and Liquors.

■ A striking porcelain tea and coffee service designed by renowned chef Thomas Keller, found at Gump's.

—Natasha Sarkisian

JEWELRY AND COLLECTIBLES

★ **San Francisco Museum of Modern Art Museum Store.** The shop is known for its exclusive line of watches and jewelry, as well as artists' monographs and artful housewares. Posters, calendars, children's art sets and books, and art books for adults round out the merchandise. Larger items include sleek, modernist furniture. ⊠ *151 3rd St., between Mission and Howard Sts., SoMa* ☎ *415/357–4035.*

SPORTING GOODS

★ **REI.** The beloved Seattle-based co-op was founded by a group of mountain climbers in 1938. In addition to carrying a vast selection of clothing and outdoor gear, the store rents camping equipment and repairs snowboards and bikes. ⊠ *840 Brannan St., between 7th and 8th Sts., SoMa* ☎ *415/934–1938.*

CIVIC CENTER

FARMERS' MARKETS

Heart of the City Farmers' Market. Held every Sunday and Wednesday near the Civic Center, this market sells heaps of cheap produce, along with occasional baked goods, potted herbs, and even live chickens. ⊠ *United Nations Plaza, between 7th and 8th Sts., Civic Center* ☎ *415/558–9455* ⊗ *Wed. 7–5:30, Sun. 7–5.*

THE TENDERLOIN

ART GALLERIES

John Pence Gallery. The 8,000-square-foot facility, San Francisco's largest gallery, can display more than 100 works. Drawings, paintings, and sculpture are all represented, with many of the works by important contemporary academic realists. ⊠ *750 Post St., between Leavenworth and Jones Sts., Tenderloin* ☎ *415/441–1138.*

Silverman Gallery. Fashion, music, performance, paintings, and photography collide here—literally. Every four to six weeks a new exhibit

18

enters the space pushing the boundaries of content, concept, and form. The gallery also hosts talks with local and international artists. ⊠ *804 Sutter St., Tenderloin* ☎ *415/255–9508.*

HAYES VALLEY

ANTIQUES

Another Time. Specializing in beautifully restored furniture from the '30s through '60s, this is the right place to come for Heywood Wakefield tambour buffets, art deco bars, or French art deco desks. There's also a wealth of jewelry, glassware, and lamps on display in well-secured cabinets. Pam, the owner, is knowledgeable and happy to answer any questions. ⊠ *1710 Market St., Hayes Valley* ☎ *415/553–8900.*

BEAUTY

Nancy Boy. This sparse white-on-white locally owned store, sells indulgent skin- and hair-care products for men, as well as a small selection of aromatherapy items, such as soy travel candles scented with essential oils. ⊠ *347 Hayes St., between Franklin and Gough Sts., Hayes Valley* ☎ *415/552–3802.*

BOOKS

The Green Arcade. For environmental, political, sustainable, and über-green books, look no further; this place will feed your head. With deep roots in the community, energetic artwork, and an atmosphere that encourages reading, this is a good place to hide away; the comfy chairs and warm vibe make it hard to leave. ⊠ *1680 Market St.,Hayes Valley* ☎ *415/431–6800.*

CLOTHING: MEN AND WOMEN

Acrimony. A handblown glass chandelier winks at you through the store's front window while DJs do their thing in the back. Sandwiched in between is a mix of styles like Mini for May zebra skirts or Shin hand-painted tops. There's something special for men, too: Gitman Brothers blue oxfords, Wings + Horns tiger fleece vests, and even chambray shorts. Think: progressive and of-the-moment. ⊠ *333 Hayes St., Hayes Valley* ☎ *415/861–1025* ⊕ *www.shopacrimony.com.*

Azalea Boutique. With a dose of global flair, this boutique blends art, fun, and fashion. The deep red walls are a flattering backdrop, especially for the extensive collection of denim (they have more than 100 different styles). The wide variety of designers from Louis Verdad to Beatrice Ong and James Perse offers a true alternative from the ubiquitous department-store brands. If you want to squeeze in a little spa time, you'll find a 300-square-foot nail bar where you can indulge in natural nail services that include formaldehyde-free polish and organic cuticle creams. ⊠ *411 Hayes St., Hayes Valley* ☎ *415/861–9888* ⊕ *www.azaleasf.com.*

Dish. Many of the women's clothes displayed within this spare, concrete-floor space are romantic, minus the frills. Look for the flowing dresses of local designer Erica Tanov, as well as clothes and accessories by more widely known brands like BCBG and Theory. ⊠ *541 Hayes St., between Laguna and Octavia Sts., Hayes Valley* ☎ *415/252–5997.*

Lemon Twist. A fashionable family affair: Dannette Scheib is known for her inspired details, such as her signature tulle petticoats that go underneath her A-line skirts. Her husband Eric's T-shirts capture an urban essence in a simply stenciled telephone-pole design. Their Lemon Drop baby line is both sweet and tart. ■TIP➜ If you see a print you like on the workshop table in back, she's happy to make you a custom piece at no additional charge and ship it to you back home. ✉ *537 Octavia Blvd., between Hayes and Grove Sts., Hayes Valley* ☎ *415/558–9699.*

RAG. To really get your pulse on the local fashion scene, seek out the Residents Apparel Gallery. Bay Area designers rent racks to showcase their deconstructed tees and socially responsible designs. Above each rack hangs a photo and a bio of the aspiring designer. ✉ *541 Octavia St., between Hayes and Grove Sts., Hayes Valley* ☎ *415/621–7718.*

VINTAGE AND RESALE CLOTHING ★ **Ver Unica.** Though you can find a few items from the psychedelic '60s, beautifully preserved fashions from the '40s and '50s are the best reason for visiting. You can even find purses and several pairs of hard-to-find vintage shoes to go along with that faux-fur-trimmed jacket. ✉ *437B Hayes St., between Gough and Octavia Sts., Hayes Valley* ☎ *415/431–0688.*

FOOD AND DRINK

★ **Miette Confiserie.** There is truly nothing sweeter than a cellophane bag tied with blue-and-white twine and filled with malt balls or chocolate sardines from this European-style apothecary. The lovely pastel-color cake stands make even window-shopping a treat. ✉ *449 Octavia Blvd., between Hayes and Linden Sts., Hayes Valley* ☎ *415/626–6221.*

WINES AND SPIRITS **Arlequin Wine Merchant.** If you like the wine list at Absinthe Brasserie, you can walk next door and pick up a few bottles from its highly regarded sister establishment. This small, unintimidating shop carries hard-to-find wines from small producers. Why wait to taste? Crack a bottle in the patio out back. ✉ *384 Hayes St., at Gough St., Hayes Valley* ☎ *415/863–1104.*

18

True Sake. Though it would be reasonable to expect a Japanese aesthetic at the first store in the United States dedicated entirely to sake, you might instead hear dance music thumping quietly in the background while you browse. Each of the many sakes is displayed with a label describing the drink's qualities and food pairing suggestions. Should these prove insufficient, simply pick up a copy of *The Sake Handbook* or another sake-related publication. ✉ *560 Hayes St., between Laguna and Octavia Sts., Hayes Valley* ☎ *415/355–9555.*

FURNITURE, HOUSEWARES, AND GIFTS

★ **Flight 001.** Über-stylish travel accessories—retro-looking flight bags, supersoft leather passport wallets, and tiny Swiss travel alarm clocks—line the shelves of this brightly lighted shop, which vaguely resembles an airplane interior. High-tech travel gear and a small collection of guidebooks speed you on your way. ✉ *525 Hayes St., between Laguna and Octavia Sts., Hayes Valley* ☎ *415/487–1001.*

Modern Artifacts. From Eames chairs and a Hans Wegner sofa covered in nubby fabric to a sensuous lamp designed by Italian architect Gae Aulenti, this store has all the accoutrements for a stylish modernist apartment. ⊠ *1639 Market St., between Franklin and Gough Sts., Hayes Valley* ☎ *415/255–9000.*

VINTAGE
HOUSEWARES
Zonal. Most of the refurbished vintage steel filing cabinets, dining-room tables, desks, and even barrister bookcases were built in the 1930s and '40s. Upholstered pieces, such as a generously sized slipper chair, are contemporary but have a sleek retro look. ⊠ *568 Hayes St., at Laguna St., Hayes Valley* ☎ *415/255–9307.*

HANDICRAFTS AND FOLK ART

F. Dorian. In addition to cards, jewelry, and other crafts from Central and South America, Africa, Asia, and the Middle East—a carved wooden candleholder from the Ivory Coast is one example—this store carries brightly colored glass and ceramic works by local artisans and whimsical mobiles. ⊠ *370 Hayes St., between Franklin and Gough Sts., Hayes Valley* ☎ *415/861–3191.*

Polanco. Devoted to showcasing the arts of Mexico, this gallery sells everything from antiques and traditional folk crafts to fine contemporary paintings. Brightly painted animal figures and a virtual village of Day of the Dead figures share space with religious statues and modern linocuts and paintings. ⊠ *393 Hayes St., between Franklin and Gough Sts., Hayes Valley* ☎ *415/252–5753.*

SHOES

Gimme Shoes. From the chunky to the sleek, the shoes carried here—including those by Robert Clergerie, Helmut Lang, Prada, and John Varvatos—are top-notch. And if $600 seems steep for pale-green pumps, perhaps you haven't seen the perfect pair by Dries Van Noten. ⊠ *416 Hayes St., at Gough St., Hayes Valley* ☎ *415/864–0691.*

Paolo Shoes. Looking for gorgeous handcrafted Italian leather shoes? (Who isn't?) This is *the* place in San Francisco to find them—and what a stunning selection it is. From knee-high boots to contoured heel pumps, Paolo Iantorno's designs will make your heart miss a beat. The prices might as well; they hover around the $300 mark; but all shoes are made in quantities of 25 pieces or fewer, which means each pair is a one of a kind. ⊠ *524 Hayes St., between Octavia and Laguna Sts., Hayes Valley* ☎ *415/552–4580* ⊕ *www.paoloshoes.com.*

FINANCIAL DISTRICT

ANTIQUES

Antonio's Antiques. The two busily packed stories of furniture and objets d'art might include an 18th-century French harp or delicate tortoiseshell miniatures. If you like the shop's pieces, which lean toward items from the 17th and 18th centuries, you may also want to visit its larger store in SoMa at 701 Bryant Street, a maze of museum-quality English and French antiques. Italian pieces are housed across the street. ⊠ *701 Sansome St., at Jackson St., Financial District* ☎ *415/781–1737.*

Hunt Antiques. Full of fine 17th- to 19th-century period English furniture, porcelains, Staffordshire pottery, paintings, and grandfather clocks, this Jackson Square shop feels like an English town house. ⊠ *478 Jack-*

son St., between Montgomery and Sansome Sts., Financial District* ☎ 415/989–9531.

Lotus Collection. The handmade pillows, tapestries depicting iconic events in Europe, and Japanese brocades make this one of the finest collections of decorative antique textiles in the States. It's also a secret source for the city's interior designers outfitting Pacific Heights mansions. ⊠ *445 Jackson St., between Montgomery and Sansome Sts., Financial District* ☎ 415/398–8115.

BOOKS

★ **William Stout Architectural Books.** Architect William Stout began selling books out of his apartment 25 years ago. Today the store sources libraries from around the world and Bay Area professionals with serious-minded tomes on architecture and design. Head down into the crumbling whitewashed basement for beautifully illustrated coffee-table books. Stout is also the sole distributor of the über-popular IDEO method cards, which offer and inspire design solutions. ⊠ *804 Montgomery St., at Jackson St., Financial District* ☎ 415/391–6757.

CLOTHING: MEN AND WOMEN

Carrots. The former location of Ernie's (the historic restaurant made famous in Hitchcock's *Vertigo*) was transformed by Melissa Grimm and her sister Catie into this boutique. The name points to the sisters' background as members of the Grimm family of Grimmway Farms fame (the world's largest grower of carrots). Their spacious emporium showcases Bay Area superstar designers Alexander Wang and Peter Som alongside Narciso Rodriguez and Stella McCartney. The icing on the cake (literally!) is a bar that serves mini carrot cupcakes. ⊠ *843 Montgomery St., between Gold and Jackson Sts., Jackson Square* ☎ 415/834–9040.

FARMERS' MARKETS

Fodor's Choice ★ **Ferry Plaza Farmers' Market.** The most upscale and expensive of the city's farmers' markets, in front of the restored Ferry Building, places baked goods and fancy pots of jam alongside organic basil and heirloom tomatoes. The Saturday market is the grandest, with about 100 vendors packed both in front of and behind the building. The Tuesday and Thursday markets are smaller. At the Sunday garden market, vegetable and ornamental plants crop up next to a small selection of food items. (The Thursday and Sunday markets don't operate in winter, generally December or January through March.) ■TIP➜ On Saturday, don't miss the coffee at Blue Bottle—and yes, the line is worth it. ⊠ *Ferry Plaza, Embarcadero at north end of Market St., Financial District* ☎ 415/291–3276 ⊕ *www.ferryplazafarmersmarket.com* ☉ *Tues. and Sun. 10–2, Thurs. 4–8, Sat. 8–2.*

RUSSIAN HILL

ANTIQUES

Interior Visions. The welcoming proprietor is happy to tell you about her collection of mostly 19th- and early-20th-century pieces. Among the treasures might be a French gold-velvet chaise longue from the 1930s or a turn-of-the-20th-century Belgian oak highboy. ⊠ *2206 Polk St., between Vallejo and Green Sts., Russian Hill* ☎ 415/771–0656.

18

CLOTHING: MEN AND WOMEN

Anica. This avant-garde women's clothing boutique—whose name means "charismatic" in Hindi—specializes in low-maintenance high fashion. The designs here, from serious up-and-coming designers, actually look good off the hanger. ✉ *2418 Polk St., between Filbert and Union Sts., Russian Hill* ☎ *415/447–2878.*

Eco Citizen. The men's and women's clothes here are not just green, they're also fair-trade, organic, sustainable, and trendy—yet still basic enough to wear for more than one season (so you won't have to throw them out after two months, which makes them truly green). ✉ *1488 Vallejo St., between Polk and Larkin Sts., Russian Hill* ☎ *415/614–0100.*

FURNITURE, HOUSEWARES, AND GIFTS

JAK home. Against their Golden Delicious–green backdrop, an eclectic assortment of one-of-a-kind home furnishings leaps off the shelves: cake pedestals, assorted globes, and candles are completely irresistible. It's so cozy and inviting you'll want to take a seat in one of their brightly reupholstered armchairs and ponder how to re-create the look. ✉ *2423 Polk St., between Union and Filbert Sts., Russian Hill* ☎ *415/839–8264.*

COOKWARE   **City Discounts.** This small restaurant-supply store sells commercial-grade pans, knives, and microplanes at a fraction of the price you'd pay at a national kitchenware chain store. There's a nice selection of imported Italian food, and the Italian proprietress is a great help in making selections. ✉ *1542 Polk St., between Sacramento and California Sts., Russian Hill* ☎ *415/771–4649.*

JEWELRY AND COLLECTIBLES

Velvet da Vinci. Each contemporary piece of jewelry here is one-of-a-kind or limited edition. The beautiful, unusual items might be sculpted out of resin, hammered from copper, or woven with silver wires. ✉ *2015 Polk St., between Broadway and Pacific Ave., Russian Hill* ☎ *415/441–0109.*

NORTH BEACH

ANTIQUES

Aria Antiques. Get a gift for your favorite globe-trotter at this oasis for the unordinary. You'll find maps, boxes, vases, and vintage furniture—as well as European artifacts. ✉ *1522 Grant Ave., Nobles Alley and Union St., North Beach* ☎ *415/433–0219.*

Schein & Schein. This tiny, sunny spot houses thousands of antique maps and engraved prints, many with a local focus. Whether you're looking for a chart of the world from the 13th century or a map of the Barbary Coast—they have it all, from very inexpensive small prints to genuine collector pieces. Even if you're no cartographer, the helpful owners will enthrall you with their historical anecdotes and educate you with their vast knowledge. ✉ *1435 Grant Ave., between Green and Union Sts., North Beach* ☎ *415/399–8882.*

BOOKS

Fodor's Choice   **City Lights Bookstore.** The city's most famous bookstore is where the Beat
★   movement of the 1950s was born. Neal Cassady and Jack Kerouac hung out in the basement, and now regulars and tourists while hours away

in this well-worn space. The upstairs room highlights impressive poetry and Beat literature collections. Poet Lawrence Ferlinghetti, the owner, remains active in the workings of this three-story shop. Since publishing Allen Ginsberg's *Howl* in 1956, City Lights Publishers continues to issue a dozen new titles each year. ⊠ *261 Columbus Ave., at Broadway, North Beach* ☎ *415/362–8193.*

CLOTHING: MEN AND WOMEN

AB fits. The friendly staff can help guys and gals sort through the jeans selection, one of the hippest in the city (check out the Del Forte organic denim). Salespeople pride themselves on being able to match the pants to the person. There are two locations in the city, but the Union Square branch leans toward slightly dressier designs. ⊠ *1519 Grant Ave., between Filbert and Union Sts., North Beach* ☎ *415/982–5726.*

Ooma. The delicious fashions, many made by local designers, tend toward the feminine and flirty (no masculine stuff here). A wide range of jewelry and accessories complements the colorful clothes. ⊠ *1422 Grant Ave., between Green and Union Sts., North Beach* ☎ *415/627–6963.*

FOOD AND DRINK

Graffeo Coffee Roasting Company. Forget those fancy flavored coffees if you're ordering from this North Beach emporium, open since 1935. This shop, one of the best-loved coffee stores in a city that's truly devoted to its java, sells dark roast, light roast, and dark roast decaf beans only. ⊠ *735 Columbus Ave., at Filbert St., North Beach* ☎ *415/986–2420.*

Fodor'sChoice ★ **Molinari Delicatessen.** Billing itself as the oldest delicatessen west of the Rockies, the store has been making its own salami, sausages, and cold cuts since 1896. Other homemade specialties include meat and cheese ravioli, tomato sauces, and fresh pastas. ■TIP➔ In-the-know locals grab a made-to-order sandwich for lunch and eat it at one of the sidewalk tables. ⊠ *373 Columbus Ave., at Vallejo St., North Beach* ☎ *415/421–2337.*

Victoria Pastry Co. In business since the early 1900s, and a throwback to the North Beach of old, this bakery has display cases full of Italian pastries, cookies, and St. Honoré cakes. ⊠ *1362 Stockton St., at Vallejo St., North Beach* ☎ *415/781–2015.*

FURNITURE, HOUSEWARES, AND GIFTS

Biordi Art Imports. Hand-painted Italian pottery, mainly imported from Tuscany and Umbria, has been shipped worldwide by this family-run business since 1946. Dishware sets can be ordered in any combination. ⊠ *412 Columbus Ave., at Vallejo St., North Beach* ☎ *415/392–8096.*

JEWELRY AND COLLECTIBLES

BEADS **Yone.** In business since 1965, the store carries so many types of beads that the owner has lost track (though it's probably somewhere between 5,000 and 10,000). Individual beads, made of glass, wood, plastic, bone, sterling silver, and countless other materials, can cost up to $100. ⊠ *478 Union St., at Grant Ave., North Beach* ☎ *415/986–1424.*

MUSIC

MEMORABILIA **San Francisco Rock Posters and Collectibles.** The huge selection of rock-and-roll memorabilia, including posters, handbills, and original art, takes you back to the 1960s. Also available are posters from more recent shows—many at the legendary Fillmore Auditorium—featuring such musicians as George Clinton, Porno for Pyros, and the late Johnny Cash. ✉ *1851 Powell St., between Filbert and Greenwich Sts., North Beach* ☎ *415/956–6749.*

PAPER AND STATIONERY

Lola of North Beach. For a card that is anything but Hallmark, snap up something from local letterpresses; many have San Francisco themes. A section of this intimate North Beach store is devoted to the various stages of a relationship: friendship, I like you, I love you, I miss you, I'm sorry, and I'm here for you. It also carries an impressive collection of baby clothes, including some adorable tees. ✉ *1415 Grant Ave., at Green St., North Beach* ☎ *415/781–1817.*

THE WATERFRONT

FISHERMAN'S WHARF
CLOTHING: MEN AND WOMEN

VINTAGE AND RESALE CLOTHING

Helpers' Bazaar. Arguably the city's best-dressed philanthropist, Joy Bianchi, along with other volunteers, runs this store to benefit the mentally disabled. A red Bill Blass cocktail dress, a Chanel suit, or a Schiaparelli hat are among the vintage masterpieces you might expect to find here—to see the good stuff, all you have to do is ask nicely. Don't miss a look at Bianchi's "mouse couture," a clever fund-raiser display in which designers like Armani and Carolina Herrera dress up 4-inch stuffed mice. ✉ *900 N. Point St., Ghirardelli Square, Fisherman's Wharf* ☎ *415/441–0779.*

FOOD AND DRINK

WINES AND SPIRITS

Cellar 360. If you can't make it to Napa, come here to browse through 6,000 square feet of wine retail space in the historic Woolen Mill building. During happy hour, tourists and locals alike pack the longest bar in the city to taste the 250 wines available. After a few glasses you might be sold on a case . . . and if you're not, a Copia education class in their fully equipped classroom will probably do the trick. ✉ *900 Northpoint St., Suite F301, Ghirardelli Square, Fisherman's Wharf* ☎ *415/440–0772.*

SPORTING GOODS

Patagonia. Technical wear for serious outdoors enthusiasts is the specialty. Along with sportswear and casual clothing, it carries active wear for backpacking, fly-fishing, kayaking, and the like. ✉ *770 N. Point St., at Hyde St., Fisherman's Wharf* ☎ *415/771–2050.*

EMBARCADERO
BOOKS

Book Passage. Windows at this modest-size bookstore frame close-up views of the Ferry Building docks and San Francisco Bay. Commuters snatch up magazines by the front door as they speed off to catch their ferries, while leisurely shoppers thumb through the thorough selection of cooking and travel titles. Author events typically take place several times a month. ✉ *1 Ferry Bldg., #42, Embarcadero at foot of Market St., Embarcadero* ☎ *415/835–1020.*

FOOD AND DRINK

Cowgirl Creamery Artisan Cheese. Fantastic organic-milk cheeses—such as the mellow, triple-cream Mt. Tam and *bocconcini* (small balls of fresh mozzarella)—are produced at a creamery an hour north of the city. These and other carefully chosen artisanal cheeses and dairy products, including a luscious, freshly made crème fraîche, round out the selection at the in-town store. ⊠ *1 Ferry Bldg., #17, Embarcadero at foot of Market St., Embarcadero* ☎ *415/362–9354.*

McEvoy Ranch. The only retail outpost of this ranch in Sonoma County, a producer of outstanding organic, extra-virgin olive oil. Depending on seasonal availability, the store also gets olive trees, plants, and flowers in from the ranch. ■**TIP→** If you stop by in fall or winter, don't miss the Olio Nuovo, the days-old green oil produced during the harvest. ⊠ *1 Ferry Bldg., #30, Embarcadero at foot of Market St., Embarcadero* ☎ *415/291–7224.*

★ **Recchiuti Confections.** Michael and Jacky Recchiuti began making otherworldly chocolates in 1997, using traditional European techniques. Now considered among the best confectioners in the world, they stock their only stand-alone store with their full chocolate line, including several unique items inspired by the surrounding gourmet markets. ⊠ *1 Ferry Bldg. #30, Embarcadero at foot of Market St., Embarcadero* ☎ *415/834–9494.*

THE MARINA AND THE PRESIDIO

THE MARINA
CLOTHING: MEN AND WOMEN

18

dress. Neatly tucked alongside buzzing Chestnut Street, this quaint boutique is easy to overlook. It offers up dozens of designers like Halston Heritage and Aiko. The clothes are thoughtfully selected with entire wardrobes in mind. Clothes don't crowd the racks, and the service is friendly without being overwhelming. You can find some bargains here, too, on a good day. ⊠ *2271 Chestnut St., at Union St., Marina* ☎ *415/440–3737* ⊕ *www.shopdressonline.com.*

OUTLET AND DISCOUNT CLOTHING **My Roommate's Closet.** Fed by more than 25 boutiques in San Francisco, New York, and Los Angeles, the Closet carries clothing and accessories by designers like Vera Wang, Chaiken, and Theory, all at less than 50% of their retail price. ⊠ *3044 Fillmore St., at Union St., Marina* ☎ *415/447–7703.*

FOOD AND DRINK

Lucca Delicatessen. At this bit of Old Italy in the upscale Marina District, take a number and wait your turn to choose from a wide selection of homemade pastas, Italian sausages, prepared salads, and imported cheeses and olive oils. ⊠ *2120 Chestnut St., at Steiner St., Marina* ☎ *415/921–7873.*

SPORTING GOODS

★ **Lululemon Athletica.** This yoga-inspired company makes all kinds of athletic gear with their Luon fabric—it's non-chafing, moisture-wicking, preshrunk, and best of all it can be washed in warm water. Their pants are known for being the best thing in town for a yogi's derriere. ✉ *1981 Union St., between Laguna and Buchanan Sts., Marina* ☎ *415/776–5858.*

TOYS AND GADGETS

Exploratorium. The educational gadgets and gizmos sold here are so much fun that your kids—whether they're in grade school or junior high—might not realize they're learning while they're playing with them. Space- and dinosaur-related games are popular, as are science videos and CD-ROMs. ✉ *3601 Lyon St., at Marina Blvd., Marina* ☎ *415/561–0360.*

THE PRESIDIO

CLOTHING: WOMEN

Sarah Shaw. Specializing in cocktail and party dresses, this boutique racks up American designers like Wendy Hil, Trina Turk, and Robert Rodriguez. Businesswomen looking to give their corporate suits a feminine spin take their cues from Sarah's inspired outfits. ✉ *3095 Sacramento St., at Baker St., Presidio Heights* ☎ *415/929–2990.*

COW HOLLOW

CLOTHING: MEN AND WOMEN

★ **Blues Jean Bar.** With more than a dozen different brands of jeans on tap, this Western-themed shop takes the pain out of finding the perfect pair of denims. Simply tell the "bartender" the size and style you're looking for and he or she will load you up with several trendy pairs by designers such as Carpe Denim and True Religion to try on in either the "Him," "Her," or "Them" dressing rooms. ✉ *1827 Union St., between Octavia and Laguna Sts., Cow Hollow* ☎ *415/346–4280.*

TAILORED **Red Lantern.** Chinese fashions of centuries past get a modern updating at this pretty little boutique where luxe fabrics—silk, brocade, and faux fur—give each item a sumptuous feel. If none of the mandarin-style jackets or *cheongsams* (traditional formfitting Chinese dresses) suits you, owner Fong Chong can make clothing to order. ✉ *2030-A Union St., between Webster and Buchanan Sts., Cow Hollow* ☎ *415/776–8876.*

FOOD AND DRINK

WINES AND **PlumpJack Wines.** A small selection of imported wines complements the
SPIRITS well-priced, well-stocked collection of hard-to-find California wines here. Gift baskets—such as the Italian market basket, containing wine, Italian foods, and a cookbook—are popular hostess gifts. You can find its sister branch in Noe Valley on 24th Street. ✉ *3201 Fillmore St., at Greenwich St., Cow Hollow* ☎ *415/346–9870.*

JEWELRY AND COLLECTIBLES

Union Street Goldsmith. Open since 1976, this local favorite prides itself on its wide selection of rare gemstones, such as golden sapphires and violet tanzanite. Custom work is a specialty, and a number of no-pressure design consultants are happy to talk with you about how to make the jewelry you're dreaming of a reality. ✉ *1909 Union St., at Laguna St., Cow Hollow* ☎ *415/776–8048.*

TOYS AND GADGETS

ATYS. Gadgets for the home and office with a sleek modern design are imported from Scandinavia, Italy, Germany, and Japan. Among the eye-catching items are a digital watch designed by Philippe Starck and Japanese knives that could be displayed as sculptures. ⊠ *2149-B Union St., between Fillmore and Webster Sts., Cow Hollow* ☎ *415/441–9220.*

THE HAIGHT, THE CASTRO, AND NOE VALLEY

THE HAIGHT
BOOKS

Booksmith. Founded in 1976, this fine bookshop sells current releases, children's titles, and offbeat periodicals. Authors passing through town often make a stop at this neighborhood institution. ⊠ *1644 Haight St., between Cole and Clayton Sts., Haight* ☎ *415/863–8688.*

Bound Together Anarchist Book Collective. This old-school collective, in operation since 1976, stocks books on anarchist theory and practice, as well as an array of books on other forms of radicalism, gender issues, and other left-leaning topics. A portion of the revenue goes to the support of anarchist projects and the Prisoners' Literature Project. ⊠ *1369 Haight St., at Masonic Ave., Haight* ☎ *415/431–8355.*

CLOTHING: MEN AND WOMEN

Behind the Post Office. There's no "return to sender" here, as covetable women's clothes fill this little shop. In spite of its limited size, this store attracts a devoted clientele for its casual clothing, including slinky knits by Ella Moss and jeans by Citizens of Humanity. ⊠ *1510 Haight St., at Ashbury St., Haight* ☎ *415/861–2507.*

Loyal Army. This locally based graphic design company creates hilarious graphic tees inspired by Japanese kawaii or cutesy comics. Think a stack of pancakes with the inscription "I'm a hot mess." Their designs embellish supersoft tees, hoodies, and totes. ⊠ *1728 Haight St., between Cole and Shrader Sts., Haight* ☎ *415/221–6200.*

VINTAGE
AND RESALE
CLOTHING

Buffalo Exchange. Both men and women can find fashionable, high-quality used clothing at this national chain. Among the items: a wide selection of Levi's, leather jackets, sunglasses, and vintage lunch boxes. Some new clothes are available, too. ⊠ *1555 Haight St., between Clayton and Ashbury Sts., Haight* ☎ *415/431–7733.*

Held Over. The extensive collection of clothing from the 1920s through 1980s is organized by decade, saving those looking for flapper dresses from having to wade through lime-green polyester sundresses of the '70s. Shoes, hats, handbags, and jewelry complete the different looks. ⊠ *1543 Haight St., between Ashbury and Clayton Sts., Haight* ☎ *415/864–0818.*

MUSIC

Fodor's Choice
★

Amoeba Music. With more than 2.5 million new and used CDs, DVDs, and records, this warehouselike store (and the original Berkeley location) carries titles you can't find on Amazon at bargain prices. No niche is ignored—from electronica and hip-hop to jazz and classical—and

18

the stock changes daily. Weekly in-store performances attract large crowds. ⊠ *1855 Haight St., between Stanyan and Shrader Sts., Haight* ☎ *415/831–1200.*

Recycled Records. A Haight Street landmark, this store buys, sells, and trades a vast selection of used records, including hard-to-find imports and sides by obscure alternative bands. The CD collection is large, but the vinyl is the real draw. ⊠ *1377 Haight St., between Masonic and Central Aves., Haight* ☎ *415/626–4075.*

SHOES

★ **John Fluevog.** The selection of trendy but sturdily made footwear for men and women is one of the best in the city. Club kids go for the Canadian brand's boots, handing over a pretty penny for dramatic styles such as the popular 5-inch-heel knee-highs made out of red pony fur. ⊠ *1697 Haight St., at Cole St., Haight* ☎ *415/436–9784.*

TOYS AND GADGETS

Giant Robot. This superhip spot feeds San Franciscans' passion for Asian pop-cultural fluff, from Gama-Go Ninja Kitty bike messenger bags and Uglydoll keychains and figurines to Astro Boy stationery sets. Of course, the store also carries *Giant Robot* magazine, as well as a large selection of T-shirts. ⊠ *618 Shrader St., at Haight St., Haight* ☎ *415/876–4773.*

THE CASTRO

CLOTHING: MEN

Rolo. Selling hard-to-find men's and women's denim, sportswear, shoes, and accessories with a distinct European influence, this store includes clothes designed by Comme des Garçons, Corpus Denim, and Fred Perry. Another location in SoMa also carries women's wear. ⊠ *2351 Market St., at Castro St., Castro* ☎ *415/431–4545.*

FURNITURE, HOUSEWARES, AND GIFTS

Under One Roof. Profits from the home and garden necessities, gourmet foods, bath products, books, frames, cards, and silly gift items sold here go to Northern California HIV/AIDS organizations, which makes it easy to justify buying such playful objects as an Oscar Wilde action figure or a bath mat shaped like a T-bone steak. ⊠ *518A Castro St., between 18th and 19th Sts., Castro* ☎ *415/503–2300.*

JEWELRY AND COLLECTABLES

Brand X Antiques. The vintage jewelry, mostly from the early part of the 20th century, includes a wide selection of estate pieces and objets d'art. With rings that range from $5 to $30,000, there's something for everyone. ⊠ *570 Castro St., at 18th St., Castro* ☎ *415/626–8908.*

BEADS **Bead Store.** More than a thousand kinds of strung and unstrung pieces include such stones as lapis and carnelian, Czech and Venetian glass, African trade beads, Buddhist and Muslim prayer beads, and Catholic rosaries. Silver jewelry is another specialty. ⊠ *417 Castro St., between 17th and 18th Sts., Castro* ☎ *415/861–7332.*

Giant Robot features toys for tots and too-cool-for-school hipsters.

MUSIC

Streetlight Records. Thousands of used CDs, with an emphasis on rock, jazz, soul, and R&B, are bought and sold here. But there's plenty of vinyl for purists. The Noe Valley branch has been a neighborhood staple since 1973. ⊠ *2350 Market St., at Castro St., Castro* ☎ *415/282–8000.*

NOE VALLEY

BOOKS

Omnivore. Love to eat? Love to read? Then this place is paradise. The shelves are bursting with books on growing and cooking food. They have cookbooks on such diverse subjects as colonial Jamaica and Victorian England cuisine or 1940s Creole cooking. And if you're after a signed first-edition book by Julia Child or James Beard, they have those, too. ⊠ *3885 Cesar Chavez St., at Masonic Ave., Noe Valley* ☎ *415/282–4712* ⊕ *www.omnivorebooks.com.*

CHILDREN'S CLOTHING

Small Frys. The colorful cottons carried here are mainly for infants, with some articles for older children. Brands include OshKosh and many Californian and French labels. A few shelves of toys and whimsical finger puppets round out the store's selection. ⊠ *4066 24th St., between Castro and Noe Sts., Noe Valley* ☎ *415/648–3954.*

CLOTHING: WOMEN'S

Ambiance. A well-loved destination for fashion-conscious locals, this is a fun place to find 1920s-inspired dresses, velvet scarves, and dangling silver jewelry. They also have jaw-dropping sales. ⊠ *3985 and 3989 24th St., between Castro and Noe Sts., Noe Valley* ☎ *415/647–7144* ⊕ *www.ambiancesf.com.*

HANDICRAFTS AND FOLK ART

Global Exchange. A branch of the well-known nonprofit organization, the store carries handcrafted items from more than 40 countries. The staff works directly with village cooperatives and workshops. Whether you buy a Nepalese sweater, a South African wood carving, or Balinese textiles, employees can explain the origin of your purchase. ⊠ *4018 24th St., between Noe and Castro Sts., Noe Valley* ☎ *415/648–8068.*

Xela Imports. Africa, Southeast Asia, and Central America are the sources for these handicrafts, which include jewelry, religious masks, fertility statuary, and decorative wall hangings. (Note: the name of the store is pronounced *shay*-la.) ⊠ *3925 24th St., between Sanchez and Noe Sts., Noe Valley* ☎ *415/695–1323.*

TOYS AND GADGETS

Ark Toys, Books & Crafts. The stock here emphasizes high-quality toys, many of which have an educational bent (books, science kits) or encourage imaginative play (dress-up costumes, paper dolls). Numerous toys are manufactured in Europe, with a range from toddlers through 12-year-olds. ⊠ *3845 24th St., between Church and Sanchez Sts., Noe Valley* ☎ *415/821–1257.*

MISSION DISTRICT

ART GALLERIES

Southern Exposure. One of the city's most established venues for cutting-edge art is this artist-run, nonprofit gallery. Exhibitions and events as well as accompanying lectures, performances, and films change frequently in the custom-designed spaces. ⊠ *3030 20th St., at Alabama St., Mission* ☎ *415/863–2141.*

BOOKS

Dog Eared Books. An eclectic group of shoppers—gay and straight, fashionable and practical—wanders the aisles of this pleasantly ramshackle bookstore. The diverse selection of publications, about 85% of them used, includes quirky selections like vintage children's books, remaindered art books, and local zines. A bin of free books just outside the front door is fun to browse, if only to see the odd assortment of out-of-date titles. ⊠ *900 Valencia St., at 20th St., Mission* ☎ *415/282–1901.*

Get Lost Travel Books, Maps & Gear. Here travel literature is mixed in for inspiration amid the guidebooks—totaling more than 9,000 titles. You can also find language-instruction materials, luggage, and other travel accessories. ⊠ *1825 Market St., at Guerrero St., Mission* ☎ *415/437–0529.*

Modern Times Bookstore. Named after Charlie Chaplin's politically subversive film, the store stocks high-quality literary fiction and nonfiction, much of it with a political bent. There are also sections for children's books, Spanish-language titles, and magazines and local subversive zines. Author readings and public forums are held regularly. ■ TIP➜ If you're looking to kill a little time in the Mission before hooking up with dinner companions, this is a low-key and inviting place to hide out in the stacks. ⊠ *888 Valencia St., between 19th and 20th Sts., Mission* ☎ *415/282–9246.*

San Francisco shoppers are spoiled for choice on Haight Street.

CLOTHING: MEN AND WOMEN

ADS Hats. Traditionalists will find a beautiful selection of cloche hats for women and fedoras and porkpie hats for men, while outdoorsy types can shop for sun hats, rain hats, or whimsically styled wool and cashmere caps for colder climes. Knitted caps for kids and babies are frightfully cute. ⊠ *418 Valencia St., at 15th St., Mission* ☎ *415/503–1316.*

Bell Jar. Their tag line is "Gorgeous Little Things," and they certainly do have them. Flowing dresses, dangling turquoise earrings, cat prints, and pineapple vases, this wonderfully diverse shop sells just about everything—everything gorgeous that is. The owner is former art director Sasha Wingate, and she's made the atmosphere romantic, bright, and whimsically beautiful. ⊠ *3187 16th St., between 21st and 22nd Sts., Mission* ☎ *415/626–1749* ⊕ *www.shopbelljarsf.com.*

Dema. Dema Grim's classically cut clothes in ethnic and vintage fabrics really pop and truly capture the spirit of the Mission. Deep reds with rosebuds and rich purple leopard prints are just a few of the patterns you'll see hanging from the lively rails. ⊠ *1038 Valencia St., between 21st and 22nd Sts., Mission* ☎ *415/206–0500.*

Self Edge. Hanging from metal rods on perfectly separated wooden hangers are dozens of pairs of Japanese selvage denim. The industrial-weight fabric that makes up these jeans will run you between $160 and $450, but they'll hem them for free with their vintage chain-stitching machine. ⊠ *714 Valencia St., at 18th St., Mission* ☎ *415/558–0658.*

VINTAGE
AND RESALE
CLOTHING

Schauplatz. Vintage clothing from the 1920s to the 1980s can be unearthed on the racks of this narrow little store on a hip block in the Mission. Some of the dramatic women's wear—go-go boots, pillbox hats, faux Chanel suits—is suitable for street wear or dress-up, depending on your style, while the menswear tends more toward fashionably retro jackets and button-up shirts from the classic to the gaudy. ✉ *791 Valencia St., between 18th and 19th Sts., Mission* ☎ *415/864–5665.*

FURNITURE, HOUSEWARES, AND GIFTS

Aldea. A visit to this shop is like being in someone's home and being able to buy everything you see, from the sheets to the chairs to the shampoo in the shower. The aesthetic is modern, with bright references to Mexico, India, Turkey, and Japan. It's the perfect place to find a hostess gift or to deck out that corner missing something special. ✉ *3338 17th St., Suite 100B, between Valencia and Mission Sts., Mission* ☎ *415/865–9807.*

★ **Paxton Gate**. Elevating gardening to an art, this serene shop offers beautiful earthenware pots, amaryllis and narcissus bulbs, decorative garden items, and coffee-table books such as *An Inordinate Fondness for Beetles*. The collection of taxidermy and preserved bugs presents more unusual gift ideas. ✉ *824 Valencia St., between 19th and 20th Sts., Mission* ☎ *415/824–1872.*

Therapy. Housewares range from ever-practical refrigerator magnets to downright silly items such as a soap-on-a-rope tribute to the cartoon character Strawberry Shortcake. A retro theme runs to stationery and other reasonably priced items, and the adjacent annex sells retro-style furniture. ✉ *545 Valencia St., between 16th and 17th Sts., Mission* ☎ *415/865–0981.*

VINTAGE
HOUSEWARES

The Curiosity Shoppe. This intimate shop is all about old-school collecting—we're talking flowers and butterflies, waaaay further back in the day than your father's shot glasses or your mother's charm bracelets. Meticulous organization and careful selection is what makes this a collection, not a horde. ✉ *855 Valencia St., between 19th and 20th Sts., Mission* ☎ *415/671–5384.*

HANDICRAFTS AND FOLK ART

Ruby Gallery. A pooch named Ruby presides over this small artists' cooperative where the jewelry, clothing, handbags, candleholders, intricately crafted cards, and other gift items are made by local artists. Hair accessories—from elegant clips studded with vintage Czech glass to barrettes fashioned out of buttons—are especially charming. You'll find a second branch on Haight Street. ✉ *3602 20th St., at Valencia St., Mission* ☎ *415/550–8052.*

Studio 24. The gift shop of the acclaimed Galería de la Raza sells crafts from Mexico and Central and South America. Prints and calendars by Latino artists, Day of the Dead folk art, and masks and wood carvings from Latin America are a few of the objects for sale. ✉ *2857 24th St., at Bryant St., Mission* ☎ *415/826–8009.*

MUSIC

Aquarius Records. Owner Windy Chien carries on the tradition in this space, which was *the* punk-rock store in the 1970s. These days it carries a variety of music, including a large selection of experimental electronica, all of it handpicked by staffers, so you can be sure you're getting the latest and hippest. ⊠ *1055 Valencia St., between 21st and 22nd Sts., Mission* ☎ *415/647–2272.*

PAPER AND STATIONERY

★ **Flax.** In addition to paints, brushes, and various art supplies, this sprawling creators' playground sells beautifully made photo albums and journals, fine pens and pencils, crafts kits, scads of stationery, and inspiring doodads for kids. ⊠ *1699 Market St., near Valencia St., Mission* ☎ *415/552–2355.*

TOYS AND GADGETS

☺ **826 Valencia.** The brainchild of author Dave Eggers is primarily a center
★ established to help kids with their writing skills via tutoring and storytelling events. But the storefront is also "San Francisco's only independent pirate supply store," a quirky space filled with eye patches, spyglasses, and other pirate-themed paraphernalia. Eggers's quarterly journal, *McSweeney's,* and other publications are available here. Proceeds benefit the writing center. ⊠ *826 Valencia St., between 18th and 19th Sts., Mission* ☎ *415/642–5905.*

POTRERO HILL

ANTIQUES

★ **Forgotten Shanghai.** The Asian antiques for sale here are both beautiful and practical, with camphor-wood trunks and beautifully aged leather boxes among the treasures. ⊠ *245 Kansas St., near 16th St., Potrero Hill* ☎ *415/701–7707.*

FURNITURE, HOUSEWARES, AND GIFTS

Dandelion. The variety of housewares, bath items, books, and tchotchkes includes something for everyone on your gift list. Cocktail paraphernalia, golf-related books, luxury bath products, and indulgent food items such as Fauchon-brand black-fig preserves are only a sample of what's here. ⊠ *55 Potrero Ave., at Alameda St., Potrero Hill* ☎ *415/436–9500.*

SPORTING GOODS

Sports Basement. This sprawling store rewards intrepid shoppers with significant discounts on name-brand sportswear, accessories, and camping and outdoor gear. Helpful salespeople, more knowledgeable than you would expect at a discount warehouse, will help you find just the right running shoes, biking shorts, or yoga tights. ⊠ *1590 Bryant St., between 15th and 16th Sts., Potrero Hill* ☎ *415/437–0100.*

PACIFIC HEIGHTS AND JAPANTOWN

PACIFIC HEIGHTS

BEAUTY

★ **BeneFit.** You can find the locally based BeneFit line of cosmetics and skin-care products at Macy's and Sephora, but it's much more fun to come to one of the eponymous boutiques. No-pressure salespeople dab you with whimsical makeup such as Ooh La Lift concealer and Tinted Love, a stain for lips and cheeks. ⊠ *2117 Fillmore St., between California and Sacramento Sts., Pacific Heights* ☎ *415/567–0242.*

18

Kiehl's. Perhaps because it started out in 1851, Kiehl's has a no-nonsense appeal. Fans swear by its high-quality, simply packaged skin- and hair-care products. This spacious store stocks a wide variety of its lotions, potions, and soaps. Not sure whether the Formula 133 Hair Conditioner and Grooming Aid is right for you? Ask for a sample. ✉ *2360 Fillmore St., between Washington and Clay Sts., Pacific Heights* ☎ *415/359–9260.*

CHILDREN'S CLOTHING

Dottie Doolittle. Pacific Heights mothers shop here for charming silk dresses and other special-occasion outfits for their little ones. Less pricey togs for infants, boys to size 12, and girls to size 16, are also on hand. ✉ *3680 Sacramento St., at Spruce St., Pacific Heights* ☎ *415/563–3244.*

CLOTHING: MEN AND WOMEN

Elizabeth Charles. Parlaying the city's current obsession with the land down under, this intimate boutique stocks only Australian and New Zealand designers, with an emphasis on flowing frocks in the very finest fabrics. ✉ *2056 Fillmore St., between California and Pine Sts., Pacific Heights* ☎ *415/440–2100.*

Erica Tanov. The designer's background in lingerie and bedding guides the delicate designs here: wispy cashmere, silk organza and charmeuse, and linen. Sweaters tend to drape and wrap; skirts and pajama-wide pants are often brightened with florals or stripes. ✉ *2408 Fillmore St., between Jackson and Washington Sts., Pacific Heights* ☎ *415/674–1228.*

HeidiSays. Fanciful windows brimming with bright and festive prints draw passersby into this store. Perky salespeople help you choose between Catherine Malandrino, Trina Turk, and Rebecca Taylor frocks. To complete your emblematic San Fran chic outfit, head down the street, where the Heidi empire continues with HeidiSays Casual and HeidiSays Shoes, where you can pick up lingerie, loungewear, bags, and pumps. ✉ *2426, 2416, and 2105 Fillmore St., Pacific Heights* ☎ *415/749–0655.*

TAILORED **Mrs. Dewson's Hats.** Although this shop was the famous purveyor of hats to nattily dressed former San Francisco mayor Willie Brown, Ruth Garland Dewson has been selling chapeaus—some of her own design—since 1978. The popular "Willie Brim" is a fur felt fedora; the brim comes in three sizes. ✉ *2050 Fillmore St., at California St., Pacific Heights* ☎ *415/346–1600.*

Three Bags Full. Everything here is hand-knit—whether it be a featherweight cashmere shrug or a chunky wool cable sweater. Local businesswomen come here to replace their stuffy suit jackets with a cozy-but-sleek wool or cotton blazer. There's an additional branch on Sutter Street. ✉ *3314 Sacramento St., near Fillmore St., Pacific Heights* ☎ *415/923–1454.*

FOOD AND DRINK

WINES AND **D&M Wines and Liquors.** This family-owned liquor store appears to be like
SPIRITS any neighborhood liquor store at first glance, but it's actually a rare and wonderful specialist. In a city obsessed with wine, these spirit devotees distinguished themselves by focusing on rare, small-production Armagnac, Calvados, and Champagne. ✉ *2200 Fillmore St., at Sacramento St., Pacific Heights* ☎ *415/346–1325.*

FURNITURE, HOUSEWARES, AND GIFTS

Nest. A mix between a Parisian antiques show and a Jamaican flea market, this cozy store could get even the most monochrome New Yorker excited about color. You can turn up the volume on your SF souvenirs with vibrant handmade quilts, Chan Luu jewelry, Les Indiennes hand-blocked cotton fabrics, and M. Sasek's cheerfully illustrated book *This Is San Francisco.* ⊠ *2300 Fillmore St., at Clay St., Pacific Heights* ☎ *415/292–6199.*

Sue Fisher King Company. When Martha Stewart or the buyers at Williams-Sonoma need some inspiration they come to see how Sue has set her sprawling table or dressed her stately bed. (Her specialty is opulent linens for every room.) And when Pacific Heights residents are looking for an impeccable hostess or bridal gift, they come by for a hand-embroidered velvet pillow or a piece of Astier de Villatte white pottery. ⊠ *3067 Sacramento St., between Baker and Broderick Sts., Pacific Heights* ☎ *415/922–7276.*

PAPER AND STATIONERY

Paper Source. Beautiful handmade papers, cards, envelopes, ribbons, and bookbinding materials line the walls of this shop, which embodies the Bay Area's do-it-yourself spirit. Assembly is required here and that's the fun of it. ⊠ *1925 Fillmore St., at Pine St., Pacific Heights* ☎ *415/409–7710.*

JAPANTOWN

BOOKS

★ **Kinokuniya Bookstore.** The selection of English-language books about Japanese culture—everything from medieval history to origami instructions—is one of the finest in the country. Kinokuniya is the city's biggest seller of Japanese-language books. Dozens of glossy Asian fashion magazines attract the young and trendy, and books and DVDs related to the Japanese anime director Hayao Miyazaki are the latest trend. ⊠ *Kinokuniya Bldg., 1581 Webster St., 2nd fl., Japantown* ☎ *415/567–7625.*

CLOTHING: MEN AND WOMEN

VINTAGE AND RESALE CLOTHING

Shige Nishiguchi Kimonos. Though cotton *yukatas* (casual, lightweight kimonos) are the biggest sellers, vintage silk kimonos—some of them hand-painted—and vintage *obis* (kimono sashes) are the reason this tiny shop in the Japan Center is a destination for aficionados of Japanese dress. ⊠ *1730 Geary Blvd., Suite 203, Japantown* ☎ *415/346–5567.*

HANDICRAFTS AND FOLK ART

Ma-Shi'-Ko Folk Craft. Beautiful Mashiko pottery, rustic pieces fired in a wood kiln and coated with a natural glaze, are the specialty here. The wealth of unique pottery and antiques, including many ceramic vases and wooden chests, makes a visit here worth the somewhat chilly reception from the proprietor. ⊠ *Kinokuniya Bldg., 1581 Webster St., 2nd fl., Japantown* ☎ *415/346–0748.*

Soko Hardware. Run in Japantown by the Ashizawa family since 1925, this shop specializes in beautifully crafted Japanese tools for gardening and woodworking. In addition to the usual hardware-store items, you can find seeds for Japanese plants and books about topics such as making shoji screens. ⊠ *1698 Post St., at Buchanan St., Japantown* ☎ *415/931–5510.*

18

MALL

☺ **NEW PEOPLE.** Japanese pop culture has never been so neatly organized as it is here at this state-of-the-art, 20,000-square-foot mini mall. NEW PEOPLE is divided into four shiny levels: the cinema/café downstairs; the Store (selling trinkets, toys, books and DVDs) on the first floor; clothing shops like Baby, the Stars Shine Bright, and Sou-Sou on the second floor; and the Superfrog Gallery at the third floor. Expect to see a rotation of emerging artists in the gallery and make sure you try the superstrong coffee and vegan donuts on sale in the café. ⌧ *1746 Post St., at Webster St., Japantown* ☎ *415/525–8631* ⊕ *www.newpeopleworld. com.*

WESTERN ADDITION

FURNITURE, HOUSEWARES, AND GIFTS

COOKWARE

Fodor'sChoice

★

Cookin': Recycled Gourmet Appurtenances. People trek here from all over the world for the impressive collection of indestructible vintage Le Creuset in discontinued colors. If you can't make sense of this store's jumble of used cookware—stacked ceiling-high in some places—ask the helpful owner, who will likely interrogate you about what you're preparing to cook before leading you to the right section, whether that be the corner with hundreds of ramekins or the bewildering selection of garlic presses. ⌧ *339 Divisadero St., between Oak and Page Sts., Western Addition* ☎ *415/861–1854.*

INGLESIDE

FOOD AND DRINK

WINES AND SPIRITS

San Francisco Wine Trading Company. Owner and noted wine expert Gary Marcaletti provides the only place in the city with well-known Bay Area importer Kermit Lynch's line of wines. It also has Saturday-afternoon tastings. ⌧ *250 Taraval St., between Funston and 12th Aves., Ingleside* ☎ *415/731–6222.*

Marin County, Berkeley, and Oakland

WORD OF MOUTH

"We . . . caught the ferry over to Sausalito. A stroll along the sheltered waterfront and a close-quarters view of Alcatraz on the way back rounded out a perfect stay in the City by the Bay."
                                                                —kiwi_rob

WELCOME TO MARIN COUNTY, BERKELEY, AND OAKLAND

TOP REASONS TO GO

★ **Walk among giants:** Walking into Muir Woods, a mere 12 mi north of the Golden Gate Bridge, is like entering a cathedral built by God.

★ **Attend a reading:** Chances are, an author you admire will be reading somewhere in the Bay Area during your trip. Berkeley draws an especially erudite crowd; Q&A sessions can feel like a grad-school discussion.

★ **Bite into the "Gourmet Ghetto":** Eat your way through this area of Berkeley, starting with a slice of pizza from the Cheeseboard.

★ **Sit on a dock by the bay:** Admire the beauty and tranquillity of the Bay Area from the rocky, picturesque shores of Sausalito.

★ **Find solitude at Point Reyes National Seashore:** Head here to hike beautifully rugged—and deserted—beaches.

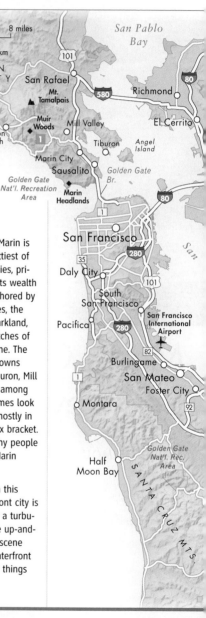

1 Marin County. Marin is considered the prettiest of the Bay Area counties, primarily because of its wealth of open space. Anchored by water on three sides, the county is mostly parkland, including long stretches of unmolested coastline. The picturesque small towns here—Sausalito, Tiburon, Mill Valley, and Bolinas among them—may sometimes look rustic, but they're mostly in a dizzyingly high tax bracket. There's a reason why people call BMWs "basic Marin wheels."

2 Oakland. Life in this tight-knit, harbor-front city is strongly defined by a turbulent history. But the up-and-coming downtown scene and rejuvenated waterfront are signals of good things ahead.

3 **Berkeley.** This college town has long been known for its liberal ethos, stimulating university community (and perhaps even more stimulating coffee shops), and activist streak. But these days the booming restaurant and arts scenes are luring even those who wouldn't be caught dead in Birkenstocks.

GETTING ORIENTED

Cross the Golden Gate Bridge and head north to reach Marin County's rolling hills and green expanses, where residents enjoy an haute-suburban lifestyle. Farther afield, the wild landscapes of the Marin Headlands, Muir Woods, Mt. Tamalpais, Stinson Beach, and Point Reyes National Seashore await.

East of the city, across the San Francisco Bay, are Berkeley and Oakland, which most Bay Area residents refer to as the East Bay. These two towns have distinct personalities, but life here feels more relaxed than in the city—though every bit as vibrant.

19

3
Berkeley
24
Redwood Regional Park
580
Oakland
2
880
Oakland International Airport
San Leandro
580
Hayward
92
San Francisco Bay
880
Union City
680
Fremont
Belmont
101
84
San Francisco Bay National Wildlife Refuge
Redwood City
84
880
35
Palo Alto
101
Stanford University ◆
Milpitas
237
Mountain View
280
85
Santa Clara
101
San Jose
85
280

Updated by
Fiona G.
Parrott

It's rare for a metropolis to compete with its suburbs for visitors, but the view from any of San Francisco's hilltops shows that the Bay Area's temptations extend far beyond the city limits. To the north is Marin County, the beauty queen, with small but chic villages like Tiburon and Mill Valley, plus dramatic coastal scenery. East of town are two energetic urban centers, Berkeley and Oakland. Formerly radical Berkeley is getting more glam, while Oakland is shaking off its image as San Francisco's ugly stepsister and transforming into an epicenter of hipness.

Up in Marin, the birthplace of mountain biking, trail-veined Mt. Tamalpais and the woods below draw hikers and cyclists. Beaches lure families and thrill seekers, while little towns offer urbanites respite from busy city streets. In the mid-1960s and '70s alternative lifestyle seekers established Marin's reputation as ground zero for gurus, granola, and redwood hot tubs. Despite the influx of stock-market millionaires and chic boutiques, the counterculture identity still sticks. Immediately after crossing the Golden Gate Bridge on Highway 101 northbound, you'll pass through a tunnel whose archway is painted with a rainbow that welcomes you to magical Marin, "Land of Oz."

Meanwhile, the town often referred to as the People's Republic of Berkeley retains its liberal image, though it's drastically tamer than it was in the late 1960s. It's now as famous for chef and food activist Alice Waters (and her pricey restaurant Chez Panisse) as it is for its role as the birthplace of the Free Speech movement. Oakland is polishing some of its rough edges, too, with a successful port and a revitalized downtown, an alternative arts scene, and hipster cafés and boutiques.

PLANNING

WHEN TO GO

Berkeley is a university town, and the rhythm of the school year might affect your visit. It's easier to navigate the streets and find parking near the university between semesters, but there's also less buzz around town. Surprisingly, summer is chock-full of students attending the many summer sessions on campus. Moving-in weeks before the fall semester bring a massive influx of students *and* parents and other family members—definitely not the best time to take a campus tour.

BART trains can be packed during traditional morning and evening rush hours, but things are much less congested at other times. BART can get you from downtown San Francisco to a coffee shop in Rockridge in about 25 minutes. (It's closer to 30 minutes for farther points in Berkeley.)

It'll take about the same amount of time by car to reach Tiburon if traffic is clear on the Golden Gate Bridge (also depending, of course, on what part of the city you're departing from).

GETTING HERE AND AROUND

BART TRAVEL

If you don't want to worry about finding a parking space, using public transportation to reach Berkeley or Oakland is ideal. BART (Bay Area Rapid Transit) has several central stops in both towns. The under- and above-ground trains make stops in downtown Berkeley and in several parts of Oakland, including Rockridge. Use the Lake Merritt Station for the Oakland Museum and southern Lake Merritt; the Oakland City Center–12th Street Station for downtown, Chinatown, and Old Oakland; and the 19th Street Station for the Paramount Theatre and the north side of Lake Merritt. From the Berkeley (not North Berkeley) Station, walk a block up Center Street to get to the western edge of campus. Both trips take 30 to 45 minutes one way from the center of San Francisco.

19

Contacts BART (☎ 510/465–2278 ⊕ www.bart.gov).

BOAT AND FERRY TRAVEL

For sheer romance, nothing beats the ferry; there's service from San Francisco to Sausalito and Tiburon in Marin County, and to Alameda and Oakland in the East Bay.

The Golden Gate Ferry crosses the bay to Sausalito from the south wing of San Francisco's Ferry Building (at Market Street and the Embarcadero). Blue & Gold Fleet ferries depart daily for Sausalito and Tiburon from Pier 41 at Fisherman's Wharf; weekday commuter ferries leave from the Ferry Building for Tiburon. The trip to Sausalito takes 30 minutes; to Tiburon, it takes 20 minutes. Expect more crowds on weekends and during peak commute times.

The Angel Island–Tiburon Ferry sails across the strait to the island daily April through September and weekends the rest of the year.

The Alameda/Oakland Ferry runs several times daily between San Francisco's Ferry Building or Pier 39, Alameda, and the Clay Street dock near Oakland's Jack London Square; one-way tickets are $6.25. The trip lasts 30 to 45 minutes, depending on your departure point, and leads to the heart of Oakland's gentrified shopping and restaurant district. Arriving in Oakland by boat conveys a historic sense of the city's heyday as a World War II–era shipbuilding center. Purchase tickets on board.

Boat and Ferry Lines Alameda/Oakland Ferry (☎ 510/522–3300 ⊕ www.eastbayferry.com). **Angel Island–Tiburon Ferry** (☎ 415/435–2131 ⊕ www.angelislandferry.com). **Blue & Gold Fleet** (☎ 415/705–8200 ⊕ www. blueandgoldfleet.com). **Golden Gate Ferry** (☎ 415/923–2000 ⊕ www. goldengateferry.org).

BUS TRAVEL

Golden Gate Transit buses travel to Sausalito, Tiburon, and Mill Valley from 1st and Mission streets as well as from other points in San Francisco. For Mt. Tamalpais State Park and West Marin (e.g., Stinson Beach, Bolinas, and Point Reyes Station), take Bus 10, 70, or 80 to Marin City; in Marin City transfer to the West Marin Stagecoach; call or check online for routes and schedules. San Francisco MuniBus 76 runs hourly from 4th and Townsend streets to the Marin Headlands Visitor Center on Sunday and major holidays only. The trip takes roughly 45 minutes.

AC Transit buses run frequently between San Francisco's TransBay Terminal (at 1st and Mission streets) and the East Bay. AC Transit's F and FS lines stop near the university and 4th Street shopping in Berkeley. Lines C and P travel to Piedmont in Oakland. The O bus stops at the edge of Chinatown near downtown Oakland.

Bus Lines AC Transit (☎ 511 ⊕ www.actransit.org). **Golden Gate Transit** (☎ 415/455–2000 ⊕ www.goldengate.org). **San Francisco Muni** (☎ 415/701–2311 ⊕ www.sfmuni.com). **West Marin Stagecoach** (☎ 415/526–3239 ⊕ www. marintransit.org/stage.html).

CAR TRAVEL

To visit the outer reaches of Marin, a car is essential (unless you want to spend all day on the bus). Head north on U.S.101 and cross the Golden Gate Bridge. For Sausalito, take the first exit, Alexander Avenue, just past Vista Point; after winding all the way down the hill to the water, the road becomes Bridgeway. Continue north on Bridgeway to the municipal parking lot near the center of town—but expect the lot to be full on weekends, in which case you should continue north and hunt for street spots. For Tiburon, exit at Tiburon Boulevard. For Mill Valley, exit at East Blithedale, continue west on East Blithedale to Throckmorton Avenue, and turn left to reach Lytton Square. All three trips take 20 to 45 minutes one way, depending on traffic.

The Marin Headlands are a logical stop en route to Sausalito, but reaching them can be tricky. After exiting on Alexander Avenue, take the first left (signs read "San Francisco/U.S. 101 South"), pass through a tunnel under the freeway, and make a hard right up the steep hill just before the road merges back on to the bridge toward San Francisco. You should see a small sign that says "Forts Barry and Cronkhite."

Conzelman Road follows the cliffs that face the ocean and becomes one-way before a spectacular drop toward Point Bonita; Bunker Road is a less spectacular inland route through Rodeo to the forts.

For Muir Woods and Mt. Tamalpais, take the Route 1–Stinson Beach exit off U.S. 101 and follow Route 1 west and then north. Both trips may take from 30 minutes to more than an hour, depending on traffic. Allow plenty of extra time on summer weekends.

To reach the East Bay from San Francisco, take I–80 East across the Bay Bridge. For most of Berkeley, take the University Avenue exit through downtown Berkeley to the campus or take the Ashby Avenue exit and turn left on Telegraph Avenue to the traditional campus entrance; there's a parking garage on Channing Way. For Oakland, take I–580 off the Bay Bridge to the Grand Avenue exit for Lake Merritt. To reach downtown and the waterfront, take I–980 from I–580 and exit at 12th Street. Both trips take about 30 minutes unless it's rush hour or a weekend afternoon, when you should count on an hour.

SIGHTSEEING GUIDES

Blue & Gold Fleet has a one-hour narrated tour of the San Francisco Bay, for $22, with frequent daily departures from Pier 39 in San Francisco. Super Sightseeing offers a four-hour bus tour of Muir Woods. The tour, which stops in Sausalito en route, leaves at 9 am and 2 pm daily from North Point and Taylor Street at Fisherman's Wharf and costs $50 ($47 senior citizens, $26 ages 5–11); 24-hour advance reservations are recommended. Great Pacific Tour Co. runs four-hour morning and afternoon tours of Muir Woods and Sausalito for $55 ($53 senior citizens, $43 ages 5–11), with hotel pickup in 14-passenger vans with excellent interpretation.

By Bus and Van Blue & Gold Fleet (☎ *415/705–8200* ⊕ *www. blueandgoldfleet.com*). **Great Pacific Tour Co.** (☎ *415/626–4499* ⊕ *www.greatpacifictour.com*). **Super Sightseeing** (☎ *415/353–5310* ⊕ *www.supersightseeing.com*).

19

RESTAURANTS

The Bay Area is home to some of the most popular and innovative restaurants in the country, including Chez Panisse Café & Restaurant, in Berkeley, and Lark Creek Inn, in Larkspur—for which reservations must be made well in advance. Expect an emphasis on locally grown produce, hormone-free meats, and California wine. The coast provides a spectacular waterfront setting for dining as well as lodging; in many instances the views are the most important part of the experience. Keep in mind that many Marin cafés don't serve dinner, and that dinner service ends on the early side. (No 10 pm reservations in this neck of the woods.)

HOTELS

There aren't many hotels in Berkeley or Oakland, but Marin is a destination where hotels package themselves as cozy retreats. Summer is often booked well in advance, despite weather that is often mercurial and sometimes downright chilly. Check for special packages during this season.

Hotel reviews have been condensed for this book. Please go to Fodors. com for expanded reviews of each property.

DINING AND LODGING PRICE CATEGORIES				
¢	$	$$	$$$	$$$$
Restaurants	under $10	$10–$14	$15–$22	$23–$30	over $30
Hotels	under $90	$90–$149	$150–$199	$200–$250	over $250

Restaurant prices are per person for a main course at dinner, or the equivalent. Hotel prices are for two people in a standard double room in high season.

VISITOR INFORMATION

Contact Marin Convention & Visitors Bureau (✉ *1 Mitchell Blvd., Suite B, San Rafael* ☎ *415/925–2060* ⊕ *www.visitmarin.org*).

MARIN COUNTY

Marin is quite simply a knockout—some go so far as to call it spectacular and wild. This isn't an extravagant claim, since more than 40% of the county (180,000 acres), including the majority of the coastline, is parkland. The territory ranges from chaparral, grassland, and coastal scrub to broadleaf and evergreen forest, redwood, salt marsh, and rocky shoreline.

Regardless of its natural beauty, what gave the county its reputation was Cyra McFadden's 1977 book *The Serial*, a literary soap opera that depicted the county as a bastion of hot-tubbing and "open" marriages. Indeed old-time bohemian, but also increasingly jet-set, Marinites still spend a lot of time outdoors, and surfing, cycling, and hiking are common after-work and weekend activities. Adrenaline junkies mountain bike down Mt. Tamalpais, and those who want solitude take a walk on one of Point Reyes's many empty beaches. The hot tub remains a popular destination after hours, but things have changed since the boho days. Artists and musicians who arrived in the 1960s have set the tone for mellow country towns, but Marin is now undeniably chic, with BMWs supplanting VW buses as the cars of choice.

Most cosmopolitan is Sausalito, the town just over the Golden Gate Bridge from San Francisco. Across the inlet from Sausalito, Tiburon and Belvedere are lined with grand homes that regularly appear on fund-raising circuits, and to the north, landlocked Mill Valley is a hub of wining and dining and tony boutiques.

In general, the farther you get from the Golden Gate Bridge the more country things become, and West Marin is about as far as you can get from the big city, both physically and ideologically. Separated from the inland county by the slopes and ridges of giant Mt. Tamalpais, this territory beckons to mavericks, artists, ocean lovers, and other free spirits. Stinson Beach has tempered its isolationist attitude to accommodate out-of-towners, as have Inverness and Point Reyes Station. Bolinas, on the other hand, would prefer you not know its location.

SAUSALITO

2 mi north of Golden Gate Bridge.

Bougainvillea-covered hillsides and an expansive yacht harbor give Sausalito the feel of an Adriatic resort. The town sits on the northwestern edge of San Francisco Bay, where it's sheltered from the ocean by the Marin Headlands; the mostly mild weather here is perfect for strolling and outdoor dining. Nevertheless, morning fog and afternoon winds can roll over the hills without warning, funneling through the central part of Sausalito once known as Hurricane Gulch.

South on Bridgeway (toward San Francisco), which snakes between the bay and the hills, a waterside esplanade is lined with restaurants on piers that lure diners with good seafood and even better views. Stairs along the west side of Bridgeway climb the hill to wooded neighborhoods filled with both rustic and opulent homes. As you amble along Bridgeway past boutiques, gift shops, and galleries, you'll notice the absence of basic services. If you need an aspirin or some groceries (or if you want to see the locals), you'll have to head to Caledonia Street, which runs parallel to Bridgeway, north of the ferry terminus and inland a couple of blocks. The streets closest to the ferry landing flaunt their fair share of shops selling T-shirts and kitschy souvenirs. Venture into some of the side streets or narrow alleyways to catch a bit more of the town's taste for eccentric jewelry and handmade crafts.

■ **TIP→** The ferry is the best way to get to Sausalito from San Francisco; you get more romance (and less traffic) and disembark in the heart of downtown.

Like much of San Francisco, Sausalito had a raffish reputation before it went upscale. Discovered in 1775 by Spanish explorers and named Sausalito (Little Willow) for the trees growing around its springs, the town served as a port for whaling ships during the 19th century. By the mid-1800s wealthy San Franciscans were making Sausalito their getaway across the bay. They built lavish Victorian summer homes in the hills, many of which still stand. In 1875 the railroad from the north connected with ferryboats to San Francisco, bringing the merchant and working classes with it. This influx of hardworking, fun-loving folk polarized the town into "wharf rats" and "hill snobs," and the waterfront area grew thick with saloons, gambling dens, and bordellos. Bootleggers flourished during Prohibition, and shipyard workers swelled the town's population in the 1940s.

Sausalito developed its bohemian flair in the 1950s and '60s, when a group of artists, led by a charismatic Greek portraitist named Varda, established an artists' colony and a houseboat community here. Today more than 450 houseboats are docked in Sausalito, which has since also become a major yachting center. Some of the houseboats are ragged, others deluxe, but all are quirky (one, a miniature replica of a Persian castle, even has an elevator inside). For a close-up view of the community, head north on Bridgeway—Sausalito's main thoroughfare—from downtown, turn right on Gate Six Road, and park where it dead-ends at the public shore. Keep a respectful distance; these are homes, after all, and the residents become a bit prickly from too much ogling.

19

ESSENTIALS

Visitor Information Sausalito Chamber of Commerce (✉ *780 Bridgeway* ☎ *415/332-0505 or 415/331-7262* ⊕ *www.sausalito.org*).

GETTING HERE AND AROUND

From San Francisco by car or bike, follow U.S. 101 north across the Golden Gate Bridge and take the first exit, Alexander Avenue, just past Vista Point; continue down the winding hill to the water to where the road becomes Bridgeway. Buses 10 and 22 will drop you off in downtown Sausalito, and the ferries dock downtown as well. The center of town is flat, with plenty of sidewalks and bay views. It's a pleasure and a must to explore on foot.

EXPLORING

☺ **Bay Area Discovery Museum.** Sitting at the base of the Golden Gate Bridge, this indoor-outdoor museum offers entertaining and enlightening hands-on exhibits for children under eight. Kids and their families can fish from a boat at the indoor wharf, imagine themselves as marine biologists in the Wave Workshop, and play outdoors at Lookout Cove (made up of scaled-down sea caves, tidal pools, and even a re-created shipwreck). At Tot Zone, toddlers and preschoolers can dress up in animal costumes and crawl through miniature tunnels. From San Francisco, take the Alexander Avenue exit from U.S. 101 and follow signs to East Fort Baker. ✉ *557 McReynolds Rd., at East Fort Baker* ☎ *415/339-3900* ⊕ *www.baykidsmuseum.org* 🖃 *$10; children under 1 free* ⊙ *Tues.–Fri. 9–4, weekends 10–5.*

☺ **Bay Model.** An anonymous-looking World War II shipyard building holds one of Sausalito's great treasures: the sprawling (more than 1½ acres) Bay Model of the entire San Francisco Bay and the San Joaquin–Sacramento River delta, complete with flowing water. The U.S. Army Corps of Engineers uses the model to reproduce the rise and fall of tides, the flow of currents, and the other physical forces at work on the bay. *2100 Bridgeway, at Marinship Way* ☎ *415/332-3870 recorded information, 415/332-3871 operator assistance* ⊕ *www.spn.usace.army.mil/bmvc* 🖃 *Free* ⊙ *Memorial Day–Labor Day, Tues.–Fri. 9–4, weekends 10–5; Labor Day–Memorial Day, Tues.–Sat. 9–4.*

Drinking Fountain. On the waterfront between the Hotel Sausalito and the Sausalito Yacht Club is an unusual historic landmark—a drinking fountain. It's inscribed with "Have a drink on Sally" in remembrance of Sally Stanford, the former San Francisco madam who later became the town's mayor in the 1970s. Sassy Sally, as they called her, would have appreciated the fountain's eccentric custom attachment: a knee-level basin that reads "Have a drink on Leland," in memory of her beloved dog.

QUICK BITES

Judging by the crowds gathered outside Hamburgers (✉ *737 Bridgeway* ☎ *415/332-9471*), you'd think someone was juggling flaming torches out front. They're really gaping at the juicy hand-formed beef patties sizzling on a rotating grill. Brave the line (it moves fast), get your food to go, and head for the esplanade to enjoy the sweeping views. Hours are 11 am–5 pm.

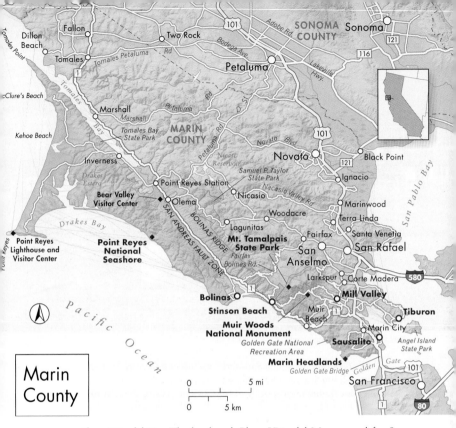

Marin County

Plaza Viña del Mar. The landmark Plaza Viña del Mar, named for Sausalito's sister city in Chile, marks the center of town. Flanked by two 14-foot-tall elephant statues (created in 1915 for the Panama-Pacific International Exposition), the fountain is a great setting for snapshots and people-watching. ⊠ *Bridgeway and Park St.*

Sausalito Visitors Center and Historical Exhibit. Get your bearings and find out what's happening in town at the Sausalito Visitors Center and Historical Exhibit, operated by the town's historical society. It's closed Monday. ⊠ *780 Bridgeway* ☎ *415/332–0505*

WHERE TO EAT

$$
SEAFOOD
☾
Fodor's Choice
★

✕ Fish. If you're wondering where the locals go, this is the place. For fresh seafood, you can't beat this gleaming dockside fish house a mile north of downtown. Order at the counter and then grab a seat by the floor-to-ceiling windows or at a picnic table on the pier, overlooking the yachts and fishing boats. Most of the sustainably caught fish is hauled in from the owner's boats, right at the dock outside. Try the ceviche, crab Louis, cioppino, barbecue oysters, or anything fresh that day that's being grilled over the oak-wood fire. Outside, kids can doodle with sidewalk chalk on the pier. ⊠ *350 Harbor Dr.* ☎ *415/331–3474* ☝ *Reservations not accepted.*

The crowded piers and rolling hillside of the Sausalito waterfront.

$$ ✕ **Le Garage.** When Sausalito executives and entrepreneurs want a stylish lunch with a bay-side setting, they head to Chef Olivier Souvestre's local lunch hot spot. Brittany-born Souvestre serves traditional French bistro fare in a relaxed, sidewalk café–style setting. The menu is small, but the dishes are substantial in flavor and presentation. Standouts include frisée salad with poached egg, bacon, croutons, and pancetta vinaigrette; steak frites with a shallot confit and crispy fries; and a chef's selection of cheese or charcuterie with soup and mixed greens. The restaurant only seats 35 inside and 15 outside, so to avoid a long wait for lunch, arrive before 11:30 or after 1:30. ⊠ *85 Liberty Ship Way, Suite #109* ☎ *415/332–5625* ☽ *No dinner Sun.*

FRENCH BISTRO

$ ✕ **Lighthouse Cafe.** A cozy spot with a long coffee bar and dose of Scandinavian flair, this local establishment has been a favorite brunch destination for nearly two decades. The hearty Norwegian salmon omelet with spinach and cream cheese or fruit pancakes, as well as a wide selection of grilled burgers, sandwiches, and Danish specials like meatballs with potato salad always hit the spot, especially on chilly days. They don't take reservations, which means you might need to join the crowd (there normally is one) and wait in line for a table. ⊠ *1311 Bridgeway* ☎ *415/331–3034* ⊕ *www.lighthouse-restaurants.com* ✍ *Reservations not accepted* ☽ *3 pm onward*

SCANDINAVIAN

$–$$ ✕ **Paradise Bay.** The views from this gem of a restaurant—which is a five-minute walk north of the tourist hub—will make you feel like you're in a secluded paradise; boats, sea kayaks, and the beautiful bay stretch before you. Outdoor seating in the Bay Area doesn't get much better than this, and the inventive, well-balanced, local- and organic-based menu won't disappoint either. Try the Paradise Bay cioppino in a rich

AMERICAN

tomato-fennel broth or the grilled organic lamb sirloin with goat cheese and garlic flan. The trio crème brûlée—espresso, mango, and coconut—is divine, as is the extensive cocktail list. This is also the perfect place for weekend brunch—the buttermilk ginger pancakes topped with banana and mango are out of this world. ⊠ *1200 Bridgeway* ☎ *415/331–3226.*

$$–$$$ ✕ **Poggio.** One of the few restaurants in Sausalito to attract both food-
ITALIAN savvy locals and tourists, Poggio serves modern Tuscan cuisine in a
★ handsome, open-wall space that spills onto the street. Expect dishes such as grilled lamb chops with roasted eggplant, braised artichokes with polenta, feather-light gnocchi, and pizzas from the open kitchen's wood-fired oven. ⊠ *777 Bridgeway* ☎ *415/332–7771* ⌔ *Reservations essential.*

$$–$$$ ✕ **Sushi Ran.** Sushi aficionados swear that this is the Bay Area's best for
JAPANESE raw fish, but don't overlook the excellent Pacific Rim fusions, a result
★ of Japanese ingredients and French cooking techniques, served up in unusual presentations. Because Sushi Ran is so highly ranked among area foodies, book two to seven days in advance for dinner. Otherwise, expect a long wait, which you can soften by sipping one of the 45 by-the-glass sakes from the outstanding wine-and-sake bar. ■**TIP**➔ If you wander in after a day of sightseeing and can't get a table, you can dine in the noisy bar. ⊠ *107 Caledonia St.* ☎ *415/332–3620* ⊙ *No lunch weekends.*

WHERE TO STAY

$$$–$$$$ ⛺ **Casa Madrona.** What began as a small inn in a 19th-century land-mark house has expanded over the decades to incorporate a variety of lodgings and a full-service spa, all tiered down the hill in the center of town. **Pros:** elegant new furniture; spacious rooms; central location. **Cons:** rooms in older section don't have air-conditioning or full elevator access; parking is pricey. **TripAdvisor:** "service was top notch," "absolutely perfect," "very comfortable." ⊠ *801 Bridgeway* ☎ *415/332–0502 or 800/567–9524* ⊕ *www.casamadrona.com* ⇲ *60 rooms, 6 suites* ⌂ *In-room: Wi-Fi. In-hotel: restaurant, spa.*

$$$$ ⛺ **Cavallo Point.** Set in Golden Gate National Park, this luxury hotel and resort's location is truly one of a kind, featuring turn-of-the-20th-century buildings converted into well-appointed yet eco-friendly rooms. **Pros:** stunning views and numerous activities: a cooking school, yoga classes, and nature walks; spa with a tea bar; art gallery. **Cons:** landscaping feels incomplete; isolated from urban amenities. **TripAdvisor:** "excellent location," "beautiful view," "the most comfortable bed." ⊠ *601 Murray Circle, Fort Baker* ☎ *415/339–4700* ⊕ *www.cavallopoint.com* ⇲ *68 historic and 74 contemporary guest rooms* ⌂ *In-room: no a/c (some), Internet, Wi-Fi. In hotel: restaurant, room service, bar, gym, spa, water sports, parking, some pets allowed.*

$$ ⛺ **Hotel Sausalito.** Handmade furniture and tasteful original art and reproductions give this well-run inn the feel of a small European hotel. **Pros:** great staff; excellent central location; feels like home away from home. **Cons:** no room service; some rooms feel cramped. **TripAdvisor:** "reminiscent of the cheap Paris hotels," "great location," "very clean." ⊠ *16 El Portal* ☎ *415/332–0700 or 888/442–0700* ⊕ *www.hotelsausalito.com* ⇲ *14 rooms, 2 suites* ⌂ *In-room: Wi-Fi.*

19

$$$$ ⬚ **The Inn Above Tide.** This is the only hotel in the Bay Area with balconies literally hanging over the water, and each of its rooms has a perfect-10 view that takes in wild Angel Island as well as the city lights across the bay. **Pros:** great complimentary breakfast; minutes from restaurants/attractions; free in-room binoculars let you indulge in the incredible views. **Cons:** costly parking; some rooms are on the small side. **TripAdvisor:** "very comfortable," "stunning view," "wonderful service." ⬚ *30 El Portal* ☎ *415/332–9535 or 800/893–8433* ⊕ *www.innabovetide.com* ➷ *29 rooms, 3 suites* ⬚ *In-room: a/c, Wi-Fi.*

SPORTS AND THE OUTDOORS

Specializing in sea kayaking, **Sea Trek Ocean Kayaking Center** (⬚ *Schoonmaker Point Marina, off Libertyship Way* ☎ *415/488–1000* ⊕ *www.seatrekkayak.com*) offers guided half-day trips underneath the Golden Gate Bridge and full- and half-day trips to Angel Island, both for beginners. Starlight and full-moon paddles are particularly popular. Trips for experienced kayakers, classes, and rentals are also available. Prices start at $20 per hour for rentals; $65 for a three-hour guided trip.

SF Bay Adventures (⬚ *60 Liberty Ship Way, Suite 4* ☎ *415/331–0444* ⊕ *www.sfbayadventures.com*) lead specialized nautical tours out and around the bay. Their expert skippers give sunset and full-moon sails as well as fascinating eco and great-white-shark tours. If you're interested, they can arrange for you to spend the night in a lighthouse or even barbecue on Angel Island.

THE ARTS

The annual **Sausalito Art Festival** (☎ *415/332–3555 or 415/331–3757* ⊕ *www.sausalitoartfestival.org*), held over Labor Day weekend, attracts more than 50,000 people to the northern waterfront area; Blue & Gold Fleet ferries from San Francisco dock at the pier adjacent to the festival. Tickets are $20.

SHOPPING

Sausalito Ferry Co. This somewhat eccentric but fun local shop is a great place to buy trendy T-shirts, wallets, and clocks. There are plenty of solar-powered bobbleheads, outrageous cocktail napkins, even one-of-a-kind key chains. There's often a crowd huddled in front of the store admiring the window display. ⬚ *688 Bridgeway* ☎ *415/332–9590* ⊕ *www.sausalitoferry.com.*

Something/Anything Gallery. Right where Broadway ends and curves toward the dock, this gallery has a huge array of jewelry and gifts, from unique watches to humorous pendants. With friendly service and carefully crafted mementos of Sausalito, it's easy to find an inexpensive souvenir. ⬚ *20 Princess St.* ☎ *415/339–8831.*

TIBURON

2 mi north of Sausalito, 7 mi north of Golden Gate Bridge.

On a peninsula that was called Punta de Tiburon (Shark Point) by the Spanish explorers, this beautiful Marin County community retains the feel of a village, despite the encroachment of commercial establishments from the downtown area. The harbor faces Angel Island across Raccoon

Strait, and San Francisco is directly south across the bay—which makes the views from the decks of harbor restaurants a major attraction. Tiburon is slightly more low-key than Sausalito, and the community favors Sunday brunch and cocktail hour. Since its incarnation, in 1884, when ferries from San Francisco connected the point with a railroad to San Rafael, the town has centered on the waterfront. ■TIP→ The ferry is the most relaxing (and fastest) way to get here whenever the weather is pleasant, particularly in summer, allowing you to skip traffic and parking problems. Think about avoiding a midweek visit to Tiburon. Although there will be fewer strollers on the street, most shops close either Tuesday or Wednesday, or both.

ESSENTIALS
Visitor Information Tiburon Peninsula Chamber of Commerce (✉ 96-B Main St. ☎ 415/435–5633 ⊕ www.tiburonchamber.org).

GETTING HERE AND AROUND
By car, head north from San Francisco on U.S.-101 and take the CA 131 exit toward Tiburon Boulevard/East Blithedale Avenue. Tiburon Boulevard goes briefly inland, then hugs the bay with remarkable views; it's just over 4 mi from the freeway to downtown. Golden Gate Transit buses 8 and 19 will also take you from San Francisco to downtown Tiburon, as will the Blue & Gold Fleet Ferry service. Tiburon's Main Street is made for wandering down, as are the footpaths that frame the water's edge.

EXPLORING
Ark Row. Past the pink-brick bank building, Main Street is known as Ark Row, and has a tree-shaded walk lined with antiques and specialty stores. Look closely, and you can see that some of the buildings are actually old houseboats. They floated in Belvedere Cove before being beached and transformed into stores. If you're curious about architectural history, the Tiburon Heritage & Arts Commission prints a self-guided walking-tour map, which you can pick up at local businesses. ✉ Ark Row, parallel to Main St. ⊕ www.landmarks-society.org

Main Street. Tiburon's narrow Main Street is on the bay side; you can browse the shops and galleries or relax on a restaurant's deck jutting out over the harbor.

Old St. Hilary's Landmark and Wildflower Preserve. The stark-white Old St. Hilary's Landmark and Wildflower Preserve, an 1886 Carpenter Gothic church barged over from Strawberry Point in 1957, overlooks the town and the bay from its hillside perch. ■TIP→ The church is surrounded by a wildflower preserve that's spectacular in May and June, when the rare black jewel flower blooms. Expect a steep walk uphill to reach the preserve. ✉ 201 Esperanza St., off Mar West St. ☎ 415/435–1853 ⊕ www.landmarks-society.org ⫎ $2 suggested donation ☉ Apr.–Oct., Wed. and Sun. 1–4 and by appointment.

Windsor Vineyards. Remodeled in 2007, this vineyard gives free tastings of its Sonoma County wines (head for the chardonnay) in a converted 19th-century rooming house on Ark Row. ✉ 72 Main St. ☎ 415/435–3113 ⊕ www.windsorvineyards.com ☉ Fri. and Sat. 10–7, Sun.–Thurs. 10–6.

19

WHERE TO EAT

$$$
AMERICAN

✗ **The Caprice.** For more than 50 years this Tiburon landmark has been the place to come to mark special occasions. Perched on a cliff overlooking the bay, it boasts views that are truly spectacular. Looking out from your table it almost feels as if you're eating on water. The soft-yellow walls and starched white tablecloths help to make the space bright and light. Elegant comfort food is their premise, with choices like seared day boat scallops or pan-roasted filet mignon. Polishing off the warm chocolate cake with almond ice cream while gazing out at the sunset and porpoises bobbing in the waves below is a near perfect end to the evening. ⊠ *2000 Paradise Dr.* ☎ *415/435–3400*⊕ *www.thecaprice.com* ◉ *Closed Mon.*

$$–$$$
MEXICAN

✗ **Guaymas.** The festive Guaymas restaurant at the ferry terminal claims a knockout view of the bay, handsome whitewashed adobe walls, tile floors, and a heated terrace bar—and it serves a top-notch margarita. A large open kitchen churns out fairly authentic Mexican dishes such as ceviche, *carnitas uruapan* (slow-roasted pork with salsa and black beans), mesquite-grilled fish, tamales, and a long list of others. ■**TIP**➜ Sunday lunch is very popular, so make a reservation. ⊠ *5 Main St.* ☎ *415/435–6300* ⚞ *Reservations essential.*

¢–$
AMERICAN

✗ **New Morning Cafe.** If you ran straight for the morning ferry and didn't have time to eat, nab breakfast at this homey café with cozy booths and bright tablecloths. Omelets and scrambles are served all day long alongside more innovative egg dishes such as the "Scrumptious," which mixes in vegetables. If you're past morning treats, choose from the many soups, salads, and sandwiches. It's open 6:30 am–2:30 pm weekdays and 6:30 am–4 pm weekends. ⊠ *1696 Tiburon Blvd.* ☎ *415/435–4315* ◉ *No dinner.*

$$–$$$
AMERICAN

✗ **Sam's Anchor Cafe.** Open since 1921, this casual dockside restaurant with mahogany wainscoting is the town's most famous eatery. Today most people flock here for the deck, where out-of-towners and old salts sit shoulder to shoulder for bay views, beer, seafood, and Ramos fizzes. The lunch menu has the usual suspects—burgers, sandwiches, salads, fried fish with tartar sauce—and you'll sit on plastic chairs at tables covered with blue-and-white-checked oilcloths. At night you can find standard seafood dishes with vegetarian and meat options. Expect a wait for outside tables on weekends (there are no reservations for deck seating or weekend lunch). Mind the seagulls; they know no restraint. ⊠ *27 Main St.* ☎ *415/435–4527.*

$
PIZZA

✗ **Waypoint Pizza.** A nautical decor theme and a tasty "between the sheets" pizza-style sandwich are signatures of this creative pizzeria that also serves slices and whole gourmet pies. Booths are brightened with blue-checked tablecloths, and a playful air is added by indoor deck chairs, a picnic table complete with umbrella, and lighthouse salt-and-pepper shakers. If you're dining alone, peruse the aluminum rack for an excellent selection of magazines and newspapers. ⊠ *15 Main St.* ☎ *415/435–3440.*

WHERE TO STAY

$$–$$$ ⬚ **Waters Edge Hotel.** Checking into this elegant hotel feels like tucking
★ away into a inviting retreat by the water—the views are stunning and
the lighting is perfect. **Pros:** complimentary wine and cheese for guests
every evening; restaurants/sights are minutes away. **Cons:** no room service; fitness center is off-site; not a great place to bring small children.
TripAdvisor: "very helpful," "a breakfast to die for," "view and staff
are wonderful." ✉ *25 Main St.* ☎ *415/789–5999 or 877/789–5999*
⊕ *www.marinhotels.com* ⤵ *23 rooms* ⚐ *In-room: Wi-Fi.*

SHOPPING

☞ **The Candy Store on Main Street.** If you long for sheets of candy dots or
chewy wax bottles, come here to score the retro candy of your childhood. There's also ice cream, freshly made fudge, and a space-age-
looking dispenser for pucker powder. ✉ *7 Main St.* ☎ *415/435–0434.*

Ruth Livingston Studio. The namesake owner of this design showcase and
walk-in shop will greet you and explain the concepts behind her neo-
modern pieces. Find everything from striking vases to one-of-a-kind
furniture. ✉ *74 Main St.* ☎ *415/435–5264.*

Schoenberg Guitars. Small, narrow, and chockablock with handmade
guitars, this shop is a treat even for those who don't play music. Dozens, if not hundreds, of guitars varying in size, shape, and color hang
from the walls and stand against the polished wood floor. There is an
organized beauty to the layout of this place and a comforting sense of
musical harmony. ✉ *106 Main St.* ☎ *415/789–0846.*

MILL VALLEY

2 mi north of Sausalito, 4 mi north of Golden Gate Bridge.

One of just a few towns that are simultaneously woodsy and chic, Mill
Valley has a dual personality. Here, as elsewhere in the county, the
foundation is a superb natural setting. Virtually surrounded by parkland, the town lies at the base of Mt. Tamalpais, the Bay Area's tallest
mountain, and includes dense redwood groves traversed by countless
creeks. But this is no lumber camp. Smart restaurants and chichi boutiques line the streets, and more rock stars than one might suspect make
their homes here.

19

The rustic village flavor is not a modern conceit but a holdover from
the town's early days as a logging camp. In 1896 the Mill Valley and
Mt. Tamalpais Scenic Railroad—called "the crookedest railroad in the
world" because of its curvy tracks—began transporting visitors from
Mill Valley to the top of Mt. Tam and down to Muir Woods, and the
town soon became a vacation retreat for joyriding city slickers. The
trains stopped running in the 1940s, but you can see the old railway
depot: the 1924 building has been transformed into the popular Depot
Bookstore & Cafe, at 87 Throckmorton Avenue.

The small downtown area, no more than five blocks square, has the
constant bustle of a leisure community; even at noon on a Tuesday,
people are out shopping for fancy cookware and lacy pajamas.

ESSENTIALS

Visitor Information Mill Valley Chamber of Commerce (⊠ *85 Throckmorton Ave.* ☎ *415/388–9700* ⊕ *www.millvalley.org*).

GETTING HERE AND AROUND

By car, from San Francisco head north on U.S. 101 then exit at East Blithedale, continue west on East Blithedale to Throckmorton Avenue; turn left to reach Lytton Square, then park. The Golden Gate Transit Route 4 bus leaves for Mill Valley from 8th and Folsom (downtown San Francisco) every 30 minutes during commute hours. Check their schedule for details. Once here, explore the streets on foot; the town is great for strolling.

EXPLORING

Lytton Square. In the center of it all is this square, at the corner of Miller and Throckmorton avenues, where locals and visitors congregate on weekends to socialize in the many coffeehouses.

Old Mill Park. To see one of the numerous outdoor oases that make Mill Valley so appealing, follow Throckmorton Avenue ¼ mi south from Lytton Square to Old Mill Park, a shady patch of redwoods that shelters a playground and reconstructed sawmill. From the park, Cascade Drive winds its way past creek-side homes to the trailheads of several forest paths.

OFF THE BEATEN PATH

Marin County Civic Center. This wonder of arches, circles, and skylights was Frank Lloyd Wright's last major architectural undertaking. You can wander about on your own or take a docent-led tour of the complex. Tours ($5) leave from the gift shop, on the second floor, on Wednesday mornings at 10:30. If you can't make it on a Wednesday, pick up the self-guided tour map for 50¢ at the gift shop. Don't miss the photographs on the first floor, which show Marin County homes designed by Wright. There's also an excellent California library here for bibliophiles and oral-history buffs. ⊠ *3501 Civic Center Dr., on San Pedro Rd., San Rafael* ☎ *415/499–7009* ⊠ *Free* ⊙ *Weekdays 8–5.*

WHERE TO EAT

$$–$$$
AMERICAN
✕ **The Balboa Café.** With intimate lighting, rich wood accents, and fresh-pressed white linens, this café offers an upscale dining experience. Hanging on the walls are old black-and-white photos depicting Mill Valley in its lumber years. The bar is so busy that you'll be lucky if your elbow gets anywhere near it. Although the cocktails are not as stiff as their price tags, the food is creative, local, and beautifully presented. Try the Black Angus rib eye, wild-mushroom risotto, or seared sea scallops—and be sure to save room for the blueberry brioche bread pudding. The wine list is extensive, and even offers wines from Marin County. If you prefer something on the lighter side, they purify and carbonate their own water. ⊠ *38 Miller Ave.* ☎ *415/381–7321* ⋈ *Reservations essential.*

$$–$$$
AMERICAN
✕ **Buckeye Roadhouse.** This is Mill Valley's secret den of decadence, where house-smoked meats and fish, grilled steaks, and old-fashioned dishes such as brisket bring the locals coming back for more. They also serve beautiful organic, locally grown salads and desserts so heavenly—like their rich but light crème brûlée—you'll just about melt into

the floor. The look of the 1937 roadhouse is decidedly hunting-lodge chic, with trophy heads and a river-rock fireplace dominating one wall. Marin County's Jaguar-driving bon vivants pack the place every night. The busy but cozy bar with elegant mahogany paneling and soft lighting is a good place to quench your thirst for a Marin martini or Californian merlot. ⊠ *15 Shoreline Hwy.* ☎ *415/331–2600* ⚞ *Reservations essential.*

$ ✕ **Champagne.** This adorable little bakery/café on Mill Valley's main
FRENCH/ street is a nice place to pop into for breakfast, a light lunch,
AMERICAN dinner, or afternoon pick-me-up. Filled with light, authentic French decor and only a dozen tables, Champagne serves amazing crepes with roasted chicken, creamed spinach, and Swiss cheese, as well as an assortment of savory flat breads—try the pesto-and-tomato version. It's a popular place for breakfast, too, with a wide selection of omelets, as well as the perennial favorite: brioche French toast with bacon. The afternoon crowd keeps the tables busy as they chat over cappuccinos, raspberry-almond croissants, and meringue cookies. There's also a tempting assortment of baked goods to take home with you. ⊠ *41 Throckmorton Ave.* ☎ *415/380–0410.*

$$ ✕ **The Dipsea Cafe.** There is no better place for breakfast than the Dipsea,
AMERICAN which is named after the gorgeous trail that stretches from Mill Valley to Stinson Beach. Locals crowd its cozy interior most mornings, but weekends are especially popular. Choose from huge plates of French toast, eggs Benedict, and huevos rancheros; the homemade fries and jam that accompany the breakfast entrées are to die for. The café also serves hearty lunches, like Chinese salad with seared salmon and enormous BLTs. This is a great spot to fuel up on your way to Muir Woods or Stinson Beach. ⊠ *200 Shoreline Hwy.* ☎ *415/381–0298* ☉ *No dinner Sun.–Thurs.*

$ ✕ **Joe's Taco Lounge.** A funky, bright lounge (and it really does feel like
MEXICAN someone's lounge), this is a fun place to go for a casual, cheap, and delicious Mexican meal. There are all sorts of colorful relics on the walls, and chili-pepper lights adorn the windows. The signature dishes are fish tacos and snapper burritos—which are generous in both size and flavor. The organic burger with spicy fries and the fire-grilled corn on the cob are also yummy. Choose from a wide selection of Mexican beers or go for a wine-based margarita, which is refreshingly tasty. This is a popular place for families between 5 and 7 pm. ⊠ *382 Miller Ave.* ☎ *415/383–8164.*

$$–$$$ ✕ **Lark Creek Inn.** Occupying a refurbished 100-year-old house sur-
NEW AMERICAN rounded by lush, mature gardens and towering redwoods, this is one of
★ Marin's prettiest—and best—restaurants, especially for Sunday brunch. The menu, which changes daily, highlights top-notch meats and organic produce from local farmers. Try the Caesar salad, which boasts a secret ingredient and is succulently presented with whole leaf spears. Butterscotch pudding, their signature dessert, sounds humble, but has deep flavor. Sit outside on the patio or inside the country-elegant dining room beneath a dramatic greenhouse ceiling. Be mindful that all this beauty of place and its plates comes at a price. ⊠ *234 Magnolia Ave., Larkspur* ☎ *415/924–7766* ⚞ *Reservations essential* ☉ *No lunch Mon.–Sat.*

19

$$–$$$
FRENCH

✗ **Left Bank.** Provincial France meets Northern California at this convivial, bustling brasserie with a gigantic stone hearth and whimsical French posters. The menu packs in hearty dishes such as bouillabaisse, braised oxtail with homemade noodles, steak and french fries, and a succulent fondue of local goat, Brie, and blue cheeses. For dessert, you'll have to go to Lyon to find better profiteroles. The service can be erratic, and the plank floors and high ceilings can make things noisy, but this place is fun. ■TIP→ For quieter conversation and maximum romance, sit outside on the wraparound veranda. Check the Web site for special event dinners, such as tie-ins to celebrations of cookbooks by local writers or evenings that include live music. ⊠ *507 Magnolia Ave., Larkspur* ☎ *415/927–3331.*

$$–$$$
ITALIAN

✗ **Piazza D'Angelo.** In the heart of downtown, busy D'Angelo's is known for its osso buco and veal saltimbocca, as well as pastas and delicious crème brûlée. The food is authentic and fresh; another draw is the scene, especially in the lounge area, which hosts a lively cocktail hour packed with beautiful people and serves food until 10 or 11 pm—late for Mill Valley. The sprawling space encompasses a bright front room, romantic booths, and a warm patio. ⊠ *22 Miller Ave.* ☎ *415/388–2000.*

WHERE TO STAY

$$$–$$$$

🏨 **Mill Valley Inn.** The only hotel in downtown Mill Valley has smart-looking rooms done up in Tuscan colors of ocher and olive, with hand-crafted beds, armoires, and lamps by local artisans. **Pros:** minutes from local shops and restaurants; great complimentary continental breakfast. **Cons:** dark in winter months because of surrounding trees; some rooms are not accessible via elevator. **TripAdvisor:** "beautiful view," "great location," "great service." ⊠ *165 Throckmorton Ave.* ☎ *415/389–6608 or 800/595–2100* ⊕ *www.marinhotels.com* ⤴ *25 rooms, 1 suite, 2 cottages* ⚭ *In-room: a/c, Wi-Fi.* ▯◯▯ *Breakfast.*

$$$–$$$$
★

🏨 **Mountain Home Inn.** Abutting 40,000 acres of state and national parks, the inn sits on the skirt of Mt. Tamalpais, where you can follow hiking trails all the way to Stinson Beach. **Pros:** amazing deck and views; peaceful, remote setting. **Cons:** nearest town is a 20-minute drive away; restaurant can get very crowded on sunny weekend days. **TripAdvisor:** "stunning view," "great location," "outstanding service." ⊠ *810 Panoramic Hwy.* ☎ *415/381–9000* ⊕ *www.mtnhomeinn.com* ⤴ *10 rooms* ⚭ *In-room: no a/c, no TV, Wi-Fi. In-hotel: restaurant, bar* ▯◯▯ *Breakfast.*

NIGHTLIFE AND THE ARTS

The well-regarded **Mill Valley Film Festival** (☎ *415/383–5256* ⊕ *www.mvff.com*), held annually in early October, shows everything from features and documentaries to experimental works.

The **Mill Valley Fall Arts Festival** (☎ *415/383–5256* ⊕ *www.mvfaf.org*) takes place in mid-September in Old Mill Park, with live music, a kids' stage, and artisans selling crafts, jewelry, and art.

Beerworks. Serving more than 100 local, national, and international beers, from ale to port to lager, Beerworks truly has a beer for everyone at its long polished bar. They also serve tapas-style foods: cheese plates, olives, homemade pretzels, and sandwiches. It's the perfect place to rest your feet after wandering the town or hiking Mt. Tamalpais. ⊠ *173 Throckmorton Ave.* ☎ *415/336–3596.*

SHOPPING

The area around Throckmorton Avenue in downtown Mill Valley brims with stylish and quirky stores—indies as well as chains. One of the chains, Banana Republic, actually began life here as a small safari-focused retailer.

Book Passage. This sprawling independent bookstore in nearby Corte Madera is a magnet for book lovers. The calendar of author events is packed with readings by such big names as Alice Walker, Calvin Trillin, Michael Connelly, and Peter Mayle. Pick-me-up snacks are available at the in-store café. ⊠ *The Marketplace, 51 Tamal Vista Blvd., Corte Madera* ☎ *415/927–0960 or 800/999–7909.*

Jay Lina's. Budget fashionistas are lured into this chic consignment store, where Prada dresses, Seven jeans, even Channel bags are offered at reasonable prices. The items are carefully selected and easy to find; no need to rummage crowded racks. ⊠ *19 E. Blithedale Ave.* ☎ *415/388–4682.*

Maison Rêve. French farmhouse meets contemporary style here. Clusters of interesting objects, such as vintage glass bottles, gather gracefully in vignettes. The price range is admirable, with unique finds possible at a reasonable cost. They also have charming children's gifts. ⊠ *108 Throckmorton Ave.* ☎ *415/383–9700.*

Summer House. All sorts of surprises pile up here. For the home: lavish pillows and decorative objects. For the body: scented potions and soaps. To decorate both: stunning jewelry, tableware, and tempting shirts. Ask about their warehouse for furniture, or better yet, their warehouse sales. ⊠ *21 Throckmorton Ave.* ☎ *415/383–6695.*

The Tyler Florence Shop. Stock up here on everything you need for cooking—even kitchen gadgets you didn't know existed. This celebrity chef shop has the works, from chicken-shape hard-boiled-egg holders to charms for crystal flutes, even copper frying pans. And if you want to escape into one of Florence's many cookbooks, there's a little library in the back with leather sofas and animal heads hanging from the wall. ⊠ *59 Throckmorton Ave.* ☎ *415/380–9200* ⊕ *www.tylerflorence.com.*

19

THE MARIN HEADLANDS

★ The term "Golden Gate" may now be synonymous with the world-famous bridge, but it originally referred to the grassy, poppy-strewn hills flanking the passageway into San Francisco Bay. To the north of the gate lie the Marin Headlands, part of the Golden Gate National Recreation Area (GGNRA) and the most dramatic scenery in these parts. The raw beauty of the headlands, which consist of several small but steep bluffs, is particularly striking if you've just come from the enclosed silence of the nearby redwood groves. Windswept hills plunge down to the ocean, and creek-fed thickets shelter swaying wildflowers.

The headlands stretch from the Golden Gate Bridge to Muir Beach. Photographers flock to the southern headlands for shots of the city, with the Golden Gate Bridge in the foreground and the skyline on the horizon.

Equally remarkable are the views north along the coast and out to sea, where the Farallon Islands are visible on clear days. ■**TIP**➔ Almost any of the roads, all very windy, offer great coast views, especially as you drive at higher elevations. You'll see copious markers for scenic spots.

The headlands' strategic position at the mouth of San Francisco Bay made them a logical site for World War II military installations. Today you can explore the crumbling concrete batteries where naval guns protected the approaches from the sea; kids especially love climbing on these structures. The headlands' main attractions are centered on Forts Barry and Cronkhite, which lie just across Rodeo Lagoon from each other. Fronting the lagoon is Rodeo Beach, a dark stretch of sand that attracts sand-castle builders and dog owners.

⚠ Note: The beaches at the Marin Headlands are not safe for swimming. The giant cliffs are steep and unstable, so hiking down them can be dangerous. Stay on trails. Head farther north, to Muir Beach and beyond, for better ocean access.

GETTING HERE AND AROUND

Driving from San Francisco, head north on U.S. 101, then exit on Alexander Avenue. From there take the first left (signs read "San Francisco/U.S. 101 South"), go through the tunnel under the freeway, and turn right up the hill where the sign reads: "Forts Barry and Cronkhite." The MuniBus 76 runs hourly from 4th and Townsend streets to the Marin Headlands Visitor Center on Sunday and major holidays only. Once here, it's important to get out of your car or bus and explore this beautiful countryside.

EXPLORING

Green Gulch Zen Center. Giant eucalyptus trees frame the long winding road that leads to this tranquil retreat. There are mediation programs on Sunday, workshops, and events, as well as an extensive organic garden. Visitors are welcome to roam freely through the acres of gardens that reach down toward Muir Beach. If you follow the main dirt road it will take you to a walking path that brings you to the beach. It's a peaceful walk surrounded by trees, birds, and the ocean breeze. ✉ *1601 Shoreline Hwy., Muir Beach* ☎ *415/383–3134* ⊕ *www.sfzc.org* ➩ *Free* ☉ *Tues.–Sat. 9–noon and 2–4, Sun. 9–10 am.*

Headlands Center for the Arts. If you're an art lover, stop by the Headlands Center for the Arts, where you can see contemporary art in a rustic natural setting. All but one of the center's nine converted military buildings are usually closed to the public, but you can visit the main building (the former barracks) to see several changing installations. The downstairs "archive room" features an odd assortment of objects found and created by residents, such as natural rocks, interesting glass bottles filled with collected items, and unusual masks. Stop by the industrial gallery space, two flights up, to see what the resident visual artists are up to—most of the work is quite contemporary. The center also hosts biweekly public programs, from artist talks to open studios. Call for current schedules. ✉ *944 Fort Barry* ☎ *415/331–2787* ⊕ *www.headlands.org* ☉ *Weekdays 10–5, Sun. noon–5.*

Shutterbugs rejoice in catching a scenic Muir Beach sunset.

Marin Headlands Visitor Center. The Marin Headlands Visitor Center, open daily 9:30–4:30, sells a useful guide to historic sites and wildlife, and has exhibits on the area's history and ecology. Pick up the park newspaper, which has a calendar of events, including a schedule of guided walks. Kids will enjoy the "please touch" educational sites and small play area inside. ⊠ *Fort Barry, Field and Bunker Rds., Bldg. 948* ☎ *415/331–1540* ⊕ *www.nps.gov/goga/marin-headlands.htm.*

🕒 **Marine Mammal Center.** If you're curious about the rehabilitation of sea life in the Pacific, stop by this hospital for rescued seals, sea lions, dolphins, and otters. You can glimpse the mammals convalescing in the pool out front, then visit the small gift shop. You can still look in on the preserved military base mess hall, pet a sealskin inside the gift shop, or watch the seal cam. ⊠ *2000 Bunker Rd., Fort Cronkhite* ☎ *415/289–7325* ⊕ *www.tmmc.org.*

🕒 **Muir Beach.** Small but scenic, this beach—a rocky patch of shoreline off Route 1 in the northern headlands—is a good place to stretch your legs and gaze out at the Pacific. Locals often walk their dogs here; families and cuddling couples come for picnicking and sunbathing. At one end of the sand is a cluster of waterfront homes, and at the other are the bluffs of Golden Gate National Recreation Area. The beach also has an interesting history—Janis Joplin's ashes are scattered here among the sands and this is where Ken Kesey hosted his second Acid Test.

🕒 **Point Bonita Lighthouse.** At the end of Conzelman Road, in the southern ★ headlands, is the Point Bonita Lighthouse, a restored beauty that still guides ships to safety with its original 1855 refractory lens. Half the fun of a visit is the steep ½-mi walk from the parking area down to the lighthouse, which takes you through a rock tunnel and across a suspension bridge. Signposts along the way detail the bravado of surfmen, as the early lifeguards were called, and the tenacity of the "wickies," the first keepers of the light. ⊠ *End of Conzelman Rd.* ☎ *Free* ⊙ *Sat.–Mon. 12:30–3:30.*

WHERE TO STAY

¢ 🏨 **Marin Headlands Hostel.** As hostels go, it's hard to beat this beautifully situated, well-maintained property in a valley on the north side of the headlands, the only lodging in the GGNRA that isn't a campsite. **Pros:** plenty of peace and quiet; great prices; rural setting. **Cons:** no Wi-Fi; difficult to get to without a car or bike; far from restaurants and shops. **TripAdvisor:** "warm and welcoming," "a hidden gem," "cool location." ⊠ *941 Fort Barry* ☎ *415/331–2777* ⊕ *www.norcalhostels.org/ marin* ⤵ *7 private rooms, 8 dormitory rooms; all with shared bath* ⚐ *In-room: no a/c, no TV.*

$$$–$$$$ 🏨 **Pelican Inn.** From its slate roof to its whitewashed plaster walls, this
★ inn looks so Tudor that it's hard to believe it was built in the 1970s. **Pros:** five-minute walk to beach; great bar and restaurant; peaceful setting. **Cons:** 20-minute drive to nearby attractions; no Wi-Fi or wheelchair access to bedrooms. **TripAdvisor:** "quiet and beautifully decorated," "old world English charm," "food was perfect." ⊠ *10 Pacific Way, off Rte. 1, Muir Beach* ☎ *415/383–6000* ⊕ *www.pelicaninn.com* ⤵ *7 rooms* ⚐ *In-room: no a/c, no TV. In-hotel: restaurant, bar* ⎟⊙⎟ *Breakfast.*

MUIR WOODS NATIONAL MONUMENT

⟳ *12 mi northwest of the Golden Gate Bridge.*

Fodor's Choice
★

GETTING HERE AND AROUND

To get here from San Francisco by car, take U.S. 101 north across the Golden Gate Bridge to the Mill Valley/Stinson Beach exit, then follow signs to Highway 1 north. On weekends and holidays, Memorial Day through Labor Day, Golden Gate Transit operates a shuttle ($3 round-trip) from Mill Valley every half hour. Park in Marin City at the Gateway Shopping Center (look for lighted signs directing you from U.S. 101) or at the Manzanita Park-and-Ride, at the Highway 1 exit off U.S. 101 (look for the lot under the elevated freeway), or take connecting bus service from San Francisco with Golden Gate Transit. Once here, you need to explore the wilderness. Get out of your machine and wander through this pristine patch of nature.

EXPLORING

Muir Woods National Monument. One hundred fifty million years ago, ancestors of redwood and sequoia trees grew throughout the United States. Today the *Sequoia sempervirens* can be found only in a narrow, cool coastal belt from Monterey to Oregon. The 550 acres of Muir Woods National Monument contain some of the most majestic redwoods in the world—some nearly 250 feet tall and 1,000 years old. The stand was saved from destruction in 1905, when it was purchased by a couple who donated it to the federal government. Three years later it was named after naturalist John Muir, whose environmental

DID YOU KNOW?

The gorgeous old-growth redwood trees in Muir Woods are often enveloped in fog, a useful dampness for the trees, especially to counteract the dry summers.

campaigns helped to establish the national park system. His response: "This is the best tree lover's monument that could be found in all of the forests of the world. Saving these woods from the ax and saw is in many ways the most notable service to God and man I have heard of since my forest wandering began."

Muir Woods, part of the Golden Gate National Recreation Area, is a pedestrian's park. The trails vary in difficulty and length. Beginning from the park headquarters, a 2-mi, wheelchair-accessible **loop trail** crosses streams and passes ferns and azaleas, as well as magnificent redwood groves. Among the most famous are **Bohemian Grove** and the circular formation called **Cathedral Grove**. On summer weekends visitors oohing and aahing in a dozen languages line the trail. If you prefer a little more serenity, consider the challenging **Dipsea Trail,** which climbs west from the forest floor to soothing views of the ocean and the Golden Gate Bridge. For a complete list of trails, check with rangers, who can also help you pick the best one for your ability level.

■TIP➔ The weather in Muir Woods is usually cool and often wet, so wear warm clothes and shoes appropriate for damp trails. Picnicking and camping aren't allowed, and pets aren't permitted. Parking can be difficult here—the lots are small and the crowds are large—so try to come early in the morning or late in the afternoon. The **Muir Woods Visitor Center** has a wide selection of books and exhibits on redwood trees and the history of Muir Woods. ⊠ *Panoramic Hwy. off Hwy. 1, approximately 12 mi north of Golden Gate Bridge* ☎ *415/388–2595 park information, 415/925–4501 shuttle information* ⊕ *www.nps.gov/muwo* ⛝ *$5* ⊙ *Daily 8 am–sunset.*

MT. TAMALPAIS STATE PARK

16 mi northwest of Golden Gate Bridge.

GETTING HERE AND AROUND

By car, take the Route 1–Stinson Beach exit off U.S. 101 and follow Route 1 west and then north. From San Francisco the trip can take from 30 minutes up to an hour, depending on traffic. By bus, take the 10, 70 or 80 to Marin City; in Marin City transfer to the West Marin Stagecoach. Call or check online for routes and schedules (☎ *415/226–0855* ⊕ *www.marintransit.org/stage.html*). Once here, the only way to explore is on foot or by bike.

EXPLORING

Mt. Tamalpais State Park. Although the summit of Mt. Tamalpais is only 2,571 feet high, the mountain rises practically from sea level, dominating the topography of Marin County. Adjacent to Muir Woods National Monument, Mt. Tamalpais State Park affords views of the entire Bay Area and the Pacific Ocean to the west. The mountain was sacred to Native Americans, who saw in its profile—as you can see today—the silhouette of a sleeping Indian maiden. Locals fondly refer to it as the "Sleeping Lady." For years the 6,300-acre park has been a favorite destination for hikers. There are more than 200 mi of trails, some rugged but many developed for easy walking through meadows, grasslands, and forests and along creeks. Mt. Tam, as it's called by locals, is also the birthplace (in the 1970s) of mountain biking, and today many spandex-clad bikers whiz down the park's winding roads.

The park's major thoroughfare, the Panoramic Highway, snakes its way up from U.S. 101 to the **Pantoll Ranger Station** (⊠ *3801 Panoramic Hwy., at Pantoll Rd.* ☎ *415/388–2070* ⊕ *www.parks.ca.gov*). The office is staffed sporadically, depending on funding, but if you leave a phone message, a ranger will call you back (within several days) during business hours. From the ranger station, the Panoramic Highway drops down to the town of Stinson Beach. Pantoll Road branches off the highway at the station, connecting up with Ridgecrest Boulevard. Along these roads are numerous parking areas, picnic spots, scenic overlooks, and trailheads. Parking is free along the roadside, but there's a fee at the ranger station and at some of the other parking lots.

ᘓ The **Mountain Theater,** also known as the Cushing Memorial Theater, is a natural amphitheater just off Ridgecrest Boulevard. Constructed in the 1930s, the theater has terraced stone seats for 3,750 people. Every May and June hundreds of locals tote overstuffed picnic baskets up the short trail to the Mountain Theater to see the **Mountain Play** (☎ *415/383–1100* ⊕ *www.mountainplay.org*), a presentation of popular musicals such as *The Music Man* and *My Fair Lady*. Depending on the play, this can be a great family activity. The **Rock Spring Trail** starts at the Mountain Theater and gently climbs about 1¾ mi to the **West Point Inn,** once a stop on the Mt. Tam railroad route. Relax at a picnic table and stock up on water before forging ahead, via Old Railroad Grade Fire Road and the Miller Trail, to Mt. Tam's Middle Peak, about 2 mi uphill.

Starting from the Pan Toll Ranger Station, the precipitous **Steep Ravine Trail** brings you past stands of coastal redwoods and, in the springtime, numerous small waterfalls. Take the connecting **Dipsea Trail** to reach the town of Stinson Beach and its swath of golden sand. If you're too weary to make the 3½-mi trek back up, Golden Gate Transit Bus 63 (Saturday, Sunday, and holidays from mid-March through early December) takes you from Stinson Beach back to the ranger station.

19

STINSON BEACH

20 mi northwest of Golden Gate Bridge.

GETTING HERE AND AROUND

If you're driving, take the Route 1–Stinson Beach exit off U.S. 101 and follow Route 1 west and then north. The journey from San Francisco can take from 30 minutes to more than an hour, depending on traffic. By bus, take the 10, 70, or 80 to Marin City; in Marin City transfer to the West Marin Stagecoach. Call or check online for routes and schedules. The town is intimate and perfect for casual walking.

EXPLORING

ᘓ **Stinson Beach.** Stinson Beach is the most expansive stretch of sand in Marin County. It's as close (when the fog hasn't rolled in) as you can get to the stereotypical feel of a Southern California beach.

⚠ Swimming here is recommended only from early May through September, when lifeguards are on duty, because the undertow can be strong and shark sightings, although infrequent, aren't unusual. There are several clothing-optional areas (such as Red Rock Beach). On any hot summer weekend every road to Stinson Beach is jam-packed, so factor this into your plans. The town itself is very down to earth—like tonier Mill Valley, but more relaxed.

WHERE TO EAT AND STAY

$$–$$$ ✕ **Parkside Cafe.** Most people know the Parkside for its beachfront snack
AMERICAN bar (cash only), but inside is the best restaurant in Stinson Beach. The food is classic Cal cuisine, with appetizers such as day-boat scallops, ceviche, and mains such as lamb with goat-cheese-stuffed red peppers. Breakfast, a favorite among locals, is served until 2 pm. Eat on the sunny patio, which is sheltered from the wind by creeping vines, or by the fire in the contemporary dining room. ✉ *43 Arenal Ave.* ☎ *415/868–1272.*

$$–$$$ ✕ **Sand Dollar.** The town's oldest restaurant still attracts all the old salts
AMERICAN from Muir Beach to Bolinas, but these days they sip whiskey over an up-to-date bar or beneath market umbrellas on the spiffy deck. The food is good—try the panfried sand dabs (small flatfish) and pear salad with blue cheese—but the big draw is the lively atmosphere. Musicians play on weekends in summer, and on sunny afternoons the deck gets so packed that people sit on the fence rails sipping beer. ✉ *3458 Rte. 1* ☎ *415/868–0434* ⊘ *No lunch Tues. Nov.–Mar.*

$–$$ ⌷ **Stinson Beach Motel.** Built in the 1930s, this motel surrounds three courtyards that burst with flowering greenery, and rooms are immaculate, simple, and summery, with freshly painted walls, good mattresses, and some kitchenettes. **Pros:** minutes from the beach; cozy, unpretentious rooms. **Cons:** smaller rooms feel a little cramped; not much to do once the sun sets. **TripAdvisor:** "tiny but nice," "well-maintained," "great value." ✉ *3416 Hwy. 1* ☎ *415/868–1712* ⊕ *www.stinsonbeachmotel.com* ⤳ *7 rooms* ⌂ *In-room: no a/c, kitchen (some), Wi-Fi (some).*

BOLINAS

7 mi north of Stinson Beach.

The tiny town of Bolinas wears its 1960s idealism on its sleeve, attracting potters, poets, and peace lovers to its quiet streets. With a funky gallery, a general store selling organic produce, a café, and an offbeat saloon, the main thoroughfare, Wharf Road, looks like a hippie-fied version of Main Street USA.

GETTING HERE AND AROUND

Although privacy-seeking locals openly dislike tourism and have torn down signs to the town, Bolinas isn't difficult to find: heading north from Stinson Beach follow Route 1 west and then north. Make a left at the first road just past the Bolinas Lagoon (Bolinas–Olema Road), and then turn left at the stop sign. The road dead-ends smack-dab in the middle of the tiny town, so drive slowly lest you find yourself in a confrontation with an angry local. By bus, take the 10, 70, or 80 to Marin City; in Marin City transfer to the West Marin Stagecoach. Call or check online for routes and schedules. The town is small; walking is the only way to see it.

WHERE TO EAT

$$–$$$ ✕ **Coast Cafe.** Decked out in a nautical theme with surfboards and buoys, AMERICAN the dining room at the Coast serves dependably good American fare, including specials such as shepherd's pie, pot roast, local fresh fish, grass-fed steaks, and gorgeous salads. It's also open for breakfast on weekends. ✉ *46 Wharf Rd.* ☎ *415/868–2298.*

POINT REYES NATIONAL SEASHORE

Fodor's Choice *Bear Valley Visitor Center is 12 mi north of Bolinas.*
★

GETTING HERE AND AROUND

Take the Route 1–Stinson Beach exit off U.S. 101 if you're driving, and follow Route 1 west and then north toward McKennas Gulch Fire Road. Turn left at Sir Francis Drake Boulevard. If you're going by bus, take the 10, 70, or 80 to Marin City; in Marin City transfer to the West Marin Stagecoach. Call or check online for routes and schedules. Once you arrive, the best way to get around is on foot.

EXPLORING

Point Reyes National Seashore. One of the Bay Area's most spectacular treasures and the only national seashore on the West Coast, the 66,500-acre Point Reyes National Seashore (⊕ *www.nps.gov/pore*) encompasses hiking trails, secluded beaches, and rugged grasslands as well as **Point Reyes** itself, a triangular peninsula that juts into the Pacific. The town is a quaint, one-main-drag affair, with a charming bakery, some good gift shops with imported goods, and a few places to eat. It's nothing fancy, but that's part of its relaxed charm.

The infamous San Andreas Fault runs along the eastern edge of the park and up the center of Tomales Bay; take the short **Earthquake Trail** from the visitor center to see the impact near the epicenter of the 1906 earthquake that devastated San Francisco. A ½-mi path from the visitor center leads to **Kule Loklo,** a brilliantly reconstructed Miwok village that sheds light on the daily lives of the region's first inhabitants. From here trails also lead to the park's free campgrounds (camping permits are required).

19

■TIP➜ In late winter and spring, wildlife enthusiasts should make a stop at Chimney Rock, just before the lighthouse, and take the short walk to the Elephant Seal Overlook. Even from up on the cliff, the males look enormous as they spar for the resident females.

Bear Valley Visitor Center. The Bear Valley Visitor Center, open weekdays 9–5 and weekends 8–5, has informative exhibits about the park wildlife. Rangers here dispense information about beaches, whale-watching, hiking trails, and camping. ✉ *Bear Valley Rd. west of Rte. 1* ☎ *415/464–5100* ⊕ *www.nps.gov/pore/planyourvisit/visitorcenters.htm.*

Duxbury Reef. Mile-long Duxbury Reef is the largest shale intertidal reef in North America. Look for starfish, barnacles, sea anemones, purple urchins, limpets, sea mussels, and the occasional abalone. But check a tide table (⊕ *www.wrh.noaa.gov/mtr/marine.php*) or the local papers if you plan to explore the reef—it's accessible only at low tide. To get here, take Mesa Road and turn left onto Overlook Drive and then right on Elm Avenue.

Point Reyes Bird Observatory. In the southernmost part of Point Reyes National Seashore, accessed through Bolinas, is the free Point Reyes Bird Observatory. Those not interested in birds might find it ho-hum, but birders adore it. The compact visitor center, open daily 9–5, is small yet has excellent interpretive exhibits, including a comparative display of real birds' talons. What really warrants a visit, though, are the surrounding woods, which harbor nearly 225 bird species. As you hike the quiet trails through forest and along ocean cliffs, you're likely to see biologists banding birds to aid in the study of their life cycles. ⊠ *Mesa Rd.* ☎ *415/868–0655* ⊕ *www.prbo.org*

☺ ★ **Point Reyes Lighthouse.** In operation since December 1, 1870, this lighthouse is one of the premier attractions of the Point Reyes National Seashore. It occupies the tip of Point Reyes, 22 mi from the Bear Valley Visitor Center, a scenic 45-minute drive over hills scattered with old cattle ranches. The lighthouse originally cast a rotating beam lighted by four wicks that burned lard oil. Keeping the wicks lighted and the lens soot-free in Point Reyes's perpetually foggy climate was a constant struggle that reputedly drove the early attendants to alcoholism and insanity. On busy whale-watching weekends (late December through mid-April), parking at the forged-iron-plate lighthouse may be restricted by park staff; on these days buses shuttle visitors from the Drakes Beach lot to the top of the stairs leading down to the lighthouse (bus $5, admission free). Once there, consider whether you have it in you to walk down—and up—the 308 steps to the lighthouse. The view from the bottom is worth the effort, but the whales are visible from the cliffs above the lighthouse. ⊠ *Western end of Sir Francis Drake Blvd.* ☎ *415/669–1534* ☻ *Thurs.–Mon. 10–4:30; weather lens room 2:30–4, except during very windy weather*

WHERE TO EAT

¢–$
AMERICAN
☺
✗ **Pine Cone Diner.** For California country-kitchen cooking, the Pine Cone is where it's at. A block off the main drag, this oh-so-cute diner serves great traditional breakfasts as well as Mexican specialties such as huevos rancheros. At lunch expect hearty homemade soups, fresh salads, and thick sandwiches, all made with local, organic ingredients. The dinner menu has a good selection of comfort food. ■TIP➔ Kids love the outdoor picnic tables. ⊠ *60 4th St., Point Reyes Station* ☎ *415/663–1536* ☻ *No dinner.*

$$–$$$
AMERICAN
✗ **Station House Cafe.** In good weather hikers fresh from the park fill the garden to enjoy alfresco dining, and on weekends there's not a spare seat on the banquettes in the wide-open dining room. The focus is on traditional American food—fresh popovers hit the table as soon as you arrive—and there's a little of everything on the menu. Grilled salmon, barbecued oysters, and burgers are all predictable hits. The place is also open for breakfast, and there's a full bar, too. ⊠ *11180 Rte. 1, Point Reyes Station* ☎ *415/663–1515* ☻ *Closed Wed.*

¢–$ ✕**Tomales Bay Foods.** A renovated hay barn off the main drag houses this
AMERICAN   collection of food shops, a favorite stopover among Bay Area foodies.
★   Watch workers making Cowgirl Creamery cheese; then buy some at a
counter that sells exquisite artisanal cheeses from around the world.
Tomales Bay Foods showcases local organic fruits and vegetables and
premium packaged foods, and the kitchen turns the best ingredients
into creative sandwiches, salads, and soups. You can eat at a small café
table or on the lawn or take it away for a picnic. The shops are open
until 6 pm. ✉ *80 4th St., Point Reyes Station* ☎ *415/663–9335 cheese
shop, 415/663–8478 deli* ⊘ *Closed Mon. and Tues.*

WHERE TO STAY

$$ ⌂ **Inverness Valley Inn.** Nestled within a 15-acre valley on the north end
of town, this secluded getaway offers private cabins with plenty of room
and peace and quiet. **Pros:** spacious accommodations; great place to
bring kids. **Cons:** over 3 mi from downtown Inverness; don't expect
to swim laps in the pool. **TripAdvisor:** "location is perfect," "incred-
ible surroundings," "very friendly owners." ✉ *13275 Sir Francis Drake
Blvd., Inverness* ☎ *415/669–7250* ⊕ *www.invernessvalleyinn.com* ⟿ *20
cabins* ⌂ *In-room: no a/c, kitchen, Wi-Fi. In-hotel: tennis courts, pool,
spa, some pets allowed.*

$$$–$$$$ ⌂ **Olema Druids Hall.** Set on a quiet hill beneath towering eucalyptus
trees, the inn was built in 1885 as a meeting hall for the Ancient Order
of Druids. **Pros:** heated hardwood floors; wood-burning fireplaces.
Cons: not much to do at night; some traffic noise. ✉ *9870 Shoreline
Hwy., Box 96, Olema* ☎ *415/663–8727 or 866/554–4255* ⊕ *www.
olemadruidshall.com* ⟿ *3 rooms, 1 suite, 1 cottage* ⌂ *In-room: no a/c,
kitchen (some), Wi-Fi.* ⏣ *Breakfast.*

$$ ⌂ **Olema Inn & Restaurant.** Built in 1876, this inn retains all its 19th-
century architectural charm but has been decorated in a sophisticated,
uncluttered style. **Pros:** great restaurant; magnificent scenery. **Cons:** no
elevator means carrying your luggage up the stairs; the carpets need
to be replaced. **TripAdvisor:** "very good food," "quiet and comfortable bedroom," "service was great." ✉ *10000 Sir Francis Drake Blvd.,
Olema* ☎ *415/663–9559* ⊕ *www.theolemainn.com* ⟿ *6 rooms* ⌂ *In-
room: no a/c, Wi-Fi. In-hotel: some pets allowed* ⊘ *Closed Tues. No
lunch weekdays.*

$$ ⌂ **Ten Inverness Way.** This is the kind of down-to-earth place where
you sit around after breakfast and share tips for hiking Point Reyes or
linger around the living room with its stone fireplace and library. **Pros:**
great base for exploring nearby wilderness; peaceful garden and friendly
staff. **Cons:** overly folksy decor; some rooms are on the small side; poor
cell-phone reception. **TripAdvisor:** "warm and cozy," "a magical spot,"
"romantic and friendly." ✉ *10 Inverness Way, Inverness* ☎ *415/669–
1648* ⊕ *www.teninvernessway.com* ⟿ *4 rooms, 1 suite* ⌂ *In-room: no
a/c, no TV. In-hotel: restaurant, some age restrictions.*

SPORTS AND THE OUTDOORS

Blue Waters Kayaking (✉ *12938 Sir Francis Drake Blvd., Inverness*
☎ *415/669–2600* ⊕ *www.bwkayak.com*) rents kayaks and offers tours
and lessons. **Five Brooks Stable** (✉ *8001 Hwy. 1, Olema* ☎ *415/663–1570*

19

⊕ *www.fivebrooks.com*) rents horses and equipment. Trails from the stables wind through Point Reyes National Seashore and along the beaches. Rides run from one to six hours and cost $40 to $240.

THE EAST BAY

When San Franciscans refer to it, the East Bay often means nothing more than what you can see across the bay from the city—mainly Oakland and Berkeley, both of which are in Alameda County. In fact, the East Bay stretches north and east of Alameda to Contra Costa County, which itself has emerged as a powerful business nexus. East Bay towns south of Alameda and Contra Costa counties have become bedroom communities for workers in the high-tech industry. These begin to run into one another, reaching critical mass on the edge of Silicon Valley.

OAKLAND

Directly east of Bay Bridge.

Often overshadowed by San Francisco's beauty and Berkeley's storied counterculture, Oakland's allure lies in its amazing diversity. Here you can find a Nigerian clothing store, a beautifully renovated Victorian home, a Buddhist meditation center, and a lively salsa club, all within the same block. Oakland's multifaceted nature reflects its colorful and often tumultuous history. Once a cluster of Mediterranean-style homes and gardens that served as a bedroom community for San Francisco, the city became a hub of shipbuilding and industry almost overnight when the United States entered World War II. New jobs in the city's shipyards and factories attracted thousands of workers, including some of the first female welders, and the city's neighborhoods were imbued with a proud but gritty spirit. In the 1960s and '70s this intense community pride gave rise to such militant groups as the Black Panther Party and the Symbionese Liberation Army, but they were little match for the economic hardships and racial tensions that plagued Oakland. In many neighborhoods the reality was widespread poverty and gang violence—subjects that dominated the songs of such Oakland-bred rappers as the late Tupac Shakur.

Today Oakland is a mosaic of its past. The affluent have once again flocked to the city's hillside homes as a warmer, more spacious, and more affordable alternative to San Francisco, and a constant flow of newcomers—many from Central America and Asia—ensures continued diversity, vitality, and growing pains. Many neighborhoods to the west and south of downtown remain run-down and unsafe, but a renovated downtown area—including one of the most vibrant arts scenes in the Bay Area—and the thriving though sterile Jack London Square have injected new energy into the city.

Everyday life here revolves around the neighborhood, with a main business strip attracting both shoppers and strollers. In some areas, such as high-end Piedmont and Rockridge, you'd swear you were in Berkeley or San Francisco's Noe Valley or Cow Hollow. These are perfect places for browsing, eating, or just relaxing between sightseeing trips to Oakland's

19

architectural gems, rejuvenated waterfront, and numerous green spaces. Between Rockridge and Piedmont and to the west, you can find the Temescal District, along Telegraph Avenue just south of 51st Street, which is beginning to attract a small collection of eateries and shops.

ESSENTIALS

Visitor Information Oakland Convention and Visitors Bureau (✉ *463 11th St.* ☎ *510/839–9000* ⊕ *www.oaklandcvb.com*).

GETTING HERE AND AROUND

Driving from San Francisco, take I–80 East across the Bay Bridge, then take I–580 to the Grand Avenue exit for Lake Merritt. To reach downtown and the waterfront, take I–980 from I–580 and exit at 12th Street. By BART, use the Lake Merritt Station for the Oakland Museum and southern Lake Merritt; the Oakland City Center–12th Street Station for downtown, Chinatown, and Old Oakland; and the 19th Street Station for the Paramount Theatre and the north side of Lake Merritt. By bus, take the AC Transit's C and P lines to get to Piedmont in Oakland. The O bus stops at the edge of Chinatown near downtown Oakland. Once you arrive, be aware of how quickly neighborhoods can change. Walking is safe and advised downtown as well as in the Piedmont and Rockridge areas, but avoid walking west and south of downtown.

EXPLORING

Chinatown. Across Broadway from Old Oakland but worlds apart, Chinatown is a densely packed, bustling neighborhood. Unlike its San Francisco counterpart, Oakland's Chinatown makes no concessions to tourists; you won't find baskets of trinkets lining the sidewalk and souvenir displays in the shop windows. But supermarkets such as **Yuen Hop Noodle Company and Asian Food Products** (✉ *824 Webster St.*), open since 1931, overflows with goodies. And the line for sweets, breads, and towering cakes snakes out the door of **Napoleon Super Bakery** (✉ *810 Franklin St.*).

College Avenue. The main shopping drag in Rockridge, College Avenue is a busy thoroughfare. By day it's crowded with shoppers buying fresh flowers, used books, and clothing; by night the same folks are back for dinner and locally brewed ales in the numerous restaurants and pubs. The hub of College Avenue life in Rockridge is **Market Hall** (✉ *5655 College Ave.* ☎ *510/250–6000* ⊕ *www.rockridgemarkethall.com*), an airy European-style marketplace with pricey specialty-food shops. The avenue ends at the California College of the Arts campus.

Jack London Square. Shops, restaurants, small museums, and historic sites line Jack London Square, which is named after one of California's best-known authors; London wrote *The Call of the Wild and The Sea Wolf,* among many other books. When he lived in Oakland, he spent many a day boozing and brawling in the waterfront area. The tiny, wonderful **Heinold's First and Last Chance Saloon** (✉ *48 Webster St.* ☎ *510/839–6761*) was one of London's old haunts. It has been serving since 1883, although it's a little worse for the wear since the 1906 earthquake. The Klondike cabin in which London spent a summer in the late 1890s was moved from Alaska and reassembled here, next door to Heinold's saloon, in 1970. The square also contains a bronze bust of

A fun place to wet your whistle, Heinold's First and Last Chance Saloon.

London. ■ **TIP** → Since it's on the waterfront, the square is an obvious spot for tourists to visit and it's worth a peek if you take a ferry that docks here; to really get a feel for Oakland, though, you're better off browsing downtown, or at least in Rockridge. ⊠ *Embarcadero at Broadway* ☎ *866/295–9853* ⊕ *www.jacklondonsquare.com.*

Lake Merritt. Centering the middle of downtown Oakland is this 155-acre natural saltwater lake. Joggers and power-walkers charge along the 3-mi path that encircles the lake, crew teams often glide across the water, and boatmen guide snuggling couples in authentic Venetian gondolas. **Gondola Servizio** (⊠ *1520 Lakeside Dr., Lake Merritt* ☎ *510/663–6603* ⊕ *www.gondolaservizio.com*) is by the sign that says "Sailboat House, Gondola Servizio." Fares start at $40 per couple for 30 minutes.

☾ **Oakland Museum of California.** One of Oakland's top attractions, the
★ Oakland Museum of California is an excellent introduction to a tour of California, and its detailed exhibits on the state's art, history, and natural wonders can help fill the gaps on a brief visit. You can travel through the state's myriad ecosystems in the Natural Sciences Gallery, from the sand dunes of the Pacific to the coyotes and brush of the Nevada border. Kids love the lifelike wild-animal exhibits, especially the snarling wolverine, big-eyed harbor seal, and trove of hidden creatures. The rambling Cowell Hall of California History includes everything from Spanish-era armor to a small but impressive collection of vintage vehicles, including a gorgeous, candy-apple-red "Mystery" car from the 1960s and a gleaming red, gold, and silver fire engine that battled the flames in San Francisco in 1906. The Gallery of California Art

holds an eclectic collection of modern works and early landscapes. Of particular interest are paintings by Richard Diebenkorn, Joan Brown, Elmer Bischoff, and David Park, all members of the Bay Area Figurative School, which flourished here after World War II. Fans of Dorothea Lange won't want to miss the gallery's comprehensive collection of her work. The museum also has a sculpture garden with a view of the Oakland and Berkeley hills in the distance. ⊠ *1000 Oak St., at 10th St.* ☎ *510/238–2200* ⊕ *www.museumca.org* ⊠ *$12, free 1st Sun. of month* ⊙ *Wed.–Sun. 11–5.*

Old Oakland. Bordered by 7th, 10th, Clay, and Washington streets in the shadow of the convention center and towering downtown hotels, Old Oakland was once a booming business district. Today the restored Victorian storefronts lining these four blocks house restaurants, cafés, shops, galleries, and a lively three-block farmers' market, which takes place Friday morning. Architectural consistency distinguishes the area from surrounding streets and lends it a distinct neighborhood feel. **Ratto's International Market** (⊠ *827 Washington St.* ☎ *510/832–6503*), the Italian grocer that's been dishing up meat, cheese, imported sweets, and liquor to the neighborhood since 1897, has fresh deli sandwiches. **Pacific Coast Brewing Company** (⊠ *906 Washington St.* ☎ *510/836–2739*) is a homey place for some pub grub or a microbrew on the outside patio.

★ **Paramount Theatre.** Given Oakland's reputation for Victorian and Craftsman homes, newcomers are generally surprised by the profusion of art-deco architecture in the downtown neighborhood around the 19th Street BART station. Some of these buildings have fallen into disrepair, but the Paramount Theatre, perhaps the most glorious example of art-deco architecture in the city, if not the entire Bay Area, still operates as a venue for concerts and performances of all kinds, from the Oakland Ballet to Tom Waits and Elvis Costello. You can take a two-hour tour of the building, which starts near the box office on 21st Street at 10 am on the first and third Saturday of each month. Just behind the Paramount on Telegraph Avenue, the Fox Theater, another art-deco landmark, was saved from the wrecking ball and is being lovingly restored. ⊠ *2025 Broadway* ☎ *510/465–6400* ⊕ *www.paramounttheatre.com* ⊠ *Tour $5.*

Rockridge. The upscale neighborhood of Rockridge is one of Oakland's most desirable places to live. Explore the tree-lined streets that radiate out from College Avenue just north and south of the Rockridge BART station for a look at California bungalow architecture at its finest.

Rotary Nature Center and Waterfowl Refuge. Lakeside Park, which surrounds the north side of Lake Merritt, has several outdoor attractions, including a children's park. The Rotary Nature Center and Waterfowl Refuge is the nesting site of herons, egrets, geese, and ducks in spring and summer. Migrating birds pass through from September through February, and you can watch the birds being fed daily at 3:30 (year-round). ⊠ *600 Bellevue Ave.* ☎ *510/238–3739* ⊕ *www.oaklandnet.com/parks/facilities/rnc.asp* ⊠ *Free* ⊙ *Daily 10–5.*

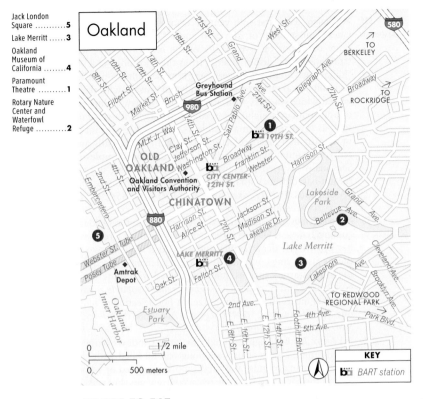

KEY

b *BART station*

WHERE TO EAT

$
MEDITERRANEAN
✕ **À Côté.** This is the place for Mediterranean food in the East Bay. It's all about small plates, cozy tables, and family-style eating here—and truly excellent food. The butternut-squash ravioli, Alsatian goose sausage, and pear-and-walnut flat bread are all lovely choices. And you won't find a better plate of pommes frites anywhere. The restaurant offers more than 40 wines by the glass from an extensive, ever-changing wine list. Desserts here are tempting: try the warm crème-fraîche pound cake with apple confit, vanilla ice cream, and huckleberry sauce or a tangy pomegranate sorbet. The heavy wooden tables, cool tiles, and natural light make this a coveted destination for students, families, couples, and after-work crowds. ⊠ *5478 College Ave., Rockridge* ☎ *510/655–6469* ⌂ *Reservations not accepted* ⊘ *No lunch.*

$
AMERICAN
✕ **Brown Sugar Kitchen.** Chef and owner Tanya Holland uses local, organic, and seasonal products in the menu that incorporates her African-American heritage together with her culinary education in France. She blends sweet and savory flavors like no one else, and offers up a wine list that is both unique and wide-ranging. The dining room is fresh and bright, with a long sleek counter, red leather stools, and spacious booths and tables. This is *the* place to come for chicken and waffles. ⊠ *2534 Mandela Pkwy.* ☎ *510/839–7685* ⊕ *www.brownsugarkitchen. com* ⊘ *Closed Mon. No dinner.*

19

$$$

AMERICAN

✕ **Camino.** This first solo venture from chef-owner Russell Moore (a Chez Panisse alum of 21 years) and co-owner Allison Hopelain was quite the labor of love. Many of the menu's simple, seasonal, and straightforward dishes emerge from the enormous crackling camino (Italian for "fireplace"). Everything is made with top-notch ingredients, including local sardines; grilled lamb and sausage with shell beans; and grilled white sea bass with green beans and new potatoes. The menu of approximately eight dishes rotates nightly, with vegetarian options such as eggplant gratin available as well. The restaurant is decorated in a craftsman-meets-refectory style, with brick walls and two long redwood communal tables filled with East Bay couples and friends. Seasonally inspired cocktails from the small bar are not to be missed; the gin-based drink with house-made cherry and hibiscus bitters is notably delicious. ✉ *3917 Grand Ave.* ☎ *510/547–5035* ☉ *Closed Tues. No lunch (weekend brunch 10–2).*

$$

MEXICAN

✕ **Doña Tomás.** A neighborhood favorite, this spot in Oakland's up-and-coming Temescal District serves seasonal Mexican fare to a hip but low-key crowd. Mexican textiles and art adorn walls in two long rooms; there's also a vine-covered patio. Banish all images of taquería grub and tuck into starters such as quesadillas filled with butternut squash and goat cheese and entrées such as *albondigas en sopa de zanahoria* (pork-and-beef meatballs in carrot puree). A fine selection of tequilas rounds out the offerings. ✉ *5004 Telegraph Ave.* ☎ *510/450–0522* ☉ *Closed Sun. and Mon. No lunch.*

¢–$

CAFÉ

✕ **L'Amyx Tea Bar.** Light through the large windows bathes the blond-wood tables, comfy chairs, and long bar, all filled with absorbed students, chatting friends, and tired shoppers in need of a boost. A small area in the back sells first-rate tea accoutrements, but sink into a couch or private nook to bask in much more than the usual cuppa. Try a tea smoothie or an herbal remedy such as Tealaxation. ✉ *4179 Piedmont Ave.* ☎ *510/594–8322.*

¢–$

VIETNAMESE

✕ **Le Cheval Restaurant.** A longtime favorite Vietnamese restaurant in Oakland, Le Cheval is known for large parties and boisterous family-style dining. This is a good place to try *pho*, Hanoi-style beef noodle soup fragrant with star anise. Other entrées include lemon chicken, cubed beef steak, clay-pot snapper, and shark in coconut milk. It's hard to spend more than $20 for an entire meal unless you order the special crab (about $30). The complementary mini-bowls of soup that are placed on the table as soon as you sit down are a great balm to hungry diners although service is lightning-quick anyway. ✉ *1019 Clay St.* ☎ *510/763–8495* ☉ *No lunch Sun.*

$–$$

FRENCH

✕ **Luka's Taproom & Lounge.** Luka's is a real taste of downtown Oakland: hip and urban, with an unpretentious vibe. Diners nibble on *frites* any Belgian would embrace and entrées like *choucroute garni* (sauerkraut with duck confit, ham hock, and pork shoulder). The brews draw 'em in, too—you'd be hard-pressed to find a larger selection of Belgian beer this side of the pond—and the DJs in the adjacent lounge keep the scene going late. ✉ *2221 Broadway, at West Grand Ave.* ☎ *510/451–4677* ☉ *No lunch Sat.*

$$–$$$ ✕**Oliveto Cafe & Restaurant.** Respected chef Jonah Rhodehamel is at
MEDITERRANEAN the helm of this locally renowned eatery that anchors Market Hall in
the Rockridge neighborhood. The first-class dining room ($$–$$$$)
upstairs serves straightforward Italian cuisine; the menu changes daily,
but might include house-made duck prosciutto, pan-seared swordfish,
or spit-roasted leg of lamb. Downstairs, in the terra-cotta-wall café
($–$$), everything from a morning espresso to pizza to a full-blown
Italian meal (at half the upstairs price) can be enjoyed at one of the
small tables or at the bar. ⊠ *5655 College Ave.* ☎ *510/547–5356* ⊗ *No
lunch weekends in restaurant.*

WHERE TO STAY

$–$$ ⊞ **Executive Inn & Suites.** This two-building hotel is convenient to both
the Oakland airport and downtown Oakland, and to make up for its
removed location, the property offers free shuttle service to the Oakland airport, BART stations, and Jack London Square. **Pros:** free parking; west-facing rooms overlook the peaceful waters of the Oakland
Estuary; all rooms have microwaves and fridges. **Cons:** east-facing
rooms look out onto the freeway and can be noisy; the decor is overly
bright and busy. **TripAdvisor:** "very friendly and helpful," "huge room
and comfy bed," "good customer service." ⊠ *1755 Embarcadero, off
I–880 at 16th St. exit* ☎ *510/536–6633 or 800/346–6331* ⊕ *www.
executiveinnoakland.com* ⮌ *143 rooms, 81 suites* ⚘ *In-room: a/c,
Internet, Wi-Fi (some). In-hotel: restaurant, bar, pool, gym, laundry
facilities, parking* ⦿ *Breakfast.*

$–$$ ⊞ **Washington Inn Hotel.** This stylish four-story brick hotel sits across the
street from the convention center, in the heart of Old Oakland. **Pros:**
central location; old-fashioned charm. **Cons:** some rooms feel cramped
and need to be freshened up. **TripAdvisor:** "wonderful customer service," "extremely comfortable room," "great location." ⊠ *495 10th
St., at Washington St.* ☎ *510/452–1776* ⊕ *www.thewashingtoninn.com*
⮌ *47 rooms, 6 suites* ⚘ *In-room: Wi-Fi. In-hotel: restaurant, bar, gym,
parking* ⦿ *Breakfast.*

$$–$$$ ⊞ **Waterfront Hotel.** One of Oakland's more appealing neighborhoods is
home to this thoroughly modern waterfront hotel. **Pros:** great location;
dog-friendly. **Cons:** passing trains can be noisy; some rooms have yet to
be renovated. **TripAdvisor:** "very friendly and helpful," "hospitable and
accommodating." ⊠ *10 Washington St., Jack London Sq.* ☎ *510/836–
3800 or 800/729–3638* ⊕ *www.waterfrontplaza.com* ⮌ *143 rooms*
⚘ *In-room: a/c, Wi-Fi. In-hotel: restaurant, room service, bar, pool,
gym, parking.*

NIGHTLIFE AND THE ARTS

Oakland is where practicing artists have found cheaper rent and loft
spaces. Oakland's underground arts scene—visual arts, indie music,
spoken word, film—is definitely buzzing.

Fodor'sChoice **Café van Kleef.** When Dutch artist Peter van Kleef first opened his gallery
★ in this downtown space, the booze flowed freely—and free, for lack
of a liquor license. That gallery has morphed into this candle-strewn,
funky café-bar that crackles with creative energy. Van Kleef has a lot
to do with the convivial atmosphere; the garrulous owner loves sharing

19

tales about his quirky, floor-to-ceiling collection of mementos, including what he claims are Cassius Clay's boxing gloves and Dorothy's ruby slippers. The café also has a consistently solid calendar of live music, heavy on the jazz side. And the drinks may not be free anymore, but they're quite possibly the stiffest in town. ⊠ *1621 Telegraph Ave., between 16th and 17th Sts.* ☎ *510/763–7711* ⊕ *www.cafevankleef.com.*

Mama Buzz Café. At this well-worn café-gallery, a kind of living room for the indie arts crowd, you can get the lowdown on one of the most diverse arts communities around. In addition to coffee and light fare, the calendar includes poetry readings, live-music events, art exhibits, and hard-to-categorize events such as Punk Rock Haircut Night (get a new 'do, cheap), the Knitty Gritty knitting circle, and the Left-Wing Letter Bee. The owners publish the 'zine *Kitchen Sink.* ⊠ *2318 Telegraph Ave.* ☎ *510/465–4073*

Fodor'sChoice ★ **Yoshi's.** Oma Sosa and Charlie Hunter are among the musicians who play at Yoshi's, one of the area's best jazz venues. Monday through Saturday shows start at 8 pm and 10 pm; Sunday shows usually start at 2 pm and 8 pm. The cover runs from $16 to $30. ⊠ *510 Embarcadero St., between Washington and Clay Sts.* ☎ *510/238–9200* ⊕ *www.yoshis. com.*

SPORTS AND THE OUTDOORS

BASEBALL The American League's **Oakland A's** (⊠ *McAfee Coliseum, 7000 Coliseum Way, off I–880, north of Hegenberger Rd.* ☎ *510/638–4900* ⊕ *oakland.athletics.mlb.com*), formally the Oakland Athletics, play at the **McAfee Coliseum.** Same-day tickets can usually be purchased at the stadium box office (Gate D), but advance purchase is recommended. On Wednesday, entry is a bargain at $2, and you can buy a hot dog for a dollar. To get to the game, take a BART train to the Coliseum/Oakland Airport Station.

BASKETBALL The National Basketball Association's **Golden State Warriors** (⊠ *Oakland Arena, 7000 Coliseum Way, off I–880, north of Hegenberger Rd.* ☎ *510/986–2200 or 888/479–4667* ⊕ *www.nba.com/warriors*) play at the **Oakland Arena** from November through April. Basketball tickets are available through **Ticketmaster** (☎ *415/421–8497* ⊕ *www. ticketmaster.com*). You can take a BART train to the game. Get off at the Coliseum/Oakland Airport Station.

FOOTBALL The National Football League's **Oakland Raiders** (⊠ *McAfee Coliseum, 7000 Coliseum Way, off I–880, north of Hegenberger Rd.* ☎ *510/864–5000* ⊕ *www.raiders.com*) play at **McAfee Coliseum.** Tickets, sold through **Tickets.com** (☎ *510/762–2277* ⊕ *www.tickets.com*), are usually available, except for high-profile games.

SHOPPING

College Avenue is great for upscale strolling, shopping, and people-watching. The streets around Lake Merritt and Grand Lake have more casual fare and smaller boutiques.

Diesel. Wandering bibliophiles collect armfuls of the latest fiction and nonfiction here. The loftlike space, with its high ceilings and spare design, encourages airy contemplation, and on chilly days (a rarity) there's a fire going in the hearth. Keep an eye out for their excellent reading series. ✉ *5433 College Ave.* ☎ *510/653–9965.*

Maison d'Etre. Close to the Rockridge BART station, this store crystallizes the funky-chic shopping scene of Rockridge. Look for impulse buys like whimsical watches, imported fruit tea blends, and a basket of funky slippers near the back. ✉ *5640 College Ave.* ☎ *510/658–2801.*

BERKELEY

2 mi northeast of Bay Bridge.

The birthplace of the Free Speech Movement, the radical hub of the 1960s, the home of arguably the nation's top public university, and the city whose government condemned the bombing of Afghanistan—Berkeley is all of those things. The city of 100,000 facing San Francisco across the bay is also culturally diverse, a breeding ground for social trends, a bastion of the counterculture, and an important center for Bay Area writers, artists, and musicians. Berkeley residents, students, and faculty spend hours nursing various coffee concoctions while they read, discuss, and debate at any of the dozens of cafés that surround the campus. Oakland may have Berkeley beat when it comes to cutting-edge arts, and the city may have forfeited some of its renegade 1960s spirit, as some residents say, but unless a guy in a hot-pink satin body suit, skullcap, and cape rides a unicycle around *your* town, you'll likely find that Berkeley remains plenty offbeat.

It's the quintessential university town, and many who graduated years ago still bask in daily intellectual conversation, great weather, and good food. Residents will walk out of their way to go to the perfect bread shop or consult with their favorite wine merchant. And every September, residents gently lampoon themselves during the annual "How Berkeley Can You Be?" parade and festival where they celebrate their tie-dyed past and consider its new incarnations.

19

ESSENTIALS

Visitor Information Berkeley Convention and Visitors Bureau (✉ *2030 Addison St. #102* ☎ *510/549–7040* ⊕ *www.visitberkeley.com*).

GETTING HERE AND AROUND

BART is the easiest way to get to Berkeley from San Francisco. Alight at the Berkeley (not North Berkeley) Station, and walk a block up Center Street to get to the western edge of campus. AC Transit buses F and FS lines stop near the university and 4th Street shopping in Berkeley. By car, take I–80 east across the Bay Bridge then take the University Avenue exit through downtown Berkeley to the campus or take the Ashby Avenue exit and turn left on Telegraph Avenue to the traditional campus entrance. Once you arrive, explore on foot. There's a lot to see, and the city is very pedestrian friendly.

EXPLORING

4th Street. An industrial area on 4th Street north of University Avenue has been converted into a pleasant shopping stretch, with popular eateries and shops selling handcrafted and eco-conscious goods. About six blocks long, this compact area is busiest on bright weekend afternoons.

Berkeley's Political History

Those looking for traces of Berkeley's politically charged past need go no farther than Sather Gate. Both the Free Speech Movement and the fledgling political life of actor-turned-politician Ronald Reagan have their roots here. It was next to Sather Gate, on September 30, 1964, that a group of students defied the University of California–Berkeley chancellor's order that all organizations advocating "off-campus issues" (such as civil rights and nuclear disarmament) keep their information tables off campus. Citation of the tablers brought more than 400 sympathetic students into Sproul Hall that afternoon. They stayed until 3 am, setting a precedent of protest that would be repeated in the coming months, with students jamming Sproul Hall in greater numbers each time.

Conservative U.C. president Clark Kerr eventually backed down and allowed student groups to pass out information on campus. By then, the Free Speech Movement had gathered momentum, and the conflict had made a national hero of student leader Mario Savio. Political newcomer Ronald Reagan played on Californians' unease about the unruly Berkeley students in his successful 1966 bid for governor, promising to rein in the "unwashed kooks."

By the end of the 1960s, the cohesion of the groups making up the Free Speech Movement had begun to fray. Some members began questioning the efficacy of sit-ins and other nonviolent tactics that had, until then, been the hallmark of Berkeley student protests. The Black Panthers, headquartered just over the border in Oakland, were ascending into the national spotlight, and their "take no prisoners" approach appealed to some Berkeley activists who had seen little come of their efforts to affect national policy.

By 1969 both Robert Kennedy and Martin Luther King Jr. were dead, and the issue of the day—stopping the flow of troops heading to Vietnam—was not as easy as overpowering a school administration's resistance to free speech. But a more dramatic clash with the university came when it brought in police units to repossess People's Park, a university-owned plot of land at Telegraph Avenue and Haste Street that students and community members had adopted as a park. On the afternoon of May 15, 1969, nearly 6,000 students and residents moved to reclaim the park. In the ensuing riot, police and sheriff's deputies fired both tear gas and buckshot, blinding one observer and killing another. Governor Ronald Reagan ordered the National Guard into Berkeley. Despite a ban on public assembly, crowds continued to gather and march in the days after the first riot. The park changed hands several times in the following tear-gas-filled months, with the fence coming down for the last time in 1972.

A colorful mural on the side of Amoeba Records (Haste Street at Telegraph Avenue) offers the protestors' version of park history. Although the area around People's Park and Sather Gate may seem quiet now, issues such as affirmative action and tuition increases still bring protests to the steps of Sproul. Protests over civil rights, war, and other inequities march through the center of the campus, though students also gather to rally for sports events, social gatherings, and shows of school spirit.

–Chris Baty

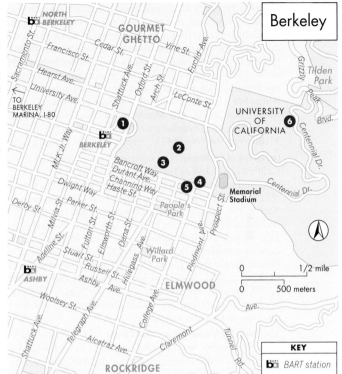

Popular destinations are the Stained Glass Garden, Hear Music, and the Crate and Barrel Outlet, along with a mini-slew of upscale boutiques and wonderful paper stores.

QUICK BITES

With a jazz combo playing in the storefront and a long line snaking down the block, Cheeseboard Pizza (✉ *151 Shattuck Ave.* ☎ *510/549–3055* ⏱ *Tues.–Fri. 11:30–2 and 4:30–7, Sat. 11:30–3*) taps into the pulse of the Gourmet Ghetto. This cooperatively owned take-out spot draws devoted customers with the smell of just-baked garlic, fresh vegetables, and perfect sauces. Next door at the bakery–cheese shop, customers take a playing card instead of a number and are served in suites.

Elmwood. South of campus, along College Avenue between Ashby Avenue and Claremont, shops and cafés pack the area known as Elmwood, a local favorite for browsing. **Nabolom Bakery** (✉ *2708 Russell St.* ☎ *510/845–2253*), which has been around since 1976, is a workers' collective where politics and delicious pastries collide. Shingled houses line tree-shaded streets nearby.

Telegraph Avenue. Berkeley's student-oriented thoroughfare, Telegraph Avenue is also the best place to get a dose of the city's famed counter-culture. On any given day you might encounter a troop of chanting

Hare Krishnas or a drumming band of Rastafarians. First and foremost, however, Telegraph is a place for socializing and shopping, the only uniquely Berkeley shopping experience in town and a definite don't-miss. ■TIP→ Take care when wandering the street at night, as things can feel a bit edgy. The nearby People's Park, mostly harmless by day, is best avoided at night. Cafés, bookstores, poster shops, and street vendors line the avenue. T-shirt vendors and tarot-card readers come and go on a whim, but a few establishments—**Rasputin Music** (No. 2401), **Amoeba Music** (No. 2455), and **Moe's Books** (No. 2476)—are neighborhood landmarks. Allen Ginsberg wrote his acclaimed poem "Howl" at **Caffe Mediterraneum** (No. 2475), a relic of 1960s-era café culture.

University of California. The state legislature chartered the University of California in 1868 as the founding campus of the state university system, and established it five years later on a rising plain of oak trees split by Strawberry Creek. Frederick Law Olmsted, who designed New York City's Central Park, proposed the first campus plan. University architects over the years have included Bernard Maybeck as well as Julia Morgan, who designed Hearst Castle at San Simeon. The central campus occupies 178 acres, bounded by Bancroft Way to the south, Hearst Avenue to the north, Oxford Street to the west, and Gayley Road to the east. With more than 30,000 students and a full-time faculty of 1,400, the university, known simply as "Cal," is one of the leading intellectual centers in the United States and a major site for scientific research. ⊕ *www.berkeley.edu.*

The **Berkeley Visitor Information Center** (⊠ *University Hall, Room 101, 2200 University Ave., at Oxford St.* ☎ *510/642–5215* ⊙ *Weekdays 8:30–4:30*) is the starting point for the free, student-guided tours of the campus, which last 1½ hours and start at 10 on weekdays. (Weekend tours depart from Sather Tower, *see below.*)

Student-guided campus tours leave from **Sather Tower,** the campus landmark popularly known as the Campanile, at 10 on Saturday and 1 on Sunday. The 307-foot structure, modeled on St. Mark's Tower in Venice and completed in 1914, can be seen for miles. The carillon is played daily at 7:50 am, noon, and 6 pm and for an extended 45-minute concert Sunday at 2. Take the elevator up 175 feet; then walk another 38 steps to the observation deck for a view of the campus and a close-up look at the iron bells, each of which weighs up to 10,500 pounds. ⊠ *South of University Dr.* 🗐 *$2* ⊙ *Weekdays 10–4, Sat. 10–5, Sun. 10–1:30 and 3–5.*

Sproul Plaza (⊠ *Telegraph Ave. and Bancroft Way*), just inside the U.C. Berkeley campus border on Bancroft Way, was the site of several free-speech and civil-rights protests in the 1960s. Today a lively panorama of political and social activists, musicians, and students show off Berkeley's flair for the bizarre. Preachers orate atop milk crates, amateur entertainers bang on makeshift drum sets, and protesters distribute leaflets about everything from marijuana to the Middle East. No matter what the combination, on weekdays when school is in swing, it always feels like a carnival. ■TIP→ Walk through at noon for the liveliest show of student spirit.

The collection of the **Phoebe A. Hearst Museum of Anthropology** counts almost 4 million artifacts, of which fewer than 1% are on display at any time. The Native Californian Cultures gallery showcases items related to the native peoples of California. Changing exhibits may cover the archaeology of ancient America or spotlight the museum's especially strong ancient Egyptian holdings. Mood music enhances the experience. ✉ *Kroeber Hall, Bancroft Way, at end of College Ave.*☎ *510/642–3682* ⊕ *hearstmuseum.berkeley.edu* ✉ *Free; guided tour $5* ⊗ *Wed.–Sat. 10–4:30, Sun. noon–4.*

The **University of California, Berkeley Art Museum & Pacific Film Archive** has an interesting collection of works that spans five centuries. Changing exhibits line the spiral ramps and balcony galleries. Look for the museum's enormous orange-red statue of a man hammering, which can be seen from the outside when strolling by its floor-to-ceiling windows. Don't miss the museum's series of vibrant paintings by abstract expressionist Hans Hofmann. On the ground floor, the Pacific Film Archive has a library and hosts programs about historic and contemporary films, but the exhibition theater is across the street at 2575 Bancroft Way, near Bowditch Street. The downstairs galleries, which house rotating exhibits, are always free. The museum's raw foods café is famous, and you can also find some cooked options, too. ✉ *2626 Bancroft Way, entrance to theater at 2575 Bancroft Way, between College and Telegraph*☎ *510/642–0808, 510/642–1124 film-program information* ⊕ *www.bampfa.berkeley.edu* ✉ *$10, free 1st Thurs. of month* ⊗ *Wed.–Sun. 11–5, Fri. 11–9.*

⟲ Thanks to Berkeley's temperate climate, about 13,500 species of plants from all over the world flourish in the 34-acre **University of California Botanical Garden.** Free garden tours are given Thursday, Saturday, and Sunday at 1:30. Benches and shady picnic tables make this a relaxing place to take in breathtaking views. ✉ *200 Centennial Dr.* ☎ *510/643–2755* ⊕ *botanicalgarden.berkeley.edu* ✉ *$9, free 1st Thurs. of month* ⊗ *Daily 9–5. Closed 1st Tues. of month.*

⟲ At the fortresslike **Lawrence Hall of Science,** a dazzling hands-on science center, kids can look at insects under microscopes, solve crimes using chemical forensics, and explore the physics of baseball. On weekends there are special lectures, demonstrations, and planetarium shows. The museum runs a popular (and free) stargazing program, which is held on the first and third Saturday of each month, weather permitting. (Call for times.) ✉ *Centennial Dr. near Grizzly Peak Blvd.* ☎ *510/642–5132* ⊕ *www.lawrencehallofscience.org* ✉ *$12* ⊗ *Daily 10–5.*

Vine Street. Another top culinary destination is this street, an offshoot of the "Gourmet Ghetto." In a historic building, **Vintage Berkeley** (✉ *2113 Vine St.* ☎ *510/665–8600*) gathers locals in its large front garden for nightly wine-tastings of California wines from smaller vineyards. Take the stairs up to the top floor of Walnut Square to find **Love at First Bite** (✉ *1510 Walnut St., Suite G* ☎ *510/848–5727*) a cupcakery showcasing scrumptious confections. **Twig & Fig** (✉ *210 Vine St., Suite B* ☎ *510/848–5599*) invites you in for a peek at its three rhythmically clacking letterpresses. Stop in for one-of-a-kind papery gifts and publications such as

19

Inside the Brambles, a local's guide to Tilden Park. Of all the coffee-houses in caffeine-crazed Berkeley, the one that deserves a pilgrimage is **Peet's** (✉ *2124 Vine St.* ☎ *510/841–0564*). When this spot, the original, opened at Vine and Walnut streets in 1966, the unparalleled coffee was roasted in the store and brewed by the cup. Named after the Dutch last name of the founder, Peet's has since expanded, but this isn't a café where you can sit on sofas or order quiche. It's strictly coffee, tea, and sweets to go.

> **A TASTING TOUR**
>
> For an unforgettable foodie experi-ence, take Lisa Rogovin's **Culinary Walking Tour** (☎ *510/540-6444* ⊕ *www.gourmetghetto.org*). You'll taste your way through the Gour-met Ghetto, learn some culinary history, and meet the chefs behind the food. Tours run Thursday 11 am–2:15 pm and cost $75 per person.

Walnut Square. Northwest of the U.C. Berkeley campus, Walnut Square, at Walnut and Vine streets, has coffee shops and an eclectic assortment of boutiques proffering such goodies as holistic products for your pet, African masks, and French children's clothing. Around the corner on Shattuck Avenue is Chez Panisse Café & Restaurant, at the heart of what is locally known as the **Gourmet Ghetto**, a three-block stretch of specialty shops and eateries. Your senses will immediately perk up as you enter the upscale market **Epicurious Garden** (✉ *1509–1513 Shattuck Ave.*), which has everything from impeccable sushi to gelato. Outside, you can find a terraced garden—the only place to sit—that winds up four levels and ends at the Imperial Tea Court. The restaurant Taste anchors this zone; it offers a rechargeable wine-tasting card that guests use to help themselves to 1-ounce automated pours from new wine selections.

WHERE TO EAT

Dining in Berkeley is a low-key affair; even in the finest restaurants—and some are quite fine—most folks dress casually. Late diners be fore-warned: Berkeley is an "early to bed" kind of town.

¢–$
AMERICAN
× **Bette's Oceanview Diner.** Buttermilk pancakes are just one of the spe-cialties at this 1930s-inspired diner complete with checkered floors and burgundy booths. Huevos rancheros and lox and eggs are other break-fast options; kosher franks, generous slices of pizza, and a slew of sand-wiches are available for lunch. The wait for a seat can be quite long; thankfully, 4th Street was made for strolling. ■**TIP→** If you're starving, head to Bette's to Go, next door, for takeout. ✉ *1807 4th St.* ☎ *510/644–3230* ⌣ *Reservations not accepted* ☉ *No dinner.*

$$$–$$$$
AMERICAN
× **Café Rouge.** You can recover from 4th Street shopping in this spacious two-story bistro complete with zinc bar, skylights, and festive lanterns. The short, seasonal menu ranges from the sophisticated, such as rack of lamb and juniper-berry-cured pork chops, to the homey, like spit-roasted chicken or pork loin, or cheddar-topped burgers. If you visit by day, be certain to peek at the meat market in the back. ✉ *1782 4th St.* ☎ *510/525–1440* ☉ *No dinner Mon.*

The pioneer restaurant Chez Panisse focuses on seasonal local ingredients.

$–$$
SPANISH
✕ **César.** Suitably keeping near-Spanish hours for the Spanish cuisine here, dinners are served late at César, whose kitchen closes at 11:30 pm on Friday and Saturday and at 11 pm the rest of the week. Couples spill out from its street-level windows on warm nights, or rub shoulders at the polished bar or center communal table. Founded by a trio of former Chez Panisse chefs, César is like a first cousin to Chez Panisse, each restaurant recommending the other if there's a long wait ahead. For tapas and perfectly grilled *bocadillos* (small sandwiches), there's no better choice. The bar also makes a mean martini and has an impressive wine list. ■TIP➜ Come early to get seated quickly and also to hear your tablemates; the room gets loud when the bar is in full swing. ⊠ *1515 Shattuck Ave.* ☎ *510/883–0222* ⌔ *Reservations not accepted.*

$$$–$$$$
AMERICAN
Fodor'sChoice
★
✕ **Chez Panisse Café & Restaurant.** At Chez Panisse even humble pizza is reincarnated, with innovative toppings of the freshest local ingredients. The downstairs portion of Alice Waters's legendary eatery is noted for its formality and personal service. The daily-changing multicourse dinners are prix-fixe ($$$$), with the cost slightly lower on weekdays. Upstairs, in the informal café, the crowd is livelier, the prices are lower ($$–$$$), and the ever-changing menu is à la carte. The food is simpler, too: penne with new potatoes, arugula, and sheep's-milk cheese; fresh figs with Parmigiano-Reggiano cheese and arugula; and grilled tuna with Savoy cabbage, for example. Legions of loyal fans insist that Chez Panisse lives up to its reputation and delivers a dining experience well worth the price. Visiting foodies won't want to miss a meal here; be sure to make reservations a few weeks ahead of time. ⊠ *1517 Shattuck Ave., north of University Ave.* ☎ *510/548–5525 restaurant, 510/548–5049 café* ⌔ *Reservations essential* ☉ *Closed Sun. No lunch in the restaurant.*

$$–$$$ ✕**Lalime's.** Inside a charming, flower-covered house, this restaurant
MEDITERRANEAN serves dishes that reflect the entire Mediterranean region. The menu,
★ constantly changing and unfailingly great, depends on the availability
of fresh seasonal ingredients. Choices might include grilled ahi tuna
or creamy Italian risotto. Light colors used in the dining room, which
has two levels, help to create a cheerful mood. A star in its own right,
Lalime's is a good second choice if Chez Panisse is booked. ✉ *1329 Gil-*
man St. ☏ *510/527–9838* ✍ *Reservations essential* ⊘ *No lunch.*

¢–$ ✕**Picante.** A barnlike space full of cheerful Mexican tiles and folk-art
MEXICAN masks, Picante is a find for anyone seeking good Mexican food for a
song. The *masa* (flour) is freshly ground for the tortillas and tamales,
the salsas are complex, and the flavor combinations are inventive. Try
tamales filled with butternut squash and chilies or a simple taco of
roasted poblanos and sautéed onions; we challenge you to finish a plate
of supernachos. ✉ *1328 6th St.* ☏ *510/525–3121* ✍ *Reservations not*
accepted.

$–$$ ✕**Rick & Ann's.** Haute comfort food is the focus here. The brunches are
AMERICAN legendary for quality and value, and customers line up outside the door
before the restaurant opens on the weekend. If you come during prime
brunch hours, expect a long wait, but their soft-style eggs are worth
it. Pancakes, waffles, and French toast are more flavorful than usual,
with variations such as potato-cheese and orange-rice pancakes. Lunch
and dinner offer burgers, favorites such as Mom's macaroni and cheese,
and chicken potpie, but always with a festive twist. Reservations are
accepted 48 hours in advance for dinner and for lunch parties of six or
more, but, alas, you can't reserve a table for brunch. ✉ *2922 Domingo*
Ave. ☏ *510/649–8538* ⊘ *No dinner Mon.*

$–$$ ✕**Saul's.** Well known for its homemade sodas and enormous sand-
AMERICAN wiches, the Saul's of today also uses sustainably sourced seafood, grass-
fed beef, and organic eggs. The restaurant is a Berkeley institution, and
has a loyal clientele that swears by their pastrami sandwiches, stuffed
cabbage rolls, and tuna melts. For breakfast, the challah French toast is
so thick it's almost too big to bite and the deli omelets are served pancake style. The high ceilings and red-leather booths add to the friendly
atmosphere. Don't overlook the glass deli case where you can order
food to go. ✉ *1475 Shattuck Ave.* ☏ *510/848–3354* ⊕ *www.saulsdeli.*
com ✍ *Reservations not accepted* ⊘ *Closed Thanksgiving and Yom*
Kippur.

WHERE TO STAY

For inexpensive lodging, investigate University Avenue, west of campus. The area is noisy, congested, and somewhat dilapidated, but does
include a few decent motels and chain properties. All Berkeley lodgings,
except for the swanky Claremont, are strictly mid-range.

$$$$ 🖼 **Claremont Resort and Spa.** Straddling the Oakland–Berkeley border,
Fodor's Choice the hotel beckons like a gleaming white castle in the hills, luring trav-
★ eling executives that come for the business amenities, including T-1
Internet connections, guest email addresses, and oversize desks. **Pros:**
amazing spa; supervised child care; some rooms have great views of
the bay. **Cons:** parking is pricey; additional facilities charge for use of
spa, tennis courts, pool, gym etc.; no Wi-Fi in rooms; breakfast is an

additional fee. **TripAdvisor:** "staff was pleasant," "room was spacious and clean," "great view." ✉ *41 Tunnel Rd., at Ashby and Domingo Aves.* ☎ *510/843–3000 or 800/551–7266* ⊕ *www.claremontresort.com* 🛏 *249 rooms, 30 suites* ♿ *In-room: a/c, Internet. In-hotel: restaurants, bars, tennis courts, pools, gym, spa, children's programs, parking.*

$ 🏨 **French Hotel.** The only hotel in north Berkeley, one of the best walking neighborhoods in town, this three-level brick structure has a certain *pensione* feel—guests check in at a counter at the back of the café, and the only public space in the hotel is the hallway to the elevator. **Pros:** great location; reasonable price. **Cons:** nearby trains and delivery trucks can be noisy; rear rooms are small and dark. **TripAdvisor:** "conveniently located," "overpriced for the facilities," "not particularly clean or cozy." ✉ *1538 Shattuck Ave.* ☎ *510/548–9930* 🛏 *18 rooms* ♿ *In-room: no a/c, Wi-Fi. In-hotel: restaurant, parking.*

$ 🏨 **Holiday Inn Express.** Convenient to the freeway and 4th Street shopping, this inviting, peach-and-beige hotel offers lots of bang for the buck. **Pros:** newly decorated rooms; good breakfast. **Cons:** area can get noisy and congested with traffic during commute hours; a 15-minute drive to UC campus. **TripAdvisor:** "sketchy location at night," "fairly comfortable and definitely clean," "great value." ✉ *1175 University Ave.* ☎ *510/548–1700 or 866/548–1700* ⊕ *www.hiexberkeley.com* 🛏 *69 rooms, 3 suites* ♿ *In-room: a/c, Wi-Fi. In-hotel: gym, laundry facilities, parking.* 🍽 *Breakfast.*

$$ 🏨 **Hotel Durant.** Long a mainstay of parents visiting their children at U.C. Berkeley, this boutique hotel is also a good option for those who want to be a short walk from Telegraph Avenue. **Pros:** blackout shades; organic bathrobes. **Cons:** downstairs bar can get a little noisy during Cal games; pricey parking. **TripAdvisor:** "extremely friendly and helpful," "bed was comfortable," "room service food was tasty." ✉ *2600 Durant Ave.* ☎ *510/845–8981* ⊕ *www.hoteldurant.com* 🛏 *139 rooms, 5 suites* ♿ *In-room: a/c (some), Wi-Fi. In-hotel: restaurant, room service, bar, Wi-Fi, parking.*

$–$$ 🏨 **Hotel Shattuck Plaza.** In 2009 this elegant boutique hotel in the heart
★ of Berkeley underwent a major multimillion renovation, which successfully combined turn-of-the-20th-century glamour (the hotel was built in 1910) with all the contemporary amenities. **Pros:** central location; modern facilities; great views; great restaurant. **Cons:** pricey parking; limited fitness center. **TripAdvisor:** "staff was helpful and friendly," "very clean and comfortable," "newly renovated and modern." ✉ *2086 Allston Way* ☎ *510/845–7300* ⊕ *www.hotelshattuckplaza.com* 🛏 *199 rooms, 17 suites* ♿ *In-room: a/c, Wi-Fi. In-hotel: restaurant, room service, bar, gym, parking.*

NIGHTLIFE AND THE ARTS

Berkeley Repertory Theatre. One of the region's highly respected resident professional companies and a Tony Award winner for Outstanding Regional Theatre (in 1997), the theater performs classic and contemporary plays from autumn to spring. Well-known pieces such as *Mother Courage* and *Oliver Twist* mix with edgier fare. The theater's complex is near BART's Downtown Berkeley Station. ✉ *2025 Addison St.* ☎ *510/647–2949* ⊕ *www.berkeleyrep.org.*

Berkeley Symphony Orchestra. Under artistic director Kent Nagano, this ensemble has risen to considerable prominence. The works of 20th-century composers are a focus, but traditional pieces are also performed. The orchestra plays a handful of concerts each year, in Zellerbach Hall and other locations. ⊠ *1942 University Ave., Suite 207* ☎ *510/841–2800* ⊕ *www.berkeleysymphony.org.*

★ **Cal Performances.** The series, running from September through May at various U.C. Berkeley venues, offers the Bay Area's most varied bill of internationally acclaimed artists in all disciplines, from classical soloists to the latest jazz, world-music, theater, and dance ensembles. Look for frequent campus colloquiums or preshow talks featuring Berkeley's professors. ⊠ *University of California, 101 Zellerbach Hall, Suite 4800, Telegraph Ave. and Bancroft Way* ☎ *510/642–9988* ⊕ *www.calperfs. berkeley.edu.*

Fodor'sChoice **Freight & Salvage Coffee House.** Some of the most talented practitioners of
★ folk, blues, Cajun, and bluegrass perform in this alcohol-free space, one of the finest folk houses in the country. Most tickets are less than $20. ⊠ *2020 Addison St.* ☎ *510/644–2020* ⊕ *www.thefreight.org.*

SHOPPING

Fodor'sChoice **Amoeba Music.** Heaven for audiophiles, this legendary Berkeley favor-
★ ite is *the* place to go to for new and used CDs, records, cassettes, and DVDs. The dazzling stock includes thousands of titles for all music tastes—no matter what you're looking for, you can probably find it here. The store even has its own record label. There are now branches in San Francisco and Hollywood, but this is the original. ⊠ *2455 Telegraph Ave., at Haste St.* ☎ *510/549–1125.*

Body Time. Founded in Berkeley in 1970, this local chain emphasizes the premium-quality ingredients it uses in its natural perfumes and skin-care and aromatherapy products. Sustainably harvested essential oils that you can combine and dilute to create your own personal fragrances are the specialty. Its distinct Citrus, Lavender-Mint, and China Rain scents are all popular. ⊠ *1942 Shattuck Ave.* ☎ *510/841–5818.*

Kermit Lynch Wine Merchant. Lynch's newsletters describing his finds are legendary, as is his friendship with Alice Waters of Chez Panisse. Credited for taking American appreciation of French wine to another level, this shop is a great place to peruse as you educate your palate. The friendly salespeople can direct you to the latest French bargains. ⊠ *1605 San Pablo Ave., at Dwight Way* ☎ *510/524–1524.*

Moe's Books. The spirit of Moe—the cantankerous, cigar-smoking late proprietor—lives on in this four-story house of books. Students and professors come here for used books, including large sections of literary and cultural criticism, art books, and literature in foreign languages. ▪TIP→ Wear good shoes and eat lunch first; you won't want to come out for hours. ⊠ *2476 Telegraph Ave., near Haste St.* ☎ *510/849–2087.*

Rasputin Music. A huge selection of new music for every taste draws crowds. In any other town its stock of used CDs and vinyl would certainly be unsurpassed. ⊠ *2403 Telegraph Ave., at Channing Way* ☎ *510/848–9004.*

The Wine Country

WORD OF MOUTH

"Both Napa and Sonoma are great. Napa is almost wall-to-wall wineries, Sonoma is more rural. The further north you go in either valley, the less busy it gets."

— zootsi

WELCOME TO WINE COUNTRY

TOP REASONS TO GO

★ **Biking:** Cycling is one of the best ways to see the Wine Country—the Russian River and Dry Creek valleys are particularly beautiful.

★ **Browsing the farmers' markets:** Almost every town in Napa and Sonoma has a seasonal farmers' market, each rounding up an amazing variety of local produce.

★ **Wandering di Rosa:** Though this art and nature preserve is just off the busy Carneros Highway, it's a relatively unknown treasure. The galleries and gardens are filled with hundreds of artworks.

★ **Canoeing on the Russian River:** Trade in your car keys for a paddle and glide down the Russian River. May through October is the best time to be on the water.

★ **Touring Wineries:** Let's face it: this is the reason you're here, and the range of excellent sips to sample would make any oenophile giddy.

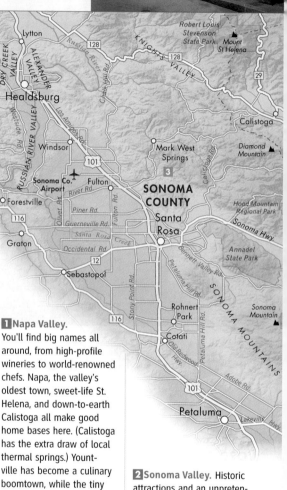

1 Napa Valley. You'll find big names all around, from high-profile wineries to world-renowned chefs. Napa, the valley's oldest town, sweet-life St. Helena, and down-to-earth Calistoga all make good home bases here. (Calistoga has the extra draw of local thermal springs.) Yountville has become a culinary boomtown, while the tiny communities of Oakville and Rutherford are surrounded by major vintners like Robert Mondavi and Francis Ford Coppola. Rutherford in particular is the source for outstanding cabernet sauvignon.

2 Sonoma Valley. Historic attractions and an unpretentious attitude prevail here. The town of Sonoma, with its atmospheric central plaza, is rich with 19th-century buildings. Glen Ellen, meanwhile, has a special connection with author Jack London.

GETTING ORIENTED

The Napa and Sonoma valleys run roughly parallel, northwest to southeast, and are separated by the Mayacamas Mountains. Northwest of the Sonoma Valley are several more important viticultural areas in Sonoma County, including the Dry Creek, Alexander, and Russian River valleys. The Carneros region, which spans southern Sonoma and Napa counties, is just north of San Pablo Bay, and the closest of all these wine regions to San Francisco.

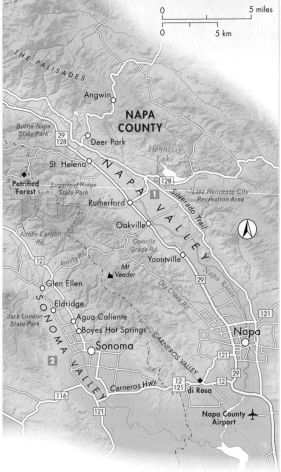

20

3 Elsewhere in Sonoma. The winding, rural roads here feel a world away from Napa's main drag. The lovely Russian River, Dry Creek, and Alexander valleys are all excellent places to seek out pinot noir, zinfandel, and chardonnay. The small town of Healdsburg gets lots of attention, thanks to its terrific restaurants, bed-and-breakfasts, and chic boutiques.

Updated by
Sharron Wood

Life is lived well in the California Wine Country. Eating and, above all, drinking are cultivated as high arts. If you've been daydreaming about driving through vineyards, stopping here and there for a wine tasting or a picnic, well, that fantasy is just everyday life here.

It's little wonder that so many visitors to San Francisco take a day or two—or five or six—to unwind in the Napa and Sonoma valleys. They join the locals in the tasting rooms, from serious wine collectors making their annual pilgrimages to wine newbies who don't know the difference between a merlot and mourvèdre but are eager to learn.

The state's wine industry is booming, and the Napa and Sonoma valleys have long led the field. For instance, in 1975 Napa Valley had no more than 20 wineries; today there are more than 275. A recent up-and-comer is the Carneros region, which overlaps Napa and Sonoma counties at the head of the San Francisco Bay. (Chardonnay and pinot noir grapes thrive on its cool, windy hillsides.)

Great dining and wine go hand in hand, and the local viticulture has naturally encouraged a robust passion for food. Several outstanding chefs have taken root here, sealing the area's reputation as one of the best restaurant destinations in the country. The lust for fine food doesn't stop at the doors of the bistros, either. Whether you visit an artisanal olive-oil producer, nibble locally made cheese, or browse the fresh vegetables in the farmers' markets, you'll soon see why Napa and Sonoma are a food-lover's paradise.

Napa and Sonoma counties are also rich in history. In the town of Sonoma, for example, you can explore buildings from California's Spanish and Mexican past. Some wineries, such as Napa Valley's Beringer, have cellars or tasting rooms dating to the late 1800s. The town of Calistoga is a flurry of Steamboat Gothic architecture, gussied up with the fretwork favored by late-19th-century spa goers. Modern architecture is the exception rather than the rule, but one standout example is the postmodern extravaganza of Clos Pegase winery in Calistoga.

Binding all these temptations together is the sheer scenic beauty of the place. Much of Napa Valley's landscape unspools in orderly, densely planted rows of vines. Sonoma's vistas are broken by rolling hills or stands of ancient oak and madrone trees. Even the climate cooperates, as the warm summer days and refreshingly cool evenings that make the area one of the world's best grape-growing regions make perfect weather for traveling, too. If you're inspired to dig further into the Wine Country, grab a copy of *Fodor's InFocus Napa & Sonoma* or the in-depth *Compass American Guide: California Wine Country.*

PLANNING

WHEN TO GO

"Crush," the term used to indicate the season when grapes are picked and crushed, usually takes place in September or October, depending on the weather. From September until November the entire Wine Country celebrates its bounty with street fairs and festivals. The Sonoma County Harvest Fair, with its famous grape stomp, is held the first weekend in October. Golf tournaments, wine auctions, and art and food fairs occur throughout fall.

In season (April through November), Napa Valley draws crowds of tourists, and traffic along Route 29 from St. Helena to Calistoga is often backed up on weekends. The Sonoma Valley, Santa Rosa, and Healdsburg are less crowded. In season and over holiday weekends it's best to book lodging, restaurant, and winery reservations at least a month in advance. Many wineries give tours at specified times and require appointments.

To avoid crowds, visit the Wine Country during the week and get an early start (most wineries open around 10). Because many wineries close as early as 4 or 4:30—and almost none are open past 5—you'll need to get a reasonably early start if you want to fit in more than one or two, especially if you're going to enjoy the leisurely lunch customary in the Wine Country. Summer is usually hot and dry, and autumn can be even hotter, so dress appropriately if you go during these times.

GETTING HERE AND AROUND

AIR TRAVEL

If you'd like to bypass San Francisco or Oakland, you can fly directly to the small Charles M. Schulz Sonoma County Airport (STS) in Santa Rosa on Horizon Air, which has direct flights from Los Angeles, Portland, Las Vegas, and Seattle. Rental cars are available from Avis, Budget, Enterprise, and Hertz at the airport.

BUS TRAVEL

Bus travel is an inconvenient way to explore the Wine Country. Service is infrequent and buses from San Francisco can only get you to Santa Rosa or the town of Vallejo, south of Napa—neither of which is close to the vineyards. Sonoma County Transit offers daily bus service to points all over the county. VINE (Valley Intracity Neighborhood Express) provides bus service within the city of Napa and between other Napa Valley towns.

20

Bus Lines Greyhound (☎ *800/231–2222*). **Sonoma County Transit** (☎ *707/576–7433 or 800/345–7433*). **VINE** (☎ *707/251–2800*).

CAR TRAVEL

Driving your own car is by far the best way to explore the Wine Country. Well-maintained roads zip through the centers of the Napa and Sonoma valleys, while scenic routes thread through the backcountry. Distances between towns are fairly short, and you can often drive from one end of the Napa or Sonoma valley to the other in less than an hour—if there's no significant traffic. This may be a relatively rural area, but the usual rush hours still apply, and high-season weekend traffic can be excruciatingly slow, especially on Route 29.

Five major roads cut through the Napa and Sonoma valleys. U.S. 101 and Routes 12 and 121 travel through Sonoma County. Route 29 heads north from Napa. The 25-mi Silverado Trail, which runs parallel to Route 29 north from Napa to Calistoga, is Napa Valley's more scenic, less-crowded alternative to Route 29.

■ **TIP→** Remember, if you're wine-tasting, either select a designated driver or be careful of your wine intake. (When you're taking just a sip or two of any given wine, it can be hard to keep track of how much you're drinking.) Also, keep in mind that you'll likely be sharing the road with cyclists; keep a close eye on the shoulder.

When calculating the time it will take you to drive between the Napa and Sonoma valleys, remember that the Mayacamas Mountains are between the two. If it's not too far out of your way, you might want to travel between the two valleys along Highway 12/121 to the south, or along Highway 128 to the north, to avoid the slow, winding drive on the Oakville Grade, which connects Oakville, in Napa, and Glen Ellen, in Sonoma.

From San Francisco to Napa: Cross the Golden Gate Bridge, then go north on U.S. 101. Next go east on Route 37 toward Vallejo, then north on Route 121, also called the Carneros Highway. Turn left (north) when Route 121 runs into Route 29. This should take about 1½ hours when traffic is light.

From San Francisco to Sonoma: Cross the Golden Gate Bridge, then go north on U.S. 101, east on Route 37 toward Vallejo, and north on Route 121, aka the Carneros Highway. When you reach Route 12, take it north. If you're going to any of the Sonoma County destinations north of the valley, take U.S. 101 all the way north through Santa Rosa to Healdsburg. This should take about an hour, not counting substantial traffic.

From Berkeley and other East Bay towns: Take Interstate 80 north to Route 37 west, then on to Route 29 north. To head up the Napa Valley, continue on Route 29; to reach Sonoma County, turn off Route 29 onto Route 121 heading north. Getting from Berkeley to Napa will take at least 45 minutes, from Berkeley to Sonoma at least an hour.

RESTAURANTS

Star chefs from around the world have come into the Wine Country's orbit, drawn by the area's phenomenal produce, artisanal foods, and wines. These days, many visitors come to Napa and Sonoma as much for the restaurants' tasting menus as for the wineries' tasting rooms.

Although excellent meals can be found virtually everywhere in the region, the small town of Yountville has become a culinary crossroads under the influence of chef Thomas Keller. If a table at Keller's famed French Laundry is out of reach, keep in mind that he's also behind a number of more modest restaurants in town. In St. Helena the elegant Restaurant at Meadowood has just as much critical acclaim as the French Laundry, yet is considerably easier to get into. And the buzzed-about restaurants in Sonoma County, including Cyrus and Farmhouse Inn, offer plenty of mouthwatering options.

Inexpensive eateries include high-end delis that serve superb picnic fare, and brunch is a cost-effective strategy at pricey restaurants, as is sitting at the bar and ordering a few appetizers instead of sitting down to a full-blown meal.

With few exceptions (which are noted in individual restaurant listings), dress is informal. Where reservations are indicated as essential, you may need to make them a week or more ahead. In summer and early fall you may need to book several weeks ahead.

HOTELS

Napa and Sonoma know the tourism ropes well; their inns and hotels range from low-key to utterly luxurious, and generally maintain high standards. Most of the bed-and-breakfasts are in historic Victorian and Spanish buildings, and the breakfast part of the equation often involves fresh local produce. The newer hotels tend to have a more modern, streamlined aesthetic and elaborate, spalike bathrooms. Many hotels and B&Bs have excellent restaurants on their grounds, and those that don't are still just a short drive away from gastronomic bliss.

However, all of this comes with a hefty price tag. As the cost of vineyards and grapes has risen, so have lodging rates. Santa Rosa, the largest population center in the area, has the widest selection of moderately priced rooms. Try there if you've failed to reserve in advance or have a limited budget. In general, all accommodations in the area often have lower rates on weeknights, and prices are about 20% lower in winter.

On weekends, two- or even three-night minimum stays are commonly required, especially at smaller inns and B&Bs. If you'd prefer to stay a single night, though, innkeepers are usually more flexible in winter. Many B&Bs book up long in advance of the summer and fall seasons. Many B&Bs and small inns also discourage the presence of children though fall short of actually prohibiting them. If you're traveling with children, be sure to ask about them when booking to make sure they will receive a warm welcome.

Hotel reviews have been condensed for this book. Please go to Fodors. com for expanded reviews of each property.

BED-AND-BREAKFAST ASSOCIATIONS

Bed & Breakfast Association of Sonoma Valley (☎ 800/969–4667 ⊕ www. sonomabb.com). The Wine Country Inns of Sonoma County (☎ 800/946–3268 ⊕ www.winecountryinns.com).

DINING AND LODGING PRICE CATEGORIES					
	¢	$	$$	$$$	$$$$
Restaurants	under $10	$10–$14	$15–$22	$23–$30	over $30
Hotels	under $200	$200–$250	$251–$300	$301–$400	over $400

Restaurant prices are per person for a main course at dinner, or for a prix fixe if a set menu is the only option. Hotel prices are for two people in a standard double room in high season.

TOURS

Full-day guided tours of the Wine Country generally include lunch, and cost about $60–$100 per person. Reservations are usually required.

Beau Wine Tours (✉ 21707 8th St. E, Sonoma ☎ 707/938–8001 or 800/387–2328 ⊕ www.beauwinetours.com) organizes personalized tours of Napa and Sonoma in their limos, vans, and shuttle buses. **Gray Line** (✉ Pier 43½, Embarcadero, San Francisco ☎ 415/434–8687 or 888/428–6937 ⊕ www.grayline.com) has a tour that covers both the southern Napa and Sonoma valleys in a single day, with a stop for lunch in Yountville. **Great Pacific Tour Co.** (✉ 518 Octavia St., Hayes Valley, San Francisco ☎ 415/626–4499 ⊕ www.greatpacifictour.com) operates full-day tours of Napa and Sonoma, including a restaurant lunch, in passenger vans that seat 14. In addition to renting bikes by the day, **Wine Country Bikes** (✉ 61 Front St., Healdsburg ☎ 707/473–0610 ⊕ www.winecountrybikes.com) organizes both one-day and multiday trips throughout Sonoma County.

THE NAPA VALLEY

When it comes to wine production in the United States, Napa Valley rules the roost, with more than 275 wineries and many of the biggest brands in the business. Vastly diverse soils and microclimates give Napa winemakers the chance to make a tremendous variety of wines. But what's the area like beyond the glossy advertising and boldface names?

The handful of small towns strung along Highway 29 are where wine-industry workers live, and they're also where most of the area lodging is. Napa—the valley's largest town—lures with its few cultural attractions and accommodations that are (relatively) reasonably priced. A few miles farther north, compact Yountville is a culinary boomtown, densely packed with top-notch restaurants and hotels, including a few luxury properties. Continuing north, St. Helena teems with elegant boutiques and restaurants; mellow Calistoga, known for spas and hot springs, feels a bit like an Old West frontier town, and has a more casual attitude.

Napa Valley

Mount St Helena 38
Robert Louis Stevenson State Park
THE PALISADES
Aetna Springs
Pope Valley
POPE VALLEY
Lake Berryessa
Calistoga 33
128
37
Petrified Forest Rd.
Dunaweal Ln.
Howell Mtn Rd.
Angwin
Angwin Airport
Lake Berryessa Recreation Area
Larkmead Ln.
36 35 34
Diamond Mountain
Bothe-Napa State Park
29 128
NAPA COUNTY
Chiles Pope Valley Rd.
SONOMA COUNTY
Bale Grist Mill State Historic Park
28
31 30 Silverado Trail
Hennessy Lake
Sage Canyon Rd.
128
32 29
Saint Helena
27
Lake Hennessy City Recreation Area
Atlas Peak
FOSS VALLEY
Sugarloaf Ridge State Park
23
24 26
22 25 18
Rutherford 21
20 17
19 16 Oakville
Oakville Cross Rd.
Hood Mountain Regional Park
Bald Mountain
Mt St. John
Oakville Grade Rd.
14 15
Yountville Hills
Yountville Cross Rd.
11
Annadel State Park
Kenwood
Sonoma Hwy.
Adobe Canyon Rd.
12
Trinity Rd.
Mt Veeder
13 12 10
9 8
Yountville
Napa River
Silverado Trail
Glen Ellen
VALLEY OF THE MOON
Eldridge
12
Agua Caliente
Sonoma Mountain
Jack London State Park
Boyes Hot Springs
REDWOOD CANYON
Dry Creek Rd.
Oak Knoll
7 6
El Verano
5
Redwood Rd.
Browns Valley Rd.
CARNEROS VALLEY
Trancas St.
Pueblo
Lincoln
Napa
4
SONOMA MOUNTAINS
Sonoma
Napa Rd.
3
Henry Rd.
Old Sonoma Rd.
121
Imola Ave.
Temelec
Dealy La.
Washington
Adobe Rd.
12 121
1 2
29
Petaluma
116
Carneros Hwy.
Bonness Rd.
121
Lakeville Hwy.
101
Napa County Airport

0 — 4 mi
0 — 4 km

Artesa Vineyards & Winery . **3**
Beaulieu Vineyard **22**
Beringer Vineyards **28**
Cakebread Cellars **19**
Castello di Amorosa **35**
Caymus Vineyards **25**
Charles Krug Winery **31**
Clos du Val **8**
Clos Pegase **36**
Crushpad **7**

Culinary Institute **29**
di Rosa **2**
Domaine Carneros **1**
Domaine Chandon **9**
Far Niente **14**
Frog's Leap **24**
Hess Collection Winery ...**5**
Indian Springs **33**
Joseph Phelps Vineyards .**30**
Luna Vineyards **6**

Mumm Napa **26**
Napa Valley Museum **13**
Oakville Grocery **15**
Opus One **17**
Oxbow Public Market **4**
PlumpJack **18**
Robert Louis Stevenson State Park **38**
Robert Mondavi **16**
Robert Sinskey **11**

Round Pond **23**
Rubicon Estate **20**
Rutherford Hill Winery ...**27**
Schramsberg **34**
Spring Mountain **32**
St. Supéry **21**
Stag's Leap Wine Cellars .**10**
Storybook Mountain **37**
V Marketplace **12**

Wine and contemporary art find a home at di Rosa.

ESSENTIALS

Contacts Napa Valley Destination Council (☎ 707/226–7459 ⊕ *www. legendarynapavalley.com*).

NAPA

46 mi from San Francisco via I–80 east and north, Rte. 37 west, and Rte. 29 north.

The town of Napa is the valley's largest, and visitors who get a glimpse of the strip malls and big-box stores from Highway 29 often speed right past on the way to smaller and more seductive Yountville or St. Helena. But Napa doesn't entirely deserve its dowdy reputation. After many years as a blue-collar town that more or less turned its back on the Wine Country scene, Napa has spent the last few years attempting to increase its appeal to visitors, with somewhat mixed results. A walkway that follows the river through town, completed in 2008, makes the city more pedestrian-friendly, and in the last two years a surprising number of high-profile new restaurants have popped up, but you'll still find a handful of empty storefronts among the wine bars and tasting rooms.

Many visitors choose to stay in Napa after experiencing hotel sticker shock; prices in Napa are marginally more reasonable than elsewhere. If you set up your home base here, you'll undoubtedly want to spend some time getting out of town and into the beautiful countryside, but don't neglect taking a stroll to see what Napa's least pretentious town has to offer, or checking out the culinary landscape, which seems to be changing faster here than anywhere else in the valley.

GETTING HERE AND AROUND

To get to downtown Napa from Route 29, take the 1st Street exit and follow the signs for Central Napa less than a mile through town until you reach the corner of 2nd Street and Main Street. Most of the town's sights and many of its restaurants are clustered in an easily walkable area around this intersection.

EXPLORING

Artesa Vineyards & Winery. With its modern, minimalist look in the tasting room, which is dug into a Carneros hilltop, and contemporary sculptures and fountains on the property, Artesa Vineyards & Winery is a far cry from the many faux French châteaus and rustic Italian-style villas in the region. Although the Spanish owners once made only sparkling wines, now they produce primarily still wines, mostly chardonnay and pinot noir, but also cabernet sauvignon and a smattering of other limited-release wines such as syrah and albariño. Call ahead to reserve a spot on one of the specialty tours, such as a wine-and-cheese pairing or the walk through the vineyard ($45). ☒ *1345 Henry Rd., north off Old Sonoma Rd. and Dealy La.* ☎ *707/224–1668* ⊕ *www.artesawinery. com* ☲ *Tasting $10–$15, tour $20* ☉ *Daily 10–5; tour daily at 11 and 2.*

Clos du Val. Although this austere winery doesn't seduce you with dramatic architecture or lush grounds, it doesn't have to: the wines, crafted by winemaker John Clews, have a wide following, especially among those who are patient enough to cellar the wines for a number of years. Though Clews's team makes great pinot noir and chardonnay (grown in the nearby Carneros region), the real claim to fame is the intense reserve cabernet, made with fruit from the Stags Leap District. The few picnic tables fill up early on summer weekends, and anyone is welcome to try a hand at the boccie-style French game of pétanque. ☒ *5330 Silverado Trail* ☎ *707/259–2200* ⊕ *www.closduval.com* ☲ *Tasting $15–$25* ☉ *Daily 10–5; tour by appointment.*

Fodor'sChoice
★

di Rosa. While you're driving along the Carneros Highway on your way to Napa from San Francisco, it would be easy to zip by one of the region's best-kept secrets: di Rosa. Metal sculptures of sheep grazing in the grass mark the entrance to this sprawling, art-stuffed property. Thousands of 20th-century artworks by hundreds of Northern California artists crop up everywhere—in galleries, in the former di Rosa residence, on every lawn, in every courtyard, and even on the lake. Some of the works were commissioned especially for the preserve, such as Paul Kos's meditative *Chartres Bleu,* a video installation in a chapel-like setting that replicates a stained-glass window of the cathedral in Chartres, France. If you stop by without a reservation, you'll only gain access to the Gatehouse Gallery, where there's a small collection of riotously colorful figurative and abstract sculpture and painting. ■**TIP➜ To see the rest of the property and artwork, you'll have to sign up for one of the various tours of the grounds (from 1 to 2½ hours).** Reservations for the tours are recommended, but they can sometimes accommodate walk-ins. ☒ *5200 Sonoma Hwy./Carneros Hwy.* ☎ *707/226–5991* ⊕ *www. dirosaart.org* ☲ *Free, tour $10–$15* ☉ *Wed.–Fri. 9:30–3, Sat. by reservation; call for tour times.*

20

★ **Domaine Carneros.** The majestic château here looks for all the world like it belongs in France, and in fact it does: it's modeled after the Château de la Marquetterie, an 18th-century mansion owned by the Taittinger family near Epernay, France. Carved into the hillside beneath the winery, Domaine Carneros's cellars produce delicate sparkling wines reminiscent of those made by Taittinger, using only grapes grown locally in the Carneros wine district. The winery sells full glasses, flights, and bottles of their wines, which also include still wines like a handful of pinot noirs and a merlot, and serves them with cheese plates or caviar to those seated in the Louis XV–inspired salon or on the terrace overlooking the vineyards. Though this makes a visit here a tad more expensive than some stops on a winery tour, it's also one of the most opulent ways to enjoy the Carneros District, especially on fair days, when the views over the vineyards are spectacular. ✉ *1240 Duhig Rd.* ☎ *707/257–0101* ⊕ *www.domainecarneros.com* ✉ *Tasting $6.75–$25, tour $25* ☉ *Daily 10–6; tour daily at 11, 1, and 3.*

Fodor's Choice **Hess Collection Winery.** Nine miles northwest of the city of Napa, up a
★ winding road ascending Mt. Veeder, this winery is a delightful discovery. The simple limestone structure, rustic from the outside but modern and airy within, contains Swiss owner Donald Hess's personal art collection, including mostly large-scale works by such contemporary European and American artists as Robert Motherwell, Andy Goldsworthy, and Frank Stella. Cabernet sauvignon is the real strength here, though Hess also produces some fine chardonnays. Self-guided tours of the art collection and guided tours of the winery's production facilities are both free. On weekdays, ask to borrow an iPod for the free audio tour, which includes commentary by Donald Hess and some of the artists featured in the collection. ✉ *4411 Redwood Rd., west of Rte. 29* ☎ *707/255–1144* ⊕ *www.hesscollection.com* ✉ *Tasting $10–$30* ☉ *Daily 10–5:30; guided tours daily, usually hourly 10:30–3:30.*

Luna Vineyards. Established in 1995 by veterans of the Napa wine industry, this spot on the southern end of the Silverado Trail originally focused on Italian varieties such as sangiovese and pinot grigio. Though these days you're just as likely to taste a merlot or a cabernet blend, it's still well worth visiting its Tuscan-style tasting room with a coffered ceiling, especially for a nip of late-harvest sauvignon blanc and semillon dessert wine called Mille Baci ("a thousand kisses" in Italian). ✉ *2921 Silverado Trail* ☎ *707/255–5862* ⊕ *www.lunavineyards.com* ✉ *Tasting $15–$25* ☉ *Daily 10–5.*

Oxbow Public Market. Though it's not terribly large, this collection of about 25 small shops, wine bars, and artisanal food producers is a fun place to begin your introduction to the wealth of food and wine available in the Napa Valley. Swoon over the decadent charcuterie at the Fatted Calf, slurp down some oysters on the half shell at Hog Island Oyster Company, sample a large variety of local olive oils at the Olive Press, or get a whiff of the hard-to-find seasonings at the Whole Spice Company before sitting down to a glass of wine at one of the wine bars. A branch of the retro fast-food joint Gott's Roadside tempts those who prefer hamburgers to duck-liver mousse. ✉ *610 and 644 1st St.* ☎ *No phone* ⊕ *www.oxbowpublicmarket.com* ✉ *Free* ☉ *Generally weekdays 9–9, weekends 10–9; hrs of some merchants vary.*

Climbing ivy and lily pads decorate the Hess Collection's rustic exterior.

WHERE TO EAT

$$$
FRENCH
✕ **Angèle.** An 1890s boathouse with a vaulted wood-beam ceiling sets the scene for romance at this cozy French bistro. Though the style is casual—tables are close together, and the warm, crusty bread is plunked right down on the paper-top tables—the food is always well executed. Look for classic French dishes like duck breast accompanied with confit, guinea hen wrapped in house-cured pancetta, or a starter of *ris de veau* (veal sweetbreads) with a poached duck egg. In fair weather, ask for one of the charming outdoor tables. ⊠ *540 Main St.* ☎ *707/252–8115* ⊕ *www.angelerestaurant.com.*

$
AMERICAN
✕ **BarBersQ.** Hardly a down-home ramshackle barbecue shack, this temple to meat in the middle of a shopping center has a clean, modern aesthetic, with black-and-white photos on the wall and brushed aluminum chairs. The menu of barbecue favorites includes a half or full rack of smoked baby back ribs and a Memphis-style pulled-pork sandwich, all served with your choice of three different sauces. The supremely juicy fried chicken, made with free-range chicken and served with mashed potatoes and vinegary collard greens, is also popular. If you can save any room, the root-beer float or chocolate bourbon pecan pie is a fitting end to a homey meal. Outside seating (on a patio facing the parking lot) is available on fair days. ⊠ *3900D Bel Aire Plaza* ☎ *707/224–6600* ⊕ *www.barbersq.com.*

$$$
ITALIAN
★
✕ **Bistro Don Giovanni.** Co-owner and host Giovanni Scala might be around to warmly welcome you to this lively bistro, where you can peek past the copper pots hanging in the open kitchen to see the 750-degree wood-burning oven. The Cal-Italian food is simultaneously inventive

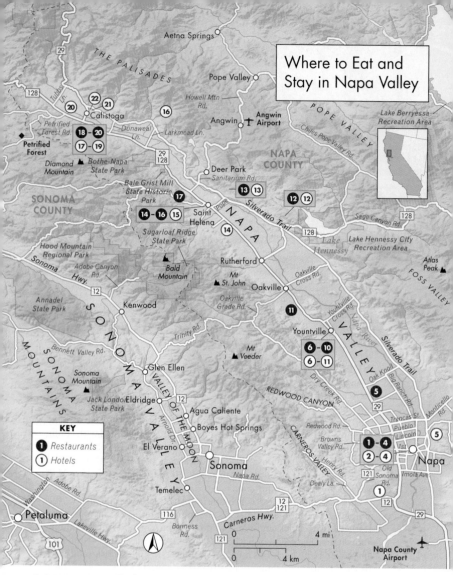

Where to Eat and Stay in Napa Valley

KEY

1️⃣ Restaurants
① Hotels

Restaurants ▼

Ad Hoc 6
All Seasons Bistro 19
Angèle 1
Auberge du Soleil 12
BarBersQ 3
Barolo 20
Bistro Don Giovanni 5
Bottega 7
Bouchon 9
Bounty Hunter 2
Calistoga Inn Restaurant and Brewery 18
Étoile 10
French Laundry 8
Go Fish 15
Press 14
Morimota Napa 4
Mustards Grill 11
Terra 16
The Restaurant at Meadowood 13
Wine Spectator Greystone Restaurant ... 17

Hotels ▼

Auberge du Soleil 12
Bardessono 6
Blackbird Inn 2
Brannan Cottage Inn 17
Calistoga Ranch 16
Carneros Inn 1
Cottage Grove Inn 18
El Bonita Motel 14
Hotel Luca 10
Indian Springs 21
Maison Fleurie 7
Meadowlark Country House 20
Meadowood Resort 13
Milliken Creek Inn 5
Mount View Hotel & Spa ... 19
Napa River Inn 3
Napa Valley Railway Inn ... 11
Solage 22
Villagio Inn & Spa 8
Vintage Inn 9
Westin Verasa 4
Wine Country Inn 15

and comforting: an excellent fritto misto of onions, fennel, calamari, and plump rock shrimp; pizza with caramelized onions and Gorgonzola; and whole roasted fish. Children are unusually welcome here, catered to with crayons and paper-topped tables and a menu with items like pizza topped with cheese, french fries, and "no green stuff." Fodors. com Forum users suggest snagging a table on the covered patio for a "more intimate and quiet" experience. ⊠ *4110 Howard La./Rte. 29* ☎ *707/224–3300* ⊕ *www.bistrodongiovanni.com.*

$$
AMERICAN
★

✕ **Bounty Hunter.** A triple threat, Bounty Hunter is a wine store, wine bar, and restaurant in one. You can stop by for just a glass of wine from their impressive list—a frequently changing list with 40 available by the glass in both 2- and 5-ounce pours, and 400 by the bottle—but it's best to come with an appetite. A miniscule kitchen means the menu is also small, but every dish is a standout, including the pulled-pork and beef brisket sandwiches served with three types of barbecue sauce, the signature beer-can chicken, and meltingly tender St. Louis–style ribs. The space is whimsically rustic, with stuffed game trophies mounted on the wall and leather saddles standing in for seats at a couple of tables. ■**TIP→** It's open until midnight on Friday and Saturday, making it a popular spot among locals for a late-night bite. ⊠ *975 1st St.* ☎ *707/226–3976* ⊕ *www.bountyhunterwinebar.com* ⌂ *Reservations not accepted.*

$$$$
JAPANESE

✕ **Morimoto Napa.** Masuharu Morimoto, known to many as the star of Iron Chef but also well regarded for his eponymous restaurants around the world, is the big name behind this hot restaurant that opened in downtown Napa in 2010. Organic materials like twisting grapevines above the bar and rough-hewn wooden tables seem simultaneously earthy and modern, which seems a fitting setting for the gorgeously plated Japanese fare, from superfresh sashimi served with grated fresh wasabi to more-elaborate concoctions like sea-urchin carbonara, made with udon noodles. For the full experience, consider the omakase menu ($110). If no tables are available, you can still order many dishes in the lounge, where a young and lively crowd drinks specialty cocktails along with appetizers like a tempura calamari salad and pork gyoza. ⊠ *610 Main St.* ☎ *707/252–1600* ⊕ *www.morimotonapa.com* ⊙ *No lunch Mon. or Tues.*

20

WHERE TO STAY

$–$$

🏨 **Blackbird Inn.** Arts and Crafts style infuses this 1905 building, from the lobby's enormous fieldstone fireplace to the lamps that cast a warm glow over the impressive wooden staircase to the attractive guest rooms, with sturdy turn-of-the-20th-century oak beds and matching night tables. **Pros:** gorgeous architecture and period furnishings; convenient to downtown Napa; free afternoon wine service. **Cons:** must be booked well in advance; some rooms are on the small side. **TripAdvisor:** "breakfast was surprisingly good," "charming arts and crafts style," "fantastic location." ⊠ *1755 1st St.* ☎ *707/226–2450 or 888/567–9811* ⊕ *www. blackbirdinnnapa.com* ⌂ *8 rooms* ⌂ *In-room: a/c, Wi-Fi. In-hotel: some pets allowed.*

$$$$
Fodor's Choice
★ **Carneros Inn.** Freestanding board-and-batten cottages with rocking chairs on each porch are simultaneously rustic and chic at this luxurious property. **Pros:** cottages have lots of privacy; beautiful views from the hilltop pool and hot tub; heaters on each private patio encourage lounging outside in the evening. **Cons:** a long drive from destinations up-valley; smallish rooms with limited seating options. **TripAdvisor:** "setting was top notch," "rooms are luxurious," "restaurant was brilliant." ⊠ *4048 Sonoma Hwy.* ☎ 707/299–4900 ⊕ *www.thecarnerosinn.com* ⚲ 76 *cottages, 10 suites* ⚐ *In-room: a/c, Wi-Fi. In-hotel: restaurants, room service, bar, pool, gym, spa, some pets allowed.*

> **MAKING TRACKS IN NAPA**
>
> Turn the driving over to someone else—a train conductor. The **Napa Valley Wine Train** (⊠ *1275 McKinstry St.* ☎ *707/253–2111 or 800/427–4124* ⊕ *www.winetrain. com*) runs a scenic route between Napa and St. Helena with several restored 1915–17 Pullman railroad cars. The ride often includes a meal, such as brunch or dinner. While it's no bargain (starting at around $90 for lunch, $100 for dinner) and can feel a bit hokey, the train gives you a chance to enjoy the vineyard views without any driving worries.

$$$$ **Milliken Creek Inn.** Wine and cheese at sunset set a romantic mood in the intimate lobby, with its terrace overlooking the Napa River and a lush lawn, while chic rooms take a page from the stylebook of British-colonial Asia, with a khaki-and-cream color scheme and gauzy canopies over the beds in some rooms, alongside hydrotherapy spa tubs and some of the fluffiest beds in the Wine Country. **Pros:** soft-as-clouds beds; serene hotel-guests-only spa; breakfast delivered to your room (or wherever you'd like to eat on the grounds); gratuities are not accepted (except at the spa). **Cons:** expensive; road noise can be heard from the admittedly beautiful outdoor areas. **TripAdvisor:** "service was superb," "modern chic with a cozy charm," "extraordinarily luxurious." ⊠ *1815 Silverado Trail* ☎ *707/255–1197 or 800/835–6112* ⊕ *www.millikencreekinn.com* ⚲ *12 rooms* ⚐ *In-room: a/c, Wi-Fi. In-hotel: spa, some age restrictions.*

$$–$$$ **Napa River Inn.** Almost everything's close here: this waterfront inn is part of a complex of restaurants, shops, a gallery, and a spa, all within easy walking distance of downtown Napa. **Pros:** a pedestrian walkway connects the hotel to downtown Napa; unusual pet-friendly policy; wide range of room sizes and prices. **Cons:** river views could be more scenic; some rooms get noise from nearby restaurants. **TripAdvisor:** "very professional and accommodating," "amenities are generous," "beds were comfortable." ⊠ *500 Main St.* ☎ *707/251–8500 or 877/251–8500* ⊕ *www.napariverinn.com* ⚲ *65 rooms, 1 suite* ⚐ *In-room: a/c, Wi-Fi. In-hotel: restaurants, bar, gym, spa, business center, some pets allowed.*

$$$–$$$$ **Westin Verasa.** Across the street from the Wine Train depot and just behind the Oxbow Public Market, this spacious hotel-condo complex, opened in 2008, is sophisticated and soothing, with pristine white bedding and furniture in warm earth tones. **Pros:** pool is heated year-round; most rooms have well-equipped kitchenettes; spacious double-headed showers. **Cons:** $20 "amenities fee" charged in addition to room rate. **TripAdvisor:** "very pleasant and helpful," "well-run and top notch," "modern and comfortable rooms." ✉ *1314 Mckinstry St.* ☎ *707/257–1800* ⊕ *www.westin.com/napa* ⇴ *130 rooms, 50 suites* ⌂ *In-room: a/c, kitchen (some), Internet, Wi-Fi. In-hotel: restaurants, room service, bar, pool, gym, some pets allowed.*

NIGHTLIFE AND THE ARTS

The interior of the 1879 Italianate Victorian **Napa Valley Opera House** isn't quite as majestic as the facade, but the intimate 500-seat venue is still an excellent place to see all sorts of performances, from Pat Metheny and Mandy Patinkin to the Napa Valley Film Festival and, yes, even the occasional opera. ✉ *1030 Main St.* ☎ *707/226–7372* ⊕ *www. napavalleyoperahouse.org.*

SPORTS AND THE OUTDOORS

BICYCLING Thanks to the scenic country roads that wind through the region, bicycling is a practically perfect way to get around the Wine Country. And whether you're interested in an easy spin to a few wineries or a strenuous haul up a mountainside, there's a way to make it happen. ■**TIP**➔ There are almost no designated bike lanes in the Wine Country, though, so be sure to pay attention to traffic.

Napa Valley Bike Tours (✉ *6795 Washington St., Yountville* ☎ *707/944–2953*) will deliver the bikes, which go for $35 to $70 a day, to many hotels in the Napa Valley if you're renting at least two bikes for a full day. In addition to hourly rentals, a variety of guided and self-guided winery tours are available.

YOUNTVILLE

13 mi north of the town of Napa on Rte. 29.

These days Yountville is something like Disneyland for food-lovers. It all started with Thomas Keller's French Laundry, simply one of the best restaurants in the United States. Now Keller is also behind two more-casual restaurants a few blocks from his mother ship—and that's only the tip of the iceberg. You could stay here for a week and not exhaust all the options in this tiny town with a big culinary reputation.

Yountville is full of small inns and high-end hotels that cater to those who prefer to walk (not drive) after an extravagant meal. It's also well located for excursions to many big-name Napa wineries, especially those in the Stags Leap District, where big, bold cabernet sauvignons helped put the Napa Valley on the wine-making map.

GETTING HERE AND AROUND

To get to Yountville from Highway 29 traveling north, take the Yountville exit and then take the first left, onto Washington Street. Almost all of Yountville's business and restaurants are clustered along Washington Street in the first half mile. Yountville Cross Road connects tiny downtown Yountville to the Silverado Trail, along which many of the area's best wineries are located.

20

CLOSE UP

A Quick Wine Glossary

Like any activity, wine making and wine tasting have specialized vocabularies, and most of the terms are actually quite helpful, once you have them down. Here are some core terms to know:

American Viticultural Area (AVA). More commonly termed an "appellation," this is a region with unique soil, climate, and other grape-growing conditions. When a label lists an appellation—Napa Valley or Mt. Veeder, for example—at least 75% of the grapes used to make the wine must come from that region.

Aroma and bouquet. Aroma is the fruit-derived scent of young wine. It diminishes with fermentation and becomes a more complex **bouquet** as the wine ages.

Corked. Describes wine that is flawed by the musty, wet-cardboard flavor imparted by cork mold.

Estate bottled. A wine entirely made by one winery at a single facility. The grapes must come from the winery's own vineyards within the same appellation (which must be printed on the label).

Horizontal tasting. A tasting of several different wines of the same vintage.

Library wine. An older vintage that the winery has put aside to sell at a later date.

Méthode champenoise. The traditional, time-consuming method of making sparkling wines that are fermented in individual bottles.

Oaky. A vanilla-woody flavor that develops when wine is aged in oak barrels. Too much overpowers the other flavors.

Reserve wine. Fuzzy term applied by vintners to indicate that a wine is better in some way (through aging, source of the grapes, etc.) than others from their winery.

Table wine. Any wine that has at least 7% but not more than 14% alcohol by volume. The term doesn't necessarily imply anything about the wine's quality or price—both super-premium and jug wines can be labeled as table wine.

Tannins. These natural grape compounds produce a sensation of drying or astringency in the mouth and throat.

Terroir. French for "soil." Typically used to describe the soil and climate conditions that influence the quality and characteristics of grapes and wine.

Varietal. A wine that takes its name from the grape variety from which it is predominantly made. California wines that qualify are almost always labeled with the variety of the source grape.

Vertical tasting. A tasting of several wines of different vintages.

Vinification. Wine making, the process by which grapes are made into wine.

Vintage. The grape harvest of a given year, and the year in which the grapes are harvested. A vintage date on a bottle indicates the year in which the grapes were harvested rather than the year in which the wine was bottled.

Viticulture. The cultivation of grapes.

EXPLORING

Domaine Chandon. On a knoll west of downtown dotted with whimsical sculptures and shaded with ancient oak trees, this French-owned winery claims one of Yountville's prime pieces of real estate. Basic tours of the sleek, modern facilities are available for $12 (not including a tasting), but other tours ($30 each), which focus on various topics (food-and-wine pairing or pinot production, for example), end with a seated tasting. The top-quality sparklers are made using the laborious *méthode champenoise*. For the complete experience, you can order hors d'oeuvres to accompany the wines in the tasting room, which can be ordered either by tasting flights or by the glass. Although Chandon is best known for its bubblies, still wines like their chardonnay, pinot noir, and pinot meunier are also worth a try. ⊠ *1 California Dr., west of Rte. 29* ☎ *707/944–2280* ⊕ *www.chandon.com* 🍷 *Tasting $5.50–$25 by the glass, $16–$22 by the flight* ⊙ *Daily 10–6; tours daily at 1:30.*

Napa Valley Museum. Although it's not worth a long detour, if you need a break from wine tasting you can visit this small museum, next to Domaine Chandon on the grounds of the town's Veterans Home. Downstairs its permanent exhibit, The Land and People of Napa Valley, focuses on the geology and history of the area, from the Native Americans who once lived here through the pioneer period to the modern winemakers who made it famous. The rotating fine-arts shows upstairs feature the work of Napa Valley artists. ⊠ *55 Presidents Circle* ☎ *707/944–0500* ⊕ *www.napavalleymuseum.org* 🍷 *$5* ⊙ *Wed.–Mon. 10–5.*

Robert Sinskey Vineyards. Although the winemaker here produces well-regarded cabernet blends, as well as a variety of aromatic white wines, from their all-organic, certified biodynamic vineyards, Sinskey is best known for its intense, brambly pinot noirs, grown in the cooler Carneros District, where the grape thrives. The influence of Rob's wife, Maria Helm Sinskey—a chef and cookbook author and the winery's culinary director—is evident during the tastings, which come with a few bites of food paired with each wine (her books and other culinary items are also available in the gift shop, next to the open kitchen). But for the best sense of how Sinskey wines pair with food, reserve a spot on the culinary tour, which takes you through the winery's gardens and ends with a seated pairing of foods and wine. ⊠ *6320 Silverado Trail, Napa* ☎ *707/944–9090* ⊕ *www.robertsinskey.com* 🍷 *Tasting $25, tour $60* ⊙ *Daily 10–4:30; tour by appointment.*

Stag's Leap Wine Cellars. It was the 1973 cabernet sauvignon produced by Stag's Leap Wine Cellars that put the winery—and the California wine industry—on the map by placing first in the famous Paris tasting of 1976. A visit to the winery is a no-frills affair; visitors in the tasting room are clearly serious about tasting wine, and aren't interested in distractions like a gift shop. It costs $30 to taste the top-of-the-line wines, including their limited-production estate-grown cabernets, a few of which sell for well over $100. If you're interested in more-modestly priced wines, try the $15 tasting, which usually includes a sauvignon blanc, chardonnay, merlot, and cabernet. ⊠ *5766 Silverado Trail, Napa*

20

Continued on page 446

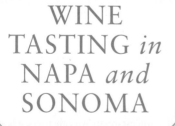

WINE
TASTING *in*
NAPA *and*
SONOMA

The tantalizing pop of a cork. Roads unspooling through hypnotically even rows of vines. Sun glinting through a glass of sparkling wine or ruby colored cabernet. If these are your daydreams, you won't be disappointed when you get to Napa and Sonoma. The vineyard-blanketed hills, shady town squares, and ivy-draped wineries—not to mention the luxurious restaurants, hotels, and spas—really *are* that captivating.

(opposite page) Carneros vineyards in autumn, Napa Valley. (top) Pinot Gris grapes (bottom) Bottles from Far Niente winery.

VISITING WINERIES

Napa and Sonoma are outstanding destinations for both wine newcomers and serious wine buffs. Tasting rooms range from modest to swanky, offering everything from a casual conversation over a few sips of wine to in-depth tours of winemaking facilities and vineyards. And there's a tremendous variety of wines to taste. The one constant is a deep, shared pleasure in the experience of wine tasting.

Wineries in Napa and Sonoma range from faux châteaux with vast gift shops to rustic converted barns where you might have to step over the vintner's dog in the doorway. Many are regularly open to the public, usually daily from around 10 am to 5 pm. Others require advance reservations to visit, and still others are closed to the public entirely. When in doubt, call ahead.

There are many, many more wineries in Napa and Sonoma than we could possibly include here. Free maps pinpointing most of them are widely available, though; ask the staff at the tasting rooms you visit or look for the ubiquitous free tourist magazines.

Pick a designated driver before setting out for the day. Although wineries rarely advertise it, many will provide a free nonalcoholic drink for the designated driver; it never hurts to ask.

Fees. In the past few years, tasting fees have skyrocketed. Most Napa wineries charge $10 to $20 to taste four or so wines, though $30 or even $40 fees aren't unheard of. Sonoma wineries are often a bit cheaper, in the $5 to $15 range, and you'll still find the occasional freebie.

Some winery tours are free, in which case you're usually required to pay a separate fee if you want to taste the wine. If you've paid a fee for the tour—often $15 to $30—your wine tasting is usually included in that price.

MAKING THE MOST OF YOUR TIME

(top) Sipping and swirling in the De Loach tasting room. (bottom) Learning about barrel aging at Robert Mondavi Winery.

■**Call ahead.** Some wineries require reservations to visit or tour. If you have your heart set on visiting a specific place, double-check their availability.

■**Come on weekdays,** especially if you're visiting during high season (May to November), to avoid traffic-clogged roads and crowded tasting rooms. For more info on the best times of year to visit, see this chapter's Planner.

■**Get an early start.** Tasting rooms are often deserted before 11 am or so, when most visitors are still lingering over a second cup of coffee. If you come early, you'll have the staff's undivided attention. You'll usually encounter the largest crowds between 3 and 5 pm.

■**Consider skipping Napa.** If you've got less than two days to spend in the Wine Country, dip into the Carneros area or the Sonoma Valley rather than Napa Valley or northern Sonoma County. Though you might find fewer big-name wineries and critically acclaimed restaurants, these regions are only about an hour and half away from the city . . . if you don't hit traffic.

■**Divide your attention.** If you're lucky enough to have three nights or more here, split your overnights between Napa and Sonoma to easily see the best that both counties have to offer.

A tasting at Heitz Cellar.

AT THE BAR
In most tasting rooms, you'll be handed a list of the wines available that day. The wines will be listed in a suggested tasting order, starting with the lightest-bodied whites, progressing to the most intense reds, and ending with dessert wines. If you can't decide which wines to choose, tell the server what types of wines you usually like and ask for a recommendation.

The server will pour you an ounce or so of each wine you select. As you taste it, feel free to take notes or ask questions. Don't be shy—the staff are there to educate you about their wine. If you don't like a wine, or you've simply tasted enough, feel free to pour the rest into one of the dump buckets on the bar.

TOURS
Tours tend to be the most exciting (and the most crowded) in September and October, when the harvest and crush-

ing are underway. Tours typically last from 30 minutes to an hour and give you a brief overview of the winemaking process. At some of the older wineries, the tour guide might focus on the history of the property.

■ TIP➜ If you plan to take any tours, wear comfortable shoes, since you might be walking on wet floors or dirt or gravel pathways or stepping over hoses or other equipment.

MONEY-SAVING TIPS
■ Many hotels and B&Bs distribute coupons for free or discounted tastings to their guests—don't forget to ask.

■ If you and your travel partner don't mind sharing a glass, servers are happy to let you split a tasting.

■ Some wineries will refund all or part of the tasting fee if you buy a bottle, making it so much easier to rationalize buying that $80 bottle of cabernet.

■ Almost all wineries will also waive the fee if you join their wine club program. However, this typically commits you to buying a certain number of bottles of their wine for a period of time, so be sure you really like their wines before signing up.

Preston Vineyards bottles only estate-grown grapes.

TOP 2-DAY ITINERARIES

First-Timer's Napa Tour

Start: Oxbow Public market, Napa. Get underway by browsing the shops selling wines, spices, locally grown produce, and other fine foods, for a taste of what the Wine Country has to offer.

Rubicon Estate, Rutherford. The tour here is a particularly fun way to learn about the history

of Napa winemaking—and you can see the old, atmospheric, ivy-covered château.

Frog's Leap, Rutherford. Friendly, unpretentious, and knowledgeable staff makes this place great for wine newbies. (Make sure you get that advance reservation lined up.)

Dinner and Overnight: St. Helena. Spluge at Meadowood Resort and you won't need to leave the property for an

Domaine Carneros

○ **di Rosa Preserve**

121

12

Old Sonoma Rd.

Oxbow Public Market

● **Napa**
29

N A P A
C O U N T Y

Robert Mondavi

Far Niente

🏠✕
Yountville

Oakville

KEY
━━ *First-Timer's Napa Tour*
━━ *Wine Buff's Tour*

Silverado Trail

Stag's Leap Wine Cellars

Wine Buff's Tour

Start: Stag's Leap Wine Cellars, Yountville. Famed for its cabernet sauvignon and Bordeaux blends.

Beaulieu Vineyard, Rutherford. Pony up the extra fee to visit the reserve tasting room to try their flagship cabernet sauvignon.

Caymus Vineyards, Rutherford. The low-key tasting room is a great place to learn more about Rutherford and Napa cabernet artistry. Reserve in advance.

Dinner and Overnight: Yountville. Have dinner at one of the Thomas Keller restaurants. Splurge at

Bardessono; save at Maison Fleurie.

Next Day: Robert Mondavi, Oakville. Spring for the reserve room tasting so you can sip the top-of-the-line wines, especially the stellar cabernet. Head across Highway 29 to the Oakville Grocery to pick up a picnic lunch.

extravagant dinner at their restaurant. Save at El Bonita Motel with dinner at Taylor's.

Next Day: Poke around St. Helena's shops, then drive to Yountville for lunch.

di Rosa, Napa. Call ahead to book a one- or two-hour tour of the acres of gardens and galleries, which

are chock-full of thousands of works of art.

Domaine Carneros, Napa. Toast your trip with a glass of outstanding bubbly.

Sonoma Backroads

20

Start: Iron Horse Vineyards, Russian River Valley.
Soak up a view of vine-covered hills and Mount St. Helena while sipping a sparkling wine or pinot noir at this beautifully rustic spot.

Hartford Family Winery, Russian River Valley.
A terrific source for pinot noir and chardonnay, the stars of this valley.

Dinner and Overnight: Forestville. Go all out with a stay at the Farmhouse Inn, whose award-winning restaurant is one of the best in all of Sonoma.

Next Day: Westside Road, Russian River Valley.
This scenic route, which follows the river, is crowded with worthwhile wineries like Gary Farrell and Rochioli—but it's not crowded with visitors. Pinot fans will find a lot to love. Picnic at Rochioli and enjoy the lovely view.

Matanzas Creek Winery, near Santa Rosa.
End on an especially relaxed note with a walk through their lavender fields (best in June).

Far Niente, Oakville. You have to reserve in advance and the fee for the tasting and tour is steep, but the

payoff is an especially intimate winery experience. You'll taste excellent cabernet and chardonnay, then end your trip on a sweet note with a dessert wine.

WINE TASTING 101

TAKE A GOOD LOOK.
Hold your glass by the stem, raise it to the light, and take a close look at the wine. Check for clarity and color. (This is easiest to do if you can hold the glass in front of a white background.) Any tinge of brown usually means that the wine is over the hill or has gone bad.

BREATHE DEEP.
1. **Sniff the wine once or twice** to see if you can identify any smells.

2. **Swirl the wine gently in the glass.** Aerating the wine this way releases more of its aromas. (It's called "volatilizing the esters," if you're trying to impress someone.)

3. **Take another long sniff.** You might notice that experienced wine tasters spend more time sniffing the wine than drinking it. This is because this step is where the magic happens. The number of scents you might detect is almost endless, from berries, apricots, honey, and wildflowers to leather, cedar, or even tar. Does the wine smell good to you? Do you detect any "off" flavors, like wet dog or sulfur?

AT LAST! TAKE A SIP.
1. **Swirl the wine around your mouth** so that it makes contact with all your taste buds and releases more of its aromas. Think about the way the wine feels in your mouth. Is it watery or rich? Is it crisp or silky? Does it have a bold flavor, or is it subtle? The weight and intensity of a wine are called its body.

2. **Hold the wine in your mouth** for a few seconds and see if you can identify any developing flavors. More complex wines will reveal many different flavors as you drink them.

SPIT OR SWALLOW.
The pros typically spit, since they want to preserve their palate (and sobriety!) for the wines to come, but you'll find that swallowers far outnumber the spitters in the winery tasting rooms. Whether you spit or swallow, notice the flavor that remains after the wine is gone (the finish).

Swirl

Sniff

Sip

DODGE THE CROWDS

To avoid bumping elbows in the tasting rooms, look for wineries off the main drags of Highway 29 in Napa and Highway 12 in Sonoma. The back roads of the Russian River, Dry Creek, and Alexander valleys, all in Sonoma, are excellent places to explore. In Napa, try the northern end. Also look for wineries that are open by appointment only; they tend to schedule visitors carefully to avoid a big crush at any one time.

HOW WINE IS MADE

1. CRUSHING
Harvested grapes go into a stemmer-crusher, which separates stems from fruit and crushes the grapes to release "free-run" juice.

2. PRESSING
Remaining juice is gently extracted from grapes. Usually done by pressing grapes against the walls of a tank with an inflatable bladder.

3. FERMENTING
Extracted juice (and also grape skins and pulp, when making red wine) goes into stainless-steel tanks or oak barrels to ferment. During fermentation, sugars convert to alcohol.

4. AGING
Wine is stored in stainless-steel or oak casks or barrels to develop flavors.

5. RACKING
Wine is transferred to clean barrels; sediment is removed. Wine may be filtered and fined (clarified) to improve its clarity, color, and sometimes flavor.

6. BOTTLING
Wine is bottled either at the winery or at a special facility, then stored again for bottle-aging.

WHAT'S AN APPELLATION?

A specific region with a particular set of grape-growing conditions, such as soil type, climate, and elevation, is called an appellation. What makes things a little confusing is that appellations, which are defined by the Alcohol and Tobacco Tax and Trade Bureau, often overlap. California is an appellation, for example, but so is the Napa Valley. Napa and Sonoma counties are each county appellations, but they, too, are divided into even smaller regions, usually called subappellations or AVAs (American Viticultural Areas). You'll hear a lot about these AVAs from the staff in the tasting rooms; they might explain, for example, why the Russian River Valley AVA is such an excellent place to grow pinot noir grapes.

By law, if the label on a bottle of wine lists the name of an appellation, then at least 85% of the grapes in that wine must come from that appellation.

☎ *707/265–2441* ⊕ *www.cask23.com* ✎ *Tasting $15–$30, tour $40*
☼ *Daily 10–4:30; tour by appointment.*

V Marketplace. In between bouts of eating and drinking, you might stop
by V Marketplace. The vine-covered brick complex, which once housed
a winery, livery stable, and a brandy distillery, contains a smattering
of clothing boutiques, art galleries, and gift stores. NapaStyle, a large
store, deli, and wine bar, sells cookbooks, luxury food items, and kitchenware, as well as an assortment of prepared foods perfect for picnics.
The complex's signature restaurant, Bottega, features the food of celebrity chef Michael Chiarello. ⊠ *6525 Washington St.* ☎ *707/944–2451.*

WHERE TO EAT

$$$$
AMERICAN
Fodor's Choice
★

✕ **Ad Hoc.** When superstar chef Thomas Keller opened this relatively
casual spot in 2006, he meant to run it for only six months until he
opened a burger joint in the same space—but locals were so charmed
by the homey food that they clamored for the stopgap to stay. Now a
single, seasonal fixed-price menu ($52)is served nightly, with a small
menu of decadent brunch items served on Sunday. The selection might
include a juicy pork loin and buttery polenta, served family style, or
a delicate *panna cotta* with a citrus glaze. The dining room is warmly
low-key, with zinc-top tables, wine served in tumblers, and rock and
jazz on the stereo. If you just can't wait to know what's going be served
before you visit, you can call a day in advance for the menu. ⊠ *6476
Washington St.* ☎ *707/944–2487* ⊕ *www.adhocrestaurant.com* ☼ *No
lunch Mon.–Sat. No dinner Tues. and Wed.*

$$$
ITALIAN
Fodor's Choice
★

✕ **Bottega.** At this lively trattoria the menu is simultaneously soulful and
inventive, transforming local ingredients into regional Italian dishes
with a twist. The antipasti in particular shine: you can order olives
grown on chef Michael Chiarello's own property in St. Helena, house-
made charcuterie, or an incredibly fresh fish crudo. Potato gnocchi
might be served with duck and a chestnut ragu, and hearty main courses
like braised short ribs could come on a bed of spinach prepared with
preserved lemons. The vibe is more festival than formal, with exposed
brick walls, an open kitchen, and paper-topped tables, but service is
spot on, and the reasonably priced wine list offers lots of interesting
choices from both Italy and California. This is one of the hottest spots
on Yountville at the moment, so try to reserved well in advance, or visit
at lunch, when it tends to be a little less crowded. ⊠ *6525 Washington
St.* ☎ *707/945–1050* ⊕ *www.botteganapavalley.com* ☼ *No lunch Mon.*

$$$
FRENCH

✕ **Bouchon.** The team that brought French Laundry to its current pinnacle is also behind this place, where everything—the lively and crowded
zinc bar, the elbow-to-elbow seating, the traditional French onion
soup—could have come straight from a Parisian bistro. Roast chicken
with mustard greens and fingerling potatoes and steamed mussels served
with crispy, addictive *frites* (french fries) are among the hearty dishes
served in the high-ceilinged room. ■**TIP→** Late-night meals from a limited menu are served until 12:30 am—a rarity in the Wine Country, where
it's often difficult to find a place to eat after 10. ⊠ *6534 Washington St.*
☎ *707/944–8037* ⊕ *www.bouchonbistro.com.*

$$$
AMERICAN
✕ **Étoile.** Housed at Domaine Chandon, this quietly elegant stunner seems built for romance, with delicate orchids on each table and views of the beautiful wooded winery grounds from the large windows. After a few years of being off the radar of many local critics, the restaurant has gotten more attention lately under the young chef Perry Hoffman, who turns out sophisticated California cuisine. Starters like lobster carpaccio with picked carrots play with a variety of textures, and luxe ingredients like shavings of black truffle dress up pappardelle with mai-take mushrooms. Four- and six-course tasting menus can be ordered with or without wine pairings. The wine list naturally features plenty of Domaine Chandon sparklers, but it's strong in wines from throughout California as well. ✉ *1 California Dr.* ☎ *888/242–6366* ⊕ *www.chandon.com/etoile-restaurant* ⊗ *Closed Tues. and Wed. and Jan.*

$$$$
AMERICAN
Fodor's Choice
★
✕ **French Laundry.** An old stone building laced with ivy houses the most acclaimed restaurant in Napa Valley—and, indeed, one of the most highly regarded in the country. The restaurant's two nine-course prix-fixe menus (both $250), one of which is vegetarian, vary, but "oysters and pearls," a silky dish of pearl tapioca with oysters and white sturgeon caviar, is a signature starter. Some courses rely on luxe ingredients like foie gras, while others take humble foods like fava beans and elevate them to art. Reservations at French Laundry are hard-won, and not accepted more than two months in advance. ■**TIP**➜ Call two months ahead to the day at 10 am on the dot. Didn't get a reservation? Call on the day you'd like to dine here to be considered if there's a cancellation. ✉ *6640 Washington St.* ☎ *707/944–2380* ⊕ *www.frenchlaundry.com* ⊜ *Reservations essential* ⋔ *Jacket required* ⊗ *Closed 1st 2 or 3 wks in Jan. No lunch Mon.–Thurs.*

$$
AMERICAN
✕ **Mustards Grill.** There's not an ounce of pretension at Cindy Pawlcyn's longtime Napa favorite, despite the fact that it's filled every day and night with fans of her hearty cuisine. The menu mixes updated renditions of traditional American dishes (what they like to call "deluxe truck stop classics"), such as barbecued baby back pork ribs and a lemon-lime tart piled high with browned meringue, with a handful of more innovative choices such as sweet corn tamales with tomatillo-avocado salsa and wild mushrooms. A black-and-white marble tile floor and upbeat artwork set a scene that one Fodors.com reader describes as "pure fun, if not fancy." ✉ *7399 St. Helena Hwy./Rte. 29, 1 mi north of town* ☎ *707/944–2424* ⊕ *www.mustardsgrill.com* ⊜ *Reservations essential.*

20

WHERE TO STAY

$$$$
🛏 **Bardessono.** Although Bardessono bills itself as the "greenest luxury hotel in America," there's nothing spartan about its large, spare rooms, arranged around four landscaped courtyards, which have luxurious organic white bedding, gas fireplaces, and huge bathrooms with walnut floors. **Pros:** large rooftop lap pool; exciting restaurant on-site; polished service. **Cons:** expensive; the view from many rooms is uninspiring. **TripAdvisor:** "very warm and friendly," "landscape is just perfect," "quiet and very peaceful." ✉ *6526 Yount St.* ☎ *707/204–6000* ⊕ *www.bardessono.com* ⇘ *50 rooms, 12 suites* ⚿ *In-room: a/c, Internet, Wi-Fi. In-hotel: restaurant, room service, bar, pool, spa, some pets allowed.*

$$$–$$$$ 🏨 **Hotel Luca.** Although this 20-room newcomer to Yountville opened in December 2009, the property embodies a rustic Tuscan style through and through, with dark-wood furniture and soothing decor in brown and sage. **Pros:** extremely comfortable beds; attentive service; breakfast, included in rates, is served in the restaurant or delivered to your room. **Cons:** rooms are soundproofed, but outdoor areas get some traffic noise. **TripAdvisor:** "best customer service experience," "romantic and relaxing," "appointments were first class." ⊠ *6774 Washington St.* 🕿 *707/944–8080* ⊕ *www.hotellucanapa.com* 🛏 *20 rooms* ♿ *In-room: a/c, Wi-Fi. In-hotel: restaurant, room service, bar, pool, gym, spa* ¶⊙¶ *Breakfast.*

$–$$ 🏨 **Maison Fleurie.** If you'd like to be within easy walking distance of
★ most of Yountville's best restaurants, and possibly score a great bargain, look into this casual, comfortable inn. **Pros:** smallest rooms are some of the most affordable in town; free bike rental; refrigerator stocked with free soda. **Cons:** breakfast room can be crowded at peak times; bedding could be nicer. **TripAdvisor:** "very friendly and attentive," "cozy atmosphere," "a great experience." ⊠ *6529 Yount St.* 🕿 *707/944–2056 or 800/788–0369* ⊕ *www.maisonfleurienapa.com* 🛏 *13 rooms* ♿ *In-room: a/c, no TV (some), Wi-Fi. In-hotel: pool* ¶⊙¶ *Breakfast.*

¢ 🏨 **Napa Valley Railway Inn.** Budget-minded travelers and those with kids appreciate these very basic accommodations—inside actual railcars— just steps away from most of Yountville's best restaurants. **Pros:** central Yountville location; guests have access to adjacent gym. **Cons:** minimal service, since the office is often unstaffed; rooms on the parking-lot side get some noise. **TripAdvisor:** "so cute and comfortable," "great location," "amazing value." ⊠ *6523 Washington St.* 🕿 *707/944–2000* ⊕ *www.napavalleyrailwayinn.com* 🛏 *9 rooms* ♿ *In-room: a/c, Wi-Fi.*

$$$–$$$$ 🏨 **Villagio Inn & Spa.** The luxury here is quiet and refined, not flashy as
★ is evident in a stroll along fountains and clusters of low buildings to the pool, where automated misters cool the sunbathers. **Pros:** amazing buffet breakfast; no extra charge for hotel guests to use the spa facilities; steps away from Yountville's best restaurants. **Cons:** can be bustling with large groups; you can hear the highway from many of the room's balconies or patios. **TripAdvisor:** "quite friendly," "spa is extremely relaxing," "grounds are beautiful." ⊠ *6481 Washington St.* 🕿 *707/944–8877 or 800/351–1133* ⊕ *www.villagio.com* 🛏 *86 rooms, 26 suites* ♿ *In-room: a/c, Internet, Wi-Fi. In-hotel: room service, tennis courts, bar, pool, spa.* ¶⊙¶ *Breakfast.*

$$$–$$$$ 🏨 **Vintage Inn.** Rooms in this lavish inn are housed in two-story villas scattered around a lush, landscaped 3½-acre property. **Pros:** spacious bathrooms with spa tubs; lavish breakfast buffet; luscious bedding. **Cons:** some exterior rooms get highway noise; pool area is smaller than the one at its sister property, the Villagio Inn & Spa. **TripAdvisor:** "very nice and professional," "location is very convenient," "beautiful grounds." ⊠ *6541 Washington St.* 🕿 *707/944–1112 or 800/351–1133* ⊕ *www.vintageinn.com* 🛏 *68 rooms, 12 suites* ♿ *In-room: a/c, Internet, Wi-Fi. In-hotel: room service, tennis courts, bar, pool, some pets allowed* ¶⊙¶ *Breakfast.*

OAKVILLE

2 mi west of Yountville on Rte. 29.

There are three reasons to visit the town of Oakville: its gourmet grocery store; its scenic mountain road; and its magnificent, highly exclusive wineries.

GETTING HERE AND AROUND

Those driving along Route 29 will know they're reached Oakville when they see the Oakville Grocery Store on the east side of the road. Here the Oakville Cross Road provides access to the Silverado Trail, which runs parallel to Route 29. Oakville wineries are scattered along Route 29, Oakville Cross Road, and the Silverado Trail in roughly equal measure.

EXPLORING

Fodor's Choice ★ **Far Niente.** Though the fee for the combined tour and tasting is at the high end, Far Niente is especially worth visiting if you're tired of elbowing your way through crowded tasting rooms and are looking for a more personal experience. Here you're welcomed by name and treated to a glimpse of one of the most beautiful Napa properties. Small groups are shepherded through the historic 1885 stone winery, including some of the 40,000 square feet of caves, for a lesson on the labor-intensive method for making Far Niente's two wines, a cabernet blend and a chardonnay. (The latter is made without undergoing malolactic fermentation, so it doesn't have that buttery taste that's characteristic of many California chards.) The next stop is the Carriage House, where you can see the founder's gleaming collection of classic cars. The tour ends with a seated tasting of wines and cheeses, capped by a sip of the spectacular Dolce, a late-harvest dessert wine made by Far Niente's sister winery. ☒ *1350 Acacia Dr.* ☎ *707/944–2861* ⊕ *www.farniente. com* ☑ *$50* ☾ *Tasting and tour by appointment.*

Oakville Grade. Along the mountain range that divides Napa and Sonoma, the Oakville Grade is a twisting half-hour route with breathtaking views of both valleys. Although the surface of the road is good, it can be difficult to negotiate at night, and the continual curves mean that it's not ideal for those who suffer from motion sickness. ☒ *West of Rte. 29.*

Oakville Grocery. Built in 1881 as a general store, this popular spot carries a surprisingly wide range of unusual and chichi groceries and prepared foods. Unbearable crowds pack the narrow aisles on weekends, but it's still a fine place to sit on a bench out front and sip an espresso between winery visits. ☒ *7856 St. Helena Hwy./Rte. 29* ☎ *707/944–8802.*

Opus One. The combined venture of the late California winemaker Robert Mondavi and the late French baron Philippe de Rothschild, Opus One produces only one wine: a big, inky Bordeaux blend that was the first of Napa's ultra-premium wines, fetching unheard-of prices before it was overtaken by cult wines like Screaming Eagle. The winery's futuristic limestone-clad structure, built into the hillside, seems to be pushing itself out of the earth. Although the tour, which focuses on why it costs so much to produce this exceptional wine, can come off as "stuffy" (in the words of one Fodors.com reader), the facilities

20

Far Niente's wine cellars have a touch of ballroom elegance.

are undoubtedly impressive, with gilded mirrors, exotic orchids, and a large semicircular cellar modeled on the Château Mouton Rothschild winery in France. You can also taste the current vintage without the tour ($30), as long as you've called ahead for a reservation. ■ TIP→ Take your glass up to the rooftop terrace if you want to appreciate the views out over the vineyards. ⊠ *7900 St. Helena Hwy./Rte. 29* ☎ *707/944–9442* ⊕ *www.opusonewinery.com* ✉ *Tour $40* ☉ *Daily 10–4; tasting and tour by appointment.*

PlumpJack. If Opus One is the Rolls-Royce of the Oakville District—expensive, refined, and a little snooty—then PlumpJack is the Mini Cooper: fun, casual, and sporty. With its metal chandelier and wall hangings, the tasting room looks like it could be the stage set for a modern Shakespeare production. (The name "PlumpJack" is a nod to Shakespeare's Falstaff.) The reserve chardonnay has a good balance of baked fruit and fresh citrus flavors, while a merlot is blended with a bit of cabernet sauvignon, giving the wine enough tannins to ensure it can be aged for another five years or more. If the tasting room is crowded, take a breather under the shady arbor on the back patio, where you can enjoy a close-up view of the vines. ⊠ *620 Oakville Cross Rd.* ☎ *707/945–1220* ⊕ *www.plumpjack.com* ✉ *Tasting $10* ☉ *Daily 10–4.*

Robert Mondavi. The arch at the center of the sprawling Mission-style building at Robert Mondavi perfectly frames the lawn and the vineyard behind, inviting a stroll under the lovely arcades. If you've never been on a winery tour before, the comprehensive Signature Tour and Tasting ($25), which concludes with a seated tasting, is a good way to learn about enology, as well as the late Robert Mondavi's role in California wine making (shorter and longer tours are also available). And those new to tasting and mystified by all that swirling and sniffing should consider the 45-minute Wine Tasting Basics experience ($25). You can also head straight for one of the two tasting rooms. Serious wine lovers should definitely consider springing for the $30 reserve-room tasting, where you can enjoy four tastes of Mondavi's top-of-the-line wines, including both the current vintage and several previous vintages of the reserve cabernet that cemented the winery's reputation. Concerts, mostly jazz and R&B, take place in summer on the lawn; call ahead for tickets. ⊠ *7801 St. Helena Hwy./Rte. 29* ☎ *888/766–6328* ⊕ *www.robertmondaviwinery.com* 🍷 *Tasting $20–$30, tour $15–$50* ☉ *Daily 10–5; tour times vary.*

RUTHERFORD

2 mi northwest of Oakville on Rte. 29.

From a fast-moving car, Rutherford is a quick blur of vineyards and a rustic barn or two, but don't speed by this tiny hamlet. With its singular microclimate and soil, this is an important viticultural center, with more big-name wineries than you can shake a corkscrew at. Cabernet sauvignon is king here. The well-drained, loamy soil is ideal for those vines, and since this part of the valley gets plenty of sun, the grapes develop exceptionally intense flavors. The late, great winemaker André Tchelistcheff claimed that "it takes Rutherford dust to grow great cabernet."

GETTING HERE AND AROUND

Wineries around Rutherford are dotted along Route 29 and the parallel Silverado Trail just north and south of Rutherford Road/Conn Creek Road, which connect these two major thoroughfares.

EXPLORING

Beaulieu Vineyard. The cabernet sauvignon produced at the ivy-covered Beaulieu Vineyard is a benchmark of the Napa Valley. The legendary André Tchelistcheff, who helped define the California style of wine making, worked his magic here from 1938 until his death in 1973. This helps explain why Beaulieu's flagship, the Georges de Latour Private Reserve Cabernet Sauvignon, still garners high marks from major wine publications. The wines being poured in the main tasting room, which might include anything from a zesty gewürztraminer to a lush petite syrah are notably good. Still, it's worth paying the extra money to taste that special cabernet in the more luxe, less-crowded reserve tasting room. ⊠ *1960 St. Helena Hwy./Rte. 29* ☎ *707/967–5200* ⊕ *www.bvwines.com* 🍷 *Tasting $15–$35, tour $40* ☉ *Daily 10–5.*

Cakebread Cellars. Jack and Dolores Cakebread snapped up the property at Cakebread Cellars in 1973, after Jack fell in love with the area while visiting on a photography assignment. Since then, they've been making luscious chardonnays, as well as merlot, a great sauvignon blanc, and a beautifully complex cabernet sauvignon. You must make an appointment for a tasting, for which there are several different options. The most basic usually involves a stroll through the winery's barrel room and crush pad and past Dolores's kitchen garden before ending in a taste

20

of current releases. Other options focus on red, reserve, or library wines, and might take place in the winery's modern wing, where an elevator is crafted out of a stainless-steel fermentation tank and the ceiling is lined with thousands of corks. ⊠ *8300 St. Helena Hwy.* ☎ *707/963–5221* ⊕ *www.cakebread.com* ⊒ *Tasting $15–$40, tour $25* ⊙ *Daily 10–4:30; tasting and tour by appointment.*

Caymus Vineyards. Wine master Chuck Wagner, who started making wine on the property in 1972, runs this well-regarded winery. His family, however, had been farming in the valley since 1906. Though they make a fine zinfandel and sauvignon blanc, cabernet is the winery's claim to fame, a ripe, powerful wine that's known for its consistently high quality. ■TIP➜ There's no tour, and you have to reserve to taste, but it's still worth planning ahead to visit, because the low-key seated tasting (limited to 10 guests) is a great opportunity to learn about the valley's cabernet artistry. ⊠ *8700 Conn Creek Rd.* ☎ *707/967–3010* ⊕ *www. caymus.com* ⊒ *Tasting $25* ⊙ *Sales daily 10–4; tasting by appointment.*

♻ **Frog's Leap.** The owner, John Williams, maintains a goofy sense of humor
Fodor's Choice about wine that translates into an entertaining yet informative experi-
★ ence, making Frog's Leap the perfect places for wine novices to begin their education. You'll also find some fine zinfandel, cabernet sauvignon, merlot, chardonnay, sauvignon blanc, rosé, and also their take on the German dessert wine Trockenbeerenauslese. The winery includes a red barn built in 1884, 5 acres of organic gardens, an ecofriendly visitor center, and, naturally, a frog pond topped with lily pads. The fun tour is highly recommended, but you can also just do a seated tasting of their wines, which takes place on a porch overlooking the garden. ⊠ *8815 Conn Creek Rd.* ☎ *707/963–4704* ⊕ *www.frogsleap.com* ⊒ *Tasting $20, tour $20.* ⊙ *Daily 10–4; tour by appointment.*

Mumm Napa. Although this is one of California's best-known sparkling-wine producers, enjoying the bubbly from the light-filled tasting room—available in either single flutes or by the flight—isn't the only reason to visit Mumm. There's also an excellent photography gallery with 30 Ansel Adams prints and rotating exhibits. You can even take that glass of wonderfully crisp Brut Rosé with you as wander. For a leisurely tasting of a flight of their library wines while seated on their outdoor terrace ($30), reserve in advance. ⊠ *8445 Silverado Trail* ☎ *707/967–7700* ⊕ *www.mummnapa.com* ⊒ *Tasting $6–$30, tour free–$20* ⊙ *Daily 10–5; tour daily at 10 (free; tasting not including), 11, 1, and 3 ($20, tasting including).*

★ **Round Pond.** It's not all grapevines here—you can switch your fruit focus to olives at Round Pond. This small farm grows five varieties of Italian olives and three types of Spanish olives. Within an hour of being handpicked, the olives are crushed in the mill on the property to produce pungent, peppery oils that are later blended and sold. Call at least a day or two in advance to arrange a tour of the mill followed by an informative tasting, during which you can sample several types of oil, both alone and with Round Pond's own red-wine vinegars and other tasty foods. ■TIP➜ If you can arrange to visit between mid-November and the end of December, you might be lucky enough to see the mill in

Frog's Leap's picturesque country charm extends all the way to the white picket fence.

action. ✉ *886 Rutherford Rd.* ☎ *888/302–2575* 🌐 *www.roundpond.com* 🎫 *Tour $25* ⏲ *Tour by appointment.*

Rubicon Estate. It's the house *The Godfather* built. Filmmaker Francis Ford Coppola began his wine-making career in 1975, when he bought part of the historic, renowned Inglenook estate. He eventually reunited the original Inglenook land and snagged the ivy-covered 19th-century château to boot. In 2006 he renamed the property Rubicon Estate, intending to focus on his premium wines, including the namesake cabernet sauvignon–based blend. (The less expensive wines are showcased at the Francis Ford Coppola Winery in Sonoma County's Geyserville.) A variety of tours and seminars cover topics that include the history of the estate, the Rutherford climate and geology, and the sensory evaluation of wine, but many just come to taste in the opulent, high-ceilinged tasting room. The wine bar, Mammarella, has seating in a picturesque courtyard. ✉ *1991 St. Helena Hwy./Rte. 29* ☎ *707/963–9099* 🌐 *www.rubiconestate.com* 🎫 *Tasting $15–$50, tours free (included in the $25 and $50 tastings)–$45* ⏲ *Daily 10–5; call for tour times.*

Rutherford Hill Winery. A merlot lover's paradise in a cabernet sauvignon world. When the winery's founders were deciding what grapes to plant, they discovered that the climate and soil conditions of their vineyards resembled those of Pomerol, a region of Bordeaux where merlot is king. The wine caves here are some of the most extensive of any California winery—nearly a mile of tunnels and passageways. You can get a glimpse of the tunnels and the 5,000 barrels inside on the tours, then cap your visit with a picnic in their oak or olive groves. With views over the valley from a perch high on a hill, the picnic grounds are more charming than many others in Napa, which tend to be rather close to one of the busy thoroughfares. ✉ *200 Rutherford Hill Rd., east of Silverado Trail* ☎ *707/963–1871* ⊕ *www.rutherfordhill.com* ☞ *Tasting $15–$30, tour $25* ☉ *Daily 10–5; tour daily at 11:30, 1:30, and 3:30.*

St. Supéry. Your instinct may be to enter the beautifully restored 1882 Queen Anne Victorian at St. Supéry looking for the tasting room; actually the wines are being poured in the building behind it, a bland, unappealing, officelike structure. But you'll likely forgive the atmospheric lapse once you taste their fine sauvignon blancs, merlots, and chardonnays, as well as a couple of unusual wines that are made primarily of either cabernet franc or petit verdot, both of which are usually used for blending with cabernet sauvignon. An excellent, free self-guided tour also allows you a peek at the barrel and fermentation rooms, as well as a gallery of rotating art exhibits. At the "Smell-a-Vision" station you can test your ability to identify different smells that might be present in wine, and a small demonstration vineyard allows you to see the differences between different types of vines and even taste the grapes when they're in season. ✉ *8440 St. Helena Hwy. S/Rte. 29* ☎ *707/963–4507* ⊕ *www.stsupery.com* ☞ *Tasting $10–$25* ☉ *Daily 10–5.*

WHERE TO STAY

$$$$
★
🏨 **Auberge du Soleil.** Taking a cue from the olive-tree-studded landscape, this renowned hotel cultivates a luxurious Mediterranean look: earth-tone tile floors, heavy wood furniture, and terra-cotta colors. **Pros:** stunning views over the valley; spectacular pool and spa areas; the most expensive suites are fit for a superstar. **Cons:** stratospheric prices; the two least expensive rooms (in the main house) get some noise from the bar and restaurant. **TripAdvisor:** "food is amazing," "truly beautiful," "the ultimate romantic escape." ✉ *180 Rutherford Hill Rd., off Silverado Trail north of Rte. 128* ☎ *707/963–1211 or 800/348–5406* ⊕ *www.aubergedusoleil.com* 🛏 *31 rooms, 21 suites* ☖ *In-room: a/c, Internet, Wi-Fi. In-hotel: restaurants, room service, tennis court, bar, pool, gym, spa* ¶◎| *Breakfast.*

ST. HELENA

2 mi northwest of Oakville on Rte. 29.

Downtown St. Helena is a symbol of how well life can be lived in the Wine Country. Sycamore trees arch over Main Street (Route 29), a funnel of outstanding restaurants and tempting boutiques. At the north end of town looms the hulking stone building of the Culinary Institute of America. Weathered stone and brick buildings from the late 1800s give off that gratifying whiff of history.

By the time pioneer winemaker Charles Krug planted grapes in St. Helena around 1860, quite a few vineyards already existed in the area. Today the town is hemmed in by wineries, and you could easily spend days visiting vintners within a few miles.

GETTING HERE AND AROUND

Downtown St. Helena stretches along Route 29, which is called Main Street here. Many of the shops and restaurants are clustered on two pleasant pedestrian-friendly blocks of Main Street, between Pope Street and Adams Street. Wineries in the area are found both north and south of downtown along both Route 29 and the Silverado Trail, but some of the less touristed and more scenic spots are on the slopes of Spring Mountain, which rises southwest of town.

EXPLORING

Beringer Vineyards. Arguably the most beautiful winery in Napa Valley, the 1876 Beringer Vineyards is also the oldest continuously operating property. In 1884 Frederick and Jacob Beringer built the Rhine House Mansion to serve as Frederick's family home. Today it serves as the reserve tasting room, where you can sample wines surrounded by Belgian art-nouveau hand-carved oak and walnut furniture and stained-glass windows. The assortment includes a limited-release chardonnay, a few big but very drinkable cabernets, and a luscious white dessert wine named Nightingale. Another, less expensive tasting takes place in the less photogenic original stone winery. ■ TIP➔ If you're looking for an undiscovered gem, pass this one by, but first-time visitors to the valley will learn a lot about the history of wine making in the region on the introductory tour. Longer tours, which might pass through a demonstration vineyard or end with a seated tasting in the Rhine House, are also offered a few times a day. ⊠ 2000 Main St./Rte. 29 ☎ 707/963–4812 ⊕ www.beringer. com ☞ Tasting $15–$25, tour $20–$30 ⊙ May 29–Oct. 22, daily 10–6; Oct. 23–May 28, daily 10–5; call for tour times.

Charles Krug Winery. The first winery founded in the Napa Valley, Charles Krug Winery, opened in 1861 when Count Haraszthy lent Krug a small cider press. Today the Peter Mondavi family runs it. Though the tasting room is fairly modest, the knowledgeable and friendly servers ensure a relaxed visit. The winery is best known for its lush red Bordeaux blends, but its zinfandel is also good—or go for something unusual with the New Zealand–style sauvignon blanc. Its zingy flavor of citrus and tropical fruit is rare in wines from this area. The picnic area behind the tasting room has a view of the redwood cellar (not open to the public), where their wines are aged. ⊠ 2800 N. Main St. ☎ 707/963–5057 ⊕ www.charleskrug.com ☞ Tasting $10–$20 ⊙ Daily 10:30–5.

Culinary Institute of America. The West Coast headquarters of the Culinary Institute of America, the country's leading school for chefs, are in the **Greystone Winery,** an imposing building that was the largest stone winery in the world when it was built in 1889. On the ground floor you can check out the quirky corkscrew display and shop at a well-stocked culinary store that tempts aspiring chefs with gleaming gadgets and an impressive selection of cookbooks. Attached to the store, at the Flavor Bar, you can experience a guided tasting of certain types of ingredients (for example, chocolate or olive oil) to gain a greater understanding of them ($10 to $15). Upstairs, if there are no special events going on, you can browse their Vintners Hall of Fame, where winemakers past and present are commemorated on plaques fastened to 2,200-gallon redwood wine barrels. One-hour cooking demonstrations ($15) take

20

place on Saturday and Sunday; call or visit the Web sites for time and reservations, or to get information on longer, hands-on cooking classes on a variety of subjects. ⊠ *2555 Main St.* ☎ *707/967–1100* ⊕ *www. ciachef.edu* ✉ *Free* ☉ *Restaurant Sun.–Thurs. 11:30–9, Fri. and Sat. 11:30–10; store and museum daily 10–6.*

Fodor's Choice
★

Joseph Phelps Vineyards. Although an appointment is required to taste here, it's worth the trouble. In fair weather the casual, self-paced wine tastings are held on the terrace of a huge, modern barnlike building with stunning views down the slopes over oak trees and orderly vines. Though the sauvignon blanc and viognier are good, the blockbuster wines are reds. The 2002 vintage of their flagship wine, a Bordeaux-style blend called Insignia, was selected as *Wine Spectator*'s wine of the year, immediately pushing up prices and demand. Luckily, you'll get a taste of the current vintage of Insignia (which goes for around $200 a bottle). A variety of 90-minute tasting seminars, available by appointment, are $40. The popular blending seminar, during which you get to try your hand at mixing the various varietals that go into their Insignia blend, is $60. ⊠ *200 Taplin Rd.* ☎ *707/963–2745* ⊕ *www.jpvwines. com* ✉ *Tasting $25* ☉ *Weekdays 10–3:30, weekends 10–2:30; tasting by appointment.*

★

Spring Mountain Vineyard. Hidden off a winding road behind a security gate, Spring Mountain Vineyard has the feeling of a private estate in the countryside, even though it's only a few miles from downtown St. Helena. Though some sauvignon blanc, pinot noir, and syrah is produced, the calling card here is cabernet—big, chewy wines that demand some time in the bottle but promise great things. A tasting of their current releases ($25) gives you a good sense of the charms of their wines, but consider springing for the estate ($35) or reserve tasting ($50), both of which include a meander through the beautiful property, from the cellars to the beautifully preserved 1885 mansion. The latter two conclude in either the mansion's dining room or their wine cellar for a seated tasting. ⊠ *2805 Spring Mountain Rd.* ☎ *707/967–4188* ⊕ *www. springmountainvineyard.com* ✉ *Tour and tasting $25–$50* ☉ *Tour and tasting by appointment.*

WHERE TO EAT

$$
SEAFOOD
★

✕ **Go Fish.** Prolific restaurateur Cindy Pawlcyn is the big name behind this bustling bistro, one of the first restaurants in the Wine Country to specialize in seafood. You can either sit at the long marble bar and watch the chefs whip up inventive sushi rolls and raw-bar bites, or head into the dining room to study the mouthwatering menu, with listings that include a French-inflected sole almondine and Asian-inspired dishes like miso-marinated black cod. Hearty sandwiches like the bigeye tuna Reuben are popular at lunch. The large, lively space works a modern-chic look, with stainless-steel lamps and comfortable banquettes, and tables on the terrace are popular on fair evenings. ⊠ *641 Main St.* ☎ *707/963–0700* ⊕ *www.gofishrestaurant.net.*

¢–$
AMERICAN
★

✕ **Gott's Roadside.** A slick 1950s-style outdoor hamburger stand goes upscale at this hugely popular spot, where locals are willing to brave long lines to order juicy burgers, root-beer floats, and garlic fries. There are also plenty of choices you wouldn't have found 50 years ago, such as the ahi tuna burger and chicken club with pesto mayo. Try to get here early or late for lunch, or all the shaded picnic tables on the lawn might be filled with happy throngs. Lines are usually shorter at the Gott's in downtown Napa's Oxbow Public Market. ⊠ *933 Main St.* ☎ *707/963–3486* ⊕ *www.gottsroadside.com.*

$$$$
AMERICAN
Fodor'sChoice
★
✕ **The Restaurant at Meadowood.** Chef Christopher Kostow has garnered rave reviews for transforming seasonal local products (some grown right on the property) into elaborate, elegant fare. The "composition of carrots," constructed of the tiniest carrots imaginable accompanied by delicate shavings of chocolate, foie gras, and candied tangerine (it sounds odd, but it works) is just one example of Kostow's inventiveness and playfulness. The slow-cooked black cod with chorizo and lamb demonstrates an earthier approach. The chef's menu ($175, $300 with wine pairings), composed of seven or so courses, is the best way to appreciate the experience, but the gracious and well-trained servers provide some of the best service in the valley even if you're ordering a less extravagant three-, four-, or five-course menu. The warm lighting and well-spaced tables in the dining room, which looks out onto a lovely stand of trees and the property's golf course, makes it a top choice for a romantic tête-à-tête. ⊠ *900 Meadowood La.* ☎ *707/967–1205* ⊕ *www. meadowood.com* ⊘ *Closed Sun. No lunch.*

$$$$
MEDITERRANEAN
★
✕ **Terra.** St. Helena may have newer, flashier, and more dramatic restaurants, but for old-school romance and service, many diners return year after year to this quiet favorite in an 1884 fieldstone building. Since 1988, chef Hiro Sone has been giving unexpected twists to Italian and southern French cuisine in dishes such as the mussel soup with caramelized onions and garlic croutons, heavily perfumed with the scent of saffron. A few, like the signature sake-marinated black cod in a *shiso* broth, draw on Sone's Japanese background. Homey yet elegant desserts, courtesy of Sone's wife, Lissa Doumani, might include a chocolate caramel tart topped with fleur de sel. The gracious staff unobtrusively attends to every dropped fork or half-full water glass. ⊠ *1345 Railroad Ave.* ☎ *707/963–8931* ⊕ *www.terrarestaurant.com* ⊘ *Closed Tues. and 1st 2 wks in Jan. No lunch.*

$$$
MEDITERRANEAN
✕ **Wine Spectator Greystone Restaurant.** The Culinary Institute of America runs this place in the handsome old Christian Brothers Winery. Century-old stone walls house a spacious restaurant that bustles at both lunch and dinner, with several cooking stations in full view. On busy nights you may find the hard-at-work chefs more entertaining than your dining companions. The tables on the terrace, shaded by red umbrellas, are away from the action, but on fair days they're even more appealing, providing a panoramic view down the hillside. The menu has a Mediterranean spirit and emphasizes locally grown produce. Typical main courses on the frequently changing menu include prosciutto-wrapped cod and house-made pasta with trumpet mushrooms and a sherry cream sauce. ⊠ *2555 Main St.* ☎ *707/967–1010* ⊕ *www.ciachef.edu.*

20

WHERE TO STAY

¢–$
🏠 **El Bonita Motel.** Only in St. Helena would a basic room in a roadside motel cost around $200 a night in high season, but for budget-minded travelers the tidy rooms here are pleasant enough, and the landscaped

grounds and picnic tables elevate this property over similar places. **Pros:** cheerful rooms; hot tub; microwaves and mini-refrigerators. **Cons:** road noise is a problem in some rooms. **TripAdvisor:** "great value and location," "staff is great," "beautifully kept up." ⊠ *195 Main St./Rte. 29* ☎ *707/963–3216 or 800/541–3284* ⊕ *www.elbonita.com* ⤳ *38 rooms, 4 suites* ⌂ *In-room: a/c, Wi-Fi. In-hotel: pool, business center, some pets allowed* ⎟○⎟ *Breakfast.*

$$$$
Fodor's Choice
★

⌾ **Meadowood Resort.** A rambling lodge and several gray clapboard bungalows are scattered across this sprawling property, giving it an exclusive New England feel, and every unit runs seamlessly—starting with the gatehouse staff who alert the front desk to arrivals. **Pros:** site of one of Napa's best restaurants; lovely hiking trail on the property; the most gracious service in all of Napa. **Cons:** very expensive; most bathrooms are not as extravagant as at other similarly priced resorts. **TripAdvisor:** "peaceful paradise," "very comfortable rooms," "lots of light." ⊠ *900 Meadowood La.* ☎ *707/963–3646 or 800/458–8080* ⊕ *www.meadowood.com* ⤳ *40 rooms, 45 suites* ⌂ *In-room: a/c, Internet, Wi-Fi. In-hotel: golf course, restaurants, room service, tennis courts, bar, pools, gym.*

$$$–$$$$

⌾ **Wine Country Inn & Gardens.** A pastoral landscape of vine-covered hills surrounds this retreat, which was styled after the traditional New England inns its owners liked to visit in the 1970s. **Pros:** free shuttle to some restaurants (reserve early); lovely grounds; swimming pool is heated year-round. **Cons:** some rooms let in noise from neighbors; some areas could use updating. **TripAdvisor:** "so helpful," "amazing breakfast," "truly beautiful view." ⊠ *1152 Lodi La., east of Rte. 29* ☎ *707/963–7077* ⊕ *www.winecountryinn.com* ⤳ *24 rooms, 5 suites* ⌂ *In-room: a/c, no TV, Wi-Fi. In-hotel: pool* ⎟○⎟ *Breakfast.*

SHOPPING

Dean & Deluca (⊠ *607 St. Helena Hwy. S/Rte. 29* ☎ *707/967–9980*), a branch of the famous Manhattan store, is crammed with everything you need in the kitchen—including terrific produce and deli items—as well as a large wine selection. The **Spice Islands Marketplace** (⊠ *Culinary Institute of America, 2555 Main St.* ☎ *888/424–2433*) is the place to shop for cookbooks, kitchenwares, and everything else related to cooking and preparing food. Elaborate confections handmade on the premises are displayed like miniature works of art at **Woodhouse Chocolate** (⊠ *1367 Main St.* ☎ *707/963–8413*), a lovely shop that resembles an 18th-century Parisian salon.

CALISTOGA

3 mi northwest of St. Helena on Rte. 29.

With false-fronted, Old West–style shops, 19th-century hotels, and unpretentious cafés lining Lincoln Avenue, the town's main drag, Calistoga has a slightly rough-and-tumble feel that's unique in the Napa Valley. It comes across as more down-to-earth than some of the polished towns to the south. And it's easier to find a bargain here, making it a handy home base for exploring the surrounding vineyards and back roads.

Ironically, Calistoga was developed as a swell, tourist-oriented getaway. In 1859 maverick entrepreneur Sam Brannan snapped up 2,000 acres of prime property and laid out a resort, intending to use the area's natural hot springs as the main attraction. Brannan's gamble didn't pay off as he'd hoped, but the hotels and bathhouses won a local following. Many of them are still going, and you can come for an old-school experience of a mud bath or a dip in a warm spring-fed pool.

GETTING HERE AND AROUND

To get to downtown Calistoga from anywhere farther south in the valley, take Route 29 north and then turn right on Lincoln Avenue. Most of the town's sights are found along a five-block stretch of Lincoln Avenue, or just off one of the side streets that intersect it. After about a mile, Lincoln Avenue (which changes names to Lake County Highway) intersects with the Silverado Trail.

EXPLORING

★ **Castello di Amorosa.** Possibly the most astounding sight in Napa Valley is your first glimpse of the Castello di Amorosa, which looks for all the world like a medieval castle, complete with drawbridge and moat, chapel, stables, and secret passageways. Some of the 107 rooms contain replicas of 13th-century frescoes, and the dungeon has an actual iron maiden from Nuremberg, Germany. You must pay for the tour to see the most of the extensive eight-level property, though paying for a tasting allows you access to a small portion of the astounding complex, as well as a taste of several of their excellent Italian-style wines, including a "super Tuscan," which is a blend of sangiovese and merlot with cabernet sauvignon, which gives it a bit more heft than your average Italian red. ⊠ *4045 N. Saint Helena Hwy.* ☎ *707/967–6272* ⊕ *www. castellodiamorosa.com* ☜ *Tasting $16–$26, tour $31–$41* ☯ *Mar.– Oct., daily 9:30–6; Nov.–Feb., daily 9:30–5; tour by appointment.*

Clos Pegase. Designed by postmodern architect Michael Graves, the Clos Pegase winery is a one-of-a-kind "temple to wine and art" packed with unusual art objects from the collection of owner and publishing entrepreneur Jan Shrem. After tasting the wines, which include a bright sauvignon blanc, fruity chardonnays, and mellow pinot noir, merlot, and cabernet (they're made in a soft, approachable style and meant to be drunk somewhat young), be sure to check out the surrealist paintings near the main tasting room, which include a Jean Dubuffet painting you may have seen on one of their labels. Better yet, bring a picnic and have lunch in the courtyard, where a curvaceous Henry Moore sculpture is one of about two dozen works of art. ⊠ *1060 Dunaweal La.* ☎ *707/942–4981* ⊕ *www.clospegase.com* ☜ *Tasting $7.50–$15, tour free* ☯ *Daily 10:30–5; tour daily at 11:30 and 2.*

20

Indian Springs. Even before Sam Brannan constructed a spa and mud baths here in the 1860s, the Wapoo Indians were building sweat lodges over the thermal geysers at this, the oldest continually operating pool and spa in California. You can choose from the various spa treatments and volcanic-ash mud baths, after which you can relax in the small Zen-inspired garden out back. Best of all, clients of the spa and guests of the lodge rooms or bungalows ($–$$$) have access to the

Floor-to-ceiling stacked bottles are no exaggeration in Schramsberg's cellars.

Olympic-size mineral-water pool, kept at 92°F in summer and a toasty 102°F in winter. ⊠ *1712 Lincoln Ave./Rte. 29* ☎ *707/942–4913* ⊕ *www. indianspringscalistoga.com* ⊗ *Daily 9–8.*

Robert Louis Stevenson State Park. Encompassing the summit of Mt. St. Helena, this state park was where Stevenson and his bride, Fanny Osbourne, spent their honeymoon in an abandoned bunkhouse of the Silverado Mine. This stay in 1880 inspired the writer's travel memoir *The Silverado Squatters,* and Spyglass Hill in *Treasure Island* is thought to be a portrait of Mt. St. Helena. The park's approximately 3,600 acres are mostly undeveloped except for a trail leading to the site of the bunkhouse—which is marked with a marble memorial in the form of a open book on top of a pedestal—and a fire trail to the summit beyond. ■TIP→ If you're planning on attempting the hike to the top, a 10-mi round-trip, bring plenty of water and dress appropriately: the trail is steep and lacks shade in spots, but the summit is often cool and breezy. ⊠ *Rte. 29, 7 mi north of Calistoga* ☎ *707/942–4575* ⊕ *www.parks.ca.gov* ⊠ *Free* ⊗ *Daily sunrise–sunset.*

Fodor's Choice
★

Schramsberg. Founded in the 1860s, Schramsberg, one of Napa's old-est wineries, produces a variety of bubblies made using the traditional méthode champenoise (which means, among other things, that the wine undergoes a second fermentation in the bottle before being "riddled," or turned every few days over a period of weeks, to nudge the sediment into the neck of the bottle). If you want to taste, you must tour first, but what a tour: in addition to getting a glimpse of the winery's historic architecture, you get to tour the cellars dug in the late 19th century by Chinese laborers, where a mind-boggling 2 million bottles are stacked in gravity-defying configurations. The tour fee includes generous pours of several very different sparkling wines. ⊠ *1400 Schramsberg Rd.* ☎ *707/942–4558* ⊕ *www.schramsberg.com* ⊡ *Tasting and tour $40* ⊘ *Tasting and tour by appointment.*

Storybook Mountain Vineyards. Tucked into a rock face in the Mayacamas range, Storybook Mountain Vineyards is one of the more beautiful wineries in Napa, with vines rising steeply from the winery in dramatic tiers. Zinfandel is king here, and they even make a Zin Gris, an unusual dry rosé of zinfandel grapes. (In Burgundy, *vin gris*—pale rosé—is made from pinot noir grapes.) Tastings are preceded by a low-key tour, during which you take a short walk up the hillside into the picture-perfect vineyard and then visit the atmospheric tunnels, parts of which have the same rough-hewn look as they did when Chinese laborers painstakingly dug them around 1888. ⊠ *3835 Hwy. 128* ☎ *707/942–5310* ⊕ *www.storybookwines.com* ⊡ *Free* ⊘ *Tour and tasting by appointment Mon.–Sat.*

WHERE TO EAT

$$
AMERICAN
✕ **All Seasons Bistro.** Bistro cuisine takes a California spin in this cheerful sun-filled space, where tables topped with flowers stand on an old-fashioned black-and-white checkerboard floor. The seasonal menu might include risotto with shiitake mushroom and duck confit or fettuccine puttanesca. Homey desserts include crème brûlée and pear-and-golden-raisin bread pudding. You can order reasonably priced wines from their extensive list, or buy a bottle at the attached wineshop and have it poured at your table. Attentive service contributes to the welcoming atmosphere. ⊠ *1400 Lincoln Ave.* ☎ *707/942–9111* ⊕ *www.allseasonsnapavalley.net* ⊘ *Closed Mon.*

$$
ITALIAN
✕ **Barolo.** With red-leather seats, artsy light fixtures, and a marble bar indoors and café seating out, this Italian-inflected wine bar is a stylish, modern spot for a glass of wine, with many from small producers you probably haven't heard of. Small plates that could have come straight from Tuscany—fried calamari, risotto croquettes, a selection of *salumi*—are great for sharing. A handful of well-executed large plates, like the *pappardelle* with shrimp and braised short ribs, round out the menu. ⊠ *Mount View Hotel, 1457 Lincoln Ave.* ☎ *707/942–9900* ⊕ *www.barolocalistoga.com* ⊘ *No lunch.*

$$$
AMERICAN
✕ **Calistoga Inn Restaurant and Brewery.** On pleasant days this riverside restaurant and its sprawling, tree-shaded patio come into their own. At lunchtime, casual plates like a grilled-turkey-and-Brie sandwich or a vegetarian black-bean chili are light enough to leave some energy for an afternoon of wine tasting. And at night, when there's often live jazz played on the patio during the warm months, you'll find heartier dishes such as braised lamb shank or Sonoma duck breast with a fennel-and-Parmesan stuffing. Service can be a bit lackadaisical, so order one of the house-made brews and enjoy the atmosphere while you're waiting. ⊠ *1250 Lincoln Ave.* ☎ *707/942–4101* ⊕ *www.calistogainn.com.*

WHERE TO STAY

¢–$
⊡ **Brannan Cottage Inn.** Housed inside the only one of Sam Brannan's 1860 resort cottages still standing on its original site, this inn, a pristine Victorian house with lacy white fretwork, large windows, and a shady

20

porch, is on the National Register of Historic Places. **Pros:** innkeepers go the extra mile; most rooms have fireplaces; a five-minute walk from most of Calistoga's restaurants. **Cons:** owners' dog may be a problem for those with allergies; beds may be too firm for some. **TripAdvisor:** "great service," "friendly host," "relaxed charm." ⊠ *109 Wapoo Ave.* ☎ *707/942–4200* ⊕ *www.brannancottageinn.com* ➸ *6 rooms* △ *In-room: a/c, no TV (some), Wi-Fi. In-hotel: some pets allowed* ¶◎¶ *Breakfast.*

$$$$
★ 🔲 **Calistoga Ranch.** Spacious cedar-shingle bungalows throughout this posh, wooded property have outdoor living areas, and even the restaurant, spa, and reception space have outdoor seating areas and fireplaces. **Pros:** almost half the cottages have private hot tubs on the deck; lovely hiking trails on the property; guests have reciprocal privileges at Auberge du Soleil. **Cons:** innovative indoor-outdoor organization works better in fair weather than in rain or cold; staff, though friendly, sometimes seems inexperienced compared to similarly priced places. **TripAdvisor:** "very efficient with room service requests," "service is top notch," "down to earth and friendly." ⊠ *580 Lommel Rd.* ☎ *707/254–2800 or 800/942–4220* ⊕ *www.calistogaranch.com* ➸ *48 rooms* △ *In-room: a/c, Wi-Fi. In-hotel: restaurant, room service, bar, pool, gym, spa, some pets allowed.*

$$$
🔲 **Cottage Grove Inn.** A long driveway lined with 16 freestanding cottages, each shaded by elm trees and with rocking chairs on the porch, looks a bit like Main Street, U.S.A., but inside the skylighted buildings are all the perks you could want for a romantic weekend away. **Pros:** bicycles available for loan; freestanding cottages offer lots of privacy; bathtubs so big you could swim in them. **Cons:** no pool; decor may seem a bit frumpy for some. **TripAdvisor:** "generous professional staff," "all sorts of cute little amenities," "beautiful décor." ⊠ *1711 Lincoln Ave.* ☎ *707/942–8400 or 800/799–2284* ⊕ *www.cottagegrove.com* ➸ *16 rooms* △ *In-room: a/c, Internet, Wi-Fi. In-hotel: business center* ¶◎¶ *Breakfast.*

$–$$
★ 🔲 **Indian Springs.** Since 1861, this old-time spa has welcomed clients to its mud baths, mineral pool, and steam room, all of them supplied with mineral water from its four geysers. **Pros:** lovely grounds with outdoor seating areas; stylish for the price; enormous mineral pool. **Cons:** lodge rooms are small; service could be more polished. **TripAdvisor:** "beautiful decorated," "pool is unparalleled," "private patio was a great plus." ⊠ *1712 Lincoln Ave.* ☎ *707/942–4913* ⊕ *www.indianspringscalistoga. com* ➸ *24 rooms, 17 suites* △ *In-room: kitchen (some), Wi-Fi. In-hotel: tennis court, pool, spa.*

$–$$
Fodor's Choice
★ 🔲 **Meadowlark Country House.** Twenty hillside acres just north of downtown Calistoga surround this decidedly laid-back but sophisticated inn, and each of the rooms in the main house and guest wing has its own charms: one has a deep whirlpool tub looking onto a green hillside, and others have a deck with a view of the mountains. **Pros:** sauna next to the pool and hot tub; welcoming vibe attracts diverse guests; some of the most gracious innkeepers in Napa. **Cons:** clothing-optional pool policy isn't for everyone. **TripAdvisor:** "very clean and nicely appointed," "beautiful and perfectly maintained," "cozy

All it needs is a fair maiden: Castello di Amorosa's re-created castle.

and warm." ✉ *601 Petrified Forest Rd.* ☎ *707/942–5651 or 800/942–5651* ⊕ *www.meadowlarkinn.com* ⤳ *5 rooms, 5 suites* ♨ *In-room: a/c, kitchen (some), Wi-Fi. In-hotel: pool, business center, some pets allowed* ❡○❘ *Breakfast.*

$–$$ 🏨 **Mount View Hotel & Spa.** A National Historic Landmark built in 1917 in the Mission Revival style, the Mount View nevertheless feels up-to-date, after renovations in 2008 resulted in repainted rooms (some are a dramatic red and black), feather duvets, and high-tech touches like iPod alarm clocks. **Pros:** convenient location; excellent spa treatments. **Cons:** ground-floor rooms dark; mediocre continental breakfast; some bathrooms could use updating. **TripAdvisor:** "very relaxing," "good staff," "great location." ✉ *1457 Lincoln Ave.* ☎ *707/942–6877 or 800/816–6877* ⊕ *www.mountviewhotel.com* ⤳ *18 rooms, 13 suites* ♨ *In-room: a/c, Wi-Fi. In-hotel: restaurant, bar, pool, spa* ❡○❘ *Breakfast.*

$$$$ 🏨 **Solage.** The cottages at this Calistogan, which spreads over 22 acres, don't look particularly luxurious from the outside, but inside they flaunt a Napa-Valley-barn-meets-San-Francisco-loft aesthetic, with high ceilings, polished concrete floors, recycled walnut furniture, and all-natural fabrics in soothing muted colors. **Pros:** great service; bike cruisers parked at every cottage for guests' use; separate pools for kids and adults. **Cons:** new landscaping needs some more time to fill out; some rooms don't have tubs. **TripAdvisor:** "room service was lightning fast," "food at Solbar was really good," "beautiful facilities." ✉ *755 Silverado Trail* ☎ *866/942–7442* ⊕ *www.solagecalistoga.com* ⤳ *89 rooms* ♨ *In-room: a/c, Internet, Wi-Fi. In-hotel: restaurant, room service, bar, pools, gym, spa.*

Best Wine Country Spas

Spas in Napa and Sonoma have two special angles. First, there are the local mud baths and mineral-water sources, concentrated particularly around Calistoga. Admittedly, it can seem really strange to lower yourself into a vat of thick, muddy paste, but once you've had a few minutes to get used to the intense heat and peaty smell, you may never want to leave your cocoon. Second, there are all those grapes: their seeds, skins, and vines are credited with all sorts of antioxidant and other healthful properties by those who use them in scrubs, lotions, and other spa products.

Below are some of the best spas of the bunch.

■ **Dr. Wilkinson's**. The oldest spa in Calistoga. Although it's the least chic of the bunch, it's still well loved for its reasonable prices and its friendly, unpretentious vibe. Their mud baths are a mix of volcanic ash and peat moss. ✉ 1507 Lincoln Ave., Calistoga ☎ 707/942–4102 ⊕ www.drwilkinson.com.

■ **Fairmont Sonoma Mission Inn & Spa**. The largest spa of its type in the Wine Country. The vast complex covers every amenity you could want in a spa, including several pools and Jacuzzis fed by local thermal mineral springs. ✉ 100 Boyes Blvd./Rte. 12, Boyes Hot Springs ☎ 707/938–9000 ⊕ www.fairmont.com/sonoma.

■ **Kenwood Inn & Spa**. The prettiest spa setting in the Wine Country, thanks to the vineyards across the road and the Mediterranean style of the inn. The "wine wrap" body treatment is finished off with a slathering of lotion made from various grape-seed oils and red-wine extract. ✉ 10400 Sonoma Hwy./Rte. 12, Kenwood ☎ 707/833–1293 ⊕ www.kenwoodinn.com.

■ **Spa at Villagio**. This 13,000-square-foot spa with fieldstone walls and a Mediterranean theme has all the latest gadgets, including men's and women's outdoor hot tubs and showers with an extravagant number of showerheads. Huge spa suites—complete with flat-panel TV screens and wet bars—are perfect for couples and groups. ✉ 6481 Washington St., Yountville ☎ 707/948–5050.

SPORTS AND THE OUTDOORS

Calistoga Bikeshop (✉ 1318 Lincoln Ave. ☎ 707/942–9687) offers a self-guided Calistoga Cool Wine Tour package ($79), which includes free tastings at a number of small wineries. Best of all, they'll pick up any wine you purchase along the way if you've bought more than will fit in the handy bottle carrier on your bike.

SHOPPING

Enoteca Wine Shop (✉ 1348B Lincoln Ave. ☎ 707/942–1117), on Calistoga's main drag, displays almost all their wines with extensive tasting notes. This makes it easier to choose from among this unusually fine collection, which includes both hard-to-find bottles from Napa and Sonoma and many rare French wines. The **Wine Garage** (✉ 1020 Foothill Blvd. ☎ 707/942–5332) is the stop for bargain hunters, since all their bottles go for $25 or less. It's a great way to discover the work of smaller wineries producing undervalued wines. The unusually helpful staffers are happy to share information on all the wines they stock.

THE SONOMA VALLEY

Although the Sonoma Valley may not have quite the cachet of the neighboring Napa Valley, wineries here entice with their unpretentious attitude and smaller crowds. The Napa-style glitzy tasting rooms with enormous gift shops and $25 tasting fees are the exception here. Sonoma's landscape seduces, too, its roads gently climbing and descending on their way to wineries hidden from the road by trees.

The scenic valley, bounded by the Mayacamas Mountains on the east and Sonoma Mountain on the west, extends north from San Pablo Bay nearly 20 mi to the eastern outskirts of Santa Rosa. The varied terrain, soils, and climate (cooler in the south because of the bay influence and hotter toward the north) allow grape growers to raise cool-weather varietals such as chardonnay and pinot noir as well as merlot, cabernet sauvignon, and other heat-seeking vines. The valley is home to dozens of wineries, many of them on or near Route 12, which runs the length of the valley.

ESSENTIALS

Contacts Sonoma County Tourism Bureau (✉ *3637 Westwind Blvd., Santa Rosa* ☎ *707/522–5800 or 800/576–6662* ⊕ *www.sonomacounty.com*). **Sonoma Valley Visitors Bureau** (✉ *453 1st St. E, Sonoma* ☎ *707/996–1090 or 866/996–1090* ⊕ *www.sonomavalley.com*).

SONOMA

14 mi west of Napa on Rte. 12; 45 mi from San Francisco, north on U.S. 101, east on Rte. 37, and north on Rte. 121/12.

Founded in the early 1800s, Sonoma is the oldest town in the Wine Country, and one of the few where you can find some attractions not related to food and wine. The central Sonoma Plaza dates from the Mission era; surrounding it are 19th-century adobes, atmospheric hotels, and the swooping marquee of the 1930s Sebastiani Theatre. On summer days the plaza is a hive of activity, with children blowing off steam in the playground while their folks stock up on picnic supplies and browse the boutiques surrounding the square.

On your way into town from the south, you pass through the Carneros wine district, which straddles the southern sections of Sonoma and Napa counties.

GETTING HERE AND AROUND

To get to the town of Sonoma from San Francisco, cross the Golden Gate Bridge, then go north on U.S. 101, east on Route 37 toward Vallejo, and north on Route 121, aka the Carneros Highway. When you reach Route 12, take it north. It turns into Broadway, which dead-ends at Sonoma's Central Plaza. If you park here, a pleasant stroll around the plaza will take you by many of the town's restaurants and shops. Many of the town's most interesting wineries are a mile or less east of this downtown area. If you drive east from the plaza on East Spain Street or East Napa Street, signs will direct you to most of them.

20

EXPLORING

Fodor's Choice
★ **Bartholomew Park Winery.** Although this winery was founded only in 1994, grapes were grown in some of its vineyards as early as the 1830s. The emphasis here is on handcrafted, single-varietal wines—cabernet, merlot, zinfandel, syrah, and sauvignon blanc. The wines themselves, available only at the winery, make a stop worth it, but another reason to visit is its small museum, with vivid exhibits about the history of the winery and the Sonoma region. Another plus is the beautiful, slightly off-the-beaten-path location in a 375-acre private park about 2 mi from downtown Sonoma. Pack a lunch to enjoy on the woodsy grounds, one of the prettier picnic spots in Sonoma. ⊠ *1000 Vineyard La.* ☎ *707/939–3026* ⊕ *www.bartpark.com* ✉ *Tasting $10, tour $20* ☉ *Daily 11–4:30; tour Fri.–Sat. at 11:30 by reservation.*

Buena Vista Carneros Winery. It was here in 1857, at California's oldest premium winery, that Count Agoston Haraszthy de Mokcsa laid the basis for modern California wine making, bucking the conventional wisdom that vines should be planted on well-watered ground by instead planting on well-drained hillsides. Chinese laborers dug tunnels 100 feet into the hillside, and the limestone they extracted was used to build the main house, which is now surrounded by redwood and eucalyptus trees and a picnic area. Their best wines are their chardonnay, pinot noir, syrah, and merlot grown in the Ramal Vineyard in the Carneros District. ⊠ *18000 Old Winery Rd., off Napa Rd.* ☎ *800/678–8504* ⊕ *buenavistacarneros.com* ✉ *Tasting $10* ☉ *Daily 10–5.*

Cline Cellars. Although many Carneros wineries specialize in pinot noir and chardonnay, Cline Cellars goes its own way by focusing on Rhône varietals, such as syrah, roussanne, and viognier, all grown here in Carneros, as well as mourvèdre and carignane, which are cultivated in Contra Costa County. They're also known for their Ancient Vines Zinfandel, produced from vines that are around 100 years old. The 1850s farmhouse that houses the tasting room has a pleasant wrap-around porch for enjoying the weeping willows, ponds, fountains, and thousands of rosebushes on the property. Pack a picnic and plan to stay for a while. ⊠ *24737 Hwy. 121/Arnold Dr.* ☎ *707/940–4030* ⊕ *www.clinecellars.com* ✉ *Tasting free–$1 per reserve wine, tour free* ☉ *Daily 10–6; tour daily at 11, 1, and 3.*

★ **De Loach Vineyards.** Just far enough off the beaten track to feel like a real find, this winery produces a variety of old-vine zinfandels, chardonnays, and a handful of other varietals, but it is best for known for its pinot noir, some of which is made using open-top wood fermentation vats that are uncommon in Sonoma but have been used in France for centuries. (Some think they intensify a wine's flavor.) Tours focus on the estate vineyards outside the tasting room door, where you can learn about the labor-intensive biodynamic and organic farming methods used, and take you through their culinary garden. Call a day or two in advance if you want to taste their wines paired with regional cheeses ($20) or purchase a picnic basket to enjoy in their attractive picnic area. ⊠ *1791 Olivet Rd.* ☎ *707/526–9111* ⊕ *www.deloachvineyards.com* ✉ *Tasting $10, tour free* ☉ *Daily 10–5; tours by appointment.*

Ravenswood. Housed in a stone building covered in climbing vines, Ravenswood's tasting room lives up to the winery's punchy mission statement: "no wimpy wines." They generally succeed, especially with their signature big, bold zinfandels, which are sometimes blended with petit syrah, carignane, or other varietals that grow in the same field (this is called a "field blend"). Also be sure to taste the Bordeaux-style blends, early-harvest gewürztraminer, and lightly sparkling moscato, too. Tours that focus on their viticultural practices, held 10:30 daily, include a barrel tasting of wines in progress in the cellar. ✉ *18701 Gehricke Rd., off E. Spain St.* ☎ *707/938–1960* ⊕ *www.ravenswood-wine. com* 🍷 *Tasting $10–$15, tour $15* ⊘ *Daily 10–4:30.*

Robledo Family Winery. Founded by Reynaldo Robledo Sr., a former migrant worker from Michoacán, Mexico, Robledo Family Winery is truly a family affair. You're likely to encounter one of the charming Robledo sons in the tasting room, where he'll proudly tell you the story of the immigrant family while pouring tastes of their sauvignon blanc, pinot noir, merlot, cabernet sauvignon, and other wines, including a chardonnay that comes from the vineyard right outside the tasting room's door. All seven Robledo sons and two Robledo daughters, as well as matriarch Maria, are involved in the winery operations. If you don't run into them on your visit to the winery, you'll see their names and pictures on the bottles of wine, such as the Dos Hermanas late-harvest dessert wine, or one of the ports dedicated to Maria Robledo. ✉ *21901 Bonness Rd.* ☎ *707/939–6903* ⊕ *www.robledofamilywinery. com* 🍷 *Tasting $5–$10* ⊘ *Mon.–Sat. 10–5, Sun. 11–4, by appointment.*

WHERE TO EAT

$$
AMERICAN
★

✕ **Cafe La Haye.** In a postage-stamp-size open kitchen, skillful chefs turn out about half a dozen main courses that star on a small but worthwhile seasonal menu emphasizing local ingredients. Chicken, beef, pasta, and fish get deluxe treatment without fuss or fanfare. The daily roasted chicken and the risotto specials are always good. Butterscotch pudding is a homey signature dessert. The dining room is also compact, but the friendly owner, who is often there to greet diners, gives it a particularly welcoming vibe. ✉ *140 E. Napa St.* ☎ *707/935–5994* ⊕ *www. cafelahaye.com* ⊘ *Closed Sun. and Mon. No lunch.*

$
ITALIAN

✕ **Della Santina's.** This longtime favorite, with a charming heated brick patio out back, serves the most authentic Italian food in town. (The Della Santina family, which has been running the restaurant since 1990, hails from Lucca, Italy.) Daily fish and veal specials join classic northern Italian pastas such as linguine with pesto and lasagna Bolognese. Of special note are the roasted meat dishes and, when available, petrale sole and sand dabs. ✉ *133 E. Napa St.* ☎ *707/935–0576* ⊕ *www. dellasantinas.com.*

$$
FRENCH

✕ **The Girl & the Fig.** Chef Sondra Bernstein has turned the historic barroom of the Sonoma Hotel into a hot spot for inventive French cooking. You can always find something with the signature figs in it here, whether it's a fig-and-arugula salad or an aperitif of sparkling wine with a fig liqueur. Also look for duck confit with French lentils, a burger with matchstick fries, or wild boar braised in red wine. The wine list is notable for its emphasis on Rhône varietals, and a counter in the bar

20

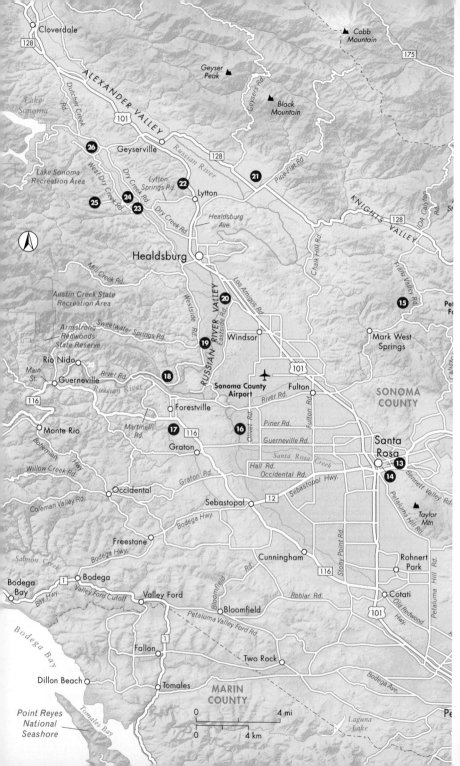

Sonoma County

20

CLOSE UP

A Grape Primer

Well more than 50 varieties of grapes are grown in the California Wine Country. Although you don't need to be on a first-name basis with them all, you'll see the following dozen again and again as you visit the wineries.

WHITES

■ **Chardonnay.** Now as firmly associated with California wine making as it is with Burgundy, where it's used extensively. California chardonnays spent many years chasing big, buttery flavor, but the current trend is toward more restrained wines.

■ **Gewürztraminer.** Cooler California climes such as the Russian River valley are great for growing this German-Alsatian grape, which is turned into a boldly perfumed, fruity wine.

■ **Riesling.** This cool-climate German grape has a sweet rep in America. When made in a dry style, as it more and more often is, it can be crisply refreshing, with lush aromas.

■ **Sauvignon Blanc.** Hails from Bordeaux and the Loire Valley. Wines made from this grape vary widely, from herbaceous to tropical-fruity.

■ **Viognier.** Once rarely planted outside of France's Rhône Valley, it's one of the hottest white-wine varietals in California today. The best viogniers have an intense fruity or floral bouquet; they're usually dry.

REDS

■ **Cabernet Franc.** Most often used in blends, often to add complexity to cabernet sauvignon, this French grape can produce aromatic, soft, and subtle wine.

■ **Cabernet Sauvignon.** The king of California reds, this Bordeaux grape grows best in austere, well-drained

soils. At its best, the California version is dark, bold, and tannic, with black-currant notes. It's often blended with cabernet franc, merlot, and other red varieties to soften the resulting wine and make it ready for earlier drinking.

■ **Merlot.** A blue-black Bordeaux variety that in California makes soft, full-bodied wine. Was well on its way to being the most popular red until anti-merlot jokes in the movie *Sideways* damaged its rep, but it's staged for a comeback.

■ **Pinot Noir.** The darling of grape growers in cooler parts of Napa and Sonoma, such as the Carneros region and the Russian River valley. At its best it has a subtle but addictive earthy quality.

■ **Sangiovese.** The main red grape of Italy's Chianti District and of much of central Italy. It can be made into vibrant, light- to medium-bodied wines, as well as into long-lived, very complex reds. Increasingly planted in California.

■ **Syrah.** A big red from France's Rhône Valley. With good tannins it can become a full-bodied beauty, but without them it can be flabby and forgettable. Also known as shiraz, particularly when it's grown in Australia.

■ **Zinfandel.** A quintessential California grape. Rich, jammy, and often spicy, zinfandel wines can be quite high in alcohol.

area sells artisanal cheese platters for eating here as well as cheese by the pound to go. Sunday brunch brings rib-sticking dishes such as steak and eggs and a Basque frittata with potatoes, onions, and tomatoes. ⊠ *Sonoma Hotel, Sonoma Plaza, 110 W. Spain St.* ☎ *707/938–3634* ⊕ *www.thegirlandthefig.com.*

$$
AMERICAN
★

✕ **Harvest Moon Cafe.** It's easy to feel like one of the family at this little restaurant with an odd, zigzagging layout. Diners seated at one of the two tiny bars chat with the servers like old friends, but the husband-and-wife team in the kitchen is serious about the food, much of which relies on local produce. The daily menu sticks to homey dishes like half a grilled chicken served with polenta and tapenade, rib-eye steak with a red-wine sauce, and a marinated-beet-and-frisée salad. Everything is so perfectly executed and the vibe so genuinely warm that a visit here is deeply satisfying. In fair weather a spacious back patio, with seats arranged around a fountain, more than doubles the number of seats. ⊠ *487 W. 1st St.* ☎ *707/933–8160* ⊕ *www.harvestmooncafesonoma. com* ☉ *Closed Tues. No lunch Mon.–Sat.*

$$
PORTUGUESE

✕ **LaSalette.** Chef-owner Manuel Azevedo, born in the Azores and raised in Sonoma, serves dishes inspired by his native Portugal in this warmly decorated spot, where the best seats are on the patio, along a pedestrian alleyway off Sonoma Plaza. Boldly flavored dishes such as *pork tenderloin recheado,* stuffed with olives and almonds and topped with a port sauce, or one of the daily seafood specials might be followed by a dish of rice pudding with Madeira-braised figs or a port from the varied list. ⊠ *452 E. 1st St.* ☎ *707/938–1927* ⊕ *www.lasalette-restaurant.com.*

$$$$
AMERICAN
Fodor's Choice
★

✕ **Santé.** Under the leadership of chef Andrew Cain, this elegant dining room in the Sonoma Mission Inn has gained a reputation as a destination restaurant through its focus on seasonal and locally sourced ingredients. The room is understated, with drapes in rich earth tones and softly lighted chandeliers, but the food is anything but. Dishes on the frequently changing menu, such as a roasted Sonoma duck breast with braised Swiss chard and duck confit, are complex without being fussy, while some dishes, like the butter-poached Maine lobster with flageolet beans and lardons, are pure decadence. Brunch is also served in summer. ⊠ *Fairmont Sonoma Mission Inn & Spa, 100 Boyes Blvd./ Rte. 12, at Boyes Blvd., 2 mi north of Sonoma, Boyes Hot Springs* ☎ *707/939–2415* ☉ *Closed 1st 2 wks in Jan. No lunch.*

20

$
AMERICAN

✕ **Sunflower Caffé.** Although you wouldn't realize it as you walk by, this casual café has one of Sonoma's prettiest patios. Equipped with both heating lamps and plenty of shade, it's comfortable in all but the most inclement weather. On dreary days, cheerful artworks brighten up the interior, where locals hunker over their computers and take advantage of the free Wi-Fi. The menu, composed mostly of salads and sandwiches (as well as omelets and waffles for breakfast), is simple but satisfying, and it relies largely on local ingredients. It's also a comfortable spot to take a quick break with an excellent coffee drink or something from the well-stocked outdoor wine bar. ⊠ *421 W. 1st St.* ☎ *707/996–6645* ⊕ *www.sonomasunflower.com* ☜ *Reservations not accepted* ☉ *No dinner fall and winter.*

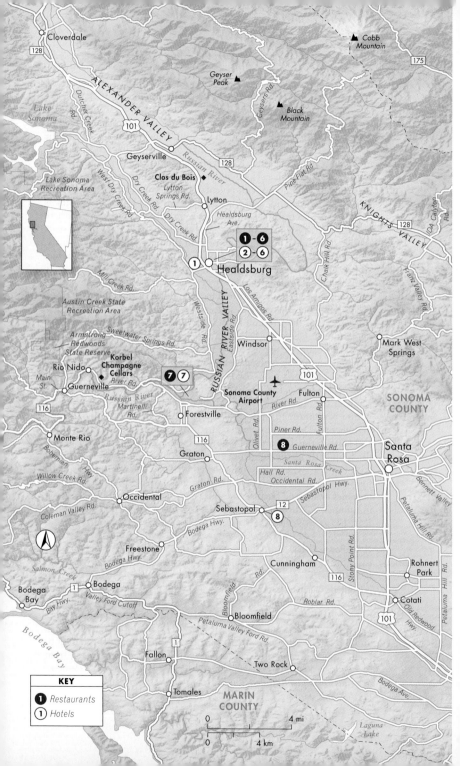

KEY

① Restaurants

① Hotels

Where to Eat and Stay in Sonoma County

Restaurants ▼

Hotels ▼

20

WHERE TO STAY

¢ 🏨 **El Dorado Hotel.** Rooms in this remodeled 1843 building strike a spare, modern pose, with rectilinear four-poster beds and pristine white bedding, but the Mexican-tile floors hint at Sonoma's mission-era past. **Pros:** stylish for the price; hip restaurant downstairs; central location. **Cons:** rooms are small; lighting could be better; noisy. **TripAdvisor:** "rooms are very comfortable," "home away from home," "great location." ✉ *405 1st St. W* ☎ *707/996–3030* ⊕ *www.eldoradosonoma.com* ⤶ *27 rooms* ♿ *In-room: a/c, Wi-Fi. In-hotel:restaurants, bar, pool.*

$$$–$$$$ 🏨 **The Fairmont Sonoma Mission Inn & Spa.** The real draw at this Mission-style resort is the extensive, swanky spa, easily the biggest in Sonoma, with a vast array of massages and treatments, some using locally sourced grape and lavender products. **Pros:** enormous spa; excellent, well-reviewed restaurant on-site; free shuttle to downtown. **Cons:** rooms on the smaller side; not as intimate as some similarly priced places. **TripAdvisor:** "very friendly and attentive," "grounds are beautiful," "close to downtown Sonoma." ✉ *100 Boyes Blvd./Rte. 12, 2 mi north of Sonoma, Boyes Hot Springs* ☎ *707/938–9000* ⊕ *www. fairmont.com/sonoma* ⤶ *168 rooms, 60 suites* ♿ *In-room: a/c, Internet, Wi-Fi (some). In-hotel: restaurants, room service, bars, golf course, pools, gym, spa, some pets allowed.*

¢ 🏨 **Sonoma Creek Inn.** The small but cheerful rooms at this roadside inn
☺ with a sunny yellow exterior are individually decorated with painted wooden armoires, cozy quilts, and brightly colored contemporary artwork, elevating this bargain option well above your average motel. **Pros:** clean, well-lighted bathrooms; a lot of charm for the low price. **Cons:** office not staffed 24 hours a day; slightly out-of-the-way location (about a 10-minute drive from Sonoma Plaza). **TripAdvisor:** "very clean," "comfortable and quaint," "friendly service." ✉ *239 Boyes Blvd.* ☎ *707/939–9463* ⊕ *www.sonomacreekinn.com* ⤶ *16 rooms* ♿ *In-room: a/c, Wi-Fi. In-hotel: restaurant, some pets allowed.*

NIGHTLIFE AND THE ARTS

The **Sebastiani Theatre** (✉ *476 1st St. E* ☎ *707/996–2020*), built on Sonoma Plaza in 1934 by Italian immigrant and entrepreneur Samuele Sebastiani, schedules first-run films, as well as the occasional musical or theatrical performance.

Hit the bar at the **Swiss Hotel** (✉ *18 W. Spain St.* ☎ *707/938–2884*) to sip a Glariffee, a cold and potent cousin to Irish coffee that's unique to this 19th-century spot.

SHOPPING

Sonoma Plaza is the town's main shopping magnet, with tempting boutiques and specialty food purveyors facing the square or just a block or two away.

Sign of the Bear (✉ *Sonoma Plaza, 435 1st St. W* ☎ *707/996–3722*) sells the latest and greatest in kitchenware and cookware, as well as a few Wine Country–themed items, like lazy Susans made from wine barrels.

Although their Sonoma Jack cheese and tangy Sonoma Teleme are no longer made on the premises, the **Sonoma Cheese Factory** (✉ *Sonoma Plaza, 2 Spain St.* ☎ *707/996–1931*) does offer samples of many local cheeses. They also have everything you need for a picnic, from sandwiches to wine to about a dozen types of homemade fudge.

A block east of Sonoma Plaza, the **Vella Cheese Company** (✉ *315 2nd St. E* ☎ *707/938–3232*) has been making superb cheeses, such as rawmilk cheddars and several varieties of jack, since 1931.

GLEN ELLEN

7 mi north of Sonoma on Rte. 12.

Craggy Glen Ellen embodies the difference between the Napa and Sonoma valleys. In small Napa towns such as St. Helena well-groomed sidewalks are lined with upscale boutiques and restaurants, but in Glen Ellen the crooked streets are shaded with stands of old oak trees and occasionally bisected by the Sonoma and Calabasas creeks.

Jack London, who represents Glen Ellen's rugged spirit, lived in the area for many years; the town commemorates him with place-names and nostalgic establishments.

GETTING HERE AND AROUND

To get to tiny Glen Ellen from Sonoma's Plaza, drive west on East Spain Street. After about a mile, turn right onto Route 12. Drive about 7 mi, then take the Arnold Drive exit and turn left. Many of Glen Ellen's few restaurants and inns are along a half-mile stretch of Arnold Drive. Though distances in town are short, the road is winding and lacks a sidewalk in most spots, so it might be safer to drive than to walk between spots.

EXPLORING

Arrowood Vineyards & Winery. Although it's neither as famous or as old as some of its neighbors, Arrowood still produces well-regarded wines, especially the chardonnays, syrahs, and age-worthy cabernets. A wraparound porch with wicker chairs invites you to linger outside the tasting room, built to resemble a New England farmhouse. In fact, if you're more interesting in lounging than learning about their wines, you can pay $5 for a glass to enjoy outside. Tours, offered daily at 10:30 by appointment, conclude with a seated tasting. ■TIP→ If you're doing a reserve tasting on a weekend, and you're interested in discovering what Arrowood wines taste like after several years in the bottle, ask whether they happen to have any library wines open they can pour. ✉ *14347 Sonoma Hwy./Rte. 12* ☎ *707/935–2600* ⊕ *www.arrowoodvineyards.com* ☕ *Tasting $5–$10, tour $25* ⊙ *Daily 10–4:30; tour by appointment.*

★ **Benziger Family Winery.** One of the best-known local wineries is Benziger Family Winery, on a sprawling estate in a bowl with 360-degree sun exposure. Benziger is noted for its merlot, pinot noir, cabernet sauvignon, chardonnay, and sauvignon blanc. The tram tours here are especially interesting (they're first come, first served). On a ride through

20

the vineyards, guides explain the regional microclimates and geography and give you a glimpse of the extensive cave system. Tours depart several times a day, weather permitting. Reservations are needed for smaller tours that conclude with a seated tasting ($40). ■ TIP→ Arrive before lunch for the best shot at joining a tour—and bring a picnic, since the grounds here are lovely. ⊠ *1883 London Ranch Rd.* ☎ *707/935–3000* ⊕ *www.benziger.com* ⊠ *Tasting $10–$20, tour $15–$40* ☉ *Daily 10–5.*

Jack London Saloon. Built in 1905, the Jack London Saloon is decorated with photos of London and other London memorabilia. ⊠ *13740 Arnold Dr.* ☎ *707/996–3100* ⊕ *www.jacklondonlodge.com.*

Jack London State Historic Park. In the hills above Glen Ellen—known as the Valley of the Moon—lies Jack London State Historic Park, where you could easily spend the afternoon hiking along the edge of vineyards and through stands of oak trees. Several of the author's manuscripts and a handful of personal effects are on view at the House of Happy Walls museum, once the home of London's widow. A short hike away from Happy Walls are the ruins of Wolf House. Designed by London, it mysteriously burned down just before he was to move in. Also open to the public are a few restored farm outbuildings, and on weekends you can visit the Cottage, a restored wood-framed building where he wrote many of his later works. London is buried on the property. ⊠ *2400 London Ranch Rd.* ☎ *707/938–5216* ⊠ *Parking $8, admission to buildings free* ☉ *Park and museum daily 10–5, cottage weekends 10–4.*

WHERE TO EAT

$$
FRENCH
Fodor's Choice
★
✕ **The Fig Cafe.** Pale sage walls, a high, sloping ceiling, and casual but very warm service set a sunny mood in this little bistro that's run by the same team behind Sonoma's The Girl & the Fig. The restaurant's eponymous fruit shows up in all sorts of places, from salads to the wintertime apple-and-fig bread pudding. The small menu focuses on California and French comfort food, like steamed mussels served with terrific crispy fries, and a roast quail served with faro and olives. Don't forget to look on the chalkboard for frequently changing desserts, such as butterscotch pots de crème. ■ TIP→ The unusual no-corkage-fee policy makes it a great place to drink the wine you just discovered down the road. ⊠ *13690 Arnold Dr.* ☎ *707/938–2130* ⊕ *www.thegirlandthefig.com* ⊠ *Reservations not accepted* ☉ *No lunch weekdays.*

$$
ECLECTIC
✕ **Glen Ellen Inn Oyster Grill & Martini Bar.** Tucked inside a creek-side 1940s cottage, this cozy restaurant exudes romance, especially if you snag a seat in the shady garden or on the patio strung with tiny lights. After taking the edge off your hunger with some oysters on the half shell and an ice-cold martini, order from the eclectic, frequently changing menu that plucks elements from California, French, and occasionally Asian cuisines. For instance, you might try ginger tempura calamari with mango salsa or grilled rib-eye steak with Gorgonzola mashed potatoes. Desserts tend toward the indulgent; witness the warm pecan bread pudding with a chocolate center that sits in a puddle of brandy sauce. ⊠ *13670 Arnold Dr.* ☎ *707/996–6409* ⊕ *www.glenelleninn.com* ☉ *No lunch Wed. or Thurs.*

Horseback riding tours loop around Jack London State Historic Park.

WHERE TO STAY

¢–$ ⊞ **Beltane Ranch.** On a slope of the Mayacamas range a few miles from
★ Glen Ellen, this 1892 ranch house, shaded by magnificent oak trees,
contains charmingly old-fashioned rooms, each individually decorated
with antiques and thick old-fashioned bedcovers. **Pros:** casual, friendly
atmosphere; reasonably priced; beautiful grounds with ancient oak
trees. **Cons:** downstairs rooms get some noise from upstairs rooms;
cooled with ceiling fans instead of air-conditioning. **TripAdvisor:** "very
clean and comfortable," "cozy and charming," "quiet and peaceful
setting." ⊠ 11775 Sonoma Hwy./Rte. 12 ☎ 707/996–6501 ⊕ www.
beltaneranch.com ⤳ 3 rooms, 3 suites ⌂ In-room: no TV, Wi-Fi. In-
hotel: tennis court ⋈ Breakfast.

$$$–$$$$ ⊞ **Gaige House.** Gorgeous Asian objets d'art and leather club chairs
Fodor's Choice cozied up to the fireplace in the lobby are just a few of the graceful
★ touches in this luxurious but understated B&B. **Pros:** beautiful lounge
areas; cottages are very private; excellent service. **Cons:** sound carries
in the main house; the least expensive rooms are on the small side. **Tri-
pAdvisor:** "calming and peaceful," "charming Ryokan feel," "breakfast
is gourmet." ⊠ 13540 Arnold Dr. ☎ 707/935–0237 or 800/935–0237
⊕ www.gaige.com ⤳ 10 rooms, 13 suites ⌂ In-room: a/c, Wi-Fi. In-
hotel: pool, spa ⋈ Breakfast.

¢ ⊞ **Glenelly Inn and Cottages.** On a quiet side street a few blocks from
☙ the town center, this sunny little establishment has a long history as a
getaway. **Pros:** children are welcome; quiet location; hot tub in a pretty
garden. **Cons:** some may not appreciate the presence of children; a few
of the rooms could be freshened up. **TripAdvisor:** "beautiful retreat,"
"very friendly," "charming and well-located." ⊠ 5131 Warm Springs

Hitching a ride on the Benziger Family Winery tram tour.

Rd. ☎ *707/996–6720* ⊕ *www.glenellyinn.com* ⥾ *8 rooms, 2 suites* ♿ *In-room: a/c (some), Wi-Fi. In-hotel: laundry facilities, some pets allowed* ⏹ *Breakfast.*

KENWOOD

3 mi north of Glen Ellen on Rte. 12.

Blink and you might miss tiny Kenwood, which consists of little more than a few restaurants and shops and a historic train depot, now used for private events. But hidden in this pretty landscape of meadows and woods at the north end of Sonoma Valley are several good wineries, most just off the Sonoma Highway.

GETTING HERE AND AROUND

To get to Kenwood from Glen Ellen, drive 3 mi north on Route 12. Most of the wineries in Kenwood are strung along Route 12, a short drive from one another.

EXPLORING

Family Wineries. Many wineries around the Kenwood area are small, so tiny that they don't have tasting rooms of their own. At Family Wineries you can sample the output of several such spots. Though the lineup of participating wineries occasionally changes, look for sweet flavored sparklers produced by SL Cellars and still wines from Sonoma producers such as David Noyes and Collier Falls. ⊠ *9380 Sonoma Hwy.* ☎ *888/433–6555* ⊕ *www.familywines.com* ⤬ *Tasting $5* ⏱ *Daily 10:30–5.*

Kunde Estate Winery & Vineyards. On your way into Kunde Estate Winery & Vineyards you pass a terrace flanked with fountains, virtually coaxing you to stay for a picnic with views over the vineyard. The tour of the grounds includes its extensive caves, some of which stretch 175 feet below a syrah vineyard. Kunde is perhaps best known for its toasty chardonnays, although tastings might include sauvignon blanc, cabernet sauvignon, and zinfandel as well. If you skip the tour, take a few minutes to wander around the demonstration vineyard outside the tasting room. Reserve in advance if you want to take advantage of the Mountain Top Tasting, a tour that ends with a sampling of their reserve wines at the highest point on their property, overlooking their vineyards ($25). ✉ *9825 Sonoma Hwy./Rte. 12* ☎ *707/833–5501* ⊕ *www.kunde. com* 🍷 *Tasting $10–$20, tour free* ☉ *Daily 10:30–5; tours Mon.–Thurs. at 11, Fri.–Sun on the hr 11–3; Mountain Top Tasting Mon.–Thurs. at 12:30 and 2:30, Fri.–Sun. hourly 11:30–2:30.*

★ **St. Francis Winery.** Named for St. Francis of Assisi, founder of the Franciscan order, which established missions and vineyards throughout California, St. Francis Winery has one of the most scenic locations in Sonoma, nestled at the foot of Mt. Hood. The visitor center beautifully replicates the California Mission style, with its red-tile roof and dramatic bell tower (a plaque explains that the bell was actually blessed in the Basilica di San Francesco in Assisi, Italy). Out back, a slate patio overlooks vineyards, lavender gardens, and hummingbirds flitting about the flower beds. The charm of the surroundings is matched by the wines, most of them red, including rich, earthy zinfandels from both the Russian River and Sonoma valleys. In addition to the usual wine tastings, there are a variety of food and wine pairings available ($20 to $35); call or check their Web site for times and details. ✉ *100 Pythian Rd.* ☎ *800/543–7713* ⊕ *www.stfranciswinery.com* 🍷 *Tasting $10, tour $25, food and wine pairings $20–$35* ☉ *Daily 10–5; tour weekdays at 11 and 2.*

WHERE TO EAT AND STAY

$
ITALIAN ✕ **Café Citti.** Classical music in the background and a friendly staff (as well as a roaring fire when the weather's cold) keep this no-frills roadside café from feeling too spartan. Order dishes such as roast chicken and slabs of tiramisu from the counter and they're delivered to your table, a few of which are on an outdoor patio. An ample array of prepared salads and sandwiches means they do a brisk business in takeout for picnic packers, but you can also choose pasta made to order, mixing and matching linguine, penne, and other pastas with sauces like pesto or marinara. ✉ *9049 Sonoma Hwy./Rte. 12* ☎ *707/833–2690* ⊕ *www.cafecitti.com.*

$$$$
★ 🛏 **Kenwood Inn and Spa.** Buildings resembling graceful old haciendas and mature fruit trees shading the courtyards make it seem like this inn has been here for more than a century (it was actually built in 1990). **Pros:** large rooms; lavish furnishings; extremely romantic. **Cons:** Wi-Fi can be spotty in some areas; expensive. **TripAdvisor:** "extremely friendly and helpful," "bed was comfy," "views were beautiful." ✉ *10400 Sonoma Hwy.* ☎ *707/833–1293* ⊕ *www.kenwoodinn.com* 🛏 *25 rooms, 4 suites* ⚘ *In-room: a/c, no TV, Internet, Wi-Fi. In-hotel: restaurant, bar, pool, spa, some age restrictions* ❝❞ *Breakfast.*

20

ELSEWHERE IN SONOMA COUNTY

At nearly 1,598 square mi, there's much more to Sonoma County than the day-tripper favorites of Sonoma, Glen Ellen, and Kenwood. To the north is Healdsburg, a lovely small town with a rapidly rising buzz. The national media have latched onto it for its swank hotels and remarkable restaurants, and many Fodors.com readers recommend it as an ideal home base for wine tasting.

Within easy striking distance of Healdsburg are some of the Wine Country's most scenic vineyards, in the Alexander, Dry Creek, and Russian River valleys. And these lookers also happen to produce some of the country's best pinot noir, cabernet sauvignon, zinfandel, and sauvignon blanc. Though these regions are hardly unknown names, their quiet, narrow roads feel a world away from Highway 29 in Napa.

The western stretches of Sonoma County, which reach all the way to the Pacific Ocean, are sparsely populated in comparison to the above destinations, with only the occasional vineyard popping up in between isolated ranches. Guerneville, a popular destination for weekending San Franciscans, who come to canoe down the Russian River, is a convenient place for picking up River Road, then Westside Road, which passes through pinot noir paradise on its way to Healdsburg.

SANTA ROSA

8 mi northwest of Kenwood on Rte. 12.

Santa Rosa, the Wine Country's largest city, isn't likely to charm you with its office buildings, department stores, and frequent snarls of traffic along U.S. 101. It is, however, home to a couple of interesting cultural offerings. Its chain motels and hotels are also handy if you're finding that everything else is booked up, especially since Santa Rosa is roughly equidistant from Sonoma, Healdsburg, and the Russian River valley, three of the most popular wine-tasting destinations.

GETTING HERE AND AROUND

To get to Santa Rosa from San Francisco, drive north over the Golden Gate Bridge and continue north on U.S. 101 to the downtown Santa Rosa exit. To get to Santa Rosa from Sonoma Valley, take Route 12 north. After passing through Santa Rosa's outskirts it will deposit you at U.S. 101. Santa Rosa's hotels, restaurants, and wineries are spread over a fairly wide area, and you should factor in a little extra time whenever driving around Santa Rosa, especially during morning and evening commute hours.

EXPLORING

Charles M. Schulz Museum. Fans of Snoopy and Charlie Brown should head to the Charles M. Schulz Museum, dedicated to the cartoonist who lived in Santa Rosa for the last 30 years of his life, until his death in 2000. Permanent installations such as a re-creation of the artist's studio share the space with temporary exhibits, which often focus on a particular theme in Schulz's work. Both children and adults can try their hand at creating cartoons in the Education Room or wander through the labyrinth in the form of Snoopy's head. Check the Web site or call for information about occasional kid-friendly workshops and events. ⊠ *2301 Hardies La.* ☎ *707/579–4452* ⊕ *www.schulzmuseum.org* 🖃 *$10* ⊙ *Labor Day–Memorial Day, Wed.–Fri. and Mon. 11–5, weekends 10–5; Memorial Day–Labor Day, weekdays 11–5, weekends 10–5.*

Luther Burbank Home and Gardens. The Luther Burbank Home and Gardens commemorates the great botanist who lived and worked on these grounds and single-handedly developed the modern techniques of hybridization. The 1.6-acre garden and a greenhouse show the results of some of Burbank's experiments to develop spineless cactus, fruit trees, and flowers such as the Shasta daisy. Instructions for accessing the free self-guided garden tour using visitors' own cell phones is posted near the carriage house. In the music room of his house, a modified Greek Revival structure that was Burbank's home from 1884 to 1906, a dictionary lies open to a page on which the verb "burbank" is defined as "to modify and improve plant life." (To see the house, you'll need to join one of the docent-led tours, which leave from the gift shop every half hour.) ⊠ *Santa Rosa and Sonoma Aves.* ☎ *707/524–5445* ⊕ *www. lutherburbank.org* 🖃 *Gardens free, tour $7* ⊙ *Gardens daily 8–dusk; museum and gift shop Apr.–Oct., Tues.–Sun. 10–4.*

Fodor's Choice ★ **Matanzas Creek Winery.** The visitor center at this beautiful winery sets itself apart with an understated Japanese aesthetic, extending to a tranquil fountain and a koi pond. Best of all, huge windows overlook a vast field of lavender plants. ■ TIP➜ The ideal time to visit is in May and June, when the lavender blooms and perfumes the air. The winery specializes in sauvignon blanc, merlot, and chardonnay, although they also produce a popular dry rosé as well as some syrah, pinot noir, and cabernet. Guided tours range from an hour-long intro to the Bennett Valley, the tiny AVA where the winery is located, to a more expensive one that concludes with a taste of limited-production and library wines paired with artisanal cheeses. If you'd like to go it on your own, ask for a printed vineyard tour guide, which will point you toward a stroll through their merlot, Grenache, and malbec vineyards. ⊠ *6097 Bennett Valley Rd.* ☎ *707/528–6464 or 800/590–6464* ⊕ *www.matanzascreek.com* 🖃 *Tasting $5, tour $10–$35* ⊙ *Daily 10–4:30; tour by appointment.*

20

☺ **Safari West.** An unexpected bit of wilderness in the Wine Country, this African wildlife preserve covers 400 acres on the outskirts of Santa Rosa. Reserve in advance and set aside an entire morning or afternoon for a visit, which begins with a stroll around various enclosures housing lemurs, cheetahs, giraffes, and many varieties of rare birds, like the brightly colored scarlet ibis. Next, guests climb onto open-air vehicles that spend about two hours driving around the expansive property, where more than 80 species, such as African cape buffalo, gazelles, wildebeests, and zebras make their home on the hillsides. All the while you're accompanied by a staff member who informs you about the animals, their behavior, and the threats they face in the wild. If you'd like to extend your stay, lodging in well-equipped tent cabins ($–$$) is also available. ⊠ *3115 Porter Creek Rd.* ☎ *707/579–2551* ⊕ *www. safariwest.com* 🖃 *$68, $30 children 3–12* ⊙ *By reservation only.*

WHERE TO EAT

$$$

ITALIAN

Fodor's Choice

★

✕ **Zazu.** A low wooden ceiling, rustic copper tables, and rock music on the stereo create a casual vibe at this roadhouse. It's a few miles from downtown Santa Rosa, but the hearty, soulful cooking of owners Duskie Estes and John Stewart brings passionate fans from all over the Wine Country. About 30% of the produce comes from their own garden, and the meats are house-cured, so the antipasto plate or a pizza with house-made pepperoni are both excellent choices. The small seasonal menu—a mix of Italian-influenced dishes and updated American classics—tends toward rich flavors, with choices like rabbit braised in red wine and served with a mushroom risotto. On Saturday and Sunday mornings hearty brunch dishes like cornmeal waffles and corned-beef hash lay the foundation for a busy day of wine tasting. ✉ *3535 Guerneville Rd.* ☎ *707/523–4814* ⊕ *www.zazurestaurant.com.*

RUSSIAN RIVER VALLEY

10 mi northwest of Santa Rosa.

The Russian River flows all the way from Mendocino to the Pacific Ocean, but in terms of wine making, the Russian River valley is centered on a triangle with points at Healdsburg, Guerneville, and Sebastopol. Tall redwoods shade many of the two-lane roads that access this scenic area, where, thanks to the cooling marine influence, pinot noir and chardonnay are the king and queen of grapes.

ESSENTIALS

Contacts Russian River Wine Road (✉ *Box 46, Healdsburg* ☎ *707/433–4335 or 800/723–6336* ⊕ *www.wineroad.com*).

GETTING HERE AND AROUND

Many people visit the Russian River valley while based in nearby Healdsburg. To get to the wineries along Westside Road from Healdsburg's central plaza, head south on Center Street and turn right at Mill Street, which turns into Westside Road after it crosses U.S. 101. Keep heading west on River Road toward Guerneville if you want to explore the western reaches of the Russian River valley. Or, for a shorter day trip, from Westside Road turn left on Wohler Road and left again on Eastside Road to loop back to U.S. 101 just south of Healdsburg. Wineries are somewhat more widely spaced in this rural area than in other parts of the Wine Country, and you should plan on spending some leisurely time driving along the winding roads. This is also a particularly scenic area for biking.

EXPLORING

Gary Farrell Winery. Pass through an impressive metal gate and wind your way up a steep hill to reach Gary Farrell, a spot with knockout views over the rolling hills and vineyards below. Although the winery has changed hands a few times since Farrell sold it in 2004, it's managed to continue producing well-regarded bottles under Susan Reed, who worked alongside him. Though their earthy, full-bodied zinfandels and Carneros and Russian River chardonnays are winners, the winery has built its reputation on its pinot noirs. ✉ *10701 Westside Rd., Healdsburg* ☎ *707/473–2900* ⊕ *www.garyfarrellwines.com* 🍷 *Tasting $10–$15, tour $25* ☼ *Daily 10:30–4:30; tour by appointment.*

Hartford Family Winery. Fans of pinot noir will surely want to stop at this surprisingly opulent winery off a meandering country road in Forestville. Here grapes from the cooler areas of the Russian River valley, Sonoma coast, and other regions are turned into crisp chardonnays, old-vine zinfandels, and a wide variety of pinots, many of which are single-vineyard wines. Call ahead if you're interested in scheduling a tour of the barrel room ($10, not including tasting) or a seated tasting of library wines ($25). ✉ *8075 Martinelli Rd., Forestville* ☎ *707/887–1756* ⊕ *www.hartfordwines.com* 🍷 *Tasting $5–$15* ☼ *Daily 10–4:30.*

Fodor's Choice **Iron Horse Vineyards.** Down a one-lane country road from Forestville,
★ Iron Horse Vineyards makes a wide variety of sparkling wines, from the bright and austere to the rich and toasty, as well as estate chardonnays and pinot noirs. Three hundred acres of rolling, vine-covered hills, barnlike winery buildings, and a beautifully rustic outdoor tasting area with a view of Mt. St. Helena set it apart from stuffier spots. (Instead of providing buckets for you to dump out the wine you don't want to finish, they ask you to toss it into the grass behind you.) Tours are available by appointment on weekdays at 10 am. ✉ *9786 Ross Station Rd., Sebastopol* ☎ *707/887–1507* ⊕ *www.ironhorsevineyards. com* 🍷 *Tasting $10, tour $20* ☼ *Daily 10–4:30; tour weekdays at 10 by appointment.*

J Vineyards and Winery. Behind the bar in the tasting room is a dramatic steel sculpture studded with illuminated chunks of glass that suggests a bottle of bubbly. It's a big clue to what's most important here. The dry sparkling wines, made from pinot noir and chardonnay grapes planted in Russian River vineyards, have wonderfully complex fruit and floral aromas and good acidity. Still best known for its sparklers, J also makes fine still wines, often from pinot and chardonnay grapes, as well as brandy-fortified dessert wine and a pear eau-de-vie. Although you can sample wines on their own at the tasting bar, for a truly indulgent experience make a reservation for the Bubble Room, where you should set aside a couple of hours for a selection of top-end still and sparkling wines served with different foods. Tours are offered twice daily by appointment. ✉ *11447 Old Redwood Hwy., Healdsburg* ☎ *707/431–3646* ⊕ *www.jwine.com* 🍷 *Tasting $20–$60* ☼ *Daily 11–5; Bubble Room hrs vary.*

20

Rochioli Vineyards and Winery. Claiming one of the prettiest picnic sites in the area, with tables overlooking vineyards, this winery also has an airy little tasting room hung with modern artwork. Production is small—about 12,000 cases annually—and fans on the winery's mailing list snap up most of the bottles, but the wines are still worth a stop. Because of the cool growing conditions in the Russian River valley, the flavors of their chardonnay and sauvignon blanc are intense and complex. It's their pinot, though, that is largely responsible for the winery's stellar reputation; it helped cement the Russian River's status as a

People often refer to the Wine Country as having a Mediterranean climate. The temperature year-around and precipitation patterns are very similar to those found in Italy and Greece. But there are also a number of micro-climates that provide the prime conditions for a variety of wines.

pinot powerhouse. ■TIP➔ Though Rochioli typically pours only a couple of wines for visitors, it's one of the few wineries of its stature that doesn't charge for a tasting. ✉ *6192 Westside Rd., Healdsburg* ☎ *707/433–2305* ⊕ *www.rochioliwinery.com* ✆ *Tasting free* ⊘ *Thurs.–Mon. 11–4, Tues. and Wed. by appointment; closed mid-Dec.–early Jan.*

WHERE TO EAT

$$$$
FRENCH
Fodor's Choice
★

✕ **The Farmhouse Inn.** From the personable sommelier who arrives at the table to help you pick wines from the excellent list to the servers who lovingly describe the provenance of the black truffles shaved over your pasta stuffed with salt-roasted pears and Parmesan, the staff match the quality of the outstanding French-inspired cuisine. The signature dish, "rabbit, rabbit, rabbit," a rich trio of confit of leg, rabbit loin wrapped in applewood-smoked bacon, and roasted rack of rabbit with a whole-grain mustard sauce, is typical of the dishes that are both rustic and refined, and the starters often include a seared Sonoma foie gras served with an apple cider sauce. ■TIP➔ The inn's a favorite of local foodies in the wine industry, who also know that their head sommelier is one of only about a hundred Master Sommeliers working in the United States, so reserve well in advance.

If you've forgotten to call ahead, a few tables in the small lounge area can often accommodate walk-ins. The small dining room, which has casual country yet elegant appeal, is warmed by a fireplace in winter. ✉ *7871 River Rd., Forestville* ☎ *707/887–3300 or 800/464–6642* ⊕ *www.farmhouseinn.com* ⚜ *Reservations essential* ⊘ *Closed Tues. and Wed. No lunch.*

WHERE TO STAY

$$$–$$$$
Fodor's Choice
★

▦ **The Farmhouse Inn.** Inside a pale yellow 1873 farmhouse and its adjacent cottages, this hotel maintains individually decorated guest rooms with comfortable touches such as down comforters and whirlpool tubs, and most of the cottages have wood-burning fireplaces and even their own private saunas, which make this place especially inviting during the rainy months. **Pros:** one of Sonoma's best restaurants is on-site; free snacks, games, movies, and luxury bath products available; full-service spa uses many products made from local ingredients. **Cons:** rooms closest to the street get a bit of road noise. **TripAdvisor:** "so friendly and helpful," "location was secluded," "ridiculously comfortable bed." ✉ *7871 River Rd., Forestville* ☎ *707/887–3300 or 800/464–6642* ⊕ *www.farmhouseinn.com* ⇆ *12 rooms, 6 suites* ⚐ *In-room: a/c, Wi-Fi. In-hotel: restaurant, pool, spa* ▥ *Breakfast.*

¢
☾

▦ **Sebastopol Inn.** Simple but cheerful rooms, freshly painted a sunny yellow and equipped with blue-and-white striped curtains, have a spare California country style at this reasonably priced inn. **Pros:** friendly staff; just steps from a café, wine bar, and spa. **Cons:** at least a 30-minute drive from most Russian River wineries; some will find the beds too firm. **TripAdvisor:** "excellent location," "well-appointed rooms," "comfortable and inexpensive." ✉ *6751 Sebastopol Ave., Sebastopol* ☎ *707/829–2500* ⊕ *www.sebastopolinn.com* ⇆ *29 rooms, 2 suites* ⚐ *In-room: a/c, Wi-Fi. In-hotel: restaurant, pool, laundry facilities.*

Annual barrel tasting along Russian River's wine road.

SPORTS AND THE OUTDOORS

At **Burke's Canoe Trips** (⊠ *River Rd. and Mirabel Rd., 1 mi north of Forestville* ☎ *707/887–1222*) you can rent a canoe for a leisurely paddle 10 mi downstream to Guerneville. A shuttle bus will return you to your car at the end of the day. Late May through mid-October is the best time for boating.

HEALDSBURG

17 mi north of Santa Rosa on U.S. 101.

Just when it seems that the buzz about Healdsburg couldn't get any bigger, there's another article published in a glossy food or wine magazine about posh properties like the restaurant Cyrus and the ultra-luxe Hôtel Les Mars. But you don't have to be a tycoon to stay here and enjoy the town. For every ritzy restaurant there's a great bakery or relatively modest B&B. A whitewashed bandstand on Healdsburg's plaza hosts free summer concerts, where you might hear anything from bluegrass to Sousa marches. Add to that the fragrant magnolia trees shading the square and the bright flower beds, and the whole thing is as pretty as a Norman Rockwell painting.

The countryside around Healdsburg is the sort you dream about when you're planning a Wine Country vacation. Alongside the relatively untrafficked roads, country stores offer just-plucked fruits and vine-ripened tomatoes. The wineries here are barely visible, since they're tucked behind groves of eucalyptus or hidden high on fog-shrouded hills.

GETTING HERE AND AROUND

To get to Healdsburg from San Francisco, cross the Golden Gate Bridge and continue north on U.S. 101. About 65 mi from San Francisco, take the Central Healdsburg exit and follow Healdsburg Avenue a few blocks to the town's central plaza. Many of the town's hotels and restaurants ring the scenic town square and the few blocks radiating out from here.

WHERE TO EAT

$$$
AMERICAN

✕ **Barndiva.** This hip joint abandons the homey vibe of so many Wine Country spots for a younger, more urban feel. Electronic music plays quietly in the background while hipster servers ferry inventive seasonal cocktails. The food is as stylish as the well-dressed couples cozying up next to one another on the banquette seats. Make a light meal out of starters like goat-cheese croquettes or "The Artisan," a bountiful plate of cheeses and charcuterie, or settle in for the evening with dishes like pork tenderloin with tarragon risotto or rosemary roasted leg of lamb. During warm weather the patio is the place to be. ✉ *231 Center St.* ☎ *707/431–0100* ⊕ *www.barndiva.com* ☾ *Closed Mon. and Tues.*

$
ITALIAN

✕ **Bovolo.** Husband-and-wife team John Stewart and Duskie Estes serve what they call "slow food . . . fast." Though you might pop into this casual café at the back of Copperfield's Books for half an hour, the staff will have spent hours curing the meats that star in the menu of salads, pizzas, pastas, and sandwiches. For instance, the Salumist's Salad mixes a variety of cured meats with greens, white beans, and a tangy vinaigrette; and a thin-crust pizza might come topped with house-made Italian pork sausage and roasted peppers. House-made gelato served with a dark chocolate sauce or *zeppole* (Italian donuts) are a simply perfect ending to a meal. Their closing hours sometimes vary according to the season and what's taking place on Healdsburg's plaza, so call ahead if you're planning an evening visit. ✉ *106 Matheson St.* ☎ *707/431–2962* ⊕ *www.bovolorestaurant.com* ⌾ *Reservations not accepted* ☾ *No dinner Sun.–Thurs. fall–spring. Often no dinner Wed.–Tues.*

$$$$
AMERICAN
Fodor's Choice
★

✕ **Cyrus.** Hailed as the best thing to hit the Wine Country since French Laundry, Cyrus has collected lots of awards and many raves from guests. From the moment you're seated to the minute your dessert plates are whisked away, you'll be carefully tended by gracious servers and an expert sommelier. The formal dining room, with its vaulted Venetian-plaster ceiling, is a suitably plush setting for chef Douglas Keane's creative, subtle cuisine. Each night (and at some Saturday lunchtimes as well), diners have their choice of four set menus: five- and eight-course extravaganzas ($102 and $130), for both omnivores and vegetarians. Set aside three hours to work your way from savory starters like the terrine of foie gras with curried apple compote, through fragrant dishes like the truffled wine risotto with Parmesan broth, to desserts such as the hazelnut *dacquoise* (layers of hazelnut and buttercream). If you've failed to make reservations, you can order à la carte at the bar, which also has the best collection of cocktails and spirits in all of the Wine Country. ✉ *29 North St.* ☎ *707/433–3311* ⊕ *www.cyrusrestaurant.com* ⌾ *Reservations essential* ☾ *Closed Tues. and Wed. in winter. No lunch, except some Sat. Call to confirm.*

$$ ✕**Scopa.** At this tiny eatery chef Ari Rosen cooks up rustic Italian spe-
ITALIAN cialties such as house-made ravioli stuffed with ricotta cheese, braised
chicken with greens and polenta, and *polpette Calabrese* (spicy meat-
balls served with smoked mozzarella in a tomato sauce). Simple thin-
crust pizzas are worth ordering, too. Locals love the restaurant for
its lack of pretension: wine is served in juice glasses, and the friendly
hostess visits guests frequently to make sure all are satisfied. You'll be
packed in elbow-to-elbow with your fellow diners, but for a convivial
evening over a bottle of nebbiolo, there's no better choice. Though
they're often booked weeks in advance, patient diners can often get a
seat at the bar by putting their name on the waiting list. ✉ *109A Plaza
St.* ☎ *707/433–5282* ⊕ *www.scopahealdsburg.com* ⊘ *Closed Mon. No
lunch.*

$$ ✕**Spoonbar.** Cantina doors that open wide onto Healdsburg Avenue
MEDITERRANEAN make this newcomer especially appealing in summer, when the warm
breeze wafts into the stylish space. Concrete walls, mid-century modern chairs, and a long communal table fashioned from rough-hewn
acacia wood make an urbane setting for the modern Mediterranean
fare. "Small bites" like the marinated quail eggs, spicy lamb meatballs,
and house-cured olives are standouts, and several of the dishes demonstrate a Moroccan flair (the Moorish-style chicken with grilled lemon
and couscous is especially popular). Though the fare is simultaneously
inventive and satisfying, the perpetually packed bar, where celebrity
bartender Scott Beattie and his staff mix inventive seasonal cocktails, is
the real draw for many locals. Show up early or late for your best shot
at a seat at the bar. ✉ *219 Healdsburg Ave.* ☎ *707/433–7222* ⊕ *www.
h2hotel.com/spoonbar* ⊘ *No lunch Mon.–Thurs.*

$$ ✕**Zin Restaurant and Wine Bar.** Concrete walls and floors and large can-
AMERICAN vases on the walls make the restaurant casual, industrial, and slightly
artsy. The American cuisine—such as grilled pork chop with homemade
applesauce or the wine-braised lamb shank—is hearty and highly sea-
soned. Portions are large, so consider sharing if you hope to save room
for desserts like the brownie sundae with house-made coffee ice cream.
As you might have guessed, zinfandel is the drink of choice here: the
varietal makes up roughly half of the 100 or so bottles on the wine
list. From Sunday through Thursday, blue-plate specials featuring their
homiest fare (like pot roast and chicken and dumplings) make this place
a particular bargain. ✉ *344 Center St.* ☎ *707/473–0946* ⊘ *No lunch
weekends.*

20

WHERE TO STAY

¢–$ ⊞**Camellia Inn.** In a well-preserved Victorian constructed in 1869, this
colorful B&B is on a quiet residential street a block from the town's
main square. **Pros:** reasonable rates for the neighborhood; a rare
family-friendly inn; within easy walking distance of dozens of restau-
rants. **Cons:** a few rooms have a shower but no bath; the only TV
on the property is in the common sunroom. **TripAdvisor:** "charming
and welcoming," "friendly owners," "terrific location." ✉ *211 North
St.* ☎ *707/433–8182 or 800/727–8182* ⊕ *www.camelliainn.com* ⤳ *8
rooms, 1 suite* ⟐ *In-room: a/c, no TV, Wi-Fi. In-hotel: pool, some pets
allowed* ⦿�‖ *Breakfast.*

$　　h2hotel. There are lots of eco-friendly touches at this LEED-certified newcomer to downtown Healdsburg, from the undulating plant-covered "green roof" to wooden decks made from salvaged lumber. **Pros:** stylish modern design; Healdsburg's most popular bar on the ground floor; king beds can be converted to two twins. **Cons:** least expensive rooms lack bathtubs; no fitness facilities on-site. **TripAdvisor:** "bed was super comfortable," "responsible and stylish comfort," "bathroom was clean and spacious." ⊠ *219 Healdsburg Ave.* ☎ *707/922–5251* ⊕ *www.h2hotel.com* ⤵ *34 rooms, 2 suites* ⚘ *In-room: a/c, Wi-Fi. In-hotel: restaurant, room service, bar, pool, business center, some pets allowed* ⦿ *Breakfast.*

$$$　　**The Honor Mansion.** An 1883 Italianate Victorian houses this photoge-
★　　nic hotel, and rooms in the main house preserve a sense of the building's heritage, while the larger suites are comparatively understated. **Pros:** spacious grounds with boccie and tennis courts, a putting green, and half-court for basketball; homemade sweets available at all hours; spa pavilions by pool available for massages in fair weather. **Cons:** almost a mile from Healdsburg's plaza; on a moderately busy street. **TripAdvisor:** "breakfasts were impeccably served," "staff are very helpful," "quaint and charming." ⊠ *14891 Grove St.* ☎ *707/433–4277 or 800/554–4667* ⊕ *www.honormansion.com* ⤵ *5 rooms, 8 suites* ⚘ *In-room: a/c, Wi-Fi. In-hotel: tennis court, pool, business center* ⊘ *Closed 2 wks around Christmas* ⦿ *Breakfast.*

$$$–$$$$　　Hotel Healdsburg. Across the street from Healdsburg's tidy town plaza, this spare, sophisticated hotel caters to travelers with an urban sensibility. **Pros:** several rooms overlook the town plaza; comfortable lobby with a small attached bar; extremely comfortable beds. **Cons:** exterior rooms get some street noise; rooms could use better lighting. **TripAdvisor:** "clean and comfortable," "staff were top notch," "sophisticated and modern feel." ⊠ *25 Matheson St.* ☎ *707/431–2800 or 800/889–7188* ⊕ *www.hotelhealdsburg.com* ⤵ *45 rooms, 10 suites* ⚘ *In-room: a/c, Internet, Wi-Fi. In-hotel: restaurant, room service, bar, pool, gym, spa, some pets allowed* ⦿ *Breakfast.*

$$$$　　Hôtel Les Mars. In 2005 posh Healdsburg got even more chichi with the opening of this opulent Relais & Châteaux hotel, featuring guest rooms spacious and elegant enough for French nobility, with 18th- and 19th-century antiques and reproductions, canopied beds, and gas-burning fireplaces. **Pros:** large rooms; just off Healdsburg's plaza; Bulgari bath products. **Cons:** very expensive. **TripAdvisor:** "true elegance," "exquisite rooms," "incredible service." ⊠ *27 North St.* ☎ *707/433–4211* ⊕ *www.lesmarshotel.com* ⤵ *16 rooms* ⚘ *In-room: a/c, Internet, Wi-Fi. In-hotel: restaurant, bar, pool, gym* ⦿ *Breakfast.*

$$$–$$$$　　Madrona Manor. The oldest continuously operating inn in the area, this 1881 Victorian mansion is surrounded by 8 acres of wooded and landscaped grounds, and rooms in the three-story mansion, the carriage house, and the three separate cottages are splendidly ornate, with mirrors in gilt frames and paintings covering every wall. **Pros:** old-fashioned and romantic; pretty veranda perfect for a cocktail. **Cons:** pool heated May through October only; decor might be too fussy for some. **TripAdvisor:** "incredible customer touch," "a tranquil escape," "very romantic." ✉ *1001 West-side Rd., central Healdsburg exit off U.S. 101, then left on Mill St.* ☎ *707/433–4231 or 800/258–4003* ⊕ *www.madronamanor.com ⌁ 17 rooms, 5 suites & In-room: a/c, no TV, Wi-Fi. In-hotel: restaurant, bar, pool* ❡❍❙ *Breakfast.*

SHOPPING

Oakville Grocery (✉ *124 Matheson St.* ☎ *707/433–3200*) has a bustling Healdsburg branch filled with wine, condiments, and deli items. A terrace with ample seating makes a good place for an impromptu picnic, but you might want to lunch early or late to avoid the worst crowds. You'll have to get in your car to head north on Healdsburg Avenue to **Tip Top Liquor Warehouse** (✉ *90 Dry Creek Rd.* ☎ *707/431–0841*), a nondescript spot that stocks an interesting selection of wines and spirits at fair prices. Though it's strongest in bottles from Sonoma, you'll also find a few Napa wines, including some rare cult cabernets.

> ## FARMERS' MARKET
>
> During two weekly **Healdsburg farmers' markets** you can buy locally made goat cheese, fragrant lavender, and olive oil in addition to the usual produce. On Saturday from May through November the market takes place one block west of the town plaza, at the corner of North and Vine streets, 9 am–noon. The smaller Tuesday market, which runs from June through October, takes place two blocks northwest of the plaza, in a parking lot off North Street, 4–7 pm.

DRY CREEK AND ALEXANDER VALLEYS

On the west side of U.S. 101, Dry Creek Valley remains one of the least-developed appellations in Sonoma. Zinfandel grapes flourish on the benchlands, whereas the gravelly, well-drained soil of the valley floor is better known for chardonnay and, in the north, sauvignon blanc. The wineries in this region tend to be smaller, which makes them a good bet on summer weekends, when larger spots and those along the main thoroughfares fill up with tourists.

The Alexander Valley, which lies northeast of Healdsburg, is similarly rustic, and you can see as many folks cycling along Highway 128 here as you can behind the wheel of a car. The largely family-owned wineries often produce zinfandel and chardonnay.

20

GETTING HERE AND AROUND

The Dry Creek Valley is to the west of downtown Healdsburg, across U.S. 101. To get here from the plaza, drive north on Healdsburg Avenue and turn left on Dry Creek Road. This takes you under the freeway and veers north. Many of the region's wineries are along Dry Creek Road or on West Dry Creek Road, which runs roughly parallel about a mile to the west, accessible by the cross streets Lambert Bridge Road and Yoakim Bridge Road.

The Alexander Valley is just northeast of Healdsburg. To get here from the plaza, drive north on Healdsburg Avenue and veer right on Alexander Valley Road. Although there are a few wineries on Alexander Valley

Best Wine Country Festivals

■ **February–March: Napa Valley Mustard Festival.** When Napa is at its least crowded, and wild mustard blooms in between the vines, locals celebrate wine, food, and art with exhibitions, auctions, dinners, and cooking and photography competitions. (⊕ www.mustardfestival.org)

■ **March: Wine Road Barrel Tasting Weekends.** For two weekends in March more than 100 wineries in the Russian River, Dry Creek, and Alexander valleys open their cellars to visitors who want to taste the wine in the barrels, getting a preview of what's to come. (⊕ www.wineroad.com)

■ **Late May: Sonoma Jazz + Festival.** Headlining jazz, rock, and world music performers play in a large tent in downtown Sonoma, while smaller music, food, and wine events take place around town. (⊕ www.sonomajazz.org)

■ **Early June: Auction Napa Valley.** The world's biggest charity wine auction is one of Napa's glitziest gatherings. Events hosted by various wineries culminate in a hotly contested auction followed by an opulent dinner and party. (⊕ www.napavintners.com)

■ **Early October: Sonoma County Harvest Fair.** This festival celebrates agriculture in Sonoma County, with wine tastings, cooking demos, livestock shows, crafts, carnival rides, and local entertainers filling the Sonoma County Fairgrounds in Santa Rosa. (⊕ www.harvestfair.org)

■ **Mid-November: Napa Valley Film Festival.** Film premieres, pre-movie wine tastings, and food- and wine-related events where you can meet some of the filmmakers whose works are being shown take place in downtown Napa and St. Helena. (⊕ www.napavalleyfilmfest.org)

Road itself, most of them on are on Highway 128, which intersects is after about 3.3. mi.

EXPLORING

Dry Creek Vineyard. Fumé blanc is king here, where they have been making this refreshing white wine in the style of those made in Sancerre, France, since the beginning of the 1970s. But Dry Creek also makes well-regarded zinfandels, a zesty dry chenin blanc, a pinot noir, and a handful of cabernet sauvignon blends. Since many of their quality wines go for less than $20 or $30 for a bottle, it's a popular stop for those who want to stock their cellars for a reasonable price. After picking up a bottle you might want to picnic on the lawn, next to the flowering magnolia tree. Conveniently, a general store and deli with plenty of picnic fixings is just steps down the road. ⊠ 3770 Lambert Bridge Rd., Healdsburg ☎ 707/433–1000 ⊕ www.drycreekvineyard.com ☜ Tasting $5–$10 ⊙ Daily 10:30–4:30.

Francis Ford Coppola Winery. In 2006 filmmaker-winemaker Francis Ford Coppola snapped up a majestic French-style château, formerly Château Souverain, to showcase his less-expensive wines. (His Napa winery, Rubicon Estate, focuses on the high-end vintages). After years of renovation the château has been turned into an impressive fantasyland where you could easily spend all day. In addition to tasting their wines or ordering a cocktail at the full bar, you can select from a variety of tours, from a vineyard walk to an opportunity to watch the bottling facility in action. Scattered throughout the gift shop are mementos of Coppola's film career, from his Oscars to Don Corleone's desk in *The Godfather,* to a display on the filming of *Apocalypse Now.* Kids (and some adults), though, will be most excited by the large pool on the terrace, where you'll also see a band shell that is a replica of the one that appears in *Godfather II.* Guests rent cabines to shower and change into their swimsuits before spending the afternoon lounging under the striped umbrellas, perhaps even ordering food from the poolside café. The winery's restaurant, Rustic, serves a more elaborate menu from a spacious dining room and a terrace overlooking the vineyards. Prices, pool hours, and tour times are still being finalized, so check the winery's Web site or call ahead for the latest. ✉ *300 Via Archimedes (formerly Souverain Rd.), Geyserville* ☎ *707/857–1400* ⊕ *www. franciscoppolawinery.com* 🖃 *Tasting free–$10; tour $20; pool pass $15. See prices and family plans online.* ☉ *Tasting room daily 11–6, restaurant daily 11–9; pool hrs vary seasonally.*

Fodor'sChoice   **Michel-Schlumberger.** Down a narrow road at the westernmost edge of the ★   Dry Creek Valley, Michel-Schlumberger is one of Sonoma's finest producers of cabernet sauvignon. A spin through their organically farmed vineyard is like taking a walk through France, and though they're best known for their Bordeaux varietals, you'll also find Burgundian grapes next to ones from Alsace and the Rhône. The tour is unusually casual and friendly. Weather permitting, you'll wander up a hill on a gravel pathway to the edge of their lovely terraced vineyards before swinging through the barrel room in the California Mission–style building that once served as the home of the winery's founder, Jean-Jacques Michel. To taste older vintages of their cabernet and learn what their wines will taste like after 10 or so years in the bottle, reserve in advance for a vertical library tasting ($30). Wine and cheese pairings ($35) are also available by reservation. ✉ *4155 Wine Creek Rd., Healdsburg* ☎ *707/433–7427 or 800/447–3060* ⊕ *www.michelschlumberger.com* 🖃 *Tasting $10–$15, tour $20* ☉ *Daily 11–5; tours at 11 and 2, by appointment.*

Fodor'sChoice   **Preston Vineyards.** Once you wind your way down Preston Vineyards' ★   long driveway, flanked by vineyards and punctuated by the occasional olive tree, you'll be welcomed by the sight of a few farmhouses encircling a shady yard prowled by several friendly cats. In summer a small selection of organic produce grown in their gardens is sold from an impromptu stand on the front porch, and house-made bread and olive oil are available year-round. Their down-home style is particularly in evidence on Sunday, the only day of the week that tasting-room staffers sell a 3-liter bottle of Guadagni Red, a primarily zinfandel blend filled from the barrel right in front of you. Owners Lou and Susan Preston are committed to organic growing techniques, and use only estate-grown grapes in their wines, like sauvignon blanc, and Rhône varietals such as syrah and viognier. ✉ *9282 W. Dry Creek Rd., Healdsburg* ☎ *707/433–3372* ⊕ *www.prestonvineyards.com* 🖃 *$5 tasting* ☉ *Daily 11–4:30.*

20

Quivira. An unassuming winery in a modern wooden barn topped by solar panels, Quivira produces some of the most interesting wines in Dry Creek Valley. It's known for its dangerously drinkable reds, including a petite syrah, and a few hearty zinfandel blends. The excellent tour provides information about their biodynamic and organic farming practices and also offers a glimpse of their beautiful garden and the pigs, chickens, and beehives kept on the property. Redwood and olive trees shade the picnic area. ⊠ *4900 W. Dry Creek Rd., Healdsburg* ☎ *707/431–8333* ⊕ *www.quivirawine.com* 🍷 *Tasting $5, tour $15* ⊙ *Daily 11–5; tour by appointment.*

★ **Stryker Sonoma.** Inside the tasting room at Stryker Sonoma, vaulted ceilings and seemingly endless walls of windows onto the vineyards suggest you've entered a cathedral to viniculture. The wines are almost as impressive as the architecture: most of their bottles are single varietals, such as chardonnay, merlot, zinfandel, and cabernet sauvignon. An exception, however, are a few Bordeaux-style blends, including the powerful E1K, which, unfortunately, is not usually poured in the tasting room (though it never hurts to ask whether they have a bottle open). The picnic tables are a particularly lovely way to enjoy the quiet countryside of the Alexander Valley. Call ahead at least a day in advance to book a spot on a tour that concludes on the observation deck overlooking the vineyards. ⊠ *5110 Hwy. 28, Geyserville* ☎ *707/433–1944* ⊕ *www.strykersonoma.com* 🍷 *Tasting $10, tour $15* ⊙ *Daily 10:30–5.*

**OFF THE
BEATEN
PATH**

Though it's certainly possible to get a great drink in downtown Healdsburg at either Cyrus or Spoonbar, those who want to feel a million miles away from the bustle of downtown Healdsburg should drive the 6 mi to the **Alexander Valley Bar** (⊠ *3487 Alexander Valley Rd.* ☎ *707/431–1904*), a dimly lighted Victorian-style speakeasy where you'll find historic photos on the walls and a vintage photo booth to document the occasion. A mostly local crowd gathers to enjoy fine cocktails, some using produce grown in their own gardens. The place is poorly marked; to get there from Healdsburg's plaza, drive 3 mi north on Healdsburg Avenue and then turn right on Alexander Valley Road. The bar, which is attached to the Medlock Ames tasting room, is in another 3 mi, at the intersection of Alexander Valley Road and Sausal Lane.

Travel Smart

GETTING HERE AND AROUND

San Francisco encompasses 46.7 square mi. As a major metropolitan hub it has a fantastic public transportation system; however, if you stray from the main thoroughfares public transport can get tricky, and renting a car becomes a more practical option.

All the city's major attractions are easily accessible via Muni (light-rail vehicles), BART (Bay Area Rapid Transit) trains, taxis, and cable cars; or if you have a comfy pair of shoes, you can always walk. It's exactly 8 mi from the west side of the city to the east side. The streets are neatly arranged along two grids that come together at Market Street, and with the area's well-known landmarks—the Golden Gate Bridge (north), Twin Peaks (south), the Bay Bridge (east), and the Pacific Ocean (west)—as a physical compass, it's difficult to lose your way.

The East Bay is also extremely accessible via public transport; BART is a good way to get where you want to go. And the North Bay is only a boat or bike ride away. Both are good choices, depending on the weather. A car only becomes necessary when you want to go farther north, for example, to Napa or Sonoma County. Keep in mind that rush-hour traffic isn't pleasant, so if you do rent a car try to take to the streets between 10 am and 3 pm, or after 7 pm.

▮ AIR TRAVEL

The least expensive airfares to San Francisco are priced for round-trip travel and should be purchased in advance. Airlines generally allow you to change your return date for a fee; most low-fare tickets, however, are nonrefundable. (But if you cancel, you can usually apply the fare to a future trip, within one year, to any destination the airline flies.)

Nonstop flights from New York to San Francisco take about 5½ hours, and with the 3-hour time change, it's possible to leave JFK by 8 am and be in San Francisco by 10:30 am. Some flights may require a midway stop, making the total excursion between 8 and 9½ hours. Nonstop times are approximately 1½ hours from Los Angeles, 3 hours from Dallas, 4½ hours from Chicago, 4½ hours from Atlanta, 11 hours from London, 12 hours from Auckland, and 13½ hours from Sydney.

Airline Contacts American Airlines (☎ 800/433-7300 ⊕ www.aa.com). **Continental Airlines** (☎ 800/523-3273 for U.S. and Mexico reservations, 800/231-0856 for international reservations ⊕ www.continental.com). **Delta Airlines** (☎ 800/221-1212 for U.S. reservations, 800/241-4141 for international reservations ⊕ www.delta.com). **Southwest Airlines** (☎ 800/435-9792 ⊕ www.southwest.com). **United Airlines** (☎ 800/864-8331 for U.S. reservations, 800/538-2929 for international reservations ⊕ www.united.com).

Smaller Airlines Frontier Airlines (☎ 800/432-1359 ⊕ www.frontierairlines.com). **jetBlue** (☎ 800/538-2583 ⊕ www.jetblue.com).

AIRPORTS

The major gateway to San Francisco is San Francisco International Airport (SFO), 15 mi south of the city. It's off U.S. 101 near Millbrae and San Bruno. Oakland International Airport (OAK) is across the bay, not much farther away from downtown San Francisco (via I–80 east and I–880 south), but rush-hour traffic on the Bay Bridge may lengthen travel times considerably. San Jose International Airport (SJC) is about 40 mi south of San Francisco; travel time depends largely on traffic flow, but plan on an hour and a half with moderate traffic.

Depending on the price difference, you might consider flying into Oakland or San Jose. Oakland's an easy-to-use alternative, since there's public transportation between the airport and downtown San

Francisco. Getting to San Francisco from San Jose, though, can be time-consuming and costly via public transportation. Heavy fog is infamous for causing chronic delays into and out of San Francisco. If you're heading to the East or South Bay, make every effort to fly into Oakland or San Jose Airport, respectively.

At all three airports security check-in can take 15 to 30 minutes at peak travel times.

■ TIP➜ Count yourself lucky if you have a layover at SFO's International Terminal. During its 2005 renovation SFO brought in branches of some top local eateries. The food's far better than standard airport fare; you'll find Italian pastries from Emporio Rulli, burgers from Burger Joint or Lori's Diner, sushi from Ebisu, and much more.

Long layovers don't have to be only about sitting around or shopping. These days they can be about burning off vacation calories. Check out www.airportgyms.com for lists of health clubs that are in or near many U.S. and Canadian airports.

Airport Information San Francisco International Airport (*SFO* ☎ *800/435–9736* or *650/821–8211* ⊕ *www.flysfo.com*). **Oakland International Airport** (*OAK* ☎ *510/563–3300* ⊕ *www.flyoakland.com*). **San Jose International Airport** (*SJC* ☎ *408/392–3600* ⊕ *www.sjc.org*).

GROUND TRANSPORTATION

From San Francisco International Airport Transportation signage at the airport is color-coded by type and is quite clear. A taxi ride to downtown costs $35 to $45. Airport shuttles are inexpensive and generally efficient. Lorrie's Airport Service and SuperShuttle both stop at the lower level near baggage claim and take you anywhere within the city limits of San Francisco. They charge $15 to $17, depending on where you're going. Lorrie's also sells tickets online, at a $2 discount each way; you can print them out before leaving home. SuperShuttle offers some discounts for more than one person traveling in the same party ($17 per person and $10 for each additional passenger),

but only if you're traveling to a residential address.

Shuttles to the East Bay, such as BayPorter Express, also depart from the lower level; expect to pay between $35 to $40. Inquire about the number of stops a shuttle makes en route to or from the airport; some companies, such as East Bay Express, have nonstop service, but they cost a bit more. Marin Door to Door operates van service to Marin County for $30 to $40 for the first passenger, and $12 for each additional person; you must make reservations by noon the day before travel. Marin Airporter buses cost $20 and require no reservations but stop only at designated stations in Marin; buses leave every 30 minutes, on the half hour and hour, from 5 am to midnight.

You can take BART directly to downtown San Francisco; the trip takes about 30 minutes and costs less than $9. (There are both manned booths and vending machines for ticket purchases.) Trains leave from the international terminal every 15 minutes on weekdays and every 20 minutes on weekends.

Another inexpensive way to get to San Francisco is via two SamTrans buses: No. 292 (55 minutes, $2 from SFO, $4 to SFO) and the KX (35 minutes, $5; only one small carry-on bag permitted). Board the SamTrans buses on the lower level.

To drive to downtown San Francisco from the airport, take U.S. 101 north to the Civic Center/9th Street, 7th Street, or 4th Street/Downtown exits. If you're headed to the Embarcadero or Fisherman's Wharf, take I–280 north (the exit is to the right, just north of the airport, off U.S. 101) and get off at the 4th Street/King Street exit. King Street becomes the Embarcadero a few blocks east of the exit. The Embarcadero winds around the waterfront to Fisherman's Wharf.

From Oakland International Airport A taxi to downtown San Francisco costs $35 to $40. By airport regulations, you must make reservations for shuttle service.

BayPorter Express and other shuttles serve major hotels and provide door-to-door service to the East Bay and San Francisco. SuperShuttle operates vans to San Francisco and Oakland. Marin Door to Door serves Marin County for a flat $45 for the first passenger, and $12 for each additional person; make reservations by noon the day before travel.

The best way to get to San Francisco via public transit is to take the AIR BART bus ($3) to the Coliseum/Oakland International Airport BART station (BART fares vary depending on where you're going; the ride to downtown San Francisco from here costs $3.80).

If you're driving from Oakland International Airport, take Hegenberger Road east to I–880 north to I–80 west over the Bay Bridge. This will likely take at least an hour.

From San Jose International Airport A taxi to downtown San Jose costs about $15 to $20; a trip to San Francisco runs about $140 to $150. South & East Bay Airport Shuttle transports you to the South Bay and East Bay; a ride to downtown San Jose costs $20 for the first passenger, $8 for each additional, and a van to San Francisco costs $79 for the first passenger, $10 for each additional. Reservations are required to the airport, but not from the airport; call from baggage claim before you collect your luggage. Reservations are also required for VIP Airport Shuttle, which has service to downtown San Francisco for $81 for the first passenger, $6 for each additional passenger; to downtown San Jose costs $24, $6 for each additional passenger.

To drive to downtown San Jose from the airport, take Airport Boulevard east to Route 87 south. To get to San Francisco from the airport, take Route 87 south to I–280 north. The trip will take roughly two hours.

At $8 for a one-way ticket, there is no question that Caltrain provides the most affordable option for traveling between San Francisco and San Jose's airport. However, the Caltrain station in San Francisco at 4th and Townsend streets is not in a conveniently central location. It's on the eastern side of the South of Market (SoMa) neighborhood and not easily accessible by other public transit. You'll need to take a taxi or walk from the nearest bus line. From San Francisco it takes 90 minutes and costs $8 to reach the Santa Clara Caltrain station, from which a free shuttle runs every 15 minutes, whisking you to and from the San Jose International Airport in 15 minutes.

Contacts American Airporter (☎ 415/202–0733 ⊕ www.americanairporter.com). **Bay-Porter Express** (☎ 415/467–1800 ⊕ www.bayporter.com). **Caltrain** (☎ 800/660–4287 ⊕ www.caltrain.com). **East Bay Express Airporter** (☎ 877/526–0304 ⊕ www.eastbaytransportation.com). **Lorrie's Airport Service** (☎ 415/334–9000 ⊕ www.gosfovan.com). **Marin Airporter** (☎ 415/461–4222 ⊕ www.marinairporter.com). **Marin Door to Door** (☎ 415/457–2717 ⊕ www.marindoortodoor.com). **SamTrans** (☎ 800/660–4287 ⊕ www.samtrans.com). **South & East Bay Airport Shuttle** (☎ 800/548–4664 ⊕ www.southandeastbayairportshuttle.com). **SuperShuttle** (☎ 800/258–3826 ⊕ www.supershuttle.com). **VIP Airport Shuttle** (☎ 408/986–6000 or 800/235–8847 ⊕ www.viptransportgroup.com).

▌ BART TRAVEL

Bay Area Rapid Transit (BART) trains, which run until midnight, travel under the bay via tunnel to connect San Francisco with Oakland, Berkeley, Pittsburgh/Bay Point, Richmond, Fremont, Dublin/Pleasanton, and other small cities and towns in between. Within San Francisco, stations are limited to downtown, the Mission, and a couple of outlying neighborhoods.

Trains travel frequently from early morning until evening on weekdays. After 8 pm weekdays and on weekends there's often a 20-minute wait between trains on the same line. Trains also travel south from

San Francisco as far as Millbrae. BART trains connect downtown San Francisco to San Francisco International Airport; a ride is $8.10.

Intracity San Francisco fares are $1.75; intercity fares are $3.10 to $5.95. BART bases its ticket prices on miles traveled, and does not offer price breaks by zone. The easy-to-read maps posted in BART stations list fares based on destination, radiating out from your starting point of the current station.

During morning and evening rush hour, trains within the city are crowded—even standing room can be hard to come by. Cars at the far front and back of the train are less likely to be filled to capacity. Smoking, eating, and drinking are prohibited on trains and in stations.

Contacts Bay Area Rapid Transit (*BART* ☎ 415/989–2278 or 650/992–2278 ⊕ www. bart.gov).

∎ BOAT TRAVEL

Several ferry lines run out of San Francisco. Blue & Gold Fleet operates a number of routes, including service to Sausalito ($10 one-way) and Tiburon ($10 one-way). Tickets are sold at Pier 41 (between Fisherman's Wharf and Pier 39), where the boats depart. Alcatraz Cruises, owned by Hornblower Yachts, operates the ferries to Alcatraz Island ($22 including audio tour and National Park Service ranger-led programs) from Pier 33, about a half mile east of Fisherman's Wharf ($3 shuttle buses serve several area hotels and other locations). Boats leave 10 times a day (14 times a day in summer), and the journey itself is 30 minutes. Allow roughly 2½ hours for a round-trip jaunt. Golden Gate Ferry runs daily to and from Sausalito and Larkspur (each costs $8.25 one-way), leaving from Pier 1, behind the San Francisco Ferry Building. The Alameda/Oakland Ferry operates daily between Alameda's Main Street Ferry Building, Oakland's Jack London Square, and San Francisco's Pier 41 and the Ferry Building

($6.25 one-way); some ferries go only to Pier 41 or the Ferry Building, so ask when you board. Purchase tickets onboard.

Information Alameda/Oakland Ferry (☎ 510/522–3300 ⊕ www.eastbayferry.com). **Alcatraz Cruises** (☎ 415/981–7625 ⊕ www. alcatrazcruises.com). **Blue & Gold Fleet** (☎ 415/705–8200 ⊕ www.blueandgoldfleet. com). **Golden Gate Ferry** (☎ 415/923–2000 ⊕ www.goldengateferry.org). **San Francisco Ferry Building** (✉ 1 Ferry Bldg., at foot of Market St. on Embarcadero ☎ 415/983–8030 ⊕ www.ferrybuildingmarketplace.com).

∎ BUS TRAVEL

Greyhound, the only long-distance bus company serving San Francisco, operates buses to and from most major cities in the country, terminating at the bus depot on Mission Street, near the Financial District. Service in California is limited to hub towns and cities only. Reservations are not accepted; seating is on a first-come, first-served basis. Cash, traveler's checks, and credit cards are accepted. Smoking is prohibited on all buses in California.

Greyhound (✉ 425 Mission St., between Fremont and 1st Sts., SoMa ☎ 415/495–1569 ⊕ www.greyhound.com)

∎ CABLE-CAR TRAVEL

Don't miss the sensation of moving up and down some of San Francisco's steepest hills in a clattering cable car. Jump aboard as it pauses at a designated stop, and wedge yourself into any available space. Then just hold on.

The fare (for one direction) is $5 (Muni Passport holders only pay a $1 supplement). You can buy tickets on board (exact change isn't necessary) or at the kiosks at the cable-car turnarounds at Hyde and Beach streets and at Powell and Market streets.

The heavily traveled Powell–Mason and Powell–Hyde lines begin at Powell and Market streets near Union Square and terminate at Fisherman's Wharf; lines for these routes can be long, especially in summer. The California Street line runs east and west from Market and California streets to Van Ness Avenue; there is often no wait to board this route.

▌CAR TRAVEL

Driving in San Francisco can be a challenge because of the one-way streets, snarly traffic, and steep hills. The first two elements can be frustrating enough, but those hills are tough for unfamiliar drivers.

Be sure to leave plenty of room between your car and other vehicles when on a steep slope. This is especially important when you've braked at a stop sign on a steep incline. Whether with a stick shift or an automatic transmission, every car rolls backward for a moment once the brake is released. So don't pull too close to the car ahead of you. When it's time to pull forward, keep your foot on the brake while tapping lightly on the accelerator. Once the engine is engaged, let up on the brake and head uphill.

▌TIP→ Remember to curb your wheels when parking on hills—turn wheels away from the curb when facing uphill, toward the curb when facing downhill. You can get a ticket if you don't do this.

Market Street runs southwest from the Ferry Building, then becomes Portola Drive as it nears Twin Peaks (which lie beneath the giant radio-antennae structure, Sutro Tower). It can be difficult to drive across Market. The major east–west streets north of Market are Geary Boulevard (it's called Geary Street east of Van Ness Avenue), which runs to the Pacific Ocean; Fulton Street, which begins at the back of the Opera House and continues along the north side of Golden Gate Park to Ocean Beach; Oak Street, which runs east from Golden Gate Park toward downtown, then flows into northbound Franklin Street; and Fell Street, the left two lanes of which cut through Golden

TRACKING CHEAP GAS

Determined to avoid the worst prices at the pump? Check the Web site ⊕ *www.sanfrangasprices.com,* which tracks the lowest (and highest) gasoline costs in the Bay Area. It also has a handy price-mapping feature and a master list of local gas stations.

Gate Park and empty into Lincoln Boulevard, which continues to the ocean.

Among the major north–south streets are Divisadero, which becomes Castro Street at Duboce Avenue and continues to just past César Chavez Street; Van Ness Avenue, which becomes South Van Ness Avenue when it crosses Market Street; and Park Presidio Boulevard, which empties into 19th Avenue.

GASOLINE

Gas stations are hard to find in San Francisco; look for the national franchises on major thoroughfares such as Market Street or California Street. Once you find one, prepare for sticker shock—the fuel is notoriously expensive here.

Aside from their limited numbers and high costs, everything else is standard operation at these service stations. All major stations accept credit and ATM cards; self-service pumps are the norm. Most gas stations are open seven days a week until 11 pm or midnight. Many national franchises on well-traveled streets are open 24/7.

PARKING

San Francisco is a terrible city for parking. In the Financial District and Civic Center neighborhoods parking is forbidden on most streets between 4 pm and 6 pm. Check street signs carefully to confirm, because illegally parked cars are towed immediately. Downtown parking lots are often full, and most are expensive. The city-owned Sutter-Stockton, Ellis-O'Farrell, and 5th-and-Mission garages have the most reasonable rates in the downtown area. Large hotels often have parking available, but it doesn't come cheap; many charge in excess of $40 a day for the privilege.

Garages 766 Vallejo Garage (✉ 766 Vallejo St., at Powell St., North Beach ☎ 415/989–4490). **Ellis-O'Farrell Garage** (✉ 123 O'Farrell St., at Stockton St., Union Square ☎ 415/986–4800 ⊕ www.eofgarage.com). **Embarcadero Center Garage** (✉ 1–4 Embarcadero Center, between Battery and Drumm Sts., Financial District ☎ 415/772–0670 ⊕ www.embarcaderocenter.com). **5th-and-Mission Garage** (✉ 833 Mission St., at 5th St., SoMa ☎ 415/982–8522 ⊕ www.fifthandmission.com). **Opera Plaza Garage** (✉ 601 Van Ness Ave., at Turk St., Civic Center ☎ 415/771–4776 ⊕ www.sfopera.com). **Pier 39 Garage** (✉ Embarcadero at Beach St., Fisherman's Wharf ☎ 415/705–5418 ⊕ www.pier39.com). **Portsmouth Square Garage** (✉ 733 Kearny St., at Clay St., Chinatown ☎ 415/982–6353 ⊕ www.portsmouthsquaregarage.com). **Sutter-Stockton Garage** (✉ 444 Stockton St., at Sutter St., Union Square ☎ 415/982–8370). **Wharf Garage** (✉ 2801 Leavenworth St., Fisherman's Wharf ☎ 415/775–5060).

ROAD CONDITIONS

Although rush "hours" are 6–10 am and 3–7 pm, you can hit gridlock on any day at any time, especially over the Bay Bridge and leaving and/or entering the city from the south. Sunday-afternoon traffic can be heavy as well, especially over the bridges.

The most comprehensive and immediate traffic updates are available through the city's 511 service, either online at ⊕ *www.511.org* (where webcams show you the traffic on your selected route) or by calling 511. On the radio, tune in to an all-news radio station such as KQED 88.5 FM or KCBS 740 AM/106.9 FM.

Be especially wary of non-indicated lane changes.

San Francisco is the only major American city uncut by freeways. To get from the Bay Bridge to the Golden Gate Bridge, you'll have to take surface streets, specifically Van Ness Avenue, which doubles as U.S. 101 through the city.

TAKE THE 511

The city's 511 service is operated by a partnership of government and public agencies. In this case, several transportation organizations—the Metropolitan Transportation Commission, the California Highway Patrol, the California Department of Transportation, and more—pool their data into a free, one-stop telephone and Web resource for all nine Bay Area counties. It gives the latest info on traffic conditions, route and fare information for all public transit, bicyclist info, and a host of other options. The telephone line can be called 24/7 toll-free.

RULES OF THE ROAD

To encourage carpooling during heavy traffic times, some freeways have special lanes for so-called high-occupancy vehicles (HOVs)—cars carrying more than one or two passengers. Look for the white-painted diamond in the middle of the lane. Road signs next to or above the lane indicate the hours that carpooling is in effect. If you're stopped by the police because you don't meet the criteria for travel in these lanes, expect a fine of more than $340.

Drivers are banned from using handheld mobile telephones while operating a vehicle in California. The use of seat belts in both front and back seats is required in California. The speed limit on city streets is 25 mph unless otherwise posted. A right turn on a red light after stopping is legal unless posted otherwise, as is a left on red at the intersection of two one-way streets. Always strap children under 80 pounds or under age eight into approved child-safety seats.

CAR RENTALS

When you reserve a car, ask about cancellation penalties, taxes, drop-off charges (if you're planning to pick up the car in one city and leave it in another), and surcharges (for being under or over a certain age, for additional drivers, or for driving across state or country borders or beyond a specific distance from your point of rental). All these things can add substantially to your costs. Request car seats and extras such as GPS when you book.

Rates are sometimes—but not always—better if you book in advance or reserve through a rental agency's Web site. There are other reasons to book ahead, though: for popular destinations, during busy times of the year, or to ensure that you get certain types of cars (vans, SUVs, exotic sports cars).

■TIP➡ Make sure that a confirmed reservation guarantees you a car. Agencies sometimes overbook, particularly for busy weekends and holiday periods.

Car-rental costs in San Francisco vary seasonally, but generally begin at $30 a day and $150 a week for an economy car with air-conditioning, automatic transmission, and unlimited mileage. This doesn't include tax on car rentals, which is 9.5%. If you dream of driving with the top down, or heading out of town to ski the Sierra, consider renting a specialty vehicle. Most major agencies have a few on hand, but the best overall service is with two locally owned agencies: Specialty Rentals and City Rent-a-Car. The former specializes in high-end vehicles and arranges for airport pickup and drop-off. City Rent-a-Car likewise arranges airport transfers, and also delivers cars to Bay Area hotels. Both agencies also rent standard vehicles at prices competitive with those of the major chains.

In San Francisco you must be at least 20 years old to rent a car, but some agencies won't rent to those under 25; check when you book. Super Cheap Car Rental is near the airport and rents to drivers as young as 20.

ALTERNATIVE RENTALS

City Car Share and Zipcar are membership organizations for any person over 21 with a valid driver's license who needs a car only for short-term use. You must join their clubs beforehand, which you can do via their Web sites. They're especially useful if you only want to rent a car for part of the day (say four to six hours), find yourself far from the airport, or if you're younger than most rental agencies' 25-years-or-older requirement. The membership fee often allows you to use their service in several metropolitan areas. If using such a service, you can rent a car by the hour as well as by the day.

GoCar rents electric vehicles at Fisherman's Wharf and Union Square. These cars can travel between 25 and 35 mph and are very handy for neighborhood-based sightseeing, but they're not allowed on the Golden Gate Bridge. GoCars are electric, two-seater, three-wheeled, open convertibles with roll bars (so drivers must wear helmets) with GPS audio tours of the city. You can pick up a GoCar at three locations: two in Fisherman's Wharf and one in Union Square.

Automobile Associations U.S.: **American Automobile Association** (AAA ☎ 415/565–2141 ⊕ www.aaa.com); most contact with the organization is through state and regional members. **National Automobile Club** (☎ 800/622–2136 ⊕ www.thenac.com); membership is open to California residents only.

Local Agencies City Car Share (☎ 415/995–8588 or 877/363–0710 ⊕ www.citycarshare. org). **City Rent-a-Car** (☎ 415/359–1331 or 866/359–1331 ⊕ www.cityrentacar.com). **GoCar** (☎ 800/914–6227 ⊕ www.gocartours. com). **Specialty Rentals** (☎ 800/400–8412 ⊕ www.specialtyrentals.com). **Super Cheap Car Rental** (☎ 650/777–9993 ⊕ www. supercheapcar.com). **Zipcar** (☎ 415/495–7478 ⊕ www.zipcar.com).

Major Agencies Alamo (☎ 800/462–5266 ⊕ www.alamo.com). **Avis** (☎ 800/331–1212 ⊕ www.avis.com). **Budget** (☎ 800/527–0700 ⊕ www.budget.com). **Hertz** (☎ 800/654–3131 ⊕ www.hertz.com). **National Car Rental** (☎ 800/227–7368 ⊕ www.nationalcar.com).

▌MUNI TRAVEL

The San Francisco Municipal Railway, or Muni, operates light-rail vehicles, the historic F-line streetcars along Fisherman's Wharf and Market Street, trolley buses, and the world-famous cable cars. Light rail travels along Market Street to the Mission District and Noe Valley (J line), the Ingleside District (K line), and the Sunset District (L, M, and N lines); during peak hours (Monday through Friday, 6 am–9 am and 3 pm–7 pm) the J line continues around the Embarcadero to the Caltrain station at 4th and King streets. The T line light rail runs from the Castro, down Market Street, around the Embarcadero, and south past Hunters Point and Monster Park to Sunnydale Avenue and Bayshore Boulevard. Muni provides 24-hour service on select lines to all areas of the city.

On buses and streetcars the fare is $2. Exact change is required, and dollar bills are accepted in the fare boxes. For all Muni vehicles other than cable cars, 90-minute transfers are issued free upon request at the time the fare is paid. These are valid for two additional transfers in any direction. Cable cars cost $5 and include no transfers (*see Cable-Car Travel, above*).

One-day ($13), three-day ($20), and seven-day ($26) Passports valid on the entire Muni system can be purchased at several outlets, including the cable-car ticket booth at Powell and Market streets and the visitor information center downstairs in Hallidie Plaza. A monthly ticket, called a Fast Pass, is available for $70, and can be used on all Muni lines (including cable cars) and on BART within city limits. The San Francisco CityPass, a discount ticket booklet to several major city attractions, also covers all Muni travel for seven consecutive days.

The San Francisco Municipal Transit and Street Map ($3) is a useful guide to the extensive transportation system. You can buy the map at most bookstores and at

the San Francisco Visitor Information Center, on the lower level of Hallidie Plaza at Powell and Market streets.

▐ **TIP →** During football season Muni runs a special weekend shuttle to Candlestick Park for $10 round-trip.

BUS OPERATORS

Outside the city, AC Transit serves the East Bay, and Golden Gate Transit serves Marin and Sonoma counties.

Bus and Muni Information AC Transit (☎ 510/839–2882 ⊕ www.actransit.org). **Golden Gate Transit** (☎ 511 or 415/455–2000 ⊕ www.goldengate.org). **San Francisco Municipal Railway System** (*Muni* ☎ 311 or 415/701–3000 ⊕ www.sfmta.com).

▌TAXI TRAVEL

Taxi service is notoriously bad in San Francisco, and hailing a cab can be frustratingly difficult in some parts of the city, especially on weekends. Popular nightspots such as the Mission, SoMa, North Beach, the Haight, and the Castro have a lot of cabs but a lot of people looking for taxis, too. Midweek, and during the day, you shouldn't have much of a problem—unless it's raining. In a pinch, hotel taxi stands are an option, as is calling for a pick-up. But be forewarned: taxi companies frequently don't answer the phone in peak periods. The absolute worst time to find a taxi is Friday afternoon and evening; plan well ahead, and if you're going to the airport, make a reservation or book a shuttle instead. Most taxi companies take advance reservations for airport and out-of-town runs but not in-town transfers.

Taxis in San Francisco charge $3.10 for the first 1/5 mi (one of the highest base rates in the United States), 45¢ for each additional 1/5 mi, and 45¢ per minute in stalled traffic. There is no charge for additional passengers; there is no surcharge for luggage. For trips outside city limits, multiply the metered rate by 1.5.

Taxi Companies DeSoto Cab (☎ 415/970–1300). Luxor Cab (☎ 415/282–4141). Veteran's Taxicab (☎ 415/648–1313). Yellow Cab (☎ 415/626–2345).

Complaints San Francisco Police Department Taxi Complaints (☎ 415/553–1447).

▎ TRAIN TRAVEL

Amtrak trains travel to the Bay Area from some cities in California and the United States. The *Coast Starlight* travels north from Los Angeles to Seattle, passing the Bay Area along the way, but contrary to its name, the train runs inland through the Central Valley for much of its route through Northern California; the most scenic stretch is in Southern California, between San Luis Obispo and Los Angeles. Amtrak also has several routes between San Jose, Oakland, and Sacramento. The *California Zephyr* travels from Chicago to the Bay Area, and has spectacular alpine vistas as it crosses the Sierra Nevada mountains. San Francisco doesn't have an Amtrak train station but does have an Amtrak bus station, at the Ferry Building, which provides service to trains in Emeryville, just over the Bay Bridge. Shuttle buses also connect the Emeryville train station with downtown Oakland, the Caltrain station, and other points in downtown San Francisco.

Caltrain connects San Francisco to Palo Alto, San Jose, Santa Clara, and many smaller cities en route. In San Francisco, trains leave from the main depot, at 4th and Townsend streets, and a rail-side stop at 22nd and Pennsylvania streets. One-way fares are $2.75 to $11.50, depending on the number of zones through which your travel tickets are valid for four hours after purchase time. A ticket is $6 from San Francisco to Palo Alto, at least $8 to San Jose. You can also buy a day pass ($5.25–$22.75) for unlimited travel in a 24-hour period. It's worth waiting for an express train for trips that last 1 to 1¾ hours. On weekdays, trains depart three or four times per hour during the morning and evening, twice per hour during daytime non-commute hours, and as little as once per hour in the evening. Weekend trains run once per hour. The system shuts down at midnight. There are no onboard ticket sales. You must buy tickets before boarding the train or risk paying a $250 fine for fare evasion.

INFORMATION

Amtrak (☎ 800/872–7245 ⊕ www.amtrak. com). **Caltrain** (☎ 800/660–4287 ⊕ www. caltrain.com). **San Francisco Caltrain station** (✉ 700 4th St., at King St. ☎ 800/660–4287).

ESSENTIALS

▪ COMMUNICATIONS

INTERNET

All public libraries provide Internet access and most hotels have a computer stationed in the lobby with free (if shared) high-speed access for guests. Some hotels can charge up to $10 a day to provide a high-speed connection in the room, others offer it free of charge. In addition, many cafés throughout San Francisco, Marin County, and the East Bay now offer free Wi-Fi, but a few continue to charge a $5 to $7 fee. For a list of free Wi-Fi spots in San Francisco, check ⊕ *www. openwifispots.com.*

Contacts Cybercafes (⊕ *www.cybercafes. com*) lists more than 4,000 Internet cafés worldwide.

▪ DAY TOURS AND GUIDES

For walking-tour recommendations, see the Experience San Francisco chapter or the pull-out On-the-Go map.

BOAT TOURS

Blue & Gold Fleet operates a bay cruise that lasts about an hour. Tickets may be purchased at Pier 39, near Fisherman's Wharf. The tour, on a ferryboat with outside seating on the upper deck, loops around the bay taking in the Bay Bridge, Alcatraz Island, and the Golden Gate Bridge. An audiotape tells you what you're seeing. Discounts are available for tickets purchased online.

Information Blue & Gold Fleet (☎ *415/705–8200* ⊕ *www.blueandgoldfleet.com*).

BUS AND VAN TOURS

In addition to bus and van tours of the city, most tour companies run excursions to various Bay Area and Northern California destinations, such as Marin County and the Wine Country, as well as to farther-flung areas, such as Monterey and Yosemite. City tours generally last 3½

hours and cost $48 to $49 per person. The bigger outfits operate large buses, which tend to be roomy. Service is more intimate with the smaller companies, however, because they can fit only about 10 people per vehicle; the vans can be a little tight, but with the driver-guide right in front of you, you're able to ask questions easily and won't have to worry about interrupting someone on a microphone, as is the case with the big companies.

Great Pacific Tours is the best small company and conducts city tours in passenger vans (starting at $49). Super Sightseeing is also locally owned and operates tours in 28- and 50-passenger buses. For $18 to $19 more, both companies can supplement a city tour with a bay cruise. Super Sightseeing can also add a trip to Alcatraz for $28.

Information Great Pacific Tours (☎ *415/626–4499* ⊕ *www.greatpacifictour. com*). **Super Sightseeing** (☎ *415/777–2288* ⊕ *www.supersightseeing.com*).

▪ MONEY

San Francisco often finds itself near the top of lists rating the most expensive cities in the United States. Don't let that scare you off; those ratings are usually based on the cost of living. Local real-estate prices are out of this world—but a trip here doesn't have to cost the moon.

Payment methods are those standard to major U.S. cities. Plastic is king; hotels and most stores and restaurants accept credit cards. Small, casual restaurants, though, may be cash-only operations. You can easily find ATMs in every neighborhood, either in bank branches (these have security vestibules that are accessed by your bank card), convenience stores, drugstores, supermarkets, and even some Starbucks coffee shops. Some performing-arts venues, hotels, and fine-dining spots will also accept traveler's checks.

ITEM	AVERAGE COST
Cup of Coffee (Not a Latte!)	$2
Glass of Wine	$8
Glass of Beer	$8
Sandwich	$7
One-Mile Taxi Ride	$5
Avg. Museum Admission	$11

Prices throughout this guide are given for adults. Substantially reduced fees are almost always available for children, students, and senior citizens.

CREDIT CARDS

It's a good idea to inform your credit-card company before you travel. Otherwise, the credit-card company might put a hold on your card owing to unusual activity—not a good thing halfway through your trip. Record all your credit-card numbers—as well as the phone numbers to call if your cards are lost or stolen—in a safe place, so you're prepared should something go wrong. Both MasterCard and Visa have general numbers you can call (collect if you're abroad) if your card is lost, but you're better off calling the number of your issuing bank, since MasterCard and Visa usually just transfer you to your bank; your bank's number is usually printed on your card.

Reporting Lost Cards American Express (☎ 800/528–4800 in U.S. ⊕ www. americanexpress.com). **Diners Club** (☎ 800/234–6377 in U.S. ⊕ www.dinersclub. com). **Discover** (☎ 800/347–2683 in U.S. ⊕ www.discovercard.com). **MasterCard** (☎ 800/627–8372 in U.S. ⊕ www.mastercard. com). **Visa** (☎ 800/847–2911 in U.S. ⊕ www. visa.com).

▌ RESTROOMS

Public facilities are in forest-green kiosks at Pier 39, on Market Street at Powell Street, at Castro and Market streets, and at the Civic Center. The fee to use the facilities is 25¢, although it's free at some places. Since they're self-cleaning, they're usually tolerable. Most public garages have restrooms, and large hotels usually have lobby-level facilities, and chain bookstores are another good bet.

Find a Loo The Bathroom Diaries (⊕ www. thebathroomdiaries.com) is flush with unsanitized info on restrooms the world over—each one located, reviewed, and rated.

▌ SAFETY

San Francisco is generally a safe place for travelers who observe all normal urban precautions. First, avoid looking like a tourist. Dress inconspicuously, remove badges when leaving convention areas, and know the routes to your destination before you set out. Use common sense and, unless you know exactly where you're going, steer clear of certain neighborhoods late at night, especially if you're walking alone. Below are certain areas to stay on alert, or avoid:

The Tenderloin. Named for a cut of steak, this neighborhood west of Union Square and above Civic Center can be a seedy part of town, with drug dealers, homeless people, hustlers, and X-rated joints. It's roughly bordered by Taylor, Polk, Geary, and Market streets. Avoid coming here after dark, especially if you're walking.

Western Addition. Gang activity makes this a sketchy neighborhood, even in daytime, with occasional outbreaks of gun violence. Don't stray too far off Fillmore Street.

Civic Center. After a show here, walk west to Gough Street; don't head north, east, or south from the Civic Center on foot, and avoid Market Street between 6th and 10th.

Parts of the Mission District. The flat blocks of the Mission range from a bit scruffy to edgy to truly sketchy, with some gang activity. Steer clear of the areas east of Mission Street and south of 24th Street, especially after dark. If you're walking between 16th and 24th streets, head west to Valencia, which runs parallel to Mission.

Some areas in Golden Gate Park. These include the area near the Haight Street entrance, where street kids often smoke and deal pot, and around the pedestrian tunnels on the far west end of the park.

Parts of SoMa: Drift a few blocks south of Market and you'll either be near the ballpark, in a high-rise jungle, or exploring the slow transformation of formerly industrial neighborhoods.

Like many larger cities, San Francisco has many homeless people. Although most are no threat, some are more aggressive and can persist in their pleas for cash until it feels like harassment. If you feel uncomfortable, don't reach for your wallet.

■TIP➔ Distribute your cash, credit cards, IDs, and other valuables between a deep front pocket, an inside jacket or vest pocket, and a hidden money pouch. Don't reach for the money pouch once you're in public.

If you use common sense and follow basic precautions (sticking to well-lighted streets after dark, holding on to your bags rather than leaving them next to you), all should be fine.

▌TAXES

The sales tax in San Francisco is 8.5%. Nonprepared foods (from grocery stores) are exempt. The tax on hotel rooms is 14%.

▌TIME

San Francisco is on Pacific Time. Chicago is 2 hours ahead of San Francisco, New York is 3 hours ahead, and, depending on whether daylight saving time is in effect, London is either 8 or 9 hours ahead and Sydney is 17 or 18 hours ahead.

▌TIPPING

TIPPING GUIDELINES FOR SAN FRANCISCO	
Bartender	About 15%, starting at $1 a drink at casual places
Bellhop	$1 to $5 per bag, depending on the level of the hotel
Hotel concierge	$5 or more, if he or she performs a service for you
Hotel doorman, room service, or valet	$2–$3
Hotel maid	$2–$3 a day (either daily or at the end of your stay, in cash)
Taxi Driver	15%–20%, but round up the fare to the next dollar amount
Tour Guide	10% of the cost of the tour
Waiter	15%–20%, with 20% being the norm at high-end restaurants; nothing additional if a service charge is added to the bill

▌VISITOR INFORMATION

The San Francisco Convention and Visitors Bureau can mail you brochures, maps, and festivals and events listings. Once you're in town, you can stop by their info center near Union Square. Information about the Wine Country, redwood groves, and northwestern California is available at the California Welcome Center on Pier 39.

The Berkeley Convention and Visitors Bureau provides an extensive events calendar and detailed suggestions, which you can download online by going to www.visitberkeley.com.

Oakland's Convention and Visitors Bureau also has an extensive Web site; you must call their offices or email info@oaklandcvb.com to order your 60-page guide by mail.

Information on Marin tends to be listed as a day trip in San Francisco guides. For more specific information on the many small communities in Marin County, plus the state and national parks within it, visit the Marin County, California Visitors Bureau in Larkspur or online at www.visitmarin.org.

Contacts San Francisco Visitor Information Center (✉ *Hallidie Plaza, lower level, 900 Market St., Union Sq.* ☎ *415/391–2000 TDD* ⊕ *www.onlyinsanfrancisco.com*).

Metro Area Berkeley Convention and Visitors Bureau (✉ *2015 Center St., Berkeley* ☎ *800/847–4823 or 510/549–7040* ⊕ *www.visitberkeley.com*). **Marin County, California Visitors Bureau** (✉ *1013 Larkspur Landing Circle, Larkspur* ☎ *866/925–2060 or 415/925–2060* ⊕ *www.visitmarin.org*). **Oakland Convention and Visitors Bureau** (✉ *463 11th St., Oakland* ☎ *510/839–9000* ⊕ *www.oaklandcvb.com*). **San Jose Convention and Visitors Bureau** (✉ *408 Almaden Blvd., San Jose* ☎ *800/726–5673 or 408/295–9600* ⊕ *www.sanjose.org*).

State California Travel and Tourism Commission (✉ *980 9th St., Suite 480, Sacramento* ☎ *800/862–2543 or 916/444–4429* ⊕ *www.visitcalifornia.com*); free visitor information and itinerary planners. **California Welcome Center** (✉ *2nd level, Pier 39, San Francisco* ☎ *415/981–1280* ⊕ *www.visitcwc.com*).

ONLINE RESOURCES

Start your search for all things SF by following the links option from **www.sfcityscape.com**. This comprehensive Web site posts a link to every local publication,

---

THE FODORS.COM CONNECTION

Before your trip, be sure check out what fellow travelers are saying in Talk on www.fodors.com.

---

cultural institution, and government agency in the Bay Area.

For a snappy view of city trends, with gossip on everything from the city's best ice cream to concerts, check out **www.sfist.com**. For local politics and news, there's the online presence of the major daily newspaper, **www.sfgate.com/chronicle** as well as **www.fogcityjournal.com**. Current arts and cultural events are detailed on the extensive events calendar of **www.sfstation.com** or the *San Francisco Chronicle*'s online entertainment Web site, **www.sfgate.com/eguide**.

You can browse articles from *San Francisco*, a monthly glossy, at **www.sanfran.com**. The annual summer issues on "bests" (restaurants, activities, and so on) are handy overviews. *SF Weekly*'s site, **www.sfweekly.com**, makes for good browsing.

Where's the Wi-Fi? Click on **www.wifi-freespot.com** to see where you can log on in the Bay Area for free.

INDEX

PHOTO CREDITS

1, Som Vembar, Fodors.com member. 2, Philip Dyer/iStockphoto. 5, travelstock44/Alamy. Chapter 1: Experience San Francisco: 8-9, Robert Holmes. 10, Brett Shoaf/Artistic Visuals Photography. 11 (left), elvis santana/iStockphoto. 11 (right), Brett Shoaf/Artistic Visuals Photography. 14-17, Brett Shoaf/ Artistic Visuals Photography. 18 (left), Eli Mordechai/Shutterstock. 18 (top right), Andresr/Shutterstock. 18 (bottom center), Rostislav Glinsky/Shutterstock. 18 (bottom right), Chee-Onn Leong/Shutterstock. 19 (top left), Chris Pancewicz/Alamy. 19 (bottom left), FloridaStock/Shutterstock. 19 (right), Klaas Lingbeek- van Kranen/iStockphoto. 20 (left), Robert Holmes. 20 (top right), Tim Griffith. . 20 (bottom right), Brett Shoaf/Artistic Visuals Photography. 21, Lisa M. Hamilton. 22, Brett Shoaf/Artistic Visuals Photography. 23, Hal Bergman/iStockphoto. 26, wili_hybrid /Flickr. 27 (left), Brett Shoaf/Artistic Visuals. 27 (right), Corbis Photography. 28-29, Brett Shoaf/Artistic Visuals Photography. 30, Janet Fullwood. 31, travelstock44/Alamy. 33, Brett Shoaf/Artistic Visuals Photography. 34, San Francisco Municipal Railway Historical Archives. Chapter 2: Union Square & Chinatown: 35, Rubens Abboud/ Alamy. 37, Chee-Onn Leong/Shutterstock. 38, Steve Rosset/Shutterstock. 40, Brett Shoaf/Artistic Visuals Photography. 44, Robert Holmes. 47, Brett Shoaf/Artistic Visuals Photography. 48 (top), Arnold Genthe. 48 (bottom), Library of Congress Prints and Photographs Division. 49 (left), Sandor Balatoni/ SFCVB. 49 (right), Detroit Publishing Company Collection, Photography Collection, Miriam and Ira D. Wallach Division of Art, Prints and Photographs, The New York Public Library, Astor, Lenox and Tilden Foundation. 50, Brett Shoaf/Artistic Visuals Photography. 51 (top), Gary Soup/Flickr. 51 (bottom), Albert Cheng/Shutterstock. 52 (top), Sheryl Schindler/SFCVB. 52 (center), Ronen/Shutterstock. 52 (bottom), Robert Holmes. Chapter 3: SoMa and Civic Center: 53, Walter Bibikow/age fotostock. 55, Robert Holmes. 56, Rafael Ramirez Lee/Shutterstock. 58, stephenrwalli/Flickr. 60, Brett Shoaf/ Artistic Visuals. Chapter 4: Nob Hill and Russian Hill: 67, Robert Holmes. 69 and 70, Brett Shoaf/ Artistic Visuals Photography. 76-77, POPPERFOTO/Alamy. 78 and 79 (top), Library of Congress Prints and Photographs Division. 79 (bottom), North Wind Picture Archives/Alamy. 80, Library of Congress Prints & Photographs Division. 81, Bettmann/CORBIS. Chapter 5: North Beach: 83, Andrea Benassi/Flickr. 85-86, Brett Shoaf/Artistic Visuals Photography. 88, William Fawcett fotoVoyager.com/

iStockphoto. Chapter 6: On the Waterfront: 93, Jon Arnold Images/Alamy. 95, Musee Mecanique in San Francisco. 96, Robert Holmes. 100-101. Chee-Onn Leong/Shutterstock. 107, Lewis Sommer/SFCVB. 108, Daniel DeSlover/Shutterstock. 109 (left), POPPERFOTO/Alamy. 109 (center and right), wikipedia. org. 111, Eliza Snow/iStockphoto. 112, Steve Rosset/Shutterstock. Chapter 7: The Marina and the Presidio: 113, Carolina Garcia Aranda/iStockphoto. 115, Brett Shoaf/Artistic Visuals Photography. 116, javarman/Shutterstock. Chapter 8: The Western Shoreline: 123 and 125, Robert Holmes. 126, Brett Shoaf/Artistic Visuals Photography. 129, Chee-Onn Leong/Shutterstock. Chapter 9: Golden Gate Park: 131, Brett Shoaf/Artistic Visuals Photography. 132, Robert Holmes. 133 and 134 (top), Brett Shoaf/ Artistic Visuals Photography. 134 (center), Robert Holmes. 134 (bottom), Brett Shoaf/Artistic Visuals Photography. 135, Natalia Bratslavsky/iStockphoto. 136, Robert Holmes. 137 (top), Jack Hollingsworth/SFCVB. 137 (center), Robert Holmes. 137 (bottom), Brett Shoaf/Artistic Visuals Photography. 138 (top and bottom), Robert Holmes. 139 (top and bottom), Janet Fullwood. 140 (top), Donna & Andrew/Flickr. 140 (center and bottom), Robert Holmes. Chapter 10: The Haight, the Castro, and Noe Valley: 141, Robert Holmes. 143, Brett Shoaf/Artistic Visuals Photography. 144, SFCVB. 145, Brett Shoaf/Artistic Visuals Photography. 149, aprillilacs, Fodors.com member. 151, AP Photo/Noah Berger/ Newscom. Chapter 11: Mission District: 155 and 157, Robert Holmes. 158, Brett Shoaf/Artistic Visuals Photography. 159, Held Jürgen/Prisma/age fotostock. 162, Robert Holmes. Chapter 12: Pacific Heights and Japantown: 165, Robert Holmes. 167, ryan + sarah/Flickr. 168, Brett Shoaf/Artistic Visuals Photography. 170, Rafael Ramirez Lee/iStockphoto. 175, Robert Holmes. 176 (top), rick/Flickr. 176 (center), Danita Delimont/Alamy. 176 (bottom), iStockphoto. 177 (top), Beata Jancsik/Shutterstock. 177 (center), Rafael Ramirez Lee/Shutterstock. 177 (bottom), Susanne Friedrich/iStockphoto. 178 (top), orphanjones/ Flickr. 178 (center), Bruce Damonte. 178 (bottom), Janet Fullwood. Chapter 13: Where to Eat: 179 and 180, Lisa M. Hamilton. 186, Nikolay Bachiyski/Flickr. 187 (top), miss karen/Flickr. 187 (bottom), Audrey Chong/Shutterstock. 188, Atwater Village Newbie/Flickr. 189 (top), Jason Riedy/Flickr. 189 (bottom), Clemson/Flickr. 190, Rough Guides/Alamy. 191 (top), Liv friis-larsen/Shutterstock. 191 (bottom), Bill Helsel/Alamy. 192, Robert Holmes. 193 (top), Yodel Anecdotal/Flickr. 193 (bottom), SFCVB. 194, rick/Flickr. 195 (top), Ei-Lun Tsai/Flickr. 195 (bottom), Cathleen Clapper/Shutterstock. 196, moonlightbulb/Flickr. 197 (top), P_R_/Flickr. 197 (bottom), mashe/Shutterstock. 198, rick/Flickr. 199 (top), mark noak/iStockphoto. 199 (bottom), jessicafm/Flickr. Chapter 14: Where to Stay: 245, George Apostolidis/Mandarin Oriental Hotel Group. 246, Clift Hotel. 254 (top), George Apostolidis/Mandarin Oriental Hotel Group. 254 (bottom), David Phelps/Argonaut Hotel. 260 (top), The Ritz-Carlton, San Francisco. 260 (center left), Joie de Vivre Hospitality. 260 (center right), Joie de Vivre Hospitality. 260 (bottom), Cris Ford/Union Street Inn. 265 (top), Rien van Rijthoven/InterContinental Hotels & Resorts. 265 (bottom left), Starwood Hotels & Resorts. 265 (bottom right), Four Seasons. 270 (top), Hotel Nikko San Francisco. 270 (bottom left), Orchard Hotel. 270 (bottom right), Hotel Monaco. Chapter 15: Performing Arts: 275, Erik Tomasson. 276, San Francisco Symphony by Max Kiesler www.flickr.com/ photos/maxkiesler/3979025521/ Attribution License. Chapter 16: Nightlife and the Arts: 287, irene./ Flickr. 288, Robert Holmes. 299, Rough Guides/Alamy. 310, Evanne Grate/rick/Flickr. Chapter 17: Sports and the Outdoors: 315, Jack Hollingsworth/SFCVB. 316, Robert Holmes. Chapter 18: Shopping: 331 and 332, Robert Holmes. 334, The Archive. 335, Macy's Union Square by Denmark www.flickr. com/photos/tekniks/3084387641/ Attribution License. 336, Mila Zinkova/Wikimedia Commons. 337, Amoeba Music by Mack Male www.flickr.com/photos/mastermaq/4995219816/ Attribution-ShareAlike License. 338, Jessica Watson. 339, IMG_0821 by John Martinez Pavliga www.flickr.com/photos/virtualsugar/5552991843/ Attribution-License. 348, Lisa M. Hamilton. 361, besighyawn/Flickr. 363, besighyawn/Flickr. Chapter 19: Marin County, Berkeley, and Oakland: 369, Robert Holmes. 371 (top), Robert Holmes. 371 (bottom), Jyeshern Cheng/iStockphoto. 372, Brett Shoaf/Artistic Visuals Photography. 380, Robert Holmes. 391, Mark Rasmussen/iStockphoto. 393, Robert Holmes. 400, S. Greg Panosian/ iStockphoto. 403 and 415, Robert Holmes. Chapter 20: The Wine Country: 419, Robert Holmes. 420, iStockphoto. 421, Robert Holmes. 422, Warren H. White. 428, Robert Holmes. 431, Robert Holmes. 438, Robert Holmes. 439 (top), kevin miller/iStockphoto. 439 (bottom), Far Niente+Dolce+Nickel & Nickel. 440 (top and bottom) and 441 (top), Robert Holmes. 441 (bottom), star5112/Flickr. 442 (top left), Rubicon Estate. 442 (top right and bottom) and 443 (top and bottom), Robert Holmes. 444 (top), Philippe Roy/Alamy. 444 (center), Agence Images/Alamy. 444 (bottom), Cephas Picture Library/Alamy. 445 (top), Napa Valley Conference Bureau. 445 (second and third from top), Wild Horse Winery (Forrest L. Doud). 445 (fourth from top), Napa Valley Conference Bureau. 445 (fifth from top), Panther Creek Cellars (Ron Kaplan). 445 (sixth from top), Clos du Val (Marvin Collins). 445 (seventh from top), Panther Creek Cellars (Ron Kaplan). 445 (bottom), Warren H. White. 450, Far Niente+Dolce+Nickel & Nickel. 453, Terry Joanis/Frog's Leap. 460, Chuck Honek/Schramsberg Vineyard. 463, Castello di Amorosa. 477, 478, 484-485, and 487, Robert Holmes.

ABOUT OUR WRITERS

San Francisco writer Michele Bigley spends most of her days exploring her favorite city with her kiddo and husband. When not hunting for sand dollars, hiking through eucalyptus groves, or munching on Italian pastries, she writes articles, books, iPhone apps and essays about her travels around the globe. Michele updated our Where to Stay chapter.

Marcia Gagliardi is a freelance food writer who has been eating her way through San Francisco since 1994. She publishes a weekly e-column about the local restaurant scene called "the tablehopper" (at tablehopper.com), which is chock-full of insider news and gossip, reviews, and culinary events. She is also the author of *The Tablehopper's Guide to Dining and Drinking in San Francisco*. Marcia updated the Where to Eat chapter.

A veteran Fodor's writer, Berkeley-based writer and editor Denise M. Leto roams the city out of sheer love for SF, peeking down overgrown alleyways and exploring tucked-away corners from the Tenderloin to the Richmond, often with her two homeschooled sons in tow. She updated all the neighborhood chapters and the Experience chapter in this edition. She also wrote our special features on cable cars, Chinatown, Golden Gate Park, and Alcatraz.

Fiona G. Parrott is a Californian native. She spent her childhood exploring the raw wilderness of Marin County and her later years exploring the culinary and musical delights of San Francisco, Berkeley, and Oakland. At present she divides her adventure time between wilderness and cityscape, writing about the Bay Area's cutting edge hotspots. She's been a veterinarian, actor, bartender, watermelon picker, latrine builder and university lecturer, but writing for Fodor's has been one of her most exciting jobs. For this edition she updated the Sports and Outdoors and Marin, Berkeley, and Oakland chapters, as well as the Travel Smart and Shopping chapters. In recent years Fiona also contributed to *Fodor's Scotland* and *Fodor's Great Britain*.

A longtime Fodor's contributor, Sharron Wood simply adores San Francisco, from its flourishing food, wine, and cocktail culture to its perpetually perfect weather. When she's not exploring the Wine Country, she's writing about the city's nightlife, editing cookbooks, developing recipes, or plying her friends with cocktails in her Mission District apartment. For this edition, Sharron updated our Wine Country chapter.

Bay Area writer Sura Wood lost her heart in San Francisco when she was eight, and she's never stopped loving the city. An arts journalist for the last fifteen years, she's written with gusto about San Francisco's food, fashion, hotels, nightlife, art, and architecture for the Fodor's Web site. She updated our Nightlife and Performing Arts chapters and Eye on Architecture feature for this year's guide.